DIETRICH BONHOEFFER WORKS, VOLUME 15

Theological Education Underground: 1937–1940

This series is a translation of
DIETRICH BONHOEFFER WERKE
Edited by
Eberhard Bethge†, Ernst Feil,
Christian Gremmels, Wolfgang Huber,
Hans Pfeifer, Albrecht Schönherr†,
Heinz Eduard Tödt†, Ilse Tödt

This volume has been made possible through the generous support of the Lilly Endowment, Inc.; the Thrivent Financial Foundation for Lutherans; the New England Synod, ELCA; the Bowen H. and Janice Arthur McCoy Charitable Foundation; the Lutheran Theological Seminary at Philadelphia; the Goethe-Institut; the German Lutheran Church of Washington, D.C.; and the gifts of numerous members and friends of the International Bonhoeffer Society.

DIETRICH BONHOEFFER WORKS, VOLUME 15

DIETRICH BONHOEFFER

Theological Education Underground: 1937–1940

Translated from the German Edition
Edited by
DIRK SCHULZ

English Edition
Edited by
VICTORIA J. BARNETT

Translated by
VICTORIA J. BARNETT, CLAUDIA D. BERGMANN,
PETER FRICK, AND SCOTT A. MOORE

Supplementary Material Translated by
DOUGLAS W. STOTT

FORTRESS PRESS MINNEAPOLIS

DIETRICH BONHOEFFER WORKS, Volume 15

Originally published in German as *Dietrich Bonhoeffer Werke*, edited by Eberhard Bethge, et al., by Chr. Kaiser Verlag / Gütersloher Verlagshaus, Gütersloh, in 1998; Band 15, *Illegale Theologenausbildung: Sammelvikariate 1937–1940*, edited by Dirk Schulz. First English-language edition of *Dietrich Bonhoeffer Works*, Volume 15, published by Fortress Press in 2012.

The translation of this work was subsidized in part by a grant from the Goethe-Institut Inter Nationes, Munich.

Jacket design: Cheryl Watson
Cover photo: Christian Gremmels/Renate Bethge (eds.), *Dietrich Bonhoeffer: A Life in Pictures* © 2005 Gütersloher Verlagshaus, Gütersloh, a division of Random House.
Book design: HK Scriptorium, Inc.
Typesetting: Ann Delgehausen, Trio Bookworks

Library of Congress Cataloging-in-Publication Data

Bonhoeffer, Dietrich, 1906–1945.
[Illegale Theologen-Ausbildung. English]
Theological education underground, 1937–1940 / Dietrich Bonhoeffer ; translated from the German edition edited by Dirk Schulz ; English edition edited by Victoria J. Barnett ; translated by Victoria J. Barnett . . . [et al.] ; supplementary material translated by Douglas W. Stott.
p. cm. — (Dietrich Bonhoeffer works ; v. 15)
Includes bibliographical references and indexes.
ISBN 978-0-8006-9815-7 (alk. paper)
1. Bonhoeffer, Dietrich, 1906–1945—Correspondence. 2. Theologians—Germany—Correspondence. 3. Sermons, German. 4. Meditations.
I. Barnett, Victoria, 1950– II. Title.
BX4827.B65A3 2011
230'.044092—dc23

2011034419

ISBN 978-0-8006-9815-7

Contents

Part 3
Sermons and Meditations

General Editor's Foreword to Dietrich Bonhoeffer Works

The German theologian and pastor Dietrich Bonhoeffer has become one of the most influential Christian thinkers of all time. Barely twenty-seven years of age when the Nazi regime came to power in Germany, Bonhoeffer emerged immediately as a radical Protestant voice against the ideological co-optation of his church. He was one of the earliest critics of the Nazi regime and an outspoken opponent of the pro-Nazi "German Christians." From 1933 to 1935, he served as pastor of two German-speaking congregations in England, leading them to join the Confessing Church—the faction within the German Protestant Church that opposed the nazification of the Christian faith. He returned to Germany to become director of a small Confessing Church seminary and, after the Gestapo closed it, continued to work illegally to educate Confessing clergy. Throughout the 1930s, he attended ecumenical meetings, effectively becoming the voice of the Confessing Church throughout the European and American ecumenical world. In 1939, his ecumenical friends urged him to accept a position in New York. Rejecting the security of a life in exile, Bonhoeffer chose instead to join the ranks of the German conspiracy to overthrow the regime, like his brother Klaus and his brothers-in-law Hans von Dohnanyi and Rüdiger Schleicher. He was arrested and imprisoned in April 1943 and executed in the Flossenbürg concentration camp in April 1945.

In a eulogy published shortly after Bonhoeffer's death, his former professor and friend Reinhold Niebuhr wrote that Bonhoeffer's story "is worth recording. It belongs to the modern acts of the apostles. . . . Not only his martyr's death, but also his actions and precepts contain within them the hope of a revitalised Protestant faith in Germany. It will be a faith religiously more profound than that of many of its critics; but it will have learned to overcome the one fateful error of German Protestantism, the complete dichotomy between faith and political life."[1]

In the ensuing decades, Niebuhr's prescient insight that Bonhoeffer's life and work offered lasting insights for modern Christian experience and witness has been more than fulfilled. Bonhoeffer wrote hundreds of letters, sermons, and biblical reflections in addition to his published theological works. After 1945, Bonhoeffer's former student and close friend Eberhard Bethge worked with publishers to reissue and translate the books Bonhoeffer had published in his lifetime. In translation, these works—*Discipleship*, *Ethics*, and *Letters and Papers from Prison*—became classics, finding a wide readership among Christians throughout the world.

Yet there was a growing sense that these works should not stand alone—a realization of the significance of the biographical and historical context of his thought. Bonhoeffer's papers also included lecture notes that had been made by his students, documents from the German Church Struggle and ecumenical meetings, circular letters that were sent to his seminarians, sermons, extensive correspondence with theologians and religious leaders in Europe and the United States, and prison writings. Bethge published several early compilations of some of these documents (*Gesammelte Schriften* and *Mündige Welt*) and incorporated additional material into his magisterial biography of Bonhoeffer, which first appeared in English in 1970 and then, in a revised and unabridged edition, in 2000.

Bethge and leading Bonhoeffer scholars in Germany decided to publish new annotated editions of Bonhoeffer's complete theological works, together with most of the documents from the literary estate, including historical documents and correspondence to Bonhoeffer. The *Dietrich Bonhoeffer Werke* series was published by Chr. Kaiser Verlag, now part of Gütersloher Verlagshaus. The first German volume, a new edition of Bonhoeffer's dissertation, *Sanctorum Communio*, appeared in 1986; the final volume, Bonhoeffer's complete prison writings, appeared in April 1998. A seventeenth volume, an index for the entire series, appeared in 1999; this volume also included documents discovered after their respective volumes had been published. Whenever possible these documents have been included in the appropriate volumes of the English edition; documents that continue to be discovered are published in the *Dietrich Bonhoeffer Jahrbuch*, a series published by Gütersloher Verlagshaus.

[1.] Reinhold Niebuhr, "The Death of a Martyr," *Christianity and Crisis* 5, no. 11 (1945): 6–7.

Discussion about an English translation of the entire series began as soon as the first German volumes appeared. In 1990, the International Bonhoeffer Society, English Language Section, in agreement with the German Bonhoeffer Society and Fortress Press, undertook the English translation of the German *Dietrich Bonhoeffer Werke.* The project began with an initial grant from the National Endowment for the Humanities with Robin Lovin serving as project director, assisted by Mark Brocker. An editorial board was formed for the Dietrich Bonhoeffer Works, English Edition, staffed by Wayne Whitson Floyd Jr., as general editor, and Clifford J. Green of Hartford Seminary as executive director. Wayne Whitson Floyd Jr., at that time director of the Dietrich Bonhoeffer Center at the Lutheran Theological Seminary in Philadelphia, served as general editor from 1993 to 2004, overseeing publication of the first seven volumes as well as volume 9. Victoria J. Barnett, director of church relations at the U.S. Holocaust Memorial Museum, joined the project as associate general editor in 2002 and became general editor in 2004, joined by Barbara Wojhoski, a professional editor who prepared the manuscripts of the final volumes for publication.

The *Dietrich Bonhoeffer Works, English Edition* (*DBWE*) is the definitive English translation of Bonhoeffer's theological and other writings. It includes a great deal of material that appears for the first time in English, as well as documents discovered only after the publication of the original German volumes. *DBWE* is a significant contribution to twentieth-century theological literature, church history, and the history of the Nazi era. Particularly in their portrayal of the daily implications of the Protestant Church Struggle in Nazi Germany and the response of Christians outside Germany, these volumes offer a detailed and unique glimpse of Bonhoeffer's historical context and its great challenges for the churches and for all people of conscience.

The translators of the *DBWE* volumes have attempted throughout to render an accurate and readable translation of Bonhoeffer's writings for contemporary audiences, while remaining true to Bonhoeffer's thought and style. Particular attention has been paid to the translation of important theological, historical, and philosophical terms. Bonhoeffer's language and style are often reflective of his age, particularly with regard to gendered language, and this is reflected in the historical and church documents. Nonetheless, in the translations of the early volumes of his theological writings (*DBWE* volumes 1–7), the decision was made to use gender-inclusive language, insofar as this was deemed possible without distorting Bonhoeffer's meaning or unjustifiably dissociating him from his own time.

Each volume includes an introduction written by the *DBWE* volume editor(s), footnotes provided by Bonhoeffer, editorial notes added by the German and English editors, and the original afterword written by the editor(s) of the German edition. Additions to or revisions of the German editors' notes are enclosed within square brackets and initialed by the editor of the respective volume. When any previously translated material is quoted within an editorial note in altered form—indicated by the notation [trans. altered]—such changes should be assumed to be the responsibility of the translator(s). Where available, existing English translations of books and articles in German and other languages are cited in the notes.

Bonhoeffer's own footnotes—which are indicated in the body of the text by plain, superscripted numbers—are reproduced in precisely the same numerical sequence as they appear in the German critical edition, complete with his idiosyncrasies of documentation. In these, as in the accompanying editorial notes, the edition of a work that was consulted by Bonhoeffer himself can be determined by consulting the bibliography at the end of each volume.

Each volume also contains a list of abbreviations frequently used in the editorial notes, as well as a bibliography of archival sources, sources used by Bonhoeffer, literature consulted by the editors, and other works relevant to that respective volume. Each volume also includes a chronology of important dates relevant to that volume, an index of scriptural references, an index of persons with relevant biographical information, and an index of subjects. Bibliographies at the end of each volume provide the complete information for each written source that Bonhoeffer or the various editors have mentioned in the current volume.

Bonhoeffer's literary estate—the notes, sermons, and other writings, as well as correspondence, and the personal library of materials that belonged to him and survived the war—was cataloged by Dietrich Meyer and Eberhard Bethge; this catalog has been published as the *Nachlaß Dietrich Bonhoeffer*. Most of the documents cited in the *Nachlaß* are collected in the Berlin Staatsbibliothek, although some documents remain in other archives. All documents listed in the *Nachlaß*, however, have been copied on microfiches that are now at the Staatsbibliothek in Berlin and in the Bonhoeffer collection at Burke Library, Union Theological Seminary, New York. References to any of these documents are indicated within the *DBWE* by the abbreviation *NL*, followed by the corresponding catalog number. Books in the bibliography from Bonhoeffer's own library are indicated by the abbreviation *NL-Bibl.*

Volumes 1–7 of the English edition, which contain only Bonhoeffer's own writings, retain his original organization of the material, either as chapters or as sections or unnumbered manuscripts. Volumes 8–16 contain collected writings from a particular period of Bonhoeffer's life, including correspondence from others and historical documents. With the exception of volume 8, these final volumes are divided into three sections, with the documents in each section arranged chronologically: (1) Letters, Journals, Documents; (2) Essays, Seminar Papers, Papers, Lectures, Compositions; (3) Sermons, Meditations, Catechetical Writings, Exegetical Writings. Documents are numbered consecutively within the respective sections. In editorial notes these items are labeled by the *DBWE* volume number, followed by the section number, document number, and finally the page number; for example, *DBWE* 9 (1/109), p. 179, ed. note 1, would refer to the English edition, volume 9, section 1, document 109, page 179, editorial note 1.

The *DBWE* also reproduces Bonhoeffer's original paragraphing (exceptions are noted by a ¶ symbol to indicate any paragraph break added by the editors of the English edition or by conventions explained in the introductions written by the editor[s] of specific volumes). The pagination of the *DBW* German critical edition is indicated in the outer margins of the pages of the translated text. Where it is important to give readers a word or phrase in its original language, a translated passage is followed by the original, set within square brackets. All biblical citations come from the New Revised Standard Version (NRSV) unless otherwise noted. Where versification of the Bible used by Bonhoeffer differs from the NRSV, the verse number in the latter is noted in the text in square brackets.

The publication of the *Dietrich Bonhoeffer Works, English Edition* would not have been possible without the generous support of numerous individuals and institutions. The verso of the half-title page of each volume provides a list of supporters of that particular volume. The series as a whole is indebted to many individual members and friends of the International Bonhoeffer Society, and to family foundations, congregations, synods, seminaries, and universities. Special thanks are due to the following foundations and donors for major grants: the National Endowment for the Humanities; the Lilly Endowment, Inc.; the Thrivent Financial for Lutherans Foundation; the Aid Association for Lutherans; the Stiftung Bonhoeffer Lehrstuhl; the Bowen H. and Janice Arthur McCoy Charitable Foundation; and Dr. John Young and Mrs. Cleo Young. The Lutheran Theological Seminary at Philadelphia and its former auxiliary have provided space and ongoing support. We have been extraordinarily fortunate to work with Fortress Press as the publisher of *DBWE*, and particular gratitude goes to Will Bergkamp, publisher and managing director, as well as to his predecessors, editorial directors Michael West and Marshall Johnson.

The existence of this series in English and other languages is testimony to the international community of those who have found Dietrich Bonhoeffer to be a profoundly important companion in their own journey. That community would not exist without the wisdom, generosity, and dedication of Eberhard Bethge (1909–2000) and his wife, Renate. Bethge was himself a pastor in the Confessing Church. After 1945, he was convinced that the future of a living church in Germany depended on its addressing its failures under Nazism and on a new understanding of Bonhoeffer's lasting question, Who is Christ for us today?

The editors of this English edition are particularly grateful to the original editorial board of the German edition—composed of Eberhard Bethge†, Ernst Feil, Christian Gremmels, Wolfgang Huber, Hans Pfeifer, Albrecht Schönherr†, Heinz Eduard Tödt†, and Ilse Tödt. As liaison between the German and English editorial boards, Hans Pfeifer has given steadfast and congenial support to his colleagues on both sides of the Atlantic. The editors of the individual German volumes have been generous with their time and expertise. As work on *DBWE* has proceeded, a new generation of Bonhoeffer scholars in Germany has assisted us as well: Christine Kasch, Andreas Pangritz, Holger Roggelin, Christiane Tietz, and Ralf Wuestenberg.

We remain grateful to those whose original translations of Bonhoeffer's words introduced most of us to his work. It is only fitting, however, that this English edition be dedicated, finally, to the remarkable group of scholars who over the years have devoted their time, their insights, and their generous spirit to the translation, editing, and publication of these volumes. That dedication should begin with a special acknowledgment of the capable editorial leadership of Wayne Whitson Floyd Jr., who brought eight volumes to publication, and to Clifford J. Green, whose steady hand has guided the project throughout its existence and ensured the financial foundation for its completion.

The translators who have brought Bonhoeffer's words to new life in these volumes are Victoria Barnett, Douglas Bax, Claudia Bergmann, Isabel Best, Daniel W. Bloesch, James H. Burtness†, Lisa Dahill, Peter Frick, Barbara Green, David Higgins, Nick Humphrey, Reinhard Krauss, Peter Krey, Nancy Lukens, Scott Moore, Mary Nebelsick, Marion Pauck, Martin Rumscheidt, Anne Schmidt-Lange, Douglas W. Stott, and Charles West.

The following individuals serve on the editorial board of the Dietrich Bonhoeffer Works, English Edition: H. Gaylon Barker, Victoria Barnett, Mark Brocker, Keith Clements, Peter Frick, Clifford J. Green, John W. de Gruchy, Barry Harvey, Reinhard Krauss, Michael Lukens, Larry Rasmussen, and Barbara Wojhoski. In addition, James H. Burtness†, Wayne Whitson

Floyd Jr., Barbara Green, James Patrick Kelley, Geffrey B. Kelly, Robin W. Lovin, Nancy Lukens, Paul Matheny, Mary Nebelsick, F. Burton Nelson†, and H. Martin Rumscheidt all previously served on the board, and many of them continue to serve the project through its advisory committee.

In September 1943, Dietrich Bonhoeffer wrote his parents from prison: "In normal life one is often not at all aware that we always receive infinitely more than we give, and that gratitude is what enriches life. One easily overestimates the importance of one's own acts and deeds, compared with what we become only through other people."[2] Everyone who has worked on this project will, I believe, find meaning in those words and feel gratitude for Bonhoeffer's life and witness. It is a privilege to have been part of this long, deep, and rich conversation with Bonhoeffer's thought, and to extend that conversation to the readers of these volumes.

Victoria J. Barnett

[2.] Letter of September 13, 1943, *DBWE* 8, 2/57, p. 154.

Abbreviations

BA	Bundesarchiv
BWV	Bach-Werke-Verzeichnis
CC	Confessing Church
CCSL	Corpus Christianorum: Series latina (Turnhout, 1953–)
DB-ER	*Dietrich Bonhoeffer: A Biography* (Fortress Press, rev. ed., 2000)
DBW	*Dietrich Bonhoeffer Werke*, German edition
DBWE	*Dietrich Bonhoeffer Works*, English edition
DIN	Deutsche Industrie-Normen
GC	German Christians
EG	*Evangelisches Gesangbuch*
EOK	Evangelischer Oberkirchenrat
Ev. Theol.	*Evangelische Theologie*
GEC	German Evangelical Church
GS	*Gesammelte Schriften*
LKA EKvW	Landeskirchliches Archiv der Evangelischen Kirche in Westfalen, Bielefeld
Lic.	Licentiate
LPL BP	Lambeth Palace Library, Bell Papers
LW	*Luther's Works*, American edition
NIV	New International Version
NL	*Nachlaß Dietrich Bonhoeffer*
NL-Bibl.	Restbibliothek Bonhoeffers in *Nachlaß Dietrich Bonhoeffer* (supplement to the literary estate of Dietrich Bonhoeffer)
NRSV	New Revised Standard Version
NSDAP	Nationalsozialistische Deutsche Arbeiterpartei; the Nazi Party
NT	New Testament

OT	Old Testament
PAM	*Predigten—Auslegungen—Meditationen* (Chr. Kaiser, 1984–85)
RM	reichsmarks
SA	Sturmabteilung (Nazi storm troopers)
SS	Schutzstaffel
WA	Martin Luther, *Werke*, Weimarer Ausgabe (Weimar edition)
WA.Br	Weimarer Ausgabe, *Briefe*
WA.Tr	Weimarer Ausgabe, *Tischreden*
YMCA	Young Men's Christian Association

Victoria J. Barnett

Editor's Introduction to the English Edition

This volume documents the course of Dietrich Bonhoeffer's life and work from November 1937 to March 1940—a brief but decisive span of history that included the March 1938 *Anschluß* of Austria; the Evian refugee conference in France, at which thirty-two nations decided against easing immigration restrictions on Jewish refugees; the Sudeten crisis and Munich agreement, which led to the ceding of the Sudetenland to Nazi Germany; the November 1938 pogrom in Nazi Germany (*Kristallnacht*); and finally the beginning of the Second World War with the German invasion of Poland on September 1, 1939. Although the death camps were not yet in operation, the mass killings of Jews in eastern Europe began immediately with the German invasion of the east, and the "euthanasia" program—the Nazi murders of institutionalized patients—began in late 1939. Throughout this period there was a steady intensification not only of Nazi anti-Jewish laws but of open violence against Jews throughout Europe.

For the Confessing Church, it was a bleak period that exposed both the church's lack of internal unity and its utter failure to oppose National Socialism. The early unanimity against the extreme "Aryan" theology of the German Christians had dissolved by the October 1934 Dahlem synod. Even most of those who hewed to the "radical" Dahlem line were not necessarily opponents of National Socialism. Nonetheless, in the wake of Dahlem the more radical members of the Confessing Church found themselves in a precarious political position—particularly in the Prussian churches, where

German Christians held governing positions and a state church commissioner (August Jäger) had been appointed to oversee the churches and was watching closely for any sign of potential political opposition that might emerge from Confessing Church circles.[1]

In the immediate wake of the Dahlem synod, such opposition seemed possible. In March 1935, seven hundred Prussian pastors were arrested briefly after reading a Confessing Church pulpit proclamation that criticized Nazi racial ideology. The most explicit church condemnation of Nazi anti-Jewish policies came in May 1936 with the "Hitler memo," a statement written by the Confessing Church's provisional church government that openly criticized the regime's anti-Semitic policies. After the memo was sent to foreign journalists, those immediately involved were imprisoned, and Friedrich Weissler, a Jewish lawyer who had worked on the memo, was murdered.[2]

Yet these incidents did not lead to a more sustained and broad resistance against the state; instead, they alarmed clergy throughout the country and further polarized the different church factions. Those who had declared themselves "neutral" in the Church Struggle, including the leading Lutheran bishops, urged greater caution in the public sphere and the avoidance of open conflict with the Nazi state to avoid persecution; several of them viewed the outspoken Confessing Christians as extremists who were as much of a threat to church unity as the German Christians. Within the Confessing Church itself, there were increasingly sharp divisions between those who agreed with the "neutrals" and others who urged the church to speak out in political opposition against the regime, particularly in response to the growing persecution of the Jews. It is important to recall that at this stage even someone like Martin Niemöller—who was furious at the "neutral" bishops and considered himself part of the radical Dahlem group—nonetheless urged his Confessing colleagues to refrain from open political criticism of Nazism.[3] The Gestapo's own estimation, according to

[1.] Although Jäger was forced to resign in late 1934 following the uproar over the house arrest of Lutheran pastors, the state continued to pressure the churches through the Ministry for Church Affairs, headed by Hanns Kerrl. See Helmreich, *German Churches under Hitler*, 169–72 and 193–94.

[2.] One of those imprisoned was Werner Koch, a former Finkenwalde seminarian who was sent to Sachsenhausen for several months. This volume includes a note of solidarity sent to his fiancée (1/16) as well as a mention of him on the prayer list (1/21) and a telegram upon his release in December 1938 (1/39). See also Barnett, *For the Soul of the People*, 81–85, for descriptions of both incidents.

[3.] See Barnett, *For the Soul of the People*, 57. The entire chapter (pp. 47–74) deals with this period and the divisions within the Confessing Church.

a 1935 report, was that the church disputes were primarily internal and that even the Confessing Church was not opposed to the state—although the potential for such opposition remained because for Confessing Christians "the church [was] more important than the state."[4]

The push for political opposition and resistance against Nazism came only from isolated individuals, who found little support from the Confessing leadership.[5] In general, the Confessing Church between 1935 and 1939 remained focused on internal matters, particular the legalization issue for seminarians, which would become the focus of Bonhoeffer's own activism in early 1938 and is a dominant topic in this volume. A few of these issues, such as the loyalty oath controversy and the prayer liturgy controversy that followed the Sudeten crisis, touched on larger political issues.[6] But the Confessing Church remained largely quiescent about the growing persecution of the German Jews, including the November 1938 pogrom—and as readers of the present volume will discover, Bonhoeffer, too, not only remained largely silent about what was happening to the Jews but even warned his seminarians in early 1939 against subverting the state-required "Aryan certificate" process after seminarian Gerhard Vibrans suggested issuing such certificates to anyone who asked.[7] While Bonhoeffer showed considerable fervor and resolve when it came to the education of his seminarians and the related battles within the Confessing Church about legalization, he did not speak out during this period on any of the major political issues mentioned in the first paragraph, including the violent events of *Kristallnacht*. There is only a passing and oblique reference to it in his letter of November 20 to his seminarians: "In the last few days I have thought much about Ps. 74, Zech. 2:8, Rom. 9:4–5, and 11:11–15. That leads deeply into prayer."[8] Compared to Elisabeth Schmitz's letter to Helmut Gollwitzer urging the church to speak out[9] or the outspoken and courageous sermons preached by Julius

---

[4.] Ibid., 68.

[5.] One such individual whose history has only recently come to light is the laywoman Elisabeth Schmitz, who is now acknowledged as the author of the 1935 memorandum calling upon the Confessing Church to speak out on behalf of German Jews; she also urged the Confessing Church to speak out after *Kristallnacht*. See Gailus, *Elisabeth Schmitz und ihre Denkschrift gegen die Judenverfolgung*; her story is also the focus of a recent documentary film, *Elisabeth of Berlin*.

[6.] See Barnett, *For the Soul of the People*, 88–89 and 156–58.

[7.] See 1/59, esp. ed. note 3 and the reference to the related correspondence between Vibrans and Bonhoeffer in Andersen, *So ist es gewesen*.

[8.] See 1/36, p. 84, esp. ed. note 9.

[9.] The full text can be found in Gailus, *Elisabeth Schmitz*, 223–28.

von Jan and Otto Möricke[10] in Württemberg, Bonhoeffer's reaction was a remarkably passive one to an event that caused horrific suffering among Germany's Jews and sent shock waves through German society.

The reasons for this reaction may well include the Gestapo's increased pressure on the Confessing Church seminarians and its surveillance of Bonhoeffer, who was now under police restrictions on publishing, public speaking, and travel (see below). Yet like so much of the material included in these volumes, the details of Bonhoeffer's words and deeds throughout this period serve as a corrective to any easy assumptions that Bonhoeffer was always at the forefront of resistance throughout the 1930s or that he loudly protested against the Nazi measures during that period. In many ways, the period between 1935 and 1939 is almost like the calm between two storms, beginning at the conclusion of the early Church Struggle and Bonhoeffer's outspoken role in London and concluding with his entry into the resistance circles.

The portrait of Bonhoeffer that emerges from the present volume shows a man focused almost exclusively on the task of mentoring his seminarians and then, as war loomed, wrestling with decisions about his own personal future. Bonhoeffer had returned from London in April 1935 to direct Finkenwalde, one of the five newly founded Confessing Church seminaries in the Prussian churches. By offering a different path to theological examination and ordination that avoided the official (and largely German Christian–controlled) committees, these seminaries were the direct outcome of the divisions within the church after the Dahlem synod. Under the German Christian–led church consistories, the official church viewed these seminaries as "illegal" and refused to admit their seminarians to the subsequent theological examination and ordination process. From 1935 to 1939, more than five hundred seminarians chose to attend the Confessing seminaries. From the beginning it was clear to them that they were placing their careers, and perhaps much more, at risk. Having abandoned the official church procedure toward ordination, they could not count on receiving a regular salary, a pension, and other forms of job security; given the political pressures within the Prussian churches, they knew they would be under additional surveillance. Confessing parishes supported their "illegal" clergy with independent collections and the generosity of some patrons.

For those who nonetheless chose the "illegal" path to ministry, the result was a different understanding of ministry, vocation, and community—one that Bonhoeffer himself articulated in his books *Discipleship* (*DBWE* 4; writ-

---

[10.] See Barnett, *For the Soul of the People*, 142–43.

ten at Finkenwalde and published in 1937) and *Life Together* (*DBWE* 5; written in 1938). This period proved to be a remarkably fruitful and significant one in Bonhoeffer's brief life, one during which his two vocations—as pastor and as teacher—truly converged as he educated these young men for a ministry in an uncertain time.

At the end of August 1937, Heinrich Himmler, the head of the secret police, banned the Confessing seminaries, as well as related activities such as the taking up of church collections. The Gestapo closed Finkenwalde on September 28, and the first document in this volume—a report from Gestapo director Reinhard Heydrich to Minister of Church Affairs Hans Kerrl confirming the closure of Finkenwalde—sets the tone for this new period in the life of the Confessing Church and for Bonhoeffer's own career. In the weeks that followed, Gestapo surveillance of Confessing Church activities and its members increased. By November 1937, twenty-seven of Bonhoeffer's seminarians were in prison, and in January 1938 Bonhoeffer himself was banned from traveling to Berlin and the surrounding regions of Brandenburg. In February 1938, the trial of Martin Niemöller began, which would culminate with his imprisonment in Sachsenhausen and Dachau until 1945.

Theological Education Underground

Despite the closure of the Confessing Church seminaries, the training of illegal seminarians continued. From 1937 to 1939, sixty-seven seminarians completed their theological education with Bonhoeffer. Most of them were moved to Confessing parishes around the country, where their education continued in the form of apprenticeships to the pastors serving those churches. Two centers, in the districts of Köslin and Schlawe (at Groß-Schlönwitz, later called Sigurdshof), were founded in the Pomeranian countryside for "collective pastorates," where seminarians came together for brief meetings and seminars. With the support of the respective church district superintendents (Friedrich Onnasch and Eduard Block), Bonhoeffer was able to travel and teach in these centers. But most communications took the form of circular letters that included reports on the work of the seminarians, meditations, and Bible studies.

Although most of Bonhoeffer's theological lecture and teaching notes from this period have been lost, part 2 includes several Bible studies, particularly a series on key New Testament concepts (2/2), and several sermons and meditations that were distributed to his seminarians through the circular letters. Yet in this volume it is mostly the circular letters and correspondence that give a rare portrayal of "theological education underground," depicting the impact of this turbulent period on the lives of these seminarians—at the same time giving a highly personal portrait of Bonhoeffer as teacher, pastor, and mentor. The anxieties of his seminarians about their decisions and their futures are the theme of many of the letters.[11] The Confessing Church seemed to be falling apart, the threats on the churches growing, the regime tightening its hold on German society, and war was in the air. The circular letters include the names and numbers of those in prison and, after September 1, 1939, those who had died in the war. In their letters to Bonhoeffer, his seminarians wrote openly about depression, the struggles and pressures on them, and their worries about the future. Some were confident and tried to encourage Bonhoeffer; others were uncertain, torn, and anguished.

Bonhoeffer's commitment to them and his understanding of the challenges they faced are expressed in the second letter in this volume, a circular letter sent to the Finkenwalde seminarians in December 1937, where in the aftermath of the seminary closure he wrote: "Particularly now, the great task is to ensure that those among us who are isolated are not left alone."[12] Here, as throughout this period, Bonhoeffer emphasized the importance of the community members for one another—but the replies of his students illustrate his centrality as a mentor. "You are a spiritual father to me," wrote one of them.[13] Another wrote, "It was so urgent for me to write this letter to you; perhaps you will gather from this that your work in Finkenwalde has not been for nothing. I could imagine that because of the events in Pomerania your spirits are low. If it would be possible for you to write me, I should be so very grateful. I have to struggle so much with myself; that is the hardest thing."[14] Another student described the spirit of Finkenwalde:

> Instead of coming into the stuffy air of theological bigotry, I entered a world that united many things that I love and need: accurate theological work on the common ground of fellowship, in which one's own inabilities were never noticed in a hurtful fashion, but rather which turned work into pleasure; true fellowship under the Word that united all "without respect to person"—and nonetheless with open-mindedness and love for everything that makes even this fallen creation still worthy of love: music, literature, sports, and the beauty of the earth; a generous style of life that favorably combined the culture

---

[11.] See, for example, 1/50, 1/60, and 1/66.

[12.] 1/2, p. 21.

[13.] 1/46, p. 96.

[14.] 1/60, p. 121.

> of old homes with the uninhibited forms of a community of young men—last, not least, a man in charge whom one can indeed admire without reservation.[15]

Such letters testify to the close bond that had developed between Bonhoeffer and his students during this period—which made the controversy over legalization and the defection of some of his seminarians all the more bitter.[16] After the Confessing Church opened its illegal seminaries in 1935, the official church consistories offered a "legalization" process to the illegal seminarians, which cleared the path for formal ordination and ministry in the official church. Legalization, however, entailed taking the theological examinations from church committees that were dominated by German Christians—in effect, abandoning the Confessing Church. To Bonhoeffer, this was a betrayal of everything the Confessing Church had fought for—so much so that it was on this point he made his famous statement, "Whoever breaks from the Confessing Church separates himself from salvation."[17] Yet especially after the Gestapo closed the Confessing seminaries in autumn 1937, the temptations for the young "illegals" were understandable, particularly for those who were married and had started families. The Confessing path was becoming riskier and more uncertain. *DBWE* 15 documents Bonhoeffer's dogged and eloquent attempts to keep his seminarians on the Confessing side, beginning with 1/7, a lengthy circular letter to the seminarians in Pomerania that includes a point-by-point rebuttal of the arguments for legalization.[18] But the volume also includes letters from students who disagree with his position, showing how deep the divisions were even within the close community of Bonhoeffer's seminarians.[19]

In 1938 the legalization controversy overlapped with another hot issue: the swearing of a loyalty oath to Hitler. In the spring of 1938, with nationalistic fervor running high after the Austrian *Anschluß*, the Prussian church

---

[15.] 1/66, p. 128.

[16.] For a general description of the controversy, including statements from some Finkenwalde seminarians who decided to break with Bonhoeffer, see Barnett, *For the Soul of the People*, 94–98.

[17.] Bonhoeffer said this in his 1936 lecture on church fellowship (*DBW* 14, 2/19, p. 676): "Whoever consciously parts with the Confessing Church in Germany parts from salvation." See also *DBW* 14, 1/41, and pp. 992–94, as well as *DB-ER*, 607–20. See also Bonhoeffer's lecture of October 26, 1938, in this volume, "Our Path according to the Testimony of Scripture" (2/5), which is a theological argument against legalization.

[18.] The issue is a running theme in the circular letters sent to the seminarians, including 1/21, 1/24, and 1/36.

[19.] Cf. 1/59, 1/74, 1/76, and 1/163.

authorities ordered all clergy to take the following oath on the occasion of Hitler's birthday: "I will be loyal and obedient to the Führer of the German Reich and nation, Adolf Hitler." There was an immediate uproar within the Confessing Church that just as quickly died down, as church leaders fretted about the possible repercussions of refusal. The Confessing Church leadership vacillated for several weeks, first suggesting that clergy take it and then advising them not to; by summer, a number of clergy had taken the oath—only to be humiliated after Hitler deputy Martin Bormann declared it an "internal church matter" not required by the state.[20]

Bonhoeffer wrote his brother Karl-Friedrich in January 1939:

> It has been at times very depressing in the last few weeks, when one must see how many people are seeking quiet and security at all costs and using all kinds of pretexts and reasons. . . . It is entirely certain to me that for the church it all depends upon whether we now hold on, even with great sacrifices. The greatest sacrifices are now small compared to what we would lose by wrongly giving in. I wouldn't know anything worth a full commitment today if not this. It matters not how many there are but rather only that there are still some who are steadfast.[21]

Leaving Germany in the Face of Impending War

By early 1939, when Bonhoeffer wrote those words, it was clear that Germany was actively preparing for another war. On January 23, 1939 (1/56), his mother wrote him that men born in his birth year were being called to register for the military. (Bonhoeffer received his own summons in May 1939.) Bonhoeffer's focus turned increasingly to his own personal future. In March, shortly after the conclusion of the winter session for his seminarians, he took a short trip to London and met there with his old ecumenical friends George Bell, Willem Visser 't Hooft, and Reinhold Niebuhr, as well as with his brother-in-law Gerhard Leibholz, who had emigrated to London with Bonhoeffer's sister and their children in 1938. The conversations there, particularly those with Niebuhr, led to an invitation to Bonhoeffer from Henry Smith Leiper at the Federal Council of Churches in New York.[22] Leiper began consulting with Henry Coffin at Union Theological Semi-

---

[20.] See Bonhoeffer's commentary on the oath in 1/22 and 1/24, as well as the letter of September 14, 1938, from Ruth von Kleist-Retzow to Eberhard Bethge (1/28).

[21.] 1/57, p. 115.

[22.] See 1/87 and 1/90.

nary, Paul Lehmann, and others to put together a combination of teaching and lecturing possibilities for Bonhoeffer. As the ecumenical liaison to the European ecumenical movement, Leiper hoped that Bonhoeffer would take a post at the Federal Council of Churches helping European refugees.

It was not the first time that Bonhoeffer, uncertain about his own course and dismayed and frustrated by events within his church, had decided to go abroad. His decision in the fall of 1933 to accept a pastoral call to the German-speaking London congregations had also come at the end of a period of great turmoil within his church. Yet in 1939 he was torn from the beginning about the decision to go abroad, and during the few weeks he was in New York, he wrestled constantly with whether to stay or return to Germany.

The main difference between his circumstances then and his 1933 decision to go to London was what he had left behind: his seminarians and his ministry to them. The period of training seminarians, from 1935 to 1939, was a time during which Bonhoeffer's many abilities came most coherently together, years in which he truly seems to have found his vocation. It is a period in which we see his closest friendships develop, particularly with Eberhard Bethge, and in these documents we find perhaps the most personal side of Bonhoeffer anywhere in the *DBWE* series, with the exception of his later letters to Maria von Wedemeyer and some of his prison letters.[23] Surely one of the most moving passages in this volume is Bonhoeffer's opening and concluding comments in his short directive of May 28, 1939, to his "successor" who will take up the task of directing collective pastorates: "To my successor: He will find . . . one of the most gratifying tasks in the CC. . . . Spend as much time as possible together with the brothers."[24]

The Days in New York

Bonhoeffer arrived in New York on June 2, 1939, and departed for Germany on July 8. As Eberhard Bethge later wrote in the biography, Bonhoeffer's brief sojourn in New York was marked by "his own experience of existential insecurity."[25] Bonhoeffer came to New York because of his uncertainty about what would happen to him in Germany and his fears of military conscription. From the moment he arrived, however, he was haunted by the sense that he had abandoned his students and fled to safety while they confronted a precarious future. His New York diary (1/137) is filled with

[23.] See *DBWE* 8 and Bismarck, *Love Letters from Cell 92.*

[24.] 1/98.2, p. 171.

[25.] *DB-ER*, 658.

passages of doubt and remorse. "Have I indeed evaded the place where God is?"[26] he asked himself on June 9. On June 15, he wrote: "Since yesterday evening my thoughts cannot get away from Germany. I would not have thought it possible that one at my age after so many years abroad can become so agonizingly homesick. . . . I would have liked to take the next ship. This inactivity, or rather activity spent on trivialities, is simply no longer bearable for us, thinking of the brothers and the precious time. The full force of self-reproaches about a wrong decision comes back up and is almost suffocating. I was filled with despair."[27] The days that followed were restless and unhappy, spent talking with friends, reading voraciously, writing, and searching Scripture for signs that might help his decision. On June 20, he finally made the decision to return to Germany, but he continued to wrestle with the forces pulling him in both directions. His New York colleagues at Union and the Federal Council of Churches were disappointed and uncomprehending. On June 21, he wrote:

> Regarding my decision, the thoughts naturally continue. One might, of course, have justified it entirely differently: the fact is, one is here (perhaps the very misunderstanding was a guidance?); one is told that when I was announced it was as if prayers had been heard; they particularly want to have me; they don't understand why I am turning this down; it is upsetting all plans for the future; I have no news from home; perhaps everything is going just as well without me etc. Or one could ask: did I simply act out of yearning for Germany and the work there? And is this lingering homesickness, which is almost incomprehensible to me and till now remains almost completely unfamiliar, an accompanying sign from above, which should make the refusal easier? Or is it not irresponsible in light of so many other people, simply to say no to one's own future and that of many others? Will I regret it? I may not do so, that is for certain.[28]

His closest American friends, particularly Paul Lehmann, were dismayed by his decision to return. Lehmann traveled all the way from Illinois to New York just to see him before his return to Germany; they met on July 7, the day before Bonhoeffer was to sail back. Yet by the time they met, Bonhoeffer had become clear. As he explained to Lehmann on June 30, 1939

[26.] P. 218.
[27.] P. 222.
[28.] P. 228.

(1/128): "The political situation is dreadful, and I must be with my brothers when things become serious. We will then often think of one another and be with one another in prayer, and we will leave it to God as to whether and when he will lead us back together again in a way we can see. In such 'final' times everyone should be found at the place where he belongs. May God grant us that we stand firm there."[29]

After Bonhoeffer's departure, the Calvin scholar John McNeill moved into the room at Union where Bonhoeffer had stayed: "He was surprised by the amount of illegible sheets of paper left by his unknown predecessor, and at the quantities of cigarettes he had smoked. . . . Only later did he realize who had lived there before him and had made the most difficult of all his decisions in that room."[30]

Despite the emotional turmoil of the New York weeks, Bonhoeffer also immersed himself in the study of U.S. church life, and his readings and reflections led him to write a remarkable essay, "Protestantism without Reformation," after his return to Europe. This volume includes the first publication of his reading notes for that essay (1/137a) as well as a new complete translation of the essay. Bonhoeffer's personal reflections enter into this essay as well. During his studies in New York (*DBWE* 10) in 1930–31, he had been quite critical of American theology, preaching, and church life. But by 1939, the course of the Church Struggle had left him profoundly disappointed in the failures of German church leadership, even in the Confessing Church, and his writings in the summer of 1939 show new insights and sometimes even appreciation for the American church differences. In his June 13, 1939, diary entry, Bonhoeffer noted his earlier differences with Henry Van Dusen, commenting on the changes he saw in American theology: "He was a poor and self-righteous theologian of the American mold. Here for the first time I realize graphically the great change in American theology in the last eight years. The cause for which we were engaged in 1930, apparently utterly hopelessly, has come to prevail in the course of the years."[31] But had American theology really changed? Or had Bonhoeffer's own experiences with his church in Germany given him a new perspective on the relative merits of the U.S. churches and the failures of those in Germany?

This particularly emerges in "Protestantism without Reformation" in his reflections on the U.S. churches as the historical product of religious

[29.] P. 209.

[30.] *DB-ER*, 655.

[31.] P. 221.

refugees, for Bonhoeffer had arrived in New York well aware that he might indeed become a refugee. Yet his appreciation for the resulting tolerance and compassion of U.S. Christianity was ambivalent, and his reflections here read quite personally. He wrote that in fleeing, the refugee had abandoned the fight for the truth back home, and his words about this may well have been an admonition to himself that he needed to return to Germany: "For the Christian refugee, the renunciation of the fight to the end for the truth remains a most troubling and lifelong issue. Only the deep sincerity and unlimited scope of compassion and the right to asylum in his country of refuge can be convincing in Christian terms. His yearning to decide for the truth against its distortion remains unfulfilled and must remain so."[32]

Bonhoeffer was changing his mind about many things in the United States, and his reading notes (1/137a) refer almost entirely to the series in *The Christian Century* titled "How My Mind Has Changed in This Decade."[33] Appearing for the first time in 1929, this series invited prominent theologians, church leaders, and other leaders in the religious world to comment on how the decade that had passed had influenced their own theology. The 1939 series included thirty-four essays by a wide range of authors, including James Luther Adams, Karl Barth (Barth's two-part contribution appeared on September 13 and 20, 1939—too late for Bonhoeffer to have read it), Georgia Harkness (the only woman), and the prominent pacifist A. J. Muste.

In his reading notes Bonhoeffer cites eight essays from the 1939 series: the essays by Edward Ames, Walter Horton, E. Stanley Jones, Edwin Lewis, Reinhold Niebuhr, Willard Sperry, George C. Stewart, and Henry Wieman. At the conclusion there are also references to works by George Herbert Betts, Henry Sloane Coffin, Josiah Strong, and Thomas Huxley. It is unclear whether Bonhoeffer read other essays in the series (it is interesting that he doesn't comment on Muste's antiwar essay, "The True International," which appeared in the May 24 issue), but the common themes addressed in these eight essays include the tension between liberalism and orthodoxy, the theological and philosophical movements that were shaping the U.S. church scene, and the role of the church in the world. It would seem, then, that Bonhoeffer had his topic—an examination of the differences between

[32.] 2/6, p. 448.

[33.] Edited by a Disciples of Christ clergyman, Charles Clayton Morrison, *The Christian Century* was established in 1900 (it actually emerged from a previous weekly titled *The Christian Oracle*) as a nondenominational weekly paper. The following commentary on this essay and many of the editorial notes were first published in the *Dietrich Bonhoeffer Jahrbuch* 4:17–20.

the churches of the Reformation in Europe and the U.S. churches that had not undergone a Reformation—clearly in mind and selected his readings accordingly.

Bonhoeffer concluded "Protestantism without Reformation" with the sentence: "The decisive task today is the conversation between the Protestantism without Reformation and the churches of the Reformation."[34] The reading notes reveal Bonhoeffer's brief but intensive attempt, in the summer of 1939, to carry on that conversation.

The Return to Germany and the Beginning of the War

Given the intensity of the final years of the Church Struggle and his days in New York, the months after his return seem almost anticlimactic. The crucial decision had been made, but what followed remained a transitional period. Bonhoeffer returned to his students and the collective pastorates, but with the onset of the war, that life changed completely. The first circular letter following the outbreak (1/160) included the announcement of the first death of one of his seminarians, Theodor Maaß. More than eighty of Bonhoeffer's seminarians—over half of those who had studied with him—would die as soldiers in the war.

His letters to them, particularly to the families of those who were killed, were strictly pastoral,[35] yet the circular letters in these early years of the war are striking in their careful distinction between God's will and the desires and deeds of human beings. The first one (1/160), dated September 20, 1939, shows his attempt to ponder the significance of the war:

> We are preachers of justification through grace alone. What [does] this mean today? Very simply it means that we no longer equate human ways and goals with divine ways and goals. God is beyond all human plans and deeds. Everything must be judged by God. . . . I do not know whether this time we will experience the outbreak of the theodicy question in as agonizing a fashion as in the previous war. It almost seems to me as though something here has changed. Christians today may know more of the biblical judgment on the world and history; thus they will perhaps be confirmed in their faith by the present events rather than afflicted. . . . Nonetheless under the force of these events the question will not be completely absent, and we will

[34.] 2/6, p. 462.

[35.] See, for example, 1/164; there are also several such letters in *DBWE* 16.

> like the author of Ps. 42 still often have to hear: "Where is your God?" [Ps. 42:3]. Is it true, that God is silent? It is only true for those whose God is the God of their own ideals and thoughts.[36]

The work of the collective pastorates would continue until they were finally closed by the Gestapo in March 1940; thereafter (during the period covered by *DBWE* 16), Bonhoeffer and Bethge traveled to visit the remaining seminarians until the summer of 1940. During these early war months, Bonhoeffer continued to seek alternatives to military service, including applying to the chaplaincy. The issue was finally resolved with the help of his brother-in-law Hans von Dohnanyi, who obtained a special classification for Bonhoeffer through which he was assigned to the Abwehr military intelligence office. His assignment there—in reality his move into the German resistance—began in October 1940.

In the clarity of that step, it is easy to lose sight of the aspects of Bonhoeffer we find in the pages of this volume, particularly his uncertainty as he confronted the momentous decisions about his future. In his New York diary entry of June 20, 1939, Bonhoeffer himself noted: "It is strange that in all my decisions I am never completely clear about my motives. Is that a sign of lack of clarity, inner dishonesty, or is it a sign that we are led beyond that which we can discern, or is it both?"[37] Yet the lack of clarity was gone by the time he wrote Eberhard Bethge from his prison cell on December 22, 1943: "You should know, by the way, that not for a single moment have I regretted my return in 1939, nor anything of what has then followed. That took place in full clarity and with the best conscience."[38] He repeated this in another letter, adding that he felt his life "had gone in a straight line, uninterrupted, at least with regard to how I've led it."[39]

This Volume

The general editor's introduction to the *DBWE* series at the beginning of this volume gives a history and overview of this series and general editorial policies. This volume is divided into three sections, each organized chronologically: Letters and Documents, Diary (part 1); Exercises, Lectures, and Essays (part 2); and Sermons and Meditations (part 3). As a complete translation of the German *DBW* volume 15, it includes the contents of that volume, the edi-

[36.] P. 275.
[37.] P. 227.
[38.] *DBWE* 8:236.
[39.] Letter of April 11, 1944, to Eberhard Bethge (*DBWE* 8:352).

torial notes, a translation of the afterword by German editor, Dirk Schulz, as well as the appendices (including a chronology for the period and a list of Bonhoeffer's seminarians during this time), the bibliography, and a biographical index of all persons mentioned in the text and the notes. The volume, however, does not reproduce all documents from this period in Bonhoeffer's literary estate; the unpublished material is listed in appendix 3.

DBWE 15 also includes several new documents that were discovered after the publication of *DBW* 15. Most of these are letters (23a; 32a; 113a; 129a; 142a); the two other new documents are the reading notes attached to the New York diary (137a) and recently discovered student notes of Bonhoeffer's lectures on pastoral counseling (2/1a).

Whenever citations document other volumes in this series, the reference is to the English translation (*DBWE*) or to the German edition (*DBW*). For other bibliographical citations in the notes, English editions are cited when available.

Throughout *DBW* the use of vertical lines in text (|) indicates either a new page or new line in Bonhoeffer's handwritten notes. While the usual *DBWE* practice is to delete those lines, we have in some instances retained them here in the biblical studies in part 2/1–3, for improved readability.

The *DBWE* series has been blessed with a team of skillful translators, each of whom brings particular expertise to his or her work. Several translators worked on this volume. As he has done for most of the *DBWE* volumes, Douglas W. Stott translated the German editor's afterword and chronology. I translated the letters. Peter Frick, the series expert on Greek and Hebrew, translated the theological and biblical studies in part 2. Claudia Bergmann and Scott Moore brought their unique pastoral gifts and understanding of the ministry to the translation of the meditations and sermons in part 3. In agreement with the German *DBW* editorial team, each of these volumes has a German reader who reviews the translation and makes suggestions. For this volume the reader was Ilse Tödt, who in addition to remarkable language skills has a comprehensive knowledge of the German *DBW* series. I am indebted to her not only for her careful review of the translation but for providing numerous cross-references to related passages elsewhere in the series. My German *DBW* colleagues Christiane Tietz and Hans Pfeifer were generous with their time and suggestions for particularly difficult passages. The German editor of this volume, Dirk Schulz, was extremely gracious in all correspondence.

Special thanks are also due to Kenneth Woodrow Henke, reference archivist at Princeton Theological Seminary, and Ruth Tonkiss Cameron, archivist at Burke Library at Union Theological Seminary, for their help with queries. As always, Clifford Green and Barbara Wojhoski, my colleagues on the *DBWE* team, have been immensely helpful at each step of the way. The *DBWE* series continues to owe gratitude to the publishing and production teams at Augsburg Fortress Publishers and at Trio Bookworks for their fine work in bringing these volumes to print. During the work on this volume, two of our key partners at Fortress Press left to take positions elsewhere: production manager Tim Larson and editor in chief Michael West. I would be remiss if I did not express our deep appreciation for the expertise, dedication, and work of both, particularly for Michael West, who worked closely with the *DBWE* team over the years and has been a wonderful colleague and partner in this endeavor. His role has been capably assumed by Will Bergkamp, publisher and managing director of Fortress Press.

Finally, I would like to express gratitude to the German Lutheran Church of Washington, D.C., whose congregation made an early financial contribution to the work of this particular volume. It is fitting that this congregation—a German *Auslandsgemeinde*, just like the ones Bonhoeffer served in London—has supported the work of *DBWE* 15, since among other things it tells the story of how, at a crucial turning point in his life, Bonhoeffer came once more to the United States and discovered new ways in which the church heritage of Germany and of this country enriched each other.

Victoria J. Barnett
April 2011

PART 1
Letters and Documents, Diary

1. From the Office of the Gestapo, Berlin, to Reich Church Minister Hanns Kerrl[1] 13

Berlin, November 30, 1937

To the Reich and Prussian Minister for Church Affairs, Berlin W 8, Leipziger Strasse 3

Re: Preachers' seminary in Finkenwalde

Dossier: none

In accordance with the decree of August 29, 1937, from the SS Reichführer and head of the German Police[2]–S–PP (II B) 4431/37—the preachers' seminary in Finkenwalde, under the leadership of Director of Studies *D. Bonhoeffer* has been closed.[3] Decisive for my decision was the fact that the entire teaching staff of the seminary[4] belonged to the confessional front and the purpose of this teaching institution clearly was to educate the vicars in the spirit of the confessional front and to equip them with the tools to complete the second theological exam before the examination offices of the confessional front.

In order to prevent the influence of the Confessing Church on theological education, I find it necessary that above all the preachers' seminaries that are under the direction of the confessional front and guided by its spirit should be closed.

May I request notification as to whether you consent to my position on this matter and, in particular, support the closing of the Finkenwalde preachers' seminary.

[1.] BA Potsdam, file 51.01, vol. 22522; typewritten with handwritten signature and stamp: "German Secret State Police, Office of the Gestapo"; return address "Berlin SW 11, Prince-Albrecht-Strasse 8"; stamped with date received: "Reich Minister Kerrl Berlin, Central Office, received: December 3, 1937"; previously unpublished.

[2.] Heinrich Himmler.

[3.] This announces the closing of the Finkenwalde preachers' seminary on September 28, 1937, based on the Himmler Decree of August 29, 1937 (see Beckmann, *Kirchliches Jahrbuch 1933–1944*, 205–6); see *DB-ER*, 584, and *DBW* 14:298–99. [After the October 1934 Dahlem synod, the Confessing Church established its own seminaries (Finkenwalde was one of five) and examination committees for candidates for the ministry, largely because most of the German theological faculties and regional church theological examination committees were under the leadership of the German Christians. These new preachers' seminaries were considered "illegal" by the official church authorities. In August 1937, the Himmler Decree banned most activities of the Confessing Church, thereby making Finkenwalde and the four other preachers' seminaries illegal under state law.—VB]

[4.] The other teacher besides Bonhoeffer was inspector of studies Wilhelm Rott.

I refer to the written notification of November 11, 1937—B.S. 18.36—of your decision regarding the preachers' seminary in Elberfeld.[5]

I would appreciate rapid enforcement.

Signed: Heydrich[6]
Notarized: [illegible signature]
Chancellery staff member

14 **2. To the Finkenwalde Brothers**[1]

December 20, 1937

Dear Brothers,

In these days my thoughts go out especially to you all. At the very least, a Christmas letter should be the sign of our fellowship. It will reach you amid the fullness and joy of your work. Most of you are in parish work, and it is a great joy to me that letters from the various regions of our church in which you work have continued to reach us. Others are in the final phase of tranquil scholarly work, which they undoubtedly will relish to the utmost. Four brothers are in prison.[2] We remember them daily.

The balance sheet for this year is rather clear and unambiguous. Twenty-seven from your circle have been in prison; for some it lasted several months. Some are still detained at present and have spent the entire Advent in prison.[3] Among the others there won't be a single person who has not experienced the impact, in his work and his personal life, of the increas-

---

[5.] The police also closed the Confessing Church preachers' seminary in Wuppertal-Elberfeld on the basis of the Himmler Decree (*DB-ER*, 589).

[6.] Reinhard Heydrich.

[1.] *NL*, A 48,3 (2); mimeographed with handwritten signature; no address is given, but probably written in Groß-Schlönwitz. Previously published in *GS* 2:524–30; cf. also *PAM* 2:81–88. After Reich propaganda minister Joseph Goebbels declared that all newsletters and mimeographed materials fell under the [1933—VB] editorial laws, Bonhoeffer's circular letters to the former Finkenwalde seminarians had to be labeled as "personal letters" and personally signed by Bonhoeffer (cf. *DB-ER*, 593) to avoid censorship. The letter exhibits a fair number of minor spelling and other errors, which were corrected in *DBW* 15 without being noted in each case.

[2.] [It is unclear which four students Bonhoeffer meant; as the following passage makes clear, twenty-seven seminarians who had studied under him in Finkenwalde had been arrested since the Himmler Decree, including Fritz Onnasch, Erich Klapproth, and Wilhelm Rott.—VB]

[3.] Regarding the wave of arrests by state authorities that affected the Confessing Church during 1937, see *DB-ER*, 577–86, and Niesel, *Kirche unter dem Wort*, 137–59.

ingly impatient attacks of the anti-Christian forces.[4] Now, even the place where we could gather for quiet work and brotherly help and reinforcement 15
has been taken from us.[5] This has made it more difficult to maintain our community, and some work can no longer be done. Perhaps this should teach us to ground our community even more strongly by listening together to the Word and by prayer. This is a time of testing for us all. Particularly now, the great task is to ensure that those among us who are isolated are not left alone. More than ever, the responsibility for this falls upon each of you. Please don't neglect it. We have said farewell to Finkenwalde in great thankfulness for everything that God gave us in the two and a half years of seminar work, and we are prepared to fulfill the new tasks we face. What we have learned will stay with us; what was ineffectual will fall aside. And already today we can say that the new paths along which we are being led will also give us reason for deep gratitude. Pray that the service to our young brothers will be done properly; lend a hand wherever you can.

I would have liked to give each of you a copy of my book[6] for Christmas. When it was published I often dedicated it in spirit to you all. I did not do this on the title page, because I did not want to claim you for my thinking and theology. Our fellowship is grounded in something else. The thought of giving the book to each of you for Christmas unfortunately had to be dropped due to finances. Anyway, you know what is in the book.

What we now want to say to one another on the occasion of Christmas and the end of the year I will attempt to say for us all, following the Daily Text[7] for the last week of the year:

Christmas Eve: Ps. 41:5 [4] "O Lord, be gracious to me; heal me, for I have sinned against you." This is a text of confession. The manger of the son of God who became flesh is the proper place for our confession. The 16

[4.] After the resignation of the Reich Church Committee on February 12, 1937, the radical anti-Christian forces in the state and the party around Joseph Goebbels, Alfred Rosenberg, and Martin Bormann intensified their ideological and administrative pressure on the churches, under the slogan of "deconfessionalization of public life." Cf. Scholder, "Politics and Church Politics," in *Requiem for Hitler*, 155.

[5.] See 1/1. During the two months between the closing of Finkenwalde and the beginning of the collective pastorates in Köslin and Groß-Schlönwitz on December 5, 1937, Bonhoeffer and Eberhard Bethge lived with Bonhoeffer's parents in Berlin (see E. Bethge, "Marienburger Alle 43," in *Friendship and Resistance*, 73). In October they left Berlin for a vacation trip to southern Germany (see Bethge's letter of October 26, 1937, to their friends, in Andersen et al., *So ist es gewesen*, 316–18).

[6.] Bonhoeffer's book *Discipleship* (*DBWE* 4) had appeared in November 1937.

[7.] These were the daily devotions (*Losungen*) published by the Moravian (Herrnhut) brotherhood.

one who bore our flesh and blood knows our heart. We are all wounded and torn by our manifold sin.

Where else should we seek grace for all disloyalty, all lack of faith, all failure, but in God's lowliness in the manger? Where else would we seek salvation for our souls, for our lives, but in the one who has appeared for our salvation? Despite all the work and unrest, may no one enter the Christmas season without seeking time to make his confession to our Lord Jesus. So will he make us partake of both his humility and his innocence. Whoever is alone and must do without the grace of brotherly fellowship and reinforcement, may God reveal to him all the more gloriously what true fellowship is. Wherever we may be, we speak in one spirit, as we did often at the same table of the Lord's Supper: Heal my soul, for I have sinned against you. Thus on Christmas Eve we will become grateful anew for the great mercy of God, our savior.[8]

Christmas day: Mal. 3:1 "See, I am sending my messenger to prepare the way before me, and the Lord whom you seek will soon[9] come to his temple. The messenger of the covenant in whom you delight—indeed, he is coming." The fact that this Advent text encounters us today teaches us that even the fulfillment of all promise and all proper expectation has only begun. Even the time of fulfillment is a long time of waiting. Thank God for this—so we say, regarding our sin. May this waiting soon end, and the time be shortened—so we pray, regarding the cross that burdens Christendom throughout the world. May the work of the messenger, who is coming to prepare us to stand before Christ, be done soon. May Christ come to his temple, to his church in the hour when it is ready and awaits him as the adorned bride awaits her bridegroom.[10] May the divine "soon" be fulfilled at the hour of mercy.

17 Second day of Christmas: Ps. 104:13 and 14 "From your lofty abode you water the mountains; the earth is satisfied with the fruit of your work. You cause the grass to grow for the cattle, and plants for people to use." God, who has given us the savior, is also willing to provide for our bodily life, as long as we are on this earth. Indeed, it is his earth. It must serve his purposes. The father will give his dear children in Jesus Christ what they need.[11] Whoever has placed belief in Christ must not worry about the

[8.] Regarding Bonhoeffer's understanding and practice of confession, see the section on confession in the 1936 Finkenwalde lectures on pastoral care (*DBW* 14:589–91), the 1936/37 Finkenwalde session on confession (*DBW* 14:749–55), and *DBWE* 5:108–18); cf. also *DB-ER*, 465–66.

[9.] [NRSV here reads "suddenly."—VB]

[10.] Cf. Rev. 21:2.

[11.] Cf. Matt. 6:8.

coming day.[12] In the middle of the cold winter, we are to see God's earth already full of fruits, grass, and seed. This should not be too difficult for us, should it, since we saw the eternal light enter the deep night, since we know of the blossom that in the middle of the winter night bloomed? "I know a rose-tree springing." Through God's power and love the heavenly spring has already dawned—"Amid the cold of winter, when half-spent was the night."[13]

December 27, 1937: Ezek. 16:6 "I passed by you, and saw you flailing about in your blood. As you lay in your blood, I said to you, 'Live!'" Have we truly understood the greatness of the miracle that happened to us? Resurrection of the dead has occurred. We lay in our blood, struck and cast down by our own sin. We could not raise ourselves again. Then God had mercy and spoke in the authority of his love: Live! And we stood up, held and strengthened through God's mercy. Live!—God has begun a new life in us; he commands us now really to live this life, the life of his grace and help. Let us not disobey this command of God. God wants not dead Christians but Christians who live to their Lord.[14] If we do not hear this Word, Christmas has passed us by.

December 28, 1937: Zech. 2:8 "For thus said the Lord of hosts . . . : Truly, one who touches you touches the apple of my eye." Just as the innocent children of Bethlehem, whom the church remembers today,[15] were the
first who had to give their lives for Jesus's sake, so in all ages the church- 18
community of Jesus has suffered persecution and death for the sake of its Lord. But the same Lord for whose sake we suffer disgrace, hatred, and imprisonment has promised to protect us like the apple of his eye. It is not we who protect him through our sacrifice; it is he who protects us. He stands up for us—this is the Christmas message. Whoever touches us for Christ's sake will be dealt with by our Lord himself. Nothing can befall us if we suffer injustice for Christ's sake. Thus we want to leave those who do us injustice in his hand alone—his hand of judgment and of mercy. This is the lesson of the murder of the children of Bethlehem, namely, that Christ is not in the hand of his enemies, but that the enemy is in the hand of God.

December 29, 1937: Ps. 25:10 "All the paths of the Lord are steadfast love and faithfulness, for those who keep his covenant and his decrees." Are

---

[12.] Cf. Matt. 6:25–34.

[13.] From the first stanza of the pre-Reformation Advent hymn, "I know a rose-tree springing" (*Es ist ein Reis [Ros] entsprungen*). [The English is taken from *The Hymnal of the Protestant Episcopal Church of the United States of America*, 17.—VB]

[14.] Cf. Rom. 14:8.

[15.] In the church calendar, December 28 is traditionally the Feast of the Holy Innocents (see Matt. 2:16–18).

you, who have experienced hardship in this year, able to speak today with all your heart that the paths of the Lord are pure goodness and truth? Did you know that God was good to you when he sent you misery and imprisonment? Has God made himself known to you as the true and faithful one when he took so much from you? No one who says No to God's promises and commandments is able to say Yes to his paths. Agreement with God's will occurs in daily submission to his word. Something may appear to us as minor disobedience, and yet it will take from our hearts the gratefulness and praise for God's paths. It is painful and difficult to walk under Christ's yoke when we do it against our will. It is easy and gentle,[16] when God at Christmas has overcome and won our hearts for it.

December 30, 1937: Ps. 20:5[17] "May we shout for joy over your help,[18] and in the name of our God set up our banners." In the past times of crisis for the church, we have received several offers of human help.[19] Yet they have only brought us into temptation, particularly when they were well intentioned. For how should even the best human intentions help the church in a struggle with the devil? We have celebrated Christmas. Jesus
19 is born. He is our help. He alone. Here is God's help for human beings in temptation and crisis. Do we think this help insufficient? Are we becoming impatient? Let us meet all temptations with the joyful confession: May we shout for joy over your help. We unfold our banner for the struggle. Upon it is inscribed: Jesus, the helper.

December 31, 1937, New Year's Eve: Ps. 71:18 "So even to old age and gray hairs, O God, do not forsake me, until I proclaim your might to all the generations to come." With astonishment we stand at the end of the year. For some time now we have grown accustomed to the fact that we cannot count on having long periods of time. We neither could nor should do so. Learning obedience on each new day is enough for us. But time moves on, and our text today speaks to us about growing old. Thus, despite everything, it

---

[16.] Cf. Matt. 11:30.

[17.] [In the German Bible this is verse 6.—VB]

[18.] [NRSV has "victory."—VB]

[19.] [Bonhoeffer is clearly referring here to the legalization procedure presented by official church leaders, which offered those trained at the illegal Confessing Church seminaries a "legal" route to ordination and ministry. Legalization, however, required that they take their theological and ordination examinations under the official church committees, which were dominated by German Christians. In the wake of the Himmler Decree and the arrests of many illegal pastors, this was even more tempting for Bonhoeffer's students. Bonhoeffer was bitterly opposed, and in fact this letter marks the beginning of a new, intense phase of his efforts to convince his students to withstand the temptation. See esp. *DB-ER*, 607–20, and Barnett, *For the Soul of the People*, 94–98.—VB]

is good to turn our eyes, for once, to the prospect that perhaps a long life still lies before us, that the day of judgment perhaps will not arrive tomorrow or the day after. "Houses and fields and vineyards shall again be bought in this land" (Jer. 32:15). So perhaps we will become gray during this time of struggle for the church, and new generations will bear new burdens on their shoulders. Therefore we pray to God, for whom a thousand years are as one day,[20] for the grace that he may let us, throughout the years, remain proclaimers of his might. Years and generations pass away, but God's word does not.[21] Indeed, we are merely one link in the chain. Yet the question, anxious and joyful, remains: which generation will live to see the day of judgment? Amen. Come, Lord Jesus![22]

The meditation texts for the coming weeks are[23]

December 26–January 1, 1938: John 1:1–18
January 2–January 8: Luke 2:21–40
January 9–January 15: Eccles. 50:24–26 or Ps. 1
January 16–January 22: Hag. 1
January 23–January 29: Hag. 2 20
January 30–February 5: Mal. 1
February 6–February 12: Mal. 2
February 13–February 19: Mal. 3

Eberhard's[24] address is Groß-Schlönwitz via Schlawe/East Pomerania. In the event of any changes, please also let us know your addresses. Albrecht Schönherr is pastor in Brüssow, at the estate of General Field Marshall von Mackensen.[25] We are currently seeing more of Brother Maechler.[26] Are the brothers in Berlin keeping up their monthly meetings?

[20.] Ps. 90:4.

[21.] Isa. 40:8.

[22.] Rev. 22:20.

[23.] Regarding the sense and significance of the daily practice of meditation that was observed in the seminary for the brothers' life together, with its elements of personal contemplation of Scripture, prayer, and intercession, see *DBWE* 5:85–91, and the 1936 "Introduction to Daily Meditation," *DBW* 14:945–50.

[24.] The reference is to Eberhard Bethge, who was inspector of studies for the collective pastorate in Groß-Schlönwitz after December 1937.

[25.] For an account of Schönherr's time as a pastor in Brüssow under the patronage of August von Mackensen, see Schönherr, . . . *Aber die Zeit war nicht verloren*, 115–27.

[26.] Since 1936 Winfried Maechler had been assistant pastor of the Confessing Church in Schlawe, under Superintendent Eduard Block; see Maechler, *Ein Christ in den Wirren des 20. Jahrhunderts*, 32–33.

God bless your work in the congregations, and may God fill you with joy. Heartfelt greetings to you and your households from all the brothers, Fritz[27] in prison, Eberhard from his work, and your ever-faithful

Dietrich Bonhoeffer

3. To Paula Bonhoeffer[1]

December 21, 1937

Dear Mama,

Many thanks for your letter[2] and the package for me to open on Christmas Eve! Unfortunately, I received the wrong delivery from Chr. Kaiser,[3] so I would like to ask you to send Franz[4] the book from Berlin. I am going to
21 send it to Karl-Friedrich[5] myself. Fritz O.[6] was released yesterday. That is a very great joy. Christmas otherwise would have been difficult indeed. Could you send me several white shirts for the holidays? I'm very sorry to trouble you even more. Here we're doing splendidly. From Iwand, unfortunately, we hear otherwise.[7] The good weather will surely hold until New

[27.] Friedrich (Fritz) Onnasch had been arrested during the state measures against the Confessing Church in November 1937, and spent four weeks in prison in Stettin. After December 1937 he became inspector of studies for the collective pastorate in Köslin.

[1.] *NL*, A 44,1 (6); handwritten postcard, postmarked Stolp. Partially reproduced in *GS* 6:433.

[2.] Letter not extant.

[3.] Chr. Kaiser Publishers in Munich, which published Bonhoeffer's book *Discipleship* in 1937.

[4.] Bonhoeffer's friend Franz Hildebrandt, who was considered "non-Aryan" under National Socialist law. In August 1937, he emigrated to England after three weeks' imprisonment for "collection misdemeanors" (he had repeatedly forwarded the collections from Confessing Church services not to the regional church consistory but to the Council of Brethren [the governing body for the Confessing Church—VB], defying a law forbidding this, "Law regarding the administration of wealth in the Protestant regional churches," passed on March 11, 1935. With this law the church authorities sought to destroy the Confessing Church's financial autonomy. For more information on this, see Kersting, *Kirchenordnung und Widerstand*, 242–49. Until the fall of 1938, Hildebrandt lived as a refugee in the parsonage of Julius Rieger in London-Sydenham.

[5.] Bonhoeffer's eldest brother, Karl-Friedrich.

[6.] Fritz Onnasch.

[7.] The Confessing Church preachers' seminary in Bloestau (East Prussia), led by Hans Joachim Iwand, had been closed by the police. Iwand provisionally continued to

Year's Day. Here, of course, some Christmas preparations are going on. We treated ourselves to real beeswax candles as a present for the entire group. Many greetings to Papa and you, dear Mama, from your grateful

Dietrich

4. Inscription in the Copy of *Discipleship* for Martin Niemöller[1]

To Pastor Martin Niemöller at Advent 1937
in brotherly thanks.
A book that he himself could have written better than
the author.

5. To Paula Bonhoeffer[1] 22

Dear Mama,

On your birthday I am thinking a great deal about you all.[2] I wish you a good new year. Once more I am traveling, and so only today am I getting around to this greeting. After New Year's, hopefully it will be quieter, so that I can write in more detail. Thank all of you very much for the lovely Christmas things! Here all is going well. Greetings to you from your grateful

Dietrich

---

train seminarians for three months in Jordan (Neumark). See H. J. Iwand, *Von der Gemeinschaft christlichen Lebens*, 3 and 17. Under the auspices of Superintendent Fritz Heuner, Iwand then attempted to found a new preachers' seminary in Dortmund. On December 18, 1937, Iwand, Heuner, and the candidates were arrested (see Iwand, *Theologie in der Zeit*, 118, and *DB-ER*, 589).

[1.] *NL*, A 45 (42); later typewritten copy; according to information received from Jan Niemöller, the original has been lost (letter to the German editor, October 22, 1994). The inscription gives no date or address, but the book was probably sent from Groß-Schlönwitz. Previously published in *GS* 2:307. Martin Niemöller had been arrested on July 1, 1937, by the Gestapo at his home in Berlin-Dahlem (see *DB-ER*, 654–57) and was in pretrial confinement in Berlin-Moabit prison until his trial began on February 7, 1938. Bonhoeffer's *Discipleship* reached him there.

[1.] *NL*, A 44,1 (7); handwritten postcard; no date or address given. It was probably sent en route from Köslin to Groß-Schlönwitz. Partially reproduced in *GS* 6:433–34.

[2.] Bonhoeffer's mother's birthday was December 30.

6. To Franz Hildebrandt[1]

January 3, 1938

Dear Franz,

Heartfelt thanks for your letter.[2] I was pleased in equal measure by the agreement with and critique of my book.[3] I am very willing to admit that Asmussen's commentary on Galatians[4] doesn't fit with my exegesis of Matt. 5:17f.[5] With Luther's commentary on Galatians,[6] though, things stand
23 *very* differently. Just don't end up establishing a law of humanity, you antinomist![7] I eagerly await your work and meet it by reciprocating your agreement with and critique of mine.[8] Now for the *third* attempt: Julius[9] should please obtain for me there (with Cromwell's[10] help): *The Way of Holiness*, by Father Benson (Oxford).[11] I need it for an exegesis of Psalm 119.[12] Many thanks for the effort. Gustav[13] is still in my debt. I'll pass that on to you and Julius!

Affectionate greetings to both of you from your
Dietrich

[1.] In the personal possession of Gottfried Rieger; handwritten postcard; stamped in Groß-Schlönwitz/Schlawe. Cf. *NL*, Anh. D 1,1 (2); cf. also *NL*, A 45 (43); a later typewritten copy, partially reproduced in *GS* 6:434. The postcard (to London) has been stamped: "Reichsparteitag [Reich Party Day—VB] commemorative postcard. Price 25 R[eich]p[ennies] including cultural donation" and portrays a parade of SA troops carrying swastika flags.

[2.] Letter not extant.

[3.] Bonhoeffer is referring to *Discipleship*.

[4.] Asmussen, *Theologisch-kirchliche Erwägungen zum Galaterbrief* (1935).

[5.] Cf. *DBWE* 4:115–20.

[6.] Martin Luther, *In epistolam sancti Pauli ad Galatas commentarius*, 1531/1535 (*WA* 40/1 and 40/2).

[7.] This is an allusion to the first and fundamental theological dispute between Bonhoeffer and Hildebrandt about Marcion and the relative importance of the Hebrew Bible for Christian proclamation and theology (see *DB-ER*, 138).

[8.] After 1937 Hildebrandt worked on a study, "The Gospel and Humanity," for which he received his doctorate from Cambridge in 1941; except for brief excerpts, it remained unpublished. In it he attempted a new evaluation of humanity, human rights, and pacifism on the foundation of Luther's distinction between law and gospel. He took natural law, reason, and freedom to be necessary components of a state order that would preserve community for the sake of the weakness of the flesh. See Hildebrandt, "Kirche und Recht," 502–3.

[9.] Julius Rieger.

[10.] Philipp Cromwell, a lawyer in London.

[11.] This is the title of a book that appeared in 1901, by R. M. Benson, who founded the Anglican community "Society of St. John the Evangelist" in Oxford in 1865. See Rieger, *Dietrich Bonhoeffer in London*, 29.

7. To the Young Brothers in Pomerania[1]

Dear Brother,

In recent weeks, I have received letters and personal messages that make it clear that our church and our young theologians, particularly in Pomera- 24
nia, are encountering an hour of severe temptation.[2] Because here it is no longer about one individual's crisis but rather about one and the same temptation that is threatening many, you will permit me, dear brother, to attempt an answer to all concerned. Nonetheless, this letter is meant for you very personally. It should address everything you have written or said to me.

We must go way back. We will agree that when we declared ourselves one with the cause of the Confessing Church, it was a step of the most certain faith and, because of that, a venture that was incomprehensible in human terms. There was a joy, a certainty of victory, a readiness for sacrifice that gave our entire personal and official life a new direction. I don't mean that there were not all kinds of secondary human considerations that played a role—who knows even his own heart?—but what made us so joyful and ready to fight and, perhaps, even prepared to suffer was one thing, namely, that we knew again that a life with Jesus Christ and his church is worth the whole effort. We believed that in the Confessing Church we not only had found the church of Jesus Christ but through God's great goodness had actually experienced it. A new life under God's joy-giving word began for individuals, for pastors and congregations. If only God's word was among us, then we no longer wanted to be afraid and worried about the future.

[12.] See 3/9.

[13.] Pastor Gustav Schönberger in London.

[1.] *NL*, A 56 (6); typewritten mimeograph with handwritten signature; no date or address given, probably sent from Groß-Schlönwitz, definitely around the end of January 1938. Previously published in *GS* 2:297–306. Bonhoeffer wrote this letter immediately before a convention of the Brotherhood of Young Theologians in Pomerania, in Stettin on January 24–25, 1938, that was to attempt to establish a common position of the "illegals" against the regional church consistory's offer to legalize them. See Ludwig, *Die "Illegalen" im Kirchenkampf*, and Klän, *An der Wegscheide*, 142–43. [After 1935 candidates for the ministry who studied and were ordained within the Confessing Church were considered "illegal" and denied jobs, salaries, and pensions by the official German Evangelical Church. After 1937 official church authorities offered "legalization" proceedings to these candidates; this meant a de facto repudiation of their examinations and ordinations by the Confessing Church.—VB]

[2.] For more on the course of the Church Struggle in Pomerania and its consequences for the illegal vicars of the Confessing Church, see *DB-ER*, 606–20, and Klän, *An der Wegscheide*.

With this word we were willing to pass through struggle, through suffering, through poverty, through sin, and through death to finally reach God's eternal kingdom. Young people and fathers of large families stood here side by side. What was it at the time that united and fortified us with such gladness? It was the one and ancient realization, given to us once more by God himself, that among us Jesus Christ wishes to build his church, which lives solely from the preaching of the pure, unadulterated gospel and by the grace of his sacraments, and which in its actions is obedient solely to him.[3] Christ wishes to hold fast to such a church; he wants to protect and lead such a church. Only such a church is permitted to be free of all fear. The confessional synods of Barmen and Dahlem bore witness to this and to nothing else.[4] Was this an illusion? Was it perhaps stated under the impression of external circumstances that appeared to favor a "realization" of this belief? No, it was the most certain faith, it was the biblical truth itself, that was then made known before the entire world. It was the witness to Christ that overcame hearts, created joy, and called to the obedient deed. Dear brother, are we not at least still in agreement that this was the case? Or do we want today to revile God's grace, which was so generously given to us?

So, then, the struggle for the true church of Christ erupted. Or do you possibly believe that the devil would take such trouble to annihilate a small band of idealists who were carried away? No, the storm arose because Christ was in the boat.[5] The struggle demanded sacrifice from the very beginning. Perhaps it has not always been clear to everyone how much personal sacrifice, how much sacrifice, too, on the part of the congregations was required for the members of the Councils of Brethren to fulfill their duty to the church. But it was a sacrifice joyfully given for the sake of the cause of Jesus Christ. Who was permitted to retreat as long as the call still came from Jesus to be the church, the church that serves him alone? Who was allowed to disengage himself, as long as *no one* had relieved him of the task of caring for the pure proclamation of the gospel and the building up of congregations in conformity with Scripture and the confessions of our church?

If we are still agreed on this, then let us ask ourselves, in all candor, what has happened between those beginnings and our present situation, or, as one might also say, what has happened between the church provinces in

[3.] Cf. Augsburg Confession, Article 7 (*Book of Concord,* 42).

[4.] The first confessional synod of the German Evangelical Church was held in Wuppertal-Barmen on May 29–31, 1934. The second confessional synod was held in Berlin-Dahlem on October 19–20, 1934. Cf. the texts of the synodal resolutions in Schmidt, *Bekenntnisse,* 2:91–98 and 157–62.

[5.] Cf. Matt. 8:23–27.

which even today they live and act and struggle on the very basis of these beginnings, and our church province? Why have voices in Pomerania com- 26
plained for months that our church lies paralyzed, as if in a spell, that an internal narrowness and stubbornness diverts us from fruitful work? How has it come about that brothers who were in the Confessing Church with full certainty say today that their gladness has been lost, that they no longer know why they could not do their work just as well under the consistory as under the Council of Brethren? And can we deny that the witness of our Pomeranian church recently has become ever weaker? That the word of the Confessing Church has to a great extent lost its faith-wakening and with that its discerning[6] power? That the true theological-ecclesiastical decisions grow more obscure behind the strategic considerations? And has all of this not had its effect upon our own preaching? We ask about the reason for all this.

I believe the answer is not as difficult as one would like it to be. The so-called paralysis in the Confessing Church, the lack of gladness, the weakness of the witness, all come from our very own disobedience. Let us think now not about the others but about ourselves and our work. What has become of the first, clear insights of the Confessing Church in our congregations? Have our congregations been truly and vividly interested in them? Is there a c[ongregation]-c[hurch]-council or a local Council of Brethren that stands in unshakable fellowship with the cause of the Confessing Church and with those of us who are confessional pastors? That carries us and helps us to take new paths in the parish? Or why do we not have it? Should the congregations alone, once again, be to blame for this? There are parish members who have the opposite opinion. Are the parishes too "immature"? As if a parish could be too immature to hear God's word and obediently act according to it, but for unchurchlike action they are "mature" enough! Who taught us to think of our congregations with such disdain? Who, then, made the cause of the Confessing Church into a matter of "maturity"? As if the maturity of a parish did not consist precisely of its plight before God! Where are the district Councils of Brethren, formed from the parish Councils of Brethren, which could help the district pastors bear their great responsibility? Where is the Pomeranian confessional synod, which could only genuinely emerge through the congrega- 27
tion, and which should have shown the way for the Pomeranian church? In other words: why did we in Pomerania not seriously implement the insights

[6.] [The German here is *scheiden* (literally, "to divide" or "to distinguish between"). —VB]

[Erkenntnisse] of the Dahlem synod?[7] And if we did not do this, did we ever take Barmen entirely seriously? Other, far more unchurched provinces fought the promising struggle for the church of the gospel, based upon clear ecclesiastical-theological decisions and, in all their suffering, rejoiced in this from their hearts. Why, so often, did we stand by? Why is the theological discussion among us so strangely quiet? In this hour it is truly not a question of one accusing the other, but rather that each person confesses that through disobedience we have often thoughtlessly scorned God's grace, which we received in the beginnings of the Confessing Church. Our word and our deed often broke apart. Now that we reap the fruits of this, however, we begin to blame one another; indeed, we grumble about the path that has been ruined by our own disobedience and thus no longer gives us gladness.

Let me try, once more, to say this differently: there is a Church Struggle as law and a Church Struggle as gospel. At present the Church Struggle, to a great extent, has become a law for us against which we rebel, an ominous, wrathful law that beats us down. No person can bear and fight the Church Struggle as law without perishing and utterly failing. Church Struggle as law means Church Struggle without gladness, without certainty, without full authority [Vollmacht]; it means Church Struggle without promise. How does this come about? It doesn't happen any differently than in personal life. The merciful word of God, from which we withdraw in disobedience, becomes a hard law for us. That which, done in obedience, is a gentle and light yoke, becomes an unbearable burden for the disobedient.[8] The more we became stubborn in disobedience against the merciful Word, the more difficult it becomes to turn around, the more willfully we rebel against God's claim. But just as there is only the one way in personal life, that of
28 turning around, of repentance under God's word, in which God again grants us the lost community, so it goes in the struggle of the church as well. We do not receive back the lost gift of a Church Struggle as gospel without repentance, that is, unless the Church Struggle itself becomes repentance for us. Even if the obedience of repentance may be harder today than it was

[7.] [The October 1934 Dahlem synod was torn by divisions between the more radical members of the Confessing Church and the more moderate leaders. The two most contentious resolutions passed at Dahlem were Article 3, which declared the Confessing Church to be the one true church in Germany, sharing no common confession with the German Christians; and the declaration of church *Notrecht*, or emergency law. Under *Notrecht*, the Confessing Church could establish its own governance structures, training, examinations of candidates for the ministry, etc.—VB]

[8.] Cf. Matt. 11:30.

previously when we failed to be obedient—only in this way does God wish to help us back to the right path.

Dear brother, if I speak in this way to you who are not yet firmly installed in ministry in the church, I know that perhaps you bear the smallest amount of guilt for all this. Indeed, you have been affected by some practices that a pastor in office could evade. But must not this very fact fill you with particular joy and gratitude, namely, the fact that the church expects you to walk the very clear path? That precisely you today have been given a responsibility that perhaps has never rested upon a young generation of theologians in our church? The Confessing Church in Pomerania must first come into being. Put in human terms, it will depend on you, too, whether it can emerge or not. Last week we were connected through our meditation text from Haggai 1.[9] There it is stated: "These people say the time has not yet come to rebuild the Lord's house. Then the word of the Lord came by the prophet Haggai, saying: Is it a time for you yourselves to live in your paneled houses, while this house lies in ruins?"[10] It cannot at all be my concern to "stand you back up," to talk you into something. But it does matter above all to reawaken in you, through God's word, courage, gladness, faith in Jesus Christ, who is and will remain with his Confessing Church, *whether you go along with it or not.* You should know that the faith that threatens to be extinguished in you still lives, as in the beginning, in many congregations and parsonages, that inside Pomerania and outside, at posts of forlorn hope, lonely brothers witness to this faith with the greatest gladness. The church of Jesus Christ that lives by his word alone and wants to be obedient in all things to him alone still lives, and will live, and calls you back out of temptation and tribulation. It calls you to repentance and warns you against the 29
disloyalty that must end in despair. It prays for you that your faith not waver.

But now, back once more to your own questions: you say that the situation today is different from that in the beginning; because of that we should act differently. I can think of only one change in the situation that could also change our action, namely, if the consistories, the EOK,[11] etc. were to relieve us of the responsibility for a church leadership in accordance with the confessions. Since, given the current makeup of church administrators, it is out of the question that this would ever happen, only those who throw sand

[9.] Cf. the list of meditation texts at the conclusion of Bonhoeffer's letter of December 12, 1937, letter to the Finkenwalde brothers, 1/2. Haggai 1 was proposed as the meditation text for the week of January 16–22, 1938.

[10.] Hag. 1:2–4.

[11.] [Evangelischer Oberkirchenrat, the governing council of the Old Prussian Union church.—VB]

in their own eyes can be in doubt. But since the situation looks more threatening from outside than before, as the nonchurch powers lay claim to the church, this can only give us more reason to close ranks even more strongly there where this intrusion [Einbruch] has not yet succeeded, namely, in the Confessing Church.

You say that the Confessing Church would surrender the possibility of finding an entry into the congregations, that is, the possibilities for proclaiming the gospel. Do you recall that the G[erman] C[hristians] made precisely the same argument and that evil fruit grew from that? Don't you see that by subordinating yourself to the consistory, you make yourself the henchman of the secular powers that intend to win the parishes not at all for the gospel but for a very different doctrine?

You say that, under the consistory, you would hold on only to the Scripture and confession. Do you recall all those who have already declared this before you? And given the case that this would be possible—which is not possible—do you forget that the church is greater than your parish? Do you forget your brothers and their parishes? Do you realize that with your step to the consistory, you give the struggle against the Confessing Church its most effective weapon? Is it clear to you that a Council of Brethren that would only practice a so-called spiritual leadership, as you wished, would be leading an illusory existence, which can be swept away in a moment? You yourself will be made responsible if the Confessing Church is crushed in this manner. Your step to the consistory is the strongest imaginable confirmation of the judgment of the anti-Christians against the Confessing Christians.

30 You complain about the Council of Brethren. Do so, if you must, to it directly as well! But please also ask yourself whether you joined the Confessing Church for the sake of a good or a miserable Council of Brethren. Ask yourself whether you would be willing to stand up for the cause of the Confessing Church even if there were no longer any Council of Brethren whatsoever, indeed, whether you are willing, isolated from any kind of church leadership or brotherly fellowship, to witness and to suffer for the Confessing Church wholly alone, before God and human beings? No, you do not simply have a choice between two church governments. You can't suddenly now reaffirm that from which you have separated yourself in faith because of some completely different reasons, without being at odds with yourself and your faith. God's word calls you to loyal participation in the Confessing Church under the leadership of the Council of Brethren, as weak as both may be.

You no longer hope for any success for the Confessing Church; you no longer see any way out. Indeed, who among us would see a way out? God alone sees it and will certainly show it to those who humbly wait for it. Perhaps we hoped once that the Confessing Church would achieve public recognition in Germany. But was this hope full of promise? Certainly not. Now we have learned to believe a church that follows its Lord under the cross.[12] That holds more promise. Finally, you say that you would be prepared for any personal and professional sacrifice if you only knew why they were necessary. Why, dear brother? Not for any humanly apparent reason, not for a flourishing church nor for a convincing church leadership, but simply because the path of the Confessing Church must be traveled, even through barren stretches of drought and desert, and because you are not meant to stay behind in the desert. That is, for the sake of the poor church, which will of course continue even without you under the leadership of its Lord, that is, for the sake of your faith and your certainty you should stay with the Confessing Church.

What should happen now? There are so many reasons, and theologians
can prove everything. Everything will depend on whether God will give his 31
witness anew into our hearts. Jesus Christ alone can break the spell. Yet we want to face several tasks clearly. We will not achieve a renewal of our Confessing Church unless we first intercede with God on its behalf in fervent prayer. An hour of prayer for our church and its leadership should unite us and cleanse and clarify our thoughts. God will then lead us again to the true path. But then we want to tackle what has been neglected. We want to struggle for full theological clarity about the insights of the Confessing Church. We are not willing to let go before we have reached firm ground. We tend to move from questions of truth to the order of the day all too easily. Yet how should a clear leadership for a parish or a church be possible without a clear theology? The false front lines in the Church Struggle arise whenever the question of truth is bypassed. Let us resume the discussion also with those who confront us with questions! But it should be a discussion in ultimate truth! The discipline in theological work, preaching, and catechism that pastors undergo in other regional churches is truly no dishonor to these churches and their pastors. Shouldn't such discipline be possible at least among the young brothers of our church, for mutual help and reinforcement? All this takes place only for better ministry to our congregations. What is finally at stake here is to prepare for the establishment of a Pomeranian confessional synod. For this we need local and district Councils of Brethren. And once we have come that far, only then will the inexhaustible field of work that is the Confessing Church's specific task

[12.] Cf. Bonhoeffer's interpretation of discipleship under the cross in *Discipleship* (*DBWE* 4), esp. 84–91 and 225–52.

begin: the ordering of church life with respect to the practice of baptism, the office of godparents, instruction, confirmation, confession and communion, visitation, etc. There are already church districts in the Confessing Church that tackle these questions seriously. But there is no authority except for the bodies of the Confessing Church that could do this work under the sole direction of the word of God. There is enough work. We must only tackle it at long last.

Before I close, one more word about the brochure by P. Schütz, *Warum ich noch ein Christ bin*.[13] This is a splendid attempt to review things again
32 and again, with new words and in great openness for the questions, from an outside perspective. Nonetheless, for some it has brought only tribulation [Anfechtung] instead of help. Why? Because ultimately it proceeds from an impossible premise. Schütz looks for the church in the attitude, in the countenance of the Christians. We, however, look for the church in God's word alone. Schütz's book has an incredibly debilitating effect, for it leaves human beings to themselves. But "it is a precious thing for the heart to *become firm*, which occurs through grace."[14] Our heart becomes firm solely by God's word and sacrament.

Let me hear from you again. Greetings from your stalwart

Dietrich Bonhoeffer

8. To His Parents[1]

Köslin, train station

My dear Parents,

Many thanks for your suggestion to meet in Stettin.[2] February 4 is not so good here, since there's work in the morning and the time is too short afterward. But I was thinking of Sunday or Saturday (February 6 or 5). Would

---

[13.] Schütz, *Warum ich noch ein Christ bin* (1937). [Bonhoeffer mentions his critique of Schütz later in one of his theological letters from prison (*DBWE* 8:430) and a 1944 letter to Maria von Wedemeyer (*Love Letters from Cell 92*, 154). Cf. also *DB-ER*, 844.—VB]

[14.] Heb. 13:9. [Italics are Bonhoeffer's. The German translation differs from the NRSV wording, which reads: "for it is well for the heart to be strengthened by grace." —VB]

[1.] *NL*, A 44,1 (8); handwritten postcard; postmarked Köslin, January 27, 1938. Previously published in *GS* 6:435.

[2.] On January 11, 1938, Bonhoeffer was arrested in Berlin-Dahlem at a meeting of the directors of theological education and leaders of the vicars' groups in the Confessing Church in the Old Prussian Union and banished from Berlin and Brandenburg. See

that suit you? I can hardly reach Stettin from Schlönwitz before 2, but I could leave on Saturday and meet you already on Sunday morning. Please write me about this.

Greetings to you from your
Dietrich

All is going well. What will the seventh[3] bring? I will write Ch.[4] after four weeks have passed. That seems better to me.

9. To His Parents[1] 33

February 10, 1938

My dear Parents,

It is truly nice that you plan to arrive already on Saturday. I'll pick you up at the station. Perhaps then we can spend some time together during the evening at the Preußenhof.[2] I will be leaving for Stettin already on Friday evening. Would it be possible, dear Mama, for you to send me my black suit, which I wanted to take with me last time from Berlin and which I still really need (c/o Mrs. von Kleist,[3] Poelitzerstr. 103), or to bring it with you? If this is too much trouble for you, I can naturally manage without it, and it could perhaps be sent to Schlawe for me. I am already looking forward eagerly to the days in Stettin.

Greetings from your grateful
Dietrich

DB-ER, 597–98, as well as Bonhoeffer's letter at the end of February 1938 to the Gestapo (1/10). After some time Karl Bonhoeffer was able to get permission for his son to visit the family in Berlin.

[3.] The trial of Martin Niemöller began on February 7, 1938, in the special court [*Sondergericht*] in Berlin-Moabit. [The Nazi regime created these special courts to try political cases.—VB]

[4.] The reference is probably to a Gestapo official named Chantré. Cf. Bonhoeffer's letter from the end of February 1938 to the Gestapo, 1/10.

[1.] *NL*, A 44,1 (9); handwritten postcard; postmarked Köslin. Partially reproduced in *GS* 6:435.

[2.] [A hotel.—VB]

[3.] The reference is to Ruth von Kleist-Retzow.

10. Request to the Gestapo[1]

In the middle of January 1938,[2] I was invited to Berlin for a discussion of church matters. Since in any case I needed to travel to Berlin at that time for personal reasons, to visit my father, I agreed to come. In the Dahlem parish hall, where the meeting was to take place, I found a group of some thirty leading Confessing pastors from throughout the Old Prussian Union. Under the chair of Pastor Lic. Niesel,[3] some important church issues were to be discussed, particularly the possibility of the subordination of Con-
34 fessing vicars and assistant pastors to the consistories.[4] After only a half hour, officials from the Gestapo appeared, took us all in large police vans to Alexanderplatz; we were interrogated; pastors who were not residents of Berlin and Brandenburg were banished from Berlin and Brandenburg, and the others were forbidden to leave Berlin and Brandenburg. No reason was given for these measures. The meeting was neither forbidden, nor was it kept particularly secret, as its location makes clear, nor could the topic of discussion offer any reason for special measures. Afterward, we learned that our gathering had been mistakenly suspected of being a theological lecture session for Confessing Church students,[5] and that [the Gestapo] had been surprised not to find a single student. Since then, I have been banished from Berlin and Brandenburg, although through my father, Privy Councillor Professor K. Bonhoeffer, I have obtained official permission for personal visits to Berlin. I am not in the position, however, to carry out any church duties for my large family and circle of acquaintances who reside in Berlin. Moreover, the State Police measure, which is still incomprehensible to me, naturally burdens me. To my mind the measure affected me only through coincidence, and it seems to me that its scale stands in no proportion to the occasion.

[Dietrich Bonhoeffer]

[1.] *NL*, A 61 (1); undated carbon copy; probably from the end of February 1938; see Bonhoeffer's January 27, 1938, letter to his parents, 1/8. Previously published in *GS* 2:295–96. The letterhead is "Pastor Lic. Dietrich Bonhoeffer, Schlawe/Pom., Koppelstr. 9." [The letter is addressed to the Geheime Staatspolizei, or Gestapo.—VB]

[2.] On January 11, 1938.

[3.] Wilhelm Niesel.

[4.] [A reference to the legalization debate.—VB]

[5.] On November 9, 1935, one day after its opening, the church college (Kirchliche Hochschule) in Berlin-Dahlem, which had been established and supported by the Confessing Church for the winter semester of 1935–36, was banned and dissolved by the Gestapo, which also sealed its rooms. Until March 1941, it continued to operate illegally in private rooms by constantly changing location. Cf. Besier, "Die Gründung der Kirchlichen Hochschule Berlin 1935/45 und ihre 'Väter.'" [For eyewitness descriptions of this situation, see Barnett, *For the Soul of the People*, 86–88.—VB]

11. To the Finkenwalde Brothers[1] 35

March 14, 1938

Dear Brothers,

You've now gone for two weeks without meditation texts. I'm especially sorry about this and beg your pardon. The enclosed sermon has been finished for a while,[2] but I couldn't get around to the letter to you. I was often on the road, and I preferred to have some quiet to write to you. First, I would like to thank all those brothers who so kindly remembered me on my birthday.[3] There were a great number of letters, and each one of them gave me great joy.[4] This sign of your faithful remembrance and prayer has greatly encouraged and strengthened me for work. Many thanks for this.

Recently the requests for gatherings of the participants from individual session groups have increased. It is painful for all of us that here, too, such great obstacles have arisen.[5] But we must somehow deal with this. I thought of inviting all the groups from the earlier sessions[6] to an estate for a gathering and then to repeat that, depending on the number of incoming registrations. It won't be possible to invite each group individually one after the other, but I think we must be satisfied with the other solution. I may be able to write more details in May. It would indeed be nice to see and talk to one another again!

We should make the effort to come together with the former brothers 36
as often as possible, so that things don't fall apart in the long period in between gatherings. In this respect we are often lax and forget that it could be an aid not only for oneself but for the other person if we could visit him sometime. It goes without saying that such time together should be not just for catching up with one another but for more than that. We need someone occasionally to ask us where we stand with our reading of the Scripture, our time for meditation, our prayer, and our work on sermons. Let us not

[1.] *NL*, A 48,3 (3); typewritten mimeograph, initialed by hand; no return address, but probably from Groß-Schlönwitz. Previously published in *GS* 2:531–33.

[2.] A sermon on Rom. 5:1–5; see 3/3.

[3.] Bonhoeffer's birthday was February 4.

[4.] None of these birthday letters from 1938 remains, with the exception of the letter from Robert Zenke to Bonhoeffer on February 4, 1938, mentioned in ed. note 9.

[5.] The Himmler Decree of August 29, 1937, which was directed against the Confessing Church's educational institutions, also banned all its theological cohorts and retreats. Cf. Beckmann, *Kirchliches Jahrbuch 1933–1944*, 205, and *DBW* 14, 1/149.

[6.] The retreat for former Finkenwaldians took place in Zingst on June 20–25, 1938. Cf. *DB-ER*, 593, and the July 18, 1938, circular letter, 1/21. Bonhoeffer held a Bible study on the sixth request of the Lord's Prayer: "Lead us not into temptation"; see 2/4.

relapse here into false courtesy; we used to know better! Help one another also in intercessory prayer. Continue to think of us as well. We all need this help today. It seems that God sends us all the external difficulties in getting together so that our spiritual life becomes stronger and more alive. I don't know whether we always consider this; for that reason, however, the troubles of our individual colleagues are almost unbearably hard. We all still look too much at that which is flesh and too little at that which is spirit.[7] We are all able to see the difficulties and allow our gaze to be captivated by them. What we must learn more and more, however, is to point to the help that God's Spirit offers us daily and hourly. But we will experience this help only when we take the step of promise and obedience, just as the waves of the Red Sea only parted when Israel set its foot in the water.[8] Thus everything is to stand on faith and obedience.

One more thing: I have thought that it could be helpful for one or another of you occasionally to send in a sermon you have given. Especially those who are all alone will perhaps be very glad to do so. It's also a pretty good discipline to do this at least once a year. I will be happy to read the sermons and send them back with my comments, as best I can. Perhaps this is also something helpful that we can offer one another.[9]

37 We think of you all a great deal and often wish we had more news from you. Fritz and Eberhard[10] have much to do and much joy in their work. Some things are different and more difficult, but others are more pleasant.[11] Soon the holidays will be here again.[12] God help us all the time and make us faithful in our ministry. Greetings to you from your faithful

D[ietrich] B[onhoeffer]

[7.] Cf. the Pauline contrast between "flesh" and "spirit" in Rom. 8:12–16, and other places.

[8.] Cf. Exod. 14:21–22.

[9.] With regard to this, see Robert Zenke's letter (*NL*, C 25) of February 4, 1938, to Bonhoeffer, which reads in part: "Many thanks for your letter [not extant] and the critique of the sermon. I accept it, although I had thought that precisely my sermon for New Year's had for once been quite respectable. But such is life. The danger of this position [i.e., the parish ministry—VB] is that the proclamation is reduced out of revivalist [*volksmissionärischen*] considerations. Due to your letter, I preached a reserved and matter-of-fact sermon on the twenty-ninth, in light of January 30 [the anniversary of Adolf Hitler's appointment in 1933 as Reich Chancellor]. Barth's exegesis of Rom. 13 [see Barth, *Epistle to the Romans*, 475–502] was good preparation for me for the sermon, which I held with great joy, notwithstanding its objective brevity and 'negativity' [Karl Barth's remarks on Rom. 11:21–13:7 were titled 'The Great Negative Possibility'—VB]—or precisely because of that. People attended, too, more than on other Sundays."

[10.] Fritz Onnasch and Eberhard Bethge.

Meditation texts:

March 13–March 19:	John 18:1–27
March 20–March 26:	John 18:28–40
March 27–April 2:	John 19:1–15
April 3–April 9:	John 19:16–30
April 10–April 16:	John 19:31–42
April 17–April 23:	John 20:1–18
April 24–April 30:	John 20:19–31
May 1–May 7:	John 21
May 8–May 14:	1 John 1–2:6
May 15–May 21:	1 John 2:7–17

12. To Else Niemöller[1] 38

Friedrichsbrunn, April 18, 1938

Dear Mrs. Niemöller,

During this Passion Week, the thoughts of many people, including many younger theologians who are attached to your husband and pray for him daily, go to you and your children. God has provided that a special blessing

[11.] [I.e., compared with the situation in Finkenwalde.—VB]

[12.] The first session of the collective pastorates in Köslin and Groß-Schlönwitz concluded at the end of March 1938. Bonhoeffer and Eberhard Bethge then left for a two-week holiday at the Bonhoeffer family vacation house in Friedrichsbrunn, until around April 25, 1938, when the summer session in the collective pastorates began. See the comment in Bethge's April 16, 1938, circular letter to his family and friends from Friedrichsbrunn: "With great thankfulness I can report that we did good work for an entire winter semester, and arrived at the end without any interference [i.e., by the Gestapo—VB]. . . . We [Bethge and Bonhoeffer] came here via Weimar and Eisenach. . . . A large swastika flag as a drapery in the church, as it was in Eisenach on the lectern there, with a large 'yes' [for the occasion of the April 10, 1938, plebiscite on the Austrian *Anschluß*—VB]. On the same evening in Eisenach, up on the Wartburg tower . . . a large golden swastika was erected, in the place of the cross, and that during Passion Week. A good example for confirmation classes!" (in Andersen, *So ist es gewesen*, 325 and 327).

[1.] LKA EKvW, file 5,1, fasc. 2, no. 431; handwritten. See also the typewritten copy in *NL*, A 45 (47). Previously published in *GS* 2:307. Martin Niemöller was tried for "misuse of the pulpit," offenses under the Malicious Practices Act (*Heimtückegesetz*), and "encouraging disobedience against state orders." His trial began on February 7, 1938, and ended on March 2, 1938, with a de facto acquittal [he was sentenced to time already served—VB]. Niemöller was taken to the Sachsenhausen concentration camp as Hitler's "personal prisoner" after Hitler's cabinet refused to consent to Hitler's demand for Niemöller's rearrest. See Niemöller, *Was würde Jesus dazu sagen?* 62–64.

should now radiate from your home to the church-community and the entire church. When those of us on the outside hear that you can remain steadfast and confident and patient in all your sadness, it truly serves only the honor of God and God's church. This is a great mercy of God for which we are thankful. It is indeed a great joy that, wherever one goes, people still ask about your husband, and that simple parishioners, when they visit the authorities, witness with great steadfastness to that for which your husband is suffering. That has a powerful effect upon the congregations. In all this, may God grant you and your children the great joy of Easter.

In the solidarity of daily intercessory prayer, greetings to you, with great admiration and gratitude, yours

Dietrich Bonhoeffer

39 13. To Spes von Bismarck[1]

Dear Spes,

At Pentecost[2] my thoughts go especially to you. I hope that your recollection of confirmation classes and confirmation day is as lively as mine. More important than the recollection, however, is to keep proceeding. And I believe that the church, despite everything, is once more on the path. Hopefully, we can see each other again soon. Please greet your parents, and warm greetings to you yourself, from your

Dietrich Bonhoeffer

14. To Martin Strege[1]

Schlawe, Koppelstrasse 9, June 9, 1938

Dear Brother Strege,

Herewith I am extending a friendly invitation to you to the first meeting of the theological committee on Wednesday, June 15, 1938, in Greifenberg (the superintendent's office) at 11:30 a.m. Agenda: 1. Constituting the com-

---

[1.] In the personal possession of Spes Pompe; handwritten postcard; postmarked Berlin-Marienburg, Bahnpost, Zug 24/28, June 5, 1938. Cf. *NL*, A 45 (48). Previously published in *GS* 6:436. Bonhoeffer confirmed Spes von Bismarck on April 9, 1938, in Kieckow; cf. *DB-ER*, 439, and Bonhoeffer's sermon on Mark 9:24, 3/3.

[2.] June 5, 1938.

[1.] *NL*, A 45 (49); later typewritten copy. Previously published in *GS* 6:437–38.

mittee. 2. Drawing up a statement concerning the message: "What divides us from the Council of Brethren" (Boeters)[2] at the wish of the Council of Br[ethren]. 3. Loyalty oath issue.[3] 4. Other.

With brotherly greetings, your
Bonhoeffer

15. To Paula Bonhoeffer[1] 40

Dear Mama,

I'm here for several days.[2] I've been on the road a great deal recently. So I didn't get around to writing. But I'm doing quite well. In the coming week I'll spend a few days vacation in Rowe by the sea.[3]

Greetings from your
Dietrich

[2.] In 1937–38, the "Pomeranian Circle of Brethren" gathered under the leadership of Stettin consistorial official Ernst Boeters; this group increasingly distanced itself from the Council of Brethren's continuation of the course taken by the confessional synod in Dahlem, with its claim to church leadership. [At the October 1934 Dahlem synod, Confessing Church leaders were divided between radicals who claimed that the Confessing Church represented the true German Evangelical Church and that there could be no compromise with the German Christians (thereby raising the specter of a schism within the GEC) and the moderate factions that sought to preserve church unity through compromise. The Dahlem declaration that emerged from the synod represented the radical viewpoint; hence Boeters's group would have represented the more moderate course.—VB] Boeters's group had outlined its position in a document, "What Divides Us from the Council of Brethren" of May 14, 1938. Cf. Meier, *Der evangelische Kirchenkampf*, 3:281.

[3.] On April 20, 1938 [Hitler's birthday—VB], Friedrich Werner ordered pastors to swear a loyalty oath to Adolf Hitler, under threat of removal from office. Regarding the controversial manner with which the leadership councils of the Confessing Church dealt with this, see *DB-ER*, 607–20, as well as Glenthøj, "Die Eideskrise in der Bekennenden Kirche 1938."

[1.] *NL*, A 44,1 (10); handwritten postcard; postmarked Zingst, June 21, 1938; previously unpublished.

[2.] Bonhoeffer was on a retreat with his former Finkenwalde seminarians in Zingst on June 20–25, 1938. See *DB-ER*, 593.

[3.] [Rowe was on the Baltic seacoast.—VB]

16. From the Finkenwalde Brothers to Gerritdina Stokmann[1]

June 23, 1938

Dear Miss Stokmann,[2]

As the brothers of Werner Koch,[3] we want to assure you of our fellowship with him. The community in the body of Jesus Christ helps transcend spatial separation—and more: it helps conquer the trial of faith.

With heartfelt prayers of intercession, yours
[signatures]

41 ### 17. To His Parents[1]

My dear Parents,

The days in Zingst, where I was together with all the former Finkenwalde brethren, were undisturbed and lovely. Now we are spending a few days vacation here[2] before the work goes on. I hear that no changes in our work are to be expected in the near future. Perhaps that has something to do with Uncle Rudi?[3]—I lie here on the beach in the sun and am reading. That is very lovely.

Greetings from your grateful
Dietrich

[1.] In the personal possession of the Koch family at the time of *DBW* publication; handwritten postcard, written by Christoph Harhausen, stamped Zingst, June 23, 1938. Signed by Bonhoeffer and forty-four participants of the retreat of former Finkenwaldians in Zingst. Cf. the subsequently typewritten copy in *NL*, A 4,45 (50). Previously unpublished.

[2.] Gerritdina Stokmann was Werner Koch's fiancée.

[3.] Werner Koch had been arrested following the publication of the May 28, 1936, memorandum from the Second Provisional Administration of the German Evangelical Church to Adolf Hitler; Koch had been imprisoned since February 13, 1937, in the Sachsenhausen concentration camp. The text of the memorandum is in Greschat, *Zwischen Widersprung und Widerstand*, 104–43. See also *DB-ER*, 531–35. [See also Barnett, *For the Soul of the People*, 83–85.—VB]

[1.] *NL*, A 44,1 (11); handwritten postcard; postmarked Stolp, June 29, 1938. Partially reproduced in *GS* 2:533 and *GS* 6:436.

[2.] Bonhoeffer was together with Eberhard Bethge in Rowe on the Baltic Sea.

[3.] "Uncle Rudi," a reference to General Rüdiger Graf von der Goltz, was the Bonhoeffer family code name for preparations for war that, in this instance, meant a reduction in the Gestapo's measures against the church's work. See *DB-ER*, 626, about this situation, as well as Bonhoeffer's September 18, 1938, letter to Erwin Sutz, 1/29.

18. To Martin Strege[1]

Schlawe, Koppelstrasse 9, July 4, 1938

Dear Brother Strege,

I hereby invite you again to the first meeting of the theological committee on Wednesday, July 13, in *Köslin*, Elisenstrasse 3, at 11:30 a.m. (the same agenda).[2] I kindly request a prompt confirmation of your coming.

With brotherly greetings, your
Bonhoeffer

19. To Friedrich-Ernst Schröter[1] 42

July 10, 1938

Dear Brother Schroeter,

Heartfelt thanks for your letter.[2] I'm very pleased that the work has had a good start.[3] We, too, can still work in peace and are very grateful for each day. We hear almost nothing from our brothers in the west.[4] I am traveling as little as possible, because to me it seems important above all that work can still proceed in peace in some places. That is also so important for our brothers. With regard to Matt. 5:34, one is happy here when one-fifth remain clear.[5] The pseudo-Lutheran exposition of the Sermon on the

---

[1.] *NL*, A 45 (51); later typewritten; previously unpublished.

[2.] Cf. Bonhoeffer's June 9, 1938, letter to Strege, 1/14.

[1.] Staatsbibliothek zu Berlin, Preußischer Kulturbesitz, Handschriftenabteilung, Autogr. I/2431; handwritten; no return address given, but probably written in Groß-Schlönwitz; previously unpublished.

[2.] Letter not extant.

[3.] Friedrich-Ernst Schröter was a seminarian in the fourth Finkenwalde session (winter 1936–37) and worked afterward as an illegal pastor of the Confessing Church in the Old Prussian Union Church.

[4.] The reference is to the former Finkenwalde seminarians in the western provinces of the Confessing Church of the Old Prussian Union Church.

[5.] Matt. 5:34–35: "But I say to you, Do not swear at all, either by heaven . . . or by the earth." The reference is to the vehement debates within the Confessing Church about the loyalty oath to Hitler, which [church chancellery director—VB] Friedrich Werner had decreed for pastors on April 20, 1938. See especially Bonhoeffer's August 11, 1938, letter (1/22) about this to the Old Prussian Union Council of Brethren, as well as his August 23, 1938, circular letter, 1/24.

Mount, and with it the theology that was taught throughout Pomerania, is once more avenging itself here.[6]

Moreover the ghost of Essen still haunts this region and is turning the
43 heads of the best people.[7] I see only new confusion and apostasy coming out of this. The planned agreement to be of one opinion about Barmen 1[8] (without calling Barmen by name, since one must almost begin to be ashamed of it in the Confessing Church!) in the spirit of Burghart[9] is simply a falsehood and a surrendering of God's grace, which God extended to us in Barmen and Dahlem. The eyes of many brethren in the Confessing Church are still captivated by numbers. If we don't get clarity soon with regard to this Essen matter, much will fall apart. Here much work is being postponed "because now the solution from Essen is coming." This is terrible. Fortunately the young brethren are clear. That is a great gift and help.

With all good wishes for you and your work and with brotherly greetings to you and the brethren, your

Dietrich Bonhoeffer

The *Discipleship* is intended for the circle of brethren, but in case of emergency for you.[10]

[6.] Bonhoeffer understood his exegesis of the Sermon on the Mount in *Discipleship* as genuinely "Lutheran" and polemicized vehemently against the distortion of Luther's teaching by Luther's "students." Cf. *DBWE* 4, esp. 49–53. Later, in *Ethics*, he particularly accuses "pseudo-Lutheranism" of fatally ripping asunder the unity of the whole of reality [*Wirklichkeitsganze*] into "two realms" and, with that, of proclaiming the "autonomy of the orders of this world" against "the law of Christ" (*DBWE* 6:56; see also 289–91).

[7.] The negotiations in Essen in the summer of 1938 attempted to unify the different factions within the Confessing Church; for Bonhoeffer's rejection of these, see especially his September 10, 1938, letter to Karl Koch and Friedrich Müller (1/26) and the letter of the same date to Wilhelm Niesel (1/27).

[8.] Among other things, the Essen negotiations focused on working out a common understanding of the May 1934 Barmen theological declaration; the first thesis of the declaration was particularly contested. [The first thesis read: "We reject the false doctrine that the church could and should recognize as a source of its proclamation, beyond and besides this one Word of God, yet other events, powers, historic figures, and truths as God's revelation." From Hockenos, *Church Divided*, 179.—VB]

[9.] Hermann Georg Burghart represented the so-called neutrals in the Essen negotiations. In Bonhoeffer's June 1936 essay, "On the Question of Church Fellowship" ("Zur Frage nach der Kirchengemeinschaft"), his judgment was that "the neutrals pose a special problem. In the first place, one must say that in reality there are no neutrals; they simply belong to the other side" [*DBW* 14:675].

[10.] Apparently Bonhoeffer had enclosed a copy of his book *Discipleship*.

20. To Martin Strege 44

20.1. Letter[1]

Groß-Schlönwitz, parsonage, July 14, 1938

Dear Brother Strege,

A final attempt to bring about the meeting. *Wednesday the twentieth of July in Labes* (superintendent's office). Please let me know soon. Hopefully, this time it will work!

Cordial greetings, your
Bonhoeffer

20.2. Telegram[2]

No meeting = Bonhoeffer

21. To the Finkenwalde Brothers

21.1. Bonhoeffer's Circular Letter[1]

(Personal letter)

Dear Brothers,

The holidays together continue to live in us.[2] It was a rich time such as I have only very seldom experienced. In the two letters of John that we meditated on at the end, John not only wanted to communicate with his brethren "with paper and ink" but also desired to speak with them "face 45
to face" "so that our joy may be complete" (2 John 12). Certainly, after our days together, we understand this better than ever. More than everything else, the spoken word is what touches us, draws us toward responsibility, strengthens us. In the conversations that went uninterrupted from morning till late in the night, the Lord Jesus Christ was among us and firmly joined us anew. We were granted to hear one another, helping our brothers think

[1.] *NL*, A 45 (52); later typewritten; previously unpublished.

[2.] *NL*, A 45 (53); later typewritten; telegram from Groß-Schlönwitz on July 18, 1938; previously unpublished.

[1.] *NL*, A 48,3 (4); typewritten mimeograph with handwritten signature; no place or date, but certainly sent from Groß-Schlönwitz on July 18, 1938. Previously published in *GS* 2:533–35.

[2.] The retreat of former Finkenwalde seminarians was held in Zingst on June 20–25, 1938.

through and bear their decisions, and we were able once more to address one another with Jesus's call, the only help to faith and obedience. Thus now we know once more how fulfilled our joy is through such encounters in fellowship. In these days many may have realized again how poor we had become, how often our prayer for one another had become empty and thoughtless during the time when we didn't see one another. It is one of the many gifts of these days that with intercession we can be there again for one another in an utterly different reality, and now hopefully after these "face to face" conversations, the conversation through "paper and ink" will be revitalized.

Once again, I thank those who attended for coming, with all my heart. Some greatly sacrificed time and money for the sake of their brothers. It was no small matter to come from the Rhine and from easternmost East Prussia. But I am certain that each of you returned home just as rewarded as the rest of us. To those who were not there, I may say: we really missed you. Many sent us faithful brotherly greetings. We thank them especially. Indeed, they were present in our community through "paper and ink." We knew that they, too, had to make a sacrifice by not coming. There were questions about some, of whom unfortunately we didn't know much. But certainly the many cards of greeting that went out to those who were absent gave to all a sign of the community that exists.

Forty-five brothers came. The photographs, which we are still awaiting, will preserve a memory for us. We will certainly do everything to come
46 together next year as well.[3] We are grateful that it was possible this year, despite everything.

I greet all of you in the fellowship of prayer for the health of your body, soul, and spirit (3 John 2), for your homes, for your ministry, and for your congregations. Don't let yourselves be confused by the multitude of negotiations and plans that we are in the midst of once again.[4] "Be on your guard, so that you do not lose what we have worked for, but may receive a full reward" (2 John 8).

Your faithful
Dietrich Bonhoeffer

[3.] A retreat of former Finkenwalde seminarians did not take place in 1939.

[4.] This refers to the Essen negotiations in the summer of 1938 about finding consensus among the different factions within the Confessing Church and the disputes about the pastors' loyalty oath to Hitler. See *DB-ER*, 599–605, and Niesel, *Kirche unter dem Wort*, 163–67.

21.2. Report by One Participant about the Zingst Retreat, June 20–25, 1938[5]

Report by a brother

It is not easy to report on our holidays together. The senior brothers can at least imagine the external surroundings, the swimming, the games on the beach, conversations behind the dunes, and everything else that this location has made so familiar to us.[6] The essential contents of these days are difficult to describe, but if I now simply enumerate what was done and discussed, you may nonetheless be able to feel some of the experience.

The day of course began with devotions in the usual form and, following breakfast, meditation, immediately followed by singing.[7] Before supper, too,
we sang for a half hour. Brother Bonhoeffer held the Bible study in the morning 47
about the concept of temptation, an exegesis of the sixth petition.[8] It is to be hoped that this study will later be made available to all the brothers. Free time was from 11:30 to 4, including the midday meal, which naturally was used by many for personal individual conversations.

After coffee, discussions were held together, introduced by short reports by individual brothers on their experience with preaching, pastoral care, confirmation classes. As to preaching, the main issue was to say one thing and yet to go through the entire text, further about the necessity of speaking concretely and about the proper way to preach paranetic texts[9] as gospel.

In the discussion about pastoral care the need of probably everyone was addressed, namely, how to help parishioners who wish to be Christians but who, out of distrust or fear, shut their eyes to the path of the Confessing Church. Both the liberating aspect of the good news and the commandment about the "first step" should be strongly impressed on the many enslaved consciences.[10] In so doing, we must consider that the red card and participation in worship services of intercession[11] are already "solid food" that not everyone can digest,

---

[5.] *NL*, A 48,3 (4); typewritten mimeographed addition to Bonhoeffer's July 18, 1938, circular letter. Partially reproduced in *GS* 2:535–37. The author is not identified.

[6.] The work of the Confessing Church preachers' seminary under Bonhoeffer's leadership began on April 26, 1935, in Zingst, before the move to Finkenwalde on June 24, 1935. See *DB-ER*, 424–28, and *DBW* 14:1043.

[7.] For more regarding the daily routine and its individual components in Finkenwalde and in the collective pastorates, see *DBWE* 5:48–80.

[8.] See 2/4. [The reference is to "Lead us not into temptation," the sixth petition in the Lord's Prayer.—VB]

[9.] [Sermons or exhortations.—VB]

[10.] Cf. *DBWE* 4:61–67.

[11.] The reference is to membership in the Confessing Church (usually signified by a red membership card) and participation in the worship services where the Confessing

whereas the individual's personal responsibility for home and parish is "the milk"[12] that must first be given to such people.

The discussion about confirmation classes included the necessity of beginning with regular devotions, introducing the children through this to the Psalter, of evaluating the aid of the monthly devotional text and hymn, of introducing them lovingly to daily Bible reading, the necessity of having them learn much and strictly, and dealing separately with those less gifted. The collection of verses for fourteen- to eighteen-year-olds, now being distributed by the VL,[13] will be very useful for our classes, next to other essential sources of help. Perhaps we have still not paid enough attention to the fact that instruction in confessing[14] belongs in the confirmation classes as well.

48 In the evenings we first received the brothers' reports from their parishes and then discussed the situation of our Confessing Church in general and that of our younger brothers[15] in particular. The report by one Saxon brother[16] about the work in his province gave us joy. Recently several brothers were retained by their congregations under explicit directive there until they were forced out by physical violence. There, too, the first attempts at regular parish evangelization, a mobile ministry of the proclamation of the Word, have been made by those brothers available for it.[17] It was clear to us that there can never be any talk of lack of work among us, even when the path to a pastorate is largely blocked for us, and that we must try everything to remain in the parishes where we have been sent, even if in some places a Council of Brethren neglects its duties of spiritual leadership, and thus our obedience to the Council of Brethren must lead this body to issue the appropriate directives to us.[18] The fact that stagnation appears to have set in among some of the church leadership, that here and there simple obedience and gladness are in danger of becoming lost and

---

Church intercessory list, with the names of those suffering under the state's repressive measures (e.g., prohibitions on public speaking, removal from parishes, confinement in prison or a concentration camp), was read.

[12.] Cf. 1 Cor. 3:2.

[13.] The reference is to *Evangelische Christenlehre: Ein Altersstufen-Lehrplan*, offered by Martin Albertz and Bernhard Forck in 1938. [The VL, or *Vorläufige Leitung*, was the Second Provisional Administration of the Confessing Church, of which Albertz and Forck were both members.—VB]

[14.] Cf. the plan for confirmation instruction in *DBW* 14, 2/27. ["Instruction in confessing" (*Beichtunterweisung*) refers to confession of sin, not the creedal confessions.—VB]

[15.] [I.e., the "illegal" Confessing Church pastors.—VB]

[16.] Probably Hans-Henning Zippel.

[17.] Regarding Bonhoeffer's distinction between the offices of ministry and of preaching, see section 1 of Bonhoeffer's lecture on homiletics (1935–36) in *DBW* 14, 2/10, as well as DB-ER, 609.

[18.] [By "appropriate directive," Bonhoeffer means the order to remain in the parishes.—VB]

that in their stead the focus on the numbers, winning over those who stand on the sidelines, the bishops, the neutrals, etc. is costing so much good energy, has moved us to write a letter to the leading men of our church,[19] which is to be delivered personally by several of the brothers. (Whoever wants the letter may write Brother Bonhoeffer.) We know that some of the brothers in leadership are grateful for such voices from the circle of brothers.

There was yet another burning task and obligation for us, namely, the service of pastoral care that we owe those brothers who have left us for the consistory.[20] In the near future, each of them will be visited by two brothers. Here it has become clear to us anew that we must take our visits to one another and to all brothers in our respective church districts as an unconditional necessity. The decisions that all of us face now and in the time to come are difficult to bear alone. One more thing we agreed upon with one another: to help one another in the time to come in evangelization [Volksmission],[21] each time with four 49
brothers who live closest to one another. The address list shows us who our neighbors are and whom we can invite to join us in this evangelization in the manner that has been worked out among us.

Several had to leave already on Friday. So Friday morning we held our communion, strengthened by the words of our meditation text: "And this is the victory that conquers the world, our faith."[22] We are not victorious, but we are allowed to participate in faith in the victory of Christ, who has conquered all that causes us such crisis and anxiety. And it is *our* belief, the belief of our entire brotherhood, to which this victory belongs. Our thanksgiving is that this belief has been strengthened anew for us in these days. For that reason we hope that such a period of fellowship will be made possible next year as well.

We very much want to tell you that we have thought of you all daily in our intercessions, particularly of our two sick brothers, Brothers Lohmann and Wichmann.[23] Likewise for our brother Koch[24] and all those imprisoned. We

---

[19.] Letter not extant.

[20.] [The reference is to those Finkenwalde seminarians who had become legalized; this was a bitter blow to Bonhoeffer. See the recollections by one of them in Barnett, *For the Soul of the People*, 97–98.—VB] Regarding the legalization controversy within the "brotherhood of young theologians in Pomerania," see DB-ER, 607–20, and Klän, *An der Wegscheide*.

[21.] Regarding the tradition of the Finkenwalde seminarians' parish mission outreach, see *DB-ER*, 542–45, and *DBW* 14, 2/10.4. [The *Volksmission* emerged in the nineteenth century in both Protestant and Catholic churches as an evangelization movement. Throughout this volume it has been translated accordingly, but readers should note that in *DBWE* 16 the editor chose to translate it as "church renewal." Cf. *DBWE* 16:27.—VB]

[22.] 1 John 5:4.

[23.] Gerhard Lohmann and Georg Wichmann.

[24.] Werner Koch; see the postcard of June 23, 1938, to Gerritdina Stokmann, 1/16.

thank you for sending your letters and greetings here. All of us send greetings to you.

Meditation texts:

July 10–July 16:	Jude
July 17–July 23:	John 4:5–42
July 24–July 30:	John 5:1–29
July 31–August 6:	John 6:1–34
August 7–August 13:	John 6:35–69
August 14–August 18:	John 8:1–36
August 21–August 27:	John 9:1–41
August 28–September 3:	John 11:1–45

50 **22. To the Council of Brethren of the Old Prussian Union**[1]

August 11, 1938

To the Old Prussian Union Council of Brethren, Berlin:

For a Confessing pastor, it is a difficult decision to have to speak out against a decision of an Old Prussian Union confessional synod,[2] particularly when he can only look back with deep gratitude and deference to the service

---

[1.] *NL*, A 45 (54); carbon copy, initialed by hand; no return address. Previously published in *GS* 2:308–15. At the peak of the nationalistic frenzy in Germany that followed the *Anschluß* of Austria (March 12–13, 1938) into the German Reich, Friedrich Werner, president of the Evangelical High Church Council in Berlin, issued a "decree regarding the loyalty oath of clergy and church officials of the Evangelical Church of the Old Prussian Union" (Beckmann, *Kirchliches Jahrbuch 1933–1944*, 232–33). The text of the required oath was "I swear: I shall be faithful and obedient to Adolf Hitler, the Führer of the German Reich and people, and shall observe the laws and conscientiously carry out the duties of my office, so help me God." Besides Bonhoeffer, Karl Barth protested vehemently against the synodal resolution that declared pastors free to swear the loyalty oath in his "open letter" "to the sixth confessional synod of the Evangelical Church of the Old Prussian Union" (Beckmann, *Kirchliches Jahrbuch 1933–1944*, 252–55). See also Gerlach-Praetorius, *Die Kirche vor der Eidesfrage*, 92–170. [See also Barnett, *For the Soul of the People*, 156–58.—VB]

[2.] The sixth confessional synod of the Old Prussian Union Church met on June 11–13, 1938, in Berlin-Nikolassee; the second meeting of the sixth confessional synod was held in Berlin-Steglitz on July 31, 1938. (Cf. *DB-ER*, 599–603, and Glenthøj, "Die Eideskrise in der Bekennenden Kirche 1938.") Only in mid-August 1938, after the overwhelming majority of pastors had taken the oath, did a circular letter of July 13, 1938, from Martin Bormann "to all *Gauleiter*" [regional party leaders—VB] of the NSDAP become known, in which he remarked that the pastors' loyalty oath to Hitler only had "internal church relevance," since church leaders had ordered it "on their own . . . without

done by this synod up to now, when he knows of God's blessing and promise that have lain upon the previous synods. But a synod that has dared to call forth a majority decision and thereby to deviate from the original Christian
[urchristlich][3] principle that synodal decisions are to be unanimous (in 51
any case where Christian faith and Christian life are affected), a synod that believes it could answer for the spiritual violation of a strong minority (in the opinion, certainly, that it performs a decisive brotherly service in such a difficult matter through a "directive"), must indeed take into account that the dissent within the synod extends far beyond the synod, into the clergy and the congregations. Nonetheless, for someone who had not borne synodal responsibility and who can therefore only judge by the outcome itself, it is difficult enough to stand as an individual against a synod that bowed in prayer for the leadership through the Holy Spirit. He must be aware of the danger of arrogance [superbia], and he must be prepared to be summoned to better knowledge and to obedience. On the basis of the synodal resolutions of the second meeting of the sixth confessional synod, I can do nothing but raise the charge against these resolutions that they are an offense against Christian fellowship, and also will be culpable for confusion and offenses to consciences.

1. From the perspective of the responsibility that has been placed upon me, I must first say that the synodal resolution must bring the young preachers of our church into difficult distress.[4] Assuming that (point 1) the question whether the state required the oath really could not have been clarified further,[5] nonetheless it remains highly unsettling that not even where it was a matter of immediate demands on Dr. Werner (points 2–4), the synod

---

obtaining the decision of the Führer beforehand" (cf. Beckmann, *Kirchliches Jahrbuch 1933–1944*, 255). The party would take no position on the matter and make no distinction "whether a member of the clergy had taken the oath to the Führer or not." Even the Prussian minister for church affairs, Hans Kerrl, saw to it that those who refused would not be disciplinarily punished—"It was a crushing blow" (*DB-ER*, 601).

[3.] [This term signifies an origin going back to early Christianity.—VB]

[4.] Neither Bonhoeffer himself nor the "illegal" Confessing Church theologians were immediately affected by the decree to take the oath, since they did not hold "legal" pastorates and consequently were not registered with the Evangelical High Church Council. The decree to take the oath primarily affected the older pastors who considered themselves part of the Confessing Church but who could now lose their "legal" pastorate if they refused to take the oath. In protesting, Bonhoeffer's concern was that the Confessing Church as a whole reject the oath requirement on theological and political grounds, so as not to endanger the cooperation and trust between the "elder" and the "younger" [i.e., "illegal"—VB] pastors.

[5.] Cf. the documentation of the Steglitz resolutions in Beckmann, *Kirchliches Jahrbuch 1933–1944*, 250–52.

insisted upon the complete clarification of its necessary demands. To point
52 2: to what extent did Dr. Werner "accept" the loyalty oath when this[6] has not publicly been determined, neither in the protocol of the oath itself nor, for example, in the official gazette [Amtsblatt] of the GEC? The very fact that the declaration[7] can be recorded in the personnel files makes it clear that matters here are being decided not ecclesially but personally. As long as the declaration of the loyalty oath is not accepted generally and publicly as a *church* declaration, no responsible church regulation has been met. It already becomes clear on this point that the overall question has not been dealt with and resolved from the perspective of what the *church* of Jesus Christ has to say and require in the matter of this oath, for the sake of the sacredness of an oath, regardless of what consequences that can have. Instead, the question has been how the individual pastor could personally take this oath without a too heavily burdened conscience. But that is a different question, and thus to this date the question has not been raised in the Confessing Church. This is where we might seek the reason why the synod was so unsuccessful in turning this affair of the oath into a clear confession to the Lord Jesus Christ. Why was the synod content with private assurances for individual cases and did not insist that Dr. Werner announce the acceptance of the loyalty oath publicly, before the eyes of the state as the actual partner to the oath? Why did people here let themselves be satisfied with an unclear situation, which led all the young brothers to ask themselves the dangerous question as to why they alone should always insist on ultimate clarity in their relationship to the consistory, when such unclear relations between the permanently appointed [beamtet] pastors and Dr. Werner are allowed to prevail, indeed are approved by the synod? The same holds true for points 3 and 4. The public recognition of the fact that the vow of ordination is binding for those who take it has, so far as I can see, simply not been stated in a clear, public, and understandable manner for everyone. To the naive reader, point 4 gives the impression that the
53 address by the EOK about the oath[8] was left unspoken. Otherwise one would not have been satisfied with some kind of oral and written declarations, as though such things suddenly had acquired some kind of value

[6.] [I.e., the oath requirement.—VB]

[7.] [I.e., that the oath has been taken.—VB]

[8.] The Evangelical Oberkirchenrat, or High Church Council, issued an address that was to be read before the oath was administered by the consistory president. The concern of this church body in decreeing the loyalty oath was explained as follows: "The pastor, in confirming the conscientious fulfillment of the duties of his ministry, testifies that he is willing to fulfill the commission he took upon himself in his ordination in its entirety, in constant awareness of the obligation toward Führer, Volk and Reich. A loyalty oath to the

in the church. If this had been considered to be a matter of the entire church and not as a private affair, then the younger brothers would have indeed been considered in this matter. Then, even for their sake, complete clarity, openness, and truthfulness would have been insisted upon, instead of giving them a rather questionable example, to say the least, for church decisions and a burden on their consciences. Precisely in light of this, one would wish that the judgment of those ordained by the Confessing Church and those colleagues who are not publicly recognized—where this indeed affects them—would not have been considered superfluous and would have been listened to. To my knowledge—and I state this explicitly and with deep regret—this was not the case in the various preliminary discussions. Never has a confessional synod left its young preachers so alone as in this irrevocable decision.

2. Personally I have the following to add: if I see this correctly, the second meeting no longer made the theological question, as to whether an oath was possible at all, the topic of discussion. Instead, it bound itself, by the rules of order, to examine whether the demands raised in the first meeting[9] had in the meantime been fulfilled—that is, it didn't have to answer a question of confession of faith, but had to make a judgment about the matter at hand. Within the synod this judgment varied. Even where common confessional prerequisites existed, no unanimity in the judgment of the matters at hand could be reached. (Here I leave aside the fact that one could raise justifiable reservations, based upon the confessions, already
against the resolutions of the first meeting, and that for this reason it was 54
deeply regrettable that the second meeting, by following its agenda disregarded or had to disregard this.) In any case, the situation in the second meeting was that interpretations of the given facts stood opposed to other interpretations. One may therefore indeed say that here a question of confession had turned into a personal question of conscience. Some believed—with an elastic conscience—to see in the matter at hand prerequisites given that would just barely suffice for a personal taking of the oath. Those with less elastic consciences feared that not everything here was as yet entirely truthful, entirely clear and pure, and that for this reason it must be seriously advised against taking the oath under these circumstances. The synod did not bow to this crisis; it did not take up discussion of this question once

Führer transcends all differences in ecclesial viewpoints. It signifies the personal attachment [*Bindung*] to the Führer under the solemn appeal to God" (Beckmann, *Kirchliches Jahrbuch 1933–1944*, 234).

[9.] Cf. the documentation of the resolutions by the synod in Berlin-Nikolassee in Beckmann, *Kirchliches Jahrbuch 1933–1944*, 239–40, esp. 244–47.

more from the very beginning in spiritual calm and patience, in the certainty that the Holy Spirit could lead even a divided synod back to unanimity. It did not venture to halt the meeting, commend the matter to God, call for the intercession of pastors and congregations, in order to come together again, after some time had passed, on the same matter and struggle for unanimity. Rather, the synod reached for a shortcut self-made solution by force. It *issued a directive to* the brethren to take the oath and with that (to be sure, in the opinion that in precisely this it was doing a brotherly service) broke the rule of brotherly love as it is given in the New Testament, and it has also made itself culpable for the confusion of consciences and of their guilt.

Rom. 14:1: "Welcome those who are weak in faith, but not for the purpose of quarreling over opinions."

Rom. 14:15: "If your brother or sister is being injured by what you eat, you are no longer walking in love. Do not let what you eat cause the ruin of one for whom Christ died."

Rom. 14:21: "It is good not to eat meat or drink wine or do anything that makes your brother or sister stumble."

Rom. 14:23: "But those who have doubts are condemned if they eat, because they do not act from faith."

1 Cor. 8:9–12: "But take care that this liberty of yours does not somehow
55 become a stumbling block to the weak. For if others see you, who possess knowledge, eating in the temple of an idol, might they not, since their conscience is weak, be encouraged to the point of eating food sacrificed to idols? So by your knowledge those weak believers for whom Christ died are destroyed. But when you thus sin against members of your family, and wound their conscience when it is weak, you sin against Christ."

There are only two possibilities. Either this is a question of confession and the majority see their decision as the decision of the Holy Spirit; then those who have strayed, after they have been instructed, must be submitted to doctrinal discipline [Lehrzucht], and, finally, in case of failure, fellowship with them must be suspended. Then, according to the opinion of the synod, the application of paragraph 4 (removal from office)[10] would quite justifiably come into effect for this errant majority.[11] With that, the dissenting brethren are expelled from the community of the Confessing Church. Or this was a matter of a different judgment of conscience; then, however, [one] offended against the weaker brethren with the *directive* to

[10.] In the oath decree, Werner had explicitly threatened removal from office if the swearing of the required oath were refused.

[11.] [Ilse Tödt believes that here, as in the first sentence of this paragraph, Bonhoeffer meant "minority."—VB]

swear ("to eat meat," "to eat the sacrifice to the gods"),[12] for in the church-community the rule is that the stronger should rather renounce their freedom than confuse the weaker and constrain them to sin. Every constraint upon weak consciences makes itself guilty against Christ, who died for the sake of the weak. The "directive" of the synod signifies the unbrotherly and guilty abandonment of the weak and the establishment of an unbearable law in the church-community. The freedom of the individual conscience that longs for complete truthfulness must be respected here, since the views of the facts differ, precisely because it is not possible for the majority to convince the dissenters to assent to the resolutions of the second meeting on the basis of Scripture and confession. It would truly be dangerous if one were to talk these dissenting brothers into consenting that their longings were Enthusiastic,[13] that we could not help being sinners and therefore were to sin more boldly [pecca fortiter].[14] That would be the most seri- 56
ous misuse of the central article of our Protestant church.[15] I can hardly escape the impression that in this synodal directive the world's judgment has prevailed over the brotherly love for the weak and over the community within the church. The synod shifts the responsibility for the lack of clarity in the oath affair to others and regards the consciences of the dissenters only as something "to work out." Where is there room in the New Testament for this latter term? (They couldn't seriously have been thinking here of Matt. 16:19?!)[16]

3. What is to be done? In the next few days the oath will have been irrevocably taken, on the responsibility of the synod, and some consciences will be burdened through this. The rift thereby brought about in the Confessing Church is—in human terms—irreparable. That is the particular gravity of this oath affair. I can only regard the guilt that the Confessing Church has taken upon itself, through the "*directive*" to take the oath, as the outcome of a path where a lack of authority, gladness in confession, courage of faith, and readiness to suffer has been evident for some time. It will be hidden from no one that this means a grave temptation for many parishioners and pastors. Will we learn from this? Will the Confessing Church be willing to confess openly its guilt and division? Will it make the room for prayer for

[12.] [Cf. Rom. 14:21 and 1 Cor. 8:10.—VB]

[13.] [The reference is to the radical Reformation group (*Schwärmer*).—VB]

[14.] This alludes to Martin Luther's statement to "sin boldly, but believe and rejoice in Christ that much more boldly" (*pecca fortiter, sed fortius fide et gaude in Christo*) (*LW* 48:282). See also *DBWE* 4:51.

[15.] The reference is to the Augsburg Confession, Article 4 (*Book of Concord*, 38–39).

[16.] ["Whatever you bind on earth will be bound in heaven, and whatever you loose on earth will be loosed in heaven."—VB]

forgiveness, and for a new beginning, which would be proper in this hour? Will it in this way honor the truth and once more console the consciences that yearn for truth alone, of those brethren who have split off, and bind their consciences to God's word? Will the confessional synods learn that it is necessary to consult and decide in the calm and patience demanded by this matter, despite all dangers and difficulties? Will they once and for all have learned that majority resolutions in matters of conscience murder the spirit? Will the confessional synod have the authority to speak once more to
57 the younger brethren? Does it see the danger into which it has brought its word through the last meeting? Today these are open questions.

I am including several quotations by Vilmar[17] that have become decisive for my view of the oath.

I request that the Council of Brethren pardon what is falsely seen and judged, and instruct me accordingly.

D[ietrich] B[onhoeffer]

23. To the Members of the Theological Committee of the Confessing Church in Pomerania[1]

Theological Committee

August 18, 1938

Dear Colleagues,

The theological committee, which has to date been unable to convene due to the fact that its members live in remote places, had to be expanded with the approval of the Council of Brethren. Our brothers Bultmann, Grude, Vedder, Voßberg[2] are hereby invited now to join the committee. Through the greater number of members, the ability of the committee to do its work is assured. I cordially ask the brothers I have named not to let us down.

The first meeting is now to take place on Thursday, August 24, at 11:30 a.m. at Elisenstrasse 3 in Köslin. I warmly invite everyone to attend. Agenda: 1. Constituting the committee. 2. The tasks of the theological committee. 3. Clarification of the theological situation in our provincial church (among

---

[17.] This enclosure is not extant, but see the enclosure to Bonhoeffer's August 23, 1938, circular letter to his Finkenwalde seminarians, 1/24.

[1.] *NL*, A 45 (55); later typewritten copy; no return address, probably sent from Schlawe. Previously published in *GS* 6:438.

[2.] Peter Bultmann, Werner Grude, Wilhelm Vedder, and Martin Voßberg.

other things, at the wish of the Council of Brethren, discussion of the letter, "What divides us from the Council of Brethren").[3] 4. Other matters.

I ask the brothers to think particularly about points 2 and 3 and to pro- 58
pose some suggestions.—Travel costs will be reimbursed.—I particularly request a reply as soon as possible to me (Koppelstrasse 9, Schlawe).

With brotherly greetings, your
Bonhoeffer

23a. To Susanne Dreß[1] 17:122

Dear Susi,

On your birthday[2] tomorrow, we will certainly all be thinking especially of you and wish for you with all our hearts that your new year has a good and joyful beginning. Hopefully, you now also take pleasure in your new apart-
ment.[3] How nice that all this was already completed before the event.[4] I 17:123
am now eagerly awaiting the telephone call from Berlin.[5] In the week after next, I am coming through Berlin[6] and already look forward to seeing you then. Warmest greetings to you all from

Your Dietrich

The cards[7] are the hint about a present that I can only give you when I come to Berlin.

[3.] Cf. Bonhoeffer's June 9, 1938, letter to Martin Strege, 1/14, ed. note 2.

[1.] Literary estate of Walter and Susanne Dreß [this collection is now in the Evangelisches Zentralarchiv in Berlin—VB]; handwritten on a card with calligraphy by Rudolf Koch with the text of Ps. 23:1, 2, 4. Probably sent from Groß-Schlönwitz (see the Chronology, p. 587); probable date is August 21, 1938. Cf. *NL*, Anh. A13. Previously unpublished. Edited by Dirk Schulz.

[2.] Susanne Bonhoeffer had been born on August 22, 1909.

[3.] In Berlin-Dahlem; Walter Dreß became the successor in the Dahlem parish of Martin Niemöller, who had been taken to the concentration camp in Sachsenhausen on March 2, 1938. Concerning the bitter dispute in the congregation about a successor [to Niemöller] and which church government was considered the right one, see 1/161, ed. note 6.

[4.] On August 26, 1938, Susanne and Walter Dreß's son Andreas was born. See also Sabine Leibholz's August 26, 1938, letter to Bonhoeffer, 1/25.

[5.] For news of the birth.

[6.] After the 1938 summer session of the collective pastorates in Köslin and Groß-Schlönwitz had ended, Bonhoeffer traveled together with Eberhard Bethge via Berlin to Göttingen, to help the Leibholz family with their flight out of Germany. See *DB-ER*, 631–33, and 1/25.

[7.] Beginning of writing on the margin of the card.

24. To the Finkenwalde Brothers

24.1 Bonhoeffer's Circular Letter[1]

August 23, 1938

Dear Brothers,

The interpretive verse [Lehrtext] for this day[2] on which I would like to send you greetings again is "Do not let anyone divert you from the goal" (Col. 2:18).[3] That is the right word that we must say to one another today. Here Paul is speaking about an umpire in a competition who cheats us of the victory medal through false directives and suggestions. Paul says, don't let yourselves be caught or lured by such people. The victory prize is sure to be yours as long as you don't let yourselves be misled in the decisive moment and reach for other means and ways to reach the goal. Then you will be cheated and lost. Why, however, should you be so foolish as to let certain victory be taken out of your hands? Stay on the right path, stay on the straight and narrow, which leads you to the goal; hold firmly to the truth that you once recognized. In three respects, this word is a clear directive for us today: first, whoever wants to tell us that today we should seek individual solutions for our difficulties, at least for us personally, is a deceitful umpire.[4]
59 It has become our firm certainty that we will either win the victory in the fellowship of our brethren or not at all. Those who look out only for themselves have been cheated of the community of the church. Second, those who press us to find a solution for all difficulties at all costs are giving us bad advice. They make us forget that our goal is not to be comfortable and free of conflict but to win the victory prize after a completed run. Do we seek solutions in this world, or do we await the redemption that Jesus Christ has won for us through his death? Third, to those who want to make us anxious and dubious, by suggesting that we should at the very least rescue what we have in our current state, since we have been beaten, deprived, and shut out enough, we must reply that from this current state we expect nothing at all. Whatever God wants to destroy, we will gladly allow to be destroyed. We have nothing to rescue. We did not set our hearts on establishments and institutions, not even on our own. The false reliance on works that

[1.] In the personal possession of Sigrid Krause; typewritten mimeograph with handwritten signature; no return address, probably sent from Groß-Schlönwitz. Cf. also *NL*, A 48,3 (5); later typewritten copy. Previously published in *GS* 2:537–41.

[2.] According to the Daily Texts published by the Moravian Church.

[3.] [This translation follows the German Luther Bible; the NRSV reads: "Do not let anyone disqualify you."—VB]

[4.] This is an allusion to the debate about the legalization of the illegal young vicars and assistant pastors in the Confessing Church. See *DB-ER*, 611–12.

depends on the church's so-called state is just as godless as any other and must deprive us of the victory prize. But we trust firmly that God will rescue his word, and with it us, in his wondrous way. That is the only state of affairs that we consider holding on to.

Dear brothers, bear with this short interpretation. We must all learn from these things each day. I look back on the past weeks with deep gratitude. The work goes on. I have received good news from you as well, personally and through letters, but unfortunately painful news too. In recent weeks brothers Hensel and Kiausch (Pomerania)[5] have left us.

I should like to repeat the offer to comment on your sermons.[6] I do it gladly, and for some who are alone, perhaps it is a help. At the moment I'm reading the new book by Althaus with interest and profit: Paul and Luther 60
on the human being (Rom. 7 and 8).[7] Brother Hofmann[8] recommends *Die höchst ergötzlichen Predigten des Jobst Sackmann* (Inselbücher 476).[9] Dear brothers, forgive me when I sincerely ask you once again to look through your bookshelves. Some things are still missing, e.g., Harnack, *History of Dogma* II.[10] Please be so good as to send the books back soon. We need them. Enclosed you will find the promised list of themes.[11]

I will think intensely of you all in the coming weeks, with all these matters still pending: "Do not let anyone divert you from the goal."

In faithful brotherly fellowship, your
Bonhoeffer

Meditation texts:

Sept. 4–Sept. 10:	Hab. 1
Sept. 11–Sept. 17:	Hab. 2
Sept. 18–Sept. 24:	Hab. 3
Sept. 25–Oct. 1:	Zeph. 1
Oct. 2–Oct. 8:	Zeph. 2
Oct. 9–Oct. 15:	Zeph. 3

[5.] Rudolf Hensel (a candidate in the fifth Finkenwalde session) and Helmut Kiausch (a candidate from the Groß-Schlönwitz session in the summer of 1938) had placed themselves under the regional church consistory in Stettin [i.e., they had gone through the legalization process—VB].

[6.] Cf. Bonhoeffer's March 14, 1938, letter to the Finkenwalde brothers, 1/11.

[7.] Althaus, *Paulus und Luther über den Menschen* (1938).

[8.] Hans Hofmann.

[9.] Sackmann, *Die höchst ergötzlichen Predigten des Jobst Sackmann* (1935). [Inselbücher 476 refers to the publisher and the number of the book.—VB]

[10.] Harnack, *Lehrbuch der Dogmengeschichte*, vol. 2.

[11.] The enclosure follows (24.2).

Oct. 16–Oct. 22: Rom. 12
Oct. 23–Oct. 29: Rom. 13
Oct. 30–Nov. 5: Rom. 14
Nov. 6–Nov. 12: Rom. 15:1–21
Nov. 13–Nov. 19: Rom. 15:22–16:27

61 **24.2. Enclosure: Quotations on the Oath from August Friedrich Christian Vilmar**

Vilmar, "*Theologische Moral*."[12] On the *oath*:

p. 182:[13] The oath, however, cannot be regarded as an act of free arbitrariness, on one's own initiative. Rather, it requires an authority that demands it. . . .

p. 183: [The oath] . . . when legitimately required by the respective authority, [is] an assurance given to that same authority for which the one who swears the oath answers with his entire godly life, with his salvation. . . .

p. 184: . . . When a Christian takes an oath, his entire soul must be directed at the same time with the clearest and objectively most complete consciousness toward God the Father and toward Christ, therewith at the same time toward the salvation that is to be held in Christ alone and toward the subject of his assurance, so that he is capable of combining in one and the same thought, with the same decisiveness and certainty: how, just as he is not in a position to alter anything with regard to God, Christ, and Christ's salvation in the slightest degree, so too should he neither want nor be able to alter the smallest thing about the subject of his assurance. Whoever is not fully clear about the one or the other of these two, swears the oath thoughtlessly. Whoever knows the subject of his assurance to be different than he presents, swears the oath falsely. Whoever loses sight of (doesn't fulfill) the subject of his assurance, insofar as this subject contains a promise, breaks the oath. . . . Thus perjury and the breaking of an oath are a qualified (having occurred under aggravating circumstances) blasphemy against God. . . .

p. 185: . . . That oath also [would similarly be] . . . blasphemy against God . . . if its object includes anything that is incompatible with the oath-taker's godly life, with God's law, with salvation. . . . Therefore, the taking
62 of an oath requires that the substance of the oath must be placed and must

[12.] Vilmar, *Theologische Moral* (1871).

[13.] The page numbers refer to the numbering in the second and third sections of Vilmar's work, which are separate from the first section.

lie in complete and utmost clarity before the eyes of the oath taker, with no doubt, not even the slightest, as to the reality (truth, possibility of fulfillment) of that substance. By the very nature of the matter, the swearing of an oath can only refer to very simple subjects. . . . On the other hand, every taking of an oath with reservations, particularly when these come from the one who takes the oath, is unconditionally reprehensible—and to take an oath with mental reservations is an unconditional perjury. . . . The one who demands the oath, not the one who takes it, is responsible for the clear posing of the oath (the wording) that leaves no room for a single doubt.

25. From Sabine Leibholz[1]

Berlin, August 26, 1938

Dear Dietrich,

I have wanted to write you so often but didn't have the peace of mind to do it. You wrote such a nice letter to us on Marianne's birthday,[2] and now you wrote another, such a lovely letter to Gert.[3] Heartfelt thanks to you for this. It also pleased me so much for Gert. In recent weeks he had no longer been able to maintain his old equanimity. Ultimately the resilience of the nerves simply gives in. At the moment it's hard to think all the way through all the decisions that need to be made, and that makes one so nervous. Unfortunately, he's simply sleeping so badly. So I must hold down the fort for two, and sometimes it's not very easy to keep in mind matters as divergent as existential questions and pressing worries alongside the large and small concerns and wishes of the children.—

This letter has been lying around since Suse gave birth in the meantime,[4] and 63
now I'm writing to you further from Göttingen, where we arrived on Saturday.[5] We are so glad that Suse now has her son, and although she has to endure so much pain, at least up to now there's no fever, thank God. Both parents were

---

[1.] *NL*, C 6; handwritten; previously unpublished. The Leibholz couple was staying with Paula and Karl Bonhoeffer in Berlin as they prepared to flee Germany, which increasingly appeared advisable (because of the August 17, 1938, order for "non-Aryans" to include the names "Israel" and "Sarah" in passports. On October 5, 1938, passports of Jews were revoked and reissued with the imprint "J").

[2.] The birthday of Marianne Leibholz, who was Dietrich Bonhoeffer's godchild, was June 30. The letter mentioned is not extant.

[3.] Gerhard Leibholz; letter not extant.

[4.] The reference is to the birth of Andreas Dreß, the son of Susanne and Walter Dreß, on August 26, 1938.

[5.] They arrived on August 27, 1938.

under quite some strain. Aunt Elisabeth[6] is staying with us and helping me some with my preparations. We would so much like to see you before we leave.[7] Are you coming here again? Many thanks for the lovely present that Marianne is to have. Unfortunately, I have not yet received the picture, and I'm sure it will be all right with you if she finds herself a nice reproduction of the *Lord's Supper* by Van Dyck.[8] We were with her at the Rijksmuseum in Amsterdam, where she was very happy and inexhaustibly able to take it all in. The lovely time at the sea now seems so long ago. We will leave around September 8. Till then there is still much to do. So please tell me whether you can still come, even if it is not as cozy in our house as it used to be. Everyone sends greetings to you. Your

Sabine

64 **26. To Karl Koch and Friedrich Müller**[1]

Lic. Bonhoeffer

At present Göttingen, September 10, 1938
Herbergerlandstrasse 55[2]

To President Dr. Koch-Oeynhausen
To President Müller-Dahlem[3]

Your letter and the proposal for "regulations for the appointment of a church government"[4] have reached me. For the sake of the Confessing Church, I must reject the proposal. The disavowal of the insights from the Barmen and Dahlem synods[5] that God granted to us has become evident

[6.] Elisabeth von Hase.

[7.] The reference is to the Leibholzes' emigration to London via Switzerland. On September 9, Bonhoeffer and Eberhard Bethge accompanied the couple and their children by car from Göttingen to Giessen on their way to the Swiss border. See Leibholz-Bonhoeffer, *Bonhoeffers*, 85–88, and *DB-ER*, 631–33.

[8.] A painting by Anthony van Dyck.

[1.] LKA EKvW, file 5,1, fasc. 1, no. L 857; typewritten with handwritten corrections and signature. Cf. *NL*, A 45 (56); later typewritten copy. Previously published in *GS* 2:315–18.

[2.] After the conclusion of the summer session of the collective pastorates (end of August 1938), Bonhoeffer spent a good six weeks in September and October 1938 (until October 12) with Eberhard Bethge at the home of his twin sister, Sabine Leibholz, in Göttingen. On September 9, 1938, Bonhoeffer and Bethge had accompanied Sabine, her husband, Gerhard, and their children on their way to their exile in London. The original plan for a longer vacation trip together in southern Europe had to be abandoned since "the intent not to remind the military enlistment offices unnecessarily of [them]

here. No promise lies on this path, because it is being entered with ingratitude against God's gifts to his church and with a lack of clarity. I see it as my duty to counteract this proposal. You request a "prompt" declaration of 65
affirmation for your plans. Moreover, you have already informed the EOK[6] and the state offices about the proposal. With that you pressure us fatally in a matter where you should be asking for the most thorough advice and consideration. Since I now may let no time pass, for the present I raise the following objections, subject to a thorough explanation and to corrections:

1. The silence about the Barmen and Dahlem synods in the new establishment of a church administration is not only a strategic maneuver, which must avenge itself in a short time, but it at the same time also signifies a theological decision that must split the Confessing Church. Every Confessing pastor must insist on knowing: Is Barmen valid (with all its theses), or is it not? Will the new church administration stand on Barmen and be committed to it, or not? Our decision will depend on this. Why does the proposal not state what it means concretely "to take the confessions . . . seriously in proclamation, regulation and action"; why is a lack of clarity permitted to prevail here? Why is it not stated explicitly what "all" must "be fended off" for the sake of the witness to Jesus Christ? This is precisely what Barmen and Dahlem achieved. Why awaken the impression that today things are self-evident that have not been self-evident for five years? Your proposal turns Barmen and Dahlem into a church episode. With that the continuity

ultimately kept [them] from all plans related to German borders" (letter of August 21, 1938, from Eberhard Bethge to his cousins and friends from Groß-Schlönwitz, in *So ist es gewesen*, 330–31). During these weeks when the danger of war intensified due to Hitler's aggressive policy against Czechoslovakia (the Sudeten crisis), Bonhoeffer wrote his book *Life Together.* See *DB-ER*, 587–88, and *DBWE* 5:3–5.

[3.] [Karl Koch was president of the Evangelical Church of Westphalia, a rank corresponding to that of bishop in the Lutheran regional churches. Fritz Müller was president of the Provisional Church Administration (Vorläufige Kirchenleitung) of the Confessing Church.—VB]

[4.] *DB-ER*, 604. On August 23, 1938, in the course of the Essen negotiations about the reorganization of the GEC, a "proposal for a regulation for the nomination of a church administration in Old Prussia" was formulated, which was circulated under the title "Essen III." See Niesel, *Kirche unter dem Wort*, 163–67, and *DB-ER*, 603–5.

[5.] See the documentation of the first confessional synod of the GEC from May 29–31, 1934, in Wuppertal-Barmen and the second confessional synod of the GEC from October 19–20, 1934, in Berlin-Dahlem in Schmidt, *Bekenntnisse*, 2:91–98 and 157–62. For Bonhoeffer's theological evaluation of the Barmen and Dahlem synod resolutions, see especially his essay "On the Question of Church Fellowship," from April or June 1936 in *DBW* 14, 2/19.1, as well as his lecture "Our Path according to the Testimony of Scripture," 2/5.

[6.] [Evangelischer Oberkirchenrat, or High Church Council.—VB]

of the Confessing Church, which goes back from Barmen through the confessions of the Reformation, the symbols,[7] etc. all the way back to the Holy Scripture, has been abandoned. With that, however, Barmen is no longer a binding confession of the church.

2. Who is eligible to vote? Will the young pastors who have been ordained by the Confessing Church, and not admitted to the ministry only because of the false church government, be eligible to vote? If not, how will the church answer for the fact that it is these very brothers, who have followed the path of the Confessing Church, who are most clearly prevented from voting? Indeed, this is not to be answered for *ecclesially*, only at most out of false consideration for those who don't know and don't wish to know anything about the Confessing Church.

66 3. Who will present the electoral proposal? A private circle of churchmen, who have no ecclesial commission to do so? On the basis of what guidelines will the electoral proposal come into being? The signatures on the proposal, which in your opinion illustrate "how extensive the circle of those already is" who stand behind your plan, make me miss the very names of those in whom particularly the younger pastors in the Confessing Church place their trust (e.g., Albertz, Niesel, Scharf, Vogel, Staemmler, Anz, de Boor, et al.).[8] Instead there are numerous names that don't seem particularly appropriate for awakening church confidence.

4. In which consistories of the Old Prussian Union, in your opinion, might such theologians and jurists be found who might be expected to give the required declaration without pernicious inner reservations?

5. The commitment to Barmen has been included in the ordination forms of the Confessing Church.[9] Is that to be left out in the future? Do you dare now to hush up Barmen, in the face of the same brothers whom you have

[7.] Bonhoeffer is referring to the confessions of faith [the "three ecumenical creeds," i.e., the Apostles' Creed, the Nicene Creed, and the Athanasian Creed—VB] from the early church. Cf. "The Three Ecumenical Creeds" (*Book of Concord*, 19–25).

[8.] Martin Albertz, Wilhelm Niesel, Kurt Scharf, Heinrich Vogel, Wolfgang Staemmler, Johannes Anz, and Werner de Boor.

[9.] For example, the ordination certificate for Otto Dudzus states: "After the candidate for the ministry . . . has sworn before God that he will practice the office of preaching in commitment [Bindung] to the word of God, as written in the Holy Scripture, witnessed in the confessions of our church and, opposing the false teachings of our times, confessed anew as binding in the Theological Declaration of the First Confessional Synod of the German Evangelical Church in Barmen, we have ordained him. . . ." Issued by the Council of Brethren of the Old Prussian Union, church province of Berlin-Brandenburg, June 21, 1938. A photocopy of the document is in the *DBW* editor's possession.

committed to Barmen publicly, before God and the church-community? Whoever still recognizes God's directive for his church in Barmen and Dahlem and gratefully stands by that up to this hour, whoever recognizes in the present crisis of the Confessing Church only the hour of trial and proof, may not acquiesce to your proposal.

6. Please don't say that for manifold reasons it would be highly unwise at present to act in opposition. None of us in this situation knows what is wise or unwise. But it is certain that it is not advisable to act against God's clear directive, against the truth we came to know, and against the conscience.
You yourselves are aware of the confusion caused by the sixth Confessing 67
Church synod.[10] After this defeat we had indeed expected a different, more spiritual statement from our church authorities. What has now been advised to us is the self-surrender of the Confessing Church. Here we will no longer follow.

Dietrich Bonhoeffer

27. To Wilhelm Niesel[1]

September 10, 1938

Dear Brother Niesel,

The new proposal[2] is the most evil document in the history of the Confessing Church. Even if one doesn't assume that it will ever become reality, it is reprehensible. It is simply the result of endless negotiations at the end of which the original intention was forgotten. I am now of the opinion that the younger brothers whom we have ordained, as well as the vicars, absolutely must be heard on this. You are perhaps the only one who could set that in motion,[3] since I don't think that provincial consultations[4] serve any purpose in this matter. Thus I sincerely ask you to take up this matter. If we

[10.] The reference is to the controversy about the loyalty oath issue; cf. Bonhoeffer's August 11, 1938, letter to the Old Prussian Union Council of Brethren, 1/22.

[1.] Literary estate of Wilhelm Niesel; handwritten; from Göttingen. Cf. *NL*, A 45 (57). Previously unpublished.

[2.] See 1/26, ed. note 4.

[3.] In the Old Prussian Union Council of Brethren, Niesel was responsible among other things for the training of new young theologians.

[4.] Bonhoeffer means separate Confessing Church consultations within each individual church province of the Old Prussian Union.

don't give warning about this in time, it will suddenly be too late and the consequences would have to be disastrous.

With brotherly greetings your
Dietrich Bonhoeffer

68 **28. From Ruth von Kleist-Retzow to Eberhard Bethge**[1]

September 14, 1938

My dear Pastor Bethge,

I thank you from the heart for your good letter. It was genuinely refreshing for me. What this fellowship with Finkenwalde means! Two of the brothers, Nithack and Sander,[2] were also here for two days, and the day before yesterday Albrecht Schönherr and his enchanting wife.[3] Throughout all this how good I have it, at a time when I feel in almost constant need of comfort! Please tell Dietrich that I almost despaired under the burden of *Discipleship*.[4] With "costly grace"[5] it seemed to me that I met with not only a lack of understanding but also a lack of interest. And then I was disheartened by the impression that there was nothing but literary interest and that no sense of belonging together grew. . . . But yesterday evening with the "Beatitudes"[6] was obviously better. The material may in general be too difficult for people who are accustomed to thinking very superficially about religious matters. Nithack and Sander, who recently attended, thought that costly grace could only move someone who had already asked seriously: how do I receive a merciful God?[7] That will be correct. They helped me very well, particularly after everyone had left. Albrecht[8] also gave me some pills to swallow. *Very* good that he did that. If only I could go back to school from the beginning. Instead, every day I get older. . . . And *still* these evenings are now my whole delight!

[1.] Literary estate of Eberhard Bethge; handwritten from Stettin. Partially reproduced in *GS* 2:318–19.

[2.] Ulrich Nithack and Erwin Sander.

[3.] Hilde Schönherr, née Enterlein.

[4.] With several friends and acquaintances from the Confessing parish in Stettin, Ruth von Kleist had started a circle to read Bonhoeffer's *Discipleship* regularly.

[5.] See *DBWE* 4:43–56.

[6.] See *DBWE* 4:100–110.

[7.] [The sentence "How do I receive a merciful God" goes back to Luther and was the starting point for him of the Reformation. According to Heinz Eduard Tödt, Bonhoeffer posed a different question: How is the word (re)claimed by God in Jesus Christ? The editor thanks Ilse Tödt for this insight.—VB]

[8.] Schönherr.

Today I was at number 17[9] and *what* did I find out! The counsel of the Old Prussian Union[10] *not* to take the oath for the time being! I froze within from outrage. Now, after everyone has sworn it, except for three who were on vacation, . . . I find it so dreadful that the blood freezes in my veins. At my request Mrs. von Mackensen[11] gave me the statement to take along. You will have it as well. It is something to think about, that one relied upon "circumstantial evidence" and acted on it! Now an "inquiry" will be sent off to the president of 69
the High Church Council![12] I feel only that Dietrich must make the Council of Brethren of the Old Prussian Union ask forgiveness in a clear statement for leading its flock astray. When I think of the crisis of conscience that the individual pastors went through until they finally swore the oath with a wounded conscience, my heart stands still. And now they simply communicate the facts and add that they have sent an "inquiry" to the irresponsible "responsible" office. They should be utterly *destroyed* by the recognition that they offered false leadership because they *thoughtlessly* relied upon "circumstantial evidence" that has now been proven wrong. Oh, it remains true: "Here we stray and err, shrouded in deep night."[13] . . . But it must be made *known* because the extent of the guilt is immeasurable. Reimer is said to have announced his resignation[14] and to have written very rudely. . . . But without yet knowing of this fact. How this will upset him and completely harden him! I had the impression that the Pomeranian Council of Brethren had communicated this counsel only to the three who didn't take the oath. (Perhaps nonetheless to the directors of the ministerial meeting groups [Pfarrkonvent].) But Mrs. von Mackensen was also very irritated. From the very beginning Koch's[15] reasoning failed to convince me; it was simply a jingle.[16] And who was right? K.B.![17] I should not be writing any of this, but I'm still seething.

[9.] The office of the Pomeranian Council of Brethren in Stettin was located at Pölitzerstrasse 17.

[10.] She means the Council of Brethren of the Confessing Church of the Old Prussian Union.

[11.] Stephanie von Mackensen-Astfeld.

[12.] Friedrich Werner.

[13.] This is the beginning of the second stanza of the chorale *Aus irdischem Getümmel* ("From earthly turmoil," by Christoph Aschenfeldt, in *Evangelisches Gesangbuch Brandenburg-Pommern*, 356).

[14.] Karl-Heinrich Reimer, a Confessing pastor under the patronage of Ewald von Kleist. [The reference is to his leaving the Confessing Church.—VB]

[15.] President Karl Koch.

[16.] [The German here, *Eselsbrücke*, literally means "donkey's bridge."—VB]

[17.] Karl Barth; see 1/22, ed. note 1. Regarding the situation, see also Rohkrämer, "Karl Barth in der Herbstkrise 1938."

And as a supplement I took the communication about Essen[18] along and just read it. I understand nothing of the legal questions, but it seems to me as though something like an "Agricultural Buying and Selling Cooperative"[19] should be newly established! Am I incorrect when I gather that in this election system German Christians can also be nominated? When do they *not* preach "Christ"?! They will swallow the "unique and fulfilled revelation" in order to get in. Oh, how must you be feeling when this is hitting even me so deeply. I'm pleased that Brandt[20] has announced his coming on Saturday–Sunday (in case he still gets leave from his barracks) so that I can talk with him about all these questions. I can understand the jurists, who determined the "circumstantial evidence," least
70 of all. The Essen proposal appears to me to be pure, downright, unvarnished unbelief, when I simply consider the salad of signatures.

In recent days I have thought so much about the "wounded conscience." It is clear, isn't it, that all actions that don't correspond down to the iota with our essential view mean an offense? As I was recently discussing the question with my son,[21] he said, "Naturally it *is* an offense." . . . I found him downhearted because he is not in a position to take these things lightly, or like my son-in-law Wedemeyer[22] to acknowledge them as "God's will." He is taking it hard. I myself believe that it is God's will to forgive but not to justify them. Today it was a comfort for me to read that Abraham committed the same sin twice (passing his wife off as his sister)[23] and nonetheless, as it is explained in the Jub[iläums] Bible,[24] remained God's "confidant."[25] "'Sin boldly'—for Luther that could be only the very last bit of pastoral advice, of consolation for those who along the path of discipleship have come to know that they cannot become sin-free, who out of fear of sin despair of God's grace."[26] Or is there still a justification in advance for actions that "offend" the conscience? The more I attempt to get

[18.] See Bonhoeffer's September 10, 1938, letter to Karl Koch and Friedrich Müller, 1/26.

[19.] [She is suggesting that the church might just as well be a commercial company, since the church leaders have lost sight of their mission.—VB]

[20.] Probably Günther Brandt.

[21.] Hans-Jürgen von Kleist-Retzow.

[22.] Hans von Wedemeyer.

[23.] See Gen. 12:10–20 and 20:1–18.

[24.] The Stuttgarter Jubiläumsbibel. [This was an extensively annotated edition of the Bible published in 1912 by the Stuttgart Bible Society. Cf. *DBWE* 16:48.—VB]

[25.] See the explanation of Gen. 20:18 in the Stuttgarter Jubiläumsbibel, 25.

[26.] This is a quotation from *Discipleship* (see *DBWE* 4:52) and Bonhoeffer's interpretation of Luther's statement: "Sin boldly, but believe and rejoice in Christ that much more boldly!" [This is from Luther's *Briefwechsel*, 3:28, lines 121ff.; also in *LW* 48:282.—VB]

clear about this, the more it seems to me that here, too, the distinction between outcome and presupposition[27] must be observed.

So the synod has been postponed due to the Essen question, as I've been told. . . . I'm glad that you apparently are having such a good vacation there.[28] In any case I want to tell you that I'll be in Krössin October 4–14. If one can think as far as the fourth. After some urging, I offered the little essay[29] to Söhlmann,[30] rather half-heartedly. It would be just as fine with me if he didn't want to have it. I have received several replies that brought me great joy. From the eldest son in Lasbeck:[31] "It is as though tailored for me." And from my eldest and first godchild, who attaches some confessions. To be allowed occasionally to be an instrument—oh, that's what makes life rewarding. But who am I telling that to— 71
both of you, for whom this is the content of your life. How well I understand it.

The letter is for you both. I'm writing it in an evening hour, following a stay in the air-raid cellar! I was told about the radio broadcast. I don't have one.[32]

My letter has really become too long, but who knows what the future brings. My son-in-law Wedemeyer must leave on Saturday.[33]

Always in complete devotion, your
Ruth Kleist

29. To Erwin Sutz[1]

September 18, 1938

Dear Brother Sutz,

It has been some time, once again—but it may well be a good sign that, despite such long interruptions, we return again and again to each other

[27.] Cf. *DBWE* 4:52.

[28.] In Göttingen.

[29.] In 1938 Ruth von Kleist composed an essay about reading the Bible: "Why should I read the Bible? A statement for my dear grandchildren, all godchildren, and for the great-grandchildren." Cf. Pejsa, *Matriarch of Conspiracy*, 233–34 and 403.

[30.] Fritz Söhlmann was the editor of *Junge Kirche*. Ruth von Kleist's essay was not published.

[31.] Jürgen von Bismarck.

[32.] The reference is to listening to the foreign radio stations during the Sudeten crisis in September 1938. On September 12, Hitler had given the Czech government an ultimatum to cede the Sudetenland to the German Reich under the threat of military action.

[33.] Hans von Wedemeyer had been drafted into the army.

[1.] In the personal possession of the Sutz family; handwritten; from Göttingen. Cf. *NL*, A 29,4 (20). Previously published in *GS* 1:48–45.

through correspondence. There are two reasons why I am writing you today, first, because I don't know how often I will still be able to write and because I want to thank you for always sending me your good devotions, as well as for your visit to Berlin and Finkenwalde, where unfortunately I missed you both times.[2] Second, I'm writing because to my great relief my sister with her husband and children are in Zurich[3] for several weeks (Kurhaus Zurichberg, Prof. Leibholz) and because you might be hearing from them sometime. Please be good to them then! If you could visit them sometime without too much difficulty, that would be especially nice.

72 At the moment I have vacation and am trying to write something.[4] But it goes slowly; I have too much else on my mind. I long greatly for a few quiet months for scholarly work. I would like to get all kind of things off my chest, but during work I don't really get to it. Too bad that you didn't bring me for a year to Zurich to stand in for Brunner![5] That would not have been bad at all. In remotest eastern Pomerania, one rather loses contact with the world. There is simply so much to do, too, that no time remains for quiet correspondence. One needs the little spare time that remains for one's own work. But the work continues to bring pleasure while continuing to grow. The only strange thing is the existence in which there can be no worries, since each day is a gift. If one forgets that, then one sometimes becomes rather stubborn and would rather choose a somewhat more settled existence, with all the "rights" that one otherwise has at this "estate"[6] and age. That would mean the abandonment of the work, however, and that simply won't do at the moment. You will know that our friend Jean Lasserre[7] married a few weeks ago! I would like to see him again and will write him in the next days as well. How nice it would be if the three of us could be together again, particularly now! There would be so much to think and talk about. Let these short lines please you and remember our cause and my own, just as I often and gladly remember yours. χάρις ὑμῖν καὶ εἰρήνη.[8]

Your devoted
Dietrich Bonhoeffer

[2.] See Bonhoeffer's October 24, 1938, letter to Sutz from Finkenwalde, in which Bonhoeffer requests a visit to Finkenwalde (*DBW* 14, 1/125).

[3.] The Leibholz family was en route to London as emigrants (see 1/25 and 1/26).

[4.] Bonhoeffer was working on his book *Life Together.*

[5.] From 1938 to 1939, Emil Brunner was a guest professor at Princeton.

[6.] [I.e., as a pastor.—VB]

[7.] Bonhoeffer, Sutz, and Lasserre had gotten to known one another during their studies at Union Theological Seminary in New York in 1930–31. See *DB-ER*, 152–54; this period is covered in *DBWE* 10.

[8.] "Grace to you and peace" (Rom. 1:7).

30. From Albrecht Schönherr to Several Finkenwalde Brothers[1] 73

Brüssow, October 7, 1938

Invitation

In the discussion about the church situation during a retreat in June of this year,[2] fifty young pastors of the Confessing Church decided that it was also necessary here in northeast Germany for a group of Confessing Church theologians to convene in order to work through the pending church questions in a theologically thorough fashion. Recently you will have realized clearly how urgent it is that such a service be performed for the church.[3]

The brothers at that time gave Pastor Dr. Bonhoeffer and myself the task of bringing such a group into being. Up to now the following have joined: Dr. Gollwitzer, Pastor Klapproth, Pastor Ebeling, all from Berlin, and Pastor Krause-Greifswald.[4]

We thought of inviting only those brothers who are not already overburdened with other church work. It is indeed urgently necessary for thorough scholarly work that these brothers manage to be free as the case arises, even for several days. We think that for the time being it is best for this association to work entirely unofficially, and try to gain a hearing only through the work it does. We would like to ask you as well to join with us in this work.

The first meeting, when various technical questions would need to be discussed, is to take place from October 31, beginning at 11 o'clock, till November 2. Location: Stettin, Pölitzerstr. 103. You will receive more information in time.

For our first topic we chose "The Public-Legal Status of the Church." We consider this topic extremely urgent, particularly in view of the new generation in the Confessing Church.[5]

It is imperative that all participating brothers prepare themselves thoroughly for this topic. I hope to be able to send all of you the theses of the papers sufficiently in advance. I expect your replies and registration by October 20 at the latest.

With brotherly greetings, your
A. Schönherr

[1.] Literary estate of Albrecht Schönherr; mimeograph with handwritten signature; previously unpublished.

[2.] The retreat of former Finkenwalde seminarians, held in Zingst on June 20–25, 1938. See 1/21.

[3.] This is an indirect reference to the issue of the loyalty oath to Hitler and the Essen negotiations ("Essen I" through "Essen III"). See 1/22, 1/25, and 1/26.

[4.] Helmut Gollwitzer, Erich Klapproth, Gerhard Ebeling, and Gerhard Krause.

[5.] This was because of the illegal status of the younger vicars and pastors in the Confessing Church.

74 **31. To Martin Fischer**[1]

Dear Brother Fischer,

Heartfelt thanks for the announcement.[2] I think of you with all good wishes and in brotherly affection.

> "May God now give me each day as much as I need to live;
> He gives this to the sparrow on the roof; how should he not give it to me."
>
> (Claudius)[3]

your humble
Dietrich Bonhoeffer

32. From Ulrich Nithack[1]

Berlin-Friedenau, October 30, 1938

Esteemed, dear Brother Bonhoeffer,

Since now finally somewhat quieter times have arrived for me, I would like to get back in touch with you. Probably Brother Sander[2] has already told you of our delightful trip through Pomerania. Afterward I waited for the assignment[3] and
75 on September 23 received the fine topic: "Vilmar's[4] teaching on the church is

---

[1.] In the personal possession of Mrs. Ilse Fischer; handwritten postcard; postmarked Göttingen, October 12, 1938; previously unpublished. That same day, Bonhoeffer and Eberhard Bethge left Göttingen and returned to Pomerania via Berlin, since the 1938–39 winter session began in the collective pastorate in Köslin on October 17, 1938, and in Groß-Schlönwitz on October 19, 1938. During his stay in Berlin, Bonhoeffer's brother-in-law Hans von Dohnanyi introduced him to the circle of Dohnanyi's colleagues around justice minister Franz Gürtner. These contacts became ever more important with the beginning of the resistance conspiracy. See Bethge's letters to his mother from Göttingen on October 8, 1938, and from Groß-Schlönwitz on October 23, 1938, in Andersen et al., *So ist es gewesen*, 334–35.

[2.] The announcement of Fischer's engagement on October 1, 1938.

[3.] This is the last stanza of the poem "Täglich zu singen" (To sing each day) by Matthias Claudius, from the third section (1777) of the *Wandsbecker Boten*, cited here with slight variations [Bonhoeffer was quoting from memory—VB]. See the 1941 Pantheon edition, 1:282 (new printing: 150). Cf. also *DBWE* 4:167.

[1.] *NL*, C 25; handwritten; previously unpublished. Nithack was a member of the collective pastorate in Groß-Schlönwitz in the summer of 1938.

[2.] Erwin Sander.

[3.] For the papers to be written for the second theological examination taken before the Confessing Church Council of Brethren.

[4.] August Friedrich Christian Vilmar.

to be described and evaluated according to Holy Scripture." The second section may indeed be quite difficult. Then on September 24 the call-up to the military arrived and for four weeks tore me away not only from work but from the entire mentality of the last half year. I wrote something about the personal difficulties that I had "on the front" in the circular letter, which may also reach Schl[awe].[5]

Now I am reading Vilmar and am happy when I am reminded of many a conversation in Schlönwitz. It is consoling when this great preacher writes of "crises," "disordered thoughts," and "conspicuous slowness" in his work on sermons;[6] but the fact that he never felt good anywhere when he hadn't stood in the pulpit on Sunday is also encouraging and a reminder for self-examination. One often experiences the reverse. I am already eager to read Vilmar's essay on church discipline in which he deals in detail with confession.[7] For him private confession is self-evident[8] on the basis of CA XI.[9] Leafing through the book, I read of massive acts of penance that Vilmar put upon a prostitute: two worship services on Sunday, reporting to the pastor, learning things by heart, etc.[10] But that cannot shake our confidence in the value of confession. I hope to be able to speak with my brothers here more often about confession. Brother Klapproth[11] wants to try to convene the brothers frequently. Since Schlönwitz and particularly after the last session, I have a particular longing for such fellowship.

In the parish I have found that everywhere there is diminishing understanding for the Confessing Church. People are weary, that means in unbelief. They are seeking a modus vivendi and forget that we should not settle here too firmly at all.

I am pleased that brothers are now there[12] again and pray for generous blessings upon the entire work.

In constant gratitude and with brotherly greetings I am your
Ulrich Nithack

[5.] This circular letter from Nithack is not extant.
[6.] See Vilmar, *Lehrbuch der Pastoraltheologie*, 69.
[7.] See Vilmar, *Von der christlichen Kirchenzucht* (1872).
[8.] Ibid., 33.
[9.] Augsburg Confession, Article 11 (*Book of Concord*, 44).
[10.] Vilmar, *Von der christlichen Kirchenzucht*, 80–81.
[11.] Erich Klapproth.
[12.] In Groß-Schlönwitz near Köslin.

17:123 **32a. To Walter and Susanne Dreß**[1]

November 4, 1938

Dear Susi, dear Walter,

You will be surprised to receive a letter from me at such an odd time. Dear Walter, I thank you for what you sent, which was not really for me, or was it? What should I do with the publication? Primarily, however, I am writing you about a matter that has become somewhat complicated in the meantime. But since I find it most sensible to discuss such matters openly, I am doing so here. It is about the English rug and the question of whether you need it urgently. I recently saw it lying, dear Walter, in all its glory in your room and once again happened to find it very lovely. Since I assume the same is true for you, I don't know whether you are capable of parting with it again or only with great difficulty? I wanted to give it to Christel for Leipzig.[2] |17:124| In reality she has no sufficiently decent rug for her salon. I realized this recently when they had company there. On the other hand, they really need one and want to return the rug borrowed from the Schleichers, so that it won't be too ruined as part of a future trousseau. I told Christel that I would write to you. She wrote me yesterday and pleaded *urgently* with me not to do so. I am therefore doing so against her will, in the opinion that it is indeed possible to talk sensibly about this. I was of the opinion that a living-room rug is actually more necessary than a rug for a man's salon. That is why I ask you to consider this and perhaps, Susi, you will be so friendly as to call Christel while she is still in Berlin and talk it over with her. She will probably hesitate, in the opinion that she is robbing you. But I did want it to at least be discussed. Mama decided very quickly at the time when you were setting up house, and there was nothing then to say against it. Only the situation is changing now due to the move and one must reconsider it. Perhaps the rug in your office doesn't matter that much to you at all, Walter, so that the matter is no problem at all. Therefore, I believe it is best if you, Susi, would telephone Christel sometime. Mama already knows about this consideration. How are things otherwise? When will the baptism be celebrated? At

[1.] Literary estate of Walter Dreß, in the personal possession of Ruprecht Dreß; handwritten letter, probably sent from Groß-Schlönwitz; previously unpublished.

[2.] Bonhoeffer's brother-in-law Hans von Dohnanyi had been appointed Reich judicial counselor in Leipzig and started his job there on October 1, 1938. [Christel was Bonhoeffer's sister Christine.—VB]

Christmas? Here everything is normal; only the province is in bad shape.[3] All the best and warm greetings from your

Dietrich

33. From Sabine and Gerhard Leibholz[1] 76

Dear Dietrich,

We've been here three days now. Since we traveled via Paris, we arrived in Dover. The ship was small, the sea stormy. I have never seen such waves. Unfortunately, I couldn't look out for long, because after ten minutes Gert was pale as a corpse and sick as a dog and only groaned about when we would be through it. Afterward in the train, too, he was still utterly useless. Mr. Böckheler[2] picked us up very nicely and took us to Miss Sharp, where we are staying.[3] Then we had supper at his house in the evening, and it was a great pleasure for me to see your old parsonage[4] and everything again. Franz[5] is traveling. Mr. Rieger[6] is coming at the end of the week. We've been invited to the Kaufmanns'.[7] They were very amicable. Otherwise nothing else. The distances are too enormous. The city takes my breath away. It must be hell to live here in the summer. It is a relief when in the evening one gets back out here to quiet again. Gert is still very self-conscious about speaking. He also doesn't yet want to visit Uncle G.[8] I doubt that he will be able to speak much better in fourteen days. I'm in favor of making visits soon, also because we must be thinking about the trip home and we still have so many invitations from people.[9] The weather is still reasonably

---

[3.] Pomerania, the church province of the Evangelical Church of the Old Prussian Union. See 1/14, ed. note 2, and 1/19.

[1.] *NL*, C 6; handwritten postcard addressed "To Pastor Berke Groß-Schlönwitz," postmarked Forest Hill [London], November 8, 1938; previously unpublished.

[2.] Martin Böckheler.

[3.] The owner of the guest house where the Leibholzes initially lived. Cf. Leibholz-Bonhoeffer, *Bonhoeffers*, 92.

[4.] After October 1933, during his work in the London congregations of Sydenham and St. Paul's, Bonhoeffer resided at the parsonage in the South London suburb of Forest Hill. See Bethge and Gremmels, *Life in Pictures*, centenary ed., 73; this period is covered in *DBWE* 13.

[5.] Franz Hildebrandt.

[6.] Julius Rieger.

[7.] Not identified.

[8.] George Bell.

[9.] Sentences such as this were written with an eye on the Gestapo's possible control of the mail, since in reality this was not just a visit, but the emigration of the Leibholz family to England.

warm, and we have not yet had fog. Gert's brother Hans[10] is here in London on business for Königs.[11] Please write us what else you would recommend to us. Warmly, your

Sabine

Dear Dietrich,

Well of course I want to visit Uncle G. and indeed soon. But I am still thinking of
77 improving my English somewhat. And whether I will manage that is also a question for me, mind you. Boeckheler received us with true hospitality. And we will call on Rieger. The most important thing is to meet together with prominent English people or in any case with those who can give introductions to others. If you think of something else that could be of use for our mission, or if someone else occurs to you of whom it seems advisable to you that we should visit them, please let us know. Our address is Honor Oak Rd. 55 SE 23. Forest Hill, Tel. Forest Hill 14-45.

The accommodations are nice enough, and our intention is to stay here—unless the heating is insufficient, which is uncomfortable on cold days. Let us hear from you again, also about how you are doing. As always, warmly

Gert

34. To Sabine and Gerhard Leibholz[1]

November 10, 1938

Dear Sabine, dear Gert,

Many thanks for your greetings from my former congregation.[2] I'm pleased that you have been received well and already have your first invitations. Once you've gotten settled there somewhat, you'll like it better than in the first days. For example, the poorly heated rooms are an English evil

[10.] Hans Leibholz.

[11.] The Koenigs family were relatives of the Bonhoeffers in the Netherlands.

[1.] *NL*, A 44,1 (12); later typewritten copy (the original has been lost); no address given, but probably sent from Groß-Schlönwitz. Previously published in *GS* 6:446–47.

[2.] From October 1933 to January 1935, Bonhoeffer had been pastor of the Sydenham and St. Paul's parishes in London. Cf. *DB-ER*, 325–417, and *DBWE* 13.

that one can't escape anywhere. But for Gert perhaps this may not be so disagreeable? Please do give Miss Sharp my greetings. She has always been so sweet, and you will surely learn good English at her place. By the way, the Behrends[3] lived with her back then. If you visit them sometime, they will certainly also be very nice. He is a terribly fat, good-humored Bavarian with a prospering antique shop. The wife is helpful and nice. I don't know whether they will be of much help to you, but perhaps there will be some 78
occasion. You, dear Sabine, would have a thoughtful and warmhearted help in Mrs. Whitburn,[4] née Lokies, a German, if you should need it. They live in straitened circumstances in the north of London. But I always enjoyed being together with the two of them. One can discuss everything with them, and they don't have many visitors. You will surely be going to visit George[5] soon. His wife knows some German. Since he does have many friends, it would be good if you don't postpone it too long. He would also be the best one to bring you together with Sir Walter Moberly; otherwise I can write Moberly as well, only then you would have to write me his address. Please write me as well about Schröder.[6] He is very ill, Parkinson's disease, but perhaps he can receive you nonetheless; he was always very friendly and helpful to me. If you want to call on him, then I will write him in advance. But then please let me know that. I would naturally be very happy to do it; I just don't want to do it unnecessarily if it's not important to you. And perhaps your time is already filled. Otherwise, please always let me know if you think that I can help you in any way.

I wish you a good time with truly nice weather. That contributes significantly to well-being in London. Dreadful that you had such a nasty boat trip.

Every day I think of you often and wish you all the best! Greetings to you from your

Dietrich

[3.] Not identified.

[4.] Cf. *DB-ER*, 328. [Mrs. Whitburn was the sister of Hans Lokies, a Confessing pastor in Berlin who headed the mission work there.—VB]

[5.] George Bell.

[6.] Baron Bruno Schröder.

79 35. From Albrecht Schönherr to the Participants of the Theological Society in Pomerania[1]

November 14, 1938

Dear Brothers,

It is difficult to communicate the outcome of our first gathering[2] to those brothers who were not there. It consists essentially of the questions listed below. I think, however, that next time we will arrive at visible developments—this time we had a more invisible achievement, namely, the fact that eight theologians could sit together in objectivity and *quiet* for a few days, simply in order to work together.

Brother Bonhoeffer and I had been commissioned to distribute the questions, which we posed to ourselves at the end, to the individual speakers for preparatory work. We thought of distributing them as follows: (the headings suggested for the presentations are to be understood as talking points for the respective questions)

Gollwitzer:[3] *Jus divinum* and *jus humanum*[4] in the church rules. Bonhoeffer: copresenter.

Traub:[5] Emergency rules of order. [Notrecht][6]

Schönherr: *Exousia*[7] in the New Testament.

Klapproth:[8] The twofold call to the ministry.

Fischer:[9] Position toward the consistories and the neutrals.

Perels:[10] Leaving the church. Church taxes.

The following is once again the formulation of the questions, the response to which, it seems to us, matters in the question of the public and legal position of the church.

1. Under what conditions can the church make legal claims upon the state? (a) on which ground? (b) under what conditions? (c) to what extent? (concerning this: is the public role of the church confined to preaching?)

[1.] Literary estate of Albrecht Schönherr; typewritten mimeograph with handwritten signature, from Brüssow; previously unpublished.

[2.] Cf. Schönherr's October 7, 1938, letter to several Finkenwalde seminarians, 1/30.

[3.] Helmut Gollwitzer.

[4.] Divine law and human law.

[5.] Hellmut Traub.

[6.] [A reference to the emergency church law adopted at the Dahlem Confessing synod in October 1934.—VB]

[7.] Authority, power, lordship.

[8.] Erich Klapproth.

[9.] Martin Fischer.

[10.] Friedrich Justus Perels.

2. The legal claims of the state upon the church.
3. Is a twofold vocation essentially necessary for the pastoral ministry? (through worldly authority and congregation) 80
4. To what degree does the Confessing Church have the commission from God's word to exercise church leadership?
5. What is the meaning of emergency law [Not-Recht]?[11]
6. What does the right suffering of injustice by the church consist of?
7. In our position toward authority, to what degree do we stand in continuity with the decisions of the Lutheran Reformation?
8. What possibilities exist for keeping up necessary forms of congregational life, independent of state recognition?
9. What paths are to be pursued (a) on principle? (b) in fact?
10. What possibilities are ruled out (a) on principle? (b) in fact?
11. What follows from this for the position (a) toward the consistories? (b) toward the undecided?
12. How can the danger be avoided that through the character of the Confessing Church as an organization the proclamation will be hindered?

We had agreed that the next meeting will be held on January 9–11 at the same location.[12] Therefore, the theses for presentations must reach me by December 15 at the latest, those of the copresenters by January 1, 1939. I request to be told as soon as possible, should there be any objections against the distribution of the presentations or different wishes with regard to the date.

With friendly greetings, your
A. Schönherr

36. To the Finkenwalde Brothers[1] 81

Personal letter!

November 20, 1938

Dear Brothers,

At the end of the old and the beginning of the new church year, I greet you with the passage from the meditation text from last week: "May the God of

---

[11.] [Many of the issues listed here were the same ones that had led to tensions between different factions at the 1934 Dahlem synod, which was also the occasion for the establishment of *Notrecht* within the Confessing Church.—VB]

[12.] Cf. Schönherr's October 7, 1938, letter, 1/30.

[1.] *NL*, A 48,3 (6); typewritten mimeograph; no return address but probably from Groß-Schlönwitz. Partially reproduced in *GS* 2:541–44. This letter of Bonhoeffer was taken by the Pomeranian Council of Brethren and sent to all Pomeranian pastors as

patient endurance[2] and encouragement grant you to live in harmony with one another, in accordance with Christ Jesus" (Rom. 15:5). Recently here we have worked a great deal and reflected together on the New Testament concept of patient endurance. In the process, it has become quite clear to me that today we have arrived right there where in essence the only issue at stake is whether we are willing to learn from the gospel what patient endurance means. I believe we needn't take the various questions, through which impatience sneaks in today, nearly as seriously as they want to be taken. The only very serious thing is that our impatience always wants to play such nasty tricks on us, in that it feigns itself to be a very special kind of obedience and diverts us to unfaithfulness. I don't quite know how, but we have widely succumbed to a thinking that is nothing short of dangerous. We think that we are acting particularly responsibly when every few weeks we reconsider the question of whether the path on which we've started was the right one. Here it's especially striking that such "responsible examination" always commences just when serious difficulties become evident. We then convince ourselves that we no longer have "the right gladness and
82 certainty for this path" or, even worse, that God is no longer with us with his word in the old clarity, and with all this we essentially are only trying to circumvent that which the New Testament calls "patient endurance" and "probation." In any case, Paul did not begin to reflect about whether his path was right when obstacles and suffering threatened, nor did Luther; instead, in the very midst of this they may have become completely certain and joyful, standing in discipleship and communion with their Lord. Dear brothers, our real crisis is not at all the doubt about the path we have begun but rather our failure of patience, of remaining below. We are still unable to imagine that God today really wants nothing new of us but solely that we stand the test in the old. That is too little for us, too monotonous, too modest. We still refuse to accept that God's cause is not always the cause of success and that we could really be "unsuccessful" even following the right path. But it is precisely here that it will become decisive whether we have started out in faith or in Enthusiasm.

---

a "Pomeranian circular letter." A mimeographed insertion (1 page) was added with excerpts from a September 1938 lecture by Johannes Hamel, "Obedience to Authority," also in *NL*, A 48,3 (6). On the one hand, the obedience "owed to *every* authority" is emphasized; on the other "the distinction between good and evil authority, between justice and injustice for the Christian" is inculcated, recalling the "church-community's public office of witness about injustice and violence," with reference to Martin Luther and the confessional writings.

[2.] [The NRSV here reads "steadfastness."—VB]

It is striking how much significance patience receives in the New Testament. Only those who endure[3] receive the good news (Matt. 24:13), only the patient one brings forth good fruit (Luke 8:15). A faith that doesn't become patient endurance is not genuine, of no use. Faith must be proven. Probation comes only through suffering. Only from suffering, only from remaining below does the "fulfilled work"[4] (James 1:3) emerge. If we remind ourselves that the word "faith"—πίστις—already contains the moment of loyalty, then the close connection between faith and patient endurance will not surprise us. There is patient endurance only "in Jesus" (Rev. 1:9), for Jesus practiced patient endurance as he bore the cross. Heb. 12:2 describes Jesus's way of the cross as remaining below, as patience. Remaining below for us means to stand in communion with the sufferings of Christ ([2][5] Cor. 1:6–7) and through that to win confidence. If we take part in the patient endurance of Jesus, we become patient ourselves, and in the end we will partake of Christ's kingdom (2 Tim. 2:12). The path to patience goes through discipline (2 Pet. 1:6). The freer we become from comfort and idleness, from personal demands, the more willing we become for patient endurance.

Our text[6] tells us that we can remain one only if we remain in patience. 83
Impatience causes division. And unfortunately it cannot be denied that all those who out of impatience go their own way or have already done so have made the struggle for probation and patience much more difficult for many a brother.[7] Impatience destroys community. In the sense of the gospel, it is not merely a small pardonable bad habit but a failure of probation when faith is put to the test. "Yet the God of patient endurance"—the God who in Jesus Christ himself remained below and helps us remain below, may that God grant you to be "of one mind"—that in this hour of testing you stand by one another, indeed pull more closely and firmly together, strengthen and help one another. Terrible, when in such times one person withdraws. But our patience depends not only on people but on Jesus Christ and his patient endurance on the cross. Christ also bore the impatience of all human beings and thus can forgive it. "Being of one mind"—indeed, that means not choosing one way today and another tomorrow, but remaining

[3.] [Bonhoeffer's word here is *Geduld*, thus those who are "patient."—VB]

[4.] [The NRSV here reads "full effect."—VB]

[5.] In the manuscript incorrectly written as "1."

[6.] Rom. 15:5.

[7.] The reference is to the problem of legalization; see *DB-ER*, 607–20, as well as Bonhoeffer's lecture of October 26, 1938, "Our Path according to the Testimony of Scripture"; see 2/5.

firm, being constant, proving oneself loyal, to what has once been acknowledged. How little value do we attach to firmness, constancy, and loyalty. In the Scriptures they stand at the very top. May God give them to us by making us patient and granting us his consolation in our remaining below. United in patience, united in consolation. We belong together in remaining below; we belong together as well in consolation and the final overcoming. No one fights the battle of probation alone. In the hour in which our patience is tested, those with whom we are of one mind are with us. Above all, however, we know that we are one in Jesus's patience and consolation. He is our patience and our consolation. So it will remain in the new church year as well.

If I may advise you, take the effort and work together with us on the concepts that we are dealing with at the moment: temptation, patience, probation, humility, thanksgiving, joy, peace, discipline.[8] In these items we must learn to hear the gospel entirely new. We are being led through
84 the Scriptures along little-traveled ways, but they offer indescribably broad and beautiful prospects. The meditation texts for the coming weeks should help us in this as well.

In the last few days, I have thought much about Ps. 74, Zech. 2:8, Rom. 9:4–5, and 11:11–15.[9] That leads deeply into prayer.

I was very happy to hear from many of you and also to receive sermons from you. May I ask those brothers to whom I return the sermons to inform me at least with a postcard whether the sermons arrived and whether they are in agreement with the evaluation. Please don't think at all that I can't be reached by mail, but write and tell me more again. I believe that in recent months I have gotten better at replying; in any case I have made some efforts in this direction, for today one really should not let such fellowship be broken off through laziness. Above all, however, keep up the connection among yourselves, write and visit each other. That would be the most important thing.

I wish you from the heart a good Advent season. God bless your preaching and all your work. May God protect you and your homes. We think of you daily.

In brotherly fellowship greetings to you from your faithful
Dietrich Bonhoeffer

[8.] Cf. 2/2.

[9.] On the night of November 9, 1938, the so-called *Reichkristallnacht*, the synagogue in Köslin was burned down as well; see Zimmermann, *I Knew Dietrich Bonhoeffer*, 152–56. Regarding Bonhoeffer's situation and reaction, see E. Bethge, "Dietrich Bonhoeffer and the Jews," 73–75, and E. Bethge, "One of the Silent Bystanders?"

Meditation texts:

Nov. 20–Nov. 26:	Matt. 24:1–14 (patience)
Nov. 27–Dec. 3:	Rev. 3:7–12 (patience)
Dec. 4–Dec. 10:	1 Pet. 5:1–11 (service and humility)
Dec. 11–Dec. 17:	Phil. 4:1–9 (joy)
Dec. 18–Dec. 24:	Isa. 9:5.6; Luke 2:14 and 19:12 (thankfulness)
Dec. 25–Dec. 31:	Ps. 75 (peace)
Jan. 1–Jan. 7:	Ps. 1
Jan. 8–Jan. 14:	1 Thess. 1
Jan. 15–Jan. 21:	1 Thess. 2
Jan. 22–Jan. 28:	1 Thess. 3
Jan. 29–Feb. 4:	1 Thess. 4
Feb. 5–Feb. 11:	1 Thess. 5

37. To Sabine and Gerhard Leibholz[1] 85

December 5, 1938

Dear Sabine, dear Gert,

Many thanks for the letter.[2] One is happy for every sign of life when we are so far apart. How nice that your invitation there is so friendly and for such a long time. Hopefully, you are finding time to work in the British Museum library. It is very quiet and lovely there, don't you think?

I was really extraordinarily happy to hear that you are going to celebrate Christmas together with our parents and the children. You will certainly spend lovely days at the home of Mucki Koenigs-Kalckreuth.[3] Mama just wrote me about it. So now you're meeting all my old friends and parishioners. Do give my greetings to Mr. Henne.[4] I will write him for Christmas. He is a very loyal man and helpful in all matters when one needs him; his wife is also very sweet. Do go there sometimes; he is always pleased and is only somewhat awkward and embarrassed. Dear Gert, he should also get you together sometime with Mr. Seagell,[5] who preaches every month at St.

[1.] Later typewritten copy in the literary estate of Eberhard Bethge (the original has been lost); no return address. Previously published in *GS* 6:447–49.

[2.] The Leibholzes' letter is not extant.

[3.] Anna Koenigs, née Countess von Kalckreuth, was a relative in the Netherlands; cf. Bonhoeffer's letter at Christmas 1938 to Christiane Leibholz, 1/45.

[4.] Gottlieb Henne was chair of the parish council at the Reformed St. Paul's parish in London.

[5.] Not identified.

Paul's and is also very nice and ready to help, an old bachelor who has given all his money to the needy and lives the life of an ascetic. He will certainly be very kind to you. Do call Henne sometime in this matter and please greet S[eagell] from me when you see him. Also the Cromwells[6] should give you the names of those whom I helped during my time there.[7] They still occasionally write a postcard, but I no longer have the addresses. I will write to George[8] again tomorrow. He is indeed a true friend. I think that
86 he will have impressed you favorably as well. Do ask him to invite you for a few days. Moreover, he should certainly bring you together with Sir Walter Moberly, who is a very cultured and fine man. I would really find that desirable. I will write to him as well and send both letters to Mama.[9]

By the way, it is a very widespread experience that for a German everything moves too slowly. The Germans are prone to catch this, and people like us become accustomed to it very slowly. But there's no reason at all for impatience. Everything just moves more slowly but usually also surely. As a German over there, you have to tell yourself this every day—until you become like this yourself! This, however, won't agree very much with your disposition! Can't Mucki speak sometime with Mr. Schröder?[10] I think that would be very nice. I can write him as well.

You asked about Tillich.[11] I know him, that is, I got to know him during his work for two days here, and perhaps he thinks of it with pleasure if he is not too forgetful. He will certainly remember. Please mention me and tell him that I recall the conference with his friends in Wannsee with pleasure. Of course, I am willing to write myself, if you want me to! Niebuhr,[12] of whom I've already told you, is of course better. I'm happy to write him; he was always very friendly to me and wanted to visit me here one year ago. But I would indeed like to know whether I should simply ask in general or already announce your visit. This would be more effective.

[6.] The family of the lawyer Philipp Cromwell in London.

[7.] Regarding Bonhoeffer's work with refugees in his London parishes, see *DB-ER*, 413–14, and *DBWE* 13:279–82 and 286–89.

[8.] George Bell.

[9.] Bonhoeffer means that he would send the letters not directly to England but rather via his mother in Berlin; this was a cautionary measure to avoid drawing the attention of police officials to his illegal training of seminarians in Pomerania. [The plan was that Paula Bonhoeffer would see the Leibholzes in Holland at Christmas; see 1/45, ed. note 2.—VB]

[10.] Baron Bruno Schröder.

[11.] Paul Tillich.

[12.] Reinhold Niebuhr.

I think of you both daily with all good wishes. If I can help in any way, I will do it, always with the greatest pleasure! Both of you must rely on that! Please just say the word! Till soon!

Heartfelt greetings to you and all the friends there, your faithful
Dietrich

Heartfelt greetings to Miss Sharp.

38. From Franz Ernst Pfisterer[1] 87

Neunkirchen, December 6, 1938

Dear Brother Bonhoeffer,

I thank you very warmly for your detailed letter of November 6.[2] I gratefully confirm that I received your letter of November 20 as well.[3] It is no small matter that such a personal exchange is still possible. Particularly now during the Christmas season my thoughts go back to the time two years ago—especially whenever I sing one of the hymns from *Der helle Ton*, perhaps "Christ we should praise indeed."[4]

But now I will try to give you a reply. I hope that I have understood your summons on the issue of "person." Put bluntly, one could perhaps express it this way: in no way may Christ for us become a means to an end. When the entire accent is put on the gifts of "grace, forgiveness of sins, righteousness," then the human being does move back into the center, without our clearly realizing this. If I recall correctly, here the theology of the Middle Ages, and Luther too, warned of such an *uti deo = deum diligere propter bona.*[5] Is not the recognition of this danger the moment of truth in the challenge of a *resignatio ad infernum?*[6]

[1.] *NL*, C 25; handwritten letter; previously unpublished. Pfisterer was a candidate in the fourth Finkenwalde session in the winter of 1936–37.

[2.] Letter not extant. In this letter Bonhoeffer probably discussed a sermon that Pfisterer had sent him in a previous letter.

[3.] See Bonhoeffer's November 20, 1938, letter to the Finkenwalde brothers, 1/36.

[4.] Hymn 18 in the hymnal *Der helle Ton* [a hymnal published by the Reich Association of Protestant Young Men; see 1/165—VB]. Originally an early church hymn, "A solis ortus cardine," it was translated by Martin Luther into German in 1524. [An English translation, "Now Praise We Christ, the Holy One," is in *Lutheran Hymnal*, 104.—VB]

[5.] The "use of God" as "loving God for the sake of God's good gifts." See the distinctions in Bernhard von Clairvaux's work "On Loving God" (*De diligendo Deo*), in A. Adam, *Lehrbuch der Dogmengeschichte II*, 77.

[6.] "Resignation to hell." This is a technical term in German mysticism, particularly in the work of Johannes Tauler, who describes the complete renunciation of salvation and

I completely agree with you that to receive Christ is much more than to receive some kind of gift—even the highest gift. Perhaps more should have been said about the Holy Spirit, which of course is not an object but the very spirit of God and of Christ. Perhaps, however, this would only be a shifting of the difficulty, unless the Holy Spirit is dissolved in some general human concept of spirit.
88 I recall well the difficulty that I felt when I had to say something about what it means to receive *Christ.* And then I nonetheless spoke about the *bona.*[7] I would, however, ask whether the New Testament does not often speak this way. Eph. 1:3–14, then especially in the Gospel of John (3:16–36; 6:35; 7:38; 11:25–26, for example). On the other hand, I think it is very significant that the decisive confession of faith by the early Christian church-community was not: Christ the σωτήρ, but rather Christ the κύριος.[8] In that, the early church-community indeed asserted that the κύριος is the σωτήρ, that the gifts of "grace, forgiveness of sins, life" come from him, and yet the confession demonstrates that Christ is more than a good fairy.

Unfortunately, I am not such a good expert on Luther as to be able to follow your reference to Luther. But I believe I recall from my reading of the Gollwitzer book[9] that Luther considered the body and blood important as symbol rather than as gift in the Lord's Supper. Perhaps this is all too schematized.

I didn't spend too much effort on the χάρις ἀντὶ χάριτος,[10] but followed W. Bauer here.[11] Perhaps at this point some of the danger of freely choosing a text from a certain viewpoint becomes evident.

Up to now I have followed the practice of memorizing my sermons almost word for word. I have some difficulty in formulating and constructing sentences. Some things simply cannot be said in a few short sentences (or more correctly, I haven't been able to up to now). Naturally it would be better to hold such a sermon on the preceding Sunday, but I was not scheduled for the service then.

the affirmation of the condemnation to hell. See A. Adam, *Lehrbuch der Dogmengeschichte II*, 185.

[7.] [(God's) good gifts.—VB]

[8.] "The savior"; "the Lord."

[9.] See Gollwitzer, *Coena Domini* (The Lord's Supper), 54–65.

[10.] "Grace upon grace" (John 1:16).

[11.] Bauer, *Griechisch-Deutsches Wörterbuch.*

By the way, some time ago a woman who is affiliated with the communal movement[12] asked me whether no one had spoken to me about this sermon. That did not happen, but she seems to have thought that some communal members had viewed it as too severe. A strange kind of liberalism concerning "free will" and the sacraments prevails here, at least among many.

My days here are now numbered. On November 18 a new pastor was elected who is a loyal member of the Confessing Church. He will probably come on January 1, 1939. It remains to be seen what will happen to me then. One can indeed be happy when one gets any kind of ministry. The Westphalian Confessing Church has rather an overflow of assistant pastors. And the possibilities for work are fewer and fewer. Previously I sometimes had the thought of going 89
abroad for a while. But today that seems to be ruled out for people like us.

Yesterday the district synod was held here, where most participants—but without enthusiasm!—accepted Essen III.[13] Those in charge tried to make this palatable for us with the comment that hopefully this would lead to a coming together with the neutrals[14] in the east. How do people there[15] think about these matters? Is there a likelihood for an agreement with those neutrals who are "loyal to the confessions"?—Finally, a request: Do give me the number of an account where I can send you something for your work. Here and there we do receive gifts.

With brotherly greetings! Your grateful
Franz Ernst Pfisterer

[12.] [This was the *Gemeinschaftsbewegung*, a movement in the late nineteenth and early twentieth century within the Protestant churches strongly influenced by pietism. See also *DBWE* 1:231 and 277, Bonhoeffer's note 139, as well as *DBW* 11:40, 122, 183, and 184 and *DBW* 14:88.—VB]

[13.] The reference is to the "Proposal for Regulation for the Appointment of a Church Administration in Old Prussia" (*Entwurf einer Ordnung zur Bestellung einer Kirchenleitung in Altpreußen*), which was passed on August 23, 1938, in the course of the negotiations in Essen for the reorganization of the GEC. Cf. Bonhoeffer's September 10, 1938, letter to Karl Koch and Friedrich Müller, 1/26.

[14.] [In the German Church Struggle, the "neutrals" were those church leaders and clergy who didn't align themselves with either the Confessing Church or the German Christians.—VB]

[15.] [I.e., with Bonhoeffer in eastern Pomerania.—VB]

39. To Werner Koch

39.1. Telegram[1]

In great rejoicing together greets = Dietrich.

39.2. Letter[2]

December 9, 1938

Dear Brother Koch,

The joy is indescribable. That which we have hoped and prayed for from day to day has become real. It is still like a dream to me. And now you
90 once more have your good bride-to-be,[3] admired by us all. It must be as though you have been granted life anew. I'm now looking forward to only one more thing, namely, to see you as soon as possible, so that it will be entirely certain for me that you are once again among us. I will be in Berlin in January too; from the ninth to the eleventh in Stettin at the home of Mrs. von Kleist-Retzow (with Gollwitzer, Fischer, Schönherr, Traub, etc.) for the theological society.[4] Couldn't you join us there? Or is that too much at present? Would you rather not see anyone now? I don't know; please do write about this. Only you must above all get some rest and get some rest again.—Here things are going well; how much longer, we don't know. There would be much to tell, but all that right now is not at all important in light of the joy that you are free! I truly don't know what else to say to you at the moment. You know better than I do what is of paramount importance. Give your fiancée heartfelt greetings.

Greetings to you in the old brotherly fellowship your
Dietrich Bonhoeffer

[1.] Literary estate of Werner Koch; the telegram was dispatched at 6:00 p.m. on December 9, 1938, in Köslin. Cf. *NL*, A 45 (58); previously unpublished. Koch was released from the concentration camp in Sachsenhausen on December 2, 1938.

[2.] Literary estate of Werner Koch; handwritten; cf. later typewritten copy in *NL*, A 45 (50). Previously published in *GS* 2:545.

[3.] Gerritdina Stokmann; see the postcard of June 23, 1938, to her from the Finkenwalde brothers, 1/16.

[4.] Cf. Albrecht Schönherr's letters of October 7 and November 14, 1938 (1/30 and 1/35).

40. To Paul Lehmann[1]

December 14, 1938

Dear Paul,

You wrote me last year at Christmas, and I was delighted to receive the
greetings![2] But without an address I couldn't reply. Now I will simply ask
R. Niebuhr[3] to forward this card. Hopefully, this will now work. There
would be so much to tell that one can't even begin. The best thing would be
if you could visit us again[4] or invite me over for a semester. That wouldn't
be bad at all! After such a long time, I would so like to see the country and 91
people again, and especially my friends. What might you be doing now?
Are you already a professor? How is the *theologia sacra*[5] doing? Probably
you have long since written the most voluminous and revolutionary books,
and here we know nothing about it. By the way, I enjoy writing books as
well, despite Eccl. 12:12.[6] If you want, I will send you my *Discipleship* from
last year. But I have no idea what interests you now. Do write me again!
How are you doing personally? What are Joe Moor, Franklin Fisher, Klein,
Dombrowski doing?[7] I visited Baillie[8] once in Edinburgh. How does
Brunner[9] come across in Princeton? I heard something about objections

---

[1.] *NL*, A 50,2 (1); later typewritten copy; no return address but probably from Groß-Schlönwitz. Previously published in *GS* 2:347–48. [A handwritten note at the top of the typewritten copy in the *Nachlaß* indicates that this is Bethge's transcription of a postcard found in a folder among Lehmann's papers that contained what Bethge described as "refugee correspondence." The original postcard is in German and is in the Paul Lehmann Collection, Special Collections, Princeton Theological Seminary, 67:11.—VB]

[2.] Letter not extant.

[3.] At the time Reinhold Niebuhr was staying for several months in London.

[4.] Lehmann had visited Bonhoeffer in Berlin in April 1933 (cf. *DB-ER*, 268–69). Regarding the friendship between Bonhoeffer and Lehmann at the beginning of the 1930s, see also Alston and Welker, "Dietrich Bonhoeffer." See also *DBWE* 10:299. [The letters published in Alston and Welker's article (the letter on this page is not among them) were then included in *DBW* 17 and have been incorporated according to date in *DBWE* vols. 11, 14, 15, and 16.—VB]

[5.] [Sacred theology.—VB]

[6.] ["Of making many books there is no end, and much study is a weariness of flesh."—VB]

[7.] These were all fellow students of Bonhoeffer at Union Theological Seminary, New York, in 1930–31.

[8.] John Baillie.

[9.] Emil Brunner; see also Bonhoeffer's September 18, 1938, letter to Erwin Sutz, 1/29.

against critical research on the Bible! What noteworthy books are being published at present over there? As you see, there's a great deal I would like to know from you!—I enjoy recalling our time together. I am still in touch with Sutz. Jean Lasserre has gotten married. People like us cannot yet afford to do so. Life is too nomadlike for it. There's much joy in the work, however. Very heartfelt greetings to you and your wife with all good wishes for the new year, yours truly

Dietrich B.

Berlin-Charlottenburg, Marienburger Allee 43.[10]

92 **41. To Walter Moberly**[1]

Dec 14th 1938

Dear Sir,

although I am afraid that you will not remember that we met in August 1936 at Chamby on the meeting of the ecumenic council—I was a delegate with D. Koch and D. Dibelius[2]—, I dare to ask a great favour from you and I hope, you will forgive me. My close friend and brother-in-law, Professor Dr. Gerhard Leibholz (Ordinarius für Staats- und Kirchenrecht)[3] with my sister and her little children is in London. The Bishop of Chichester is in contact with him and has been very kind to him. I have asked the Bishop to introduce him to you. He will be able to tell you all about him personally. Would you be good enough to give my brother-in-law a possibility of seeing you? I should be very grateful indeed for everything you would do for him. Please, excuse this question and all trouble I am causing to you. You know,

---

[10.] Bonhoeffer had to figure that the German authorities would check his correspondence abroad, in this case to the United States. For that reason he gave his parents' address as the return address, so as not to draw the officials' attention to his illegal training activities in Pomerania.

[1.] *NL*, A 46,3 (9); later typewritten copy. No return address, but probably from Groß-Schlönwitz, with enclosed visiting card: "Sir Walter Moberly, London-Lic. Theol. Dietrich Bonhoeffer, Pastor-Berlin-Charlottenburg 9, Marienburger Allee 43—introduce my brother-in-law, Professor Dr. Leibholz, London.—With kindest regards and thanks—D.B.—Dec 14th 1938." Previously published in *GS* 6:449–50. [Letter is in the original unaltered English.—VB]

[2.] The references are to Karl Koch and Otto Dibelius. Regarding the course of the August 1936 ecumenical conference in Chamby, see *DB-ER*, 551–54, and *DBW* 14, 1/114.

[3.] [Full professor of political and ecclesiastical law.—VB]

at present we can [do] nothing but ask. But I am sure, you will understand and forgive.

With many thanks I am, dear Sir, Yours very sincerely
Dietrich Bonhoeffer

42. To Martin Boeckheler[1]

Dear Brother Boeckheler,

I send heartfelt greetings to you and your parish for Christmas. May God give you all much joy, much peace, and much love, as we all ask in this season. It becomes clearer year by year what it means that the glory of God 93
was revealed in the manger, his wealth was revealed in poverty, that God was revealed in the flesh. May you all and your congregations partake of the great Christmas joy in which we may stand again as those who are poor and yet rich, as those who have been deserted and yet are loved. If you wish, please pass along to your congregations our sincere wishes and our intercessory prayers for you all.—I want to give my heartfelt thanks personally for all that you and your sister are doing so *very* kindly for my relatives.[2] They are very grateful for this, and all of us with them.—Please continue to take my relatives to heart and help them through troubled hours!—I would like to come soon myself to meet you all again! Warm greetings to you and your sister and in gratitude yours truly

D. Bonhoeffer

43. To Martin Boeckheler[1]

Dear Brother Boeckheler,

In the other postcard I forgot to ask you to kindly forward the card to Mr. Henne. I don't know his new address. I also wanted to ask you in any case to send me an invitation from the parish for Christmas and New Year, since I have made up my mind that if I indeed want to carry out the plan, I could

[1.] *NL*, A 45 (61); handwritten postcard; no return address or date; certainly Advent 1938. Previously published in *GS* 6:451–52.

[2.] The Leibholz couple in London.

[1.] *NL*, A 45 (62); handwritten postcard; no return address or date; certainly in Advent 1938. Previously published in *GS* 6:452.

best do so during the Christmas holiday.[2] I don't yet know exactly whether I can do this. But in case it is possible—I will let you know in time—it will be good to get the invitation in time. Just a few words are sufficient. The prospect of seeing and talking to you all again is very attractive. Cordial greetings and thanks your

D[ietrich] B[onhoeffer]

94 Would you please call J. Rieger and ask him to request such a brief invitation for me from Georg[3] as well. That is also better to have. My parents' address![4]

44. To Julius Rieger[1]

Dear Brother Rieger,

In these Christmas weeks my thoughts go especially to you all. It is difficult for me to think that I could have been over there right now. You will understand that. It is a comfort to me to know that you and your wife are there. I wish you much joy in your work, which certainly is becoming greater and more demanding with each year. You will be burdened with many things. I am all the more grateful to you for all the friendliness you have shown my sister and her family.[2] She will often need advice and support when the children arrive.[3] I shall be grateful to you then for each kind word that keeps her from impatience and worry. I would gladly come myself soon. I have a genuine longing for it.—My work is going normally. But I sometimes have rather enough of the nomadic life and would like to become somewhat more domestic and settled. That just comes with time. But it isn't possible now, and I am happy that I may be here in this work.—Please greet all my

---

[2.] [Bonhoeffer hoped to come to London. See 1/42.—VB]

[3.] George Bell.

[4.] In this letter to London, Bonhoeffer refers explicitly to the return address of his parents' home in Berlin. See his December 14, 1938, letter to Paul Lehmann, 1/40, ed. note 10.

[1.] *NL*, Anh. D 1,1 (3); handwritten postcard; no return address or date, certainly Advent 1938. Cf. also *NL*, A 45 (60); later typewritten copy. Previously published in *GS* 6:450–51.

[2.] The Leibholz family.

[3.] See 1/45, ed. note 2.

friends, especially Büsing[4] and his fiancée; I don't know his [address].
What is he doing? I would like to know, since I'm often asked. Tell him that
Werner has returned back home.[5]—How is the οἰκουμένη[6] doing? Pass 95
my greetings on to people there too.—Wishes for a joyous blessed Christ-
mas season to you, your wife, and your children from yours truly

Dietrich Bonhoeffer

45. To Christiane Leibholz[1]

Dear little Christiane,

Now you are celebrating Christmas and quite differently than usual.[2] That will certainly be very lovely. And until now Grandpapa and Grandmama have never spent Christmas together with you all. That is something very special indeed. You can hang the two pictures in your room. Don't you have them in Göttingen as well?[3]

Now give much joy to your parents and grandparents and celebrate a merry Christmas. Until I see you again! Your uncle

Dietrich

[4.] Wolfgang Büsing, a member of the second Finkenwalde session in the winter of 1935–36, emigrated in 1936 with his fiancée, Erika, who was affected by the "non-Aryan" laws of 1935. Bonhoeffer and the Council of Brethren of the Old Prussian Union helped him go to London, where he became assistant pastor in Julius Rieger's congregation. See *DBW* 14, 1/132.

[5.] The reference is to Werner Koch's release at the beginning of December 1938 from the Sachsenhausen concentration camp.

[6.] [Ecumenical group.—VB]

[1.] *NL*, A 44,1 (14); later typewritten copy; probably from Groß-Schlönwitz, undated; picture postcard sent for Christmas 1938 to Haarlem, the Netherlands; previously unpublished.

[2.] On their way into exile in England, the Leibholz couple had parted for a time from their two children in Switzerland. Ursula Schleicher had taken them back to stay temporarily with their Bonhoeffer grandparents in Berlin. At Christmas 1938, Paula and Karl Bonhoeffer, the Leibholz children, and their parents met at the home of their relatives, the Koenigs, in Haarlem, Holland. See Leibholz-Bonhoeffer, *Bonhoeffers*, 88 and 99–101.

[3.] [Göttingen may have been mentioned to give possible censors the impression that the Leibholz family was only temporarily away from home.—VB]

46. From Otto-Karl Lerche and Paul Henheik[1]

Dear Brother Bonhoeffer, dear Eberhard,

Please forgive us, dear Brother Bonhoeffer, if the tone and address of this letter seems more directed toward Eberhard; you are always meant too.

96 Well, now a package is really on its way from Lagendorf, not as impressive and hefty as the previous one (from [19]35), but our lively thoughts of you stand behind it.

Dear Brother Bonhoeffer, even if you hear very little from me, my gratitude does accompany you, and in these days I may be allowed to say it out loud: you are a spiritual father to me (I said this a few days ago to a brother—not from Finkenwalde—whom I told how much I enjoy using your *Discipleship*—how good that it has an index[2]—for sermon preparation, and he replied with surprise: you know, I do exactly the same. Pardon me for this awkward sentence. I said to him: Bonhoeffer would laugh at me if I told him that, and then say quietly, "Now, at most a brother in the spirit"—and yet you are more than that). It is essential to me that I know of you—simply that you are there (and that it is still day[3] for you—what a mercy).

You see, Eberhard, the package is not as festive as in the past. That, too, I think, is connected with the path (certainly with me as well: I can no longer muster the degree of belligerence).[4] The donors are Kruseberg[5] 10.–; Lüder: bacon, sausage, cookies; Kirndorf: bacon and juice (we knew we had to send that along too); Klaas: 1 tin; Mrs. Bölke: a tin and cookies and a letter; Bekes:[6] bacon and sausage; Mrs. Vahlke: 1 liverwurst; Pastors: sausage and cookies; Miss R. Lange 1.–.

What should I write you about myself? I attempt to do my work—and sometimes also to shirk it; I pray for one revival of our church-community (oh, how much patience is needed for this and how impatient we are, how we want this to be granted us instantly); at present I go along—often it is otherwise—my way quite confidently. How good that you and that I as well may continue to

---

[1.] *NL*, C 25; handwritten, from Lagendorf, undated, but very likely before Christmas 1938; previously unpublished. Lerche was a candidate in the third Finkenwalde session in the summer of 1936.

[2.] [Bonhoeffer prepared the index for the 1937 edition of *Discipleship* himself; it is reproduced in facsimile on p. 305 of the German *DBW* 4 edition.—VB]

[3.] [Cf. John 9:4: "We must work the works of him who sent me while it is day; night is coming when no one can work."—VB]

[4.] [Lerche is referring to the continuing tensions within the Confessing Church.—VB]

[5.] Difficult to decipher; may be "Krisebog."

[6.] Difficult to decipher, may be "Jakes."

work.—Forgive me that I don't write more, but I believe that whatever I "have" I need for the days to come.

Wishing that you both may grow ever more deeply—or rather, will have grown more deeply—into the great joy with which God leads us to him, your

Otto-Karl

Please give warmest greetings to Fritz[7] and Mrs. Struwe[8] and the church province of Saxony.[9]

I just read H.'s[10] lines: then I will just add "as dying, and see—we are alive!"[11]

Dear Finkenwaldians, 97

Morituri vos salutant.[12] And yet it is always so hard to have to proceed into dying. One does indeed hang onto life. That is what makes the wretchedness of these times so bitter. If only out of this the blessing would grow that, despite everything and above everything, the heart learns jubilation without ceasing: Indeed I still have Christ. Who will take him from me?[13] That is my Christmas wish for you as well. And my Christmas wish for us is that you both might have time to care about us and come to see us.

Very affectionately yours
Paul Henheik

47. From His Parents[1]

December 22, 1938

Dear Dietrich,

We will of course speak[2] the day after tomorrow, but we want to send you a written Christmas greeting as well. It would be nice if we could see you early on

[7.] Friedrich Onnasch [the younger—VB].

[8.] Erna Struwe.

[9.] [This was Bethge's home church.—VB]

[10.] Paul Henheik's comment at the end of this letter.

[11.] 2 Cor. 6:9.

[12.] "We who are about to die salute you," a reference to the gladiators' greeting as they entered the arena, addressing the emperor Claudius.

[13.] From the first stanza of the Passion hymn, "Warum sollt ich mich denn grämen?" by Paul Gerhardt, in *EG*, 370. [The English translation is "Why Should Cross and Trial Grieve Me?" in *Lutheran Hymnal*, 523.—VB]

[1.] *NL*, C 1; handwritten postcard from Haarlem, the Netherlands; previously unpublished.

[2.] [On the phone.—VB]

the third day of the holidays. Your greeting from Groß-Schlönwitz has already arrived.[3] That is really something, that you had temperatures down to minus-20 degrees.[4] It didn't go below minus-10 here. Now everything is under deep snow. Mama is doing better with her catarrh. Gert, Sabine, and the children are cheerful. My pen is making many lucky piglets.[5] Because of that I will close. Affectionate greetings from us

Father

Thinking of you in deep affection

Mother

98 **48. From Paula Bonhoeffer**[1]

Dear Dietrich,

I assume that when this card arrives, Christmas Eve will already be behind you. Mucki[2] will send a little tree over to our room. Your greetings have already arrived. But I put them aside for Sabine and Gerd.[3] Papa was in Utrecht today because of Kramer.[4] We have [minus-]12 degrees and are all snowed in; it was all supposedly very lovely, but instead of a half hour the ride took two hours! We hope to arrive early on the twenty-seventh without too much delay. I fear that I will bring my catarrh back home with me. So we will not immediately travel on, and Papa, if there are urgent cases, will hold his consultation[5] hours. Please tell that to Miss Käte.[6] We hope to still see you before your departure. Please do tell Klaus that I would love to have him with us on the evening of the twenty-seventh, naturally with Emmi. Sabine had several more wishes. Could Mr. Bethge pick up the car with the baggage and sell them in Berlin? Perhaps not? Affectionately

Mother

[3.] This probably refers to Bonhoeffer's card to Christiane Leibholz. See 1/45.

[4.] [Minus 4 degrees Fahrenheit.—VB]

[5.] I.e., his fountain pen was making inkblots.

[1.] *NL*, C 1; handwritten postcard from Haarlem, the Netherlands, postmarked December 23, 1938; previously unpublished.

[2.] Anna Koenigs.

[3.] This mailing is not extant. [Bonhoeffer obviously sent two pictures for the Leibholz daughters. Cf. 1/45.—VB]

[4.] Franz Kramer, an emigrant who lived in the Netherlands after 1938.

[5.] [Medical office hours.—VB]

[6.] The Bonhoeffers' housekeeper in Berlin.

49. To Sabine and Gerhard Leibholz[1]

January 6, 1939[2]

Dear Sabine, dear Gert,

I thank you greatly for your Christmas present, which made a very lovely ski trip possible for me. It was once again utterly wonderful in the snow. We are now thinking about installing light and central heating in the cottage,[3] so that it will also be suitable for a longer winter stay for our parents—but I find that this is much more important now than setting myself up well. That 99
can indeed come later; so I gladly wanted to help the parents somewhat through giving this up. Unfortunately, it is rather expensive, since everything in the cottage is very primitive;[4] and it will also be very agreeable for the children and for you yourselves. Otherwise it is always rather raw up there in the winter. Our parents, despite their plans, have not traveled, since the weather was somewhat too unpleasant for them. They preferred to stay home. And that was certainly better. I'm sure that you will be longing to finally travel back home. But under no circumstances may you, dear Gert, simply break off your work; the others must simply adapt themselves to that. I am somewhat familiar with the arrangements at the library of the British Museum and know that it is always difficult to get the books back out once you have handed them in. So, despite all the yearnings for a quiet time at home, you must definitely hold out, and moreover you can depend entirely on old Lina,[5] who will give the best care to your home. As a postscript to the expenses for you I am to tell you—the notes for this were not immediately at hand recently; you have already received the receipts—food for the children 50, tailor 23.5, church tax 70, underclothes for the children 10, Aunt Elisabeth's[6] trip to Göttingen 10, the garden 1.0, telephone 17, private lessons for the children 16, massage 2, x-ray 2, shoe inserts 2. Just to keep you informed about everything. I will still be visiting here for a few more days until work resumes.

By the way, I have written to Cromwell.[7] Perhaps you can call him sometime as well. I found Mama and Papa rather in need of relaxation. I hope

[1.] *NL*, A 44,1 (13); photocopy of a handwritten letter; no return address, but probably from Berlin; previously unpublished.

[2.] It was actually mailed on January 11; see the postscript.

[3.] The Bonhoeffers' vacation home in Friedrichsbrunn in the Harz Mountains.

[4.] The passage "but I find . . . is very primitive" is written in the margin.

[5.] The Leibholz family's cook in Göttingen.

[6.] Elisabeth von Hase.

[7.] Philipp Cromwell; letter not extant.

they will still travel, maybe a little later. Papa has much on his mind and seems somewhat overstrained, and I would also wish some quiet for Mama for Papa's sake as well. I haven't seen her for ten weeks, but I believe that she always undertakes too much. She always wants to do everything herself,
100 and it does often become too much for her. We think often of you all, and I was so happy to finally hear something from you personally. I was especially pleased to hear that the children had such a merry Christmas. How are they liking it now?[8] The sea air will certainly be very good for them.

I hope to see you soon. I have received a very nice invitation.[9] And woe to you if you spoil my trip by leaving too early!

Everyone sends affectionate greetings with me. Once again, many thanks for everything!

Yours truly
Dietrich

The letter unfortunately has been sitting here. Today is January 11. Forgive me! I think of all of you always! Affectionately D.[10]

50. From Herbert Liedtke[1]

Marienwalde, January 7, 1939

Dear Brother Bonhoeffer,

First, accept my heartfelt thanks for sending me such brotherly greetings at Christmas. It is almost as if you had selected the saying on your card,[2] "Lord, you are my strength and power and refuge in need,"[3] to correspond to my particular circumstances so that it could serve as warning and consolation for me.

I have sometimes thought in recent days of writing the letter that I now write to you, but only the earnest advice of my mother has led me to do so now. It is no easy thing for me to write to you now, for it will certainly not become a

---

[8.] [I.e., life in England.—VB]

[9.] This probably refers to the official invitation to London that Bonhoeffer requested in his Advent 1938 letter to Martin Boeckheler, 1/43.

[10.] Postscript written on the letterhead.

[1.] *NL*, C 25; handwritten; previously unpublished. Liedtke was a member of the fifth Finkenwalde session in the summer of 1937.

[2.] Card not extant.

[3.] See Ps. 59:17.

normal letter. I have confidence in you, however, that you know me somewhat and therefore I will dare to tell you everything that in recent weeks has almost robbed me of my clear senses and continues daily to be a burden upon my heart and soul. I know that you will receive in the face of God even that which I tell 101
you, and that you will help me, if God intends that I be helped at all.

You wrote me that I had many reasons to be thankful. This is true, as true as anything on earth can be true. God has showered me with gifts. I have parents who pray for me; I have a dear bride-to-be who belongs to me not only in the chastity of her love but who prays for me; I have here a fine possibility to work and lack nothing of the external amenities of life; I have a young brother here in the house with whom I may share daily fellowship in prayer—I have all that. Is that not grounds enough for gratitude? And nonetheless recently I have become a person for whom gratitude does not come from the heart—oh, sometimes it happens, but then it suffocates once more under a paralyzing fear that at times attacks me so strongly that my entire body trembles. This fear does not come from outside, is not connected to any recollection, nor is it because my thoughts are too worried about the future of our church. This frequent dreadful fear is the fear for my own existence as a living person, or to put it differently, the fear of my own death.

It is hard for me to have to say this to you in writing, I would much rather sit in front of you so that you could see me and then kneel down with me before God our savior, of whom I know that he alone can help here. That is also the request of my letter, that you might stand by me through your prayer and your advice. I have prayed much for this and have also been allowed to hear how the young brother here prayed for me, in the worst hours of such a misery of the heart that I can do nothing besides cry to the Lord, but I am still not free. It accompanies me like a shadow and occasionally, sometimes in the middle of a happy good thought, it strikes so that I at times can scarcely come to myself.

I have previously sometimes experienced such doubts, but it is only in the past few weeks that the experience has come with such intensity. During the day, when my thoughts are diverted through some kind of work, I can remain quiet for a long time; but I seldom succeed in the evenings while I'm trying to go to sleep. It is not at all a vague general fear but manifests itself strangely in clear comprehensible thoughts. I then stand under a barely surmountable compulsion to await the moment when my heart will beat its last beat and I must be dead. My heart beats then in a racing tempo and an enormous unrest is in me, so that I must stand up and wander around in the lit room. My thoughts are completely clear; I can even reflect on myself and my situation. Sedatives help little. I know exactly that when in such a state I would be able to concentrate my thoughts entirely on the image of Christ, then the fear would be gone, but my thoughts 102
are repeatedly driven by a demonic force to think these thoughts of mine of

death. Then there is nothing of the certainty of salvation, nothing of the joy to be allowed to be with Christ, but only the dreadful foreboding of a terrible end toward nothingness.

These thoughts are so strong that they have seeped into my subconscious and in thinking of something in the future, perhaps in thinking that I may see my fiancée again in several months, a hot terror comes over me: it will no longer be. Or as it happened in the first hour of the new year, as the housefather spoke the prayer before the gathered household community here and then said: ". . . and if it must be, that we die blessed," then suddenly this dreadful fear was there again: this year will be your last.

I try to tear myself loose from these thoughts, for they rob me of all joy, and even of all serious sense of responsibility toward the work commissioned to me here. It is almost as if the everyday life here murmurs around me like a dream; I sometimes don't stand in reality and then find no relation to the things that concern me.

But above all this, I am completely and irrefutably certain that there would be joy upon joy and jubilant gratitude if I could come free from this fear, if my thoughts would become free from this demonic shackle, if I could believe completely like a child: all that which tortures me now so severely, Jesus Christ has borne it for me, if I could accept out of whole faith: my life and my dying rest in Christ's hands. Sometimes it occurs to me that I must tell myself in astonishment: you are still alive. But I do know through all of this, yes, I know: if Christ did not hold his hands over me, then I would already be gone and have died in dreadful fear. That alone lifts me up again. But I do not find the strength to throw all these thoughts of death as my worry onto Christ; they come again and again, and sometimes it even seems to me frivolous to shake everything off and take the day joyfully and without worry from God's hand.

I have thought a great deal about why I have to suffer such hard tribulations, why I cannot be like a child, who stands with Christ in utterly simple faith and confidence. Tell me please, can this be God's school that wants to test me? In all and certainly unfeigned seriousness, I have taken up my work in Bernsee but have regarded this in my deepest heart only as a transition to a time that seemed
103 more important to me, namely, the time when I might live with my bride as a happy man in the state of marriage. My thoughts went first not in the direction of how I would have to work as a laborer in the vineyard of God but instead toward a time of yearned-for happiness. Now I am being so brutally pulled into the present that seemed so worthless to me.

But then one more thing: the burial services I must hold cause a great deal of inner misery for me. Not because I would not know what I have to say to the mourners, but because I must almost always put myself in the place of the deceased, that is, I stand once more before my own death.

I am very certain that I will not hold out much longer if the power of Christ's resurrection does not rescue me. It is as if I no longer had the strength to believe all the glorious and, as it appears even to me, saving words of promise. I shall not die, but I shall live, and recount the deeds of the Lord[4]—and all the other sayings that I seek again and again. I would like to seize these sayings with whole faith, but repeatedly the other thoughts come through.

In pondering these tribulations the question has come to me, whether in some point I had behaved disobediently to God, but I have no answer. Certainty was bestowed on me that I may have my bride according to God's will. But for the very sake of this bride and of all the other people for whom I am supposed to be there, all the unbelief, the result of which is this anxiety, seems to me to be like disobedience.

Certainly the question can't be entirely dismissed as to whether an enormous nervousness simply leaves me physically without the strength to steer my thoughts so that they are disciplined before God and hear God's word. But it is unfortunately true that I am indeed rather nervous. Sometimes I already begin to tremble during a conversation that stimulates me greatly, even when it moves me to great joy. Yet is it not indeed the case that the thoughts of our hearts influence our bodies and not the reverse?

How quiet and full of great joy so many times in my life have been. I do want to return to the gratitude that I truly owe to God, want to be free from having to think of the fear of death that could overwhelm me, want to be directed in my thoughts toward Christ alone, want to be able to go to bed and fall into a good sleep, which I so lack now, free from the fearful expectation of what will
happen, I want to be able again to look freely to the time to come, especially in 104
thinking of my bride-to-be.

I almost feel as if I could already know what you will now reply, but I will send this letter off nonetheless, for it is truly for me a matter of finding a brother before Christ who prays with me, prays for me, and who can help me in the power of the Holy Spirit. Do take my situation on, for I am no longer ashamed of saying what the truth is, that I am a beaten man who has experienced Satan's power with great fear, but who wants to become free through the blood of Jesus Christ, confidently hoping for his salvation and for joyous obedience in daily service. I want to become free from my fear, that is, from myself, and become a slave to Jesus Christ, for this is certain to me: without him there is no life for me. Jesus Christ himself, of whom I have so often spoken and preached and surely not as a liar, he must now himself come alive in my life, and as the one who has taken away the power of death.[5]

[4.] Ps. 118:17.

[5.] [Cf. 2 Tim. 1:10.—VB]

I have written many words, but I don't know how otherwise I should speak to you. Insofar as it is really Christ's will to be your and my Lord—that almost sounds like a blasphemy, but it is really now a matter of the ultimate decision—he will hear us, yes, he will hear us.

With heartfelt greetings from your
Herbert Liedtke

Address: Marienwalde Kreis Arnswalde

51. From Otto Dudzus[1]

Michendorf, January 11, 1939

Esteemed, dear Brother Bonhoeffer,

Unfortunately, I left you without any greetings for Christmas and the new year. Naturally not because of laziness. I thought a great deal about you during the entire time and often intended to write. But in the last Christmas week work piled up so high that I would have found time for a card at most, and it was sup-
105 posed to become somewhat more than that. Then right after Christmas our big move began. After searching for a half year, we have finally found a decent apartment here in Michendorf, three rooms for a reasonable price. We took care of the move ourselves, and that takes more time than one thinks and than one is happy with, in terms of the parish work. But now all that is behind us. Through the move, in any case, I didn't even get around to writing for New Year's. Your Christmas card[2] brought us great joy and fortified us greatly for the proclamation. It does indeed mean a great deal, greatly noticeable for preaching, when one can know that the brothers are praying. And I thank you very much for this. This year for the first time I was allowed to preach on Christmas. What a great joy it is indeed, that the Lord Christ has come to us in our poor, confused life and now wants to enter our lives each day anew. Hopefully, you experienced rich days with the brothers. I was with you all in my thoughts. Brother Emmerich[3] is with you, isn't he? It would be nice if we here in the countryside knew who is with you up there. One thinks differently of the brothers who are with you

[1.] *NL*, C 25; handwritten; previously unpublished. Dudzus was a candidate in the fifth Finkenwalde session in the summer of 1937.

[2.] Card not extant.

[3.] Heinz Emmerich [who was a member of the collective pastorate at Groß-Schlönwitz in the winter session of 1938–39.—VB] when one knows the names. Often one knows something more than the names. And even when one knows only the names, one knows more than a little. Or is there some difficulty in informing us of the names?[4]

The work in the parish brings me much joy, particularly preaching and the encounters here and there in the homes, when they happen. One often unexpectedly finds open doors. The Lord Christ is doing his work. There are no major events here. We can work in peace. Any kind of events and disturbances has—since I have been here—not happened. But that would of course not have been a "major thing." The truly major things usually happen quietly, in the encounter with the Word. I wrote you back then something about the internal circumstances of our congregations, about their relationship to the CC, that through the resolution of the parish council, no public intercessions naming names and no announcements were to be made.[5] This unholy resolution unfortunately has not yet come down,[6] and I notice how horribly dangerous it will become for us, how much one enjoys the quiet one has externally through this.
And yet it is not the quiet of Christ. The circular letter has just reached me on 106
its second journey.[7] One can be shocked by the uncertainty of many brothers. How suddenly the path of the CC takes away "certainty" when it stops short and becomes dangerous.[8] Oh, if it all depended upon our courage, it would be desolate! If only we don't demonstrate for the congregations with our own bodies that things also work without faith.

In October we had a mission week [Volksmissionswoche] in Rudi Kühn's congregation. R. Kühn, Br. Lerche, Br. Veckenstedt, and I were there.[9] It brought us all a great deal of joy. Perhaps we sense the blessing of such a thing best in ourselves, in how we proceed with our work in our own parishes. I have never before preached so gladly as after this week. Brother Veckenstedt, who has exactly the same kind of motorcycle as Fritz Onnasch, often comes the forty kilometers over to us. He is a great gift to me from Finkenwalde.

[4.] Because of the possible examination of the mail, it was dangerous to give the names of the participants of the illegal collective pastorates.

[5.] Behind this resolution were the conflicts within the congregation after local pastor Bruno Haese had placed himself under the state-controlled church committees and demanded that the parish council, the majority of which belonged to the Confessing Church, recall its "illegal" assistant pastor Dudzus.

[6.] He means "been rescinded" (revised).

[7.] Bonhoeffer's "personal circular letters" were circulated among the former Finkenwaldians from one to the next.

[8.] See Bonhoeffer's November 11, 1938, circular letter to the Finkenwalde brothers, 1/36.

[9.] Rudolf Kühn, Otto-Karl Lerche, and Eberhard Veckenstedt; see *DB-ER*, 543–45.

As I was straightening up some time ago, I found your lecture about the hymn[10] here after all. Hopefully, you have not missed it too much. Br. Stähler wanted to have it back then. In the meantime he was here and did attempt—but without success—to read through the manuscript.[11] I must in the coming days at any rate send something to Fritz;[12] then the lecture will go along.

Healthwise, recently I've been doing quite well. The dizzy spells still come occasionally, but haven't at all for several weeks, although I stopped taking medicine.[13] Perhaps—hopefully—they will cease completely some day.

Now I wish you, dear Brother Bonhoeffer, God's blessing for your work. Please give my greetings to Eberhard, Fritz, and Br. Emmerich. My wife sends greetings to you as well.

With heartfelt, brotherly greetings your grateful
Otto Dudzus

107 **52. To His Parents**[1]

January 16, 1939

My dear Parents,

There was much to do and discuss in the last few days; that's why I have not gotten to writing. There is not much to report either. All is going well, and I am trying to find a place for the summer.[2] I have a letter from the Leibholzes; I have also written them.[3] It was just before the departure there, and for that reason was somewhat muddled. What do you hear otherwise from them? Dear Mama, I wanted to ask you to take a look into the little cupboard where I put my files during the vacation, to see whether you can

[10.] Cf. the lecture, "The Inner Life of the German Protestant Church," which Bonhoeffer gave on August 5, 1936, during a series of public lectures organized by the Confessing Church during the Olympic games in Berlin; see *DBW* 14, 2/21, and *DB-ER*, 538–39.

[11.] [Bonhoeffer's handwriting was notoriously difficult to read.—VB]

[12.] Friedrich Onnasch [the younger.—VB]

[13.] Bonhoeffer had witnessed a particularly bad attack of dizziness in Finkenwalde, which led him to send Dudzus to be treated by his father in the Berlin Charité hospital for three to four weeks (personal letter from Dudzus to the German editor, February 20, 1994).

[1.] *NL*, A 44,1 (15); handwritten; no return address but probably from Groß-Schlönwitz; previously unpublished.

[2.] [The Groß-Schlönwitz pastorate was no longer available.—VB]

[3.] This correspondence with the Leibholzes, who at this point were probably still with their relatives in Haarlem, the Netherlands, has not been found.

find a folder in which there is an address list. Those are the names of the Finkenwalde members, which I would like to have back. Would you then please send them to Eberhard? Hopefully, this is not too much trouble for you. Are things now somewhat quieter with you or not yet? I would like to know some news. Are you still traveling?

Greetings to you from your grateful
Dietrich

53. From Herbert Liedtke[1]

At present Bernsee, January 18, 1939

Dear Brother Bonhoeffer,

God in his mercy has certainly spread much more in terms of help and gracious mercy over my life than my dulled and anxious senses are aware of. Perhaps I may say it this way, that your letter[2] and another experience in the last few days have become visible signs to me, compelling me to realize, with deep shame for all unbelief and lack of gratitude, that God's hand has been lifted for me.

I thank you very warmly for your letter. It did not come too late for me, and 108
perhaps a few days of despondent waiting were necessary for God to help me arrive at an understanding of what you had to say to me. Admittedly, this is not that easy for me. I will admit to you that I felt bitter misery when I first read your letter and only gradually do I grasp that really here a path to salvation is being shown me.

Such thoughts have tormented me terribly, that we must find a clear Yes to dying. Perhaps this was due to the fact that I could no longer think at all of death other than by placing myself momentarily in the situation of dying and indeed entirely without being able to resist. For days I repeatedly felt as if I suddenly and, so it seemed, quite unavoidably now faced the end from which there can be no reawakening to this life. But I then sometimes was simply shocked when I nonetheless noticed that life had not yet left me. I don't know whether a person can empathize with such situations without having lived through them himself. It is as if one were terrified of remaining in this life and not by having to leave it, as if one had a fear of life and not a fear of death. Both, however, are so closely connected, the sudden coming of the horrible fear: now you must go and your life is cut like a thread, and then that horrible reawakening to life. This was actually the most desolate period. Some days I had a direct physical sensation of despair.

[1.] *NL*, C 25; handwritten; previously unpublished.
[2.] Letter not extant.

This pushed me so far that one morning the mere recollection of my fiancée and my brother, who had written me a cheerful letter, brought me to unrestrained weeping. I could not help myself—and yet afterward it was enough for my pride that no one had found me in this state.

It was simply total chaos, so that sometimes only the presence of other people brought me to the comprehensible consideration that I was indeed still on this earth. I did not stop praying, I also read the Scriptures, but everything was dead. My prayer was spoken as though no one were there to hear it, even when I had my young brother with me, who has meant a great deal to me through his honest intercession and the love with which he has borne me. Everything that was not directly connected to the question of death was utterly, truly utterly, irrelevant to me. Even the confirmation class one week ago today was an hour full of unreality. It is surely not only a change in mood that today I am out of this despair.

109 But this will indeed be very difficult to learn, that I also find a joyful Yes to my dying. For that which has been so dreadful in the last few days has not yet faded away. This momentary sense of attack by the horror of death happens often, even now. It often occurs that a necessary consideration, whether it concerns the ministry or is one that affects my own life and my future, is suddenly interrupted by one thought: it makes no sense, since you must go. Above all, this thought plagues me again and again in the evening before falling asleep. It may happen, as it did last night, that I am startled more than ten times and sleep escapes me.

It is strange. I am not so horrified in this by the thoughts of the coming judgment or hell, but rather by the thoughts that I must lie in a coffin and be placed under the earth. It is almost as if I had to become an observer at my own burial. I don't know whether you will understand me. But it is a fact that sometimes the mere sight of a coffin puts me for a moment in great shock. It is as though my eyes and all my thoughts were only directed and pulled downward. The glory of Christ is then utterly invisible to me. For that reason the ministry for a burial is so difficult for me. For days I am haunted by how the coffin is sunk into the earth. It is almost as if a psychologist would have to speak here of a mania—but is not Christ the liberator, even from such manic states? Can he not make it so that even for me the coffin and the grave become nothing other than what they really are? Must this remain so for my entire life, that I shudder so before a coffin and an open grave?

Dear Brother Bonhoeffer, it becomes difficult indeed for me to speak with you this way, for there are still other things in connection with what I have related here that have tormented me. Perhaps a genuine conversation will be necessary sometime in these matters as well, so that I don't keep carrying this in seclusion, finally ending up as a person who mocks all the goodness and mercy of God through his desperation. You kindly offered to visit me sometime. Several days ago I would have very cordially asked you to do so. Now I feel as if I were recovering, and for that reason I don't really know whether I should bring such a wish to you that certainly means no small sacrifice in time and energy for you.

Here I had to let my letter sit for a few hours. During this period I repeatedly thought about whether I should not indeed ask you to visit and give me 110
the possibility to say all that is in me and which comes up again at times out of the momentary seclusion. May I express my request in this way: that in this period that has grown a tiny bit quieter, I would like to leave it up to your brotherly decision, whether you come to visit me. One thing is certain, that you will not travel for nothing when you come to me; you are not coming to someone healthy.

It is almost as if all courage to live has collapsed in me. Today again, as we started making major plans, I could not cheerfully participate in them. What I see before me are only short distances, and sometimes it appears to me to be reckless to disregard the possibility of dying soon by making a major plan. I don't know whether you can understand me here. A prayer that was spoken at midnight, as the old year passed into the new, froze my thoughts. The host said—which was certainly proper to pray before God—let us also be prepared, if it must be, to die. Then it shot through my soul with hot horror: this year will be your last. I have not gotten rid of this dreadful thought; it has tormented me incessantly, and perhaps it was the cause that so often during the day and also at night when I lay sleepless on my bed, my soul had to face the anxiety of immediate death. Now several days ago it came to me like an inspiration: God did not intend this prayer for me as a prediction, for God does not give such predictions, and surely he does give them in such a terribly tormenting manner. This filled me with great joy. Is it correct to think so?

Regarding your other offer, to be counseled by your father about what I could do to strengthen my nerves, I can say nothing other than my heartfelt thanks. I have always meant to ask a doctor whom I could trust, but I didn't know anyone. In my case it is not only a matter of a general nervousness, but that this nervousness manifests itself in a nervous heart. It reaches the point where I have an irregular heartbeat, at times am conscious of missing a beat and then afterward feel that much more powerful a throb. I already believed that I had a real heart problem, but the doctor has told me that the heart is fine, I have no heart problem and also have normal blood pressure, that everything was a symptom of nervousness. I obediently took the medicine he prescribed but have not felt any improvement. If only I could really experience something that would 111
help me, I would be very grateful for it. Above all, I would really like to know in all truth whether bicycling—which simply is part of my ministry, sometimes over twenty kilometers over sodden paths—can hurt. After such trips, I indeed note

discomfort and a pressing pain around the heart, but I am not certain whether they could be imagined and whether one can actually feel heart trouble as pain. Sleep is difficult. Usually I fall asleep quickly, but then awaken very soon with a jolt and fall into a great restlessness that can intensify into fear. Sedatives like valerian drops are unsuccessful. The pastor's wife here recommended valerian extract pills, but I don't really feel confident either. But I do notice that I cannot really perform my ministry much longer if a strengthening of my nerves isn't possible. Is it even possible for willpower to suffer under weakened nerves as well?

I must, however, give heartfelt thanks to God for yesterday and today, for I was able to be much more at peace.

I will close for today, gladly awaiting your reply. God will surely bless such pleading and such brotherly aid.

With warm greetings I am your grateful
Herbert Liedtke

54. From Herbert Liedtke[1]

January 19, 1939

Dear Brother Bonhoeffer,

As a postscript to yesterday's letter, I still have to say this today. In the midst of the worst misery, it was always entirely certain to me: if help can be brought to me, then it must come through Christ alone; Christ's resurrecting power must assert itself in my life. Now in these days, which have made me so much quieter, an apprehensive concern has come to me despite all praying, whether the turn from such despair toward a joyful and dutiful life doesn't simply occur like a natural awakening. If I now can think so much more peacefully, then it did not come
112 about because I had received a clearer vision of Christ's glory and because death had become a joyful Yes, but I simply stand at some distance from all the misery of recent days, and that which surrounds me and affects my life has become so much more natural again. Because of that my concern is now whether the devil is not once again using a new trick, by allowing me a breather so that I can enjoy my life once more, in order to bring me back into the darkness even stronger than before. Yet my plea was that I only wanted to live in Christ. I did not want to feel such a natural naive partaking in life but wanted to accept everything daily and hourly only as a gift from God. Please tell me, when I now think that I could not view this turnaround out of despair that I have experienced as the genuine

[1.] *NL*, C 25; handwritten; no return address but probably from Bernsee; previously unpublished.

help of the Lord Christ, are these thoughts of unbelief? Should I wait further? Sometimes it seems to me that I may not speak in Bible studies with such certain words about the power of Christ, because I have not yet become a completely certain witness for it myself.

I still had to say this to you today, all the misery of the past night drove me to it.

With cordial greetings your
Herbert Liedtke

55. To Theodor Litt[1]

Pastor Dr. Bonhoeffer
At present Schlawe in Pomerania
Office of the Superintendent

January 22, 1939

Esteemed Professor:

We theologians must be very grateful to you for your two recent publications.[2] They truly render the service of clarification for which they are intended. Your text on "Protestant Historical Consciousness" bears so strongly the form of a conversation that I would like to view it as your permission to join this conversation with a brief peripheral comment. I speak as a theologian, but you will of course know the language of theologians. 113
You refrained, presumably intentionally, from expressing the ultimate reason for the relationship of Christian faith to the world as we must express it, namely, with the name Jesus Christ. The objective fact of the "constant uniformity of human aberrations"[3] [Immergleichheit der menschlichen Verirrungen] as such is insufficient for Christian faith to be given its commission for the work in this world from the hereafter. According to Protestant thought, the refusal to work within the world could rather be grounded with the same right in this anthropology alone, were it not that a single fact would expose this refusal peremptorily as guilt, namely, the fact of God's becoming human. Solely because God became a poor, wretched, unknown, unsuccessful human being, and because God wants to be found from now

[1.] *NL*, A 45 (63); carbon copy, initialed by hand. Previously published in *GS* 3:31–33.

[2.] Litt, *Der deutsche Geist und das Christentum* (1938) and *Protestantisches Geschichtsbewußtsein* (1939).

[3.] Litt, *Protestantisches Geschichtsbewußtsein*, 37.

on solely in this poverty, in the cross, it is for this reason that we cannot get away from the human being and from the world, for this reason that we love our neighbors. Because the Christian faith is such that indeed the "unconditional is included in the conditional" (page 53), the "hereafter" has entered the "this-worldliness" out of a sovereign freedom of grace, for that reason the believer is not torn apart, but rather finds in this single place in this world God and human being in one, and from now on the love of God and love for one's human neighbor are indissolubly united. Here also lies, then, the relative right of the idealistic, particularly the Hegelian system: for what else does it mean that the Hegelian philosophy of religion comes to its point in the doctrine of Christ's real presence [Realpräsenz] in the Lord's Supper[4] other than the greatest secularization precisely of *this* Christian truth? And is not in turn the neglect of this origin of all Christian thought, namely, of the Word become flesh, the relative wrong of Pestalozzi's anthropology that you have presented?[5] That is, is it not manifest here that ultimately it simply does not work to express in unambiguous and clear terms the Protestant historical consciousness or the Christian understanding of
114 the world without naming the name of Jesus Christ, the name that bursts asunder both Pestalozzian as well as Hegelian anthropology?

Finally, does it not become understandable only from this point—a fact that you do not mention at all—that the Christian, for all his dedication to his brothers and all his devotion to the earth, nonetheless knows of and longs for the destruction of this earth and the future of a new earth and a new heaven,[6] for the sake of the presence of God in Christ? Indeed, that the present earth can be taken so seriously in its dignity, its glory, and its curse for the [sake of] the unity of the original, the present and the future earth as the earth of God, as the earth upon which the cross of Jesus Christ stood?

I thank you once again for the work that you have done for us up to now and will hopefully continue to do.

Respectfully, I remain your servant,
D[ietrich] B[onhoeffer]

[4.] See Hegel, *Vorlesungen über die Philosophie der Religion*, 208–15.

[5.] See Litt, *Protestantisches Geschichtsbewußtsein*, 25–30.

[6.] Cf. Rev. 21 and 22.

56. From Paula Bonhoeffer[1]

January 23, 1939

Dear Dietrich,

I hope that the papers I sent are the ones you wanted and that you have received them.—It took a little long because I first had to search for them. We were very happy that you are doing well. The letters coming from dear Sabine still sound quite depressed. Because of the complicated settlement of matters here, he[2] doesn't have his mind clear for things there. Dr. Groote[3] has taken the matter on fabulously and with great success. Now it's essential that the papers in G[öttingen] are safeguarded, and then G[erd] will make a new list of his assets and then apply for a declaration of no reservations [Unbedenklichkeitserklaerung],[4] which I think is right. All this, however, is very tedious and a long way 115
to go.—She writes that she has a lot to do because she doesn't want to cause her landlords too much work and often can't sleep at night because of the joint pain due to the damp beds. The children now are kept busy in the mornings, and that is certainly good. Naturally Gerd and Sabine will also often think of us over here with concern.—Recently they were invited for a weekend with Uncle George;[5] there was a festive meal with all kinds of people. and the old uncle, to the delight of everyone, chose little Christiane as his dinner partner. I often think about how and whether anything at all will come of your trip?![6] That would truly be a shame. On our nearby display kiosks, the military conscription was announced for those born in 6 and 7.[7] The young people would be summoned, and whoever had not been summoned by February 15 would then have to report. I don't know, however, if this is only for Berlin. Probably one can still get permission to travel in spite of this. Tomorrow Hans[8] is coming; we will

[1.] *NL*, C 1; handwritten; no return address, probably from Berlin; previously unpublished.

[2.] Gerhard Leibholz.

[3.] Wolfgang Grote was Leibholz's former assistant in Göttingen.

[4.] This is a declaration submitted by the account holder to the bank holding the account, authorizing a third person to make payments into the holder's account. [Ilse Tödt notes that Dietrich Bonhoeffer continued to receive RM 170 each month from the Leibholz account at the Commerzbank in Göttingen; cf. Bonhoeffer, *Zettelnotizen*, 74, note for Nr. 54.—VB]

[5.] George Bell.

[6.] Bonhoeffer's planned trip to England; see his letters of Advent 1938 to Martin Boeckheler and of January 6, 1939, to Sabine and Gerhard Leibholz, 1/42, 1/43, and 1/49.

[7.] The conscription into the army of men born in 1906 and 1907. [Bonhoeffer was born in 1906.—VB]

[8.] Hans von Dohnanyi.

hardly see him, because he will have too much to do. He will be very sorry about the transfer of his friend.[9] He was already quite depressed last time. What are the chances of seeing you again here?—I had already considered whether we could meet again in Stettin if necessary. Perhaps on the evening of the third, and you could then be back again on the evening of the fourth, like before.[10] We could then call Sabine on her birthday from there.—What do you think of that? We were in Leipzig for Karl Friedrich's fortieth birthday, which was very pleasant. In the evening we were all together with Heisenberg[11] and his wife. I have lost Miss Henne's address; if I cannot find it, I would request that you ask about it. What will happen with Uncle Rudi[12] is truly very worrisome. Georg Konrad[13] has now lost his job as well. Ninne[14] was here; she was very interested in the portrait of Mucki[15] at the Schönes'.[16] They are prepared to exchange it, but it isn't easy to find an equivalent for it.—*The Barn*[17] is too unfinished.
116 At Ursel's[18] there were recently three social evenings one after another. The last one was for thirty people with "performances and dance."—Now she is happy that it's all behind her. The car is still in the garage in G[öttingen]. Sabine writes that they want to sell the car right after the house. For that, though, the mortgage approval[19] has to be completed. I must be off for supper. Give my best greetings to Mr. Bethge and let us hear from you both. Papa sends warm greetings with me. Your

Mother

[9.] Regarding the contact to Fritz Wiedemann, the adjutant in the Reich Chancellery, and his transfer to San Francisco, see *DB-ER*, 626–27.

[10.] This refers to Bonhoeffer's meeting with his parents in Stettin in February 1938.

[11.] Werner Heisenberg.

[12.] "Uncle Rudi" was the Bonhoeffer family's code name for the potential beginning of war.

[13.] Georg Konrad Count von der Goltz [who was an attorney—VB].

[14.] Christine Countess Kalckreuth.

[15.] Anna Koenigs.

[16.] Regarding the friendship to the Schöne family, see *DBWE* 9:19–20.

[17.] A painting by Leopold von Kalckreuth.

[18.] Ursula Schleicher.

[19.] [I.e., for the buyer.—VB]

57. To Karl-Friedrich Bonhoeffer[1]

January 28, 1939

Dear Karl Friedrich,

This is the second attempt at a letter to you. First, I wanted to thank you very much for your Christmas letter,[2] second, to congratulate you on your fortieth birthday.[3] In some ways, I envy you for having reached this number! I wish you and all your family a good new year and in any case no more unrest than in the past one. That I didn't write in time is due to the fact that a lot is happening here at present. It has been at times very depressing in the last few weeks, when one must see how many people are seeking quiet and security at all costs and using all kinds of pretexts and reasons.[4] In such times, which come again and again, there is always a great deal to do with visits, lectures, etc. It is entirely certain to me that for the church it all depends upon whether we now hold on, even with great sacrifices. The greatest sacrifices are now small compared to what we would lose by wrongly giving in. I wouldn't know anything worth a full commitment today if not this. It matters not how many there are but rather only that there are still some who are 117
steadfast. Of course, some things are more difficult for the married people, but I think sometimes much is also easier.[5] I admire greatly the courage of the pastors' wives, who are willing to take everything on rather than to advise their husbands to give in. Often, too, the parishioners are much clearer and more resolved than their pastors. Right now in these days, some

[1.] Handwritten; no return address, but probably from Groß-Schlönwitz. Cf. also the later typewritten copy in *NL*, A 44,1 (16). Partially reproduced in *GS* 2:345–46.

[2.] Letter not extant.

[3.] January 13, 1939.

[4.] Bonhoeffer is referring to the struggle over legalization by the regional church consistory.

[5.] [The primary lure of legalization, especially as it became clear that war was imminent, was the financial and professional security offered to the young "illegals" by the official consistory; those who stayed within the Confessing Church had very little security. Married clergy, especially those with children, were very tempted to go through legalization. For a case of one of Bonhoeffer's students who did become legalized for this reason, see Barnett, *For the Soul of the People*, 94–98.—VB]

very important decisions are being made.[6]—I am doing well. I would like to visit Sabine in March if that is still possible.[7]

With best wishes to all of you, your
Dietrich

58. From Sabine Leibholz[1]

Dear Dietrich,

I don't know exactly where this letter on our birthday[2] will reach you. I wish you everything conceivably good for the next year, and thank you for all your help and thoughts for us. You wouldn't believe how much this means for Gert too. We are already looking forward to seeing you again, which hopefully will be for a very long time. I think Gert wrote you yesterday about where you will stay.[3] I would like you to stay with Hennes. The old man is a dear soul, and his wife is very sweet as well. They are doing very well and have built a lovely house equipped for German "comfortable living." I find this Lady-housekeeper[4] at the Crüsemanns'[5] not nearly as nice. She said to me, "If you can't put your brother up anywhere else, then he can come to us." Since she is German, she ought to be able to express herself better. I found it very uninviting. She seems to be an idle goose. Hopefully, we can find a place to put up Mr. Bet.,[6] whom
118 we of course would also very much like to see again. Yesterday my brother-in-law Peter arrived from Zurich. His wife is coming a month later. Then they will travel at the beginning of May to Australia. They are leaving the child for two to three years with the mother-in-law in Zurich. Also a sad thought, given these distances.

The children unfortunately are in bed with the flu. I already saw it coming. The heating conditions in the school are utterly miserable, so that I frequently

[6.] The seventh synod of the Confessing Church of the Old Prussian Union (the "Epiphany Synod") was meeting in Berlin-Nikolassee on January 29–31, 1939. Regarding the resolutions of this synod, see Niesel, *Um Verkündigung und Ordnung der Kirche*, 70–76, and *DB-ER*, 614–15.

[7.] Bonhoeffer's hoped-for visit to England was overshadowed by the fear that war would break out.

[1.] *NL*, C 6; handwritten; undated, but probably the end of January 1939; return address: "London SE 23, Honor Oak Rd. 55"; previously unpublished.

[2.] February 4, 1939.

[3.] Letter not extant.

[4.] ["Lady-housekeeper" in English in original.—VB]

[5.] The Edward Crüsemann family in London-Sydenham.

[6.] Eberhard Bethge.

kept them at home during heavy storms, which blow through all the windows. But even in our rooms we don't get above 9–10 degrees Celsius. Everyone is freezing here at the moment, and the northeast wind with clear, cold weather continues. Gert and I just had an English lesson. Marianne is making the best progress. Since she is already very fond of talking[7] in German and is very quick to speak up, her lack of inhibition serves her well. Christiane was quite obstinate for a while and didn't want to hear or learn English. She thought this was a dumb quirk of ours and somehow felt left out of things. In school she now is slowly beginning to realize that it won't work otherwise, and she is picking up some English. But when we are back in Germany again, she may quickly forget all that. Farewell and many greetings from all of us, your

Sabine

Of course, I am to pass on very many greetings to you from our weekend with the uncle.[8] I felt very well there. That is a very decent humane way of living. I also liked Aunt G.[9] very much. The children, thank God, behaved very well. Uncle and Aunt let them sing a great deal and praised Marianne's pronunciation.[10] Children simply learn this much better.

59. From Gerhard Hellmann[1]

Wustermark, January 31

My dear Brothers Dietrich, Fritz, and Eberhard,[2]

Believe me, the only reason that I have not written you for so long was the lack of time, since for a letter to you one needs time. This is certainly one of the most 119
murderous weapons of Satan, the sigh: "I don't have any time!" It hinders us pastors from performing our ministry as we should; it hinders many parishioners from coming under the Word.

Today I am finally stealing some time, although a flood of Aryans are waiting for the documenting official in me,[3] although the church tax certifications that

[7.] ["Very fond of talking" in English in original.—VB]

[8.] George Bell.

[9.] Henrietta Bell.

[10.] ["Pronunciation" in English in original.—VB]

[1.] *NL*, C 25; handwritten; certainly from 1939; previously unpublished. Hellmann was a candidate in the first course in Zingst and Finkenwalde in the summer of 1935.

[2.] Fritz Onnasch and Eberhard Bethge.

[3.] According to the orders of implementation of Paragraph 3 (the "Aryan paragraph") of the Law for the Reconstitution of the Civil Service of April 7, 1933, and the

need to be written up are also waiting for the administrator in me, although, although . . . spare me from giving a comprehensive list!

It has unfortunately now become a rule that I only find quiet for meditation and preparing my sermon on Saturday evenings around 8:00 p.m., under my desk lamp, and then half the night is spent on it regularly. Nonetheless I may experience repeatedly that out of broken vessels I may distribute God's priceless treasure,[4] which is received gratefully and gladly by the church-community. I have the hearts of the children in the Sunday school and youth meeting, and the older people forget their whining when I can testify to them what the monthly verse for January[5] says. When people visit me personally because of rent, church tax, or other reasons, I draw them into conversation, and it is astonishing how they sometimes thaw. Dear brothers, I do not want to boast, but I must boast and do it as Paul says in I Cor. 1:31.[6] One year ago I performed a wedding for a couple in their second marriage; after a half year they separated because living together was impossible. Now the woman has asked me in a letter for advice and help, and above all, to listen to her. I sometimes hear things where I ask myself, how have these people simply come to say all this to me? I am simply another
120 weak, oh so fallible—Dietrich, you know!—human being! It must simply be that

---

Reich Citizen Law (Reichsbürgergesetz) of September 15, 1935, the decisive criterion for establishing a person's "race" was religious affiliation or that of his ancestors. One means to exclude Jews from the professional and economic spheres during the Third Reich consisted of requiring proof of ancestry that confirmed "racial purity." In many cases this could be established only by referring to the church records that were kept by ministers in the individual local congregations (see Hofer, *Der Nationalsozialismus*, 269–71). Former Finkenwaldian Gerhard Vibrans frequently reported in his letters about the burden of "Aryanics"; he also discussed with Bonhoeffer whether by manipulating the issuing of "proof of Aryan identity," the "gate of Aryanism" ought to be opened for people of so-called impure blood who were deprived of their rights. Andersen et al., *So ist es gewesen*, esp. 240 and 291–92. [Beginning in 1933, enforcement of the Nazi racial laws was possible only because the vast majority of Germans filled out the state-required Aryan certifications, and these were effectively notarized by German parishes throughout the country (which held these kinds of records). As this letter and the corresponding material in the Vibrans letters (*So ist es gewesen*) indicates, Bonhoeffer's students were uncomfortable with meeting this requirement—yet as late as January 1939 they continued to do so. Bonhoeffer's reply to Vibrans's inquiry (about filling out false papers to offer some protection) is both disturbing and revealing. He wrote Vibrans: "(In my opinion,) the certificates are state matters. I believe that it is not permitted to do something about this on our own. At any rate one should consider this very carefully and discuss it with someone who has the exact information. At first I thought the plan was excellent and intended to carry it out right away. But then someone told me of this difficulty" (Andersen et al., *So ist es gewesen*, 291–92. Translation by Victoria Barnett).—VB]

[4.] Cf. 2 Cor. 4:7.

[5.] Ps. 36:9: "For with you is the foundation of life; in your light we see light."

[6.] ["Let the one who boasts, boast in the Lord."—VB]

in me they sense a person who truly means what he says, who also has strength and help at his disposal that come from above. This drives me to boast that I can and may say: "By the grace of God I am what I am!"[7] This makes me so blissful, that in the midst of all melancholy and insecurity I have become and am becoming naively cheerful like a child; this being blissful (in) God in all insecurity, indeed in spite of it, is certainly that great power that has its effect upon people. Sometimes the anxious feeling sneaks in that I speak to people in a foreign, incomprehensible language, but that only comes because I come from the other side with the good news, and we have all gone much too far astray into the cold and darkness of distance from God, so that such news seems foreign to us. How I thank God! that I may be his witness!

I am still sitting here in Wustermark as an unconfirmed assistant pastor, paid by the Confessing Church, not any more insecure than my colleagues in firm positions. The EOK[8] has planned for a year and a day to set up a superintendent's office here, but until now nothing has come of it. Only God knows, however, whether the congregation, which doesn't want to have a superintendent, will stand up for its pastor when things get tough.

Dear Brother Dietrich! I thank you for your card in December.[9] It is my special joy that until now I have always had a deaconess by my side who pulls together with me.

Dear Fritz! I thank you especially for the courageous letter that you, along with the other provincial representatives of the candidates' group, sent us on the question of the extra exam.[10] On February 3 we will again hold a large meeting in Berlin with regard to this.

[7.] 1 Cor. 15:10.

[8.] [Evangelischer Oberkirchenrat, or High Church Council.—VB]

[9.] Card not extant.

[10.] One of the controversial questions related to the legalization of illegal Confessing Church theologians and pastors by state-conformist church authorities was the consistories' demand that the Confessing Church exams, which in their eyes were illegal and invalid, be repeated. On this, see the comment in Bernhard Riemer's letter of February 3, 1939 (*NL*, C 25) to Bonhoeffer: "It will also interest you that a vicar here [in Erfurt] upon sending the records of his university exam received a reply from the consistory that will be symptomatic enough. The faculty exam is recognized without ado, as is the period served as vicar. That's what the consistory *gives*. And then it *takes*: it is assumed that the candidate recognizes the existing church ordinance in the Church of the Old Prussian Union (a signature under this declaration is not required). Further the candidate, who henceforth is on the list of candidates, must sign an attached regulation of theological training. The consistory assigns the candidate to a vicar's post as well as to a preachers' seminary. 'If the candidate leaves his vicar's post of his own accord (should of course read: to another vicar's post or preachers' seminary by the Council of Brethren) he must repay [RM] 60 per month.' The candidate is obligated to sign to obey this regulation.

121 Dear Eberhard! Where may I send you another donation? To an account or personally?

Please don't laugh at the little enthusiast who has allowed his little ego to be the subject of every sentence of this letter. But "my heart leaps and cannot be sad,"[11] and you want to know, don't you, how each one of us feels.

Remembering you in prayer, greetings from your
Gerhard Hellmann

60. From Otto Kistner[1]

End of January 1939

My dear Brother Bonhoeffer,

I had written you already once in the meantime, but burned the letter—indeed a strange manner of correspondence. But this letter will probably reach you. Several days ago I was together with the confidential council advisors[2] in the province. Occasion: Westphalia.[3] Only now do I understand your words in the circular letter correctly; I knew hardly anything about all these things.[4] We are so far removed from things up here, so overburdened with work, that these things play hardly any role. You can imagine what it meant for me to hear suddenly about Westphalia, also be told about both the Krauses.[5] This must all be very painful for you. We have tried to understand *how* it is possible for someone to take such a step. "For the sake of the congregation." How shortsighted. Fifty years from now, won't there be any congregations that still need preachers? Isn't
122 it the case, perhaps entirely unconsciously (surely also consciously for some), that the thought sneaked in: financially impossible! For all the arguments with

---

This means in plain terms: we recognize you on the condition that you dissociate yourself from the Council of Brethren and place yourselves under us."

[11.] The beginning of the thirteenth stanza of the hymn "Ist Gott für mich, so trete gleich alles wider mich," by Paul Gerhardt, in *EG*, 351. [The English version of this hymn (though the beginning of stanza 13 does not correspond to the German) is "If God Himself Be for Me," in *Lutheran Hymnal*, 528.—VB]

[1.] *NL*, C 25; handwritten; no return address; previously unpublished. Kistner was a candidate in the fifth Finkenwalde session in the summer of 1937.

[2.] [Literally, *Vertrauens-Männer*, probably the members of the Geistlicher Vertrauensrat, the Confidential Council of Clerical Advisors for the Confessing Church.—VB]

[3.] [The reference is to Westphalian church president Karl Koch's recommendation supporting legalization. See ed. note 6.—VB]

[4.] See Bonhoeffer's November 20, 1938, letter to the Finkenwalde brothers,1/36. Regarding the problem of legalization, see *DB-ER*, 607–20.

[5.] The brothers Gerhard and Winfried Krause; see 1/76. [Both decided to become legalized. See also Kistner's mention of Winfried Krause's letter later in this one.—VB]

which this step is cloaked are so untenable. It is heartening that this viewpoint of Koch's[6] hasn't penetrated here in the Rhineland; that is occasion to be grateful. Of course, I am often concerned here about what will come of it, and who wouldn't have this worry? And yet this is also the place to apply the saying about not worrying.[7] How your *Discipleship* now becomes so valuable and ever clearer to me. One must step out onto the water like Peter to experience the miracles of Christ.[8] Recently a parishioner said to me: will the young pastors remain firm? I answered: when the church-community stays firm, yes. I should have said, better: when God remains firm. But indeed, that is then no longer an irrational or conditional statement. According to the reports, around forty brothers in Westphalia did remain steadfast.

It was so urgent for me to write this letter to you; perhaps you will gather from this that your work in Finkenwalde has not been for nothing. I could imagine that because of the events in Pomerania your spirits are low. If it would be possible for you to write me, I should be so very grateful. I have to struggle so much with myself; that is the hardest thing. When is the meeting? Or can I simply arrive sometime during my vacation?

In the last few weeks, I have been given to experience that, amid the overflow of work where I might have simply lost heart and failed completely, a great gladness has come over me. This evening the text for Bible study is Matt. 9:35–38.[9] The harvest *is* plentiful.[10] Even when we think that everything has been smashed to pieces. The harvest *is* plentiful. May God give us work and himself make us capable of doing the work. In *every* respect. In speaking and in living.

In friendly solidarity
Kistner

I just saw that your birthday is on February 4. Please accept already my warmest wishes. I would like to say much more to you, but perhaps it would be better to do this when I can come up sometime. Please say hello to Mrs. Struwe[11] and send me your new address.

[6.] Westphalian church president Karl Koch advised all the illegal pastors of the Confessing Church there to register with the consistory for the reexamination. See Niesel, *Kirche unter dem Wort*, 171–72.

[7.] Cf. Matt. 6:25–34.

[8.] On this, see Bonhoeffer's exegesis, *DBWE* 4:62–69.

[9.] ["Then Jesus went about all the cities and villages . . . proclaiming the good news of the kingdom. . . . He said to his disciples, 'The harvest is plentiful, but the laborers are few; therefore ask the Lord of the harvest to send out laborers into his harvest.'"—VB]

[10.] Cf. Bonhoeffer's exegesis in *DBWE* 4:183–85.

[11.] Erna Struwe.

123 II.

Just as I wanted to send my letter, a letter arrives from W. Krause.[12] He writes: ["] I am very concerned about what to do if the CC is really at the end of its path, at least here in Pomerania. Should I look around for another profession? Or should I declare: Against my better judgment, against my understanding of the church, I go to the consistory because otherwise I cannot pursue this profession any longer." I don't know at all how he will now decide and with him the other colleagues. I have the letter that Fritz,[13] among others, has signed. Does Krause support that? If so, then he certainly cannot "against better judgment" take a step that in truth would make the continuation of his profession all the more impossible. I know from his letter that he is often together with you. Please tell him this, and if I am mistaken, he should forgive me. I am so very concerned.

What will happen when the CC is finished (is it really? can it really be or become so, if it is obedient?) I do not know either. But I know this, that under no circumstances can the path to the consistory be taken. To silently tolerate that the gospel is confused with the false gospel![14] To tolerate the restriction of Christ's lordship in his church to the "inner life" and with that the de facto removal of Christ! Impossible. Are we to suffer this? Genuine suffering leads us someplace else. But enough of that. I wish so greatly—and say it again—to receive a personal letter from you. Perhaps Fritz will be so good as to write me an objective, purely statistical report on the situation in Pomerania.

Our brother Schreiber,[15] who was imprisoned before Christmas, is free again. Reason for arrest?

I greet you and all the brothers very warmly. Your
Kistner

124 **61. To Sabine Leibholz**[1]

February 1, 1939

Dear Sabine,

I just realized that I forgot my fountain pen. That is very inappropriate for a birthday[2] letter. But if I want to be punctual, the letter must go out today.

[12.] See ed. note 5.

[13.] Fritz Onnasch.

[14.] Cf. Gal. 1:6–7.

[15.] Not identified.

[1.] *NL*, A 44,1 (17); later typewritten copy; from Köslin. Previously published in *GS* 6:453–54.

[2.] February 4, 1939.

I am thinking in these days especially of you and your family and would like to celebrate with you. How often have we intended to celebrate our birthday together once more. Now everything has changed. Recently it occurred to me that there are some laws in the research on twins—I believe only that they do not apply in our case—that certain twins often have the same life experiences, even when they don't even live near each other. I must say that to a certain degree that appears to be true, in particular when we compare ourselves with our siblings. In any case the lives of both of us have recently been different from what one had expected, even when each life has its own path. In this respect perhaps we can understand our present paths through life particularly well. It is basically one and the same thing that has so decisively determined our life and given it this unexpected turn. However that may be, in any case we will think of each other a great deal on the fourth and expect less from all kinds of good wishes than from the genuine advocacy on behalf of each other. I am already looking forward greatly to seeing you again.[3] The children will certainly help you both celebrate the fourth in a lovely and festive way. Unfortunately, I will have to do without a phone call. I have had frequent visits lately, and that makes this phone business, as you will understand, unnecessarily costly.[4] Otherwise I am doing well, and there is nothing new to report. I am going to send you—from me and Eberhard Bethge together—the book by Ludwig Richter,[5] which you perhaps will enjoy having for the children as well. It is a piece of sentimental 125
past that one must preserve. With Christel[6] we also gave it to Mama for her birthday. Hopefully, it will arrive in time.

Now be well and greet everyone! Affectionate greetings from your

Dietrich

[3.] The reference is to Bonhoeffer's plan to travel to England; he set off together with Eberhard Bethge on March 10, 1939. [See *DB-ER*, 638.—VB]

[4.] This is an allusion to the Gestapo's possible surveillance of his phone calls.

[5.] Probably a reference to the book *Die Gemälde Ludwig Richters* (1937), by K. J. Friedrich about [Adrian] Ludwig Richter.

[6.] Christine von Dohnanyi.

62. To Wilhelm Rott[1]

February 1, 1939

Dear Willi,

It is just terrible that with you I always arrive too late with my birthday greetings.[2] I wish you a good, work-filled, and not too restless new year. I heard about your skiing accident. If only for once you had not climbed into the high mountains but had come to the lower mountains of the Harz. People like us who are getting older should stay away from such undertakings. I had intended to give you my new booklet,[3] but it is not ready yet. I would like to have more free time for my greater work, such as a half year's vacation! The work is proceeding well, but at the moment one cannot be sure for how much longer. On the seventh I will come visit my parents for one evening. Could we see each other then? All the best and cordial greetings, your faithful

Dietrich

126 **63. From Paula Bonhoeffer[1]**

February 2, 1939

Dear Dietrich,

Your birthday will certainly be celebrated again very pleasantly, and you will not miss us, but our greetings should not be missing! For this new year of life, I want to entrust you entirely to our dear God, that he may give you strength to pursue your path in good spirits despite all the heavy pressure.—I just wrote to Sabine. She asked whether you were still there. Mr. Grote[2] will be flying there[3] on the fourth with greetings from us and with all kinds of other matters to discuss that aren't particularly related to birthdays. They are apparently totally preoccupied with their problems here, and he[4] is not getting farther in *his* work at all, and that is indeed sad.—I thought you might need a new house

---

[1.] *NL*, A 45 (64); later typewritten copy; return address, postmarked Köslin. Previously published in *GS* 6:443.

[2.] Rott's birthday was January 25, 1908.

[3.] *Life Together* appeared in 1939 as number 61 of the monograph series Theologische Existenz heute. See *DBWE* 5:6.

[1.] *NL*, C 1; handwritten; from Berlin; previously unpublished.

[2.] Wolfgang Grote; see 1/56.

[3.] [To London.—VB]

[4.] Gerhard Leibholz.

jacket; if that is not the case or if it doesn't fit, please send it back or rather bring it with you. I hope that you like the book by Wolfgang Schöne; I found some lovely things in it.[5] I also sent it to Sabine. How is it with your visit on Tuesday? Mrs. von Kleist,[6] who very sweetly telephoned me, said that you would be in Stettin from the sixth to the eighth. Hans[7] recently inquired by telephone and was puzzled. I guess you had written each other. I did not see him this time on Tuesday. *Everyone*[8] is in bed next door.—Hans Walter,[9] who started it, has started to get up. They all have the flu. Exchanging paintings with Schöne's is not so easy, but I still hope to achieve something.[10] I am greatly looking forward to your arrival; there is indeed much to talk about. How do you like our photos? I think they are rather good. If at all possible, please go sometime to such a photo automatic. Sabine *very much* asked for a picture of you. She has the whole series, like Papa in the cottage, and it's precisely *your* picture that's missing.

Now enjoy the cake and have a pleasant evening with one another.

Affectionately,

Your mother

We will call Saturday evening around 8.

64. From Karl Bonhoeffer[1] 127

February 2, 1939

Dear Dietrich,

It is too bad that you cannot be here on the fourth so that we could give you a preview of a celebration and tell you in person that we have many good wishes for you and that all of us hope for their fulfillment. So your candidates will probably give you a big celebration, and that will certainly be pleasant for you. Tomorrow evening we will call Sabine, whom we are naturally thinking of especially this time. It is good that the children are there.

When we see you on Tuesday, we can of course have a bit of a late celebration and tell each other what we did and thought about in the meantime. Here nothing essentially new has happened. Mama still has her head full of many

[5.] Schöne, *Die großen Meister der Niederländischen Malerei.*

[6.] Ruth von Kleist.

[7.] Hans von Dohnanyi.

[8.] [In the Schleicher family, who lived next door.—VB]

[9.] Hans-Walter von Schleicher.

[10.] See Paula Bonhoeffer's January 23, 1939, letter to Bonhoeffer, 1/56.

[1.] *NL*, C 1; handwritten from Berlin; previously unpublished.

things. She wears herself out, and I wish that we could seclude ourselves on a warm island. But that isn't possible at present, and one doesn't know at all how things will be later. It may just be utopian to believe that one can live idyllically with a large family in times of revolution. In actual fact my retirement does not exist. I have much to do, very many consultations, and am bothered constantly to write up expert opinions, so that I still am not getting around to that which at my age would be my due, to reflect peacefully and with no haste about what I have experienced in life. I just have to see to it that I manage things somewhat differently as time goes on. At the moment I am still needed; at least it is good when I can help somewhat, and that is indeed something for which one must be thankful.

Mama will write you about our practical birthday wishes and greetings. I myself was only part of this by serving as the model for your house jacket. I hope it is not too narrow for you. Your charity case[2] will call me tomorrow, and I will be glad to give him advice.

So, may the new year of life pass peacefully for you and may you be allowed to enjoy your duties that bring you joy without disturbance. Affectionate greetings to you and to Mr. Bethge as well. Your faithful

Father

128 65. From the Schleicher Family[1]

Berolinae, February 2, 1939

Rüdiger juris consultus Theodorico abbae salutem!

Quamquam influenza dejectus tibi optime gratulor. Spero te novo anno et studiis et vita generali progressurum et valetudine numquam affecta fructurum esse. Quando huc redibis animo musicali plenus et manibus bene praeparatis ad commune exercendam musicam? Ego quamquam officio absens lectionem praeparare studeo pro cursu quodam judicum militarium. Qua de causa finem factio.[2]

Rüdiger

[2.] Not identified; this may be a reference to Herbert Liedtke; see 1/53 and1/54.

[1.] *NL*, C 4; handwritten; previously unpublished.

[2.] ["From Rüdiger, the legal expert, to Dietrich, the abbot, a greeting! Although laid flat with the flu, I send you best greetings. I hope that in the new year you make headway in your studies and in life in general and that you enjoy unaffected health. When will you be coming here again, filled with a musical spirit and with hands well prepared for making music together? I am trying, although I am absent from the office, to prepare a selection of military court decisions for a session. Because of that I will close."—VB]

Dear Dietrich,

I want to [join in][3] congratulating you, for a good new year, in this lovely letter from Rüdiger. After the Führer's speech,[4] one wishes this for you in a special sense. Unfortunately, we are all in bed with the flu; I only have a mild case and was the last to decide to go to bed, whereas Rüdiger has not been to the office for a week. Because of that you won't get a package, but it will still come when we are all back on our feet. I will close so that the letter at least reaches your hands in time, since I have no one who can go later to the mailbox. So, may things go well for you, and celebrate a nice day. Affectionately

Your Ursula

Dear Uncle Dietrich, 129

I too send warm congratulations on your birthday and wish you all the best for the new year. I still think back with pleasure on the lovely winter days in the Harz. Since I was sick and cannot yet go back to school, I have a lot of time to practice cello. Since the letter has to go off, I must close. Affectionate greetings from your

Hans-Walter, Renate and Dorothee, Christine

66. From Gerhard Lehne[1]

Esteemed, dear Brother Bonhoeffer,

Now I want to finally write you the letter that I have been carrying around with me, unborn, for a year. If until now I have only let you hear from me occasionally on short postcards,[2] this was an incomplete expression of very faithful remembrance. Perhaps you know this without my having to write it.

I did not come to Schlönwitz gladly and full of hope.[3] Back then I wrote to a good lady friend: "The boundless expanse of the plains, the laughter of friends,

---

[3.] In the original erroneously written "wish."

[4.] This refers to Hitler's speech to the Reichstag on January 30, 1939, in which he defended his aggressive foreign policies of 1938, warned England and the United States against intervening, strongly attacked the Jewish people, and prophesied "the annihilation of the Jewish race in Europe." [See Arad, Gutman, and Margaliot, *Documents on the Holocaust*, 132–35.—VB]

[1.] *NL*, C 25; typewritten with handwritten corrections and signature; from Berlin-Lichterfelde, February 2, 1939. Excerpted in *DB-ER*, 592–93.

[2.] Postcards not extant.

[3.] Lehne was a member of the collective pastorate in Groß-Schlönwitz in the winter of 1937–38.

and wild songs by a burning fire are more important to me than the spiritual breath of a Prussian preachers' seminary and being together with theological brothers." I looked toward this period of physical and spiritual confinement with a shudder. To me it was a necessary evil, into which one had to enter with good grace and for the sake of self-discipline had to get through with good grace. At the same time, it was clear to me that I could only gain theologically and—devoid of all theology—should live in a circle of people each of whom would have "his theology" and would already be rich in insights and decisive in judgments. Probably the thought of being a raven among a flock of white chickens contributed to my lack of desire. Especially unpleasant were the reports that Schröder[4] had given from Finkenwalde and the impression we had of him during our short visit there: he crawled around like a beaten dog. Today I realize that all this was essentially his fault.

130 It all turned out quite differently than I had feared. Instead of coming into the stuffy air of theological bigotry, I entered a world that united many things that I love and need: accurate theological work on the common ground of fellowship, in which one's own inabilities were never noticed in a hurtful fashion, but rather which turned work into pleasure; true fellowship under the Word that united all "without respect to person"[5]—and nonetheless with open-mindedness and love for everything that makes even this fallen creation still worthy of love: music, literature, sports, and the beauty of the earth; a generous style of life that favorably combined the culture of old homes with the uninhibited forms of a community of young men—last, not least,[6] a man in charge whom one can indeed admire without reservation.

When I look back on this time today, it lies before me like a beautiful clear picture. I see myself roaming across the spring-green fields with Bluhm.[7]—I slip my long figure, head bent, through the squeaking door of the house. The doorbell rings, and after some scraping with much ado we enter the semidark dining room. Schröder[8] has turned on the radio, and the brothers are already having their afternoon coffee and bread with marmalade.—The chief has returned after a somewhat extended absence. The floor lamp throws its yellow glow on the blue plush and the copper teakettle. The tea water is boiling. And now we get the latest news; the world breaks into the stillness and simplicity of life on a Pomeranian estate.

[4.] Alfred Schröder was a member of the fifth Finkenwalde session in the summer of 1937.

[5.] Cf. 1 Pet. 1:17.

[6.] ["Last not least" in English in original.—VB]

[7.] Heinz Bluhm.

[8.] Hermann Schröder.

Dear Brother Bonhoeffer, you know that I am a romantic, so far as my reason doesn't prescribe a different attitude; that I am often more open to sensuous pleasures than to theological arguments. Does it spoil the objectivity of your theological view, when I write that it was the peripheral things that enhanced my delight in what is central? Does it perhaps spoil your opinion of me that one corner of my nature can still be grasped in terms of the psychological truth about youth: the young person believes the *bearer* of the Word?

I am very grateful that despite this[9] or even because of it, I am growing into my ministry; that the hours become fewer in which I ask myself whether the Germanic person is not broken by the Christian intellectual heritage, whether it might be my destiny to live "vitally," whether I ought to travel the path toward the beauty of the earth instead of to the cross, because on the latter path many "treasures" in me will not be dug out. There are indeed enough good and bad attempts to make Christendom palatable for idealism. Basically all they do is play down the fact that the best roots of a Christian are simply not in this world, and 131
that a Christian simply *does not* think thus: I don't know how brightly the suns will shine over there / but one day in God's eternal brightness / I will in all my blessedness / weep in longing for the dark earth.[10]—The strange thing is that I have never felt this to be a trial. I take the decade of my boyhood and youth, which awakened and encouraged this attitude, as the most beautiful gift of God, and even today hardly anything makes me happier than lying in my old leather breeches in the heat of the sun, oblivious to time, by the side of a highway in northern Sweden, and a little later roaring northward on a truck transporting ore. Romanticism? More than that! I know that however God leads me, it is good for me. And if previously I complained about many a detour that I took, today I know that it was necessary. This limitless confidence, trusting that wherever I may yet fall, I shall never fall from God's hand; the certainty that all paths lead to God's goal, whichever of them may be destined for me to travel, allows me to look confidently even into this darkness.

I must close this letter so that it doesn't arrive too late. Today is already February 2. Furthermore, I must conclude my written catechesis so that I can hand it over in Spandau[11] next week at the latest.

I am very grateful to you for everything, and I also believe that you will understand this letter correctly. After all, not everyone is called to write *Discipleship*. Please greet Brother Bethge. I think of him with great pleasure. He was a good comrade and could laugh so heartily. Say hello to Mrs. Struwe as well and to

[9.] [I.e., despite his youthful belief in Bonhoeffer.—VB]

[10.] No source for this quotation is given.

[11.] This was an assignment for the second theological exam, to be turned in to Confessing Church superintendent Martin Albertz in Berlin-Spandau.

Schutz[12] and Götz Maltusch. One year ago today, I had just returned with the Fra Angelico from Berlin; in the evening we had a great dinner. Now today you will have the latter as well, but the means for Fra Angelico were no longer possible. But Chinese war poems are worth reading too, if only for the sake of gaining insight into other people and worlds. Those are verses that I might have written if only I had been granted mastery of the lyrical form. Perhaps you sometimes read the little book[13] in memory of the tall fellow from the first Schlönwitz collective pastorate who occasionally played the harmonica in bed at night.

Greetings to you in gratitude and faithfulness as your little brother
Gerhard Lehne

132 **67. From Karl-Heinz Corbach**[1]

Göhlsdorf, February 3, 1939

Dear Brother Bonhoeffer,

Your friendly warning to return the books borrowed from you as quickly as possible gave me a mild shock, and yet nonetheless it is only being followed today. I beg your pardon, but cannot myself find any reason that would excuse me. It would be interesting to hear a man like Max Weber talk about the CC.[2]

I am doing quite well. I am grateful and happy that I do not need to live alone here in this small heathen village.[3] Some things look different when there are two of us. We live from day to day and are not suffering any want, although stupidly we are listed on the intercession list[4] [Fürbittenliste] as being without a salary. We have never received a salary from the state.

At the moment there is a strange mood in the CC. It almost looks as though people want to capitulate. And it is not surprising that this is the case. For to

[12.] Erwin Schutz.

[13.] Lehne's birthday present to Bonhoeffer was Klabund, *Dumpfe Trommel und berauschtes Gong* [a book about Chinese literature, "Thumping Drum and Dulled Gong"; "Klabund" was the pen name for Alfred Henschke—VB], with the inscription: "To his big brother! February 2, 1939. G. L."

[1.] *NL*, C 25; handwritten; previously unpublished. Corbach was a candidate in the fifth Finkenwalde session in the summer of 1937.

[2.] Possibly Marianne Weber's biography of her husband, *Max Weber: Ein Lebensbild*, was one of the books that had been borrowed. See Bonhoeffer's August 23, 1938, letter to the Finkenwalde brothers, 1/24.

[3.] Corbach had just married the theologian Ursula Duckstein. Göhlsdorf is around 20 kilometers west of Potsdam.

[4.] Regarding the Confessing Church's intercession lists, see the enclosure with the circular letter of July 18, 1938, 1/21.2, ed. note 11.

a great extent the brothers in the province—let alone in Berlin—are not prepared at all to take the simplest measures against the attacks. So much distrust among themselves, so many loveless condemnations, so much isolation, and so much church politics! I have the impression as though we in the CC have only now arrived at the point where we don't know any other way but to practice "Dahlem."[5] Until now in general it could hardly be said that we followed the way that was indicated there. Today in Berlin there is a meeting of the young brothers.[6] Unfortunately, I am prevented from going there by a cold. I think it is very good that Brother Klapproth is our representative. People will listen to some things from him. He is untiring in his service and lacking all vanity. In general we Brandenburg brothers can be pleased with our leadership. President 133
Scharf[7] is very great, and a large group depends on him and is still steadfast because of him.

I had pondered for some time whether it might be possible for you to call together all the Finkenwalde brothers in Brandenburg somewhere in Brandenburg. It seems to me that everyone would welcome it, if they could be together again without a major journey. Buckow[8] would be the suitable location. There one could be together undisturbed for two days. Such a gathering could do us good and give us new courage. One could arrive Sunday evening and leave on Tuesday evening. Perhaps there will be a possibility. For twenty-five brothers there are two possibilities for lodging. More than twenty-five would have to meet then in "Wilhelmshöhe."[9] Naturally a retreat on the Baltic is a fine thing, but quite time and money consuming.

Hopefully, you and all the brothers there[10] are well. I think a great deal about you all. May God help you in your work and bless you daily.

With warm greetings, your grateful
K. H. Corbach

[5.] The reference is to the second confessional synod of the German Evangelical Church in Dahlem on October 19–20, 1934, with its declaration of church emergency law. See Schmidt, *Bekenntnisse*, 2:157–62. [See also Barnett, *For the Soul of the People*, 65–67 and 95–96.—VB]

[6.] A meeting of young illegal theologians.

[7.] Kurt Scharf.

[8.] A town in the Märkische Schweiz [a region in the Brandenburg province—VB], about forty kilometers east of Berlin.

[9.] This suggested retreat never took place.

[10.] At the two locations of the collective pastorates.

68. From Hartmut Gadow[1]

February 3, 1939

Dear Brother Bonhoeffer,

May God preserve for you in this new year of life the possibility, here and there, to point the proclaimers of His message toward Him. May He let you not tire of admonishing us, based on the interpretation of His word, to travel the path of a true church and at the same time to lead a personal life out of discipline through the Word. Your greeting[2] was a help to me in a time of questioning. With brotherly greetings in faithful remembrance your

H. Gadow

134

69. From Hans Hofmann[1]

Lupow, February 3, 1939

Esteemed, dear Brother Bonhoeffer,

We only seem to notice how quickly a year goes by whenever certain days draw our attention to it once more. So please allow me to take your birthday as such a reminder.

Accept with the enclosed card and its biblical word my heartfelt congratulations.[2] This has become my favorite psalm, and Calvin with his sermons helps to make it even more! I ferreted the book out of our old church library and am in the process of comparing the sermons with Luther's brief comments on this psalm. A pity that I cannot look into the *WA*.[3] It would indeed be a worthwhile task to find out sometime from this how both reformers after this unique witness to the "*Word*" think about its relation to the "*Law*." (At the moment I don't recall whether Luther said anything elsewhere about this psalm outside of his "To usefully pray the 119th Psalm, to raise the word of God against his foe, the

---

[1.] *NL*, C 25; handwritten; from Berlin-Friedrichsfelde; previously unpublished. Gadow was a candidate in the fifth Finkenwalde session in the summer of 1937.

[2.] Correspondence not extant. However, it possibly refers to Bonhoeffer's November 20, 1938, circular letter to the Finkenwalde brothers, 1/36.

[1.] *NL*, C 25; handwritten; previously unpublished. Hofmann was a candidate in the fourth Finkenwalde session in the winter of 1936–37.

[2.] This card with a verse from Ps. 119 is not extant.

[3.] The Weimarer Ausgabe, or Weimar edition, of Luther's works.

Pope and anthropology . . . ,"[4] which appeared in 1521. If so, please write me when and where. Calvin's sermons come from the year 1553.)[5]

But now I have gotten away from the original purpose of this letter! Or should it be more than mere "coincidence" when we as the servants of this Word let it determine even the most personal matters and wishes of our lives?

Another year has passed, in which you, dear Brother Bonhoeffer, sheltered as if by a miracle of God, could work with brothers who are preparing themselves for the ministry. Is that not a reason each and every day to thank the one who watched over you and the brothers! Oh, this then makes you forget even all the wretchedness and the numerous shifts back and forth with all their troubles.

Things are indeed quite similar for every one of us. We yearn for full responsibility in our ministry. Here, in my estimation, lies the deep reason for all the "keeping an eye on" the consistory. It is simply more or less the case that we have enough work and do it gladly, but the ministry of the Word does want more 135
from us! I mean that now in opposition to the statement by the synod,[6] where it is stated that the brothers in office should share their ministry and house with us. Precisely here lies the difficulty: perhaps (?) they can share the house with us, but the office is simply indivisible, because there is only *one* responsibility for it.

At the end of April, my year as assistant pastor will end. Then I would like to marry. I simply cannot here in Lupow, because two parsonages in one parish are simply an absurdity. Until now I have not yet discussed this with Brother Gehlhoff,[7] but I can imagine that he will not see the matter any differently. What will then happen: the "keeping an eye on" the consistory will gain new momentum; or now to see it from the other side: I will have to request that the Council of Brethren help me somehow, after granting consent for my marriage. With that, however, the council's trouble will grow, for I will hardly be the only one in the coming months who comes with such a request! I fear the worst in this respect for Pomerania! In Brandenburg these matters seem to go better, at least judging by what Brother Giese[8] wrote me. Perhaps during the upcoming Pomeranian discussions, you will think especially about this particular Pomeranian question! Br. Dufft[9] rightfully suggested lowering the pension prices a bit in order to effect

[4.] Cf. *WA* 8:186–204. ["Der 119. Psalm nützlich zu beten, das Wort Gottes zu heben wider seinen Feind, den Papst und Menschenlehre . . ."—VB]

[5.] See Calvin, *Auslegung der Heiligen Schrift*, vol. 5, 2nd half, 425–510.

[6.] The seventh confessional synod of the Old Prussian Union (the "Epiphany synod") on January 28–31, 1939, in Berlin-Nikolassee. For the decisions of the synod, see Niesel, *Um Verkündigung und Ordnung der Kirche*, 70–76.

[7.] Gerhard Gehlhoff.

[8.] Kurt Giese.

[9.] Heinz Dufft.

a little (or perhaps essential?) financial relief for the Council of Brethren. He was notified by the Council of Brethren that no brother in office could be expected to provide food etc. for a young brother (or vicar) for [RM] 40. Yes, that is in fact the question I would ask the synod, what they then understand the sharing of ministry and house to be?! I would like to emphasize explicitly that Br. Dufft spoke out of his situation, that is, out of his *own* housekeeping. Dr. Burgwitz[10] had signed the reply! Please use this only with reservations, since it is certainly not Brother Dufft's wish to spread this around! But how typical for Pomerania!

Kierkegaard: ". . . He not only has (something most pastors have, and most often in proportion to their rank) an impartial eye for earthly gain. . . .["][11]

136 I rather like it here in Lupow, and so sometimes the thought has occurred to me: you could perhaps stay here in case Br. Gehlhoff leaves. (Which because of his Pomeranian work for the CC would not be too welcome!) And immediately the temptation to "cast an eye"[12] comes up again! From February 19 to 24, Br. Maechler[13] has requested me for his parish evangelization [Volksmission]. I'm looking forward to it.

Now I wish you, dear Brother Bonhoeffer, that your work be blessed and protected in your new year of life through our Lord.

With many greetings your
Hans Hofmann

70. From Erich Klapproth[1]

Berlin, February 3, 1939

Dear Brother Bonhoeffer,

I think of you on your birthday with the warmest wishes and blessings and in ever-increasing gratitude and solidarity. May God continue to enlighten and console you so that you can continue to guide and console your brothers.

Your faithful
Erich Klapproth

[10.] Martin Burgwitz, deputy chair of the Confessing Church Council of Brethren in Pomerania since 1938.

[11.] From Kierkegaard, "'First the Kingdom of God,'" 234.

[12.] [Toward the consistory.—VB]

[13.] Winfried Maechler.

[1.] *NL*, C 25; handwritten postcard; unpublished. Klapproth was a candidate in the fourth Finkenwalde session in the winter of 1936–37.

PS: Brother Ebeling[2] is unfortunately not in the best of health, so that his coming to St[ettin][3] is questionable. Whether I myself can take time off in these weeks of difficult decisions is not yet foreseeable. T[he] a[bove].

71. From Rudolf Lynker[1] 137

Hälver, February 3, 1939

Dear esteemed Brother Bonhoeffer,

I just want to let you know that I received the "Reflection" about our path.[2] Along with the declarations from the beginning of this week,[3] which until now I have only been told about, this has helped me to see the whole matter differently now. I hope that I receive the declarations soon in writing. As soon as I come to be completely clear about this, I will reverse my decision.[4] Think very especially of me during these days and of the many, many Westphalian brothers![5] Your

Rudi Lynker

72. From Friedrich Onnasch[1]

Köslin, Elisenstrasse 3, February 3, 1939

Dear Brother Bonhoeffer,

For your birthday I wish you with all my heart that God may give you also in this new year of life the ways and possibilities to serve His church with your gifts, and

---

[2.] Gerhard Ebeling.

[3.] Probably to a planned meeting of the "theological society." [Cf. 1/30, 1/35, and 1/39.—VB]

[1.] *NL*, C 25; handwritten postcard; return address: "R. Lynker, Schalksmühle/Westfalen, Hälver"; previously unpublished. Lynker was a candidate in the collective pastorate at Groß-Schlönwitz in summer 1938.

[2.] See Bonhoeffer's lecture, "Our Path according to the Testimony of Scripture," 2/5.

[3.] See the resolutions of the seventh confessional synod of the Old Prussian Union in Berlin-Nikolassee in January 1939, which concerned solidarity with the young illegals in the Confessing Church, in Niesel, *Um Verkündigung und Ordnung der Kirche*, 70–76.

[4.] Lynker had registered with the regional church consistory to take the required post-exam, that is, to become legalized. This is mentioned in a postcard (not reproduced here) to Bonhoeffer from Erwin Sander of February 4, 1939, *NL*, C 25.

[5.] Cf. the letter from Otto Kistner, end of January 1939 (1/60), with ed. note 4.

[1.] *NL*, C 25; handwritten card from Superintendent Friedrich Onnasch; previously unpublished.

that He may richly bless this service. May He watch over you, that your heart not become bitter, not even through grim experiences, but instead remain cheerful and confident in discipleship. The day will certainly come when His wondrous ways will be so evident that we can only give praise and thanks.

Hoping and already rejoicing today in this day with you, your
F. Onnasch

138 **73. From Hans-Jakob Büchsel**[1]

Greifenberg, February 4, 1939

My dear Dietrich,

This year's watchword is to greet you on your birthday. Even if my greeting arrives too late, you know that I remember you and your work daily, and that is more than all the warm greetings and blessings can give us. I am leaving Greifenberg in the coming week and moving to Batzwitz. I will send you another letter from there. I have placed in this text all my wishes for your life and your work and your salvation. Greet all the brothers. Commending you to God with affection in brotherly solidarity your

Jakob

74. From Werner de Boor and Gerhard Saß to the "Brotherhood of Young Theologians" in Pomerania[1]

Stolp, February 13, 1939

Dear Brothers,

I want to add a personal word to the circular letter to the brotherhood.

We all know about the weighty tensions that are running through our brotherhood. They are so hard and so dangerous precisely because they don't remain
139 theoretical opposite points of view but are becoming practical separations of the

[1.] *NL*, C 25; handwritten postcard with the devotional text drawn for the year 1939: "Do not fear, for I have redeemed you; I have called you by name, you are mine" (Isa. 43:1); previously unpublished. Büchsel was a candidate in the second Finkenwalde session in the winter of 1935–36.

[1.] *NL*, C 25; later typewritten copy; previously unpublished. In the debate about legalization, the conflicts among the assistant pastors and vicars in the Confessing Church in Pomerania intensified in the winter of 1938–39. A division among them between way "A" (consistent rejection of subordination to the consistories) and way "B" (subordination under certain conditions) had occurred. Both sides again presented

paths. But in many hearts these tensions are countered by a conviction that is just as deep of our ongoing belonging together and by the will to stay together for the very sake of the Confessing Church. The advice: "Let your brotherhood collapse only if certain measures necessary for the church are carried through!" finds no echo in our hearts. And this is not out of any sentimentality. It is much more the knowledge in all of us that precisely "brotherhood" is the essential living beginning of "church." Thus we have attempted a church administration through a "council of brethren," in conscious contrast to all church "governments" that conform to the world. (What does it matter if, after centuries of the secularization of the church, this attempt has not yet penetrated and seized the entire "church"?) Thus the knowledge is growing in us that things can only go forward in the individual congregations if there is at least a beginning of a brotherhood around the minister. (Local council of brethren, Confessing church-community as a brotherhood under the word. How can we lead the entire church through councils of brethren if this new nature of the church doesn't first begin in the parishes!) Thus in clergy circles it has long been felt that a renewal of the ministry can succeed only when the secularized forms of separation from one another in the official church [Amtskirche] are overcome by a brotherly with-one-another. And thus many of us see our "brotherhood of young theologians" as a gift from God of which we cannot let go. Perhaps here we will be given to grow beyond the great attempt of the churches of the Reformation, to win unity through the same knowledge and unanimous teaching, to a unity that admittedly, in human terms, is inconspicuous and insecure and for that reason uncanny, but nonetheless is real and powerful in the Lord and in the community of the Holy Spirit.

With this, admittedly, we stand at the beginning of questions and tasks that none of us today can easily answer and solve. Here the Prussian outcome[2] in no way means a full stop: *Roma locuta, causa finita.*[3] Here our discussion must continue, even if not with the previously narrow focus upon the one practical
question. The elaboration by Brother Saß offers us all a piece of this discussion; 140
for that reason I would like to send it to all the brothers.

---

their respective positions before the decisive meetings of the various ministeriums (*Pfarrkonvente*) in February 1939 were held. Werner de Boor, chair of the "Brotherhood of Young Theologians" in Pomerania, and Gerhard Saß advocated way "B." See *DB-ER*, 615–20, and Klän, *An der Wegscheide*.

[2.] The seventh confessional synod of the Old Prussian Union in January 1939 in Berlin-Nikolassee took a clear position against the consistories' attempts toward legalization and warned the young pastors "of upholding a false church government." See *DB-ER*, 614, and Niesel, *Kirche unter dem Wort*, 196–99.

[3.] "Rome has spoken, the matter is decided."

Dear colleagues, "make every effort to maintain the unity of the Spirit in the bond of peace" (Eph. 4:3). Your

de Boor

Stolp, February 13, 1939

Dear Brothers,

The resolutions of the Prussian synod, which have reached us in the meantime, compel us once again—like any synodal resolution—to a thorough examination of their outcomes and theological presuppositions and with that to reconsider our personal decision about the question of our path.

I submit to you the following reservations against the foundations of the synodal resolution, which have only strengthened my position, which I have held for months, of rejecting "Way A"[4] and have freed me internally to take a position against the synod, because I feel obligated to inform my brothers about the reasons that will soon compel me to leave Way A.

1. The theological rationale for Way A on the basis of the question of *vocatio*,[5] which appears to deliver such a mathematically unequivocal outcome, is questionable because the discussion about the Protestant understanding of the essence of vocation, ordination, ministry, church government [Kirchenregiment][6] cannot be seen as concluded. Certainly church action cannot always wait for theologically uncontradictory definitions. Nonetheless a church policy resolution that rests on controversial theological assumptions can never be binding as absolutely as this synodal resolution claims to be. (I only remind you of the controversies about ministry and church regime, between the opinion that the office of ministry rests within the congregation and is bestowed by the congregation on individuals [according to Thomasius,[7] v. Hofmann,[8] see Theodosius Harnack, *Die Kirche, ihr Amt, ihr Regiment: Grundlegende Sätze*, new edition 1934!]

[4.] See ed. note 1.

[5.] "Vocation"; cf. Augsburg Confession, Article 14 (*Book of Concord*, 47). On this issue see the documentation from Bonhoeffer's 1935 lecture on church constitution, *DBW* 14, 2/1.

[6.] [*Kirchenregiment* is a somewhat unusual term to describe the church governing structures (the more usual term is *Kirchenleitung*). Bonhoeffer sometimes used *Kirchenregiment* in a pejorative fashion to describe the church authorities (see, for example, a 1933 letter to his grandmother, *DBWE* 13, 1/31, p. 59), and in such instances it has been translated as "church regime." In this report by Werner de Boor, however, it does appear that he is using the term to describe the standard church governing bodies—albeit perhaps ironically—and so it is translated here as "church government."—VB]

[7.] Gottfried Thomasius.

[8.] Johann Christian Konrad von Hofmann.

and that other understanding that only the office of ministry first creates the congregation and has to continue by itself [*successio*][9] [according to Löhe,[10] and above all Vilmar].[)][11]—Furthermore: does ordination signify a sacramental (Vilmar) or only a juridical act? What is decisive for an ordination, the one who ordains, or the one who commissions him [Auftraggeber], the formulation of obligation or the "holiness" of the one who ordains or the congregation of the entire church-community? Does an ordination lack God's blessing if, while it is correctly carried out, those who ordain are not *only* in church office? What does *rite vocatus*[12] really mean? The commission that a church-community bestows to carry out a ministry within it, following the examination of the individual's capability and preparatory training? Or, *successio*—in due order—from Christ? Is the church government called for by Christian faith and the presence of a church-community of Christ in the world, or is the church government only a useful form of human-ecclesial order (*de jure humano* or *divino*?)[13]—With these questions I want only to indicate several points that show how unclarified even today the presuppositions that underlie the synod's resolution remain. Preceding the resolution is a reference to Rom. 10:15 and Eph. 4:10–11. The necessity of *vocatio* through a proper church government cannot, however, be proven from Rom. 10:15 (only the one who is sent can proclaim). Here the sending of all believers through the word of God (Rom. 10:17) is confused with the commission, to be bestowed by the congregation, to administer the word and sacrament in the congregation. (Cf., e.g., also what O. Riecker, *Das evangelische Wort*, 1935, pages 87ff., says about the sending as a pneumatic fact over against the *vocatio* according to human order. From Eph. 4:11: "*He* has set," only the Catholic Church might derive a reference to its church government.) 141

2. The singling out of one theological insight that is recognized as being correct out of the *fullness* of insights given with the gospel and the attempt to build the church upon *one* such, perhaps correct insight (here about the church government) has a destructive effect upon the church. (The mistake of all sects is their one-sided point of departure, their too-narrow theological foundation.)

Over against the narrowness of the slogan: struggle for a church government, which can in due order call and send preachers of the gospel, what is far more 142

[9.] "Succession (in the ministry)."

[10.] Wilhelm Löhe.

[11.] August Friedrich Christian Vilmar. The doctrinal development in the neo-Lutheran ecclesiology with the controversy between advocates of the "transference theory" and advocates of the "institutional theory" of the office of ministry is presented in Andresen, *Handbuch der Dogmen- und Theologiegeschichte*, 3:184–88.

[12.] "Properly called"; see ed. note 5.

[13.] "According to human law or divine law."

central for me—particularly in the present situation of the church—is Jesus's command: Matt: 28:18ff.

The historical situation of our established church as a church of the people [Volkskirche] makes it still necessary today to be obedient to this command of Jesus in the congregation (in the visible, more external congregation), that is, under the consistory. Practice shows that even the CC in Pomerania is not doing anything different, in that it must fill pastorates doubly, as it were, and tell the pastors who are retained in office by the consistory to share "office and house" with the illegal brothers. The CC, however, must leave to the middle way or to the GC those congregations in which these illegal brothers could preach.[14] However, the congregations that have understood exactly what is at stake so that they want in any event to have and support an "illegal" pastor are few.

Therefore, for the sake of a theologically theoretically clean *vocatio* (on the dubiousness of this, see above), I believe that I cannot offer support for the struggle for a pure church government, as long as congregations still want to elect and call proper preachers of the gospel and the consistories are prepared to assign such preachers to the parish. It would be more supportive for the commission given us by the Word if the number of illegal theologians *in the imprisonment* of the state-connected consistorial "church" would proclaim the Word unanimously with the CC pastors in office and the preachers of the gospel from the middle path—so long as it is still possible—in order to bear together the need and tribulation that grows out of such imprisonment.

3. The reality of the church is more extensive and greater than can be portrayed by a theoretical system about pure church government and pure church. This is evident, first, in that the system disregards the fact that even outside the CC there is proper preaching and that outside the CC there is church. Furthermore, it seems to me that the fact that the church schism practically (i.e., in our church actions) troubles us so little or warns us is an indication that we stand in the same damnation as the church-community in Corinth: We have fine knowledge. But this knowledge "puffs up" and murders love instead of edifying the congregation and creating unity of spirit. "Let all things be done for building up" (I Cor. 14:26). Where there is no building up but instead new separation and divorce and destruction of community, there we can hardly act out of the unity with the spirit of Christ. Even when marching separately it ought to be possible to maintain brotherly unity in the *proper* church of the Lord (cf. the example of Paul in his relation to Jerusalem).

4. Making the intention to preach the gospel and assume the office of a
143 preaching ministry in a congregation dependent upon authorization that has

[14.] ["GC" refers to the German Christians (in original, DC, i.e., Deutsche Christen).—VB]

been conferred by a legitimate church government overlooks the fact that the church exists in this era in the form of servant, and that its "pure" and "glorious" form, that is, the same form of the exalted Lord, can only be *believed* (3rd article).[15] The illusion of the "pure church" is always in the background wherever there is church schism instead of unity of spirit, love, and knowledge (Phil. 2:1–4). (Cf. also the Enthusiast movement;[16] parable of the weeds among the wheat.)[17] That's why the question of the earthly order of a pure church government must indeed be discussed theologically, again and again, but it can never be practiced satisfactorily, and certainly not in our era. (Certainly the realization of theological insights must be attempted ever anew, but is not the church's situation at present so serious that other tasks have become more urgent for us?) The pure church government can only be realized today in a free church (which is of course illusory for the CC), but this is the very thing that the synod obviously didn't want. For basically it is only once again giving the old slogan: wait and see! We will continue to insist on your legalization! And in this waiting period the congregation[s] are also waiting for the proper preachers of the gospel, which as things stand they can receive only via the consistories. The struggle on the frontlines for the governance of the church has long been decided, namely, it was lost by the CC.[18] The front of the Church Struggle, however, is much broader. And the decision no longer concerns the church government. Nonetheless, the synod wants to continue to fight about this and thus ties down the forces that are needed so urgently in other places and surrenders these places to the enemies in our ranks. This situation does not justify the greatness of the sacrifices being made. Way A means continually starting a new charge (with ever-diminishing strength and reasons) against a locked door. Yet according to Paul's principle we should seek the place where God—in the form of the *Volkskirche* (from which the CC too still lives with us) that has been handed down to us historically as a task and at the same time as a trouble—presently still leaves a door open for the preaching of the gospel (1 Cor. 16:9; 2 Cor.
2:12; Col. 4:3). What should be done when the previous form of the church has 144

[15.] See the third article of the Apostles' Creed (*Book of Concord*, 21–22). ["I believe in the Holy Spirit, one holy Christian church, the community of saints, forgiveness of sins, resurrection of the flesh, and eternal life."—VB]

[16.] "Enthusiasts," or "enthusiast spirits," was Martin Luther's verdict on some of those who did not share his faith convictions, such as Andreas Bodenstein (named Karlstadt), Thomas Müntzer, and others. In more recent research, these groups are characterized more neutrally as the "left wing of the Reformation" or the "radical Reformation." See the description in Andresen, *Handbuch der Dogmen- und Theologiegeschichte*, 2:27–33 and 568–81.

[17.] Matt. 13:24–30.

[18.] [See *DB-ER*, 616.—VB]

been completely destroyed—which for the time being one cannot yet say, above all in Pomerania—remains to be seen. Indeed, we can proceed into the darkness only step by step, rather than making great plans for the building up of a future new church organization.

5. The path of the church in history does not follow natural laws that one can calculate in advance. The course established in Dahlem[19] was still right at the time and had to be maintained as a claim upon the entire church as long as the possibility of and hope for a unanimous merger of congregations and pastors of the GEC existed. Today this hope—above all in Pomerania—should be buried as utterly absurd.

Therefore I am incapable of seeing the situation other than that for which we are commanded, that for the sake of the unity of the church and the command of Jesus and the congregations (which are not yet mature enough to make their own decisions), to take the path that leads into the organization: GEC, that is, into various external forms of servitude and internal torment, which the CC pastors in office have borne already for a long time.

It is not possible for me to overlook these reasons and still be convinced that Way A is correct and demanded by faith as a necessity. I once went along this path cheerfully and surely and am even now convinced that at the time such action was correct, but today I am just as convinced that further insistence on this course would be wrong for me.

The brothers who share this conviction with me—and apparently that are quite a few—would have to see two decisive questions resolved before taking the step to the consistory:

The brothers in that part of the brotherhood who for reasons of conscience have adhered to the previous path,[20] and the new Council of Brethren, which has been restructured and extended according to the Prussian resolution, must not be allowed again—as happened in many cases to brothers who joined the consistory earlier—to incur the guilt of a further destruction of brotherly community, namely, by simply "letting the renegades leave," thus forcing them into an isolation that is felt doubly harshly by one who comes from the CC and knows personally that he will always belong to the CC. Therefore, it would be necessary for the sake of the community of the CC that those brothers who now for reasons of conscience find it necessary to take the path to the consis-
145 tory, be led by their spiritual leadership, that is, the Council of Brethren (or the director of the examination office?) to the consistory, in order to document

[19.] The second confessional synod in Dahlem on October 19–20, 1934, with its declaration of church emergency law. See Schmidt, *Bekenntnisse*, 2:157–62.

[20.] [I.e., Way A.—VB]

simultaneously that the brothers under the consistory—like the CC pastors in established pastorates—belong and should belong to the CC.

The other question that we will have to ponder concerns our brotherhood. It will have to become clear whether the brotherhood was only a community formed in the church-political struggle, a community that stands or falls with the decision for or against a certain path, or a brotherhood in Christ. From such a brotherhood, only those who separate themselves from Christ, the one Word of God that we have to hear,[21] exclude themselves. We must prevent a repeated destruction and diminishment of the brotherhood, simply in view of the time when the common brotherhood will have to prove itself. Certainly a withdrawal from the CC list of candidates would be necessary, but the brotherhood ought to prove itself as the bond that transcends all external contradictions in a deeper unity.

In light of the fact that some of the older brothers in our brotherhood have also been tormented by similar reservations against Way A, I deeply deplore that not one of those who has followed Way A much longer than I myself has spoken to the brothers about these troubles, in order to challenge them to seriously examine our course, to weigh anew which questions in the current situation of the church are to be seen as central or peripheral. Since I, however, now see it as unavoidably necessary that all brothers receive knowledge of the questions that have caused me and others to advocate Way B, I have attempted here to present the arguments that seem most important to me. I would be grateful if the brothers who fundamentally agree with me could let me know this as soon as possible, and if those who have understandable reasons for their opposing position would tell me this as well. Your

G. Saß

[21.] A reference to the first thesis of the Barmen theological declaration. ["We reject the false doctrine that the church could and should recognize as a source of its proclamation, beyond and besides this one Word of God, yet other events, powers, historic figures, and truths as God's revelation." Cited in Hockenos, *Church Divided*, 179.—VB]

146 **75. To the Finkenwalde Brothers**[1]

Personal letter!

February 14, 1939

Dear Brothers,

Above all I must thank you that you responded so kindly to my brief Christmas greeting[2] with detailed letters. I am pleased to know again about you, how you are doing, about your work, and of your confidence in our cause. Your letters at the same time brought such a great number of sermons that I have not yet gotten through all of them. I thank you for these as well and have learned from this how good and valuable this kind of connection is. I would in fact even like to suggest immediately that in the letters you write to one another you also enclose sermons. That is a genuine gain for both sides, personally and objectively. Finally, I still have to thank you for the birthday greetings that I received last week. Such signs give one much new energy and joy for the work.

In my last letter I wrote to you about patient endurance in the New Testament[3] as we had worked through this concept here. I was very happy to read in many of your letters that this admonition through Scripture also appeared important to you in our time. Allow me then today to attempt to communicate to you from the same work,[4] once again as an invitation to join us in the work on another great concept from the New Testament, which we must penetrate in order to live in it: about joy.

The new beginning that has recently been given to us through God's goodness against all expectations has liberated us from a dull pressure.[5]
147 We have been called once more to the full joy in Jesus Christ our Lord. It is truly nothing but the grace of God, that he has once again allowed us to hear the witness to Christ's lordship so purely and without adulteration, for with our unjoyful, resigned, and stubborn nature, we were no longer deserving of it. Now, however, we are challenged to really grasp this gift of God anew and to be led to the full joy of Christ.

[1.] *NL*, A 48,3 (7); typewritten mimeograph with handwritten signature; probably from Groß-Schlönwitz. Previously published in *GS* 2:546–50.

[2.] Correspondence not extant.

[3.] See Bonhoeffer's November 20, 1938, circular letter, 1/36.

[4.] [A study of New Testament concepts.—VB]

[5.] The reference is to the seventh confessional synod of the Old Prussian Union in Berlin-Nikolassee, on January 28–31, 1939; see 1/74, ed. note 2.

The first thing that Scripture tells us about joy can be summarized with the beginning of the song: "Jesus, my joy. . . ."[6] This is the *continuo* of the biblical proclamation of the birth of Christ, of the dawning of God's kingdom in Christ's fellowship with the disciples, of Christ's resurrection and ascension (Luke 2:10; Mark 2:19; Luke 24:41, 52; John 20:20). God wants to make us joyful through Jesus Christ. God wants neither to oppress us nor to confront us with insoluble problems, but rather wishes us to delight in Jesus Christ and in Christ's lordship. This again is among the simplest things, which the more difficult ones make us forget, namely, that we learn to delight in Jesus Christ like children. Is it not the worst kind of ingratitude and stubbornness of our heart, when the one who came to us for the sake of salvation, of rescue, now becomes a burden? When the joy in Christ is lost for us, so too is the love for Christ and the faith in Christ. Without the joy in the Son of God, who became human and was resurrected, we fall into grumbling, into contradiction, into sadness. Where, however, do we find such joy? Solely through the firm belief: Jesus lives! When it is really true that Jesus lives, that Jesus bears witness to us, leads and helps us, how then should we not be just as joyful as the disciples were when they saw him on Easter morning? (John 20:20).

Second: Whoever has found Jesus Christ goes along Christ's path with joy, goes there with joy, and sells everything he possesses and purchases the precious pearl (Matt. 13:44). Whoever does not follow the path of Jesus will become sad like the rich young man (Matt. 19:22). Whoever entrusts himself entirely to the path of Jesus will rejoice in this. This joy also proves 148
true in the suffering that this path can bring upon us (Matt. 5:12; 1 Pet. 4:13ff; 2 Cor. 6:10; Phil. 2:17; Col. 1:24; Heb. 10:32; etc.). The reason for all such joy is the fact that Jesus is near (Phil. 4:4). "Oh, my Lord Jesus, your nearness. . . ."[7] At the same time here is the certainty that in this very way Jesus Christ's work on earth is fulfilled and completed (2 Tim. 2:10!). Thus that which should bring us sorrow and destruction must, through God's wondrous grace, only strengthen our joy. If we stand in true joy, then it is really so: "no one will take your joy from you" (John 16:22), for it remains eternally (1 Pet. 1:8).

[6.] See the chorale "Jesu, meine Freude," by Johann Franck, in *EG*, 396. [An English translation is "Jesus, Priceless Treasure," in *Lutheran Hymnal*, 347.—VB]

[7.] From the hymn "Ach mein Herr Jesu, dein Nahesein," by Christian Gregor (1767), in *Evangelisches Gesangbuch für Brandenburg und Pommern*, 206. [This was the hymnal used in Finkenwalde. This hymn is not included in the later *Evangelisches Gesangbuch*, and no English translation appears to exist.—VB]

Third: the church-community is a community of joy. All partake joyfully of the special grace that befalls one of them (1 Cor. 12:26). John knows of no greater joy than when he sees his children walking in the truth (2 John 4; 3 John 4; cf. 1 Cor. 13:6). Paul asks his church-community to participate in the joy of his suffering for the sake of Jesus Christ (Phil. 2:17). Jesus, however, calls for rejoicing together there, where someone who has been lost is found again, where a sinner repents. The entire chapter of Luke 15 stands under this call (15:6, 9, 23, 32; cf. 2 Cor. 7:9–10). Christians are an unceasing reason for joy for one another daily (1 Thess. 2:19; Phil. 4:1). Whoever has his eyes open for Christian neighbors can never lack occasion for joy. It is truly astounding to know that not only is "Jesus our joy" but our fellow Christians as well. Do we not have reason enough today to be filled with this joy?

Fourth: the origin of all true joy is God's joy in us. With God in heaven, there is joy when God's work on earth finds fulfillment, when the sinner returns to his father's house (Luke 15). Jesus is filled with joy, and it is Jesus's joy that is in us and that gives us perfect and lasting joy (John 15:11; 17:13). We are called to participate in God's joy in God's work, in the joy of Jesus over the love of God. It is our consummate joy that our prayers hence-
149 forth are heard (John 16:24). We should not distress the Holy Spirit (Eph. 4:30); rather it is our goal to enter into the joy of our Lord—Matt. 25:21.[8] For the exegesis of this verse we listen to Augustine: "Enter into everlasting joy, into the house of the Lord your God, where there are great, inscrutable, and marvelous things without number. Enter into joy without sadness, a joy that contains eternal happiness, where there will be every good and no evil, where there will be whatever you will wish for and nothing that you would not want, where there will be a full life, sweet and lovely, and forever memorable. It will be a life where there will be no enemy attacking you, nor any temptation, but rather the utmost untroubled security, secure tranquility, and tranquil pleasure, and pleasurable happiness, and happy eternity, and eternal beatitude, and the Blessed Trinity, and the unity of the Trinity, and the Godhead of the Unity, and the blessed vision of the Godhead, which is the joy of my Lord. O joy beyond joy, surpassing every joy, outside of which there is no joy. O kingdom of everlasting happiness, where you, O Lord, the hope of the saints and the crown of glory, are seen face-to-face by the saints, making them rejoice everywhere in your peace, which surpasses every sensation. There will be infinite joy, happiness without sadness, health without pain, life without labor, light without darkness, life without death,

[8.] In the manuscript this is erroneously written as "25:11."

every good with no evil. There youth never grows old, there life knows no end, where beauty never grows pale, where love never becomes tepid, where health never declines, where joy never decreases, where sorrow is never felt, where weeping is never heard, where no evil is feared because there the highest good is possessed, the good that is always to behold the face of the Lord of virtues." (In the soliloquy Cap 35.[9] Couldn't one of you attempt sometime to do a nice translation of this hymn?)

I greet you with the quotation from Ps. 100: "Serve the Lord with glad- 150
ness!"[10] God bless you, your homes, and your congregations to such service.

In the fellowship of brotherly intercession, your faithful
Dietrich Bonhoeffer[11]

[9.] "Intra in gaudium sempiternum, in domum Domini Dei tui, ubi sunt magna et inscrutabilia et mirabilia, quorum non est numerus; intra in gaudium sine tristitia, quod continet aeternum laetitiam, ubi erit omne bonum, et non erit aliquod malum; ubi erit quidquid voles, et non erit quidquid noles, ubi erit vita vitalis, dulcis et amabilis, semperque memorialis; ubi non erit hostis impugnans, nec ulla illecebra, sed summa et certa securitas, et secura tranquillitas, et tranquilla iucunditas, et iucunda felicitas, et felix aeternitas, et aeterna beatitudo, et beata Trinitas, et Trinitatis unitas, et unitatis deitas, et deitatis beata visio, quae est gaudium Domini mei! O gaudium super gaudium, vincens omne gaudium, extra quod non est gaudium. . . . O regnum beatitudinis sempiternae, ubi tu, Domine, spes sanctorum et diadema gloriae, facie ad faciem videris a sanctis, laetificans eos undique in pace tua quae exsuperat omnem sensum! Ibi gaudium infinitum, laetitia sine tristitia, salus sine dolore, vita sine labore, lux sine tenebris, vita sine morte, omne bonum sine omni malo. Ibi juventus nunquam senescit, ibi vita terminum nescit, ubi decor nunquam pallescit, ubi amor nunquam tepescit, ubi sanitas nunquam marcescit, ubi gaudium nunquam decrescit, ubi dolor nunquam sentitur, ubi gemitus nunquam auditur, . . . ubi malum nullum timetur; quoniam ibi summum bonum possidetur, quod est semper videre faciem Domini virtutum." According to the person dealing with the Augustine lexicon at the University of Giessen, the text cited here cannot be found in the works of Augustine (letter from Dr. Christof Müller to the German editor, May 11, 1994). It concerns an excerpt from the "Soliloquiorum animae ad Deum" by an unknown author, printed in Migne, *Patrologiae Latinae,* 40 (Paris, 1841), 894–95. The editor thanks the publisher, Dr. Hubert Filser, Munich. The place where Bonhoeffer found this text could not be ascertained. The somewhat erroneous transcription has been corrected here according to the citation in PL 40:894–95. [The *DBWE* editor thanks Geffrey Kelly for his translation of the Latin. Kelly notes: "Migne adds a caution before this soliloquy that what follows under the title of "From the Soliloquies about the Soul Going to God" is very different from Augustine's soliloquies. It is likely that this soliloquy quoted by Bonhoeffer was put together by a later writer, using ideas derived from the earlier writings of Augustine."—VB]

[10.] Ps. 100:2. NRSV: "Worship the Lord with gladness."

[11.] In this circular letter the list of meditation texts is missing.

76. From Gerhard Krause[1]

February 18, 1939

Dear Brother Bonhoeffer,

Now at long last I want to reply to your long and brotherly letter of December 15, 1938.[2] You must not fear that you had somehow offended me, for I love straight talk and most particularly expect it from brothers and friends. Rather, I
151 thank you that you have written to me as clearly as you felt necessary, and also that you have pointed out to me all kinds of theologically imprecise and unjustified judgments. That entire "draft" was but a quick compilation of thoughts that are in part not my own, which I submitted to friends for criticism. In the meantime, as far as possible I have followed your advice to remain silent until the church has spoken. Only at conferences and in some letters that could not be delayed did I have to convey my thoughts. In the meantime, the CC itself has moved on beyond those sketchy ideas.[3] I have been listened to in many places, but the CC did not want and was perhaps not able to go along in the slightest degree with what I suggested; the presentation of the thinking behind "B" ought to have been more thoroughly grounded and shown more readiness to take responsibility than was the case.[4] We were indeed of the opinion that we had suggested a good solution, not privately for us, but an aid to the entire CC. Since this has been rejected,[5] there remains a conflict between the CC and me: I can neither consider the continuation of the previous path as theologically correct, nor can I take responsibility for it any longer, either for others or for myself. And this is why I now write you: up to now I have gladly listened to your advice and do not wish to do without it in the future. My question here is will the brotherly community that up to now bound me to you and the Finkenwaldians continue to exist—to be sure, in a now particularly necessary openness—or not? That for my part it will not and should not collapse is certain. But will you and all those who believe they must accuse us of destroying the church and of other guilt still want to have us in your hearts and in your midst?

[1.] *NL*, C 25; typewritten with handwritten salutation and signature, with the return address: "Greifswald, Lönstrasse 2." Previously published in *GS* 6:439–42.

[2.] Letter not extant (per the letter of February 15, 1994, from Mrs. Sigrid Krause to the German editor).

[3.] See the resolutions of the seventh confessional synod of the Old Prussian Union in Berlin-Nikolassee, January 28–31, 1939 ("Epiphany synod"), in Niesel, *Um Verkündigung und Ordnung der Kirche*, 70–76.

[4.] [The reference here is to "Way B," the arrangement with provincial church consistories toward legalization. See 1/74, ed. note 1.—VB]

[5.] [The "Epiphany synod" (see ed. note 3) rejected "Way B" and the course of legalization.—VB]

The conflict[6] began so to speak with "church-political" matters. But that was always secondary to me. At times it appeared as if, and I myself thought it possible, those brothers who propagated Way "B" in Pomerania would take the leadership of the Pomeranian CC in their hands. Now, however, it has become evident that, besides all the other obstacles, these brothers themselves obviously do not have the certainty and strength that would have been required. I myself did not think it necessary to promote this path, particularly because you also had warned me not to do so, referring to the responsibility toward others that had been placed upon me. Precisely because of this, I found it necessary to express a free theological opinion that would compel individuals always to reconsider the genuineness of their decisions. That may indeed confuse some. But that, I believe, must be accepted for the sake of the truth. Here the "church-political" side is already at its end. For I can look on reassured when others decide differently about the questions laid before us today, when I recognize that the decisions here have been made in faith and in certainty. 152

But the conflict has, moreover, a theological side. It will compel me and all of you to question one another about the truth and necessity of our decisions. This questioning may not be allowed to stop—however much it be felt and characterized as a burden.—In preparation for the Prussian synod, I reread long passages from your *Discipleship*, because I wanted to leave open a reversal of my views. But you are quite right when you speak in your letter of an "abysmal theological disagreement between us." It is there, even if I cannot yet formulate it (as Brother de Boor[7] did in his letter to Fritz Onnasch: pneumatology). I simply sense errors in the doctrine of justification [Rechtfertigungslehre] and even more errors in the doctrine of the church (esp. in the "questions," *Ev. Theol.* 36:10)[8] that I otherwise know of only in Catholic theology. But such a general dictum is of no help to you, and no "heretic's hat" should be handed out either. But it must nonetheless be stated where I see the difference, even if I do not now have the leisure to expound it thoroughly and at length.

Perhaps even more important than the theological conflict is the ethical one, which of course is connected to it.[9] It is the practical question: how should Christians behave when faced by a tyrannical authority [Obrigkeit], where does 153

[6.] [This refers to his mention in the previous paragraph of the "conflict" between him and the Confessing Church.—VB]

[7.] The reference is to Werner de Boor; the letter mentioned is not extant.

[8.] This refers to the debate that erupted over Bonhoeffer's article "Zur Frage nach der Kirchengemeinschaft" (On the Question of Church Fellowship) in *Evangelische Theologie* 4 (1936): 214–33; in the October issue, Helmut Gollwitzer had raised "Comments and Reservations" (398–405), and Bonhoeffer had posed "Questions" (405–10). See *DBW* 14, 2/19.1.

[9.] [I.e., to the theological issues.—VB]

repudiation begin, where does the necessary resistance begin? That is the practical question that Christians in life today decide very differently. Unfortunately, they often turn this into a far-reaching dogmatic conflict, giving it an impact that splits the church. I am equally certain that this division, in which we are no longer at one with one another in the practical decisions, is just as much the devilish intent of our opponents as it is the personal fault of all of us. How is it possible that so many Christians who are at one in their faith draw away from one another so far that their love can only be platonic! Now I must fully acknowledge that you are right in stating that our concrete obedience in life must always have something to do with our faith and thus with our personal salvation. But I notice nonetheless that already the church of the earliest Christians very obviously set up rules of a more general kind for those life decisions for which no commandment or prohibition from the Lord exists (1 Cor. 7; Rom. 14), than for decisions where clear commandments exist. One says then that one should act ἐν κυρίῳ, or ἐν πίστει, and—it is then self-evident—ἐν ἀγάπῃ;[10] one refrains from concrete objective demands, indeed relativizes them, if only to maintain the faith and the community of the Lord. Of these two everyone should be certain.

In my opinion, today it is the decisions at this level that are at stake. Thus the question remains open what then has moved me now to change a decision that supposedly was once made in faith.

1. Here the theological opposition alluded to above can be mentioned, which impresses me more strongly from day to day. Certainly the altered circumstances had their say as well, namely, the fact that many one-time GC[11] today are fine preachers, that the church government, the consistory, today is less heretical than tyrannical, that our political situation is becoming ever more starkly conspicuous, and that in my own case the stormy times have been followed by times of reflection.

2. A very decisive contribution to this is the "certainty of the others" from whom the CC had withdrawn or was withdrawing. The existence of "neutrals" who are faithful was a shock for me, and I could not comprehend the necessity of a break with them.

3. What finally gave me pause was the insight that on this path[12] I would have to give up the established church, because my work would remain possible only within the circles of CC congregations. I believed, however, that the abandonment of the established church was not yet commanded, but rather

[10.] ["In the Lord, or in faith and . . . in love."—VB]

[11.] [German Christians.—VB]

[12.] [I.e., "Way A," which refused legalization.—VB]

that today the waiting of which Luke 13:6–9[13] speaks must still hold true. For I know that I am called to serve in these congregations for their admonition and edification, not only to serve CC circles.

4. Finally, I had to see that the "path to the consistory" would not necessarily have to be a repudiation and an acting without faith. My personal negotiations in these weeks, which are not yet completely finished, have confirmed this. Certainly the men there are "tied down" and theologically poorly qualified for church leadership. But they require nothing for legalization that I would have to reject as "against the faith" or "against the truth." If this is true, then the protest against the consistory at this point loses for me that necessity that it ought to have, if I were to renounce for its sake the ministry, the established church, the fellowship with many brothers who share my faith, etc., and to bear all the suffering. Conversely, however, it appears necessary to "preserve" these things (in the knowledge that the Lord preserves them) as long as I am hindered neither from proper preaching nor from confessing. 154

Added to this are various secondary considerations. In all of them, I am of good cheer and conscience, nor did I feel assailed in any way during my meditation on 2 Cor. 1:12 during this week. Thus I see—assuming that my negotiations with the consistory proceed unhindered—no more possibility of remaining on the previous path of the CC. Whether I remain *in* the CC is for the CC to decide; whether I remain in the Finkenwalde brotherhood, that is my request and question to you.

With warm brotherly greetings
Your Gerhard Krause

77. To Karl-Friedrich Bonhoeffer[1]

Dear Karl Friedrich,

Many thanks for your letter.[2] I am just getting ready to depart and am therefore in a hurry. I wanted to travel probably on the tenth or eleventh of March.[3] In any case, I must be over there on the fifteenth. I have the

[13.] [This is the parable of the gardener and the fig tree that took several years to bear fruit.—VB]

[1.] Letter not registered in the *NL*; handwritten postcard; postmarked Berlin-Marienburg/Westpreußen Train 24/28 [this means the card is presumably from Groß-Schlönwitz], February 19, 1939. Cf. also the later typewritten copy, previously unpublished, in *NL*, A 44,1 (18).

[2.] Letter not extant.

[3.] The reference is to the trip to London to visit the Leibholzes (see *DB-ER*, 635–48, and Rieger, *Dietrich Bonhoeffer in England*, 31–41).

semester until the eighth. It would be very nice indeed if you could arrange
155 to travel then as well. Let me know. Or would it perhaps be better if you went a month or so later, if you can do that at all? By the way, we planned perhaps to take the car to Aachen. Bethge is perhaps coming along over there.

Warm greetings
Dietrich

By the way, you hopefully did receive my *delayed* birthday letter?[4]

78. From Christine von Dohnanyi[1]

March 7, 1939

Dear Dietrich,

When you shortly travel to Sabine,[2] I would like to request two things of you. I already wrote Sabine that I would take in an English girl for a quarter of a year. Just some young girl so that Bärbel[3] learns English from her. She must only be a reasonable, not spoiled person. She will have nothing else to do. I thought that Sabine would be quite happy to see to it that someone is sent. Perhaps though she did not receive the letter. Could you take up this matter there, and if Sabine is not interested, perhaps Hildebrand[4] knows someone? Otherwise I will turn to the official exchange office. It's just that the matter is somewhat urgent for me.

2. The young Harder has now finished his *Abitur.*[5] Is only sixteen years old. Since he is too young for anything else, his parents would now like to place him in a decent home in England (or France), where he would be well taken care of and perhaps give tutoring (mathematics etc.) or make himself otherwise useful; just that he gets abroad. I believe you know the boy. He is a very well-behaved, dependable boy with good manners and a nice appearance. Would you know of anything or perhaps hear of something out there? If this worked, I would be

[4.] See Bonhoeffer's January 28, 1939, letter, 1/57.

[1.] *NL*, C 5; handwritten; no return address, probably from Leipzig; previously unpublished.

[2.] Sabine Leibholz in London.

[3.] The Dohnanyis' daughter Barbara.

[4.] Franz Hildebrandt.

[5.] Harmut Harder, son of the lawyer Dr. Hans Adolf Harder. [The *Abitur* is the concluding examination at the *Gymnasium* and the entrance examination for university study in Germany.—VB]

very grateful to you. For his parents it's very important that it's a home where he is truly in good hands, because he is simply still quite young to travel alone 156
abroad. I am eager to hear what impressions you bring of Sabine. A pity that we could not see you again before your departure. Would it perhaps work on the return trip?

Greetings to all! Warmly your
Christel

79. To Paula Bonhoeffer[1]

Dear Mama,

The trip was fine again, the water was calm, the sleeper car comfortable in every respect. We slept well and arrived here so quickly that the trip was a pleasure. This just for today.

Greetings to you from your grateful

Dietrich[2]

80. To George Bell[1]

13th March 1939

My dear Lordbishop,

May I just let you know that I have arrived in London last night. I am so happy to be here once again for a short time and I am looking forward very much to seeing you soon. A friend of mine, Pastor Bethge, has come with me and wishes to bring you a special message from the Provisional Administration.[2] There are so many things which I should like to discuss with you, that I should be very grateful, if you would let me know when and 157
where I could see you. I have found the Leibholz' well and full of gratitude for all your goodness and help. It makes me so happy to know that.—I am

[1.] *NL*, A 44,1; handwritten postcard; postmarked Forest Hill [London], March 11, 1939; previously unpublished.

[2.] Short greetings follow from Sabine, Marianne, and Christiane Leibholz and from Eberhard Bethge.

[1.] LPL, BP 42:65; handwritten letter card; return address 29 Manor Mount, SE 23, Tel. Forest Hill 14-45. Cf. also the later typewritten copy in *NL*, A 42,1 (27). Previously published in *GS* 1:279. [Letter is in the original unaltered English.—VB]

[2.] Of the Confessing Church.

afraid the political situation is just now becoming more tense and precarious.[3] In deep gratitude for all you are doing for us

Yours very sincerely
Dietrich Bonhoeffer

81. To Leonard Hodgson[1]

Dear Dr. Hodgson,

I thank you very much indeed for your kind letter and your invitation.[2] On Wednesday the 29th of March I shall come to Oxford and it would be indeed a great privilege to me if I could see you there. I have been looking forward to an occasion of seeing you ever since we had a short correspondence on the conference in Denmark two years ago,[3] and I am very happy that I shall have the opportunity of a discussion with you in a few days. The question which I should most of all like to discuss with you is concerning the regular and close contact between the Confessional Church and the "Faith and Order" movement. The more we are becoming cut off from our foreign friends the more we feel it to be necessary to find a way of a permanent representation in the oecumenic movement and particularly in the department concerning "Faith and Order." We need the theological help of other churches in order to be able to bear the burden of responsibilities which God has laid upon us, and we wish to give you a witness of the Christian
158 insights, which God has given us anew during the last years. I feel strongly that something has to be done quickly practically and effectively in order to establish new relations between you and us. Would it, for instance, not be possible to have a permanent German secretary of the Confessional Church in Geneva or in London, and if not permanent then perhaps for one year or two? Those are the questions which I should like to discuss with you from the theological and practical point of view.[4] The main difficulty might be the financial side of the matter. But I feel, there must be something wrong,

[3.] The reference is to the invasion of Czechoslovakia by German troops on March 14–15, 1939.

[1.] *NL*, A 46,3 (10); later typewritten copy; return address "Westbrook, Westwood Park, London, SE 23"; undated but certainly mid-March 1939. Previously published in *GS* 1:282–83. [Letter is in the original unaltered English.—VB]

[2.] Letter not extant.

[3.] Cf. the correspondence between Bonhoeffer and Hodgson in June and July 1935 (nearly four years earlier) on the occasion of a Faith and Order conference in Hindsgavl, Denmark. See *DB-ER*, 480–82, and *DBW* 14, 1/9, 1/11, and 1/14.

if a thing which is spiritually necessary should become impossible for financial reasons. Please excuse this long letter. I thought it better to let you know our questions and hopes before we meet.

With many thanks and best regards I am yours sincerely
Dietrich Bonhoeffer

82. To George Bell[1]

25th of March 1939

My dear Lordbishop,

Dr. Rieger just tells me that Visser 't Hooft[2] will come to London next week and stay with you at Chichester. I also understand that the next weekend does not suit you well for our visit to Chichester. May I now ask a great favour from you? Would you kindly tell Visser 't Hooft that I am very anx- 159
ious to see him during his stay in London? Any time except Wednesday when I have to be at Oxford[3] would suit me well. Would you also be so kind as to let me know any time when I could see you once more before I go back to Germany?

In order not to take too much of your time when we meet, I should like to put before you the two questions which I am very anxious to discuss with you before my return to Germany. The first question concerns the Confessional Church, the second one is very personal. Please excuse my troubling you again and again and my placing one burden after another on your shoulders.

With regard to the position of the Confessional Church we feel strongly in Germany that—mainly owing to travelling difficulties—the relationship of our church to the churches abroad is not as it ought to be. The responsibility which is placed upon us makes it more and more necessary to have a

---

[4.] In connection with the Confessing Church's interest in Germany in cooperating as closely as possible with the ecumenical organizations, Bonhoeffer's idea was that his emigrated friend Franz Hildebrandt would be available for this task. See Bonhoeffer's March 25, 1939, letter to George Bell, 1/82, and *DB-ER*, 639–42.

[1.] LPL, BP 42:66–69; handwritten; return address "Dietrich Bonhoeffer, c/o Dr. Cruesemann, Westbrook, Westwood Park, Forest Hill, London SE 23. Telephone: Forest Hill 1810"; cf. also *NL*, A 42,1 (28); later typewritten copy. Previously published in *GS* 1:279–82. [Letter is in the original unaltered English.—VB]

[2.] On the spontaneously arranged meeting between Bonhoeffer and Visser 't Hooft at the beginning of April 1939 at Paddington Station in London, see *DB-ER*, 645–47, and Visser 't Hooft, *Memoirs*, 107–9.

[3.] For a talk with Leonard Hodgson.

permanent exchange of opinion and the advice of other churches. We are fully aware of and gratefully appreciate what is continuously being done for us from individuals to individuals. But I think, we must try to go a step further and to come to some sort of regular cooperation with and to a better representation of the Confessional Church at the oecumenic movements. If we are not going to make a decisive step forward in this direction, I am afraid, we shall very soon be cut off entirely from our brethren abroad, and that would at any rate mean a tremendous loss to us. What I therefore think we should try to get, is a man, who could devote all his time to establish the necessary contacts, to cooperate in the oecumenic meetings and conferences, learning and contributing. I think we failed in earlier years to give our full assistance in advice and fellowship to the Russian Christians;[4] now a similar situation is clearly developing in Germany. Do you not think, my Lordbishop, it is urgently necessary to avoid a similar failure? Frankly and with all due respect, the German representatives in Geneva simply cannot represent the cause of the Confessional Church. So there is a real vacancy
160 which must be filled up sooner or later. This is the first question which I should like to raise and to discuss with you before I go home again to see the men of the Brethren Council. I have also an idea in my mind for the eventual financial difficulties.

The second point is of entirely personal character and I am not certain if I may bother you with it. Please, do take it quite apart from the first point. I am thinking of leaving Germany sometime. The main reason is the compulsory military service to which the men of my age (1906) will be called up this year. It seems to me conscientiously impossible to join in a war under the present circumstances. On the other hand, the Confessional Church as such has not taken any definite attitude in this respect and probably cannot take it as things are. So I should cause a tremendous damage to my brethren if I would make a stand on this point which would be regarded by the regime as typical of the hostility of our church towards the state. Perhaps the worst thing of all is the military oath which I should have to swear.[5] So

[4.] The reference is to the persecution of Christians in the Soviet Union, particularly during the massive Stalinist purges in 1936–37.

[5.] Immediately after the death of Reich president Paul von Hindenburg on August 2, 1934, Adolf Hitler appointed himself "Führer and Reich chancellor," assumed supreme command of the armed forces, and, with the help of Reich Minister of the Armed Forces Werner von Blomberg, required all officers and enlisted men to swear an oath to his person although it infringed on the Defense Law of December 1, 1933, and violated the constitution. The wording of the oath (from that point onward) was: "I swear by God this sacred oath, that I will yield unconditional obedience to the Führer of the German

I am rather puzzled in this situation, and perhaps even more, because I feel, it is really only on Christian grounds that I find it difficult to do military service under the present conditions, and yet there are only very few friends who would approve of my attitude. In spite of much reading and thinking concerning this matter I have not yet made up my mind what I would do under different circumstances. But actually as things are I should have to do violence to my Christian conviction, if I would take up arms "now and here." I have been thinking of going to the Missionfield, not as an escape out of the situation, but because I wish to serve somewhere where service is 161
really wanted. But here also the German foreign exchange situation makes it impossible to send workers abroad. With respect to British Missionary Societies I have no idea of the possibilities there. On the other hand, I still have the great desire to serve the Confessional Church as long as I possibly could.

My Lordbishop, I am very sorry to add trouble to your trouble. But I thought, I might speak freely to you and might ask your advice. You know the Confessional Church and you know me a bit. So I thought you could help me best. It was with regard to this matter that I wanted to see Visser 't Hooft too.

Please excuse this long letter. I hope to see you soon. Leibholz asks me to thank you for your letter to Dr. Lindsay.[6]

In sincere gratitude I am, my Lordbishop, Yours sincerely,
Dietrich Bonhoeffer

83. From Leonard Hodgson[1]

30th March 1939

Dear Pastor Bonhoeffer,

I was very glad indeed to have the pleasure of seeing you, and I now feel that I appreciate your situation in a manner which would have been impossible without our conversation. I had better try to put down in writing what I said yesterday.

Reich and Volk, Adolf Hitler, the Supreme Commander of the Wehrmacht, and, as a brave soldier, will be ready at any time to lay down my life for this oath." Cited in Craig, *Germany 1866–1945*, 589. See also Fest, *Plotting Hitler's Death*, 55–57.

[6.] A. D. Lindsay.

[1.] *NL*, A 46,3 (11); later typewritten copy; sent from Oxford. Previously published in *GS* 1:283–86. See also *DB-ER*, 639–44. [Letter is in the original unaltered English.—VB]

You had written to say that you wanted to discuss the possibility of maintaining contact between the Confessional Church in Germany and the Faith and Order Movement.[2]

1. I began by pointing out the impossibility of our establishing official relations with the German Evangelical Church at the present moment, the reasons being as follows:

(i) By our constitution the Churches appoint the World Conference, and the Conference then appoints its Continuation Committee, which maintains its existence by cooption until the next Conference, when it ceases to exist.
162 There is therefore no direct representation of churches on the Continuation Committee; the Committee derives its authority immediately from the churches through the Conference.

(ii) The German Evangelical Church found itself unable to be represented at the Edinburgh Conference[3] and therefore, when that Conference appointed its Continuation Committee, it could not appoint from among its members any representatives of that church. So what it did was to instruct the Committee to coopt eight representatives of that church when such action should become possible.

(iii) It is the custom of the Continuation Committee to coopt to membership those persons whom churches themselves wish to have as their representatives. For this purpose it is necessary to be able to have communication in each case with a central body having full confidence of the whole church, and able to nominate representatives in its name. We are advised that at the present time there is no such church, and that we must not attempt to treat the different groups within that church independently as if they were separate churches. Hence for the time being the filling of these places has to be left in abeyance.

2. I then told you that last summer I was approached by Dr. Wahl asking whether Dr. Krummacher and Dr. Gerstenmaier[4] might attend the 1938 meeting of the Continuation Committee. I replied in a letter explaining the position exactly as I have just set it forth in the preceding paragraph of this letter. I then added that, if they wished to come as visitors, we should be very glad to welcome them, and that they would be given a full part in all proceedings, except that they would not be able to vote on questions which the Continuation Committee alone was competent to decide, and might possibly be unable to be present at any particular session, should the Committee wish to confine it strictly to its own members. I wrote individually to Dr. Krummacher and Dr. Gerstenmaier

[2.] Cf. Bonhoeffer's letter from mid-March 1939 to Hodgson, 1/81.

[3.] The second international conference of the ecumenical movement for Faith and Order, held in Edinburgh on August 3–18, 1937.

[4.] Hans Wahl, Friedrich Krummacher, and Eugen Gerstenmaier.

explaining the situation. They both came, were welcomed by the Committee, and took a full part in its proceedings, except that they had no responsibility for any of its decisions.

3. It is quite clear that the Committee would give an equal welcome on the same conditions to any representatives of the Confessional Church who should be commended to us in a similar way. I understand that for this purpose Dr. Boehm[5] would correspond to Dr. Wahl. If therefore the names of two representatives could be communicated to me by Dr. Boehm, and those two representatives come to St. George's School, Clarens, on Monday, August 21st this year, they will be welcomed as visitors and given a full share in our proceedings.

4. I also asked whether it might not be possible for one or two younger men 163
to come as members of our Youth Group, and I suggested your consulting with the Rev. Oliver Tomkins on this subject. We welcome as visitors to our meeting whatever persons are nominated to us by Oliver Tomkins, and therefore we should welcome any of your representatives whom he included in his list.

5. We then discussed the question of finance, and you put before me the difficulty your countrymen have in obtaining foreign currency. I said that if one or two visitors representing the Confessional Church, and one or two members of the Youth Group, could get as far as Montreux station, we would be responsible for their hospitality during the period of the meeting.

6. I then pointed out that in the next few years I expect the main work of the Movement to be done by the Commissions, and expressed the hope that we should be able to have the collaboration of members of the Confessional Church in that work.

I think this covers the ground of our discussion yesterday, and I hope that it gives a satisfactory answer to the questions you raised.

Yours sincerely,
Leonard Hodgson
copies to: Archbishop of York, Temple[6]
Dr. Böhm 13.5.39
Bishop of Chichester[7] 23.5.39
Schönfeld[8] 25.6.39

[5.] Hans Böhm.
[6.] William Temple.
[7.] George Bell.
[8.] Hans Schönfeld.

84. To His Parents[1]

April 8, 1939

My dear Parents,

It has now worked out so that I can celebrate Easter[2] with the family,[3] and I'm very happy about it. Toward the end of next week, I will come visit you again. If you are not in Berlin, I would also be happy to come some-
164 where else for several days if I know where you are going. I would actually enjoy having a few very quiet days, since it has been quite nice here but not particularly quiet. I was practically always on the move, and my hosts never go to bed before 1:30 a.m. There is much to tell, including all kinds of nice news.

Very much wishing you a few quiet days, your grateful
Dietrich

85. To George Bell[1]

13th April 1939

My dear Lordbishop,

before returning to Germany I just wish to thank you once again for the great help you gave me in our talk at Chichester. I do not know what will be the outcome of it all, but it means much to me to realize that you see the great conscientious difficulties with which we are faced.[2] I will let you know as soon as I see the situation clearly. Thank you for all sympathy for our cause.

In sincere gratitude I remain, my Lordbishop, Yours ever
Dietrich Bonhoeffer

[1.] *NL*, A 44, 1 (20); handwritten postcard, from London; previously unpublished.

[2.] April 9–10, 1939.

[3.] [The Leibholzes in London.—VB]

[1.] LPL, BP 42:64; handwritten; from London. Cf. *NL*, A 42,1 (29); later typewritten copy. Previously published in *GS* 1:286. On the matter discussed here, see Bell, "Die Kirche und die Widerstandsbewegung," in *Evangelische Theologie* 17 (1957): 289–305. [Letter is in the original unaltered English.—VB]

[2.] Regarding the problem of conscientious objection, see Bonhoeffer's March 25, 1939, letter to Bell, 1/82.

86. To His Parents[1]

April 13, 1939

My dear Parents,

I just wanted to send you one more greeting before my departure. In the meantime, here the most glorious spring has arrived, and we are often in the garden. Easter was quite lovely. The children were very lively and happy. 165
Essentially, the main question that has postponed my departure somewhat is whether I should still wait for Uncle Rudi[2] here. If, however, I don't hear anything more from him, I will leave here on Saturday or Monday[3] at the latest. Where will I meet you? Aren't you going off again for a few days? Will you write this to Sabine? Until we meet again safely!

Your grateful
Dietrich

Perhaps I must go to Niebuhr already in June.[4] If this only works?!

87. From Reinhold Niebuhr to Henry Smith Leiper[1]

May 1

Dear Henry:

Sometime ago I wrote Roland Elliot and asked him to transmit the letter to you. It concerned Dr. Dietrich Bonhoeffer whom you know. My letter to Elliot wandered about and finally reached him over here in England. The proposition I wrote him about was this: Bonhoeffer is due for military service in July and will refuse to serve. The Bruederrat of the Confessional Church would like to have

[1.] *NL*, A 44,1 (21); handwritten; from London. Partially reproduced in *GS* 2:348 and *GS* 6:455.

[2.] This was the code word in letters to family and friends for the impending war and the status of Hitler's preparations for it (see *DB-ER*, 626); here the reference is to the international political tensions following the invasion of Czechoslovakia by German troops on March 15–16, 1939, and the British-French statement that followed, on March 31, 1939, regarding a guarantee for Poland's borders.

[3.] April 15 or April 17, 1939; Bonhoeffer left for Berlin on April 18 (*DB-ER*, 648).

[4.] This refers to Bonhoeffer's invitation to the United States through Reinhold Niebuhr's mediation. See the formal invitation of May 10–11, 1939, from Henry S. Leiper, 1/89 and 1/90.

[1.] *NL*, A 50,2 (2); later typewritten copy; return address: "45, Dick Place, Edinburgh, 9, Tel. 44086." Previously published in *GS* 1:287–88. Niebuhr was in Edinburgh delivering the 1939 Gifford Lectures. [Letter is in the original unaltered English.—VB]

him evade the issue and at the same time tell American Christians about their situation. To get him out they need rather formal and formidable invitations from America. I suggested in this letter that the Student movement might use him in
166 their June conferences and that afterward you might get him some engagements at church conferences and church camps during the summer. In the fall I would secure university engagements for him.

He speaks English so well and embodies the spirit of the struggle over there so well in his person that I believe his coming would be valuable for our sake as well as for his. I have also written to Dr. Coffin[2] asking him to send a formidable invitation for a lecture at Union Seminary.

Much time has been lost because of the loss of my letter. Perhaps by this time the student people have gotten in touch with you. Today I received word from Bonhoeffer[3] saying that time was short. If he is to make necessary arrangements he ought to have a cable as well as a confirming letter. If you think well of the idea of inviting him would you send him a cable if this has not been done. I shall provide a room for him at the seminary and I think nominal fees will take care of the rest.

Yours cordially,
R. Niebuhr

88. To His Parents[1]

May 4, 1939

My dear Parents,

I have received the invitation. Actually, I am awaiting yet another one for an earlier date, although the date as such is not at all disagreeable for me. But vacation[2] is not yet here! Block thought that v. K. should have passed the application on.[3] Does it make sense for me to write again after fourteen days have passed (on Monday), or could you, dear Papa, make inquiries for

[2.] Henry Sloane Coffin, at that time president of Union Theological Seminary in New York.

[3.] Letter not extant.

[1.] *NL*, A 44,1 (22); handwritten postcard; from Sigurdshof. Partially reproduced in *GS* 2:348.

[2.] Bonhoeffer had applied for a leave of absence and a statement [from the Schlawe military enlistment office—VB] certifying that there were no reservations against his spending a year in the United States. See *DB-ER*, 634. [See also 1/92, ed. note 3.—VB]

[3.] The references are to Superintendent Eduard Block and Major Dieter von Kleist at the district military enlistment office, both in Schlawe.

me in writing? I would prefer for the time being not to go there in person. That is not helpful. So everything is still uncertain. Today I am in the new 167 house.[4] Everything is very small and primitive, but wonderfully quiet up to now, and the setting is very beautiful.

Warm greetings to you from your grateful
Dietrich

89. From Henry Smith Leiper[1]

May 10, 1939

Dietrich Bonhoeffer, Marienburger Allee 43, Berlin

Central Bureau Interchurch Aid urgently requests your coming New York immediately at latest by midjune to accept important combination Post theological Lectureship and Church Work at Summer Conferences and Universities.

Leiper

90. From Henry Smith Leiper[1]

May 11, 1939

My dear Dr. Bonhoeffer:

It is my pleasure to transmit to you herewith formal invitation for you to come at once to America to undertake an important piece of service for the churches in the New York area under the general auspices of the Central Bureau of Interchurch Aid and Union Theological Seminary.

The nature of your duties would be a combination of pastoral service, preaching and lecturing in the theological summer school at Columbia and Union Seminary, to begin with, and later in the Seminary in the usual term.

[4.] The collective pastorate in Schlawe had moved into the forester's lodge in Sigurdshof because Erwin Schutz, who had the pastorate in Groß-Schlönwitz, needed the parsonage for himself and his family. See Bethge and Gremmels, *Life in Pictures*, centenary ed., 113.

[1.] *NL*, A 50,2 (3); telegram from New York. Previously published in *GS* 2:349. [Document is in the original unaltered English.—VB]

[1.] *NL*, A 50,2 (3); later typewritten copy; from New York. Previously published in *GS* 1:288. [Letter is in the original unaltered English.—VB]

168 The term of service is not now fixed although we hope that it can be a permanent thing, and expect that it will occupy you for at least the next two or three years.

The Committee has thought it best not to enter into matters such as salary and other details, but can assure you that we are prepared to meet your reasonable request with respect to salary basis and other terms of service.

We should like to have you come, if possible, to begin service by the middle of June, which will mean your reaching this country at the earliest possible date for consultation and general preparation.

Dr. Samuel McCrea Cavert and Dean Henry P. Van Dusen are associated with me in this request and share with me the very great personal hope that you will find it possible to accept and to come in the very near future, as indicated above.

Henry Smith Leiper

copies to Dr. Van Dusen and Dr. Cavert

91. From Reinhold Niebuhr to Paul Lehmann[1]

May 11

Dear Paul:

I have finished eight of my ten lectures[2] here and have done as well as could be expected I suppose. Had a good audience all through but don't know much about how my stuff has been received.

I will not bother you with personal news however. My concern is in regard to Bonhoeffer. He came to see me shortly upon our arrival[3] and is anxious to come to America to evade for the time being a call to the colours. I secured an invitation for him for the Union Seminary summer school and also asked the Federal Council to arrange for meetings in church camps etc.[4] He would like to stay through the fall and lecture in colleges and seminaries. As I will not
169 be back until November I am wondering whether you would be willing to constitute a committee with me, call me the chairman and yourself the secretary and send out a mimeographed letter offering Bonhoeffer's services to colleges

[1.] *NL*, A 50,2 (4); carbon copy (without signature); from Edinburgh. Previously published in *GS* 2:349–50. [Letter is in the original unaltered English.—VB]

[2.] In 1939 Niebuhr held the Gifford Lectures in Edinburgh, titled "The Nature and Destiny of Man," which was published in 1941.

[3.] Bonhoeffer met Niebuhr in Sussex on April 3, 1939, during his visit to England. See Fox, *Reinhold Niebuhr*, 187–88, and *DB-ER*, 639.

[4.] Cf. Niebuhr's May 1, 1939, letter to Henry S. Leiper, 1/87.

and universities. Ask them for a nominal fee of $25 to $50 for his services. You could have him give you topics and a description of his activities in behalf of the confessional synod.

I don't like to through[5] this work on you but I think you could do it best. Be sure and hire stenographers for the job and let me have the bill. Bonhoeffers present address is Marienburger Allee 43 Berlin-Charlottenburg 9. Don't write him too much but if you are willing to do this just tell him that you will get in touch with him as soon as he arrives at Union to work out plans which I have suggested. There will be some difficulty in getting him out and if he fails he will land in prison. He has done a great work for the church.

Edinburgh has been very kind to us and we have little time to ourselves. I am staying till May 23d and then will go to Oxford. After June 13 you can reach me at The Moat House, Wivelsfield, Sussex.

Love from all of us. Yours

[Reinhold Niebuhr]

92. To His Parents[1]

Saturday evening. Köslin

My dear Parents,

I just received the summons for the physical for military service from the mayor for May 22. This has nothing to do per se with my application for vacation. The mayor's office handles the conscriptions simply according to the lists. Nonetheless, the matter of the permission for leave is now urgent. Since I will not get to Schlawe during the next five days and (after consultation here) would rather not go there personally unless there is an emergency, I wanted to ask you, dear Papa, whether you could perhaps inquire of Major von Kleist per letter or, which might be even more effective, on the
telephone, how the matter stands. I happen to be at present on the road 170
and am urgently awaiting the decision, since I want to travel as soon as possible. The application was sent on April 23 and contained a request for leave from May 1, 1939, to May 1, 1940. The recommendations were in a private communication to v. K.,[2] and perhaps they have not been passed on to the other offices. The mail and telephone address is: Schlawe, Enlistment

[5.] Should be "throw."

[1.] *NL*, A 44,1 (23); handwritten; undated, but probably May 13, 1939. Previously published in *GS* 6:455–56.

[2.] Major Dieter von Kleist.

Office, Major von Kleist. Kleist can surely be reached on Monday morning. I would be very grateful to you if you could find some way to bring the matter forward.[3] If the suggestion doesn't seem good to you, please write to my Schlawe address; I must then see how I can get to it. If the permission comes in the meantime, will the arrangement in the telegram remain?—I have written Gert[4] and Niebuhr.[5]

Many thanks and many greetings from your

Dietrich

93. To the Finkenwalde Brothers[1]

Personal letter!

Dear Brothers,

Since the last time I wrote,[2] much has become better and clearer. In addition to the pain that several brothers have abandoned our cause, God has nonetheless also given the joy that after a long period we stand again in
171 clear and firm community with those who are committed to the same cause. The past months have been salutary for us all.[3] When have we been able to be more certain than today that we have been held in God's church by God's grace? Let us thank God for that. It has become evident again in these decisive weeks that the possibility for discussion ends at a certain

---

[3.] Karl Bonhoeffer's intervention and that of Ruth von Kleist-Retzow were successful. The Schlawe military enlistment office withdrew the summons and immediately issued the certificate [declaring that there were no reasons why he might not travel—VB] approving Bonhoeffer's submitted application for leave. The road to travel abroad was clear (cf. *DB-ER*, 633–35). [The process of Bonhoeffer's conscription resumed in spring 1940, and he was declared "fit for wartime service" in June 1940; at that point the efforts to have him declared "indispensable" for the military intelligence by Dohnanyi and others intensified (cf. *DBWE* 16:400–401). This was then one of the official charges against him after his arrest. Cf. *DBWE* 16:50–51, as well as the 1943 indictment against him for evading military service (*DBWE* 16, 1/230.2, p. 437).—VB]

[4.] Gerhard Leibholz; letter not extant.

[5.] Reinhold Niebuhr; letter not extant.

[1.] *NL*, A 48,3 (8); typewritten hectograph with handwritten initials of Eberhard Bethge; no return address, probably from Sigurdshof; undated, but certainly end of May 1939. Previously published in *GS* 2:550–51.

[2.] See Bonhoeffer's February 14, 1939, letter to the Finkenwalde brothers, 1/75.

[3.] Following the German Christians' "Godesberg Declaration" of April 4, 1939, and the founding of the Institute for the Study and Eradication of Jewish Influence on

point. In the back and forth of the arguments, we would have become almost worn down. We have been preserved from this. Now everyone stands and falls before his own lord.[4] But now we can also return to work in full force, and that is the most important thing. The tasks are immeasurably great, and the field is truly ripe. Gather with new courage the Christians around the word and the sacrament! Use the time that is still given to us! Do not cease to carry the word and prayer into the homes! Christ is back on the scene with all his promises. Let them be fulfilled in your church-communities through CHRIST. Let us continue to pray for one another, that our work be protected and blessed, that we ourselves grow in every way into Jesus Christ, our Lord.[5]

Our work goes on. I will now travel for several months to the seminary where I formerly studied for one year.[6] After that, I will return to this same work. But Eberhard and Fritz will take care of the meditation texts and all that is most necessary.[7]

God bless you, your work, and your homes. Your devoted D. B.

For Dietrich B: Eb.[8]

Meditation texts: 172

June 11–June 17: John 16:16–33
June 18–June 24: John 17:1–13
June 25–July 1: John 17:14–26

German Church Life in the Wartburg [the castle overlooking the city of Eisenach where Luther stayed following his excommunication; it is where he translated the Bible into German—VB] on May 6, 1939, there were theological and church-political quarrels, culminating in the "Exaudi synod" of the Confessing Church in the Old Prussian Union on May 20–22, 1939, in Berlin-Steglitz, where these measures were decisively rejected. See Niesel, *Um Verkündigung und Ordnung der Kirche,* 77–80; cf. Beckmann, *Kirchliches Jahrbuch 1933–1944,* 284–89, and Niesel, *Kirche unter dem Wort,* 199–203. [The German Christian "Godesberg Declaration" completely denied any relationship between Judaism and Christianity and called for a thorough revision of all texts and liturgies to eliminate all such references; this led to the establishment of the institute. See also Susannah Heschel's study of the institute, *Aryan Jesus.*—VB]

[4.] Cf. Rom. 14:4.

[5.] Cf. Eph. 4:15.

[6.] Union Theological Seminary, New York.

[7.] Fritz Onnasch.

[8.] Eberhard Bethge.

Cantica minora ecclesiae:[9]

July 2–July 8:	Exod. 15:1–18
July 9–July 15:	Deut. 32:1–14
July 16–July 22:	Deut. 32:15–47
July 23–July 29:	1 Sam. 2:1–10
July 30–August 5:	Isa. 12
August 6–August 12:	Isa. 38:9–20
August 13–August 19:	Hab. 3

(after this probably the Letter to the Hebrews)

94. To Master Builder [Baumeister] Korporal[1]

P. Bonhoeffer
Schlawe, Koppelstr. 9
May 22, 1939

Dear Master Builder Korporal:

Permit me, as the teacher of your son for the time being, to direct a request to you. However differently we may think about the present church situation, we do share one thing, don't we, namely, the wish, indeed the prayer to God, that your son will become a faithful and joyful witness to the gospel of Jesus Christ. Your son stands in a firm community of brothers who stand up
173 for one another; he is glad and certain of his cause; he has an abundance of work before him; he is a clear and independent-thinking theologian whom we regard highly—let us allow him to travel fully the path along which God is leading him and let us be careful [not] to take away from him the inner certainty of his ministry! Given the way your son thinks, he must not follow any other path without offending his conscience. We will stand by his side. Furthermore, the path to the consistory today is more a path of even greater uncertainty than the path of the Council of Brethren. Everything at this

[9.] "The little songs of the church." Over the course of the Middle Ages, there was a liturgical development in which a series of seven (or eight) Old Testament chants (*cantica minora*) was established, which like the three New Testament chants (*cantica majora*) were regularly sung in addition to the book of 150 psalms.

[1.] *NL*, A 45 (65); handwritten. Previously published in *GS* 6:444–45. A builder, Korporal was the father of Hinrich Korporal, a member of the collective pastorate in Sigurdshof. Korporal had pressed his son to leave Sigurdshof in the summer of 1939 and place himself under the Magdeburg consistory [i.e., to become legalized—VB].

time indicates that the consistories will collapse faster than the Council of Brethren. Who among us wants to risk forcing another person onto a path that he himself cannot survey?

I commend the matter to God, the Lord. God will make everything good,[2] and God alone.

With respectful greetings your
Dietrich Bonhoeffer

95. From Henry Smith Leiper to Reinhold Niebuhr[1]

May 22, 1939

Dear Reinie:

I acted at once upon receipt of your letter about Dietrich Bonhoeffer,[2] and was able to cable him a genuine offer of a job with the American Committee for Christian German Refugees in the City of New York,[3] where we hope very much to be able to finance a pastoral service for Germans living here which Bonhoeffer could render superbly. I know him well and am keen about him. I shall certainly be glad to do anything I can to help him.

I hope you are having a good time and that I shall see you soon. Yours fraternally

Henry Smith Leiper

Copies to Van Dusen and Cavert

[2.] Cf. Ps. 37:5.

[1.] *NL*, A 50,2 (5); later typewritten copy; from New York. Previously published in *GS* 2:350. [Letter is in the original unaltered English.—VB]

[2.] See Niebuhr's May 1, 1939, letter to Leiper, 1/87.

[3.] See Leiper's May 11, 1939, letter to Bonhoeffer, 1/90. [For a more detailed study of this committee and the U.S. churches' involvement in refugee work, see Genizi, *American Apathy*, and Nawyn, *American Protestantism's Response to Germany's Jews and Refugees, 1933–1941*.—VB]

174 **96. To Ursula Schleicher**[1]

May 23, 1939

Dear Ursel,

In the haste of events I have not even congratulated you on your birthday.[2] But hopefully Mama placed the Vials wine[3] on your birthday table to strengthen you in these rather too turbulent days. Now one more suggestion: wouldn't you find it pleasant if we could take a day trip on Whitmonday early at 8:00 a.m. to Wiesenburg or somewhere else, with three or four cars (the two Fords, ours and Walter's);[4] everyone could be seated in them, and it would surely be quite lovely. In that case I would come already on Sunday evening. Please talk it over and let me know soon, so that I can arrange my plans accordingly. Address is E. Bethge, Sigurdshof via Zollbrück, Schlawe District.

All the best for the new year of your life. Cordial greetings your

Dietrich

97. From Paul Lehmann[1]

May 27, 1939

Dear Dietrich:

The word that you have been invited to lecture in the summer session of Union Theological Seminary, New York, encourages me to make this urgent request of you. Will you not be good enough to consent and make all possible arrangements accordingly to lecture in the department of Religion here at the college during the forthcoming academic year, 1939–1940? It has long been a concern of mine that your approach to the problems of philosophy and theology should be
175 heard by my students here and by others. Accordingly, I am venturing to plan on your coming and to make arrangements for similar lectures on other campuses of my acquaintance. I am sure you will be eagerly received.

[1.] *NL*, A 44,1 (24); handwritten; no return address, probably from Sigurdshof; previously unpublished.

[2.] His sister Ursula's birthday was May 21.

[3.] Vial's tonic wine, used to stimulate the appetite and gastric juices [containing bitters, it was also said to be good for the heart—VB].

[4.] Walter Dreß.

[1.] *NL*, A 50,2 (6); typewritten; return address "Elmhurst College, Elmhurst, Illinois, Department of Religion." Previously published in *GS* 1:289. [Letter is in the original unaltered English.—VB]

More precise details can be agreed upon while you are in residence at Union Seminary. Meanwhile, I shall look forward to your arrival there. Ever sincerely yours,

Paul[2]
Paul L. Lehmann, Th. D.
Professor of Religion

98. Arrangements for Delegation of Work [Übergaberegelungen] before Departure for the United States

98.1. Appointment of the Executor of Bonhoeffer's Estate[1]

May 27, 1939

Herewith I declare that Pastor Eberhard Bethge, presently living at Sigurdshof via Zollbrück, Schlawe District, has full right of disposal over my entire possessions.

Lic. Dietrich Bonhoeffer, Pastor
Schlawe in Pomerania, Koppelstrasse 9.

98.2. Directions for the Successor[2]

May 28, 1939

To my successor

He will find

1. one of the most gratifying tasks in the CC;

2. two coworkers[3] who have stood in this work for over four years and 176
who have borne full responsibility for the leadership of the houses[4] for one and a half years, to whom therefore the leadership of the communal life can be entrusted, whenever he himself is not able to be there;

[2.] Handwritten.

[1.] *NL*, A 82,18; handwritten card; previously unpublished.

[2.] *NL*, A 82,19; handwritten card. Previously published in *GS* 2:551–52. Wilhelm Niesel, the member of the Old Prussian Union Church Council of Brethren in charge of theological training, asked Gerhard Ebeling, among others, to serve as Bonhoeffer's substitute during the period of Bonhoeffer's stay in the United States. Eberling had to refuse for personal and professional reasons (letter from Gerhard Ebeling to the German editor, December 5, 1993). During the period of Bonhoeffer's absence, Hellmut Traub was called as "acting director" of the collective pastorates.

[3.] Eberhard Bethge and Fritz Onnasch.

[4.] [I.e., the pastorates.—VB]

3. a work that has been started: *NT*: concept of ἁμαρτία,[5] soteriological concepts are to follow. *Dogmatics*: the Formula of Concord up to *de libero arbitrio.*[6] It will be necessary to continue the work on dogmatics. There is more freedom in the NT. Discussions of sermons in Köslin, several lectures on homiletics in both places.

It is requested:

1. In addition to NT and dogmatics to hold discussions on pastoral counseling, on catechetics with written drafts for catechesis in Sigurdshof, on sermons in Köslin;

2. furthermore, to take walks or otherwise spend as much time as possible together with the brothers.

With sincere thanks and in faithful remembrance
Dietrich Bonhoeffer

98.3. Transfer of Motorcycle Title[7]

May 28, 1939

Herewith I certify that on this day my motorcycle DKW 200 ccm No. I. H.[8] has been transferred to the possession of Pastor Eberhard Bethge, currently of Sigurdshof via Zollbrück.

Dr. Dietrich Bonhoeffer, Pastor

177 **99. From Ruth von Kleist-Retzow**[1]

Lasbeck, May 31, 1939

My dear Dietrich,

I don't want to let you go without saying a final greeting to you. My prayers will accompany you on your way, and the joy will be very great when you return home. This certainty will always stand by you, when perhaps sometimes in foreign lands it does become very lonely.

[5.] "Sin."

[6.] The Formula of Concord up to the section "Concerning the Free Will" (*Book of Concord*, 486–543).

[7.] *NL*, A 82,20; handwritten card; previously unpublished.

[8.] ["DKW" was the abbreviation for a motorcycle manufactured during the 1920s and 1930s, nicknamed "Das kleine Wunder" (the little miracle).—VB]

[1.] *NL*, Anh. C 4; later typewritten copy; previously unpublished.

What you have meant to me is another story, but I believe you know that you have helped me on the path to God. That is what constitutes my special gratitude and my close attachment, something of value that will not die.

Greet Eberhard. The two of us will now become even closer to each other. I am very glad that he is there. (I wonder whether he has written his friend? It makes it more difficult for me to help when our friends are neglectful.)[2]

God's blessing accompany you from morning till evening, and may what you do for God be returned to you. Someday too all our "whys" will be resolved.

Could you perhaps help our friend Go.?[3] Most faithfully yours

R[uth] v[on] K[leist]-R[etzow]

100. From Henry Smith Leiper to Samuel McCrea Cavert[1]

May 31, 1939

Dear Sam:

I want to give you the following report concerning the arrangements which have been made under considerable pressure in connection with the Rev. Dietrich Bonhoeffer of Berlin who will arrive here on June 12.

Just after the meeting of the American Christian Committee where the pre- 178
sentation was made of the need for a pastor to work with refugees and help to find appropriate church homes for them, I had word from Reinhold Niebuhr in Edinburgh that Dietrich Bonhoeffer was slated to go to a concentration camp unless we could get him out of Germany. Niebuhr stated that he had agreed to let him have residence at his apartment temporarily and would undertake to arrange some lectures for him at Union Seminary and elsewhere.[2] Knowing Bonhoeffer very well, I was struck with the peculiar fitness of the man for just the thing we had been discussing[3] and immediately called up Dr. Paul Tillich

[2.] The reference is to Major Dieter von Kleist at the military enlistment office in Schlawe, whom Ruth von Kleist had contacted on behalf of Bonhoeffer and Bethge, to prevent an immediate summons to the physical for military induction. Cf. *DB-ER*, 634. [See also 1/92, ed. note 3.—VB]

[3.] Helmut Gollwitzer. Regarding the tensions in the Berlin-Dahlem congregation over the successor to Martin Niemöller, who had been imprisoned in July 1937, see Bonhoeffer's September 23, 1938, letter to Ottonie Blanck, 1/161, ed. note 6.

[1.] *NL*, A 50,2 (7); later typewritten copy; return address "Dr. Samuel McCrea Cavert, 297 Fourth Avenue, New York City." Previously published in *GS* 1:289–90. [Letter is in the original unaltered English.—VB]

[2.] Cf. Niebuhr's May 1, 1939, letter to Leiper, 1/87.

[3.] [I.e., someone to work with refugees from Nazi Germany.—VB]

who had been appointed with me as a committee to find a man. Tillich was even more enthusiastic about Bonhoeffer than I and stated his conviction that he was exactly the right person for this delicate and difficult task.

Bonhoeffer was an exchange at Union Theological Seminary, then pastor of an Evangelical German Church in London, and latterly the director of one of the "peripatetic" theological schools of the confessional wing of the Evangelical Church in Germany. His knowledge of English is excellent and he understands the situation in American churches from firsthand contact. His skill and aptitude in pastoral work are exceptional.

May I ask you to consult with the various church bodies in New York City, which as I recall had indicated an interest in seeing that some such service was provided for the German refugees. It is my hope that we can supplement the amount made available by the Refugee Committee—$1,000—so as to underwrite a budget of about $3,000, for this undertaking. Please let me know if I can supply further data.

Yours faithfully,
[Henry Smith Leiper]
Executive Secretary

101. From Eberhard Bethge[1]

An initial greeting to you.

When I finally got together yesterday evening after all with Hans, Fritz and M.[2] (Katja)[3] at the cinema, I felt the "loneliness" after the film in the absence of the verdict of a conversation partner.

179 What a *fine* airplane you had. Now I'm leaving. Please say hello to L.[4] Your Eberhard

---

[1.] *NL*, C 1; handwritten; no location, but surely from Berlin; back of a postcard from Paula Bonhoeffer to Dietrich, written after Bonhoeffer's departure from London on June 2, 1939; previously unpublished. See *DB-ER*, 649.

[2.] Hans Bethge, Fritz Onnasch, and Margret Bethge.

[3.] *Katja, the Uncrowned Empress*, a 1938 French film directed by Maurice Tourneur, which was showing in a German version in summer 1939 in the theaters.

[4.] The Leibholz family in London.

102. To His Parents[1]

My dear Parents,

This card has just been handed to me, and I can send it off unstamped. We are just landing in Amsterdam. The flight was *very* good. In my thoughts I am entirely with you, my brothers and sisters and friends. Greet them all!

Your grateful
Dietrich

103. To Eberhard Bethge[1]

June 4, 1939

Dear Eberhard,

Now we are flying over the Channel with a wonderful glowing sunset. It is 10:00 p.m. and still very light. I am doing well. You all will now be sleepy and heading to bed. I thank you for everything. It was very good that you were there. Greet Fritz![2] and thank him too. My thoughts are between you and the future. Take care of yourself. Greet all the brothers. They are now holding the evening service! God with you all! Will you perhaps have this card tomorrow morning?

Your faithful
Dietrich

104. To Eberhard Bethge[1] 180

Dear Eberhard,

Many thanks for the first short greeting.[2] How nice that you could celebrate the departure with a movie. Today in the city I often thought of our days here together, National Gallery, portraiture, etc.[3] The Daily Texts

[1.] *NL*, A 44,1 (25); handwritten postcard; KLM [the Dutch airline—VB] postcard stamped: Amsterdam-Schipol, June 3, 1939. Partially reproduced in *GS* 6:456.

[1.] *NL*, A 44,2 (17); handwritten postcard; KLM postcard stamped Croydon, Surrey, June 4, 1939. Previously published in *GS* 1:291.

[2.] Fritz Onnasch.

[1.] *NL*, A 44,2 (18); handwritten postcard; postmarked Forest Hill [London], June 6, 1939. Previously published in *GS* 1:291.

[2.] See Bethge's June 1, 1939, card to Bonhoeffer, 1/101.

[3.] The reference is to their visit together to England in March–April 1939.

these days give me great pleasure, and I am happy to have them from you.[4] A shame that I could not buy them for you. I have initiated the necessary steps for the invitation in the autumn.[5] But you must still write me whether you would prefer to visit Sabine[6] and me for a short period or Sabine for a longer period. Greet everyone! Always

Your faithful
Dietrich

105. From George Bell[1]

5.6.39

My dear Bonhoeffer,

I am most eager to see you. I telegraphed this morning, proposing 1 pm tomorrow (Tuesday) here. I am unhappily not in Town—we have a confirmation at night in the country. *Telephone* please, to say you can!

I am affectionately
George Chichester

181 ### 106. To George Bell[1]

6.6.39.

My dear Lordbishop,

thank you once again for the talk this afternoon. I have thought the matter over on my way back and I feel the question of the German representative[2] must be considered very carefully. I forgot to tell you, that Dr. Rieger[3] is

[4.] [These would have been the Moravian Daily Texts. When possible, Bonhoeffer and Bethge gave each other copies, although as the following sentence suggests, this wasn't possible in 1939 (see also 1/119). The copy Bonhoeffer took with him seems to have been Bethge's copy, which the two might have shared in the collective pastorate. —VB]

[5.] The reference is to plans for Bethge's possible emigration to England.

[6.] Sabine Leibholz.

[1.] *NL*, A 42, 2 (12); handwritten; from Chichester; previously unpublished. [Letter is in the original unaltered English.—VB]

[1.] LPL, BP 21:9; handwritten; no return address, but surely from London; previously unpublished. [Letter is in the original unaltered English.—VB]

[2.] [For the ecumenical movement.—VB] Cf. Bonhoeffer's March 1939 correspondence with Leonard Hodgson, 1/81 and 1/83.

[3.] Julius Rieger.

going to Germany next Monday. He would certainly be a good man for examining the situation and for having the necessary preliminary conversations. My personal view would be that Otto Dibelius would be the best person for such a delicate matter. He has a long experience in Church government and works closely together with the Brethren-Councils. Of course, he is not what we should call a Confessional Theologian in the strict sense. But perhaps this is not the most important thing for your purpose. Another man of a very balanced judgement and broadmindedness and a great ability for negotiations is Pastor Held-Essen,[4] although I do not know if he has any ecumenic experience. Confidentially I should like to add that I should not approach Asmussen, Jacobi, v. Thadden[5] if the whole matter is to be kept strictly confidential. Niesel[6] would be a very good person for discussing the matter. Most important of all I should think it would be, if Visser 't Hooft could be on the meeting. He would be an invaluable help for any German representative. With regard to Rieger I have the impression that he is a clear and thoughtful man and he, of course, could do it in the less conspicuous way.

The whole matter seems to me of highest importance; but it will require much patience as far as the German situation is concerned.—

I should be very grateful to you, if you would send me a few introductions
to New York, and even more, if you would, now and then, let me know any 182
wishes you have with regard to the ecumenic situation in America. Unfortunately I forgot to discuss with you the American attitude to the refugee pastors.

With kindest regards and many thanks I remain, my Lordbishop,
Yours ever
Dietrich Bonhoeffer

107. To Eberhard Bethge[1]

Dear Eberhard,

Many thanks for your last letter,[2] which greatly delighted me just as it was! In the course of today or tomorrow, I will write you a letter. With this card

[4.] Heinrich Held.

[5.] Hans Asmussen, Gerhard Jacobi, and Reinhold von Thadden.

[6.] Wilhelm Niesel.

[1.] *NL*, A 44,2 (19); handwritten postcard; postmarked "German-American Sea, Bremen–New York, 7.6.1939. Aboard the 'Bremen.'" Previously published in *GS* 1:292.

[2.] Letter not extant.

I only want to send you a final faithful greeting, before we get out on the Atlantic and cannot send any more mail. We just departed from Southampton and will land in a few hours in Cherbourg. The cabin is very roomy, and otherwise, too, there is a wonderful amount of room on the ship. The weather is glorious, and the sea utterly still. So we are able to eat lunch without danger. Now five quiet days lie before me, in which I will be thinking very much of you and all of you. Until now I am still surprised that all this has come about. I am already looking forward to when you come for a visit! I saw Uncle George, Julius,[3] and set everything up for autumn.[4] I hope it works out. Sabine[5] sends cordial greetings and remembers our visit together with pleasure. I wish you all a joyful and blessed work. May God protect you and everyone, and give you joy! In brotherly devotion I greet you and everyone.

Your
Dietrich

183 **108. To Fritz Onnasch**[1]

Dear Fritz,

The long voyage is coming to an end. In a few hours we will be on land. Now my thoughts must once again go forward, after they were more with all of you during the quiet days on the ocean. Now I eagerly await the first news from you all. During these days I have done much reading and enjoyed that greatly. I would rather have shared the substantial meals with you all. It is too boring alone. Otherwise one could swim, play Ping-Pong etc. etc., but what is all that without all of you?—I thank you that you were in Berlin.[2] I enjoy remembering it. Greetings to the whole house, parents, and brothers.

Warm and brotherly greetings to you from your faithful
Dietrich

[3.] George Bell and Julius Rieger.

[4.] A reference to the plans for Bethge's possible emigration to England or the United States; see Bonhoeffer's June 15, 1939, letter to Henry S. Leiper, 1/111, ed. note 6.

[5.] Sabine Leibholz.

[1.] *NL*, A 45 (66); handwritten postcard; postmarked "German-American Sea, Bremen–New York, June 12, 1939. Aboard the 'Bremen.'" Previously published in *GS* 6:456–57.

[2.] For Bonhoeffer's departure from there, see 1/103.

109. From Eberhard Bethge[1]

June 12, 1939

Dear Dietrich,

Today you will just have arrived.[2] I am thinking about it a great deal and would greatly like to know how things go from here. Before you were on the open seas, you wrote me such a nice letter.[3] I thank you very much for that; I was able to make others happy with it as well. Yesterday I saw Aunt Ruth and Fritz in St[ettin].[4] For suddenly we both[5] had to go to B[erlin], since it didn't work out with Eb.[6] The two of us were even supposed to continue alone.[7] There, 184
however, I countered very energetically. And now we are waiting for confirmation from the person in Potsdam,[8] whom you know well from the work at Aunt Ruth's.[9] Through these uncertainties, of course, I have been rather consumed with work. Nonetheless, we just had our first tennis game, which went very, very well indeed. If only you could be with us. You had hardly left when we saw three fat wild boars in the twilight on the bank of the Wipper—we felt somewhat funny. Shortly before, we had already bagged an over-one-half-meter-long adder, whose stripped skin now adorns the room. Well now, tell me yourself, how should I decide? In view of the new conditions, I will hardly be able to turn to W.[10] with a request to make a longer excursion to Sabine in the fall.[11] There was really now quite some complaining about personnel difficulties.[12] One would perhaps profit more from visiting Sabine. While, of course, to visit you would bring more of a change of pace. I don't know at all what I should do. Yesterday I had intended to celebrate the Lord's Supper and had as the biblical text for Saturday from the

---

[1.] *NL*, C 26; handwritten; no return address, but surely from Sigurdshof; previously unpublished.

[2.] Bonhoeffer's arrival on the *Bremen* in New York harbor.

[3.] See Bonhoeffer's June 7, 1939, postcard to Bethge, 1/107.

[4.] Ruth von Kleist-Retzow and Fritz Onnasch.

[5.] [I.e., Bethge and Onnasch.—VB]

[6.] Gerhard Ebeling, whom Wilhelm Niesel had asked to step in for Bonhoeffer as director of the collective pastorates; see Bonhoeffer's May 28, 1939, directions to his successor, 1/98.2, ed. note 2.

[7.] Bethge was to lead the collective pastorate at Sigurdshof, Onnasch the one in Köslin.

[8.] Hellmut Traub.

[9.] This is probably a reference to a January 1939 meeting of the theological society; see Schönherr's November 14, 1938, letter to several Finkenwalde brothers, 1/35.

[10.] Wilhelm Niesel.

[11.] To visit the Leibholz family in London with plans for possible emigration.

[12.] [This refers to Niesel's difficulty finding people to lead the collective pastorates.—VB]

med.[13] John 16:8ff., and for Sunday I John 4:17a (from [the] epistle for Sunday). But now because of the citation,[14] I had to let that drop. Next Sunday I will have the wedding. Dietrich, I did have some money from you in my account, which Sabine reminded me of again; didn't we purchase my briefcase and umbrella and so forth from that? Can't you give me greetings and addresses via Karl-Friedrich? I don't have them anymore; perhaps Sabine can give them? Tell me, do you think that Mrs. von Kleist should go once more to your brother-in-law? Recently it didn't seem to have helped much, or do you think this is useless.[15] Do write her about this.

I was very happy that W.[16] in Berlin yesterday spoke so nicely about reading *Life Together* [17] with great interest and growing pleasure. That does mean a lot, doesn't it? I read it now too and am very pleased that you left it behind for us and for me. Yesterday I found exactly what I had said to Korp.[18] in a very extensive conversation the previous evening, without knowing that it was in there. That pleased me and strengthened me.

185 A letter arrived here from Professor Paul L. Lehmann, Elmhurst College, Elmhurst, Illinois; he would like you to give a lecture in winter.[19] I wonder how you are doing now. I think of you devotedly your

Eberhard

I just wrote a long thank-you letter about all kinds of things to your parents.

110. From Eberhard Bethge to Paula and Karl Bonhoeffer[1]

Sigurdshof via Zollbrück/Pomerania, June 12, 1939

Esteemed, dear Mrs. Privy Councillor, honorable Privy Councillor,

I wish to take Dietrich's departure as the occasion to say my particular thanks to you for your hospitality and home, which you extended to me so often in your family.

[13.] The inserted list of Bonhoeffer's meditation texts from the circular letter.

[14.] Bethge had to travel to Wilhelm Niesel in Berlin to discuss Bonhoeffer's possible substitute; see ed. note 6.

[15.] This reference is unclear. [It may be an allusion to the tensions in the Dahlem congregation after Niemöller's arrest; Walter Dreß, husband of Bonhoeffer's sister Susanne, was involved in these issues. See 1/99, ed. note 3, and 1/161, ed. note 6.—VB]

[16.] Wilhelm Niesel.

[17.] Bonhoeffer's book *Life Together*, which appeared in 1939 as Theologische Existenz heute 61.

[18.] Hinrich Korporal, who was facing the decision whether to leave the collective pastorate in Sigurdshof; see Bonhoeffer's May 22, 1939, letter to his father, 1/94.

[19.] See Lehmann's May 27, 1939, letter to Bonhoeffer, 1/97.

Aside from the friendship, Dietrich was my teacher as well. And I have learned a great deal from him both personally and for the ministry. With time and the frequent longer visits in his parental home, however, I realized how much of his teaching came from this home. Because I now owe you so much gratitude, I want to try to express some of it.

Esteemed Mrs. Privy Councillor, if one hardly ever encounters you unpreoccupied with the concerns of others, it may well be because one can come to you with any difficulty and any request, and in no case do you ever leave that person without advice or help. And you know how to offer this so naturally and also so appropriately that one almost has too little reluctance to approach you again and again with a request. Dietrich has preserved and used this legacy well in his work. I will not conceal that next to my admiration I have sometimes also expressed to Dietrich my wonder at how you can endure the constant mindfulness and advising in all the different directions in which you are in demand, by us and by others. And strangely, the demands placed on you by the number of your children and grandchildren seem to increase these energies instead of limiting them. Above all, I will not forget the experiences of the past half year.[2]

Dietrich once told me that there was only one point in which you, esteemed 186
Privy Councilor, have always been very stern and uncompromising in [your] children's upbringing, namely, when one of them pronounced general judgments on matters of which he or she understood nothing. Dietrich very helpfully passed on this demand for exactitude and differentiation when expressing oneself in the discipline one practices and made it important to us;[3] but then he attempted at the same time to achieve a proper correlation between this uncompromising stance and a great goodness and broad-mindedness, to listen patiently to all the so clumsy but genuine troubles and thoughts. And in this practice he referred explicitly to his father.

But your home has become very important to me in one matter that may be particularly inaccessible to people of my age. Through our schooling we have acquired a mostly insufficient and badly influenced view of Prussian Germany before the war, whose substance of almost forgotten dutifulness, selflessness, and modesty supports us even today. I can now say that through your home I have won a truly decisive and committed perspective and clarity in this matter, for which I am and will remain particularly grateful.

[1.] *NL*, C 26; handwritten; previously unpublished.

[2.] [When Bethge had stayed at the Bonhoeffer home in Berlin.—VB]

[3.] Cf. Bonhoeffer's later self-assessment in his April 22, 1944, letter to Bethge: "I don't think I have ever changed much, except perhaps at the time of my first impressions abroad, and under the first conscious influence of Papa's personality. It was then that a turning from the phraseological to the real ensued" (*DBWE* 8:358).

I know very well that for you, these things are as they are precisely through their self-evident nature, and that means through their unspoken nature; yet for once perhaps I may be permitted to express some of the various thoughts that came to my mind when Dietrich departed. And the awareness of gratitude includes a growing awareness of the gifts as well.

Now several days of your vacation have passed, and I hope very much that you have had a good trip. I was very sorry that the notification about the car didn't work out.[4] I still don't know what the reason was. Onnasch received the letter only on Tuesday afternoon, then called me, and I in turn called around on the evening of the same day. I trust that the large car doesn't let you down and makes traveling comfortable.

Yesterday I was in Berlin at the officials'. The replacement unfortunately is not working out in any way, and perhaps we will remain on our own for a while.[5] That means a great burden. Dietrich in the meantime wrote several cards according to which he was doing well and everything was working out according to his wishes.

187 I wish you a good holiday and some rest after all the lively days. In great gratitude and sincere admiration, your devoted

Eberhard Bethge

111. To Henry Smith Leiper[1]

15.6.1939

Dear Dr. Leiper,

I wish to thank you very much indeed for the reception you gave me on my arrival in New York. I felt quite at home when Mr. Macy[2] gave me your kind letter and when I met you the next morning. It is a great thing to have good friends and fellow-Christians abroad.

These beautiful days at Dr. Coffin's[3] country home are giving me some time to think about my future and I am sure you will understand that I should like to put the situation before you as I see it and ask your advice.

[4.] [Paula and Karl Bonhoeffer had hoped that Bethge could drive them to their vacation place.—VB]

[5.] See Bethge's June 12, 1939, letter to Bonhoeffer, 1/109.

[1.] *NL*, A 50,2 (12); later typewritten copy; return address: "'Coomb-Pine,' Lakeville, Connecticut." Previously published in *GS* 1:316–19. [Letter is in the original unaltered English.—VB]

[2.] Paul Macy; the letter mentioned is not extant.

[3.] Henry Sloane Coffin.

Before I left Germany I had long talks with my brethren from the Brethren-Council and pledged myself to return to Germany after about a year's time to take up the training work in the Confessional Church again, unless some unforeseen development would change the whole situation. At first they were very reluctant to let me go at all, since they are in need of teachers. It was only when I expressed my hopes that I could be of some use to them by establishing contacts with American theologians and churchmen through lectures or meetings, that they gave me leave. So from the point of view of the Confessional Church my trip to America was meant to be an ecumenic link between our isolated church in Germany and our friends over here. We all felt that to be very essential from many points of view. My personal question and difficulty with regard to military service etc. came in only as a second consideration. Of course, my colleagues were glad, that I would be
able to postpone my decision for at least one year. Now, I am sure, all that 188
could not be made quite clear in correspondence before I left Germany. But before we are going to work out my programme for the next time, however long it might be, I feel strongly, that everything ought to be quite clear between us. I deeply appreciate, and so did my friends, your readiness to invite me to come to this country and I am most happy indeed to be here again and to meet old friends. There are, however, a few questions which we have to clear up before I start my work over here and I wish, you would help me to do the right thing. The post which you are kindly intending to confer upon me attracts me from every point of view. I feel strongly the necessity of that spiritual help for our refugees. When I was pastor in London I spent most of my time with these people[4] and I felt it was a great privilege to do so. At the same time that post would offer me an unusual opportunity for getting acquainted with the life of the church in this country, which has been one of my greatest hopes for my stay over here. The only thing that makes me hesitate at the present moment of decision is the question of loyalty to my people at home. All of us, of course, were well aware of the fact that it means running a risk for a confessional pastor to go to America with the intention to go back to Germany, and we all agreed that I should take that risk and pay the price for it, if necessary, if it is of a true value to the Church of Christ there and here. But, of course, I must not for the sake of loyalty to the Confessional Church accept a post which on principle would make my return to Germany impossible. Now, my question is whether that would not be the case with any post that is officially concerned with refugee work? As a matter of fact, I am afraid, it would be so. Now, if that is true,

[4.] Regarding the refugee work in the German congregations in London, see *DB-ER*, 413–15, and *DBWE* 13, esp. 279–81 and 286–89.

what can we do about it? Is there a possibility of giving that post a somewhat larger scope? I have no particular idea, but if, for instance, it were possible to interpret that post as a sort of invitation, as a "guest-post" from the Federation of Churches as to enable me to get acquainted with the church activities in New York and to cooperate in some respect (whereby, of course,
189 some of that pastoral work of which you have been thinking might be conferred upon me on the respective occasions), I think, that would change the matter a good deal. But, of course, I have no idea under what heading such a thing could be done. This is the first point, which I should very much like to have your advice on.

Secondly, when R. Niebuhr wrote to me first in February[5] he was hoping to provide a few lectureships for me all over the country, so as to give me an opportunity of seeing a good deal of the theological schools and of getting in contact with the professors of Theology. That, of course, would be very much in the line of my work in Germany and I should be greatly interested to do that sort of work. Now, would you suppose, that the post in New York would leave the necessary time to do some investigation and some visiting of that sort?

Finally, let me add a very personal remark. My best friend in Germany,[6] a young confessional pastor, who has been working with me for many years, will be in the same conflict with regard to military service etc. at the latest by next spring, possibly in the fall of this year. I feel it would be an utmost disloyalty to leave him alone in Germany when the conflict comes up for him. I should either have to go back to stand by him and to act with him or to get him out and to share my living with him, whatever it be, though I do not know if he would be willing to leave Germany. That is a last personal, but not only personal reason, why I feel bound to keep my way-back open. I am sure, you will appreciate that this is a duty of "Bruderschaft"[7] which in these times one just has to fulfill.

Now I have put my case before you. I know, I am causing you a lot of trouble with all that. But you know us Germans and that we are sometimes a little complicated, and more than that, you know the Confessional Church and its needs. I need not assure you again how grateful I am for all that you have been doing for our cause and for me personally. It is just therefore that I feel you must know my whole case before you go on with me. If you should

---

[5.] Letter not extant; see, however, Niebuhr's May 11, 1939, letter to Paul Lehmann, 1/91.

[6.] Eberhard Bethge.

[7.] ["Brotherhood."—VB]

think it impossible to find the right post for me, after you have heard all that, please feel entirely free to tell me and then we should try to make the 190
best of the next few months and I should return to Germany, certainly very gratefully for all the friendship I have experienced over here again, in the later part of the fall. My friends at home would only be too glad, if I came back a little earlier than they expected. But if you would see a way through all these difficulties, then I shall stay here with great pleasure, interest and gratefulness.

I am going to Eaglesmere for Saturday. I am looking forward to seeing you next week. The "prophet chamber" at Union[8] is lovely and I am enjoying Union a lot.

With many thanks for everything, I remain yours ever
[Dietrich Bonhoeffer]

112. From Henry Smith Leiper to Samuel McCrea Cavert[1]

June 15, 1939

I am attaching hereto a copy of my letter of Bonhoeffer under date of May 11th,[2] which was the basis of his coming here.

I have not yet had any opportunity for a real conference with him, and when I tried to introduce him to you, I found you were out of town. He is visiting Henry Coffin at the moment, but will be back next week when we must sit down with this matter and work it out. Pit Van Dusen[3] who has had one talk with him seems to discover that he does not feel he can work with the refugees and safely go back to Germany, as he now expects to do. Of course, I thought he was coming to stay. He, apparently, is coming only on a visitor's visa and will be so hampered in his movements on that account that I seriously question whether he can do the thing we had hoped to have him do.

[8.] The guest room at Union Theological Seminary (cf. *DB-ER*, 652).

[1.] *NL*, A 50,2 (11); typewritten carbon copy. [Letter is in the original unaltered English.—VB] Previously published in *GS* 2:351. Regarding Leiper's June 15, 1939, letter to Henry P. Van Dusen, see *NL*, A 50,2 (9). [Leiper's letter to Van Dusen is a brief cover letter that reads in its entirety: "I enclose a copy of my correspondence with Bonhoeffer in which I associated Cavert and yourself with myself because of what I understood from Reinhold Niebuhr was the nature of the situation. I thought you might have this on file in the light of our conversation by telephone and the necessity of working out the future for Bonhoeffer. Yours ever, Executive Secretary HSL."—VB]

[2.] See Leiper's May 11, 1939, letter to Bonhoeffer, 1/90.

[3.] Henry P. Van Dusen.

We must talk it over at the earliest possible date which I suppose would be Tuesday, when I get back, if you are here then.

[Henry S. Leiper]

191 **113. From John Baillie**[1]

15 June 1939

My dear Dr. Bonhoeffer,

I am one of the trustees of the Croall Lectureship Trust, and I am writing to you to ask you whether you would be prepared to accept nomination as a lecturer during next winter. The duties of the lecturer are simply to deliver about six lectures on a theological subject of his own choosing, but the lectures must be published afterwards in book form. The lectures could all be given within two weeks, or could be spread over a longer period.

The fee offered would be 200 guineas (210 pounds), of which 150 guineas would be paid immediately on delivering of the lectures, and the remaining 50 guineas when the book was published.

Some suitable dates, perhaps some time between October of this year and March of next might be arranged between the lecturer and the trustees.

This letter is merely a preliminary enquiry, but if you write me indicating that you would be disposed to accept, I think the trustees will agree to invite you.

I have talked the matter over at some length with Professor Niebuhr, and he knows that I am writing you.

I shall write no more at present, but shall await an answer from you. I was most interested in all Professor Niebuhr had to tell me about you.

My wife and Jan send their warmest greetings, and so do I. Yours most sincerely,

John Baillie

[1.] *NL*, A 50,2 (10); handwritten; return address "9 Whitehouse Terrace, Edinburgh." Partially reproduced in *GS* 2:361–62. [Letter is in the original unaltered English.—VB]

113a. From Max-Peter Meyer[1]

Max-Peter Meyer (of Oberammergau)
c/o Mr. G. Henne
10 Inglemere Road
Forest Hill
London SE 23

Registered with the "Catholic Committee for Refugees from Germany"
Father Ostermann[2]
(case worker: Mr. Deechy)
123 Second Street
N[ew York] City

[1.] Lehmann Papers, Archive of the Library of Princeton Theological Seminary, box 67, folder 38; typescript. First publication in *Dietrich Bonhoeffer Jahrbuch/Yearbook 2005/2006*, 97–101; editorial notes by Hans Pfeifer. [Meyer's letter was discovered after the publication of *DBW* 17, which contains documents found after their respective volumes had already been published; discoveries after *DBW* 17 are published in the *Dietrich Bonhoeffer Jahrbuch/Yearbook*. An additional letter from Meyer to Paul Lehmann, dated July 24, 1939, was also discovered but is not included in this volume. English translations of both letters by Reinhard Krauss first appeared in the *IBS Newsletter* no. 83, Fall 2003. Krauss's translation has been revised somewhat here.—VB] Bonhoeffer passed this letter along to Paul Lehmann, and then as he passed through England on his return from New York informed Meyer of this. (Cf. Meyer's letter of July 24 to Lehmann, Lehmann Papers, Archive of the Library of Princeton Theological Seminary, box 67, folder 38.) The actual letter to Bonhoeffer follows a summary of information about Meyer, which is also included in the text here. [The following information about Meyer comes from Clifford Green. Max-Peter Meyer was a composer, organist, and music teacher from Oberammergau, Bavaria (the village internationally famous for its controversial Passion play). Married to a Catholic, he was a Jewish convert to Catholicism, and as the sole Jew in the village, referred to as "Jud Meyer." Under Nazi racial laws he was classified as a *Volljude* and thus hoped to emigrate to the United States. After being assaulted by young Nazis during *Kristallnacht*, he was imprisoned in Dachau and released after three weeks. He left Germany and received refuge in London from Gottlieb Henne, the president of St. Paul's parish council during Bonhoeffer's pastorate there. There he met Bonhoeffer, who was en route to New York. Bonhoeffer offered to help him, and so Meyer wrote him at Union giving details of his immigration application. Meyer's story is discussed in James Shapiro's book *Oberammergau*. Meyer apparently stayed in England during the war, returned to Oberammergau after 1945, and testified at the denazification trial of Alois Lang (who had played Jesus in the 1930 and 1934 productions), asserting that Lang had not been a Nazi (the court classified Lang, who had been a party member, as a "nominal" follower). More information is available in an online interview with Shapiro at http://tinyurl.com/4lcn5or.—VB]

[2.] [The director.—VB]

Under my address	Max (-Peter) Meyer. Oberammergau
	St. Gregor 1
Currently residing at	Munich
	Holbeinstrasse 16/1

1. Name of my friend who is in ongoing contact with the committee, especially with Mr. Deechy, concerning my immigration: Mr. Richard Holzner (from Munich), 596 Riverside Drive, Apt. 62, *N[ew] York City* 11.
2. Name of the gentleman with whom I am friends who obtained the first affidavit for me (the committee does not yet know of this affidavit, since it intends to procure another affidavit for me, which I will gladly accept in order to have a closer connection with the committee): Prof. Dr. Anton Lang, Georgetown University, *Washington*. (The name of the provider of the affidavit, c/o Dr. Anton Lang, is Mr. R. Putnam, mayor of the City of *Springfield, Mass.*)
3. Additional committees or persons making efforts on my behalf or being in contact with me via the Monastery Ettal, Bavaria:
   a. Father Dr. Sylvester Schaeffers
   Office of the Bishop
   Cleveland, Ohio
   605 NBC Building
   815 Superior Ave. NE
   b. Monsignor Michael I. Ready
   National Catholic Welfare Conference
   1312 Massachusetts Ave.
   Washington, D.C.

London, June 15, 1939
Pastor Dr. Dietrich Bonhoeffer
Union Theological Seminary[3]
120 Street, Broadway[4]
New York

Esteemed Pastor,

Our chance acquaintance, as well as the extraordinarily kind offer on your part, lead me to trouble you with my plans to emigrate to the United States. I do not know how much you are burdened with your own issues or more personally

[3.] "Seminary" is handwritten and replaces "University."
[4.] "Broadway" is handwritten.

pressing ones during your stay in the States. I would understand completely if you were to reply that for whatever reason you could not or would not want to deal with my concerns. It is only your kind offer during your last brief visit at the home of the Henne family, together with the need on my part to pursue all potential leads for my emigration, which prompts me to accept your kind offer. I will attempt to describe my situation to you as briefly as possible.

1. I am a *Roman Catholic* and, according to the German racial law, 100 percent Jewish [Volljude]. My wife is a *Roman Catholic*—100 percent Aryan. We lived for years undisturbed in Oberammergau. In Germany our circumstances were good. Upon my emigration, I was able to leave my wife, who is still living there, with a small sum of money, despite the expropriation of over 50 percent of our assets by the government. For the last three years, I have worked exclusively on compositions, especially the composition of masses and liturgical studies.

2. The situation of non-Aryans in Germany forced me to emigrate. I had to endure three weeks of Dachau—as part of the mass arrests [Sammelaktion] at the time.[5] Through Ettal we became acquainted with the Henne family. This family served as guarantors with the Society of Friends, Bloomsbury, for my interim stay in England. Based on this guaranty, I received my permit. We did not even try to get a permit for my wife, since as an Aryan she is still able to live in Germany without difficulty for the time being; the plan is for her to come to the United States directly some day.

3. We received the affidavit for the United States via *Professor Dr. Anton Lang, Georgetown.* I was promised another one a few months ago by the Catholic Committee in New York. However, the guarantor has since died. Another one is being sought. The committee *does not yet know anything* about the existing affidavit and *ought not to for the time being.*

4. My friend who is constantly pursuing my case with the committee is Mr. Richard Holzner from Munich—address, see reverse. Please allow him to come to you sometime; he can provide much information.

5. *My number on the Stuttgart waiting list is 25718.* Based on this number, I would not be eligible before the end of 1942 or the beginning of 1943. This is obviously impossible—to live off and impose myself on the kind Henne family for such a long time. Because of this and the need to support myself, I must thus try under all circumstances to receive permission to enter the United States as a *nonquota* immigrant.[6] Exemptions do exist for university professors and

---

[5.] [In the wake of *Kristallnacht*, approximately twenty thousand Jewish men were arrested throughout the country and sent to concentration camps. Like Meyer, most were released after several weeks.—VB]

[6.] [The 1924 U.S. immigration act created a quota system that drastically reduced the percentage of immigrants from European countries; it also required a screening of

music teachers. One has to receive an invitation from a college. (*This can be fictitious.*) With such an invitation and a significant number of teaching credentials and student certificates (from the last two to three years), there is the hope of obtaining the entry visa from the consulate. If the invitation is confirmed by the State Department, there is of course no problem at all.

Once over there, I intend to practice my profession as a music teacher, primarily for the theoretical subjects of harmony, counterpoint, and history of music, and *as an organist.* I have composed significant works, some of which have been performed. At present I am working on an a cappella Mass. It is not important to me to work in one of the major cities over there. Being used to rural living, I am just looking for a position somewhere that enables me to have my wife (there are no children) follow me in the foreseeable future.

6. I have an initial set of recommendations and references. In particular, I have found great favor with the esteemed Abbot Dr. Angelus Kupfer of the Ettal monastery. I can get a recommendation from His Eminence Cardinal von Faulhaber. For purely political reasons, His Eminence currently does not like to transmit them across the border.

7. All my personal papers are on file with the Catholic Committee.[7] If required, Mr. Holzner would assist you without reservation in this regard.

Thus I seek a position as a music teacher, primarily for theoretical subjects, in conjunction with a position as an organist in a Catholic setting. I have always combined the teaching of piano, in the many lessons that I have given with good success, with general musicology (the basics of theory as well as the historical foundation), in order to lay the foundation for a broader and deeper understanding of music. In particular I had young people play chamber music from an early age.

And now in order to practice my profession as soon as possible over there, I seek an invitation to a teaching position from a college that would bring me over.

I could imagine, most esteemed Pastor, that through some connection or other you might be able to arrange something like this for me. My only regret is that you have to do so bona fide, since I did not have the opportunity to introduce myself to you personally.

---

immigrants; the 1929 law established quotas based on national origin. For those who later sought to flee Nazi oppression, their best chance was usually to apply as a "*nonquota immigrant," meaning they either came from a country for which* there was no immigration quota (there were no quotas, for example, for countries in the Western Hemisphere) or belonged to a "nonquota" group (i.e., certain professionals or persons with relatives in the United States).—VB]

[7.] Here there is a handwritten addition at the end of the page: "At the committee, Mr. Deechy is the person in charge of my case."

If you allow Mr. Holzner to come to you sometime, he will be able to provide you with a more complete picture than is possible for me to do here in a letter. At any rate, at the top of the letter I have listed the respective addresses of those who are making efforts on my behalf.

I am extraordinarily grateful to you for whatever you do, Pastor. I have no relatives abroad and never considered leaving my native land, but am now after all forced to do so. I am thus dependent on the pure love for one's neighbor by people who know me only from a distance. Such neighborly love has in fact been extended to me in an astounding way, a case in point being the Henne family. You will surely understand, Pastor, that I do not want to unnecessarily take undue advantage of this.

I hope that you and your brother had a good passage across the Atlantic. Everything is fine here. For the next few Sundays I will serve as the temporary organist at the German Protestant Church.

With sincere greetings and most gratefully I remain
Yours respectfully
(signed) Max-Peter Meyer

Personal Data:
Name: Max(-Peter) Meyer (German address: Oberammergau, St. Gregor I)
Date and Place of Birth: born Nov. 3, 1892, in Munich
Marital Status: married since Nov. 27, 1927, to wife, Helene, neé Gutacker
Religion: Roman Catholic
Profession: composer and organist
c/o Mr. G. Henne, London etc.

114. To Paul Lehmann[1]

June 17th 1939

My dear Paul,

nun also bin ich wieder hier![2] Niebuhr[3] will have written to you about it.
There has been some misunderstanding about my trip. I am not a refugee, 192
but I must go back to Germany to take up my work over there. They are in

[1.] *NL*, A 50,2 (13); later typewritten copy; no return address, certainly from New York. Previously published in *GS* 2:351–52. [Letter in English and German. See ed. notes below.—VB]

[2.] "So now I am here again!"

[3.] Reinhold Niebuhr.

need of teachers.[4] I want to stay until late autumn or spring at the very latest. The first week in August I am delivering lectures for one week at the Summer School of Union.[5] Will I see you at all? Hopefully! Do you think that several more lectures (with salary,[6] for I have no money here!) could be arranged at other universities? Niebuhr was perhaps *too optimistic*. I spent a few days with Coffin[7] in Lakeville. Today I met Roberts,[8] whom I liked a great deal.

Let me hear from you soon! I am living at Union, Prophet's Chamber![9]

Give my regards to your wife and accept my warm greetings yourself, from your old

Dietrich Bonhoeffer

115. To Henry Smith Leiper[1]

19.6.39

Dear Dr. Leiper,

I have just received a letter from Dr. Freudenberg[2] asking me urgently not to take over the refugee-post if I wish to go back to Germany. He also calls my attention to the fact that there are many of our confessional pastors who will never be able to return to Germany and from whom, therefore, I should
193 not take away the chance of this post. I hope you will be able to spare an hour of your time to-morrow for me. We must get clear about it.

[4.] [The previous two sentences, as well as the date and the salutation, are in the original English. Bonhoeffer wrote the remainder of the letter in German, but it is translated here.—VB]

[5.] ["Summer School of Union" in English in original.—VB]

[6.] ["Salary" in English in original.—VB]

[7.] Henry Sloane Coffin.

[8.] David Roberts.

[9.] ["Prophet's Chamber" in English in original.—VB]

[1.] *NL*, A 50,2 (14a); handwritten. Previously published in *GS* 1:319. [Letter is in the original unaltered English.—VB]

[2.] Adolf Freudenberg, who because of his marriage to a "non-Aryan" woman had to emigrate to England in March 1939. [Freudenberg was a diplomat and a member of the Confessing Church.—VB] After April 1939, in London he organized the refugee work for the provisional World Council of Churches, which he later carried out from Switzerland (cf. Ludwig, "Christen dürfen zu diesem Verbrechen nicht schweigen").

With many thanks and best regards, Yours ever
Dietrich Bonhoeffer

I hope you have got my last letter.[3]

116. To Elisabeth Bethge[1]

June 20, 1939

Dear Mrs. Pastor,

I am sending you cordial greetings from here. I am doing well, and there is much to see. Unfortunately, it is dreadfully hot so that the work suffers somewhat. I was very happy to see Eberhard and your daughter[2] before my departure. Would you be so kind to pass the enclosed card on to Eberhard?[3] I would be very grateful to you.

With cordial greetings your very devoted
Dietrich Bonhoeffer

117. To Sabine and Gerhard Leibholz[1]

Dear Gert, dear Sabine,

In view of the ghastly situation over there, and since I only would have stayed until August, I have decided to travel back already with Karl-Friedrich. So I will arrive on July 13 in Southampton, unless a change for the better suddenly occurs. I cannot say at all how long I will stay with you. We must see, perhaps only briefly.[2]

Heartfelt greetings to you from your
Dietrich

[3.] See Bonhoeffer's June 15, 1939, letter to Leiper, 1/111.

[1.] *NL*, A 44, 2 (21); handwritten postcard; no return address but certainly from New York; previously unpublished.

[2.] Margret Bethge. [See 1/101.—VB]

[3.] Card not extant.

[1.] *NL*, Anh. A 28; handwritten postcard; from New York in June 1939. Partially reproduced in *GS* 6:461.

[2.] Bonhoeffer arrived in London on July 13 and remained there until July 25.

194 **118. To His Parents**[1]

June 22, 1939

My dear Parents,

Your letter[2] arrived yesterday. I thank you greatly for it. You were right in my neighborhood in Kolberg.[3] A pity that I was not there. Did you also visit the cathedral there, or did you have too little time? Now the first days here are over, and I have gotten quite used to it again. It is strange; it does take time before one relearns all the little technical things. I am living in the same house as back then, have three rooms, and am doing well. I am trying to read through the scholarly literature that has appeared in the meantime, as far as it goes, so I am occupied the entire day. I wrote you about my stay in the mountains. The landscape was very lovely, but I yearned for a time that could be really filled. Now in the meantime there have been various discussions. The outcome was that just about everything has changed. They invited me to stay as long as I wanted, but I have refused. Karl Friedrich knows more details, and he can tell you. Thus I will return already in autumn, I think. Nothing else was possible if I wanted to bring together the wishes from over there and from here. Ultimately, I am quite content with this. I am also not sure whether I could have held out in the atmosphere here for long; everything is dreadfully sensationalized and full of hatred[4] and dreadfully pharisaic.[5] Personally, everywhere I went I found the friendliest hospitality from my friends from back then, but that of course isn't enough. Now I am working hard on my lectures, which brings me much joy. It is terribly hot, however, and at the same time always so humid. But on the whole I like the heat. I will go next week to the Boerickes.[6] They send you their
195 best regards and are very friendly. Unfortunately, I have had no word until now from Eberhard. That of course is a bit unsettling. The newspapers here

[1.] *NL*, A 44:1(26); handwritten; no return address, but certainly from New York. Partially reproduced in *GS* 6:457–58.

[2.] Letter not extant.

[3.] Kolberg on the Baltic Sea is ca. fifty kilometers west of Köslin.

[4.] ["Full of hatred" in English in the original.—VB]

[5.] [An interesting comment that indicates that even though Bonhoeffer was critical of the Nazi regime, he nonetheless as a German was sensitive to the tone of foreign criticism—this was true during his first stay at Union as well; one wonders whether this, too, influenced his decision to return to Germany. Bonhoeffer's pejorative use of "pharisaic," here and elsewhere, reflects the mentality of those times.—VB]

[6.] The Boerickes were distant relatives on the Tafel side of the family who lived in Philadelphia.

are terribly upset over matters in China.[7] But people say that this is always the case.

Hopefully, I will hear again from you soon, also about how Uncle Rudi[8] is doing. Many greetings to you and my brothers and sisters from your grateful

Dietrich

I have written in detail to Sabine.[9] I will visit her some on my way back, I think. Hopefully, I will still see Karl Friedrich on the return trip!

119. From Eberhard Bethge[1]

June 23, 1939

Dear Dietrich,

I am very sorry to have left you for so long without any news; I can imagine that you watch out for news even more than we do here. But perhaps you are also so taken up with all the new things that you hardly notice it. In any case, it is a pity that it is so difficult to hear from each other.

Perhaps you can picture for yourself how I have been absorbed by matters here, which until the beginning of this week did not work out. Three times, every week on Saturday, I was in Berlin, which in the heat was not a little exhausting (counting your trip as well), and in addition took care of work and order here. But in the end everything went well, without particular disruptions; until now at least there is some help here.[2] While for the time being the two of us[3] have been given the main responsibility by Berlin, the Formula of Concord and help with concepts are indeed already quite valuable and have been a good start.[4] 196
Throughout these days I have not gotten around to writing, despite several

[7.] This is a reference to the continuation of the war that had resumed on July 7, 1937, between Japan and China, as well as to the battles between Japanese and Soviet troops on the Manchurian border and in Outer Mongolia. See Erdmann, *Die Zeit der Weltkriege*, 532–33.

[8.] The reference is to the state of the preparations for war.

[9.] Sabine Leibholz; letter not extant.

[1.] *NL*, C 26; handwritten; no return address but certainly from Sigurdshof; previously unpublished.

[2.] [Hellmut Traub had arrived to help out with the collective pastorates; see also 1/109.—VB]

[3.] [Bethge and Fritz Onnasch.—VB]

[4.] Theological work in dogmatics on the Formula of Concord and work on selected New Testament concepts; see Bonhoeffer's May 28, 1939, instructions for his successor, 1/98.2.

attempts. In fact, under no circumstances can this[5] be neglected too much. But I was nonetheless very much in conversation with you. I read a great deal and thoroughly in *Life Together*[6] and can now give you very well-founded thanks. With this you have in fact left much of yourself here and help me. It was a very great delight for me to read much in it, and it also made me happy to realize how much has become a possession in the course of time. Admittedly, the understanding of the Psalms, as I saw again today, will meet with difficulty, as briefly as it has nonetheless been stated there.[7]—Today, however, preaching about a psalm was truly good and stimulating. Over there,[8] however, where I preached the sermon yesterday about Cana,[9] it was difficult, and there was little willingness to accept, although I am perfectly certain again about the exegesis; a new suggestion is the following: regarding the striking fact that among the seven miracles in John, the first is so seemingly insignificant: wedding water to wine—the following must be considered, namely, that all the chapters on promise in the Old Testament cannot do enough to describe the concise festiveness as a sign of the last things, that is, there is a joyful community eating together, there is oil and above all wine and so forth; and now John, by giving precedence to *this* miracle ("this, the *first* of his signs . . .")[10] intends to witness precisely to this: Jesus in this first drawing back of the curtain before his disciples is pointing to this: I am *this* ultimate time [Endzeit] . . . and *thus* in this very way he revealed his glory and they believed in him.

In the Old Testament I am now in Amos. I would have liked to meditate with you about John 17 [v. 2]. What does καθὼς ἔδωκας αὐτῷ ἐξουσίαν πάσης σαρκός mean? "Authority *over* all people"[11] is really not enough, ἐξουσία here "that flesh which is taken into the lordship (of Christ)" . . . ? I find it difficult.

You can imagine how delighted I was with the plentiful mail, written on the ship and so forth, sent after your arrival there. It really was a good, long conversation with you, and you took so much trouble to write me everything that I would have particularly noticed and enjoyed on the voyage. One senses from the
197 letters the calm and contemplation. Listening to letters is indeed good for the intercession in the evenings and during the meditation period (by the way, the

[5.] [Bethge's teaching responsibilities.—VB]

[6.] Bonhoeffer's book *Life Together.*

[7.] Cf. *DBWE* 5:52–58. Regarding Bonhoeffer's understanding of the Psalter as "the prayerbook of Jesus Christ," see also his 1935 lecture "Christ in the Psalms" (*DBW* 14, 2/5) and his 1940 "Prayerbook of the Bible" (*DBWE* 5:155–77).

[8.] In the collective pastorate in Köslin.

[9.] See John 2:1–11.

[10.] John 2:11; italics are Bethge's.

[11.] [This is the NRSV wording; a closer translation of the Luther Bible German would be "power over all flesh."—VB]

day before yesterday we had a group discussion in the evening about the meditation). Fuchs[12] obtained the Daily Texts for me, and I have them again in the same form.—Now my comments on your letter will be somewhat muddled.[13] That is really incredible that Boeckheler[14] isn't preaching! Tell me, what is happening with Gert?[15] I fear that something there could fall apart. Eight days ago on Saturday I was at your sister Ursel's[16] (I slept in our room); when on Monday on my way home from the wedding[17] I called there once more, she told me that on Sunday Christel[18] had been there especially to talk about what was to be done; she and Klaus[19] and so forth had received such crazy letters.[20] They must have been harsh and been risking a breach. For my part I received very nice letters.

By the way, Julius[21] is supposed to be in Berlin now according to information from Sabine,[22] but all my attempts to find out have remained unsuccessful till now. I am extraordinarily pleased that something has worked out with George.[23] But it does not make him[24] very happy? Many thanks for obtaining the dartboard. Hopefully, it will arrive soon. You may be right about the danger of becoming a bit easygoing; in any case these days, by myself and in part with and under the eyes of strangers, are a clearly noticeable incentive to get down to business, to new thoroughness, reexamination, and so forth. That is indeed very certainly the case.

With the financial matters, that can wait; at present your parents are still away. By the way, I just paid the full price for the dictionary.[25] I am still doing quite well. The trip recently to the wedding went smoothly; I could ride there and back from Berlin with my cousin Karl-Friedrich in the BMW, which in addition was a technical pleasure. The wedding was lovely but exhausting, with many

---

[12.] A book dealer in Berlin.

[13.] Letter not extant.

[14.] Martin Boeckheler.

[15.] Gerhard Leibholz.

[16.] Ursula Schleicher.

[17.] The wedding of Dorothea (née Vibrans) and Johannes Andersen in Annarode in the eastern Harz region.

[18.] Christine von Dohnanyi.

[19.] Klaus Bonhoeffer.

[20.] [The circumstances here are unclear.—VB]

[21.] Julius Rieger [see 1/106.—VB]

[22.] Sabine Leibholz.

[23.] George Bell.

[24.] [Julius Rieger.—VB]

[25.] This refers to their joint purchase of Kittel's *Theological Dictionary of the New Testament.* [Bonhoeffer and Bethge obviously split the cost for the expensive work.—VB]

good jokes. In the morning I preached the sermon, since Gerhard[26] had shingles, and, don't laugh, I preached on "I believe, dear Lord, help my unbelief"[27] with your divisions of the verse at hand.[28] I had—there was as good as *no* time to prepare—nonetheless great fun with it. Gerhard was reasonably fit and doing all right. Perhaps next Sunday I will hold the Lord's Supper that recently had to be canceled. I must then soon look for texts!

198 Otherwise we are all doing quite well. The sun shines often, and we are frequently at the Zignitz [lake], paddling. Tennis has also come up several times. If only you could be *with us*. You would find playing it somewhat more interesting than it was in Göttingen. Recently I irretrievably lost my cigarette roller while playing, which I'm quite sorry about. Here is a letter to you in English from John Baillie, 9 Whitehouse Terrace Edinburgh, Telephone 42647, of June 15, who spoke with Niebuhr about you and would like to see you there between October '39 and March '40.[29] He wants to have your visit, as Niebuhr wanted it in America, for around fourteen days perhaps. Perhaps you should write him immediately (or to Niebuhr first?); he requested a reply. It is[30] urgent.

I would like to invite Mrs. von Kleist[31] here soon. She has now also gotten sciatica. Mrs. Struwe[32] is doing quite well; she always comes to the prayer service and is now quite amicable and nice to me. Next week I will see my Superus[33] again. Winfried[34] left for vacation after he was here two more times with me, visiting and helping, and playing tennis.

Now be very, very warmly greeted by all of us here. We think regularly of you and pray for support for your work and blessing. I look forward to your next letter. Your

Eberhard

[26.] Gerhard Vibrans.
[27.] Mark 9:24.
[28.] Cf. *DBWE* 4:65–67.
[29.] See 1/113.
[30.] Deleted: "very."
[31.] Ruth von Kleist-Retzow.
[32.] Erna Struwe.
[33.] Superintendent Eduard Block in Schlawe.
[34.] Winfried Maechler (who had a ministry in Schlawe).

120. To Martin Boeckheler[1]

June 26

Dear Brother Boeckheler,

My plans over here have changed significantly. I will return already this summer. Now my question to you is: could I not step in for you for several weeks? After all, I am on leave and would like to stay a few weeks in London without becoming a burden on anyone. I could be there on July 15 or later,
in August till September, depending on what suits you better. I can stay here 199
as long as I want. But the political circumstances are driving me somewhat toward Europe.[2] I don't want to live through a war over here. And one can quickly reach Germany from where you are. Please do let me know promptly. I would also like to be in the old parish for a few weeks again and at the same time would have time for some work. Please be so kind and send an invitation in any case for the immigration-officer![3]

With cordial greetings, your
D. Bonhoeffer

121. To Karl-Friedrich Bonhoeffer[1]

June 26, 1939

Dear Karl Friedrich,

Many thanks for your card.[2] I let the Boerickes[3] know I would like to visit them next week, but that doesn't suit; now they want to have both of us from the fifth to the seventh. That, however, neither suits me nor probably you so well. This is how things stand here: I have turned down the job they offered me, for many reasons. With that I am now completely master of my time; I can stay or travel back, as I will. Now under normal circumstances

[1.] *NL*, A 45 (67); handwritten; no return address, surely from New York; previously unpublished.

[2.] The reference is to the worsening of the international political situation in Europe, particularly following the military alliance formed on May 22, 1939, between Germany and Italy (the "Steel Pact"); see Erdmann, *Die Zeit der Weltkriege*, 484–86.

[3.] ["Immigration-officer" in English in original.—VB]

[1.] *NL*, A 44,1 (27); handwritten card; no return address, certainly from New York. Previously published in *GS* 6:458–59. Karl-Friedrich Bonhoeffer had been invited in June 1939 to Chicago for various lectures (cf. *DB-ER*, 649 and 656).

[2.] Card not extant.

[3.] See Bonhoeffer's June 22, 1939, letter to his parents, 1/118.

I would have participated here in the Summer School,[4] which lasts until August, in which they also expect my assistance. But I find the political news from Europe so dreadful that I am seriously considering whether I should not travel back earlier. In case of war I want to be not over here but back in
200 Germany. I have pondered this here in these weeks, especially since no firm work is tying me down here. So what I am considering is whether I travel on the eighth with you to England, from where I can then come home much more easily. I believe too that in one month of intensive work here, one can have seen, read, and learned a good deal. What do you think about this? It would, of course, be nice if you could come already on July 1, for there is still much we could discuss. But if you must cancel other plans, perhaps this would not be absolutely necessary. Should I register you in International House?[5]

Many greetings your
Dietrich

122. To His Parents[1]

June 17, 1939

My dear Parents,

Now I have received both your letters, one right after the other.[2] I thank you very much for them. I had not written to Anneliese,[3] because the address was not certain and I feared it would perhaps not arrive. Now you have inquired there in vain; I am very sorry. It is simply too far a distance. Now, however, in the meantime you have received all the other news and hopefully have come to terms with it, as I have. I believe that it was very well intended, but impossible.[4] After it gave me a small shock at the beginning, I am now quite content. I think that when one has already been here for as long as I was previously,[5] one can deal with many things much more

[4.] ["Summer School" in English in original.—VB]

[5.] This was a residence for international students [and visitors—VB] in the neighborhood around Union Theological Seminary and Riverside Church.

[1.] *NL*, A 44,1 (28); handwritten; no return address, certainly from New York. Previously published in *GS* 6:459–50.

[2.] Letters not extant.

[3.] Anneliese Schnurmann in Switzerland.

[4.] [Bonhoeffer is commenting on his decision to return to Germany and turn down the job offer he had received in the United States.—VB]

[5.] [I.e., as a student in 1930–31.—VB]

quickly, and there is not that much to learn academically. I now sit very often in the library. I did not get to the Boerickes yet. But something will surely still come of it. At the end of this week, I expect Karl-Friedrich, who 201
can tell you. How is Uncle Rudi doing? Did they still travel to Bühlerhöhe?[6] If he is not doing well, I do want to come earlier. A few weeks now don't matter. This is what I am planning. Moreover, I do still want to visit Sabine.[7] Will your meeting still take place?[8] I wrote to Boeckheler about whether I could substitute for him during his holidays.[9] That would be rather nice. I am doing well. The heat in recent days has relented somewhat, so that one can work better. It is otherwise always dreadfully humid here. I am living in the loveliest area of Manhattan, directly on the Hudson and somewhat above the city. But it is probably even lovelier to live high up in one of the skyscrapers (the highest is 360 meters!). Again and again, the general impression of New York is indeed stunning, the skyscrapers, the masses of people from all nations and races milling about, the host of churches and chapels. But basically I have already become so accustomed to rural life that I often really long for it.

Please give my greetings to all my brothers and sisters. I will, of course, see them all again in autumn. Greetings to you from your grateful

Dietrich

123. Letter of Recommendation from Paul Lehmann to Colleges and Seminaries in the United States[1]

June 27, 1939

Dear Sir:

A committee of which Dr. Reinhold Niebuhr, Professor of Applied Christianity at the Union Theological Seminary, New York, is the chairman, is venturing to bring to your attention, the Reverend Dietrich Bonhoeffer, Licentiate in Theology.

[6.] This is an allusion to the day of the possible beginning of the war, additionally encoded here through a suggested visit to the Bühlerhöhe sanatorium in the northern Black Forest.

[7.] Sabine Leibholz in London.

[8.] [I.e., their visit to Sabine Leibholz.—VB]

[9.] See his June 26, 1939, letter to Martin Boeckheler, 1/120.

[1.] *NL*, A 50,2 (15); typewritten mimeograph; return address "Elmhurst College, Elmhurst, Illinois, Department of Religion." Previously published in *GS* 2:352–53. [Letter is in the original unaltered English.—VB]

202 Reverend Mr. Bonhoeffer is one of the ablest of the younger theologians and one of the most courageous of the younger pastors who have undertaken the task of the faithful exposition and perpetuation of the Christian faith in the present critical time in Germany. He comes from a distinguished line of forbears both in the pulpit and in the university. He himself holds a graduate theological degree from the University at Berlin and from the Union Theological Seminary at New York. Among the more notable of Mr. Bonhoeffer's contributions to theological learning are three brilliant and profound volumes on "The Communion of Saints," "Act and Being," and one published only recently under the title, "Community Life."[2]

During the academic year, 1930–1931, Mr. Bonhoeffer was a fellow in theology at Union Seminary and after his return to Germany he began a promising theological career as Privatdozent[3] in the theological faculty at Berlin. Political circumstances have interrupted these hopes. After a pastorate in the German Church in London, Mr. Bonhoeffer returned to his country and assumed the difficult responsibility of teaching the future ministers of the Confessional Church. Some time ago his little seminary was closed by the government and he has been continuing his work since then in a private capacity in the parsonages of Pommern.

Since Mr. Bonhoeffer will be lecturing in theology at the summer session of the Union Theological Seminary, New York, we are anxious to provide for him a wider hearing in American academic and theological circles. Accordingly, we are arranging a schedule of lectures at colleges and seminaries during the academic year, 1939–1940. If your institution has a lecture foundation or lecture series on a variety of problems, will you give favorable consideration to an invitation to Mr. Bonhoeffer to appear? He is in full command of the English language and prepared to discuss in a reliable and challenging manner problems of theology, philosophy, and the contemporary situation of Christianity in Germany. The committee is venturing to suggest an honorarium of not less than twenty-five dollars and, wherever possible, of fifty dollars.

I hope very urgently that we may have some word from you at the earliest possible moment. Correspondence either for Mr. Bonhoeffer or for the committee may be addressed to me at the address below. Your active cooperation

[2.] *DBWE* 1 (1st German publication, 1930); *DBWE* 2 (1st German publication, 1931); and *DBWE* 5 (published in English as *Life Together*) (1st German publication, 1939).

[3.] [That is, as an unpaid outside lecturer.—VB]

in this venture will be a real expression of the spirit of ecumenical Christianity and deeply appreciated.

Respectfully,
Paul L. Lehmann, Th.D.
Elmhurst College,
Elmhurst, Illinois

124. From Paul Lehmann to Reinhold Niebuhr[1] 203

June 28, 1939

Dear Reinie:

Immediately upon receipt of your letter of May 11,[2] I got started. I wrote at once to Dr. Press[3] and contacted Pauck[4] and Paul Scherer. The enclosed letter which I am sending out today to some thirty or forty places will speak for itself.[5] I hope replies will not come in too slowly.

Meanwhile a letter has come from Bonhoeffer who is already at Union. I don't quite know what to make of it for he speaks already of going back. He says that he is not a refugee and must go back to Germany to take up his work over there, for Germany needs teachers. "Ich will," he writes, "bis Spätherbst oder spätestens Frühjahr bleiben."[6]

What occurred to me at once was the Eden Theological lectures at Convocation. I ventured to ask Dr. Press to invite Bonhoeffer. He replied that he knew of Bonhoeffer and that the seminary which adds him to the faculty will indeed get an able theologian. What this has to do with my request, I do not comprehend. So I have written again today asking specifically for the lectureship for Bonhoeffer and saying that you regarded the matter as urgently as I do. Since Press asked me for your address, he may want to write to you about it. Therefore I want you to know what I am doing. We are inviting Bonhoeffer for the four Lenten sermons which come just about Eden convocation time. The two would fit beautifully together. As soon as I get replies to the general letter, I shall make up a schedule.

[1.] *NL*, A 50,2 (18); later typewritten copy; return address "Elmhurst College." Partially reproduced in *GS* 2:353–54. [Letter is in the original unaltered English.—VB]

[2.] See Niebuhr's May 11, 1939, letter to Lehmann, 1/91.

[3.] Samuel D. Press, president of Eden Theological Seminary in St. Louis.

[4.] Wilhelm Pauck.

[5.] See Lehmann's June 27, 1939, letter of recommendation, 1/123.

[6.] "I want to stay until late autumn or spring at the very latest." See Bonhoeffer's June 17, 1939, letter to Lehmann, 1/114.

Richter[7] will be teaching with us next Fall. The Board seems to have been surprisingly cooperative, the faculty mildly impressed. But it will be like a cultural tornado, which is exactly what this place needs.

The Christian Century brings glowing reports of your lectures.[8] For once I can agree with something that they are responsible for. It must be pleasant if pressing to work out the second set amidst the charms of the English country side. I still insist that it is the best thing the British have had in years. The real
204 shame is that you can't take over the foreign office as well while you are there. But they seem to prefer ostriches.[9]

We shall be leaving on Saturday for Columbus for the summer. We are practically exhausted from the ridiculous pace of the past month. Carlson[10] has gone over my manuscript for stylistic touches and that has helped a great deal. The title is still hanging fire. I hope very much that you will not be bothered with the stuff at the wrong time for you.

Already we are looking forward to your January visit. Meanwhile take our continuing thoughts and good wishes to Ursula,[11] yourself and the children, and if there is any way at any time that I can do something like this, please never hesitate to write. I'm never too busy or tired for your requests.

Affectionately,
Paul

125. From Paul Lehmann[1]

June 28, 1939

My dear Dietrich,

You cannot know with what joy and relief your letter[2] was received. It came to me just when I had to be away for some days and to take part in a conference here for some days, so that I have had to wait until now to reply. Evidently my

[7.] Werner Richter.

[8.] See Niebuhr's May 11, 1939, letter to Lehmann, 1/91, ed. note 2.

[9.] This refers to the politics of British foreign minister Lord Halifax, who was still attempting in the summer of 1939 to negotiate a political arrangement with Hitler's Germany, despite the March 31, 1939, declaration by the West to defend Poland. See Hildebrand, *Das vergangene Reich*, 680–82.

[10.] Unidentified.

[11.] [Niebuhr's wife.—VB]

[1.] *NL*, A 50,2 (16); later typewritten copy; return address: "Elmhurst College." Partially reproduced in *GS* 2:354–56. [Letter is in the original unaltered English.—VB]

[2.] See Bonhoeffer's June 17, 1939, letter to Lehmann, 1/114.

letter of May 27th, sent to Berlin will not have reached you.[3] Since that time, Marion[4] and I have been eagerly awaiting word of your arrival in Union. Now that you are there, we can scarcely wait until you are here with us.

Whether or not Dr. Niebuhr has been too optimistic,[5] I do not know. But I do know that it is unthinkable that you should return before America shall have 205
had the fullest opportunity to be enriched by your contribution to its theological hour of destiny. At least, I like to think of it in this way. The tragic political occasion for these disturbed times may have one great and positive overtone in the widening of the American theological understanding by the present cross fertilization with the continental tradition. So that you must see this also as a responsibility as well as the German need for teachers.

And besides, Marion and I need very badly to see you again. Surely you would not deprive us of the hope that we have carried with us since the day when we left the café on Unter den Linden.[6] With your anticipated permission, I have already taken steps to bring this about. The enclosed letter will speak for itself.[7] But meanwhile, there is more definite word for you. I am authorized to invite you to deliver the annual series of Lenten sermons which is a part of our campus religious life program. These occur on four succeeding Wednesdays during Lent and seek to interpret the Cross to the contemporary student mind. There will be one hundred dollars at your disposal for these sermons and you will live with us. At about the same time, Eden Seminary has a theological lectureship at its annual convocation. This is usually about mid-February. I have written asking that you be invited for these. I hope it will work out.

But whatever happens, Marion and I want you to know that our home is yours in every respect for as long a time as you are able and willing to have it so. There is no limit. And you cannot afford us any greater happiness than by acting with complete freedom on this promise.

Whether or not I shall get to New York this summer, I do not yet know. I am trying very hard to arrange some kind of a brief excursion there, specially to see you. We are leaving here on Saturday for Columbus, Ohio,[8] where we are likely to be until the first of September. The address there is 931 Oakwood Avenue. It should be just about that time that you will be ready to come west and we shall await you here. You will let me hear from you in Columbus, won't you?

[3.] See Lehmann's May 27, 1939, letter to Bonhoeffer, 1/97.

[4.] Marion Lehmann.

[5.] Note Bonhoeffer's June 17 letter to Lehmann: "[Reinhold] Niebuhr was perhaps *too optimistic*" (1/114).

[6.] Regarding Lehmann's visit to Berlin in spring 1933, see *DB-ER*, 267–69.

[7.] See Lehmann's June 27, 1939, letter of recommendation, 1/123.

[8.] Residence of the Lehmann family.

Sometime between July 9 and 12th, a very good friend of mine and former student, George Kalbfleisch by name, will try to visit you in Union. He is en route to Amsterdam and expects to visit Germany. It was through him that I hoped to send you some word of reply to your earlier letter at Christmas time.[9] Since he expects to visit Germany, there may be some word that you might like to send.
206 I simply mention this in order that you may know that you can have complete confidence in him. I have told him so much of you and am anxious that you meet.

As soon as replies to the letter which I am mailing today to some thirty or forty places come to me, you will hear more. Meanwhile do keep in touch with me and remember how anxious we are to have you with us again.

Marion joins me in kindest greetings and highest regard,

Paul

126. To Paul Lehmann[1]

28.6.39

Dear Paul,

I wonder if you have received my letter last week.[2] Things have changed for me entirely. I am going back to Germany on August 2nd or even July 25th. The political situation is so terrible. But, of course, I should like to have a word from you before I leave. I am enjoying a few weeks in freedom, but on the other hand, I feel, I must go back to the "trenches" (I mean of the Church-struggle). Yours ever

Dietrich Bonhoeffer

[9.] See Bonhoeffer's December 14, 1938, letter to Lehmann, 1/40.

[1.] *NL*, A 50,2 (17); typewritten copy; return address: "Union Theological Seminary, New York." Previously published in *GS* 2:356. [Letter is in the original unaltered English.—VB]

[2.] See Bonhoeffer's June 17, 1939, letter to Lehmann, 1/114.

127. From Eberhard Bethge[1]

June 29, 1939

My dear Dietrich,

Many warm thanks for your letter[2] yesterday and the card[3] today. I am *very* sorry indeed that as late as this you must still write that you hadn't received anything. I now definitely hope that you have received our first letters. You should 207
now already have three letters from me. Apparently the delivery tempo varies considerably. My letter yesterday from you took at least ten days. Mrs. Struwe's card on the other hand only seven to eight days; it came at the same time.

I can imagine how you sometimes feel. Your letter conveys to me, I believe, a very vivid impression. But I nonetheless took great pleasure in your careful and detailed reports. Each piece interested me. How I would have liked to be there; how much I would have liked to have helped you in your considerations, to the extent help was possible. Believe me, the prospect of seeing you again sooner indeed fills me with very great joy, despite all appreciation for the tempting offers and the difficulty of giving it up. It will be good to be together again! But how will it happen? Where do I come? I must certainly pick you up somewhere! One thing, however, is clear for me. In no case can I leave Mother[4] during the days of the wedding; around September 15,[5] I *must* be there and help with planning, organizing, and so forth. That should be my obligation under any circumstances, right? But before and even more so afterward there is time! Then we will be off on a trip clear across Germany!! Yesterday I was at Koppelstrasse[6] again for the first time (even if only very briefly, because of pastoral duties) and related a few things that pleased them. As always, one is suntanned, relaxed, and in a good mood!

[1.] *NL*, C 26; handwritten; no return address, certainly from Sigurdshof; previously unpublished.

[2.] Letter not extant.

[3.] The card to Bethge has been lost; it was inserted in Bonhoeffer's June 20, 1939, card to Elisabeth Bethge; see 1/116, ed. note 3.

[4.] Elisabeth Bethge.

[5.] The wedding of Margret Bethge [Eberhard's sister—VB] and Fritz Onnasch in Kade. The wedding took place on September 17, 1939, officiated by Superintendent Friedrich Onnasch, who was imprisoned from September 9 to October 9, 1939, and received prison leave for the occasion. Bonhoeffer was able to participate as well.

[6.] In Schlawe, at the office of Superintendent Eduard Block and Winfried Maechler; the latter had been on vacation. See Bethge's June 23, 1939, letter, 1/119, ed. note 34.

As to celebrating the Lord's Supper, once more we had to postpone things a week. Aunt Ruth[7] will perhaps visit us for it. Do you sometimes get to the meditation texts? John 17 is almost too difficult, and I turn very often to the Greek text. Recently over there[8] I again had a very hard fight about the sin, which was witnessed to, and the grace, which was not to be witnessed to but rather, in a disapproving fashion, was to be proven through the portrayal of the circumstances of Christian examples. Now the work on the psalms of vengeance, which is always very fruitful, comes next.

I had a very detailed letter from your mother describing their vacation, with a personal greeting from your father, in reply to my thank-you letter back then.[9]
208 I was very pleased about it. Julius[10] has already gone back, without my having been able to reach him, nor has he sent me anything (the dartboard). He writes that he discussed the curriculum for my studies there.[11] I don't quite know what is happening now; for the time being I won't do anything on my part.

Perhaps you have enjoyed the pictures somewhat. They are meant not to increase your loneliness but on the contrary perhaps to help a bit. I hardly get around to playing music at all, due to being abundantly occupied. Yesterday afternoon I was at the manor house[12] for coffee; that always takes time, and then one also wants to use the opportunity to play tennis! Then perhaps the two of us will still play this year? Tell me, isn't it impossible for me to pick you up at the end of August? Because of here?[13] As glad as I would be to do it. It would be interesting indeed in any case.

Very heartfelt greetings and God protect you and bless your work, your
Eberhard

[7.] Ruth von Kleist-Retzow

[8.] [I.e., in the collective pastorate in Köslin.—VB]

[9.] See Bethge's June 12, 1939, letter to Paula and Karl Bonhoeffer, 1/110.

[10.] Julius Rieger.

[11.] Plans for Bethge's possible emigration to England.

[12.] The estate of the Kleist family at Wendisch-Tychow.

[13.] As "inspector of studies" for the Sigurdshof collective pastorate, with teaching responsibilities in Köslin, Bethge could not leave in midsemester.

128. To Paul Lehmann[1]

June 30, 1939

My dear Paul,

thank you so much for your good letter which is so full of friendship and
hope for the future.[2] I can hardly bring myself to tell you that in the mean-
time I have had to decide to return to Germany, already in the next few
weeks. Behind my invitation here lay the misunderstanding that I intended
to remain in America for good. They wanted to assign me the care of Chris-
tian refugees here, a job that would have prevented me from any return to
Germany, as necessary as it is in itself. It must, however, be done by a refu- 209
gee. Now in the meantime everything has been decided and has also been
settled with the Confessing Church; I shall travel back in July or August.
While I regret this for various reasons, on the other hand, I am also glad
to be given the opportunity to help again over there very soon. I am being
pulled toward the brothers in struggle. You will understand this! Now I
have one urgent request: in your very friendly letter to the Colleges[3] you
mentioned my work in Pomerania. Should such a page come into the hands
of a German official, the work that in the meantime continues would be at
an end. Will you understand my asking you sincerely and urgently to write
immediately to the same circle that I have already returned and all plans
have been canceled, perhaps also (which would be important to me) that
a misunderstanding had prevailed in the matter! I hope that the circle is
trustworthy enough not to let the letter go further. Now you have had much
work, and I thank you for this with all my heart! I am infinitely sorry that we
will not see each other. I had expected, especially from a meeting with you,
so much toward understanding the situation here and many other things.
Now this will not come to pass. It is such a pity! But there is no longer any
other way! I am now expected back there soon. The political situation is
dreadful, and I must be with my brothers when things become serious. We
will then often think of each other and be with each other in prayer, and
we will leave it to God as to whether and when he will lead us back together
again in a way we can see. In such "final" times everyone should be found
at the place where he belongs. May God grant us that we stand firm there.

[1.] *NL*, A 50,2 (19); later typewritten copy; return address "Union Theological Seminary, New York." Previously published in *GS* 2:357–58. [The first sentence of this letter is in English; Bonhoeffer wrote the remainder of the letter in German.—VB]

[2.] See Lehmann's June 28, 1939, letter to Bonhoeffer, 1/125.

[3.] Lehmann's June 27, 1939, letter of recommendation, 1/123. ["Colleges" in English in original.—VB]

Forgive the trouble I have put you to! See to it that people tacitly regard the matter as finished. From now on, please do not mention anything at all about Pomerania, etc. in your letter, nor that the matter should not reach any German official; instead it's best to just state that "the inquiry concerning Mr. D.B. in the meantime has been resolved through his return to
210 Germany and that a misunderstanding had prevailed in the matter." That would be my preference and the best thing for my work over there, which is so urgently necessary. To say more could awaken unnecessary interest. And please, do this without delay!

Do not believe that I regret the journey here. I am very happy that I was here and have seen and learned much in one month. My greatest pain is that I did not see you and your wife.

Now be well, dear Paul! May God protect you both and give you strength and joy for the work; may God preserve our fellowship as well, as he has done up to now.

Greetings to you in old faithfulness and gratitude always, your
Dietrich Bonhoeffer

PS I travel presumably already on July 8!

129. To Reinhold Niebuhr[1]

. . . Sitting here in Dr. Coffin's[2] garden I have had the time to think and to pray about my situation and that of my nation and to have God's will for me clarified. I have come to the conclusion that I have made a mistake in coming to America. I must live through this difficult period of our national history with the Christian people of Germany. I will have no right to participate in the reconstruction of Christian life in Germany after the war if I do not share the trials of this time with my people. My brothers in the Confessional Synod wanted me to go. They may have been right in urging me to do so; but I was wrong in going. Such a decision each man must make for himself. Christians in Germany will face the terrible alternative of either willing the defeat of their nation in order that Christian civilization may survive, or willing the victory of their nation and thereby destroying our civilization. I know which of these alternatives I must choose; but I cannot make that choice in security. . . .

[1.] Excerpt from a letter to Niebuhr from New York at the end of June 1939, cited by Niebuhr in "The Death of a Martyr," *Christianity and Crisis* 5, no. 11 (June 25, 1945): 6. The original of the letter has never been found. Previously published in *GS* 1:320.

[2.] Henry Sloane Coffin.

129a. Inscription to Henry Sloan Coffin[1] in *Nachfolge*

To President H. S. Coffin in sincere gratitude and respect. Dietrich Bonhoeffer.

130. To His Parents[1] 211

July 1, 1939

My dear Parents,

Karl Friedrich has already written you today to say that I have booked a room on a ship, if need arises. Since I would have come in any case in the fall, the latest news made the thought of possibly not being able to travel back in time utterly impossible for me. I will still visit Sabine,[2] as long as that can be done. Here I have seen almost all my friends, and that was very lovely. Karl Friedrich will still visit Irma Boericke. It is not yet certain whether I will still find time to visit her after everything has been arranged. Of course, I still have many plans. Would you please write to me c/o Sabine's address the date of Uncle Rudi's birthday,[3] so that I can eventually still congratulate him personally? The friends here would still like to keep me here. But I cannot decide in favor of staying. There will be much to talk about. Your vacation plans will also be very uncertain.

Warm greetings to you and all my brothers and sisters, your grateful
Dietrich

[1.] This inscription in ink ["Herrn Präsident H. S. Coffin in aufrichtiger Dankbarkeit und Verehrung. Dietrich Bonhoeffer"] appears on a recto leaf inside the front cover of a 1st edition of *Nachfolge*. It was found in the open stacks of Burke Library, Union Theological Seminary, when a collection of archival papers and memorabilia were assembled for the visit to the seminary, in May 2009, of the scientist Friedrich Bonhoeffer, Dietrich Bonhoeffer's nephew and the son of his brother Karl-Friedrich. This volume is now housed in the Special Collections at Burke Library. Note by Clifford Green. First publication, with two similar inscriptions, in the *Dietrich Bonhoeffer Jahrbuch* 4, with notes and commentary by Clifford Green ("Commentary: Three Bonhoeffer Inscriptions at Union Theological Seminary Library"). The date of the inscription would be after November 1937, likely in the summer of 1939. While it is possible that Bonhoeffer mailed a copy to Coffin when the book was first published, it is more likely that he brought some copies with him on his visit in the summer of 1939.

[1.] *NL*, A 44,1 (29); handwritten postcard; no return address, but certainly from New York. Partially reproduced in *GS* 2:359.

[2.] Sabine Leibholz in London.

[3.] This was the code word for the beginning of the war.

131. From Paul Lehmann[1]

Columbus, Ohio July 2, 1939

My dear Dietrich:

Your letter[2] was awaiting me when I arrived here this morning. It was of great help in explaining your card[3] which I received in Elmhurst on last Thursday. But I cannot tell you how deeply it troubles both Marion[4] and me. I write now, believe me, with great heaviness of spirit.

212 I shall, of course, comply immediately with your request. Please know that I do so with great reluctance and out of a full understanding of your situation. On such a basis you are not entitled to speak of effort expended and kindnesses shown. The principle matter of concern is you and the cause to which you are devoted.

Now, I have the following to propose: we must meet before your return. I simply could not think of your being here and going back without it. Therefore, you must be good enough to let me know by return mail which time will be best for my coming to New York. Since the friend about whom I wrote you[5] is planning to come to New York next Saturday, July 8, arriving Sunday morning, July 9th, I wonder whether or not you could wait long enough to make possible my coming with him. Then I could also be with him when he sails on July 12th. On the other hand, if you must sail on the 8th, as you suggest, I shall come at once. We must have some opportunity to talk together.

Will you let me have word by return mail? Do you think also that you could explain my coming to Emmanuel[6] and ask him whether I might have a bed at the Seminary for the few days, I shall be there? Please go to no trouble over this. If it cannot be, I shall arrange when I come.

Meanwhile, I shall look forward to seeing you and Marion joins me in the prayerful commitment of our ways to Him who bringeth all things to pass[7] and in continuing, affectionate regard,

Paul

[1.] *NL*, A 50,2 (20); later typewritten copy; reprinted in *GS* 2:359–60. [Letter is in the original unaltered English.—VB]

[2.] See Bonhoeffer's June 30, 1939, letter to Lehmann, 1/128.

[3.] See Bonhoeffer's June 28, 1939, card to Lehmann, 1/126.

[4.] Marion Lehmann.

[5.] George Kalbfleisch.

[6.] The house manager at Union Theological Seminary.

[7.] Cf. Ps. 37:5.

132. Circular Letter from Paul Lehmann to Colleges and Seminaries in the United States[1]

July 3, 1939

Dear Sir:

Under date of June 27th,[2] a communication was addressed to you in behalf of the Reverend Dietrich Bonhoeffer, Licentiate in Theology. It concerned the desire of a committee of which Dr. Reinhold Niebuhr is the chairman, to make Mr. Bonhoeffer's visit to America available to colleges and seminaries interested in his lectures.

Word has just come that the circumstances of Mr. Bonhoeffer's visit to the 213
United States have been entirely misunderstood and that the contemplated opportunity of inviting him cannot materialize owing to his return to Germany.

The committee appreciates the courtesy of your interest in its effort and regrets very much the error of its earlier communication.

Respectfully,
Paul L. Lehmann,
Th.D., Secretary

133. To Paul Lehmann[1]

July 3, 1939

My dear Paul,

Many, many thanks for your letter![2] Of course, I would be *very* happy to still see you, and your offer to come is more than I dared to think. Of course, I can also arrange my schedule as I wish. But I must depart on the evening of July 8. Can you really undertake the long journey for such a short time? Or is that not too much? Please don't overtax yourself! I will probably

---

[1.] *NL*, A 50,2 (21); typewritten mimeograph; return address: "Elmhurst College, Elmhurst Illinois, Department of Religion." Previously published in *GS* 2:360–61. [Letter is in original unaltered English.—VB]

[2.] See Lehmann's June 27, 1939, letter of recommendation, 1/123.

[1.] *NL*, A 50,2 (22); later typewritten copy; from New York. Previously published in *GS* 2:361.

[2.] See Lehmann's July 2, 1939, letter to Bonhoeffer, 1/131.

hear more from you. The enclosed letter[3] was exactly what I had in mind. Sincere thanks!

Always in faithfulness your
Dietrich Bonhoeffer

214 **134. To His Parents**[1]

July 3, 1939

My dear Parents,

Today your letter from Switzerland arrived.[2] Thank you very much for it. In the meantime you will have received our mail from here. Today I will try an airmail letter. An airplane is supposed to go out on the fifth. Since tomorrow is a major holiday here—Independence day[3]—I am already writing today so that the letter goes off for certain. There is not much to tell, since we wrote only two days ago.[4] The news continues to make us uneasy here, and nowhere can one learn what is really going on. In any case, I am staying at present with my plan to travel together with Karl Friedrich. Ultimately, four weeks here more or less should not be of any consequence. Of course, it is a real shame. The other decision would in any case be all too incalculable. I would be very happy to find news from you at Sabine's.[5] I will, of course, not stay there very long, and their vacation plans appear to me to be rather uncertain. Karl Friedrich is downtown all day today, at the consulate, the party,[6] etc., so we will see each other only this evening; I still hope to visit several friends. Aunt Irma[7] sent a very nice letter today.

[3.] Lehmann's July 3, 1939, circular letter to colleges and seminaries, 1/132.

[1.] *NL*, A 44,1 (30); handwritten; no return address, certainly from New York. Partially reproduced in *GS* 6:461–62.

[2.] Letter not extant.

[3.] ["Independence day" in English in the original.—VB]

[4.] See Bonhoeffer's July 1, 1939, letter to his parents, 1/130.

[5.] Sabine Leibholz in London.

[6.] The reference is to the NSDAP organization abroad, which at the time was represented at all major German consulates. Among other things, its role was to examine the political reliability of Germans who traveled abroad, and in some cases to denounce them to the regime in order to prevent them from obtaining visas for future trips abroad. [Regarding party surveillance of Bonhoeffer during his period in London, see *DBWE* 13:262, 264–66, 293.—VB]

[7.] Irma Boericke; the letter mentioned is not extant.

Karl Friedrich is decided on going there. By the way, Karl Friedrich and I had a long conversation with Gert[8] before our departure. It was necessary. I will, of course, see him soon. By the way, I would like to have a letter to Sabine from Eberhard. I have heard almost nothing from there and want to
[know] when they're taking vacation at the seaside and whether a substitute 215
is there. Karl Friedrich is also in the midst of major deliberations, as you know.[9] I wonder whether Walter[10] knows enough English to come here sometime? I could certainly procure an invitation for him. He should write me there too, if he wishes. He would have to pay for the journey himself. That's it for today. Hopefully, the letter will arrive safely. Many greetings to you and my brothers and sisters, your grateful

Dietrich

135. To Erwin Sutz[1]

Dear brother Sutz,

You will be not a little surprised to receive a card from me here. I was invited to be here at Union for one month.[2] It was good and instructive, but I am being pulled irresistibly back toward the Confessing Church. Tomorrow I will depart. I have thought of you often and spoken of you. Coffin, Bewer, and others send their regards.[3]

In old faithfulness, regards from your
Dietrich Bonhoeffer

[8.] Gerhard Leibholz.

[9.] This refers to plans to accept a professorship in the United States that had been offered to him; Karl-Friedrich turned down the call to Chicago. See *DB-ER*, 656.

[10.] Walter Dreß.

[1.] In the personal possession of the Sutz family; handwritten postcard; postmarked: New York, 5.7.1939. Cf. *NL*, A Anh. A 8 (3). Partially reproduced in *GS* 1:49.

[2.] Union Theological Seminary.

[3.] Henry Sloane Coffin and Julius A. Bewer. Sutz and Bonhoeffer had become acquainted when both were studying at Union Seminary in 1930–31. See *DB-ER*, 153, and *DBWE* 10.

216 **136. From Reinhold Niebuhr to Paul Lehmann**[1]

Dear Paul:

Thank you for your kind letter. I am sorry about all the trouble you have had at my suggestion with Bonhoeffer. A letter from Van Dusen[2] in the same mail with yours informs me that Bonhoeffer is returning on August 8. I do not understand it at all. He wanted to stay out for a year and [I] don't understand why he changed his plans after we made the arrangements.

I am working on my third lecture right now.[3] Have been at it so long that I feel the whole thing to be stale and unprofitable. I don't find it easy to get material in the libraries in London so the second series will be thin and will have to be reworked. Karl Barth's son Marcus was at the lectures and he thought them very heretical. A very nice lad but 102% Barthian. He believes that if there were no ten commandments no one would ever have known that it is wrong to kill. That kind of stuff gets me quite madly liberal.

You are right about the English countryside. We have a lovely spot in Sussex where we will be till September 1st. The children are doing well. I enclose a photo. I do hope you and Marion[4] will have a good rest this summer. For goodness sake don't do everything they ask you to do.

Terribly sorry to have increased your work futilely about Bonhoeffer. Please send me a bill for the actual expenses.

Love from Ursula[5] to Marion. Affectionately yours,

Reinie

[1.] *NL*, A 50, 2 (26); typewritten carbon copy with handwritten signature; return address "The Moat House, Wivelsfield, Sussex, July 8th [1939]"; previously unpublished. [Letter is in the original unaltered English.—VB]

[2.] Henry P. Van Dusen.

[3.] See Niebuhr's May 11, 1939, letter to Lehmann, 1/91, ed. note 2.

[4.] Marion Lehmann.

[5.] Ursula Niebuhr.

137. American Diary[1] 217

June 8, 1939[2]

Zech. 7:9: "Render true judgments, show kindness and mercy to one another."[3]

Matt. 5:7: "Blessed are the merciful, for they will receive mercy."

Yesterday evening, shortly after I had written,[4] I became acquainted with a young American theologian, a former Union man.[5] That was as if my prayers had been heard. We spoke of Christ in Germany and in America and in Sweden, from where he had just come. The task in America became great again to me.

"Render true judgments and . . ." I request that first of you, my brothers at home. I do not want to be spared in your thoughts. But what does it mean to render true judgment before the merciful God, before the cross of Jesus Christ, other than to be merciful? Not a blind mercy; for that would not be merciful, but a seeing, forgiving, fraternal mercy as the just judgment upon us.

"Render true judgments and . . ." This is a compelling warning and directive for the task in America. It forbids all overconfidence and makes the *task* great. To see brothers in the Others, who stand just as much under the mercy of Jesus Christ as all of us, who have a right to a brotherly word, without glossing over, without prejudice, without arrogance, and full of merciful love. Only when we ourselves live and speak entirely from the mercy of Christ and no longer at all out of our own and particular knowledge or experience, then we will be not sanctimonious but merciful. If only God remains merciful to *us*!

[1.] *NL*, A 50,1; typewritten copy made later by Eberhard Bethge (the original has not been found). Partially reproduced in *GS* 1:292–315. On Bonhoeffer's trip to the United States in June–July 1939, see *DB-ER*, 648–62.

[2.] Written aboard the *Bremen* en route from Southampton to New York, via Cherbourg.

[3.] This verse and the following verses throughout the diary are the daily watchwords and interpretive verses from the Moravian Daily Texts.

[4.] Cf. 1/107, Bonhoeffer's June 7, 1939, postcard to Bethge.

[5.] The man is not identified.

218 June 9, 1939

Isa. 41:9: "You are my servant, I have chosen you and not cast you off."

John 12:26: "Whoever serves me must follow me, and where I am, there will my servant be also."

God chooses the sinner as servant, in order that God's grace becomes entirely clear. The sinner is to do God's work and spread God's grace. Whomever God has forgiven, God gives this person a service to do. But this service can consist in nothing other than in discipleship. Great programs always lead us only to where we ourselves are; we, however, should be found only where God is. We cannot be anywhere other than where God is. Whether you work over there or I work in America, we are both only where God is. God takes us along. Or have I indeed evaded the place where God is? where God is *for me*? No, God says: You are my servant.

June 10, 1939

Ps.[6] 28:7: "The Lord is my strength and my shield; in him my heart trusts; so I am helped, and my heart exults, and with my song I give thanks to him."

Eph. 4:30: "And do not grieve the Holy Spirit of God, with which you were marked with a seal for the day of redemption."

Wherein can "the heart exult" except in the daily certitude that God is our loving father and Jesus Christ is our savior! With what could we grieve the Holy Spirit more than by giving way to sad thoughts rather than entrusting ourselves confidently to the Spirit's direction, his language, his comfort? until the day of redemption is there, is finally there!

219 June 11, 1939

Ps. 44:21: "For he knows the secrets of the heart."

1 Cor. 13:12: "For now we see in a mirror, dimly, but then we will see face to face."

[6.] The typescript erroneously states "Isaiah."

Today is Sunday. No worship service. Moreover, the hours have already shifted so that I cannot take part in your worship[7] as it is happening. But I am fully with you, today more than ever. If only the doubts about my own path were overcome. The own search for the secrets of the heart, which are unfathomable—"for God knows the secrets of our heart." When the confusion of reproaches and excuses, of wishes and fears makes everything in us opaque, God sees in all clarity right through to the bottom. There, however, God finds the very name that he himself has inscribed: Jesus Christ. And thus we will someday see in all clarity, right through to the bottom of the divine heart, and there will be one name to read, no, to see there: Jesus Christ.—Thus let us celebrate Sunday. Someday we will come to know and behold what we believe today, someday we will worship together in eternity.

The beginning, the end, O Lord, they are thine,
The span in between, the life, was mine.
And if I erred in the darkness and found no way out,
With you, Lord, is clearness, and light is your house. Reuter[8]

A little time still and I have won.
Then all the strife at once is done.
Then I may rest in valleys sweet,
Continually with Jesus speak.[9]

This afternoon a former student from the Harnack seminar,[10] Miss Dr. 220
Ferber,[11] addressed me. She has a job in the information office on the *Bremen.*[12] We had a good talk.

[7.] Bonhoeffer is referring to Bethge and the candidates in the collective pastorate in Sigurdshof.

[8.] This is the first verse of the epitaph written by the novelist Fritz Reuter for his own gravestone in Eisenach (Reuter, *Sämtliche Werke* 1:35); cf. also *DBWE* 10:555, ed. note 10, and *DBW* 14:777 and 925.

[9.] The inscription chosen by Søren Kierkegaard for his own grave. This is a verse from a hymn by Hans Adolf Brorson, whose hymns Kierkegaard greatly loved (Geismar, *Søren Kierkegaard,* 636. Translation by Ann R. Born; http://www.webcom.com/kierke/bio/church.html).

[10.] On Bonhoeffer's participation in Adolf von Harnack's church history seminar during the 1920s in Berlin, see *DB-ER,* 67–68, and *DBWE* 10:621–26.

[11.] Not otherwise identified.

[12.] See ed. note 2.

June 12, 1939

Deut. 6:6: "Keep these words that I am commanding you today in your heart."

Acts 15:40: "But Paul chose Silas and set out, the brothers[13] commending him to the grace of the Lord."

"Paul set out, the brothers commending him to the grace of the Lord." Arrival in New York. To know in these first hours that brothers have commended us to the grace of the Lord was decisive. Rev. Macy[14] from the Federal Council of Churches[15] welcomed me at the pier. First night in the Parkside Hotel. In the evening Dr. Sch.[16] picked me up. The entire problematic of the German [. . .][17] became evident. Great disappointment about [. . .][18] at Harvard; appears utterly resigned.

June 13, 1939

Breakfast with Leiper,[19] who welcomes me most cordially and picks me up. First consultations about the future. I state, as the clear point of departure for everything, that I intend to go back after one year at the latest. Surprise. But it is entirely clear to me that I must go back.—Visit to the office. An entire city block is filled with church offices of every kind.

221 After several preliminary conversations and appointments made by telephone, on to Union Theological Seminary and the Prophets' Chamber[20] with a lovely view of the Quadrangle. I had forgotten a great deal; but everything came back quickly, right up to the smell of the house.—Lunch with Van Dusen.[21] Earlier I quarreled with him.[22] He was a poor and self-

---

[13.] [Here the NRSV has "believers."—VB]

[14.] Paul Macy.

[15.] The Federal Council of Churches of Christ in the USA was founded in 1908 by various churches and North American Protestant associations that were close to the "social gospel" (with its emphasis on the social significance of the gospel).

[16.] Probably Paul Scherer.

[17.] A word is missing in the typescript; possibly "emigration."

[18.] A word is missing in the typescript.

[19.] Henry Smith Leiper.

[20.] This was the guest room at Union Theological Seminary.

[21.] Henry P. van Dusen.

[22.] [In 1930–31, Bonhoeffer attended the seminar on philosophical theology taught by John Baillie, Eugene Lyman, and Van Dusen (cf. *DBWE* 10:643). While Bonhoeffer does not mention Van Dusen there directly, see *DBWE* 10:308–10 for his low opinion of much of the academic theology at Union. (Bonhoeffer did not care for Van Dusen

righteous theologian of the American mold. Here for the first time I realize graphically the great change in American theology in the last eight years. The cause for which we were engaged in 1930,[23] apparently utterly hopelessly, has come to prevail in the course of the years. How this came about is not yet clear to me. Perhaps only a culture crisis? One speaks often of the human being's forlornness, of the "sins" of human beings; the optimistic evolutionism is past. But is it perhaps just the replacement of an optimistic view of humankind by a pessimistic one? What is known and proclaimed of the gospel, of Jesus Christ himself? That is the question. Meeting with President Coffin[24] at Grand Central at four o'clock. On the train, an hour and a half conversation about the American situation. Strange, how critically Coffin speaks about his own colleagues. I believe that we can no longer do that at home. There is too much that connects us, for all the difference in opinions. Continuation of the conversation with Van Dusen. Coffin is a clear, practical man. He sees the necessity of preaching the gospel. He says: "Niebuhr[25] preaches a half hour about the 'failure of man' and the last two minutes about the 'grace of God.'"[26] If this is true in general, then people here stand now where we stood fifteen years ago.—Interesting, the reports about the re-union[27] of Episcopal and Presbyterian, mutual recognition as Churches of Christ, and of ordination. (Apostolic succession among the Presbyterians recognized by the Episcopalians as acceptable through the presbyteries. Somewhat questionable, it remains an institutional understanding of succession!)

The country house in Lakeville, Connecticut, is in the mountains; it is 222
cool and lush vegetation. In the evenings thousands of fireflies in the garden, flying lightning bugs. I had never seen them. Utterly fantastic sight. Very cordial and "informal" reception. For all that, only Germany, the brothers, are missing. The first solitary hours are hard. I don't comprehend

---

personally; see the June 20, 1939, entry from this diary.) While Bonhoeffer here emphasizes how his U.S. acquaintances and their theology have changed, one wonders if his reevaluation of American theology in 1939 was not also influenced by his experiences of the failures of his church and theologians in Germany and his own changed perspective after several years under National Socialism. And he remained quite critical of U.S. theology, particularly the sermons he heard in New York; see, for example, the diary entry for July 3, 1939. See also the comments on this in my introduction to this volume.—VB]

[23.] During Bonhoeffer's studies at Union in 1930–31. Regarding this, see Bonhoeffer's 1931 report on his year of study to the Church Federation Office, *DBWE* 10, 1/181.

[24.] Henry Sloane Coffin, president of Union Seminary.

[25.] Reinhold Niebuhr.

[26.] ["Failure of man" and "grace of God" are in English in the original.—VB]

[27.] ["Re-union" is in English in the original.—VB]

why I am here, whether it was sensible, whether the outcome will be worth it. In the evenings the last thing: the Daily Texts and the thought of the work at home. Almost two weeks have passed now without my knowing anything from over there. That is hardly bearable. "It is good that one should wait quietly for the salvation of the Lord" (Lam. 3:26).[28]

June 14, 1939

Breakfast on the veranda at eight o'clock. During the night it poured. Everything is fresh and cool. Afterward devotions. The short prayer—the whole family kneels—in which we thought of the German brothers almost overwhelmed me. Then reading, writing, a drive out to deliver invitations for the evening. In the evening some twenty-five people, pastors, teachers with wives and friends. Very amicable encounters without yielding anything in particular.

June 15, 1939

Since yesterday evening my thoughts cannot get away from Germany. I would not have thought it possible that one at my age after so many years abroad can become so agonizingly homesick. In the morning a car drive that was in itself beautiful, to a woman acquaintance in the countryside, that is, in the mountains, became almost unbearable to me. One sat for an hour and chatted, not at all stupidly, but about matters that were so utterly trivial to me, whether a good musical education is possible in New York, about raising children, etc. etc., and I thought, how usefully I could
223 spend these hours in Germany. I would have liked to take the next ship. This inactivity, or rather activity spent on trivialities, is simply no longer bearable for us, thinking of the brothers and the precious time. The full force of self-reproaches about a wrong decision comes back up and is almost suffocating. I was filled with despair. In the afternoon I attempted to work somewhat. Then I was invited to a second drive to the mountains of Massachusetts. It was very ill-timed for me. I had not even found the quiet to read the Bible and for prayer. The drive was lovely. We passed through a whole stretch of laurel woods. The view from above was somewhat similar to the Harz countryside. But the pressure didn't leave me all day. In the evening the cinema: *Juarez* with P. Muni.[29] A good film. My thoughts were captured

[28.] The Daily Text for that day.

[29.] The 1939 film *Juarez* (directed by William Dieterle) with Paul Muni in the role of Benito Pablo Juarez.

for a while.—By the way, another letter to Leiper: I must return in one year at the latest.[30] How happy I was, when in the evening I opened the Daily Texts again and read: "My heart rejoices, for you have dealt bountifully with me"(Ps. 13:6).[31]

June 16, 1939

Only fourteen days ago today from Berlin, and already so filled with longing for the work again. Return to New York. Finally evening. I needed that urgently. One is less lonely when one is alone. Afternoon to evening the World's Fair.[32] The strongest impression perhaps the [. . .][33] pavilion. The Russians are too pompous, and in addition completely bourgeois. Most of the others too commercialized. Overall no particular impression. In the "Temple of Religion" Christians and Jews preach in turns. The whole building is dreadful, a movie theater. By the way: how much cleaner New York is than London. Neither on the trains nor on the street do people smoke. Also technologically more advanced or sophisticated (ventilation on every subway). But also how much more international New York is than London. 224
Of the people that I spoke to today, at least half spoke a very terrible broken English. For a good American this constant murder of the language must be an abomination!

I wait for mail! It can hardly be endured. I will probably not stay long. God's word today states: "See, I am coming soon—."[34] No time is to be lost, and here I am losing days, perhaps weeks. In any case, that's how it looks at present. Then, on the other hand, I tell myself: it is cowardice and weakness to run away from here now. But will I ever really be able to do meaningful work here?—Disturbing political news from Japan.[35] If turmoil now breaks out, I will definitely travel to Germany. I cannot be alone abroad. That is utterly clear to me. I do live over there, after all.

[30.] See Bonhoeffer's June 15, 1939, letter to Henry S. Leiper, 1/111.

[31.] [NRSV: "My heart shall rejoice. . . . I will sing to the Lord, because he has dealt bountifully with me" (Ps. 13:5–6).—VB]

[32.] The 1939–40 World's Fair in New York.

[33.] A word is missing in the typescript.

[34.] Rev. 3:11.

[35.] There was heavy fighting between Japanese and Soviet troops around the Manchurian-Mongolian border (the Lake Khasan and Nomonhan incidents) and tensions with the United States before the cancellation of the Japanese-American trade agreement on July 26, 1939.

June 17, 1939

The whole day in the library looking through *Christian Century*. Instructive essays: "How my mind has changed in the last decade."[36] Theology professors about the change in American theology since 1929. The decisive turn toward the Word appears to have not yet occurred, but rather a turn from belief in progress to nihilism, from ethicism to a philosophy of the "present," of the "concrete situation." Report on the most recent lynching of a black person. Two white persons enter the home and pray with the blacks "that the day may come when such things will not happen in America."[37] That is a good resolution of such events.—Furthermore, a report on the
225 areligiosity of college students, "disinterested."[38] That must be what comes if one doesn't finally understand that "religion" is truly superfluous.

June 18, 1939—Sunday

Worship at Riverside Church. Simply unbearable. Text: a statement by Jane James (!)[39] about "accepting an horizon,"[40] how one gains a horizon, namely, God as the necessary horizon for humankind. Preacher Luccock, Professor of Yale;[41] the whole thing a discreet, opulent, self-satisfied celebration of religion. With such an idolization of religion, the flesh, which was accustomed to being held in check by the word of God, revives. Such preaching renders people libertine, egoistic, indifferent. Do the people really not know that one can do as well or better without "religion"—if only it weren't for God himself and his word? Perhaps the Anglo-Saxons really are more religious than we, but they may not be more Christian, if they tolerate such sermons. For me there is no doubt that someday a storm will blow forcefully into this religious hand-out,[42] if God himself is still in the plan

---

[36.] A series of articles titled "How My Mind Has Changed in This Decade" appeared in the magazine *Christian Century* from January to September 1939. [See Bonhoeffer's reading notes on several of these essays (1/137a), which clearly influenced his work on the essay "Protestantism without Reformation" (2/6).—VB]

[37.] [Bonhoeffer gives the quotation in English.—VB]

[38.] Ruth Davies, "Are Students Losing Their Religion?" *Christian Century* 56 (1939): 676–69.

[39.] Bonhoeffer probably means William James, the standard representative of American pragmatism.

[40.] [Quotation in English in original.—VB]

[41.] [The German *DBW* has "Lubrook," but the reference is to Halford E. Luccock, professor of homiletics at Yale at the time; Luccock spoke at Riverside Church in 1939 as part of its "30 Good Minutes" series. "Professor of Yale" in English in original.—VB]

[42.] ["Hand-out" in English in original.—VB]

at all. In human terms the matter is not even unpleasant, but I do prefer a sermon by Brother Schutz,[43] as rustic as it may be. The tasks for a genuine theologian over here are immeasurable. But only an American can get rid of this rubble. Up to now no one appears to be there.

How good the Daily Texts for today are: Ps. 119:105; Matt. 13:8.[44] Worked in the afternoon. Didn't speak to anyone the whole day. I must now learn again how well off I have been so far, always to be in the fellowship of
the brothers. And Niemöller has been alone for two years.[45] Unthinkable. 226
What faith, what discipline, and what a palpable act of God!—Now the day has nonetheless ended well. I was in church again. As long as there are lonely Christians, there will still be worship services. It is truly a great help after a few completely lonely days to go to church and pray together, sing together, listen together there. The sermon was astounding (Broadway Presbyterian Church, Dr. Mc[Comb])[46] about "our likeness with Christ."[47] A completely biblical sermon—particularly good the sections: "*we are blameless like Christ*," "we are *tempted* like Christ!"[48] Later this will eventually be a center of resistance long after Riverside Church will have become a temple of idolatry. I was very pleased about this sermon. But why does a man who preaches this way not notice at all what dreadful music he has them play? I will ask him about it. With this sermon, an America heretofore completely unknown to me has been opened up.

By the way, I almost became ungrateful during these days for all the protection God has given to me. Over the intention and the innermost need to think unceasingly of the brothers over there and their work, I almost fled the task here. It would have almost seemed to me to be disloyalty if I am not with all my thoughts over there. I must still find the right balance. Paul writes too that he thinks of his congregation "without ceasing"[49] in
prayer and simultaneously devoted himself entirely to the task there. This 227

[43.] Erwin Schutz [one of Bonhoeffer's students in the collective pastorates—VB].

[44.] "Your word is a lamp to my feet and a light to my path" and "other seeds fell on good soil."

[45.] Martin Niemöller had been imprisoned since July 1, 1937; after the beginning of February 1938, he was in the Sachsenhausen concentration camp.

[46.] John H. McComb. The typescript erroneously has "Dr. McColm."

[47.] [Quotation in English in original.—VB]

[48.] [Quotations in English in original.—VB] A note sheet of Bonhoeffer's has been preserved (*NL, A* 54,15), possibly his notes from the sermon he had heard: "Let us never pity ourselves; let us never be tragic. There is nothing tragic about our suffering. Let us realize that through suffering God is conforming us to his likeness, that our suffering is only part of God's suffering and that finally the victory and triumph is his. So a life of suffering is the root of victorious living."

[49.] Rom. 1:9–10.

is something that must be learned. It will come only through praying. God, in the next week give me clarity about my future and keep me in the community of the prayers of the brothers.

June 19, 1939

Without news from Germany the whole day, from mail to mail, waiting in vain. It doesn't help to get angry and write letters in that mood. By the time the letter arrives, the awaited news will have long come. I want to know how the work over there is going, whether all is going well or whether they need me. I want to have a hint from over there for tomorrow's decisive consultation.[50] Perhaps good that it didn't arrive.—The news about China is disturbing.[51] Can one reach home in time if things become serious? The whole day in the library. Wrote English lectures.[52] I have much difficulty with the language. They say that I speak good English, and I find it so completely inadequate. How many years, decades did it take to learn German, and one cannot master it even now. I will never learn English. That in itself is a reason to go back home soon. Without language one is lost, hopelessly lonely. In the evening to Times Square, an escape. News Reel[53] here lasts for an hour. Early to bed. What a day. But: "the name of the Lord Jesus was praised" (Acts 19:17). It bothers me that we don't have the same time as
228 Germany. It makes common prayer more difficult and hinders it. It is the same each evening. But: "We give thanks to you, God, that your name is so near" (Ps. 75:2).

June 20, 1939

In the morning a letter from my parents in southern Germany.[54] Booklets from Stettin.[55] Visit with Leiper. With that the decision has been made.

[50.] [Bonhoeffer had an appointment to speak to Leiper, where he shared his decision to return to Germany; see the diary entry for June 20.—VB]

[51.] Bonhoeffer refers to the events of July 7, 1939; the ongoing war between Japan and China had flared up again, as well as the battles between Japanese and Soviet troops on the Manchurian border and in Outer Mongolia. Cf. Erdmann, *Die Zeit der Weltkriege*.

[52.] See the descriptions in *NL*, A 50,1:21–25, mainly notes about the series of articles "How My Mind Has Changed in This Decade," from the *Christian Century*. Bonhoeffer used most of them in the sixth section (on theology) of his essay "Protestantism without Reformation," 2/6. [These notes, which are not included in the German *DBW* 15, are included in this volume as 1/137a.—VB]

[53.] ["News Reel" in English in original.—VB]

[54.] Letter not extant.

[55.] Not identified.

I turned it down.[56] He was visibly disappointed and indeed somewhat put out. For me it may mean something more than I am able to foresee at the moment. God alone knows. It is strange that in all my decisions I am never completely clear about my motives. Is that a sign of lack of clarity, inner dishonesty, or is it a sign that we are *led* beyond that which we can discern, or is it both?

Isa. 45:19: "I am the Lord who speaks of righteousness,[57] I declare what is right."

1 Pet. 1:17: "If you invoke as Father the one who judges all people impartially according to their deeds, live in reverent fear during the time of your exile."

The Daily Text today speaks with terrible severity of God's incorruptible judgment. God certainly sees how much personal concern, how much fear is contained in today's decision, as courageous as it may appear. The reasons that one puts forward to others and oneself for an action are certainly not sufficient. One can simply give reasons for anything. In the end one acts out of a level that remains hidden from us. Because of that one can only pray that God will wish to judge us and forgive us.[58]

Visit to Dr. Bewer;[59] very cordial reception. In the afternoon David
Roberts. Long theological conversation. Criticism of the fundamentalists,
holds them in an emergency as no more dependable than the Riverside
Church people. Fosdick,[60] the Antichrist in the eyes of Broadway Pres- 229
byterian. America forty years behind Germany. Twenty years behind Scotland. It appears as though Germany is indeed still the land of spiritual discoveries.—In the evening at Van Dusen's. I don't like him; he likes himself too much. Wrote letters.[61] Nine-thirty for an hour at Bewer's. How good to speak German again. At the end of the day, I can only pray that God may hold merciful judgment over this day and all decisions. It is now in God's hand.[62]

[56.] [Bonhoeffer had turned down Leiper's offer of a position overseeing refugee work.—VB]

[57.] [Here the NRSV has "who speaks the truth."—VB]

[58.] This is similar to Bonhoeffer's letter to the young colleagues in Pomerania at the end of January 1938, 1/7, p. 35: "What should happen now? There are so many reasons, and theologians can prove everything. Everything will depend on whether God will give his witness anew into our hearts. Jesus Christ alone can break the spell."

[59.] Julius A. Bewer.

[60.] Harry E. Fosdick.

[61.] See Bonhoeffer's June 29, 1939, letter to Elisabeth Bethge, 1/116.

[62.] For more about Bonhoeffer's decision to return to Germany, see *DB-ER*, 653–55.

June 21, 1939

Worked peacefully in the morning. Very hot. In the afternoon the Metropolitan Museum; I particularly liked El Greco (landscape above Toledo entirely in green)[63] and Memling (head of Christ).[64] In the evening very warmly and generously invited to Bewer's. I notice how much more freely one behaves among these people today compared to back then.[65] It was so good to speak and think German again. I have never felt the resistance of the English language against my thoughts as strongly as here in New York. In the garb of this language, I always feel dissatisfied with myself. Bewer's judgment about America was quite important to me, as well as his experiences of war. They can yield themselves to hatred without reservation, perhaps immaturely.

Regarding my decision, the thoughts naturally continue. One might, of course, have justified it entirely differently: the fact is, one is here (perhaps the very misunderstanding was a guidance?); one is told that when I was announced it was as if prayers had been heard; they particularly want to have me; they don't understand why I am turning this down; it is upsetting
230 all plans for the future; I have no news from home; perhaps everything is going just as well without me etc. Or one could ask: did I simply act out of yearning for Germany and the work there? And is this lingering homesickness, which is almost incomprehensible to me and till now remains almost completely unfamiliar, an accompanying sign from above, which should make the refusal easier? Or is it not irresponsible in light of so many other people, simply to say no to one's own future and that of many others? Will I regret it? I may not do so, that is for certain.[66] Despite everything, for me the promise stands in the first place, then the joy in the work at home, and finally the other person whom I would be driving out.[67] Once more the Daily Text speaks so harshly: "God will sit as a refiner and purifier of silver"

[63.] El Greco's painting *View of Toledo* (ca. 1595–1610).

[64.] Probably Hans Memling's painting *Christ Giving the Blessing*; cf. Friedländer, *Early Netherlandish Painting*, vol. 6, pt. 1, 90.

[65.] [I.e., in 1930–31, during his study year in New York.—VB]

[66.] Cf. Bonhoeffer's statement in his December 22, 1943, letter to Bethge from the Military Detention Center in Berlin-Tegel: "You should know, by the way, that not for a single moment have I regretted my return in 1939, nor anything of what has then followed. That took place in full clarity and with the best conscience" (*DBWE* 8:236).

[67.] [Bonhoeffer had been offered a job helping refugees in the American Committee for Christian German Refugees. He feared this would make any return to Germany impossible and also felt that the position should be given to a refugee who did not have the option of returning to Germany, as Bonhoeffer did. Cf. *DB-ER*, 651–52.—VB]

(Mal. 3:3). It is necessary indeed. I no longer know how things stand with myself. But God knows, and in the end all actions and deeds will be clear and pure.

June 22, 1939

Without news from over there. Invitation to Boerickes.[68] I leave next week. In the morning worked, wrote.[69] I am sorry about my decision mostly because of Sabine.[70] Read in the afternoon. Niebuhr: *Interpretation of Christian Ethics.*[71] Filled with wrong and superficial statements. The formulation of the questions still entirely between orthodox and liberal critique, but no truly fundamental new approach, "myth" instead of the word of God. Evening in the News Reel Theatre, nothing special. The evening papers bring very upsetting news about Japan.[72] Bewer calms me down. For a German over here it is simply no longer to be endured; one is simply
torn apart. To be here during a catastrophe is simply unthinkable, unless 231
it is meant to be. But to be guilty of this oneself, to have to reproach oneself for having gone abroad unnecessarily, is certainly crushing. We simply cannot separate ourselves from our fate, here abroad less than ever; here it rests upon one's shoulders alone, and one has no voice and no rights in a foreign land. Moreover, here too the storm will soon break loose. There is seething unrest under the surface. Woe then to them who are here without a homeland! It is so strange, how strongly these very thoughts move me in these days and how all thoughts of the Una Sancta[73] break through only with difficulty. Terribly much is already buried in oblivion.

Since yesterday evening I write in bed. That is a very good close. What remain are only the Daily Texts and intercessory prayers. No news from Germany. In the morning discussions with Bewer, Van Dusen about the future. I intend to go back in August. They urge me to stay longer. But if nothing else intervenes, I am staying with August 12. I will then stay a while at Sabine's.[74] Lunch with David Roberts and his wife, very nice. We talked

[68.] See 1/118, ed. note 6.

[69.] Cf. Bonhoeffer's June 22, 1939, letter to his parents, 1/118.

[70.] Sabine Leibholz.

[71.] Reinhold Niebuhr's 1935 book.

[72.] See ed. note 35.

[73.] The abbreviation for the formula from the Nicene Creed (*Book of Concord,* 22–23): "Credo . . . unam, sanctam, catholicam et apostolicam ecclesiam" (I believe . . . one only, holy, Christian, apostolic church).

[74.] In London.

about the Negro question. Nothing seems to have changed, unless, at most the anti-lynching-bill.[75] He thinks that the danger of revolution in the South is great. Until now I didn't know that the blacks are being kept from exercising their right to vote. In the great unification of the Methodists (May 1939), the black churches are not included.[76] He couldn't name any recent literature. Great increase in anti-Semitism. A mountain resort: "1000 feet—too high for Jews."—Advertisement: "Gentiles preferred."[77] In the
232 afternoon visited Colvin.[78] Back home. Sat by the Hudson and thought of Sigurdshof. Why do I not hear anything?—Finished reading Niebuhr.[79] The portrayal of the inapplicability of so-called Christian principles to life, politics, etc. is still the best. Critique of liberalism. Little or rather no originality as to positive statements. (Contrast between the absolute ideal and the relative-pragmatic good. Both necessary.) This thinking does not come from the Bible, for that reason deeply unproductive. His essay in *Beyond Tragedy* about "as deceivers yet true"[80] is pure modernism.

Downstairs at the moment a conference about revising the hymnal is concluding. They are playing chorales in terribly bad tempo and with poor pedaling. For that the clavichord is better. Daily Texts and intercessory prayer.

June 24, 1939

Finally mail.[81] That is a great liberation. But it is also totally clear to me again that I must get back to the work. Today I got quite a bit done. W. A.

[75.] ["Anti-lynching" in English in original.—VB] This refers to the law against lynching that was proposed and debated in 1934 in both houses of Congress and passed in 1935. [The reference here is probably to the Wagner-Costigan bill, which was debated in 1934 but was filibustered in 1935 and never made it out of committee. The first federal antilynching law was passed in the United States in 1968, when lynching became a federal crime under the Civil Rights Act.—VB]

[76.] As a result of their different positions on slavery, the southern Methodist Episcopal Church had broken away from the northern Methodist Episcopal Church in 1844. The reunification took place in 1939.

[77.] [Quotations in English in original.—VB]

[78.] Harold Colvin.

[79.] See ed. note 71.

[80.] Reinhold Niebuhr, *Beyond Tragedy*, 1–24. Cf. 2 Cor. 6:8: ". . . as impostors, and yet are true."

[81.] Cf. Bethge's June 12, 1939, letter to Bonhoeffer, 1/109.

Brown: State and Church,[82] etc. This morning Rockwell[83] took too much of my time. I am now reflecting often on whether it is true that America is the land without Reformation.[84] If Reformation is the God-given recognition of the failure of all paths to the building of the kingdom of God on earth, then this is accurate. But does that not also hold true for England? In America the voice of Lutheranism does exist, but as one among many; it has never really been capable of challenging the other denominations. Apparently, "encounters" rarely come about at all in this vast land, where one can always evade the other. Where, however, there are no encounters, where liberty[85] [is] the only unifying force, there the community created through encounter is naturally unfamiliar. This alters the general life
together. Community in our sense can[not] grow here, neither culturally 233
nor in the churches. Is this true?—Wrote cards in the evening. Called Felix Gilbert.—The newspapers today are again dreadful. Daily Text: "Whoever believes, will not flee" [Isa. 28:16].[86] I think of the work at home. Tomorrow is Sunday. Will I hear a *sermon* tomorrow?

June 25, 1939—Sunday

Worship service at Luther Church. Church on Central Park, Dr. Scherer.[87] Sermon on Luke 15, about overcoming fear. Very forced approach to the text. Otherwise lively and original, but too much analysis and very little gospel. It hit home when he said of the life of the Christian that it is similar to the daily joy of one who is on the way home.—Again, no basic exegesis of the text. It is very pathetic.—Lunch at the Bewers. Conversation about the newspapers here, afterward about the peculiar silence of the American public about the suffering of Christians in Russia,[88] about the unfamiliarity with the Bible, about poor Sunday schools.—Afternoon and evening with Gilbert.[89] He respects Roosevelt greatly. Explained a

[82.] ["State and Church" in English in original.—VB] Brown, *Church and State in Contemporary America.*

[83.] [William Rockwell, the Union Theological Seminary librarian at the time.—VB]

[84.] See 2/6.

[85.] ["Liberty" in English in original.—VB]

[86.] [The NRSV reads: "One who trusts will not panic."—VB]

[87.] Paul Scherer. [The church was Holy Trinity Lutheran Church, where Scherer was pastor from 1920 to 1945.—VB]

[88.] Particularly during and after the large Stalinist purges in the Soviet Union in 1936–37.

[89.] Felix Gilbert.

great deal to me. Pleasant encounter since our years at school.—Today is Augustana day.[90] This makes me remember the brothers at home. Rom. 1:16.[91]

June 26, 1939

Letter from my parents in Switzerland.[92] During the day work in the library. Finished W. A. Brown.[93] Denominational praxis of training and
234 ordination.[94] It is very difficult to get a uniform picture. Tillich's formulation of the contrast between the theocratic-democratic and the autocratic-sacramental is still too formal, too sociological. Theoretically it is somehow connected to the absence of the Reformation. The word of God has never entirely shattered and entirely liberated this people. Therefore too the preference for Catholicizing concepts of humanitarianism. (J. Maritain: *True Humanism.*)[95]—Today I happened to read from 2 Tim. 4:21 "come before the winter"—Paul's plea to Timothy. Timothy is to share the suffering of the apostle[96] and not be ashamed. "Come before the winter"—otherwise it might be too late. That is haunting me the whole day. We seem to feel like the soldiers on leave from the front who, despite all that awaits them, push to return to the front. We can't come free of it. Not as if we were necessary, as if we were needed (by God!?), but simply because our life is there and because we desert our life, annihilate it, if we are not part of things there. It is not at all something pious, but something almost vital. But God acts not only through pious impulses but also through such vital stirrings as well. "Come before the winter"—it is not a misuse of the Scripture if I allow this to be said *to me.* If God gives me the grace for that.

[90.] The commemoration of the day the Augsburg Confession was given to Charles V at the Reichstag in 1530. [The Augsburg Confession was central in the theological training of Confessing Church pastors. See, for example, the section on "daily study" in *DBW* 14:151 (1/72).—VB]

[91.] ["For I am not ashamed of the gospel; it is the power of God for salvation to everyone who has faith, to the Jews first and also to the Greek."—VB]

[92.] Letter not extant.

[93.] See ed. note 82.

[94.] Bonhoeffer made notes about the different training and ordination practices of the Presbyterians, the Congregationalists, and the Baptists. See *NL*, A 54,2.

[95.] Maritain's 1938 book.

[96.] [Paul.—VB]

June 27, 1939

Letter from my parents.[97] Great joy, quite surprising. Noon and afternoon work in the library. Tillich, Niebuhr. In the evening a visit from Professor Richardson,[98] long conversation. He is English. It seems to me as if one stood closer to him than to the Americans. Do the Americans perhaps fail so utterly to understand us because they are a population of those who left Europe in order to live their faith freely on their own? That is, because they did not stand up to the ultimate decision in questions of faith. They 235
would, I believe, understand the refugee better than the one who stays. From this perspective the American tolerance or, more correctly, indifference on dogmatic questions can be understood. The encounter in battle is ruled out, but therefore the genuine passionate longing for unity in faith as well.

June 28, 1939

In the morning YMCA headquarters, tour. The chapel is the loveliest room in the entire building. Most [. . .][99] have none at all. Among other things the Roman missal lies in the chapel. Otherwise the usual picture. Afternoon work in the library. In the evening supper with Professor Richardson. Afterward read for a long time. *Kingdom of God in America*—Richard Niebuhr.

The newspaper reports become more and more disturbing. They pull the thoughts away. I cannot think that it is God's will that if war comes I should remain here without a particular assignment. I must leave at the first possible date.

June 29, 1939

Telegram from K. Fr.[100] Looked for lodging. Work till noon. Afternoon a missed appointment. In the evening a good, brotherly talk with Roberts,[101] who leaves tomorrow on vacation. I gave him two of my books. He promised to send me books when I write him. The news today is such

[97.] Letter not extant.

[98.] Cyril Richardson.

[99.] One or several words are missing in the typescript.

[100.] Karl-Friedrich Bonhoeffer; the telegram is not extant.

[101.] David Roberts.

that I am rather decided to travel back with Karl Friedrich. Tomorrow we will talk about it.

Roberts spoke very critically about the church in America. The dis-
236 tress [Not] comes from within. The utter indifference toward the message increasingly undermines the church. "Keep away from politics"[102]—says that the church should confine itself to its "religious task," in which no one has any interest. It is always difficult for me to understand how the principle of a separation between church and state is consistent with the praxis of a social, economic, societal, and political effectiveness of the church. In any case, the separation of church and state obviously does not mean that the church remains devoted to its own tasks, nor does it safeguard against secularization. Nowhere is the church more secularized than here, where it is separated on principle [from the state]. This very separation can create a counterpart that drives the church much more strongly into political-secular matters. That may be important for our own decisions over there.

June 30, 1939

Letter from Fritz.[103] Contemplative and brotherly as always. Unfortunately nothing else. At 11 a call from Karl Friedrich, who is coming from Chicago. There is much to talk about. He received an excellent offer of a professorship there; it means a permanent decision.[104] Then my questions. Since in the present situation I would have departed in any case after four weeks at the latest, under the present circumstances I have decided to leave with Karl Friedrich on the eighth. I do not want to be here in case of war, and objectively there is nothing here to learn about the situation. That was a major decision. In the morning a letter from Paul, who was so optimistic about my staying here.[105] Afternoon and evening the World's Fair,[106] the technical things. In the evening for the first time didn't write anything.

237 July 1, 1939

Moved this morning. Noon Karl Friedrich. Afternoon wrote a bit. Then with Karl Friedrich in the city, bought presents, Music Hall, cinema, the

[102.] [Quotation in English in original.—VB]

[103.] Fritz Onnasch; letter not extant.

[104.] Karl-Friedrich Bonhoeffer turned down the professorship offered in Chicago. See *DB-ER*, 656.

[105.] See Lehmann's June 28, 1939, letter to Bonhoeffer, 1/125.

[106.] See ed. note 32.

largest.[107] Horrible. Obtrusive, showy, sumptuous colors, music, and flesh. Only in such a metropolitan atmosphere can one put on such fantasies. Karl Friedrich is of a different opinion. Back home in time in the evening. The whole day, thoughts about the situation in Germany and of the church did not leave me. The Daily Texts today are so good again! Job 41:11.[108] "Who has a claim against me that I must pay? Everything under heaven belongs to me." Rom. 11:36: ". . . from him and through him and to him are all things. To him be the glory forever. Amen." The earth, the peoples, Germany, and above all the church cannot fall from God's hand. In light of the situation today, it is tremendously difficult for me to think and pray "Thy will be done."[109] But it must be. Tomorrow is Sunday. May God's word find a hearing throughout the world.

July 2, 1939—Sunday

Church, Park Avenue, Rev. Sockman[110] (radio preacher!) about "today is ours,"[111] without a text, not the faintest echo of Christian proclamation. One more disappointment. The collection with prayer and singing is always good. Noon with Karl Friedrich, afternoon work, that is, wrote something about America, *attempted* to write. Spent the day at the seminary with Karl Friedrich; spoke at length about his plans.

The Americans in their sermons speak so much about freedom. Freedom as a possession is for the church a dubious thing; freedom must be won under the constraint of necessity. The freedom of the church arises from the necessity [Muß] of God's word. Otherwise, it becomes arbitrary and ends in many a new bondage. Whether the church in America is truly "free" is very questionable to me. These are lonely Sundays over here. Only 238
the Word creates the true church-community. I yearn for a good devotional service in community in my own language.—The news is not good. Will we come in time? Daily Text: Isa. 35:10!![112] Intercessory prayer.

[107.] [Probably Radio City Music Hall.—VB]

[108.] [The German text incorrectly gives Job 41:3 for this verse. Translation here is from the NIV, which is closer to the German text.—VB]

[109.] The third verse of the Lord's Prayer, Matt. 6:10.

[110.] [The German *DBW* text and *NL* microfiche incorrectly have "Gorkmann," but the reference is certainly to Ralph Washington Sockman, a famous radio preacher of that era; the church was Christ Church, a Methodist church.—VB]

[111.] [Quotation in English in original.—VB]

[112.] "And the ransomed of the Lord shall return, and come to Zion with singing; everlasting joy shall be upon their heads; they shall obtain joy and gladness, and sorrow and sighing shall flee away."

July 3, 1939

Lectures by Coffin, Richard Niebuhr, Harris.[113] Everything confirmed my observation that theology here stands where we stood fifteen years ago. In the afternoon work at home. In the evening a long night conversation with a student, Gill.[114] A full day. I have written down the first summary thoughts for an essay.[115] But I would have to be able to continue writing it in one sitting. The morning prayer service with Coffin was very pitiful. I must watch myself, that I don't become neglectful in reading the Bible and in prayer.—Letter from Paul Lehmann.[116]

July 4, 1939

In the morning Coffin; then visit with Richard Niebuhr. Noon with Karl Friedrich Empire State Building. Film. In the evening invited to the Niebuhrs. Very long good conversation. The American separation of state and church has the sense of a "limitation of power"[117] with regard to the government, not the Reformation teaching on respective offices.[118] I suspected that. Niebuhr believes that Roger Williams[119] held God as effective
239 only in the spiritual sphere, and Williams's complete indifference toward the state can be explained in light of this perspective. Separation of church and state in America is no unambiguous phenomenon.—Daily texts, intercessory prayer.

July 5, 1939

The closer the departure approaches, the fuller the days become. In the morning, devotional service with Professor Smart.[120] Van Dusen on

---

[113.] Erdman Harris.

[114.] Theodore Gill. [Gill later published the outline for a screenplay on Bonhoeffer's life (*Memo for a Movie*), but Bonhoeffer's 1939 stay in New York is mentioned only briefly and there is no account of this conversation.—VB]

[115.] This refers to his essay "Protestantism without Reformation," 2/6. [These notes are the concluding pages of his diary, 1/137a.—VB]

[116.] See Lehmann's July 2, 1939, letter to Bonhoeffer, 1/131.

[117.] ["Limitation of power" in English in original.—VB]

[118.] [That is, the offices of state authorities, on the one hand, and the office in the church on the other.—VB]

[119.] Founder of the colony of Rhode Island and the first Baptist congregation in America; a proponent of the separation of church and state and religious toleration.

[120.] James D. Smart.

Descartes. Very superficial. Work in the library. Horton, Keller.[121] Continued in the afternoon. Noon conversation with two students from southern states about the problems of blacks. In the evening reception in the social room.[122] It would be good to stay for four more weeks. But the stakes are too high. Letter from Eberhard,[123] great joy. Good thought about John 2. Still no reply to my decisions. The Daily Text calls for gratitude.[124]

July 6, 1939

I am writing on the ship. The last two days were filled, so that I didn't get to writing. In the morning down town[125] to take care of travel preparations. On the way back the Stock exchange.[126] Errands. At 2:30 I meet Paul Lehmann in my room, who came from Columbus, Ohio, to see me while I'm still here. Great joy. From now on the entire remaining time together with him. Prepared l[ecture course].

July 7, 1939 240

Last day. Paul is still trying to keep me here. It is no longer possible. Van Dusen lecture. Packed. Before noon with Hans Wedell. Theological conversations with Paul. Farewells in the seminary. Supper with Van Dusen. Drive to the ship with Paul. Good-byes at 11:30, departure at 12:30. Manhattan at night, the moon stands above the skyscrapers.[127] It is very hot. The journey is over. I am glad that I was there, and glad that I am on my way home again. I have perhaps learned more in this month than in the entire year nine years ago; at least I have come to realize important things for all future personal decisions. Probably this journey will have a great effect upon me.

[121.] Walter B. Horton and Adolf Keller.

[122.] ["Reception" and "social room" in English in original.—VB]

[123.] See Bethge's June 23, 1939, letter to Bonhoeffer, 1/119.

[124.] Gen. 32:10: "[Jacob said:] for with only my staff I crossed this Jordan; and now I have become two companies." The interpretive verse is Eph. 3:20–21: "Now to him who by the power at work within us is able to accomplish abundantly far more than all we can ask or imagine, to him be glory in the church and in Christ Jesus to all generations, forever and ever. Amen."

[125.] ["Down town" in English in original.—VB]

[126.] ["Stock exchange" in English in original.—VB]

[127.] ["Skyscrapers" in English in original.—VB]

July 8, 1939

On the ship. It is quiet and hot. Travel by ship has lost the charm of novelty. Read much, America book[128] (which is truly bad; the style is so poor that much becomes unclear).—Practical Religion,[129] good essays.

July 9, 1939—Sunday

English worship service, which is well attended, but probably just as much for a change from the monotonous life aboard, like the cinema, among other things the text: "the sea will no longer be" (Rev. 21:1).[130] The sermon sentimental and full of hollow phrases. Conversation with Karl Friedrich about theological topics. Read much. The days are noticeably shorter through the reduction of an hour. Since I have been aboard the ship, the internal tension about the future has stopped. I can think about the abbreviated time in America without reproach.—Daily Text: "It is good for me that I was humbled, so that I might learn your statutes" [Ps. 119:71]. One of my favorite sayings from my favorite psalm.[131]

137a. Notes at the Conclusion of the Diary[1]

Church as religious province (philosophically-culturally)

As means to an end (peoples' . . . moral life, for the satisfaction of religious needs for the harmony of existence, like science, art[)].
Church submerged into the world
Religion, church, private matter, private enjoyment.
Church as an invention for forgiveness of sins
Waste of the word and the sacraments.

[128.] Not identified.

[129.] ["Practical Religion" in English in original.—VB] Not identified.

[130.] [NRSV: "and the sea was no more."—VB]

[131.] Cf. Bonhoeffer's meditation on Psalm 119, 3/9.

[1.] [The following notes are from pp. 21–25 of Bethge's typewritten transcript of Bonhoeffer's New York diary (*NL*, A 50,1). They were not included in *DBW* 15. We have chosen to include them in *DBWE* 15 because they are clearly Bonhoeffer's reading notes for his essay "Protestantism without Reformation" (2/6). Bonhoeffer's notes were made both in English and German; this is indicated only where he cites directly from an English work. The editor particularly thanks Clifford J. Green for his help with transcription and bibliographic queries. First publication in the *Dietrich Bonhoeffer Jahrbuch* 4.—VB]

Outstanding:
Problems of . . . continental theology
Doctrine and heresy.

1. Confession and damnation
2. The Church
3. The powers ordained by God
6. Christ and anti-christ[2]
   Christlike life
4. Christian life, the meaning of suffering
5. Church and synod.

Edwin Lewis: "From Philosophy to Revelation"[3]

June 14, 1939

1924: Jesus Christ and the Human Question.[4]
Based upon the philosophy of Pringle-Patterson:[5] The idea of God in the light of recent Philosophers.

1934: Christian manifesto[6]
Through study of the Bible to recognition of the independence of the biblical belief in revelation.

Willard L. Sperry: professor of practical theology, Harvard University.

Jan. 18, 1939: How my mind has changed in this decade.
General overview. First article.
Older generation. Begin with "What would Jesus do?" (Marles M. Sheldon).[7] Direct ethic. Called into question by Tolstoy and Nietzsche (English spokesman for N. was H. W. Garrod, "The

[2.] [The numbered sequence here, which is out of order, replicates what is in the typescript.—VB]

[3.] [Lewis subsequently published *A Philosophy of the Christian Revelation*, so his essay in the *Christian Century* seems to anticipate that book.—VB]

[4.] [Lewis, *Jesus Christ and the Human Quest*.—VB]

[5.] [*The Idea of God in the Light of Recent Philosophers*, by Andrew Seth Pringle-Pattison (not Patterson as in the typescript), was the publication of the 1911–13 Gifford Lectures.—VB]

[6.] [Lewis, *A Christian Manifesto*, a critique of liberal theology.—VB]

[7.] ["Marles" is a typographical error; the reference is to Charles M. Sheldon's *In His Steps: "What Would Jesus Do?"*—VB]

religion of all good men," 1906)[8] Connection between dogmatics and ethics. A turning to the God question. "American life has been, until most recently, optimistic, once-born. . . . Our once-born America is changing before our eyes."[9] In . . . the sense of L. G. Tyrell's formulation: "Christian religion is an ultimate optimism [founded] upon a provisional pessimism."[10] Repentance: provisional pessimism.

Henry Nelson Wiemann: Professor Religious Philosophy, Chicago

Jan. 25, 1939: Growth of religion.[11]
"Some blind spots removed."[12]

He sees more clearly:

1. symbol Christian
2. Sin: every ideal that positions itself above the concrete situation Therefore—he who makes ideals supreme over his life, no matter how loftily and no matter how perfectly he may live up to them, is sinning.
3. grace. The grace of God is the good word God puts into each concrete situation over and above all that man can do or plan or even imagine. Because of our ideal we do not receive the grace of God.
4. Living Christ.
   "It is the working of a process of history which used that human personality (Jesus)
   "the growth of a community"—which breaks through all groups of culture, ideal, law. That is the living Christ.
5. The Church.
   "a new way of living." Church must have a certain continuity. "Therefore ceremony and doctrine," but they change. "It is the way of life that is important."

[8.] [H. W. Garrod, *Religion of All Good Men*.—VB]

[9.] [This quotation is from Sperry's essay, p. 84; William James used the term "once-born" to describe the kind of faith "which looks on all things and sees that they are good"; W. James, "The Varieties of Religious Experience," in *Writings 1902–1910*, 85.—VB]

[10.] [The quotation from p. 84 of Sperry's essay is by the Irish Jesuit scholar George Tyrrell from his book *Christianity at the Cross-Roads*, 69. The actual phrase there is "a proximate pessimism but an ultimate optimism."—VB]

[11.] [Wieman and Horton, *Growth of Religion*.—VB]

[12.] [This was the title of Wieman's essay in the *Christian Century*.—VB]

6. The otherness of God.
   "God alone is concrete in his working." "Man must work abstractly." God travels through all conceptions of the human [Menschenbilder]

   Particular assessment of the Apostle Paul.
   For Wiemann the transition came "through recognition of the sin" (!) (Sin = nonconcreteness) (idolization of the concrete, of history. Immanentism: ideology of the "concrete situation"[)]

   "Growth of religion"[13]—1938
   "Theistic naturalism"—God is "growth of living connections of values in the universe" or *"unlimited growth."* Therefore higher than all ideas, doctrines etc. Romantic naturalism. Schleiermacher. Rejection of the personhood [Personhaftigkeit] of God, the personal immortality.
   Immanentism as philosophy of history
   Christianity: the God who is *becoming* and the history that is *becoming*!

Reinhold Niebuhr

26.IV.39: "The year that shook my world"[14]

Starting point: *liberalism.* Belief in the good of humanity, whether in the naturalistic-romantic or in the rational-idealistic sense. Optimism.

Positive aspects of liberalism:
- The liberation of exact science
- The religion
- The application of historical method to the Bible

In contrast: the Cross is the end of history.
Liberalism forgot that "the spirit of man can find a home neither in nature nor in reason, but only in God.["]
The political end of liberalism is "Munich."[15]

[13.] [Wieman's book *The Growth of Religion.*—VB]

[14.] [Niebuhr, "Ten Years That Shook My World," *Christian Century* (April 26, 1939).—VB]

[15.] [This is a reference to the 1938 Munich agreement between Nazi Germany and the governments of France, Italy, and Great Britain, in which those governments agreed

Christ for the *new-orthodoxy*: source of despair. God
Christ for the *correct liberalism* demands our ideal, our norm, and the revelation of our essential being.

Both are necessary.

W. M. Horton: Professor Oberlin College . . .

17.V.39: "Between Libertism and the New Orthodoxy"[16]

1930: "R . . . and the modern mood"[17]
1934: "Realistic Theology[")][18]
1930: Question: outright surrender to humanism—without belief in God (Lippmann)[19] and "fatalitarism" (Krutsch—without "faith in man")[20] or turning to theological tradition.

Contemporary english Theology[21]
Contemporary continental Theology.[22]

First landmark: *Augustine, Calvin, Barth*. See in everything only the theology of crisis, the transcendence appropriate for the present age; but other eras need Thomas, Schleiermacher, the Christian penetration of the world.
Second landmark: *M. W. Wiemann*[23]
Third landmark: *The social gospel*

---

to the German annexation of the Sudetenland region of Czechoslovakia for the sake of preserving the European peace. It was criticized even at the time as an act of appeasement and a betrayal of democratic values.—VB]

[16.] [The actual title of Horton's article in the *Christian Century* was "Between Liberalism and the New Orthodoxy."—VB]

[17.] [W. M. Horton, *Theism and the Modern Mood*.—VB]

[18.] [Horton, *Realistic Theology*.—VB]

[19.] [Walter Lippmann, the U.S. journalist.—VB]

[20.] [Incorrect transcription; the word Horton actually used was "futilitarianism" (the belief in the futility of all human endeavor), and the reference is to Frederick Doyle Kerschner (not "Krutsch"), a Christian educator and dean of the School of Religion at Butler University.—VB]

[21.] [Horton, *Contemporary English Theology*.—VB]

[22.] [Horton, *Contemporary Continental Theology*.—VB]

[23.] [Incorrect transcription; the reference is to H. M. Wieman.—VB]

E. S. Ames.[24]Minister in the University Church of Disciples in Chicago, Prot. Professor of Philosophy

"Liberation Confirmed"[25]
Decisive humanism. Detestation of today's theology. Atavism. Recommendation of science. "God is life as you live it." "Worship as praise and adulation does not fit with my idea of either God or man. It tends to separate them, to exalt one too much and to debase the other too much."—How can this man be a pastor?

E. Stanley Jones: India. Missionary.

May 3, 1930: *The Christ of the Kingdom*

Emphasis on the Kingdom that has its center in Christ. Overcoming of individualism. Christocentric. "Barthianism in small doses" (here, as everywhere, outrageous ignorance!)

Cl. E. Macartney[26]

March 8, 1939: *Warm hearts and steady faith*
Fundamentalist—trained in Princeton Seminary. Says that nothing essential has changed for him in the last ten years and that he is pleased by this. (Heb. 13:8)[27] Center is reconciliation. Then comes ethics, social gospel etc. on its own. The church was ethically most effective when it preached Christ. Critique of the modernists. Little interest in church-union: that doesn't hit Satan.

G. C. Stewart. Episcopal Bishop of Chicago. Anglican.

"A Bend of the River"
sees . . . rupture since the *altar* has moved to the center of worship instead of the *pulpit.*

[24.] [Associated with the Chicago School of pragmatism.—VB]
[25.] [The actual title of the article was "Liberalism Confirmed."—VB]
[26.] [Clarence E. Macartney, a Presbyterian fundamentalist.—VB]
[27.] ["Jesus Christ is the same yesterday and today and forever."—VB]

Dr. Bets: re Belief of 700 ministers[28]

> "the church against the world" (Niebuhr, Pauck, Miller 1935)[29]
> "What must we do to be saved?" is the question of the church today. Afflicted by the world from without and from within. The church has spoken and worked in the international, social, educational programs without visible success.
> Pauck: The crisis of religion[30]
> Miller: American Protestantism and the christian faith.[31]
> Sees an American national-cultural religion growing up in the sense of J. Dewey![32]
> Niebuhr: toward the independence of the church.[33]

Coffin[34]

Henry Drummonds[35]	Natural science and God
J. Fiss[36]	Assimilation. Theologians go into the laboratory.
Evolution	God of countless pulpits

[28.] [The reference is to George Herbert Betts, a Methodist professor of religious education at Northwestern University, and his book *The Beliefs of 700 Ministers*.—VB]

[29.] [Niebuhr, Pauck, and Miller coauthored *The Church against the World*, each taking one section.—VB]

[30.] [The title of part 1 of *The Church against the World*.—VB]

[31.] [The title of part 2 of *The Church against the World*.—VB]

[32.] [John Dewey, the U.S. pragmatist philosopher and educator.—VB]

[33.] [The title of part 3 of *The Church against the World*.—VB]

[34.] [In Henry Sloane Coffin's *Religion Yesterday and Today*, the first chapter is titled "Evolution"; on pp. 19–21 Coffin refers to H. Drummond, *Natural Law in the Spiritual World* (London 1883), Drummond, *The Ascent of Man* (London 1894), and John Fiske, *Through Nature to God* (Boston 1899). The editor thanks Clifford Green for these citations. Since Coffin's book wasn't published until 1940, it would seem that Coffin must have shared the manuscript with Bonhoeffer during his stay in New York.—VB]

[35.] [Henry Drummond.—VB]

[36.] [Probably the U.S. philosopher and historian John Fiske.—VB]

Josiah Strong: on the Americans as the survival of the[37]
Proverb "evil is good in the making."[38]

Huxley:[39]
1893 difference between natural and moral law.

138. From Eberhard Bethge[1] 241

July 11, 1939

Dear Dietrich,

I am at the moment somewhat disconsolate concerning how I actually should behave. On the one hand, I really have not written for quite some time. In the last week I was not doing well; I had rather severe vascular troubles that permitted me to do only the most necessary things; once I was better, I had to prepare for my two homilies on Saturday evening and then the celebration of the Lord's Supper on Sunday. When I finally wanted to write yesterday, a postcard arrived from your mother, in which she wrote me that just one letter dated the third had arrived, you both[2] were together on your way to Sabine,[3] and I should write there and no longer to the United States. Now I waited until this evening (in vain) for confirmation of this from you perhaps by the same post, which arrives here somewhat later. For this truly surprises me greatly. Now here is a letter from Aunt Ruth,[4] and moreover you have again nothing for so long that I myself am very unhappy about it. Your letters with the complaint that you didn't receive anything hurt me a great deal. The mail from you varies in the time it takes, between eight and fourteen days! I believe that I wrote a total of four longer letters over there. I am truly very sorry that you had to wait so. The reasons

[37.] [The word is missing in the *NL* transcription but is probably "fittest."—VB]

[38.] [The phrase is from Emerson's "The Conduct of Life," part 1: "Fate": "If Fate is ore and quarry, if evil is good in the making, if limitation is power that shall be, if calamities, oppositions, and weights are wings and means,—we are reconciled" (in *Selected Writings of Ralph Waldo Emerson*, 433.—VB]

[39.] [Thomas Henry Huxley. In 1893 Huxley delivered the Romanes Lecture titled "Evolution and Ethics," in which he defined "social progress" not as "the survival of the fittest" but as the survival of "those who are ethically the best" (in his *Evolution and Ethics*, 81.—VB]

[1.] *NL*, C 26; handwritten; no return address, certainly from Sigurdshof; previously unpublished.

[2.] Bonhoeffer and Karl Friedrich.

[3.] Sabine Leibholz [i.e., they were en route to London.—VB]

[4.] Ruth von Kleist-Retzow.

were of course first the overwork, and last week I was not doing so well. Now today I am already writing, as your mother writes, to England so that you don't have to wait too long. I beg you please to give me some benefit of the doubt about what the new situation here demanded and not to be angry with me, so that we can look forward, untroubled and happy, to seeing each other again. Perhaps tomorrow morning I will already have news of what is happening and what I should prepare. Here all is going well and smoothly. Sunday I held communion. Preparation of the Sunday Daily Text Psalm 119:71: "It is good for me that I was humbled, so that I might learn your statutes"[5] and the communion homily on the meditation text Exod. 15:2: "The Lord is my strength and my might,[6] and he has become my salvation." I was, as I said, initially affected in my work through the considerable health troubles, but then all went smoothly and well. Now I am completely back in shape. I couldn't explain it to myself at all, really, where this
242 came from, for I had no particular exertions immediately behind me; the fourteen days here alone, which perhaps were more of a strain on me than I initially felt, were already ten to fourteen days in the past, but perhaps it was only then that a certain exhaustion emerged. However it may be, now I am fine again, and Mrs. Struwe is feeding me especially well. So on Sunday I was doing well again, when we had visitors, the two from the estate, Aunt Ruth with her Kieckow son and his wife.[7] Aunt Ruth already for lunch, the other four for afternoon coffee. I think it was quite lively and pleasant.

Yes, Dietrich—your return. When I announced it, it naturally provoked an outburst of enthusiasm, and there is the energetic wish to have the offer come true and herewith I pass it on.[8] The only one whom this filled with ambivalent feelings is Potsdam,[9] who simply likes it here very well.[10] But that doesn't count. Should it still be as you wrote in your letters to me, then I believe that you will be in demand from many quarters upon your return, but I would nonetheless say, especially since you have offered it: please come! We are immensely pleased, especially me.

[5.] Cf. Bonhoeffer's July 9, 1939, diary entry during his trip to the U.S., 1/137, p. 238.

[6.] [Bonhoeffer's Luther Bible text reads ". . . and my praise and my salvation."—VB]

[7.] Margarethe and Ewald von Kleist from Tychow, and Ruth, Hans-Jürgen, and Maria von Kleist-Retzow.

[8.] [Bonhoeffer's offer to resume his work in the collective pastorates.—VB]

[9.] Hellmut Traub.

[10.] [Traub had substituted for Bonhoeffer during the latter's trip to the United States. See 1/109, ed. note 8.—VB]

Your letters, the last two,[11] made me very happy, and I thank you deeply, especially for all the care with which you describe and observe. In case you are not there soon, do send me at the next opportunity a brief written devotion or exegesis of a Daily Text, which I then would like to use in the foreseeable future! My plans? I don't have any at all, except that on September 15 I must be there for the wedding,[12] and Mother would be quite unhappy if I did not help her with the deliberations a few days in advance. We will make the final date[13] dependent on your commitment to come or other plans. It's not yet set. I have not yet heard anything about the winter in E[ngland].[14] I think, too, that it would be more proper to stay here. Well, in case you are in E[ngland], you will hear about this. In case you come soon, please let me pick you up somewhere with the car! That liberty must be! No trace yet of the dartboard that is supposed to arrive here. What is the cause of that? I think your 2 Timothy verses are very fine![15] By the way, on the whole I am really happy with the man from Potsdam. He is warmhearted and, for example, of one mind with me on the question of confession and says that is something *very* important to him!

At present the weather is so bad; this week I wanted at long last to go to the Baltic. Now it's stormy. Not even tennis can be played at the moment. One 243
more thing to report from here, that very suddenly Pastor Gelhoff's[16] wife died. Bleeding on the brain or something similar. Hopefully, I will know soon what will happen and can talk to you directly again. I look forward to it greatly. Did indeed have to think of you here during these weeks very much and of the particular duties that you have in such an office.[17] Overall, things are going quite well, but the inner burden is out of proportion to everything else. When I have news, I will reply at once.

We think in the intercessory prayers of you and your path *every* evening. God keep you your

Eberhard

[11.] Letters not extant.

[12.] See Bethge's June 29, 1939, letter to Bonhoeffer, 1/127, ed. note 5.

[13.] For the end of the semester in the collective pastorates.

[14.] [A reference to the discussion of Bethge's possible emigration to England.—VB]

[15.] [These have not been found; they may have been in one of the lost letters.—VB]

[16.] [The wife of Gerhard Gehlhoff.—VB]

[17.] [I.e., that of a theological instructor and supervisor.—VB]

139. To His Parents[1]

My dear Parents,

Karl Friedrich arrives on Friday in Bremen and will travel via Berlin, if that works with the trains. I will go on to Sabine;[2] I don't know yet for how long. I will await news there. Despite cutting it short, I am happy that I was over there. It was, however, under these circumstances certainly better to cut short the visit. The final days were very nice and full. So one travels home heavily laden with impressions.

Greetings to you from your grateful
Dietrich

140. To His Parents[1]

My dear Parents,

Many thanks for your news. Your plans coincide completely with those of
244 Sabine.[2] They too wanted to take an earlier vacation. Now I don't quite know yet how I should arrange my plans. I am still working on a scholarly text for which I still need several days as well as some books from here.[3] When exactly are you leaving? I would have liked to stay for several days in the Rhineland on the return trip, in order to visit several friends. Could we possibly meet somewhere there? I think I will be there somewhere around the twenty-seventh, twenty-eighth, or twenty-ninth [of July]. Please write me whether you could arrange that. Sabine will also leave on vacation around the twenty-seventh, twenty-eighth. They are doing well, but I think that they all could use some relaxation. Waiting periods are indeed often especially disagreeable. They already look forward greatly to seeing you again. Hopefully, our meeting too can be arranged beforehand.

[1.] *NL*, A 44,1 (31); handwritten postcard; postmarked: New York–Bremen, July 12, 1939. Partially reproduced in *GS* 6:462.

[2.] Sabine Leibholz in London.

[1.] *NL*, A 44,1 (32); handwritten; from London in mid-July 1939. Partially reproduced in *GS* 6:462–63.

[2.] The Bonhoeffer parents' plans for holidays together with the Leibholzes in Holland (cf. Bonhoeffer's July 21, 1939, letter to Karl Bonhoeffer, 1/144).

[3.] This is very probably a reference to the essay "Protestantism without Reformation." See 2/6.

The baggage claim is enclosed. Please don't busy yourself too much with unpacking, dear Mama. I can do it when I come, and it is already crumpled. There's nothing to declare.

Greetings to you from your grateful
Dietrich

141. To Eberhard Bethge[1]

Dear Eberhard,

Many thanks for your card,[2] which probably just crossed paths with my letter. By the way, the airmail letter with the Clipper took a rather long time! I hardly understand it. I dropped it into the mail on the evening of the sixth. It should take three to four days to Berlin, and the airplane left on the eighth. Perhaps the plane was held up again due to weather.

So I will gladly come to the Baltic![3] I am even looking forward to it 245
very much. See to it that we find someplace nice to stay. Is it again like last year?[4] Or somewhere else? I can't wait to see. It is very lovely; one can talk a lot on the beach. Well, where do you want to pick me up? I might spend several days in the Rhineland visiting a few friends. I hoped to meet my parents there, possibly around [July] twenty-seventh, twenty-eighth, twenty-ninth, since they are traveling earlier to Holland. I don't know yet if it will work. Then I think in any case I wouldn't really need to go back via Berlin. I could have some things sent after me. Can you come farther than Stettin? I wouldn't have suggested Berlin, because there one must always live up to so many demands and there is no peace for real conversation. I don't think Stettin is very *lovely*, but one could perhaps drive home along the sea. It would be around the thirtieth, thirty-first, or first, I think. I am just figuring out that the twenty-ninth is a Saturday; does that suit you better? Perhaps particularly *not*? We hoped, didn't we, to have a day and a half for the return trip. But perhaps you will take me directly to the sea? So, I will count on your picking me up in any case and send you word of the details.

[1.] *NL*, A 44,2 (22); handwritten; no return address, but certainly from London on July 13, 1939 (cf. Bethge's July 17, 1939, letter to Bonhoeffer, 1/142). Partially reproduced in *GS* 6:464–65.

[2.] Card not extant.

[3.] This refers to the planned retreat of the Sigurdshof collective pastorate, which then took place in Jershöft on August 4–14, 1939.

[4.] Reference is to the June 20–25, 1938, retreat of former Finkenwaldians in Zingst. At its conclusion Bonhoeffer and Bethge took several days' vacation together in Rowe; see Bonhoeffer's June 29, 1939, postcard to his parents, 1/17.

In the meantime, you will book the fourth to the fourteenth, won't you! By the way, Sabine[5] wants to give us a trip to Switzerland, which I find very kind. Do try as soon as possible to apply for the necessary foreign currency; I will do so as well as soon as I arrive. How should things go after the Baltic? Do you want me or not? I would really like to know. Please also see to it that Block[6] doesn't speak too much about me on the estate.[7] Officially I am still traveling.

Now a quick close; the letter must be on its way. It will probably cross again with one of yours. The dartboard is on the way. Julius[8] forgot it again! How are you doing now? Warm greetings to all. I think of you very much. Many thanks to Mrs. Struwe for the card![9]

Greetings to you from yours truly
Dietrich

246 **142. From Eberhard Bethge**[1]

S[igurdshof] July 17, 1939

Dear Dietrich,

Many thanks for your first letter that comes again from nearby.[2] For one does sense this very strongly. One knows the environments, the people, can imagine the intellectual, physical, also spiritual (admittedly not too highly concentrated) atmosphere, and that is very good. Admittedly, this cannot reduce the longing to see and talk to each other soon; on the contrary, this has become newly urgent through the new prospects. But it still is something different from utter foreignness. I fear you are being bombarded from within and from without about what you should do. Potsdam[3] preached this week in Berlin, and on that occasion I sent him to your mother. Now he tells me that you are to set yourself up there for several weeks in the house in the neighboring garden in pursuit of the old usual work.[4] One found it very important to do this. Potsdam thinks so as well,

---

[5.] Sabine Leibholz.

[6.] Eduard Block, the superintendent in Schlawe.

[7.] The guarded reference is to Major Dieter von Kleist at the military enlistment office in Schlawe.

[8.] Julius Rieger.

[9.] Card not extant.

[1.] *NL*, C 26; handwritten; previously unpublished.

[2.] From London; see Bonhoeffer's July 13, 1939, letter to Bethge from London, 1/141.

[3.] Hellmut Traub.

but that isn't so important. Now I cannot quite visualize what you yourself think, but perhaps I will hear soon. Naturally, I can't say anything about it. What my heart thinks about it, you know of course. On the other hand, here of course all is going as usual. Although in the last few days the pressure is increasing somewhat. I will have to go to Berlin after all.[5]

For the moment I have only your letter of the thirteenth. According to what it says, I would find August 1 very good for a reunion. I can come at least as far as Berlin, for I am feeling well again, especially since today it is cooler again after two very sultry days. The estate,[6] of course, should not know about this. That should be doable.

Won't it be unnecessarily expensive to come to west Germany by train? But I would gladly otherwise pick you up at an earlier station (Hanover?).

Wouldn't a vacation trip have to include a new attempt to look at a harpsichord in Nuremberg? Perhaps it will turn out that we have to finish up already by mid-August![7] Please say a very friendly hello to Gert.[8] I just received a 247
wonderful Rembrandt card,[9] which I was very pleased about. It is truly the most valuable of all my pictures to date, don't you agree? It's fine that you all were still able to get it. I was already thinking it might have been lost. Don't you judge this self-portrait as I do? It surpasses all the earlier ones. Do tell Gert that he shouldn't take so much trouble with letters to me; if he writes a brief postcard, that is quite enough and I am happy about it. I received his last letter the day before yesterday. Many thanks for all the greetings on the picture postcard. Just now a message came from your mother to Erna,[10] who wants to send your things home because of the presently convenient chance for transporting them; she (your mother) also writes that they would not travel from the end of July to mid-August. Now I will call Berlin this evening. Because then I would indeed like to talk to her beforehand. I had wanted to combine the driving with picking

---

[4.] At the Schleicher home at Marienburger Allee 42; the house was next to that of Bonhoeffer's parents. See Bethge and Gremmels, *A Life in Pictures*, centenary ed., 150.

[5.] [Possibly for discussions with those in charge of the Confessing Church's theological education.—VB]

[6.] An oblique reference to the Schlawe military enlistment office [see 1/141, ed. note 7.—VB]

[7.] [This refers to ending the courses at Sigurdshof and Köslin around August 24–25, 1939.—VB]

[8.] Gerhard Leibholz.

[9.] To circumvent the rigorous German regulations on foreign currency, Bethge periodically sent money to the Leibholz family, hidden in unopened literature on jurisprudence, the pages of which were not yet cut open. To signify the receipt of the money, Leibholz always sent Bethge an art postcard with images from the National Gallery in London. See Bethge, *Mein Freund Dietrich Bonhoeffer*, 23.

[10.] Erna Struwe.

you up at the same time. If that doesn't work, however, I will simply have to go there earlier.

Yesterday the sermon was not as good. But I was able to play the organ, and I enjoy that. In the afternoon we read the end of *Under Satan's Sun*,[11] which, however, was found to be too difficult. The weather prevented a boat trip. I would enjoy playing tennis with you again! I am practicing energetically. But I don't want to give you a heavy heart. You know things must work without you being here, and then they do work out, just as they have done up to now. With the warmest greetings your

Eberhard

A big hello from Alexander,[12] who wrote me a good letter filled with steadfastness; and one from Horst Lekszas, a true Horst (stylistically uniting Tersteegen[13] and Luther-German, as Fritz[14] put it!).

17:125 **142a. From Paul Lehmann to Timothy Lehmann**[1]

Columbus, Ohio. July 17, 1939

Dear Dad:

Thanks so much for all your bother about the mail and the check.[2] It was a great help to have it since I had finally to go to New York. By this time the letter and the denial[3] will have reached everybody so that I doubt any unfortunate circumstances will result.

[11.] George Bernanos's 1926 novel, *Sous le soleil de Satan*, had been published in Germany in 1927.

[12.] Alexander von der Marwitz. Both this letter and the one mentioned from Lekszas have been lost.

[13.] Gerhard Tersteegen.

[14.] Fritz Onnasch.

[1.] Lehmann Papers, Archive of the Library of Princeton Theological Seminary; typewritten carbon copy; unpublished. [Letter is in the original unaltered English.—VB] Lehmann had traveled on July 6, 1939, from Columbus, Ohio, to meet Bonhoeffer in New York. They spent the final day and a half together until Bonhoeffer's departure from New York harbor on July 7, 1939. See Bonhoeffer's diary (1/137, p. 237) as well as the related correspondence between him and Lehmann that summer [1/97, 1/114, 1/125, 1/126, 1/128, 1/131, 1/133.—VB]

[2.] Timothy Lehmann had financed his son Paul's trip to New York and taken on the task of sending cancellations to some forty colleges since Bonhoeffer couldn't lecture there. See 1/123 and 1/132.

[3.] This was the letter from Lehmann, 1/132.

It was really very worth my going even though I could not persuade Bonhoeffer to change his mind. I simply could not bring myself to allow him to have come and gone, perhaps without any possibility of meeting again, without seeing him while he was here. The reunion was a great joy to us both. Of the details, I must tell you when we are in Elmhurst[4] again. Meanwhile, I can only note that two important matters are likely to come from my visit. One is a rethinking of my whole theological and ethical position in the light of the current struggle of the Confessional Church; the other is a wholly new appraisal of the National Socialist movement. I am reading just now a book which Bonhoeffer gave me, written by a former Nazi,[5] and the best interpretation of the spiritual and cultural significance of what is now happening in Germany. It is called "The Nihilistic Revolution"[6] and reinforces in a remarkable way the reports from Bonhoeffer himself. I wish everyone might read the work for it makes plain what a vast difference there is between the penetrating and the surface understanding of current affairs and what is more shocking, how the end of a completely pragmatic philosophy is a pragmatic methodology which completely destroys all universal forms.

As for Dietrich himself, I can only say that I understand his position completely. He had agreed with his friends that he would come back without fail 17:126
within one year, unless a mutually agreed upon code formula came to him. This formula was to express their conviction that war was imminent. This formula came and there was no alternative. He fully expects war in September and will thus have one month to make the necessary connections so vital to the ongoing of the Confessing Church. Meanwhile, there had come to Bonhoeffer the clear perception that he who wishes to have any voice in the new Germany must live through this worst of agonies with her.[7] It was unthinkable to him to desert his friends and his task simply in order to safeguard his own life. The outstanding impression one gets from being with him and from hearing his account of the work he is doing is that the only power for living in a completely broken world is the Christian gospel. Here is a man and a group who are so completely committed to Christ in life that it has become axiomatic to them that they may have to die for Him. And they are ready. When the New Testament talks about one's "joy being full"[8] it lays down what these men are actually experiencing now.

[4.] Lehmann's father was president of Elmhurst College in Illinois.

[5.] Hermann Rauschning [see also Wilhelm Rott's mention of the book in 1/143 —VB].

[6.] [The actual title in English was *The Revolution of Nihilism*; see also 1/151, ed. note 11.—VB]

[7.] Cf. the excerpt of Bonhoeffer's letter to Niebuhr, 1/129.

[8.] Cf. John 15:11–13.

One discovers over against such a witness to the faith that the times of the end are really the time of the only possible beginning and that one's own life and faith securely pursued above these struggles of the end lack all reality. The German Confessional Church is re-enacting the book of the Acts. Therein is its power; therein is the hope for the only possible German future. . . .[9]

Marion joins me in warmest greetings and love to you all,

As ever, [Paul]

248 **143. From Wilhelm Rott**[1]

At present Jungfraujoch (in the fog), July 20, 1939

Dear Dietrich,

Your card[2] reached me in Wengen (the Bernese highlands), where I am spending the major part of my holidays. I was very pleased to get it. Less pleased, naturally, with your resigned observation re: "liberty."[3] Perhaps—I hope so—in the meantime other impressions have been added to it. In view of the world misery, which here outside Germany one overlooks in an utterly different manner (the—in my opinion—unavoidable catastrophe after the harvest!),[4] this secularized Christendom and theology! Here in Switzerland the latter has become noticeably better in the past year. With many fellow pastors whom I've encountered by chance, the same self-evident position. The clear will to defend has really increased, not only here! The unrepentant anti-German stance, generally prevalent among contemporaries outside, is distressing. In this moment you have a great and difficult task! Call them all to bow down under the Word and to pray in intercession for all the need of the times.

Basel is indeed pleasant![5] Have you read Rauschning, *The Revolution of Nihilism?*[6]—I will travel for several days to the south (Mediterranean); on July 31 I am in Zollbrück near Bern (D. v. Steiger). Do send something to the Bergli[7]

[9.] [Here a passage from Lehmann's letter has been omitted.—VB]

[1.] Previously published in *GS* 6:443–44; the original has been lost.

[2.] From New York; card not extant.

[3.] Cf. Bonhoeffer's observations on "freedom" in "Protestantism without Reformation," 2/6, pp. 448–49 [and in the June 24 and July 2 entries in his diary, 1/137—VB].

[4.] This is a reference to the constantly growing danger of war, which Hitler then began on September 1, 1939.

[5.] A reference to Karl Barth [Barth had left Germany in 1935 to teach at the university there—VB].

[6.] [Bonhoeffer had shared the book with Paul Lehmann; see 1/142a.—VB]

[7.] Rudolf Pestalozzi's vacation home, where Karl Barth met with theological and political friends in late July/early August 1939. See Busch, *Karl Barth*, 297–98.

(Dehn[8] is there at present). Finis Germaniae??[9]—CC[10] will go on! Come back soon. Your

Willi

144. To Karl Bonhoeffer[1] 249

July 21, 1939

Dear Papa,

Many thanks for your letter.[2] We have now reconsidered things and have arrived at the following conclusion: Sabine travels on Friday and wants to meet with you on Saturday; she will write about the place.[3] I didn't want to shorten your time by the sea through my suggestion of a meeting on the Rhine and think it best if I come to Berlin on July 27, that is, on Thursday. We then have time until your departure, Friday evening. Sabine also asks very much that you not shorten your time together by a few days. I will then travel to Pomerania and either work at the old place with the others or by myself on an estate. I travel on Monday to Aachen. A letter would reach me by early Tuesday there at the main post office, in case you do have other plans.

Greetings to you from your grateful
Dietrich

145. To Eberhard Bethge[1]

July 21, 1939

Dear Eberhard,

Many thanks for your letter, which, as expected, crossed with mine again.[2] [—]Forgive the handwriting. I am writing on my knees.[—]So now brief

[8.] Günther Dehn.

[9.] "The end of Germany??"

[10.] [Confessing Church.—VB]

[1.] *NL*, A 44,1 (33); handwritten; from London. Partially reproduced in *GS* 6:463.

[2.] Letter not extant.

[3.] The reference is to a planned meeting between Sabine Leibholz and her parents in Holland.

[1.] *NL*, A 44,2 (23); handwritten; no return address, but certainly from London. Previously published in *GS* 6:465–68, with excerpts published in *GS* 2:552.

[2.] See Bethge's July 17, 1939, letter to Bonhoeffer, 1/142. The next two sentences, set off with dashes, are a comment written in the upper left margin.

250 news about the plans. I am in Aachen on Tuesday (i.e., probably Monday night), if possible will visit my colleagues in Dortmund and friends in Elberfeld[3] on Tuesday and Wednesday, and am Thursday evening presumably in Berlin. On Friday evening my parents travel to Holland. Saturday I wanted to travel on to the north. Now the question is where I am to meet you. Naturally, the earlier the better. On the other hand, I would prefer that we can really talk at leisure when we meet; that may be your intention as well. I am afraid in Berlin it will not be very peaceful, because there everything will descend upon me again, and I am a bit averse to that, in light of the pleasure with which I await our meeting. At times in the past, we have not found the quiet for conversations that we would like to have had. Would not Stettin on Saturday afternoon be better, possibly so that we could still go on toward the sea and then at least travel together till Monday, perhaps back home via Krössin.[4] Naturally, I am also delighted if you are already in Berlin, but I don't quite know whether it wouldn't be better the other way. Your suggestion to come to Hanover with the car is, of course, also terribly nice and tempting. It's only that I can't tell you today which train. Also the traveling is indeed exhausting for you. Please send a telegram with your plans to Aachen *poste restante*[5] before Tuesday morning. If nothing is there, I will let you hear from me, by telephone or telegram. Now as the return is so imminent, the joy of seeing you again is already very great. So, till the twenty-ninth at the latest; I'm looking forward to the sea.

By the way, I also think the Rembrandt portrait more beautiful than all the others.[6]

Give everyone my warmest greetings. I am now eager to see whether you still want me to help or only wish a visit.

Why do you eventually want to start your vacation already on August 15? That I would really like to know.

251 Soon we will meditate again together. That is also very important to me. In recent weeks I have followed the Daily Texts much more.[7]

May God strengthen you in your work and keep you! Warmly, your faithful

Dietrich

[3.] Hans Joachim Iwand and Hermann A. Hesse. See *DB-ER*, 662.

[4.] Klein-Krössin, the estate of Ruth von Kleist-Retzow.

[5.] [To be held for pickup.—VB]

[6.] See Bethge's July 17, 1939, letter to Bonhoeffer, 1/142, ed. note 9.

[7.] Cf. his diary from his period in the United States, 1/137.

Sabine sends cordial greetings. I'm writing in her room. She is doing well and will also soon take a vacation! We could also telephone on Thursday evening (around 9:30 I would await your call) and discuss everything else, if that is still necessary. Everything will surely come out fine.

146. To John Baillie[1]

22.7.39.

Dear Professor Baillie,

I have just returned from America and received a letter from Germany with some indication of an invitation from you to Edinburgh for the purpose of lectures there next spring.[2] Thank you very much indeed for this invitation. I will come with the greatest pleasure, if I get out of Germany by that time. Since I am not yet in the possession of your letter I do not know if you have any particular wish with respect of the topic of the lectures. But I suppose, we could correspond about it later. I should be most interested to spend a short time in Edinburgh and I am looking forward to seeing you again.[3] I shall leave for Germany on Tuesday.[4] If you have any special message for me which you would rather not write to Germany, will you please send it to the above mentioned address. Professor Leibholz,[5] my brother-in-law who is living there, will find a way of passing it on to me. 252

With many thanks I remain Yours sincerely
Dietrich Bonhoeffer

[1.] *NL*, A 50,2 (23); handwritten; return address "Dietrich Bonhoeffer, 55, Honor Oak Road, SE 23, Forest Hill, London." Previously published in *GS* 2:362. [Letter is in the original unaltered English.—VB]

[2.] See Baillie's June 15, 1939, letter to Bonhoeffer, 1/113. [Bonhoeffer had been invited to give the Croall Lectures at the University of Edinburgh; cf. *DB-ER*, 661.—VB]

[3.] Bonhoeffer had met Baillie during his time at Union Seminary in 1930–31. See *DB-ER*, 157–60, and *DBWE* 10:307–9.

[4.] July 25, 1939.

[5.] Gerhard Leibholz.

147. To George Bell[1]

22.7.39

My dear Lordbishop,

when you were in London on Thursday I asked Hildebrandt[2] to tell you that I had already come back from U.S.A. and that I am on my way to Germany. Unfortunately, he forgot to tell you. Now I can only write a few words of explanation and to say "good bye" to you. I shall leave on Tuesday morning.

On my arrival in New York Dr. Leiper[3] very kindly offered me the post of a refugee pastor (I mean a pastor for the refugees) in New York. This post was to be connected with lectures in various places. Of course, I was rather surprised about this offer and told Dr. Leiper, that I had promised to the Confessional Church to come back at the latest after a year unless the political circumstances would make that impossible. So it was just a question of loyalty whether I could accept a post which by itself would make my return doubtful or even impossible. I discussed the problem with my friends very thoroughly and decided to decline the offer for three reason: I was bound by my promise to go back next year; there are many non-aryan brethren who a[re] much more entitled to such a post; I had got my leave of absence for another purpose.

It was a difficult decision, but I am still convinced, I was not allowed to decide otherwise. That meant my early return to Germany. Kindly enough, I was invited by Dr. Coffin and Van Dusen to stay at Union Seminary as long
253 as I wanted. But when news about Danzig[4] reached me I felt compelled to go back as soon as possible and to make my decision in Germany. I do not regret my trip to U.S.A., though, of course, it had been undertaken under different presuppositions. I have seen and learned much in the few weeks over there and I am looking forward to my work in Germany again. What sort of personal decisions will be asked from me I do not know. But nobody knows that now.

[1.] LPL, BP 42:70–71; handwritten; return address "Dietrich Bonhoeffer, 55, Honor Oak Road, SE 23, London." Cf. also *NL*, A 42,1 (30); later typewritten copy. Partially reproduced in *GS* 1:320–22. [Letter is in the original unaltered English.—VB]

[2.] Franz Hildebrandt.

[3.] Henry Smith Leiper.

[4.] This refers to the intensified tensions between Germany and Poland due to the Nazi foreign policy demanding that Danzig become part of the German Reich. Following the abrogation on April 28, 1939, of the German-Polish Non-Aggression Pact, the situation in July 1939 escalated dangerously. For excerpts from Hitler's speech in the Reichstag, see Snyder, *Documents of German History*, 440–45.

My passport expires next spring;[5] it is therefore uncertain when I shall be in this country again. Let me thank you today for all help and friendship and real understanding in the past and in the future. We shall never forget you during the coming events. I thank you for what you have done for my brother-in-law[6] and his family. It has meant everything to them. Will you allow me to leave them and this country with the confidence that they may approach you whenever they need advice and help?[7] Of course, their future is unsettled, too, and it will require much patience and much energy before they can start afresh. Nevertheless I am confident that they finally will not suffer more than they can bear.

May I ask you to convey my best regards to Mrs. Bell? I remain, my Lordbishop, in sincere gratitude Yours ever

Dietrich Bonhoeffer

P.S. I have just heard that my brother-in-law has applied to Magdalen-College[8] to be allowed to keep his offered grant of 100 pounds for two years in addition to the grant from the Church. That would give them 350 pounds a year which would be a sufficient basis to live on. Do you think that anything could be done to support this request? It would make a great difference. D.B.

148. From Eberhard Bethge[1] 254

July 22, 1939

Dear Dietrich,

Aleas sunt iacta.[2] I just wrote your mother (in reply) that I will be in Berlin Thursday (the twenty-seventh) evening, and would like to drive with them

[5.] Bonhoeffer's passport expired on March 4, 1940. See Bethge and Gremmels, *Life in Pictures*, centenary ed., 115.

[6.] Gerhard Leibholz.

[7.] Regarding all the help that Bell offered the Leibholz family in the years that followed, see Leibholz-Bonhoeffer, *Bonhoeffers*, esp. 113–16, and Bethge and Jaspers, *An der Schwelle zum gespaltenen Europa*. [Bell also assisted numerous German refugees in England and was responsible for helping many of the "non-Aryan" Confessing Church pastors emigrate, as well as finding them positions in England. See Gerlach, *And the Witnesses Were Silent*, 152–54.—VB]

[8.] [In Oxford.—VB]

[1.] *NL*, C 26; handwritten; unaddressed, but certainly from Sigurdshof; previously unpublished.

[2.] Mistakenly instead of *Alea iacta esto* (the die has been cast).

together toward the west, the main stretch on the twenty-eighth, then the shorter one on Saturday morning to wherever you are staying, Cologne or wherever. You can simply write to Berlin; I will find out there. Based on your letter,[3] for which I thank you very much, things have just worked out that way; I called and simply asked with this as a recommendation. Now I am looking forward very much for everything to go this way. Hopefully, you will be able to keep your promise. I have also already reserved rooms in Jeershöft.[4] That will be the best for several reasons. Rented from the fourth on. Before that, though, I would like to come back here and finish some things. Namely, we would like Potsdam[5] to bring some of his work to a close, and to take over my time for that (the conclusions I arrived at are all right), and I would then very much like to be able to sit in and listen to you and him teach. We think this is a very good idea. Now let us get going.

Some days now I lead a fantastically lazy life, during the day by the lake with games, the boat, and an old punt that constantly capsizes and then in the evening a nice easy game of tennis. I am enjoying this to the fullest, in the expectation that soon I can enjoy doing it even more with you.

I informed Block in the appropriate manner.[6] I don't see him very often now. Didn't come so often to Schlawe. Next week we will see Knorr[7] and several others.

On the whole I am doing quite well. I am getting ample exercise in the fresh air. Do you not also think that for the winter we should find the opportunity to start playing *The Art of the Fugue* on two keyboards?[8] My thoughts are somewhat preoccupied with that. Well, there is so much to tell. I look forward to the drive.

A very warm hello to your sister, brother-in-law, nieces[9] (how is the recorder practice going?) your

Eberhard

[3.] See Bonhoeffer's July 13, 1939, letter to Bethge, 1/141.

[4.] ["Jershöft."—VB] See 1/141, ed. note 3.

[5.] Hellmut Traub.

[6.] Eduard Block [see the warning in Bonhoeffer's July 13 letter, 1/141—VB].

[7.] Dr. August Knorr in Köslin, who was very active there in the Confessing Church. Cf. *DB-ER*, 590.

[8.] Bach's composition *The Art of the Fugue*, from the 1740s [BWV 1080.—VB]

[9.] The Leibholzes in London.

149. From Jean Lasserre[1] 255

July 26, 1939

My dear Friend,

Thank you for your postcards, which gave me great pleasure and revived in me very agreeable memories, including those of our camaraderie at Union and the jokes we played together.[2] I am very happy for you that you were able to make the trip again and am sure that you did a lot of good work there. Courage, brother!

Next week we are leaving for vacation in the Drôme, and the first week of September we will be in Houches (near Chamonix) before returning here.

Our work continues here, inspiring but difficult because of the discouraging atmosphere all round, the skepticism, and the embittered indifference. But those few souls who approach God are heading directly toward the heavens.

When will I see you again?—We are well; my wife and my little boy are my pride and joy. I would really like you to meet them.

I received a nice letter from Erwin,[3] who is also keeping to the straight and narrow path of celibacy.

Have no doubts, my brother in Christ, of my sincere affection. Yours ever.[4]

Jean Lasserre

150. To John Baillie[1]

30.7.39

Dear Professor Baillie,

many thanks for your letter which I found here on my return. I am writing today to confirm my letter from London[2] which you will have received in the meantime. It is indeed a great privilege and joy to me to be invited to Edinburgh for the purpose you have mentioned in your letter. I hope to 256

[1.] *NL*, C 23; handwritten postcard; stamped: Maubeuge, August 2, 1939; previously unpublished. The original letter is in French; translation here by David Higgins.

[2.] Bonhoeffer had come to know the young Frenchman during their year of study at Union Theological Seminary in 1930–31. Cf. *DB-ER*, 153–54, and the frequent references to their friendship in *DBWE* 10.

[3.] Erwin Sutz, who was also at Union Theological Seminary in 1930–31.

[4.] [These two words are in English in the original.—VB]

[1.] *NL*, A 50,2 (24); handwritten; no return address, probably from Berlin; previously unpublished. [Letter is in the original unaltered English.—VB]

[2.] See Bonhoeffer's July 22, 1939, letter to Baillie, 1/146.

hear from you soon if everything will work out as you think. October would be a most suitable time for me to come to see you. I am looking forward to this visit very much indeed.

May I ask you to give my best regards to Mrs. Baillie and to Jan. Hoping to see you soon and in sincere gratefulness for your great kindness I am

Yours most sincerely

Dietrich Bonhoeffer

151. From Paul Lehmann to Reinhold Niebuhr[1]

Columbus, Ohio
July 31, 1939

Dear Reinie:

After hearing from your mother and Hulda[2] about your tremendously crowded schedule these days, I ought to thank you for taking any time at all to write and for the additional kindness of the photo. I saw your folks, including also Helmuth,[3] when I made a dash to New York the first week of this month to see what all this was about Bonhoeffer. Your mother was kind enough also to let me have the press comments on your lectures.[4] These I have now read with great interest and care and shall return. It was almost as though I had been there myself. I have no doubt at all that the Gifford's have reached a new high. As soon as they will be published, I shall own them myself.

Perhaps you will have heard all about Bonhoeffer by now. His hope was to get a brief glimpse of you on his return through England. In case he did not succeed, I think some explanation is due you, so I shall venture to make it. My own conversation with him convinced me that he was doing the only thing he could do.

You see, his original concern was the avoidance of military duty. The oath to Hitler which this would have involved was intolerable to him. At the same time, he did not welcome the idea of imprisonment on this ground any earlier than absolutely necessary. The visit to America would have secured a postponement of this decision and left him free to continue his work, though at some distance.
257 Meanwhile anything could happen both within Germany and without and the whole problem disappear. The American invitation actually has delayed his obligation to report for duty until Spring.

[1.] *NL*, A 50,1 (27); typewritten carbon copy; previously unpublished. [Letter is in the original unaltered English.—VB]

[2.] Hulda Niebuhr, Niebuhr's elder sister.

[3.] H. R. Niebuhr.

[4.] See Niebuhr's May 11, 1939, letter to Lehmann, 1/91, ed. note 2.

Bonhoeffer arrived in New York about the tenth of June, expecting a stay for one year. Before he left Germany, he pledged himself to return without fail after this year and, if war seemed imminent, to return at once. The war news was to reach him from his friends in the confessional church by code. He was here scarcely a week when this formula came to him, whereupon he decided to return at once. He reasoned that one month of work before the hostilities would be of strategic importance for the confessional church.

Now there are three other factors which play into this decision. The first is that Bonhoeffer had no definite job over here. The post which Leiper[5] offered him with the Refugee Committee could not be accepted without excluding himself permanently from Germany, which he was pledged not to do. On the other hand, if he had had a definite teaching post, he would have regarded that as a prior obligation and not returned immediately. Occasional lectures seemed to him too dangerous in view of the imminence of war which would certainly prohibit these opportunities to aliens. The second consideration was the discovery during the short time that he was here that he could not hope to make any contribution to the German future, if it were given him to survive, unless he suffered through this present time. This had not been quite so clear to him before his trip. But from the isolation of Coffin's summer home he had looked across the seas and become convinced that voluntary exile was the path to permanent inactivity. Here was an additional ground for not endangering his return by accepting Leiper's offer. And of course, the third factor in his decision was the growing feeling that to remain here would have reduced itself to a violation of the gospel injunction that he that loseth his life shall save it.[6] On this point he could not bring his conscience to rest and in the face of the next few critical weeks, he simply had to return.

I do not feel justified in taking your time now with more than the barest comments. So I shall reserve other remarks about this whole situation until we meet, I hope in January. As for the expenses, please let this be a small contribution of mine to the decencies that still remain in this world. It was not very much and I can and do gladly assume it. If you want to get rid of the money you would have spent, give it to the society for drowning the present Prime Minister,[7] if the British still have enough virility to organize it.

[5.] Henry S. Leiper.

[6.] Cf. Matt. 10:39.

[7.] Neville Chamberlain. [This is a comment on Chamberlain's role at the September 1938 Munich conference, where both Britain and France agreed to Nazi Germany's annexation of the Czech Sudetenland. Chamberlain defended the agreement, saying it had ensured "peace for our time."—VB]

258 One specific point Bonhoeffer wanted me to mention. It concerns the Union fellowship to Germany. We visited Tryon[8] while in New York and gleaned indirectly that the German appointee was a German Christian. This really disturbed Bonhoeffer greatly. He felt it an unwarranted contradiction in the professed interest of the Seminary in the Confessional struggle, the more especially since he believes it of very great importance for Confessional Church students to have the opportunity of the freer air of foreign study for a time. Doesn't it mean that the Seminary ought to revise its German Committee? Why couldn't Bonhoeffer be asked to head such a committee for the future? The International Student Exchange in Berlin is certainly Nazi dominated. I suppose nothing can be done anymore this year. But I think that these awards out to be thoroughly altered.

Perhaps Eden[9] could help by exchanging students with the Confessional Church. Bonhoeffer says that they are prepared to provide keep over there and passage from Germany to New York for the German student. If Eden could offer keep here plus the fare from New York to St. Louis some arrangement could be made. It would be a real assistance to the Confessional Church. . . .[10]

Do you know the book by Hermann Rauschning: "Die Revolution des Nihilismus"?[11] Bonhoeffer gave it to me as the best interpretation of contemporary German affairs. I have just finished it and found it immensely illuminating. I must talk with you about that too when we meet. . . .

[Paul Lehmann]

[8.] Harold Harrison Tryon.

[9.] Eden Theological Seminary in St. Louis.

[10.] Here some comments about Lehmann's personal professional plans have been omitted; a similar omission concludes the following paragraph.

[11.] Rauschning's book (the German subtitle was *Kulisse und Wirklichkeit im Dritten Reich*, or "Stageset and Reality in the Third Reich") appeared in Zurich and New York in 1938. [The English title was *The Revolution of Nihilism: Warning to the West*.—VB]

152. From Ottonie Blanck[1]

Berlin-Steglitz, August 11, 1939
Paulsenstrasse 55

Dear Pastor Bonhoeffer,

Perhaps you will have a vague recollection that we are children of the same department and university;[2] indeed I do not turn to you today for that rea- 259
son, but I possibly do so more freely and with fewer reservations than I would have otherwise. I turn to you as the author of the pamphlet "Life Together,"[3] which, whenever I reach for it, enriches and delights me more and more. It will be familiar to you that in these turbulent times questions within the congregation come up and go around, which often don't find a path to the appointed pastor—(unfortunately or thank God?)—because he is too overburdened, or because the parishioners' sense of their own responsibility and maturity among themselves is growing?[4]—Thus during my vacation the question came to me, posed by a group of very young people: whether it is permissible or commanded to go to Holy Communion, when for those concerned the general confession[5] is no longer that "which it pretends to be," but rather a path to the attainment of cheap grace,[6] while they cannot yet travel the path to private confession. It was surely a genuine question, filled with need, from which a great thirst for the "bread of life"[7] was speaking, a resolve no longer to be satisfied with cheap commitments. Now I naturally asked them to pose this question first to the pastor in charge. However, since a cordial brotherly relationship ties me to these young people of our congregation, I had to attempt as well to reply what my own stand is on this; approximately to this effect: yes, permitted and commanded.

[1.] Letter in the personal possession of Heinz-Jürgen Blanck-Lubarsch; typewritten carbon copy; previously unpublished.

[2.] Ottonie Blanck's father, Otto Lubarsch, was professor of pathology at the Berlin University medical school during the same period as Bonhoeffer's father.

[3.] *DBWE* 5; it first appeared in 1939 as Theologische Existenz heute 61. See *DBWE* 5:6.

[4.] From summer 1933 on, Ottonie Blanck worked energetically as a voluntary deaconess for Martin Niemöller in the Berlin-Dahlem congregation, helping to build up the Confessing congregation there. See Graff et al., *Unterwegs zur mündigen Gemeinde,* 54.

[5.] [The general confession during the liturgy is spoken together by the congregation.—VB]

[6.] This was a central concept in Bonhoeffer's *Discipleship*; cf. *DBWE* 4:43–56.

[7.] Cf. John 6:35.

And attempted to ground this reply on the basis of the sacramental words of institution of the Lord's Supper[8] and Luther.[9]

Now, however, I feel greatly burdened by this responsibility, and I would be very thankful to you if you could tell me whether such a venture is forbidden to laypeople and how you would respond to such a question. The open door to private confession should have remained clearly visible in the answer.

On page 79 below you say: "From now on, the Christian gains one victory after another."[10] But what if experience can also say that the defeats "from now on" will become much harder, more numerous, and more burdensome? Could you show me a way out from being caught between these contradictions, which are a heavy burden on me?

260 In the hope that I don't burden your full schedule too terribly much with my questions—(I can also wait patiently!)—I remain with best respects

Yours truly
[Ottonie Blanck]

153. To Paula Bonhoeffer[1]

Dear Mama,

I will be here by the sea for several days, this time with the group from Köslin. I may stay up here until we finish working,[2] if Uncle Rudi[3] continues to do well. Here though the relatives had serious doubts about that. I can best be reached by telephone or otherwise via Eberhard.

Best regards from your grateful
Dietrich

[8.] Cf. Mark 14:22–24 and pars. (Matt. 26:26–29; Luke 22:14–20; 1 Cor. 11:23–25).

[9.] See especially Luther's explanation of the "sacrament of the altar" in the Small Catechism (*Book of Concord*, 362) and "A Brief Exhortation to Confession" in the Large Catechism (*Book of Concord*, 476–80).

[10.] See *DBWE* 5:112.

[1.] *NL*, A 44,1 (34); handwritten postcard; postmarked: Bauerhufen via Köslin, August 16, 1939. Partially reproduced in *GS* 6:467.

[2.] The end of the summer term in the collective pastorates at Sigurdshof and Köslin on August 24–25, 1939.

[3.] Code name for the day of the beginning of the war.

154. To John Baillie[1]

24.8.39

Dear Professor Baillie,

when I wrote my last letter to you indicating that October would be a very
suitable time for my coming to Edinburgh[2] I had not yet received your
kind letter to my address in London. Since I have not heard from you after
my last letter I supposed that it has not reacted. Today I must tell you that
it will be very difficult for me to get out in October and I should like to
ask you if any time after December 1st or 15th would be acceptable for the 261
committee. I am thinking of the following topic: "the death in the christian
message." Would you kindly let me know if you could agree to this proposal.
I thank you most sincerely for your great kindness and help and I remain
Yours ever

Dietrich Bonhoeffer

155. To Sabine and Gerhard Leibholz[1]

August 28, 1939

Dear Sabine and Gert,

Since the day before yesterday I've been with our parents. It was difficult in recent days and weeks to take longer trips.[2] You have also not heard much from me. I was very sorry about that. Nonetheless, if it is still possible for you to go to the National Museum sometime, I would like to have the colored reproduction of Raphael,[3] if that doesn't create too many difficulties for you. It is the very large painting that one sees immediately from the entrance, and the reproduction is also larger than the other cards. Perhaps you can still obtain it? Everyone is doing well, and our thoughts often go in your direction. Do drive again if possible to George[4] concerning where to

---

[1.] *NL*, A 50,2 (25); photocopy of a handwritten card; return address: "43, Marienburger Allee, Berlin-Charlottenburg 9." Partially reproduced in *GS* 2:362. [Letter is in original unaltered English.—VB]

[2.] See Bonhoeffer's July 30, 1939, letter to Baillie, 1/150.

[1.] *NL*, A 44,1 (35); later typewritten copy; from Berlin. Partially reproduced in *GS* 6:467.

[2.] This refers to the mobilization in Germany in preparation for the attack on Poland on September 1, 1939.

[3.] Cf. Bethge's July 17, 1939, letter to Bonhoeffer, 1/142, ed. note 9.

[4.] George Bell.

stay during your vacation. He will certainly be able to give you good advice and recommendations. How is Franz's[5] new cottage coming along? Don't you want to take something like that too? Our parents have spoken very happily about your days together by the sea.[6] It remains uncertain when I will come. Perhaps in December.[7]

Much love to you all from your faithful
Dietrich

262 **156. From George Bell**[1]

6.9.39

My dear Dietrich,

You know how deeply I feel for you and yours in this melancholy time. May God comfort and guide you. I think often of our talk in the summer.[2] May He keep you now. Let us pray together often by reading the Beatitudes;[3] Pax Dei quae superate omnia nos custodiat.[4]

Your affectionate
George

[5.] Franz Hildebrandt.

[6.] The reference is to their meeting in Holland; cf. Bonhoeffer's July 21, 1939, letter to Karl Bonhoeffer, 1/144, ed. note 3.

[7.] Cf. Bonhoeffer's August 24, 1939, letter to John Baillie, 1/154.

[1.] LPL, BP 9:357; handwritten; from Chichester. Cf. also *NL*, A 42,2 (13); later typewritten copy. Previously published in *GS* 6:469. [Letter is in the original unaltered English.—VB] After the September 1, 1939, German attack on Poland, Great Britain and France declared war on Germany on September 3. Regarding Bell's concerns about the fate of his friends in Germany after the war began, see *DB-ER*, 665.

[2.] See Bonhoeffer's letters of June 6 and July 22, 1939, to Bell, 1/106 and 1/147.

[3.] Matt. 5:3–12.

[4.] "May the peace of God, which surpasses all understanding, preserve us." Cf. Phil. 4:7.

157. To Johannes Radtke

157.1 Application for Army and Military Hospital Chaplaincy[1]

To Army Head Chaplain Radtke, Berlin-Spandau

September 9, 1939

My dear and esteemed Brother Radtke,

It has been more than ten years since we last saw each other. Now the connection has surprisingly been reestablished in a rather roundabout way through my cousin Mrs. v. Hase.[2] A few days ago I was at the military bishop's[3] to offer my services. On his advice I went to Schackla[4] in Stettin, who, however, cannot use me at the moment, although possibly later. 263
In the meantime, you have been informed about my intention. I would be very grateful to you if you could use my services in the military hospitals or elsewhere in some fashion, and I may expect your decision. My previous work will unfortunately have to cease for the time being, since almost all the young people have been drafted.

At the same time, [I] would like to ask you whether you see a way to use my assistant supervisor [Inspektor], an excellent young Confessing Church theologian—born in 1909.[5] You would find him a very efficient man, and I would be pleased if he could be used in a ministry of proclamation.

For your information I am enclosing the curriculum vitae that the military bishop recently asked me for.

I thank you very much for all your efforts and would be very pleased to see you again. With all best wishes for your work, greetings from your respectful

Dietrich Bonhoeffer

157.2 Enclosure: Curriculum vitae[6]

I, Dietrich Bonhoeffer, was born on February 4, 1906, in Breslau as the son of university full professor for psychiatry Karl Bonhoeffer and his wife,

---

[1.] Letter in the personal possession of Johannes Radtke; typewritten with hand signature; return address: "Pastor Lic. Dietrich Bonhoeffer, presently at Berlin-Charlottenburg 9, Marienburger Allee 43"; previously unpublished. Cf. *NL*, Anh. A 26,1. See also *DB-ER*, 666.

[2.] Klara von Hase (residing in Rostock), wife of the army chaplain Hans Christoph von Hase.

[3.] Franz Dohrmann.

[4.] Army head chaplain Schackla, the Protestant pastor in Military District II in Stettin.

[5.] Eberhard Bethge.

[6.] Document in the personal possession of Johannes Radtke; typewritten; unpublished. Cf. *NL*, Anh. A 26,1.

Paula née von Hase. After 1912 I attended the humanistic Friedrich Werder Gymnasium in Berlin, later the Grunewald Gymnasium, which I left in 1923 with my Abitur.[7] After studies in Tübingen and Berlin, I completed my Licentiate degree summa cum laude under Privy Councillor Seeberg[8] at the University of Berlin. After my first theological examination[9] before the consistory in Berlin, I was sent to Barcelona as a vicar[10] for one year—1928–29. In 1930 I received my habilitation degree in systematic theology
264 at the University of Berlin, completed my second theological examination before the consistory in Berlin, and then went on an academic scholarship to Union Theological Seminary in New York for one year. After my return I was ordained—in 1931—lectured at the university, and held the office of student chaplain at the Technical College in Charlottenburg. In October 1933 I was elected pastor of two German Protestant congregations in London. From there I was called back to Germany in April 1935 to assume the directorship of a preachers' seminary. Since the conclusion of this work—winter 1937–38—I have worked in the superintendents' offices in Schlawe and Köslin. I speak English fluently.

I have published the following books: *Sanctorum Communio: A Theological Study of the Sociology of the Church*, 1930; *Act and Being*, 1931; *Creation and Fall: A Theological Exposition of Genesis 1–3*, 1933; *Discipleship*, 1937; *Life Together*, 1939.

Under the present circumstances, I would like to place myself at the service of the military chaplaincy.

158. To Johannes Radtke[1]

To Military Head Chaplain Ra[d]tke, Berlin-Spandau

September 13, 1939

Dear Brother Ra[d]tke,

You will have received my letter from last Saturday. I don't want to press you at all. But I should inform you of the following: I have just been called by

[7.] [The German secondary school diploma that allows students to pursue university studies.—VB]

[8.] Reinhold Seeberg.

[9.] [Prospective pastors had to pass two theological examinations.—VB]

[10.] [I.e., an assistant pastor who had yet to pass the second theological exam.—VB]

[1.] Letter in the personal possession of Johannes Radtke; typewritten with hand signature; return address: "Pastor Lic. Dietrich Bonhoeffer, presently at Berlin-Charlottenburg 9, Marienburger Allee 43"; previously unpublished. Cf. *NL*, Anh. A 26,2.

the Army High Command and authorized to tell you that my wish has come to the attention of Colonel Burdach and Major General Kaufmann, who would warmly support it. The military chaplain[2] has also been informed. 265
Perhaps it is important for you to know this.

With best wishes respectfully yours
Dietrich Bonhoeffer

159. From Heinz Doebert[1]

Züllichau, September 16, 1939

Dear Brother Bonhoeffer,

When the Sunday sermon is done, one is also at ease to write letters! So I am doing quite well! I am still a civilian. Unfortunately, things didn't work out on the one Wednesday for getting together! My fiancée and I had bicycled to Bethesda Hospital in Teltow, where my fiancée held a Bible study and then visited patients. On the way back, we were caught in a thunderstorm in Lichterfelde. And to make matters worse, I didn't know Brother Grosch's[2] house number.

I had hardly arrived in Berlin when I was told that I had to go to Züllichau on the Polish border,[3] since several brothers there had been conscripted. At the same time I received my topics:[4] "the true relationship of the offices of preacher and of elder and its historical realization in the Old Prussian Protestant congregations in the western and the eastern provinces," 2 Cor. 5:14–15 and Luther's explanation of second article.[5]

At the train station I was told that everything beyond Frankfurt/Oder was uncertain. Therefore: a ticket that far, and took the bicycle along. The train went as far as Liegnitz. So in Frankfurt I paid extra while the locomotive engines were changed. One look at the road map obtained with effort (the army needed maps too!): to Sommerfeld. There I arrived around 7:20 p.m. It was dark. I

[2.] Franz Dohrmann.

[1.] *NL*, C 25; handwritten; unpublished. Doebert was a candidate in the collective pastorate at Sigurdshof in the summer of 1939.

[2.] Götz Grosch.

[3.] [This was in Silesia, which at that time was a church province in the Old Prussian Union.—VB]

[4.] The reference is to the topics he had to write for his second theological examination, taken under the Old Prussian Union Confessing Church Council of Brethren.

[5.] Cf. Martin Luther's explanation of the second article of the Apostles' Creed in his Small and Large Catechism (*Book of Concord*, 355 and 435–40). On the first topic, cf. the word πρεσβύτερος (elder) at the end of the paragraph following the next one.

had two small suitcases and a coat. I drove, lamp dimmed,[6] in total darkness through the completely strange area. Finally the moon came out. As long as the
266 road was good, things now went pretty quickly. This was true, however, of the fewest stretches. Finally it became hilly. I finally reached a telephone connection in Grünberg. Fortunately, the superintendent had just returned from guard duty, so that I awakened him at 11:30 p.m.! He informed me that tomorrow (a Sunday) had been taken care of. So I spent the night in Grünberg. I had ridden forty-five kilometers! The next morning I rode in bright sunshine to the peaceful little town of Züllichau, twenty-two kilometers behind the front. As I traveled by moonlight, I heard the thunder of the cannons: the Poles were shooting at Fraustadt on German territory.

In the meantime, the superintendent was needed to minister to the wounded and could put down the soldier's profession. Brother Röhling[7] is still here as well, unexpectedly. So just a few surrounding villages had to be tended to. That worked to the benefit of my exam. So the sermon and catechesis are done. My fiancée made excerpts from the commentaries, and so I gathered the obligatory literature for the exam with the help of the local parish libraries. After Monday I will turn πρεσβύτερος over in my mind.

Otherwise I depend on the Stabi[8] for the academic work. I have therefore requested a transfer to the area around Berlin, because from here traveling will be too expensive (185 km) and is also too problematic, since one must manage some of the connections by bicycle.

I wrote Brother Tonn[9] last week but have no answer yet. Do you know anything about the other brothers from Sigurdshof?

Here it is peaceful and rural. It is as if nothing at all were happening. In Berlin people were beside themselves. Here one scarcely notices anything of the events.

Next Sunday I am coming to Berlin to work through the literature that my fiancée obtained from the library, above all the church ordinances. I hope that I can remain in Berlin for a week. Will we see each other there?

Tomorrow morning I head through the countryside, twelve kilometers to a worship service. Outside it's raining cats and dogs, and I'm preparing myself for a wet ride.

In brotherhood respectful greetings to you from your
H. Doebert

[6.] [The wartime blackout instructions required that bicycle lamps be hooded so that only a slit of light came through.—VB]

[7.] Not otherwise identified.

[8.] Staatsbibliothek, or state library, in Berlin.

[9.] Heinz Tonn.

160. To the Finkenwalde Brothers[1] 267

September 20, 1939

Dear Brothers,

In response to an army postcard to the front, I received the news, which I must pass on to you today, that our dear brother Theodor Maaß was killed in action on September 3 in Poland. This news will be as incomprehensible for you as it was for me. But please let us thank God in remembering him. In him we had a good brother, a quiet, faithful pastor of the Confessing Church, who himself lived by the Word and sacrament, whom God has also honored with the privilege of suffering for the gospel.[2] I am certain that he was ready to go. We should not try to fill with human words those gaps that God has ripped open. They should remain open. Our own comfort is the God of the resurrection, the father of our Lord Jesus Christ, who was and is also his God. We know that our brother is with him, and that in him is the lasting fellowship of those to whom fulfillment has come and those who stand before their final hour. May God be praised for our fallen brother and be merciful to us all at our end. Brother Maaß's parents live in Stralsund, Pastor Maaß, Ketelhotstr. 8.

I know the following brothers are now soldiers: Maechler, Dobrick, von der Marwitz, Mickley, Wolfgang Schmidt, Gerhard Krause, Block, Martin Schaaf, Berg, Buchmann, Schrader, Pompe, Lynker, August, Winkelmann, Sander.[3] Despite my inquiries, I have as yet no army postal numbers for Brothers Corbach, Seydel, Harhausen, Giese, Nimz, Hofmann, Büchsel, Schröter, Winfried Krause. Others face being called up soon. I sincerely ask you to inform me as soon as someone is drafted or if someone is missing from the list about whom I have not been informed. Please let me know
every army postal number that you learn of. Take time now, as often as 268
possible, to write to the brothers out there. Above all, let us not neglect the greatest service that remains for us to do, the service of the faithful daily intercessory prayer. For our brothers among the soldiers we have so much to pray for, first and last and ever again, that they can prove themselves at all times to be Christians, that they can perform a genuine ministry to many

[1.] *NL*, A 48,3 (9); typewritten mimeographed copy. Previously published in *GS* 2:553–58. This was the first newsletter during the war. Regarding the situation after the beginning of the war, cf. *DB-ER*, 662–64.

[2.] Theodor Maaß was one of the first in the Pomeranian Confessing Church to be imprisoned for a period.

[3.] Behind each name (in parentheses) is an army postal number.

of their comrades, and that Jesus Christ be their one and only comfort in life and in death.[4]

An inner restlessness may have come over most of us in the last weeks. We know that our brothers out there are in all kinds of battles and danger; we hear of the death of one brother and this burden is like a compulsion: I must be there too, where my brothers are; I now want to have nothing else and nothing better than they have. This often depresses us completely, and then everything that we do appears superfluous; in fact at times we even tend to regard the vital questions about our church, for which we have struggled up to now, as secondary in light of worldwide events. We think that suddenly now everything must completely change; we should leave everything in the past behind us and start all over again. Who would not understand this? And yet, dear brothers, since you have not yet been called up, everything now depends upon not throwing to the winds the grace God has given us until now, upon not despising our ministry now, but learning to honor and love it, particularly in these days. We have the vocation to be preachers of the gospel and shepherds of the church-community, and as long as we are that, God will only ask us one thing, namely, whether the faithful ministry to his church-community has suffered damage due to us for even one moment, whether, for even one moment, we have paid too little attention to his church-community and the brothers he has given us.

We may still preach, and so let us continue to preach as we've done until now, with a good, free conscience, and to be faithful pastors who do not deny their church even in times of need. We know that God demands this
269 service of us today, and that we thereby perform the greatest service to human beings that can be done for them. We do not ask what our inclination [Sinn] is today or tomorrow, but ask instead for our commission. Therefore, let us not quarrel and offend, but instead rejoice in it and serve.

The Daily Text and interpretive verse for the first of September[5] were surprising and promising enough: "Seek the Lord while he may be found, call upon him while he is near" (Isa. 55[:6]), "See, now is the acceptable time; see, now is the day of salvation" (2 Cor. 6[:2]). What else does this say but this: the hour of God has struck; it is high time for conversion and prayer; the day of the good news has dawned; the harvest of God's word will be greater than the harvest of death; victory belongs not to the world but

[4.] This is an allusion to the first question of the Heidelberg Catechism of 1564, "What is thy only comfort in life and death?" Entire text online at http/www.ccel.org /creeds/heidelberg-ca.html.

[5.] The day of the German invasion of Poland.

to God. If we truly believe this, we and our congregations will have been helped.

We are preachers of justification through grace alone.[6] What [does] this mean today? Very simply it means that we no longer equate human ways and goals with divine ways and goals. God is beyond all human plans and deeds. Everything must be judged by God. Whoever evades this judgment of God must die, but whoever submits to it will live; for to be judged by God is grace for life. God judges for the sake of mercy; God humbles in order to lift up. Only the humble will succeed. God does not confirm human action, but thwarts it and with that tugs our gaze upward to God's grace. By thwarting our paths, God comes to us and speaks his merciful Yes to us, but precisely only through the cross of Jesus Christ. He has placed this cross on the earth; if under the cross he gives us back to the earth and its work and toil, so he commits us anew to the earth and the human beings who live, act, struggle, and suffer on it. "You then, my child, be strong in the grace that is in Christ Jesus" (2 Tim. 2:1). "Be strong, be courageous, and keep the charge of the Lord your God" (1 Kings 2:2–3).

I do not know whether this time we will experience the outbreak of the 270
theodicy question in as agonizing a fashion as in the previous war. It almost seems to me as though something here has changed. Christians today may know more of the biblical judgment on the world and history; thus they will perhaps be confirmed in their faith by the present events rather than afflicted. The non-Christians have done away with the question of the righteousness of a personal God too definitely to be overwhelmed by it. Nonetheless, under the force of these events the question will not be completely absent, and we will, like the author of Ps. 42, still often have to hear: "Where is your God?" [Ps. 42:3].[7] Is it true that God is silent? It is only true for those whose God is the God of their own ideals and thoughts. The biblical message of the power and terrible might [Furchtbarkeit] of the Creator and Lord of the whole world must be brought to these people. "Who can command and have it done, if the Lord has not ordained it? Is it not from the mouth of the Most High that good and bad come?" (Lam. 3:37–38). "I am the Lord, and there is no other. I form light and create darkness, I make weal and create woe" (Isa. 45[:6–]7). "Does disaster befall a city, unless the Lord has done it?" (Amos 3:6). This God, who lets the peoples drink from the cup of wrath and confuses them (Jer. 25:15ff.), is the father of our Lord Jesus Christ, whose council is wonderful and who carries it out

---

[6.] This is an allusion to the Augsburg Confession, Article 4 (*Book of Concord*, 38–39).

[7.] [In the German Bible, this is verse 42:4.—VB]

gloriously at the end (Isa. 28, 29). Is God silent? No, God speaks the tacit language of his terrible power and glory, in order that we become small and humble and pray to him alone. He speaks out of pure grace as well the clear, audible language of his mercy and blessings for his human children through the mouth of Jesus Christ, in whom we have the almighty God as a loving father. "Holy, holy, holy is the Lord of hosts; the whole earth is full of his glory" (Isa. 6:3).

Therefore, our hearts and our gaze are not trapped and captivated by the daily events, as attentively as we follow them. We seek and find through them God the Lord and see his works in awe. We seek and find our Lord
271 Jesus Christ and believe firmly in his victory and in the glory of his church-community. We seek and find God, the Holy Spirit, who makes his word win power over us, greater power than the world can ever win over us. And we pray that the work of the Trinitarian God may soon be fulfilled.

Death has once again entered into our midst, and we must think about it, whether we wish to or not. Two things have become important to me recently: death is outside ourselves, and it is in us. Death from outside is the terrible foe that approaches us when it wishes. It is the Grim Reaper, under whose blow the flower drops off. It steers the bullet so that it hits. We can do nothing against it; "[its] force is from God in the highest."[8] It is death for the entire human race, God's wrath and the end of all life. But the other is the death within us, our own death. It, too, has rested in us since Adam's fall. But it belongs to us ourselves. We die this death daily in Jesus Christ, or we refuse it. This death in us has something to do with the love for Christ and for human beings. We die this death when we love Christ and our brothers with all our heart, for to love means to give oneself wholly to the loved one. This death is grace and the fulfillment of life. This may be our prayer: that we die this death, that it be given to us that the death from without only meets us after we have been prepared for it through this death of our own; then our death is truly only the gateway to the fulfilled love of God.

When around us strife and death practice their wild dominion, then we are summoned to witness to God's love and God's peace, not only through

---

[8.] This alludes to the spiritual folk song *Es ist ein Schnitter, heißt der Tod, hat Gewalt vom großen Gott* (There Is a Reaper, Called Death, Has Power from the Great God), Regensburg 1637 (composer unknown; the song is not in German Protestant hymnals). [The song is included in *Der Zupfgeigenhansl*, the songbook of the German Youth Movement, which was already in its 60th edition by 1918. Cf. *DB-ER*, 32. The editor thanks Ilse Tödt for this information.—VB]

words and thoughts but also through the deed. Do read James 4:1–2![9] Let us daily ask ourselves where we can give witness through the deed for the 272
kingdom [Reich] where love and peace rule. Only from the peace when two or three are gathered[10] can the great peace for which we hope begin to grow. Let us put an end to all hatred, mistrust, envy, strife, wherever we can. "Blessed are the peacemakers, for they will be called children of God."[11]

I have been back from my journey for several weeks.[12] The day before yesterday was Fritz's wedding.[13] This summer's work was very rewarding. I would have liked to send you all a report on my trip,[14] but it has become too long, and I don't know how I can make it available to you. Of course it's already long ago.

I am thinking of you all and your work in intercessory prayers. May God keep and bless you, your homes, and your congregations. God grant us all his peace.

Greetings to you all from your faithful
Dietrich Bonhoeffer

Meditation texts:

September 24–September 30:	Ps. 16
October 1–October 7:	Ps. 23
October 8–October 14:	Ps. 31
October 15–October 21:	Ps. 34
October 22–October 28:	Pss. 42, 43
October 29–November 4:	Ps. 62

[9.] ["Those conflicts and disputes among you, where do they come from? Do they not come from your cravings that are at war within you? You want something and do not have it; so you commit murder. And you covet something and cannot obtain it; so you engage in disputes and conflicts. You do not have, because you do not ask."—VB] Bonhoeffer's note *NL*, A 54,16 (handwritten) contains thoughts about being a "doer" [Täter]: "James 4:11f Rom. 2:13 Matt. 7:21 and finally Matt. 21:31 Matt. 12:50 to do God's will is foundation [addition:] center of community John 7:17 John 15[:5] without me . . . [you can do nothing]—doing is the only appropriate behavior when faced by God's will. First contrast: to say Lord, Lord—confession (Matt. 7 Matt. 21:31) Second contrast: the Christian works (Matt. 7 1 Cor. 13 John 6:28) Third contrast: judging (James 4:11–12 Rom. 2:1ff.). Fourth contrast: hearing (James 1 Rom. 2:13)—doing is the exclusive orientation of the whole human being toward God—works are done in God (John 3:21!)"

[10.] [Cf. Matt. 18:20.—VB]

[11.] Matt. 5:9. Cf. Bonhoeffer's exegesis of this in *DBWE* 4:108–9.

[12.] The reference is to his trip to the United States and England.

[13.] The marriage of Margret Bethge and Fritz Onnasch on September 17, 1939; see Bethge's June 29, 1939, letter to Bonhoeffer, 1/127, ed. note 5.

[14.] Bonhoeffer is referring to his essay "Protestantism without Reformation," 2/6.

November 5–November 11:	Ps. 73
November 12–November 18:	Ps. 85
November 19–November 25:	Ps. 32
November 26–December 2:	John 5:24–29
December 3–December 9:	Luke 1:26–38
December 10–December 16:	Luke 1:39–56
December 17–December 23:	Luke 1:57–80 . . .[15]

273 **161. To Ottonie Blanck**[1]

September 23, 1939

My dear Lady:

I was very pleased to receive your letter.[2] Thank you very much for it. Since you yourself have already found it necessary to answer the question you directed to me, I may assume that to begin with we are agreed that this is one of those questions that cannot be answered with a simple yes or no. The question as you formulate it is, I believe, not a dogmatic question but a pastoral one, which must be answered differently according to the people with whom we are concerned. If one asks whether a Christian may come to communion without private confession, in general one can only say yes, for the sacrament of forgiveness may not be dependent upon a work done by me. Asking in this way one turns confession into a law. Every sinner is permitted to come to communion, therefore, certainly the one who until now either did not find the courage or the occasion for confession. On the other hand, we will have to examine in the individual case why the path to confession has not yet been taken. Here we will have to clear hindrances and misunderstandings out of the way. Above all, the misunderstanding of confession as a severe law. We cannot speak enough about the joy and the

[15.] The literature recommendations have been omitted. Besides several evangelizing writings (*volksmissionarischen Schriften*), e.g., "Biblical sayings for soldiers," they also include Kohlbrügge's *Sechs Predigten, gehalten vor der Eröffnung der Kriegsläufte im Jahre 1870*; Luther's *Ob Kriegsleute auch in seligem Stande sein können* (1526), *WA* 19:616, 623–62; Schnepel's *Als Christ und Kompanieführer im Weltkrieg* (1938). Named with "most serious reservations" are Arper and Zillessen's *Kriegsagende* (1915).

[1.] Letter is in the personal possession of Heinz-Jürgen Blanck-Lubarsch; typed with handwritten signature; previously unpublished.

[2.] See Ottonie Blanck's August 11, 1939, letter to Bonhoeffer, 1/152.

gift of confession.[3] Further, it will be important to learn the reasons why the general confession is insufficient. Finally, our advice will also depend
very much on whether the gift of communion itself has become weak and 274
ineffective for the person concerned, precisely because the full confession of sins is absent.

Only in cases of sins that have become evident must we demand a personal confession before we can extend communion. In all other cases, and this is the great majority, we must display the glory of the gift[4] tirelessly, but we may not make it compulsory, since otherwise the confession becomes an ultimate work of piety, and with that forgiveness itself is called into question. Indeed, everyone should confess, but on the other hand only the one who can do nothing else may confess. I believe that this is how Luther meant it, and that thus confession must be practiced in light of the gospel.[5]

I don't know whether with all this I have said anything that is of use to you. Otherwise, I would be happy to write again at greater length.

With thanks and all good wishes for your work in Dahlem. (How much we in the countryside outside Berlin are oppressed by what we hear from there! God grant someone there an easing and unifying word!)[6] Greetings from your respectful

Dietrich Bonhoeffer

[3.] Regarding Bonhoeffer's theological respect for and practice of confession, see especially *DBW* 14, 2/12.2 and 2/24, as well as *DBWE* 5:108–18.

[4.] [I.e., of personal confession.—VB]

[5.] Cf. *DBWE* 5:114 and its reference to Luther's Large Catechism (1529), "A Brief Exhortation to Confession" (*Book of Concord*, 460).

[6.] After Martin Niemöller was taken to the Sachsenhausen concentration camp on March 2, 1938, a bitter dispute broke out in the Berlin-Dahlem parish about his successor and the proper church authority. Pastor Eberhard Röhricht, who worked together with the Old Prussian Union church committee, and the parish council decided for Walter Dreß and achieved his official installation by the church authorities. [It is interesting that the installation of Dreß, who was married to Bonhoeffer's sister Susanne, was approved by the official (German Christian–controlled) church governance board in Berlin. This pitted Dreß against Gollwitzer, who was Niemöller's successor.—VB]. In opposition, the confessional faction of the parish, with Pastor Fritz Müller, which since Niemöller's imprisonment assembled each evening for a prayer service, refused any cooperation with the official German Christian–led church government, and demanded (as did Niemöller himself) that Helmut Gollwitzer be Niemöller's successor. See Graff et al., *Unterwegs zur mündigen Gemeinde*, 81–84. [For an account of the different factions in the Dahlem congregation, which fought even during Niemöller's time there, see Barnett, *For the Soul of the People*, 70–71.—VB]

275 **162. From Ottonie Blanck**[1]

Steglitz, September 25, 1939

Dear Pastor Bonhoeffer,

Thank you very much for your friendly and quick reply. Particularly for your word of solidarity about the crisis in Dahlem,[2] which is truly a difficult burden for us; the certainty that outside there are also people who think of this in intercessory prayer is a great comfort and we are in great need of that!—And now please do not be angry if I have further questions and additional remarks to your letter: Surely we are agreed that the question cannot be answered with a simple yes or no, and in one individual case that came to me in a letter during my holidays, it was certainly a matter of pastoral care. Since the same question is occurring more and more frequently, I would like to ask whether it might not indeed be a dogmatic question. In one case it was formulated approximately as follows: "I simply feel trapped. The path to communion, which is becoming more and more a genuine 'bread of life,'[3] through the general confession seems for the time being closed to me.[4] For this path seems to me to be a means toward attaining cheap grace.[5] The general confession leaves one so wonderfully uncommitted. And this absence of commitment naturally shatters the essential meaning of confession. A person who confesses his sins to God and asks forgiveness, but who shies away from confessing these sins also before his brother, is simply not serious in his desire for forgiveness. . . . And the noncommittal general confession is surely to blame that, again and again, the old misery starts up anew the next day. . . . My concern with all this is much more the communion than the confession, and the case is apparently solved if I just say: communion without confession. It's only that this appears to me to be running away from it."

This is essentially the tenor of all such questions as I got to hear them, and now I must confess that I only attempted and attempt a response in fear and trembling, and am ever again terribly oppressed that such things that are particu-

[1.] Letter in the personal possession of Heinz-Jürgen Blanck-Lubarsch; typewritten carbon copy; previously unpublished.

[2.] See Bonhoeffer's September 23, 1939, letter to Ottonie Blanck, 1/161, ed. note 6.

[3.] Cf. John 6:35.

[4.] [Blanck and the young parishioners turning to her were obviously familiar with Bonhoeffer's *Discipleship* and read its comments on "cheap grace" as a critique of the official church and its accommodation to the German Christians, and therefore were questioning whether they could take communion and make their confession within the official church.—VB]

[5.] See Blanck's August 11, 1939, letter to Bonhoeffer, 1/152, ed. note 6.

larly important for young people are asked solely among laypeople, burdening some of us with an immense responsibility, and we are much too immature and unripe in our faith to bear this! It could indeed be that we should be grateful 276
for these questions and appreciate that it is a fruit of our special circumstances in Dahlem that the parishioners must help themselves. But I often fear this enormous responsibility and the potential of going astray toward a sectarian community!

In my attempt to give a reply, I endeavored to keep to the biblical words of institution of the Lord's Supper and the places in Luther that are known to me,[6] but I cannot escape the feeling that I have encroached on a field that I am not entitled to enter. But much less can I leave those who asked me without an answer, as they simply don't turn to a pastor because today they are such overburdened people. I have great fear—and I believe this is even truer of the younger people among us—that the merciful gift of confession will be made a law, and it is also somewhat problematic for me in *Life Together*, whether the sentence on page 111: ". . . we refuse to carry the cross when we are ashamed to take upon ourselves the shameful death of the sinner in confession,"[7] is not also somewhat legalistic. I have also endeavored to speak of the joy and the gift of confession, in order to direct the perspective of the questioner in that direction again and again, but I simply cannot hide the fact that—in my experience—the Christian [may] indeed "gain one victory after another,"[8] but that accordingly the defeats become much harder and are more burdensome as well! The Christian must certainly consider this as well before he ventures into the abyss of confession?

Since you were friendly enough to offer me a further reply, I would indeed be grateful to you for that; it would be good if I could on occasion read your reply to such a group?! Do I perhaps express myself clumsily or unclearly, thereby troubling you more than is responsible? In any case, I thank you once more very cordially for your lines yesterday, which will certainly help me and the others further, and with the request that you continue to take us to heart in your prayers for our particular needs in Dahlem, I am

Your respectful
[Ottonie Blanck]

[6.] Cf. Bonhoeffer's September 23, 1939, letter to Blanck, 1/161, ed. note 5.
[7.] See *DBWE* 5:111.
[8.] See *DBWE* 5:112.

277 **163. From Otto Kistner**[1]

Trier, September 28, 1939

Dear Brother Bonhoeffer,

Heartfelt thanks for the newsletter,[2] which reached me here in Trier. I had to leave Saarbrücken—leaving behind all my books etc.[3] The congregation is scattered throughout Germany; here and there I hear from a few parishioners, and that is then always a great joy. I stayed the first days in Boppard with my parents, until the summons came from the council[4] to substitute here in Trier for a brother who had been drafted. One then works in a very strange situation. All preparation is only based on the Book of the church.[5] The external life circumstances are similarly confined only to the bare necessities. So the day begins with housewives' work, make beds, make coffee, wash the dishes, straighten the room a bit, and then on to the rest. In addition the uncertainty, will Trier be evacuated as well, must I take such a route once again or not? I have never before experienced so clearly what it means: we have no lasting city.[6]

What you enumerate in your letter as the questions that move the brothers basically doesn't move me at all. Other things do. Everything that I had wanted to tell you during the summer is stored up and will—if God wills and we live[7]—be said at some point. I am unable to doubt God and his righteousness, but can doubt myself. But more on that later.

Here in the Rhineland there have been some things happening. I simply don't know how I should judge it. The disciplinary proceedings and blocking of salaries have been canceled.[8] Regarding the collection question, a mixed committee is at work.[9] Even the assistant pastors are to be (?) legalized. You have certainly

---

[1.] *NL*, C 25; handwritten; unpublished. Kistner was a candidate in the fifth Finkenwalde session in the summer of 1937.

[2.] See Bonhoeffer's September 20, 1939, newsletter to the Finkenwalde brothers, 1/160.

[3.] [Directly on the French border, the Saar region was placed under French and British governance in 1920 by the Treaty of Versailles and reunited with Germany after the January 1935 Saar plebiscite. On September 7, 1939, the French army surrounded Saarbrücken and captured a number of small German villages in the region; the French withdrew after the fall of Poland.—VB]

[4.] [The Council of Brethren.—VB]

[5.] [I.e., the Bible.—VB]

[6.] Cf. Heb. 13:14.

[7.] Cf. James 4:15.

[8.] [In January 1939, Kistner had been glad that things for the Confessing Church were still going well; see 1/60, p. 121.—VB]

[9.] [The taking up of collections by the Confessing Church was banned in December 1935; cf. *DB-ER*, 496.—VB]

heard of this. It would interest me to learn whether these things have started happening where you are as well. The gentleman from Hanover has brought his name once again to public attention.[10] How lovely!

It occurs to me that the brothers in Pomerania often complain that they 278
live in such a remote region and can hardly get together with other brothers. If I want to travel here from Trier to a confidant, I need two days, one for the trip there and one for the trip back; even under normal conditions it doesn't go faster.

By the way, do you know Trier? It is indeed an astounding city. Everywhere one goes one is reminded of the Roman era and thereby also of the early Christian period as if it were alive. I don't know the date ascribed by archaeologists to the first Christian finds. But when one considers that even before the great migration of tribes, a Christian congregation existed here and indeed quite a large one, when one considers that Christians back then already went by the Porta Nigra and the Caesarean hot springs and pondered the Roman Empire and its world power, then one has very peculiar feelings. Sic transit—.[11]

And now may you and the brothers who are with you be very cordially greeted from this Trier. Your

O. Kistner

A friend of mine who also had to flee Saarbrücken found the enclosed gravestone inscription in a church in Schwäbisch Hall.[12] Perhaps it will be of interest.

[10.] [The "gentleman from Hanover" refers to Lutheran bishop August Marahrens, leader of that regional church, who as a "neutral" party in the Church Struggle was viewed as an enemy by Confessing Church radicals; of the Lutheran bishops in Germany, he was one of the most outspoken supporters of the Nazi regime.—VB] See the September 2, 1939, "Public Proclamation of the German Evangelical Church," signed by Dr. Friedrich Werner and the other members of the German Evangelical Church "Spiritual Confidential Council," which included, in addition to Marahrens, German Christian Bishop Walther Schultz (Schwerin) and High Church Council member Johannes Hymmen (Berlin). Among other things, this document stated: "Since yesterday our German Volk stands in battle for the land of its fathers, in order that German blood may return home to German blood. The German Evangelical Church always stood in loyal solidarity with the fate of the German Volk. It has offered invincible strength from the word of God to augment the weapons of steel. . . . So we unite in this hour as well with our Volk in intercessory prayer for the Führer and Reich, for the entire armed forces and all who perform their service in the homeland for the fatherland" (*Gesetzblatt der Deutsche Evangelische Kirche 1939*, 99). See also Herbert, *Der Kirchenkampf*, 226–27.

[11.] Sic transit gloria mundi, "thus the glory of the world passes." Cf. 1 John 2:17.

[12.] The grave inscription has been lost. Bonhoeffer's ancestors lived in Schwäbisch Hall after 1513. "Some of these ancestors gaze down on visitors to the St. Michael Church in Schwäbisch Hall from their baroque epitaphs on the walls" (*DB-ER*, 9).

279 **164. To the Families of Finkenwalde Brothers Drafted into the Armed Forces**[1]

October 8, 1939

Esteemed, dear Friends,

Today may I turn to you, the parents, siblings, and wives of our brothers who now stand in the field? As the former teacher of your son, your husband, I consider it a brotherly obligation to him that I write a word in these weeks not only to him but to you as well, as his closest relatives. At the same time I want to do it in accordance with the wishes of all those who consider themselves always bound to him as brothers, on the foundation of their work together. Even if we hardly know each other, we are connected by the daily remembrance of him for whom we can now do so little and whom we must commend entirely to the grace of God.

For those of us who still stand in our church ministry in the homeland, it is often hard to think of our brothers whom we know to be out there, without being able to share with them all that they must endure there. When we then hear from them through letters that they rejoice in thinking of everyone who is still doing his urgently needed ministry in the parish, then we continue in this ministry with greater joy and greater seriousness. It is indeed the same ministry into which our brothers out there hope soon to return and through which we are bound to them.

When we consider the life of the young pastors who are now in the field, it moves us to see how much their life has been a struggle until now. It is no easy life, but it is a life that they and we know is worthy of being lived. We must not feel sorry for these young pastors, but we should, wherever we can, bear their burdens, struggle, and suffer with them. Nowhere else is the peace that they have found in Jesus Christ for their entire life more wonder-
280 ful and visible than in the midst of struggle. Whoever has found this peace may be blessed as happy, despite all that may befall him.

In the past weeks I have received many letters from the field.[2] Not one of them includes a word of complaint about how they are faring personally.

[1.] *NL*, A 48,3 (10); typewritten with handwritten signature; return address: "Pastor Dietrich Bonhoeffer, Berlin-Charlottenburg 9, Marienburger Allee 43." Previously published in *GS* 6:469–71.

[2.] Letters not extant.

But they all have two things in common: the hope of being able to prove themselves as Christians even in war and thereby serve their comrades, and the yearning for the preaching ministry in their parish back home. Again and again our brothers in the field ask and remind us to do for them that for which they often lack time and quiet, namely, to pray for them and their faith, for their families, parents, wives, children, and for their congregations. Let us not leave this request unheard.

A great circle of Christians, colleagues, and parishioners surrounds your son, your husband, your brother in faithful intercession during these months. We have often heard that this prayer has become a help in difficult hours for those out there. It is God himself who turns the prayers of the church-community into a source of strength for our brothers. All those who are connected to one another through intercessory prayer know about this. But let us include in our intercessions the unknown others who are together with ours and perhaps have no one who does this service for them. Who among us knows how often in his life he has been preserved by the prayer of an unknown person! Not only we, however, but the entire church of Jesus Christ stands praying by our brothers as its true servants, for whom it thanks God and prays to God for their service in the future as well. This we may take as our great comfort.

The most important thing for us, however, may be this: we may know that our brothers have gone out there well prepared through God's word. As conscious Christians they face the future and know that all things must serve for the best of those who love God.[3] Thus we don't want to burden
them with our worries, rendering the testing of their faith even more dif- 281
ficult. Instead, we want to learn from them to entrust all worries to the one who alone can and will take care of us.

In conclusion, may I ask you to write me if there is anything that I can do for your son, your husband; and I believe it is in accord with our brothers when I ask you to let me know if I can offer any kind of service to you during this time.

God give us all his peace. Greetings from your respectful

Dietrich Bonhoeffer

[3.] Cf. Rom. 8:28.

165. To Max Mebes[1]

October 10, 1939

Dear Brother Mebes,

You will be deployed for the winter work in Pomerania.[2] I ask you to be patient a few more days before you receive exact information. In any case, the work will begin in October. You need a bicycle there and warm clothes, in addition to bedsheets, towels, etc. Bring along the Nestle NT; Lutheran confessional writings; *Der helle Ton.*[3]

Please let me know immediately the year in which you were born and what your military status is. Please give this information to Pastor Bethge, Berlin-Charlottenburg 9, Marienburger Alle 43. All other questions should be directed to him as well.

With best wishes your
Bonhoeffer

282 166. From Georg Eichholz[1]

Wuppertal-Barmen, November 6, 1939

Dear Licentiate Bonhoeffer,

I would like to request your participation for a series of interpretations (meditations) of old gospel pericopes, which are to serve in the preparation of the pastor's Sunday proclamation—the publishers will be E. Müller, Barmen.[2] Because

[1.] Letter in the personal possession of Mrs. Renate Petras; typewritten with handwritten name of recipient and signature; return address: "Lic. Bonhoeffer, Schlawe/ Pommern, Koppelstrasse 9"; previously unpublished.

[2.] Invitation to the collective pastorate in Sigurdshof in the winter of 1939–40. Due to conscriptions into the military, there could no longer be a second collective pastorate in Köslin.

[3.] *Der helle Ton* was a songbook of the Reich Association of Protestant Young Men. [Since 1871, the word "Reich" had been synonymous with "National"; while after 1933 some groups adopted "Reich" when they nationalized and became extensions of the Nazi Party, in this instance the title does not connote any association with the Nazi party.—VB]

[1.] Literary estate of Georg Eichholz; typewritten carbon copy with handwritten initials; return address: "Pastor G. Eichholz, Wuppertal-Barmen, Missionsstrasse 9." Cf. also *NL*, A 60,2; later typewritten copy. Previously published in *GS* 6:478.

[2.] The book appeared in 1941 as G. Eichholz, ed., *Herr tue meine Lippen auf* (Lord, Open My Mouth), vol. 1.

the prospectus must be sent out, I would be gratefully obliged to you if I could have your consent, which in practical terms would have to be fulfilled approximately for the season of Trinity, in principle by the end of this week. The pericopes for Advent are already being written by Brunner and Schlier, with further pericopes by Gollwitzer and Dehn.[3] I hope that the working community that this book wants to call into being will offer a new consideration of fundamental problems of proclamation, for example, that of the homily, which the present book by Diem[4] also sets as a task for further consideration.

Please pardon me for this very short notice. I ask you however to understand it in terms of the matter itself. I don't believe I need to emphasize the urgency of the task.

[G. Eichholz]

167. To Georg Eichholz[1]

November 8, 1939

Dear Brother Eichholz,

Many thanks for your letter. I agree, but would ask you to tell me the deadline and text very soon. By the way, do we not know each other from the summer of 1931?[2]

Cordially, your
Dietrich Bonhoeffer

[3.] Peter Brunner, Heinrich Schlier, Helmut Gollwitzer, and Günther Dehn.

[4.] Hermann Diem, *Warum Textpredigt?* (Why a Textual Sermon?) (1939).

[1.] Literary estate of Georg Eichholz; handwritten; from Berlin. Cf. also *NL*, A 60,2: later typewritten copy. Previously published in *GS* 6:478.

[2.] They had met during Bonhoeffer's visit to Barth in Bonn. Cf. *DB-ER*, 175–78, and *DBW* 11, 1/4, 1/5, and esp. 1/6 (which describes the visit, although Eichholz is not mentioned—VB].

283 **168. To Georg Eichholz**[1]

December 6, 1939

Dear Brother Eichholz,

Many thanks for your letter.[2] When do you need the manuscripts? A reply will have to depend on that somewhat. If the date is not too early, I would agree to do it.

Best regards, your
Dietrich Bonhoeffer

169. To the Finkenwalde Brothers[1]

Personal letter

Dear Brothers,

Sad news must come at the beginning of this Christmas letter. On December 2, 1939, our brother Emanuel Kahn had a fatal accident during his military service in the homeland. He was buried on December 6 in Sternberg, where he last worked. Brother Kahn participated in the entire Polish campaign. Out there he had the task of picking up the wounded on the front and taking them to the first-aid station. During a brief leave he visited me less than two weeks before his death. He spoke with great clarity and steadfastness about the path of our church and the ultimate decisions of faith. He asked about many brothers, and after a conversation of many hours, we parted after devotions. I am very grateful that I could still have this meeting with Brother Kahn. I am certain that God's call did not meet
284 him unprepared. In this life he was with the Word, so we may believe that the Word holds him fast in eternity. The meditation text for the week of his death was "anyone who hears my word and believes him who sent me has eternal life, and does not come under judgment, but has passed from death to life" (John 5:24).

The fact that today a Christmas letter must begin like this makes our situation utterly clear to us. Death and Christmas have moved very close to each other, and we do not at all want to avoid this. Do we not already hear

[1.] Literary estate of Georg Eichholz; handwritten; no return address; previously unpublished. Cf. *NL*, A 60,2; later typewritten copy.

[2.] Letter not extant.

[1.] *NL*, A 48,3 (11); typewritten mimeographed copy; return address: "Lic. Bonhoeffer, Schlawe, Koppelstrasse 9"; undated, but certainly during Advent 1939. Previously published in *GS* 2:559–62.

the news of the death of a Christian brother today with different ears than we did only a few months ago? Hasn't the light of the Christmas message become bright enough for us that we can genuinely rejoice when we may know that one of us may now already see this light in eternity? Indeed, that even we ourselves begin to look forward to this? Admittedly, we are sometimes seized by an indescribable anxiety, particularly in the face of this light, when we think of the many whom death meets without their being in faith, and perhaps as well when we think of ourselves, our life, and the way we carry out our ministry. Then there are times when we would like to try to force, for ourselves and for others, that which God often only wants to give us in long years of praying, seeking, and waiting, and perhaps then the comfort is sometimes rather hasty and fast, and there is therefore no lasting peace. So we then thank God that he does not yet call us away today, that he still gives us time to learn his word here and live according to it and carry out our ministry in such a way that it brings fruit, perhaps after long fruitless years. Thus the Christmas message of the great joy, of the Savior, of peace, amid all fulfillment that it brings, remains for us personally and for our ministry to people a promise that we pursue.[2]

Many of you will receive this letter amid a great burden of work. God knows all your service and knows your strength; he will allow you to stand upright as long he needs you. For most of you it will be uncertain how long you can still work in the congregation. Regarding this, one brother recently 285
wrote from the front: when God bids us to leave the congregation, then he may want to till the acre himself. Many of you are separated from your parishes, from wives and children, and you yearn for the work that threatens to suffocate the others. We think very particularly of you, dear brothers, who are out there. No one there is forgotten, not by us and most certainly not by God. We commend you each day to the grace of God and pray that you will be led back into your parishes back home. But we know of course as well, that through you a great service is being performed out there, and that your commission accompanies you, wherever you are. We have received many letters from the field in the last months, and each one truly made us happy.[3] It is one and the same witness, in which we strengthen one another; and the fact that you out there could remain steadfast in this is a great help and assurance for us here. Let us continue to pray for one another, that each of us can make that confession that God requires of him where he is, even if this becomes very difficult at some point. Only that in this time no one be left alone and that God, in addition to faith in the community of saints, may

[2.] Cf. 1 Pet. 3:11.

[3.] Letters not extant.

give us again and again to experience and see something of this! Yet God will and can only do this when we place ourselves at his disposal and seek our brother and stand by his side.

Dear brothers, when have we been able to preach the Christmas message with more confidence and joy than in this year? When would our ministry have been more necessary and glorious? When would we have had to call on God more urgently to finally, finally give the fruit that he has promised, to purify us and to brush away everything that hinders a proper ministry, and then to use us, the way we are, as his servants?

On a limited scale, our work here proceeds as before.[4] Please let us hear again from you, of your work and how you are doing. I very warmly thank all those who have written in the last weeks.

286 May God bless you this Christmas time, you personally, your homes, and your congregations. May he let you enter the new year strengthened in faith, richer in love, and confirmed in your hope.

Greetings to you all from your faithful
Dietrich Bonhoeffer

. . .[5] I am sending as an enclosure a theological letter composed for another purpose, for a quiet hour over Christmas.[6]

Meditation texts:

December 31–January 6:	Prov. 1
January 7–January 13:	Prov. 3
January 14–January 20:	Prov. 8
January 21–January 27:	Prov. 14
January 28–February 4:	Prov. 18
February 5–February 11:	Prov. 28
February 12–February 18:	Col. 1:1–20
February 19–February 25:	Col. 1:21–29
February 26–March 2:	Col. 2
March 3–March 9:	Col. 3:1–15
March 10–March 16:	Col. 3:16–25
March 17–March 23:	Col. 4

[4.] In the collective pastorate at Sigurdshof. The collective pastorate in Köslin did not take place in the winter of 1939–40 due to all the conscriptions [of young Confessing Church theologians—VB] into the military.

[5.] Omitted here is a list of the military postal numbers of several Finkenwalde brothers.

[6.] See 3/10.1.

170. To Paula Bonhoeffer[1]

December 18

Dear Mama,

With the same mail I'm sending a package in which there are a few Christmas things and some dirty laundry. I don't need it immediately, since I will of course find some at your place; all the same, I would like to have it some- 287
time during the holidays. It has become very cold here. Early today -20.[2] But the lake is frozen over, and so today we intend to go ice skating. I wanted to be in Berlin Thursday evening.[3] How is Thomas doing?[4]

Many greetings and loving thanks your
Dietrich

171. To Karl-Friedrich Bonhoeffer[1]

January 15, 1940

Dear Karl Friedrich,

I did not forget your birthday,[2] but because I was completely without help in recent days, I didn't find time for a letter. Although that remains just as much the case today, I want to at least briefly wish you a good new year, that you both can stay healthy and with each other. The period of uncertainty will now not last much longer.[3] Here we sit concerned about coal and with no petroleum,[4] so that we must light candles as long as they are in supply. We are also presently almost entirely cut off from the town. All this would be in itself quite nice if it were not accompanied by the general worries here. But we are still doing quite well.[5] By the way, I must tell you I am currently

[1.] *NL*, A 44,1 (36); handwritten postcard; postmark: Zollbrück, December 18, 1939. Previously unpublished.

[2.] [Celsius.—VB]

[3.] Presumably Thursday, December 28, 1939.

[4.] Thomas Bonhoeffer, son of Klaus and Emmi Bonhoeffer.

[1.] *NL*, A 44,1 (37); handwritten card; no address but certainly from Sigurdshof. Partially reproduced in *GS* 2:562.

[2.] January 13.

[3.] [This is a reference to the conspiracy's negotiations at the time with the Vatican. Cf. *DB-ER*, 673.—VB]

[4.] [For lamps.—VB]

[5.] Eberhard Bethge described the situation in Sigurdshof, which was snowed in, on January 1, 1940, in a letter to his cousins and friends: "At present my existence stands under the motto, freezing and in darkness. We're worried about the coal. . . . We also

with real enthusiasm reading the book *Wissenschaft bricht Monopole*[6] like a novel. If only someone had told me this in school or somewhere later! For
288 me it virtually alters my view of the world; in any case, it is making a great impression on me and much pleasure. Time and time again, I find the photographs of Mama very splendid. So, all the best to all of you!

Many greetings your
Dietrich

172. From Georg Eichholz[1]

January 16, 1940

My very dear Brother Bonhoeffer,

I thank you very much indeed for your telegram of consent, which I received on January 10.[2] The letter you mention must have been lost, since it hasn't reached me yet. I am pleased that I may expect your manuscript on Quasimodogeniti and Misericordiasdomini by February 1, the manuscript for Pentecost Sunday and the Monday after Pentecost (for these 240 typed lines per pericope, otherwise 160 typed lines) by February 20.

With cordial greetings and all good wishes your
[G. Eichholz]

173. To Georg Eichholz[1]

January 24, 1940

Dear Brother Eichholz,

Here are the meditations requested by February 1.[2] The other two will follow as we agreed before February 20. My address is Schlawe/Pomerania,

---

aren't receiving any more petroleum, so that presently we are straining our eyes with candles only, evenings almost everyone huddles in one room. Work for that reason is difficult. We play games or read something aloud" (in Andersen, *So ist es gewesen*, 359).

[6.] Zischka, *Wissenschaft bricht Monopole* (1938).

[1.] Literary estate of Georg Eichholz; typewritten carbon copy with handwritten initials; return address: "Pastor G. Eichholz, Wuppertal-Barmen, Missionstrasse 9"; previously unpublished. Cf. also *NL*, A 60,2; later typewritten copy.

[2.] See *NL*, A 60,2; this was sent from Stettin on January 10, 1940.

[1.] Literary estate of Georg Eichholz; handwritten; postmarked Stettin, January 25, 1940; previously unpublished. Cf. also *NL*, A 60,2; later typewritten copy.

[2.] See 3/11.1 and 3/11.2.

Koppelstrasse 9, or Berlin-Charlottenburg 9, Marienburger Allee 43. The mail is forwarded from both places. Since I am often on the road, the one 289
is not more convenient than the other. Please confirm receiving this letter, since I am not sure of your address.[3]

Cordially your
Dietrich Bonhoeffer

174. To His Parents[1]

Sigurdshof, January 29

My dear Parents,

Yesterday I arrived here. Despite great delay the trip was warm and tolerable. Yesterday the postal vehicle almost didn't get through due to the snow. It has been snowing for four days almost without stop. Yesterday afternoon I could not keep myself from going out right away with the skis and through the snowy woods. It was utterly beautiful, such a quiet peace, so that everything else seems uncanny. Indeed, I feel more and more that living in the countryside, particularly in times like these, is much more humanely decent than in the city. All the mass effects simply fall away here. The contrast between Berlin and this remote farmstead is now particularly great. How is Papa doing? And Christel?[2] Otherwise everyone has stayed healthy? I am fine. This afternoon I want to ski some more in the woods; unfortunately there are only two pairs of snowshoes here; therefore not everyone can come along. Many greetings and many thanks for everything! Your

Dietrich

Eberhard Bethge says hello and will send the receipt.

[3.] Eichholz acknowledged receiving the first two meditations and thanked Bonhoeffer "very cordially" in a January 31, 1940, letter. See *NL*, A 60,2.

[1.] *NL*, A 44,1 (38); handwritten postcard. Partially reproduced in *GS* 6:472.

[2.] Christine von Dohnanyi.

290 **175. From Fritz Onnasch**[1]

Stettin 7, Pölitzerstrasse 33, February 2, 1940

My dear Dietrich,

In the last four years, the fourth of February[2] is among the high points of "life together" for me as well, and it is hard for me not to be able to say my greetings to you in person. While we will also celebrate your birthday together with Aunt Ruth,[3] a celebration together by the burning fireplace or in the forester's cottage with its dark oak-beamed ceiling would be much lovelier.

May God gently guide you along his path through your new year of life, continue to transform your gifts into the ministry to his church and the brothers who are being placed on your way, and give you always the παρρησία,[4] which overcomes the unbelief and fear of this world, since it comes from his hand. On Sunday we want to think especially of you, as we used to do otherwise. With that, even the great geographical distances are overcome, so that a firm fellowship will indeed come about.

We don't want to pass over in silence one very personal wish: do come here to us in this new year as well, as often as you can. We count every visit as a gift; we hope that you feel that way as well!

Warm thanks for your letter.[5] Now we look forward very much to Eberhard. He will tell us about the party, which has a special character every year. Don't forget to talk a bit yourself about your youthful years with Harnack[6] et al. That era is so remote for us young folks. Both of us[7] send warmest greetings to you.

In steadfast fellowship, your grateful
Fritz

[1.] Literary estate of Eberhard Bethge; handwritten; previously unpublished.

[2.] Bonhoeffer's birthday.

[3.] Ruth von Kleist-Retzow, whose birthday was also February 4.

[4.] "Frank outspokenness."

[5.] Letter not extant.

[6.] Regarding Bonhoeffer's studies under Adolf von Harnack in Berlin at the beginning of the 1920s, see *DB-ER*, 66–68, and *DBWE* 10:621–26.

[7.] Fritz Onnasch and his wife, Margret, neé Bethge.

176. To Sabine Leibholz[1] 291

February 2, 1940

Dear Sabine,

We are all together on our birthday[2] evening; I came over for the evening, and we are thinking a great deal about all of you. Everyone is doing well. We were very pleased to receive your letters. Hopefully, next year we will celebrate together again. It is still very cold, and there is much snow here. Where Martin[3] is, there are one (or two) petroleum stoves, nothing else. We all wish you a good and healthy new year. I will still buy something nice for my birthday from you and write you about it. I will already thank you now. Warmest greetings to you all, your

Dietrich[4]

177. To His Parents[1]

February 14

My dear Parents,

You will be surprised that you still haven't heard anything from me. Since Saturday now we have been totally snowed in and cut off. Even the postal vehicle is not getting through anymore. Only through occasional sleds can we get anything here. (I am by the way always reachable by telegraph.) Sunday we visited a neighboring estate by sled. It was a gloriously long trip. When we returned it was -28,[2] and yet it hardly felt freezing. Under these circumstances work is proceeding well. We received two cubic meters of
wood as well as two tons of coal from the forester. So that will do for the 292
next few days. It's naturally rather difficult to get supplies, but for the time being we still have enough to eat. Dear Mama, thank you very much for taking care of things in Schlawe. I received a car. That same night everything became snowed in. Despite all the discomfort, I wish that you both could

---

[1.] Literary estate of Eberhard Bethge; handwritten; no address, but surely from Berlin; previously unpublished.

[2.] [Sabine Leibholz, of course, was Bonhoeffer's twin.—VB]

[3.] The reference is to Martin Niemöller, who was in the concentration camp in Sachsenhausen.

[4.] The signatures of their parents and other family members follow.

[1.] *NL*, A 44/1(39); handwritten; no return address, but certainly from Sigurdshof. Partially reproduced in *GS* 2:562.

[2.] [Celsius; this would be -18 degrees Fahrenheit.—VB]

spend a few days out here. If it were up to me, I believe that I would never again want to live in a city permanently. Thank you again so much for the lovely birthday present, which I found when I got here and which we are enjoying very much. How is Wilhelm doing?[3]

Greetings to you all from your grateful
Dietrich

178. To His Parents[1]

February 23, 1940

My dear Parents,

The chance just arose to send mail to Schlawe, so I want at least to send greetings from our wintry hermitage. Many thanks for the letter[2] that came today. Everything here continues to go well; today it began to thaw. Now everything is even more impassable than before. No car can get through. And soon we will have terrible floods. The ground is still frozen so hard. How do these things look elsewhere in the country? We know almost nothing. I am very pleased that Diestel[3] may stay on. In contrast I am rather disturbed with regard to Wilhelm.[4] Hopefully, all will go well. I have now been here two weeks in a row. Thus I am getting around again to some work that I have been sitting with for some time.[5] It is very wonder-
293 ful to be able to work quietly, and one cannot be thankful enough for this, truly for each day.

How are you doing? Hopefully, we will hear something soon from Sabine.[6] But with the present circumstances affecting the mail, one can't count on that at all.

Greetings to you all from your grateful
Dietrich

[3.] Wilhelm Niesel had been arrested on February 3, 1940, together with Erich Andler and Willi Praetorius. After his release on March 8, he was barred from Berlin on May 3, and forbidden to speak publicly throughout Germany [Reichsredeverbot—VB].

[1.] *NL*, A 44,1 (40); handwritten; no address, but certainly from Sigurdshof. Partially reproduced in *GS* 2:563.

[2.] Letter not extant.

[3.] Max Diestel. [In 1940 the consistory tried to force Diestel into retirement; Diestel was a member of the Berlin-Brandenburg Council of Brethren.—VB]

[4.] Wilhelm Niesel; see Bonhoeffer's February 14, 1940, letter to his parents, 1/177, ed. note 3.

[5.] The exegesis of Ps. 119; see 3/9.

[6.] Sabine Leibholz in London.

179. To His Parents[1]

February 27, 1940

My dear Parents,

The letter from the army chaplaincy[2] included the notification that according to a new regulation of the OKH[3] only those people could become wartime chaplains "who have already proven themselves as soldiers on the front" and that according to this everyone else must be ruled out, therefore me as well. (The other side of the matter is that all pastors who have already served or are wartime officers have naturally been drafted with weapons and that therefore there's nothing left for wartime chaplains!) Besides, the conscription of CC pastors[4] and the reclaiming of those in the consistories to fill CC positions in the absence of CC pastors with the consistory people is leading ever more clearly to a destruction of the still-existing church-communities.

Here we have indescribable black ice following strong flooding. The meadows up to ten meters close around our house have become the most glorious skating rink. But it is a catastrophe for the fields, as well as for the wild animals.

Papa will certainly have heard in detail about the closing of the Pomeranian mental institutions.[5]

Dear Mama, would you please purchase the soap for February on Eber- 294
hard's soap card.[6] I am sending a package with dirty laundry. We again have fuel for one week. How are things with you in this respect? How are the Dohnanyis?

Greetings from your grateful
Dietrich

Did Sabine[7] write?

[1.] *NL*, A 44,1 (41); handwritten; no address, but certainly from Sigurdshof. Partially reproduced in *GS* 6:472–73.

[2.] Letter not extant; cf. *DB-ER*, 666.

[3.] Oberkommando des Heeres, or Army High Command.

[4.] [Confessing Church pastors.—VB]

[5.] This refers to the T-4 "euthanasia" program that began in September–October 1939 (named for the central office at Berlin's Tiergartenstrasse 4)—the Nazi regime's murder of so-called life unworthy of life, under which by August 1941 ca. 80,000–100,000 people were victims. See Schleunes, *Nationalsozialistische Entschlußbildung und die Aktion T4*. Cf. also *DB-ER*, 688–89, and *DBWE* 6:189–96.

[6.] The wartime soap rationing card.

[7.] Sabine Leibholz.

180. To Paula Bonhoeffer[1]

March 1, 1940

Dear Mama,

Many thanks for the letters,[2] which I am returning with this one. Above all, I was happy to hear that Sabine is indeed so fit and healthy. The move to L.[3] will surely be worth it; they will get to know the people there, which always makes a difference. And the gentleman[4] who invited Gert there is very influential and helpful, a friend of George.[5] One can't be surprised that George himself is having some trouble.[6] But he is wise and will certainly win out. I am not worried at all about that. I thought a great deal about an art history book[7] but am not yet really clear: Amsler and Ruthhard in Berlin have a large volume (it is rather thin, however) Dürer: *Great*
295 *Passion* twelve wood engravings.[8] Also there will be some nice edition of the so-called *Green Passion* by Dürer. Otherwise one could also consider a work on the "catacombs," but the Schleichers themselves have very good reproductions of those. How would the book be that Klaus[9] gave Papa for Christmas? Or the volume by Wolfgang Schöne: Dutch painting?[10] That would additionally have a personal connection? There are fewer things of this kind, I believe. But Walter[11] will certainly be able to advise you as well.

I am writing Gert[12] during these days. Hopefully, it will arrive. I have the impression that my birthday letter did not arrive, but only the letter that followed afterward.[13]

Today everything has frozen over again, after the streets yesterday were supposedly like streams. On the neighboring estate they opened up the potato clamp; all was frozen. That rumor is spreading around here, and

---

[1.] *NL*, A 44,1 (42): handwritten; no address, but certainly from Sigurdshof. Partially reproduced in *GS* 6:473–74.

[2.] From the Leibholz family via Switzerland.

[3.] St. Leonards-on-Sea; see Leibholz-Bonhoeffer, *Bonhoeffers*, 115–21.

[4.] Canon Griffith.

[5.] George Bell.

[6.] [Because of his ties to the German resistance, George Bell during the war defended "the other Germany" (i.e., the Germans who were critical of National Socialism) and came under harsh criticism in Great Britain.—VB]

[7.] Bonhoeffer's considerations were about a confirmation gift for Renate Schleicher.

[8.] Dürer, *Die große Passion.*

[9.] Klaus Bonhoeffer.

[10.] Schöne, *Die großen Meister der Niederländischen Malerei des 15. Jahrhunderts* (1939).

[11.] Walter Dreß.

[12.] Gert Leibholz.

[13.] Letter not extant.

everyone fears for their own. But perhaps those potatoes were poorly stored. The ground is said to be frozen down to one meter deep. So it will be some time before spring begins. What will this month bring?

I will write about my coming. It is not yet firm. Many greetings to you and my brothers and sisters

Your grateful
Dietrich

181. To His Parents[1]

March 6, 1940

My dear Parents,

Many thanks for your letter[2] from Potsdam. Hopefully, you will have been able to relax a bit there. Thanks as well for the packet with the hat and the other wonderful things in it. The coffee is very useful for my work. For two 296
days now, we are again in deep snow and almost uninterrupted snowstorms. Now the thaw will have to start all over from the beginning. Agriculturally all this appears very terrible indeed. The people were already so happy about the few days of thawing; now they are quite depressed. Here the work goes until the fifteenth, and I don't know yet whether I will make it to the confirmation.[3] I sent Ursula[4] something yesterday to help with the children. Hopefully, it will arrive in good shape. She might need it now.

Eberhard has not yet been examined.[5] Dudzus wrote that he has been deferred due to the attest. He was examined by one of Papa's auditors.[6] Otherwise nothing new.

Greetings to you from your grateful
Dietrich

[1.] *NL*, A 44,1 (43); handwritten card; no address, but certainly from Sigurdshof. Partially reproduced in *GS* 6:475.

[2.] Letter not extant.

[3.] Renate Schleicher's confirmation on March 17, 1940.

[4.] Ursula Schleicher.

[5.] This is a reference to the physical examination and the possible conscription into the military.

[6.] After his summons to the military in February 1940, Otto Dudzus was able at Bonhoeffer's suggestion to show a medical attest written by Karl Bonhoeffer about his illness (Meniere's disease, with several fits of dizziness and vomiting), upon which he was released and only drafted two years later (letter from Dudzus to the *DBW* editor, April 9, 1994).

182. To Sabine and Gerhard Leibholz[1]

March 7, 1940

My dears,

It is very pleasing that we continue to receive good news from you. I am, however, unsure whether my birthday letter reached you. The book by Waetzhold[2] appears to have gotten there. Your birthday present to me is still pending, I will get it for myself when I am home again. I think it will
297 be a book as well, for like you, I also find that one right now feels especially drawn toward good books. If I only knew more exactly what would particularly interest you! I find the idea of a children's book excellent. Could not my friend Dorothee,[3] whom Julius[4] also knows quite well, help Marianne find a publisher?[5] Ask them sometime. In recent weeks I have lived totally secluded in my little forest cottage, could only reach the next village with snowshoes, without train, auto, or telephone connections. It was quite wonderful. Even up to today there is deep snow here. But it will not last much longer. I thought of you all again and again during the cold here. But you seem to have held up well without any particular illnesses.

In recent days I have again pondered and read a great deal about our old topic of discussion that we didn't bring to an end the last time we were together.[6] To continue a conversation in written form is always somewhat awkward. But I continue to think that Brunner says wise things on the matter in his ethics, "Imperative and Order,"[7] particularly in the notes. It's simply a matter of portraying thoroughly, first, the positivist and the idealist theories and then to show the limits of each, thereby advancing toward the biblical-Christian teaching based upon revelation. Here in my opinion a distinction must be drawn between the law within the creation and that within the redemption. To the first belongs the question of *jus naturale, lex*

[1.] *NL*, A 44,1 (44); handwritten; no address, but certainly from Sigurdshof. Previously published in *GS* 3:33–36. This letter was forwarded to the relatives in England by Erwin Sutz in Switzerland.

[2.] This is likely a reference to Wilhelm Waetzhold, *Dürer und seine Zeit* (1936).

[3.] Dorothy Buxton.

[4.] Julius Rieger.

[5.] Marianne Leibholz wrote and illustrated children's books.

[6.] During Bonhoeffer's visit to London, upon his return from the United States in July 1939.

[7.] Emil Brunner, *Das Gebot und die Ordnungen* (1932), published in English as *The Divine Imperative*; cf. esp. 269–74 and 629–32 in the English translation.

naturae (Tröltsch).[8] Are there principles of law in the creation that could be viewed as absolutely valid? Or is law bound to actual power? The doctrine of *lex naturae*, which underlies Catholicism, presupposes several legal entities sui generis (family, economy, etc. . . .), which all have one source, 298
the Creator of the world.[9] Protestant teaching has repeatedly critiqued this doctrine of *lex naturae*, because it fears in it a relativization of the recognition of God's will, which can only be known from revelation in the Holy Scripture. With that, the question of law becomes a question about the concept of revelation. Does God reveal himself in history (or does he remain hidden here, although present?) or solely in the Scripture that bears witness to Christ? The dangers of the first opinion are self-evident; it can lead to a complete relativization; history justifies itself (nonetheless, on this point the strict Reformation doctrine in Germany has always opposed Anglo-Saxon theology, which presumes a double revelation—in history and in Scripture). However, the danger of the second (strict Reformation thesis, although the opinions of Luther and Calvin themselves here waver!) is also clear: the risk of losing the possibility for finding some form of inner historical legal norms, which would mean a relativization of what is historical and created. So, on the one side: relativization of the revelation; on the other: relativization of the historical, the norms of creation. Both, however, must be avoided. That in my opinion is the crucial issue, and that is how the problem is posed at present. Now Karl[10] did attempt to keep to the basis of the strict Reformation thesis and yet avoid the relativization of the historical. That is tempting indeed. He relates (in proper biblical fashion) all the orders of the created world strictly to Christ and says that they are to be understood correctly only in relation to him and must find their orientation in him. One must read this. The treatment of these problems must then in my opinion be followed by the question of the relationship of law, righteousness, and love (in the sense of the Sermon on the Mount). Do they exclude one another? Do they not necessarily belong (although as antithesis!) together? (that would be my opinion). Law that is oriented toward righteousness and is a historical reality through power 299
(and not an abstract idea!) is "the pedagogue leading up to Christ," as it

[8.] Ernst Troeltsch. Above all in his work *The Social Teaching of the Christian Churches* (first German publication, 1912), Troeltsch analyzed the significance of natural law for the understanding of Christian social doctrine.

[9.] [This comment anticipates Bonhoeffer's doctrine of mandates, which he subsequently articulated in *Ethics*; see *DBWE* 6:17–22.—VB]

[10.] Karl Barth, *Church and State* (published in 1938 as *Rechtfertigung und Recht*).

says in Galatians [3:24].[11] Although with regard to content, as Brunner explains very well, love essentially differentiates itself from law (renunciation of one's own right for the sake of God and one's neighbor),[12] it[13] can be practiced only within a legal order. Here was the great contrast between Enthusiasm [Schwärmertum] and Luther. The Enthusiasts wanted to build the world upon love, upon the Sermon on the Mount. Luther saw in this a confusion of God's realm and the earthly realm, which was bound to have the most dangerous chaotic consequences. For that reason Christianity, too, has something to say about law, although its essential meaning is to proclaim love.

It now appears to me that the ultimate meaning of all law on earth is to guarantee the possibility of love in the sense of Christianity, despite all the strictness to be achieved through power, without ever willing or being able to become identical to it.[14] Law therefore is just as antithetical to love as it is necessary for its sake. (It is a strange concept of righteousness—and one that must be strictly distinguished from the ancient Aristotelian concept—when Luther, with the New Testament, characterizes our righteousness before God as "given," as "reckoning Christ's righteousness" to us out of grace. Justice here means not *suum cuique*[15] but rather submission to God, who himself is the holy righteousness [judge!] and love. Both revealed in the cross.)

Forgive this boring academic letter! But I just slid into writing! Now, however, I need to close. Say a warm hello to the children! Also to George, please.[16] Do tell him that I am doing well and that I send greetings to him. Did you get around to writing Sutz[17] in Wiesendangen? Do that sometime.

[11.] [The NRSV here reads "disciplinarian until Christ came," but the translation in the text is much closer to the German and to the original Greek, and it also anticipates Bonhoeffer's argumentation in *DBWE* 6:173 that the natural is directed toward the future coming of Christ. The editor thanks Ilse Tödt for this insight.—VB]

[12.] Cf. Brunner, *Divine Imperative*, 450–53.

[13.] [I.e., love.—VB]

[14.] ["It" here refers to love, i.e., law and love cannot be identical to each other.—VB]

[15.] This refers to the classical definition of righteousness in natural law according to the Roman jurist Ulpian: "Iustitia est constans et perpetua voluntas ius suum cuique tribuendi" (Justice is the constant and perpetual will to attribute to each his own right), Digesten I:1, 10. Cited in Brunner, *Divine Imperative*, 689.

[16.] George Bell.

[17.] Erwin Sutz.

By the way, he also has a good library. I am just writing him too. Next week 300
I will be at our parents'. Renate is being confirmed.[18] With all best wishes warmest greetings from your

Dietrich

Please also say a warm hello to Franz[19] when the occasion arises! He too has access to libraries and an overview of what has been published.[20]

[18.] Renate Schleicher's confirmation was on March 17, 1940.

[19.] Franz Hildebrandt. [Hildebrandt had emigrated to England.—VB]

[20.] Eberhard Bethge wrote a note in the margin: "One year ago we were constantly together! It is difficult now to imagine your new living conditions [since the Leibholzes had moved to St. Leonards-on-Sea—VB]. And that is truly a shame. Our thoughts of you over there lack some of the capacity to imagine details, but they are now especially intensely with you and preoccupied with everything that affects you. How are the children doing? How might they be adjusting to things? Please say hello for me. Warmest regards to you and your esteemed spouse, remembering you faithfully your Eberhard Bethge."

PART 2
Exercises, Lectures, and Essays

A. Exercises

1a. Lecture on Pastoral Counseling, First Session of the Collective Pastorate, March 3–23, 1938[1]

Pastoral Counseling.

[*Lecture Outline*:

- The commission for pastoral care
- The confession of sin (Beichte)[2]
- Law and Gospel in pastoral care

[1.] From Wolf Georgii's handwritten notes of Bonhoeffer's lecture on pastoral care during the illegal collective pastorate in the winter of 1937–38. Wolf Georgii was a vicar for Pastor Robert Zenke at St. Marien-Kirche in Köslin and was a member of the collective pastorate there (cf. 1/11, ed. note 9). Original is in the personal possession of Hans-Otto Georgii, Eichenau. First publication in the *Dietrich Bonhoeffer Jahrbuch* 3 (2007/2008), 97–112, edited by Dirk Schulz, who dedicated it "To Bishop Dr. Hans Christian Knuth, the theological teacher, on September 28, 2008." The editors thank Dr. Georgii for permission to publish here. Schulz also thanks Dr. Hans-Otto Georgii for allowing him to see excerpts of his father's letters from December 1937–March 1938 to his fiancée, Agnes-Marie Hardegen. These letters (esp. that of December 22, 1937) show that immediately before Christmas 1937 the [Confessing Church] vicars had to reckon with arrest as part of the wave of arrests of those in positions of authority in the Confessing Church at the time (cf. 1 /2, 1/3, and 1/7). They also show very clearly how shocked the group had been by the circumstances and outcome of Martin Niemöller's trial: "Friday at 11:30 came the dreadful news: Sachsenhausen concentration camp! This news shocked me so greatly that there was no more thinking of work. This is the sharpest attack on the Christian faith since [19]33. . . . This is an outrage to German justice. This challenge will probably lead many to lose their faith in loyalty and justice. It is terrible that we must go through this" (letter of March 3, 1935). [Niemöller was arrested in July 1937 and tried in February 1938 for sedition. The court sentenced Niemöller to time already served, but Hitler personally ordered that he be rearrested and sent to Sachsenhausen. He was eventually sent to Dachau and remained imprisoned until May 1945.—VB] For their help in deciphering the manuscript, Dirk Schulz thanks Maja Rudl of Sörup and Hans Pfeifer of Düsseldorf, as well as Ilse Tödt of Hanover, Ernst Feil of Gilching, and Jürgen Henkys of Berlin.

Statements about confession of sin
- Home visits
- Visiting the sick
- Visiting a deathbed
- The pastor's visit to those in tribulation
- Exorcism]

March 3, 1938

The commission for pastoral care

1. [This] is given with the proclamation. Indeed it should preach in and out of season, etc. The issue is the very same one as in the sermon: that Christ's word comes through. To that extent pastoral care and the sermon are objectively the same. The preaching ministry to the individual. Against a moralistic understanding. The pastor is not just preacher but shepherd. Difficulties in pastoral care indicate that something[3] is not right in the sermon, either. It can't just be a matter of human transformation (such as from sorrow to joy), but rather that God is proclaimed into sorrow, fear, and sickness.

   The normal parishioner does not expect the word of God. Therefore
2. The particular task of pastoral care: διακονία. It applies to the preaching ministry and nonetheless is not identical to it. It corresponds to a specific need: whoever comes to me, comes first from the Word and want to go toward the Word, but often stands in between. The task is to lead him back to the Word along the path of *diakonia. Assistance toward the Word is the essential office of pastoral care.*

Pastoral care occurs not primarily through proclaiming and hearing[4] but through the listening of the pastor and the speaking of the parishioner.

The handwritten notes contain various abbreviations that have been spelled out, with the exception of "Cath." and "Reform." Cf. also the other documents related to the lecture on pastoral care in *DBW* 14, 2/12 and 2/24, and *DBWE* 5:108–18. Translation by Victoria J. Barnett. [The topic of this lecture—*Seelsorge*—literally means "concern for the soul" and can be translated either as "pastoral care" or "pastoral counseling." Both terms are used in this lecture.—VB]

[2.] [The word "confession" can used to translate two very different German theological terms used throughout these notes: *beichten* is the act of confessing one's sins in the confessional; *bekennen* is the confession of one's faith. To avoid confusion here they are spelled out.—VB]

[3.] [The German here reads *es* (it), but the editor notes that *etwas* (something) is meant.—VB]

[4.] [The German here, *hören*, means both "to hear" and "to listen"; both nuances are present here.—VB]

Therefore a reversal: silence forbidden! *Learning to hear is of immense importance.* This is the very first and simplest act of love for one's neighbor!

The first sense of this twofold command: *to hear.*[5] A pastor who is unable to hear becomes a clericalist [Pfaffe].[6] The Holy Spirit, however, comes *only* through the proclamation. This is the presupposition between sermon and pastoral care.

Where someone who is stubborn hears the word of God, he doesn't hear it and ultimately can no longer hear it. Whoever withdraws in this way into disobedience to God's command will also no longer hear forgiveness, can't hear it. (Cf. the freedom to . . .[7] who do evil.)

The goal, the heart of pastoral care, is:

The Confession of Sin [Beichte].

There the parishioner speaks, pastor hears [=] part 1;

Pastor speaks, parishioner hears [=] absolution.

Without the ministry of confession of sin, the preaching ministry can bring the greatest devastation into the congregation. There where grace is always only preached, without helping the individual to hear that this grace is really the grace of God, a new beginning etc., there the preaching of grace is dead.

The ministry of confession of sin is the necessary corrective for the preaching ministry.

Four things make pastoral care necessary:

1. Because through unknown, hidden sins against the hearing of the word, the human being becomes *obdurate.* The unrepentant heart draws from the proclamation of grace a lack of constraint leading toward sin.
2. Because the sermon confirms this obduracy each and every time.
3. Because the sermon cannot call the individual's sin, which he uses to become obdurate, by its name and exorcise it.
4. Because precisely here it is essential that the parishioner speak.

Therefore two aspects characterize pastoral care in the narrow sense:

1. The speaking of the parishioner
2. The exposure, naming, and exorcism of the sin

This provision of pastoral care to be applied in *all* cases of pastoral care, not only for the sick. Goal *always* confession of sin (see below).

[5.] Cf. Mark 12:28–31 and Deut. 6:4–5.

[6.] [The German *Pfaffe* is a combination of the word for "pastor" (*Pfarrer*) and "monkey" (*Affe*); it was derogatory slang for the clergy and can also mean "clericalist."—VB]

[7.] Illegible in the manuscript; it may read *Vehikel* or *Deckel* ("vehicle" or "cover").

The pastor is given to do pastoral care particularly as the one who proclaims. But it can also be entrusted to the deacons and elders; cf. reform.[8] Exercise of the priesthood next to the office of proclamation; Luther has both lines.

Law and Gospel in pastoral care

1. The social ministry [Diakonie] of pastoral care stands in the service of the proclaiming pastoral care. The first should prepare the way.

Preparation for hearing:

The human being who comes to us for counsel and help in all kinds of need is the normal case. In this he is unknowingly fleeing the simple obedience to God's word. He speaks of need instead of sin. The reason for this evasion [is] unbelief. As if one could acknowledge the lordship of Christ and keep something back from him. Herein harmlessness leads to a general perplexity and uncertainty in the decisions of Christian life.

A general uncertainty enters in where on some point we don't struggle between spirit and flesh. Classic example Matt. 19 (rich young man) questions only attempt to flee.[9]

Answer: Hear God's word!

Where he feels that his condition is one of great *need*, he *must* ultimately be addressed by me as *sinner*. This is the situation in all cases.

2. The counselor [Seelsorger] understands more about the other than that person himself. Behind the unveiling of the need, he hears the not-yet-guilty plea of sin. Goal to speak to him in that: "Why do you withdraw from obedience to Jesus Christ?" "Where you become obdurate at one place you become entirely obdurate against him." Lead from the question for human help to the question for God's help.

    Service: *To take the questioner more seriously than his questions.*

    Known from the pastoral care to youth, *and more serious than he takes himself.*

    From the abstruseness of the war of words, lead back into the plain hearing of the word, confession [Bekennen] of sins and acceptance of forgiveness and the call to discipleship to Christ.

[8.] *DBW* 14:559 reads here: "elders in the reformed congregations." Cf. *DBW* 14:559, ed. note 14.

[9.] Cf. here the exegesis of Matt. 19:16–22 in *Discipleship* (*DBWE* 4:69–76, esp. 70–71). Georgii had received *Discipleship* from his parents for Christmas 1937 (letter of December 28, 1937).

March 12, 1938

Path from advice to command, from all kinds of help to God's help.

How can this path be described?

3. For the pastor, there is no counseling conversation without constant prayer to God.

There is no direct approach from two people toward each other. Even in the world of eros[10] one bumps up against the limit.

The service of social ministry knows: it's a matter of service to God, independent of my person.

Observe the mediating position of Jesus Christ himself. It extends itself not only to the relationship [from] the human being to God, but also the entire creation to God and from human to human. [He has] made peace.[11]

The pastoral counselor is free from any kind of agonizing calculation and delving into the other. This in contrast to the psychiatrist. The pastoral counselor remains fundamentally pre-psychological, pre . . . ,[12] remains naive. In that atmosphere magic, demons, enchantment dominate instead of help, love.

The psychotherapist binds the patient to his own power and person. The Christian pastoral counselor is completely different. He loves the other out of the ἀγάπη,[13] which leaves him free. When the ἄνθρωπος ψυχικός[14] nonetheless has effect, struggle against that. Yes, it's always a matter of dissolving the connection to the person.

Dominance: the Christian pastoral counselor sees every human being *beneath the cross of Jesus Christ,* that is, where a human being comes in a condition of utter depravation, the pastoral counselor knows: what comes to light here is nonetheless nowhere near what he knows about sin, depravation, etc. at the cross of Christ.

Precondition: to automatically take the other as sinner. Expect nothing else at all. This liberates the other. Books by Georges Bernanos: *Under*

[10.] "Love." On the pair of concepts "eros and agape" (see below) and on this section with the contrast between the "emotional" (*seelisch*) or "psychological" (*psychisch*) and "spiritual" (*geistlich*), see the section on "Community" in Bonhoeffer's *Life Together* (*DBWE* 5:27–47, esp. 34ff.).

[11.] Cf. Rom. 5:1–2 and Eph. 2:14.

[12.] Word missing in the manuscript.

[13.] "Love."

[14.] "Psychological person."

Satan's Sun, The Diary of a Country Priest, The Imposter.[15] Similar things can be found in Dostoevsky.[16]

Even the Christian pastoral counselor must pose trenchant questions, but this as thoroughly penultimate as a service of brotherly help. As a human being he stands just as much with empty hands. There is no difference in terms of strength, rather a *different commission.* On the other hand, not to dissolve the distance, despite the solidarity of guilt. The solidarity may not become a method in the psychological sense. We don't make any guilty pleas of our own but rather bind them to God. Whatever the pastoral counselor knows, he should know as if he didn't know it.

March 16, 1938

4. Pastoral counseling is the *accompanying* of another, not a one-time event. Normal: parishioner turns to the *pastor.*

Example: farmer confesses adultery to an unfamiliar priest and finds no peace. Timmermanns.[17] Only once he goes to his own priest!

5. Question of confidentiality

Pastoral counseling bound to the personal confidence in a particular person. Prerequisite that we are entrusted with the keeping of the *pledge of secrecy of the confessional.* Usually the congregation doesn't know of the confessional pledge at ordination. Pastoral counseling between two. There are no observers. Strict rule of Catholic practice: once something has become known, it may never become a topic of conversation for the priest and toward others!!

In general: Discretion of the pastor. He alone administers the office of preacher and pastoral counselor.

Every word of the pastor about the congregation to others must be weighed extremely carefully. Gossip the most destructive thing for the building up of a congregation. Confidence in the confidentiality of the con-

---

[15.] Several books by the French novelist Georges Bernanos (published in German as *Die Sonne Satans, Tagebuch eines Landpfarrers, Der Abtrünnige*) were read together during the collective pastorates (cf. 1/142 and *DB-ER,* 562–63). At the beginning of January 1938, the assistant pastors read together Hans Christian Andersen's fairy tale "The Snow Queen" (letter from Wolf Georgii of January 3, 1938, which includes the comment: "B[onhoeffer] is very much for fairy tales"). At the beginning of March 1938, they read from Ernst Wiechert's 1936 autobiography *Wälder und Menschen* (letter of March 9, 1938).

[16.] Cf. Dostoyevsky's novels *The Brother Karamazov* and *The Idiot.* (Cf. *DBW* 14:564, ed. note 31 and 565, ed. note 34).

[17.] In the course "Confession of Guilt (according to the Large Catechism)," Bonhoeffer in a similar context had referred in 1936 to the novel *Bauernpsalm,* by Felix Timmermanns. Cf. *DBW* 14:754, ed. note 29.

fessional when there is silence about small matters as well. During visits turn off chatter about others.

Breaking the confidentiality of the confessional must have the consequence of the loss of the office.

Even the *courts* honor the confidentiality of the confessional, unless it concerns an imminent crime. These boundaries, however, are a problem. Generally speaking, the confidentiality of the confessional must be in effect completely.

6. A man comes for a consultation who wants to be a Christian. Says that for years he has not gotten free of a particular sin. This hinders his ability to absorb the word. General confession didn't help. Forgiveness has no power. Question: Do I, who keep the word and sacrament, stand within the faith, or am I deceiving myself? Etc.

This question leads to *desperation*.

Reversed: isn't the grace of God independent of this? "Let my grace be sufficient for you."[18] *Pecca fortiter.*[19] Here *securitas*[20] looms.

Conflict between law and gospel.

(The human being in whom faith and obedience have broken apart from each other stands very normally in this condition.)

Two paths for the pastor:

1. I speak forgiveness to the parishioner in response to the confession of faith—unconditionally.

But: absolution in a vacuum is misuse. Then a deeper obduracy easily enters in under the poison of a too-cheap forgiveness.

This happens in countless cases of a false absolution, which can rob the human being of his soul's salvation.

2. Is the precondition there: contrition and the intent to improve? But precisely this question cannot be answered by a serious Christian. Here, too, perplexity.

What to do?

Every proper Christian pastoral counselor must know this *need.* Precisely here lies the promise of pastoral care. Unity of obedience and faith only there, where Christ himself speaks, where Christ himself is propelling the pastoral care. The Holy Scripture testifies to this unity; Jesus himself testifies to it. Jesus demands of his disciples that they abandon their connections.

[18.] Cf. 2 Cor. 12:9. [The NRSV here reads: "My grace is sufficient for you . . ."—VB]

[19.] "Sin boldly!" For Bonhoeffer's interpretation of Martin Luther's statement "pecca fortiter," cf. *DBWE* 4:51–53.

[20.] Cf. the inclusion of Luther's distinction between *securitas* (security) and *certitudo* (certainty) in *DBWE* 4:44 and elsewhere.

Without obedience no discipleship!

Only the obedient can believe. But just as much: *only the believer can obey.*

It concerns both these statements. Cf. parable of the prodigal son.[21]

God opens his arms and the human being surrenders himself, just as he is. But only the penitent finds forgiveness. And only the one who has forgiveness finds penitence.

So Jesus's entire sermon:

"Repent, for the kingdom of God has come near."[22] The same in the OT:

Sacrifice without law, forgiveness without obedience is nothing, but law without sacrifice is also nothing; forgiveness does not come through law. For Paul both are connected in the justification of the godless.

God wants you, but he wants you completely, that is, completely as a sinner.

Overall things bound together. The false connection replaces faith in Jesus Christ. The replaced faith in turn fortifies the false bond: *pecca fortiter*! Inevitable development. Jesus did two things: (a) rich young man,[23] (b) the woman caught in adultery.[24] Different and yet the same. (a) First obedience, then faith; (b) faith, then obedience.

Pastoral counseling concerns the realization of these two statements.

It involves leading the sinner back to the Word. The bond that divides from Christ must be named. Often a human being is so poisoned by disobedience that he is no longer aware of the bond at all.

In the pastoral letters there is a great deal about the garments in which disobedience shows itself, that alter it: for example, superficial indifference, endless problematizing, ethical rigor, secret sectarianism, addiction to innovation and restlessness of worldviews.[25]

Reason for everything: because they bear a *stigma in their conscience.*[26]

Ps. 32, Prov. 28.

Sin must be made known. By becoming a sinner, the human being is obedient.

7. *The confession of sin.*[27]

[21.] Regarding this section and the reference to the parable in Matt. 19 in general, cf. the central section "The Call to Discipleship," *DBWE* 4:57–76. See also Luke 15:11–32.

[22.] Matt. 4:17.

[23.] Matt. 19:16–22.

[24.] John 8:1–11.

[25.] Cf. 2/1, "Exercises in the Pastoral Epistles."

[26.] 1 Tim. 4:2.

[27.] Regarding this section on the confession of sin, cf. Bonhoeffer's 1936 exegeses about the confession of sin according to Luther's Large Catechism (Kolb and Wengert, *Book of Concord*, 460–65) . Documented in *DBW* 14:2/24. See also the theses on "Confession of Sin and the Lord's Supper," *DBW* 14, 2/24.1.

In the confession of sin, faith and obedience become one. What is the confession of sin? All pastoral counseling has this as its goal. Luther in the Large Catechism: "Therefore, when I urge you to go to confession, I am simply urging you to be a Christian."[28] Demarcation against the Roman practice of confession of sin.

1. Confession of sin is not compulsory, is not a law.
2. The meaning of the confession of sin is not to enumerate all sins. Rather: the confession of sin is purely a means of grace. The importance of the confession of sin is absolution.

At the time of the Reformation, the confession of sin had primarily a sacramental character (as the third sacrament). Never officially, but historically practiced in this way until pietism, which brought it down, because it became too institutionally hardened through orthodoxy.

Now statements about the confession of sin:

1. If I go to confession, I go [to] God. The pastor in God's stead. He preserves the secret as God's secret.
2. The pastor has been called as the confessor; on the other hand, the confession of faith is not bound to the person who bears that office but is a matter of the priesthood of all believers (*mutua consolatio fratrum*).[29] The actual practice was the institutional one. Confession of sin as a component of the power of the keys [Schlüsselamt]. It is a healthier thing when the pastor hears the confession.
3. Fear that we will not be understood by the confessor, because he would be so completely different, is false. No human being is exposed to such difficult tribulations as a serious Christian. The understanding of the other will come about through being spoken to. Basically every Christian understands us.
4. In the confession of sin everything depends on the *personal* absolution. To be able to be completely certain of this, I may call my sins by name and receive absolution. I confess to my sins, not my need. Confession of sin serves to strengthen faith.
5. Why is the confession of sin before God insufficient?
    (a) I am called to this for the sake of certitude that God is not a phantom, that I am not confessing to myself, [therefore] *for the sake of objectivity.*

[28.] From "A Brief Exhortation to Confession" at the end of the Large Catechism (Kolb and Wengert, *Book of Concord*, 460). Also cited by Bonhoeffer in *DBWE* 4:271.

[29.] The entire Latin phrase is *per mutuum colloquium et consolationem fratrum*, "referring to absolution by a neighbor or friend." See the Smalcald Articles, in *Book of Concord*, 319n128.

Something unhealthy, that [confession of sin] before God is easier than before human beings!

(b) Because the concealed sin must someday [come] to light. It is better that it come to light *today* than on the day of judgment. As long as it remains in darkness, it poisons my entire being. *Odor of decay*. For the sake of certitude it takes place before a witness.

(c) The root of all our sin is *arrogance*. The confession of sin is the humiliation that we experience before the brother.

It hurts us, reduces us, overloads us with disgrace. But precisely in that, we participate in the disgrace of Christ. It lies upon us (cf. Luther).[30]

6. In the confession of sin, what occurs is the human being's complete surrender to the mercy and the help and justice of God. Here in the confession of sin the essential procedure of conversion can be seen. That which is called "discipleship" in the gospels. The proper confession of sin is the proper conversion and the call into discipleship.
7. Only the one who stands in the confession of sin finds community. If one remains alone with his evil, he remains completely alone.
8. Confession of sin is grace and not law, grace of the certainty of conversion. Grace is healing sadness, divine sadness, and incomparable joy. It is followed by gratitude, freedom, and new life. Where someone has cast off all sins in the confession of sin, there he is free.
9. Because confession of sin is no law, for that reason the Christian can also live without confession of sin. But probably only theoretically true. Luther could think of no one who did not need it, and needed it until the end of his life. Don't reject the divine offer of mercy! A certain amount of *certitude* is given here.
10. The confessor himself must practice confession of sin. Otherwise highest danger! Whoever practices confession is more likely to be sought as a confessor.

    Cath.: even the pope must go to confession. Otherwise the danger of a psychological, magical power over the soul.

[30.] Cf. the theses on "Confession of Sin and the Lord's Supper" in *DBW* 14, 2/24.1.

11. It is really a path with certain stages. Aid: spiritual disciplines. Only those that are grounded in the Scripture itself.

(Cath. have penances: *contritio cordis, confession oris, satisfactio opera*, 10 *pater noster* etc.)[31]

But certain exercises within Protestant pastoral counseling practices good: prayer, meditation on the Scripture, abstinence, silence, service in humility to one's neighbor. Those are *exercises* in accordance with Scripture. To meditate on Scripture. To mention these kinds of exercises, once before the confession of sin, once after the confession of sin. For example, whoever says that he hates his father cannot come to the Lord's Supper. He could be given an exercise of service in humility to his neighbor.

For newcomers to Christian life the exercise will be a great help. They stand in twilight.

(a) As difficult law, (b) as a gentle and light yoke

Don't misunderstand Christian freedom as complete lack of law. Only the one who is willing to obedience can be seized by faith; see above.

The entire confessional conversation may not be too lengthy (perhaps in the vestment in the sacristy). Firmly decide: preach one time about the confession of sin, letting the congregation know of this possibility. Matt. 16:18–19; John 20; James 5; also OT: Ps. 32; Prov. 28.

March 22, 1938

Home visits.

Here no possibility to hide somewhere, but rather immediate facing one another. Where we come, there is nothing more important to us than that God's gospel be spoken. "For out of the abundance of the heart . . ."[32] applies here. Failure mostly one's own fault.

There are pastors for whom pastoral counseling is embarrassing, who can't speak a free prayer!

For Christians the house is the place of Christian living [Christlichkeit]; cf. Jesus.[33] Entry into a strange house means that I see the other in a world in which he is completely in his own. I notice one thousand relationships of which I could otherwise never be witness. Spying? Inspector instead of God's messenger?

[31.] Cf. *DBW* 14:751, ed. note 11. [Actually, the first three penances Bonhoeffer lists are the three traditional parts of Catholic penance (contrition of heart, oral confession, acts performed in satisfaction for sin). Saying the Lord's prayer or other prayers (e.g., "10 pater noster") is considered part of the *satisfactio opera*.—VB]

[32.] Cf. Matt. 12:34.

[33.] Cf. Mark 1:29; Mark 6:10; and elsewhere.

Permission to enter is *a very special proof of trust.* Everything that he notices in the house is included in his official discretion. (Here there is a question mark about intervention in social welfare in the conditions in the home.) Pastor is (a) not master of the house, (b) nonetheless has the responsibility to conduct the discussion.

Even *the first visit* must have the goal of getting down to business. It's false to lie in wait anxiously for a starting point. The freer and more impartial the pastor is, the more so the parishioner will be. This must be the self-evident part of the visit. The pastor comes with the Bible, not just to the pious but to all (in northern France the pastor goes with the large Bible through the town).

Naturally there are also situations in which it is imperative not to cast pearls before swine.[34] Usually, however, we tend to see this point prematurely.

The order of visits:

1. The elders and sick, elderly
   (on the first Sunday ask for the names of these)
2. The homes of confirmation students
3. Regionally, not according to social status

Visiting the sick.

1. It should be regular:
   - (a) Simply for the sake of the sick. An announced visit better than a surprise one. An announced visit that does not come to pass is a great disappointment and is *absolutely* to be avoided.
   - (b) Put on the work schedule.
   - (c) For the pastor's sake. Illness is nothing abnormal but is part of being healthy. We have barracked off the sick so that they're out of sight (different in the Orient). Therefore the illusion of a healthy people [Volk].[35]

Matt. 8:17 healing of the sick justified with Isa. 53[:4]. Among the sick, the pastor is closer to the memory of Jesus's suffering on the cross. The sick shed light on the healthy, on the sickness in the healthy, on the suffering in all creation.

[34.] Cf. Matt. 7:6.

[35.] [In the context of the times, this can certainly be read as a clear critique of Nazi ideology and policies that portrayed people with physical disabilities and illnesses as threats to the health of the *Volk*. Less than two years after this was written, the Nazi regime was murdering such people in its "euthanasia" program.—VB]

The sick asks for healing. The pastor must teach him to understand this question as the quest for salvation in Christ. Exod. 15: "I am the Lord, your physician . . ."[36] Cf. the path of pastoral care in social ministry from need to sin; see above.

The pastor brings the Sunday sermon to the sick. He tells whoever is not part of the church that he should know that the church also comes to the sick. Offer of help. Decisive that one attempts to give *tasks* to the sick. Task of this time: (a) for his own person and relationship to God; (b) intercessory prayer for the congregation. There should basically be no idle hours. (In sleepless hours: *Der helle Ton,* no. 316: "Now one goes to sleep," Tersteegen.)[37] There is no time that should just be killed. Every time *is given to you by God.*

Particular difficulty: egotistical sick persons. Tyrants. Also fights and quarrels in the wards.

The Lord's Supper for the sick . . .

The healing of the sick . . .[38]

Know many Bible verses and hymns by heart. Perhaps get a notebook in which one writes down appropriate proverbs as soon as one comes across them.

Visiting a deathbed.

There can be no reason here to keep a pastor away. Final possibility for conversion. Last boundary reached, where there is only prayer, confession of sin, and absolution. Short prayer and question whether the dying one still has something to say, whether he wants to die in faith and be certain of the forgiveness of sin.

If the person dying is not aware of his end, one must also pose these questions.

After the sick person has died, pray, perhaps sing with the relatives.

If possible, visit the relatives before the funeral, otherwise of course afterward, self-evident.

[36.] Cf. Exod. 15:26 [the NRSV here reads: "I am the Lord who heals you"—VB].

[37.] "Nun schläfet man," the 1745 evening hymn by Gerhard Tersteegen (*EG,* 480) [an English version of the hymn does not seem to exist.—VB]. *Der helle Ton* (The Clear Tone) was the hymnal of the Reich Association of Protestant Young Men's groups. Georgii wrote his fiancée shortly before the beginning of the collective pastorate: "We are to bring bedding, wool blankets, towels and napkins, as well as *Der helle Ton* and instruments, possibly warm clothing, firm shoes, the most important books" (letter of December 3, 1937). Cf. also Bonhoeffer's letter of October 10, 1939, to Max Mebes with the invitation to the winter 1939–40 collective pastorate (1/165).

[38.] Here words are missing from the text.

The pastor's visit to those in tribulation

1. There is the tribulation that is experienced and that is not experienced. It is always a matter of faith.

(a) The experienced tribulation feels the power of the devil as completely real. The devil has many ways:

(α) Inordinate drive of the flesh, passion, so that the cross vanishes. Indifference about salvation. Addiction to fame, vanity, sexual lust, etc.

The devil knows that with this, he clouds over the clear capacity to discern at the same time.

Here there is nothing else but to name the liar as liar.

(β) Sadness. (Cath.: *acedia*[39] one of the seven deadly sins). Scruples of conscience, everything in vain, everything dark. Doubt about the very existence of God. Suicide threatens at the end of this sadness.

Danger that we imagine this is divine sadness.[40]

(γ) Destruction of faith in salvation. Rejected by God, unworthy reception of the sacrament. Sin can no longer be forgiven. In all this the human being perceptibly feels in the grip of the devil's power.

(b) Even more dangerous is the imperceptible tribulation, that he no longer feels his sin, no longer has any remorse, etc. He no longer believes in the Christian terminology, even though he masters it. Here God's very wrath is hidden and hardened.

Here in pastoral counseling it is really a matter of

Exorcism.

He is only driven out by Christ. (cf. confessional sessions[41] Blumhardt).[42]

Regarding α: In the tribulation of flesh and blood, the flesh becomes "proud" (Luther),[43] succumbs to *superbia*;[44] it must be humiliated. Here

[39.] Listlessness, dejection, bitterness.

[40.] Cf. 2 Cor. 7:10.

[41.] Illegible.

[42.] Johann Christoph Blumhardt (the elder) was pastor in Bad Boll after 1852. Cf. Bonhoeffer's communion homily on 1 Cor. 15:55 on Remembrance Sunday, November 26, 1939, 3/6, esp. ed. note 6.

[43.] Luke 1:51; cf. Luther's German translation of Mary's Magnificat (Luke 1:46–55) [the German word translated as "proud" here is *hoffärtig*.—VB]

[44.] Pride or arrogance.

a clearly assigned exercise of discipline is helpful, then a making present of the crucified body of Christ. Behold *Him*! Strong help: the brother. The word of grace is heard not by the insurgent flesh but by the humiliated flesh.

Regarding β: three points are doors by which the devil can invade:

1. Ingratitude toward God.
2. Hopelessness.
3. Some unknown sin that wants to come to light.

In pastoral counseling, recognize even at these three points: God was merciful, he wants to be merciful to you, but he also wants to have you *completely*.

Regarding γ: He frequently thinks he takes God particularly seriously. The proper taking seriously is a taking seriously of grace above all sin and above all scruple. God's wrath is precisely his nearness. If God were not wrathful, then he would also not be merciful.

Those in tribulation who have little experience suffer particularly under their lack of experience. Answer: this is not where the problem lies. We have no claim on particular experience. You owe to the word of God, to prayer. "Let my grace be sufficient for you."[45] But no *cheap* comfort.

In all these questions the path points very clearly toward the *confession of sin*.[46]

[45.] 2 Cor. 12:9 [the NRSV reads: "My grace is sufficient for you . . ."—VB].

[46.] Wolf Georgii's letter of March 27, 1938, indicates that the first session of the collective pastorate in Köslin on March 25, 1938, concluded with a collective celebration of the Lord's Supper where Bonhoeffer spoke about Heb. 9:14. ["how much more will the blood of Christ, who through the eternal Spirit offered himself without blemish to God, purify our conscience from dead works to worship the living God!"—VB].

303 **1. Exercises in the Pastoral Epistles, 1938 (Fragment)**[1]

1. The Letter to Timothy. Chapter 1

Verse 1. Παῦλος ἀπόστολος Χριστοῦ Ἰησοῦ—not from his own will, but κατ' ἐπιταγὴν θεοῦ (Rom. 16:26)[2] [(] Paul refers to his authorization in his personal letter to Timothy as well. [)].

θεὸς σωτὴρ ἡμῶν—the same God, who is our Savior,[3] orders the apostle [(] cf. 2:3, 4:10; Titus 1:3; 2:10; 3:4; Jude 25 (Luke 1:47) [)] otherwise Jesus Christ σωτήρ 2 Tim. 1:10; Titus 1:3; 2:10; 3:4 [(] Old Testament Hab. 3:18; Pss. 25:5; 27:9 [)]

Χριστὸς Ἰησοῦς ἐλπὶς ἡμῶν[4]—Col. 1:27.[5] On the basis of salvation—hope, as the one who came in the flesh and the one who will come again. The letter moves into the eschatological context. *Christ* our hope—this is eschatology in utmost simplicity. Not this or that, but only one: Jesus Christ.

304 Verse 2. Τιμοθέῳ γνησίῳ τέκνῳ ἐν πίστει[6]—1. Faith creates life. I have become the son of the one who helped me to live in faith. The father-son relationship is completely genuine in faith. It is different from the relation between teacher/student or employer/employee. The birth of the new life

[1.] *NL*, A 52, 5; handwritten note, primarily in ink. Previously published in *GS* 4:358–84. Bonhoeffer's abbreviations, including those of proper names and the Greek text, are spelled out. [The German edition of this volume replicated the inconsistent abbreviations Bonhoeffer used for the names of biblical books, since such variations sometimes indicated the different reference works he consulted. This English edition uses standard abbreviations for biblical books.—VB] The designation of the discussed verses (frequently placed in the margin beside the text in Bonhoeffer's manuscript) has been standardized. The underlining of Greek expressions has not been reproduced here. Bonhoeffer's additions, often written in pencil, are indicated by parentheses enclosed in brackets, [(] [)]. The "Exercises in the Pastoral Epistles" were part of his teaching responsibilities during the second collective pastorate session in the summer of 1938. Cf. Bonhoeffer's Bible study of the letters to Timothy in 1936, "The Servant in the House of God," *DBW* 14:945–69.

[2.] 1 Tim 1:1: "Paul, an apostle of Christ Jesus by the command of God"; "according to the command" found also in Rom. 16:26.

[3.] "God . . . our Savior" is Bonhoeffer's translation of the Greek expression. In the following notes, only those Greek terms that Bonhoeffer does not explain will be translated.

[4.] "Christ Jesus our hope."

[5.] The cross-reference to Col. 1:27 is underlined in pencil in the Greek text of Bonhoeffer's Nestle New Testament, as are most of the words in vv. 1 and 2 of the Greek text. [The Nestle edition of the New Testament included the Greek and the Luther German translation. Ilse Tödt observes that Bonhoeffer often quoted Luther's translation and recommended it to his students, since at that time many parishioners still knew those familiar texts by heart.—VB]

[6.] "To Timothy, my loyal child in the faith."

is bound with the spiritual father, and the spiritual father recognizes in his true son in faith the special grace of God, which made him the father of this son. Faith does not rule out certain relations between human beings, but constitutes these in the proper manner. [(] Phil. 2:22; 1 Tim. 1:18; 2 Tim. 1:2; 2:1 [)] 1 Cor. 4:17 "beloved and faithful child" Acts 16:1ff. Timothy, the son of a Greek man and a Jewish woman; in Jewish eyes an illegitimate heritage—νόθος[7] (cf. Titus 1:4 γνήσιον τέκνον) *Philem 10* and of the church-community: Gal. 4:19 τέκνα μου, οὓς πάλιν ὠδίνω[8] 1 Cor. 4:14; 2 Cor. 6:13. Father: Phil. 2:22; 1 Thess. 2:11[–12] "like a father with his children, urging and encouraging." 2. There is a difference between Paul calling someone his son and someone calling Paul father. The question is whether Paul acknowledges his fatherhood. 3. Timothy is one with Paul in faith; he stands in the faith of Paul and the Letter to the Romans. With that, faith, *fides qua* and *quae creditur*,[9] is understood as a *prerequisite* for the relation in its entirety. Because of this, the content of faith does not need to be expounded here explicitly. It is sufficient to give an occasional reminder, the reference to the premise: "Remember"—(2 Tim. 2:8). Here is the basis for the relation between the Letters to the Romans and to Timothy.

χάρις, ἔλεος, εἰρήνη cf. 2 Tim. 1:2 (2 John 3; Jude 2)—Romans, 1 and 2 Corinthians, Galatians, Ephesians, Philippians, Colossians, 1–2 Thessalonians: χάρις καὶ εἰρήνη. Here ἔλεος—compassion, help, is inserted. ἔλεος, instead of ὑμῖν[10] (cf. Gal. 6:16) [(] *Peace before the powers.* ἔλεος—from the father. [)]

Verses 3–4. About chronology: difficult to determine. Timothy came with Paul from Ephesus. 2 Cor. 1:1; Acts 20:4. Starting from Rome? Timothy was with Paul in Rome. Philippians, Colossians, Philemon. Only after the first 305
Roman imprisonment. Ephesus: Acts 18, 19, 20. [(] (Sceva, Apollos, Demetrius, disciples of John.)[11][)] A lively church-community with great difficulties, excesses, immense mission success. Great work of Paul.—Timothy stays alone back in Ephesus. Much later, Paul still remembers the tears of farewell (2 Tim. 1:5).[12] Timothy did not ask for this task. He takes it from the hand of the apostle. The work is great and difficult, and Paul thinks

[7.] "Illegitimate." The contrasting term γνήσιος (marital), Luther translates as *rechtschaffen*, Bonhoeffer as *recht*, or "true."

[8.] "My little children, for whom I am again in the pain of childbirth."

[9.] "Faith through which" and "faith which is believed" (act and content of faith).

[10.] 1 Thess. 1:1 and 2 Thess. 1:1 reads: χάρις ὑμῖν καὶ εἰρήνη (Grace with you and peace).

[11.] [The reference is to the Jewish high priest Sceva (Acts 19:14ff.); Apollos, a Jewish follower of Jesus (Acts 18:24ff.); and the silversmith Demetrius (Acts 19:24ff.).—VB]

[12.] "Tears" are mentioned in v. 4.

of his son day and night in his intercessory prayers (2 Tim. 1:3). Timothy's task is to defend the church-community *against false doctrine* [Irrlehre].[13] He is supposed "*to command,* that others do not teach differently." Apparently, he needed special *authority* for this, a commission [Amt]. The fact that Timothy is supposed to take command indicates that the false teachers are still *within* the church-community. ἑτεροδιδασκαλεῖν, μῦθοι, γενεαλογίαι, Titus 1:14;[14] 3:9 (1 Tim. 4:7; 2 Tim. 4:4; 2 Pet. 1:16) Ἰουδαϊκοῖς[15] (Titus 1:14). Myths are stories of the gods based on speculation, a contradiction to revelation. Genealogies belong to myth [(] ἀπέραντοι unlimited, without conclusion, endless [)]. The genealogical tree is to lead today's generation back to its divine origin. (It is dubious whether the Old Testament genealogies are meant here. Preference of Jewish Christianity by virtue of its lineage?) *Decisive:* Paul does not even refer to *this.* No *discussion*! *Apologetics*! For all that leads to ἐκζητήσεις—questions, problems—instead of to the οἰκονομία θεοῦ[16]—(*stewardship,* the treasure, wealth remains only to be distributed. To distribute that which is given, that which is revealed.) ἐν πίστει—the office "which is performed in faith."[17]

Verse 5. Summary.—The aim of the command is the exhortation (of Timothy)—ἀγάπη[18] [(] 1 Cor. 8:1 [)]—"from a pure heart," "good con-
306 science," "sincere faith" [(] 2 Tim. 1:5 [)]; love only in its separation from uncleanness. The *good* conscience (1:19; 3:9; 2 Tim. 1:3)—in contrast to the defiled conscience of false teachers (1 Tim. 4:2); there is also such a thing as hypocritical faith, not genuine—not all have reached this and have, therefore, arrived at "empty talk." μάταιος[19] Eph. 4:17; Titus 1:10; 1 Tim. 5:13; 6:20.

νομοδιδάσκαλοι—ἑτεροδιδασκαλεῖν—those who do not live in faith and love become teachers of the law.

Verses 6–7. The one who has not been freed by the gospel establishes a new law. The one whose conscience is unclean hides behind a strict preach-

---

[13.] [This would have called to mind the heresies of the German Christians.—VB]

[14.] "Titus 1:14" in Bonhoeffer's Greek text is written in pencil in the margin; ἑτεροδιδασκαλεῖν (to teach differently) and μύθοις in 1 Tim. 1:3–4 are underlined. Luther translates in v. 4: "Fables and genealogies."

[15.] "Jewish" (myths).

[16.] "Householding" or "the order of God's salvation."

[17.] In Bonhoeffer's Greek text, the page that begins with πίστει is torn out. From here on, there are only a few other handwritten notations by Bonhoeffer in 1 and 2 Timothy.

[18.] "Love."

[19.] "Vain." In the previous sentence Bonhoeffer translated the word as "empty." Luther translated it as "useless."

ing of the law. θέλοντες[20]—ironically; μὴ νοοῦντες—they do not know what the law is—they use the *words* and yet know nothing of the *realities.*

Verses 8–10. The law is good (Rom. 7:12, 16), when it is used in accordance with the law.—The law is not for the δίκαιος[21] but for the ἄνομος.[22] Thus the δίκαιος is never an ἄνομος (but an ἔννομος,[23] 1 Cor. 9:21!). The law applies to those who transgress the Decalogue; this catalog of vices (unlike other such catalogs!!) is constructed according to the Decalogue. *This lawlessness is contrary to sound teaching,* that is, the law is contained in sound teaching. A teaching is unsound when it does not include the law, when it is without law, but also when the law is established even over the righteous. Sound teaching encompasses the fulfillment of the law. Sound teaching strengthens, while sick teaching weakens. Sound teaching links the recognition of sin and the separation from evil; sick teaching leads to sick holiness. Sound teaching teaches respect for the natural gifts of God, thereby worshipping the Creator alone, but sick teaching rejects the natural. Sound teaching creates a good conscience, while sick teaching originates from a branded conscience (see below).[24] [(] *Is this the case in the church-community?* [)]

Verse 11. Κατὰ τὸ εὐαγγέλιον, cf. Rom. 2:16—the law is his work— 307
"according to my gospel," that is, in unity with the gospel. For this reason it is καλός.[25] Letter to the R[omans]. Galatians.[26]

Verses 12–17. The gospel, portrayed through Paul's personal experience as the act of Christ in the life of the apostle, as an example of the sound teaching of Timothy. χάριν ἔχω—I always thank for what I have not earned! Paul names his sins in plain words.

ἀγνοῶν[27]—difference between the knowingly committed sin ἑκουσίως and the unknowingly committed (Heb. 10:26; 6:6, contrary to Luke 23:34 and Acts 3:17; 1 Cor. 2:8). Old Testament: *unknowing* and *deliberate* sin! The last one is beyond remedy.

Verse 15. The good news—help for the sinner through Jesus Christ.—ἁμαρτωλός εἰμι—Paul calls himself a sinner! The only reference to a Christian as ἁμαρτωλός.

[20.] Verse 7: θέλοντες εἶναι νομοδιδάσκαλοι (desiring to be teachers of the law).

[21.] "The righteous one."

[22.] "The lawless one."

[23.] "The one who is in the law."

[24.] See below on 1 Tim. 4:2–3.

[25.] "Good."

[26.] Cf. Rom. 7:12, 16 (referred to above by Bonhoeffer for verses 8–10); Gal. 5:22–23.

[27.] "Unknowing."

Verse 16. But it happened not for the sake of Paul but for the sake of the example, that there is no sin so great that it could be beyond mercy. In this way, guilt and grace are revealed to the church in the life of Paul. Paul remains "the first sinner" and the "first example of God's forbearance." Paul's past lies open for everyone to see, yet precisely through this God's grace is extolled.

Verse 17. Now it is expressed clearly who the God of salvation is: The king of the ages, the everlasting, invisible, unique God to whom honor and glory are due. This testimony calls for the "Amen."

Verse 18. Timothy now knows what he has to preach: *the law,* "in accordance with the law," and *the gospel,* to sinners. In whose power is he supposed to do this? τέκνον Τιμόθεε, says Paul. He calls him "child." Will Timothy be the right man? Timothy's fear of this task must be reduced. How? Paul reminds Timothy not of his former accomplishments, of his gifts in evangelization, of shared experiences and situations, but of his *ordination,* the commission conferred upon him by the church-community (2 Tim. 1:6–7;
308 1 Tim. 4:14). Paul does not provide false comfort to the servant of the Word about his ability and call to this service. He says: there were men in this church-community who selected you for this service. Their prophetic insight has appointed you for this service. There were elders who laid their hands on you and prayed for God's Spirit upon you. Therefore, have confidence. It is none other than God who called you through them. Those whom God calls to service will not be left lacking in power for it. Do not grumble at your task, do not doubt, but be confident, and take up the *struggle* in the power of your divine charge, for it is not a humiliating but a *beautiful* struggle. Proclamation urges the struggle on, necessarily, outwardly, inwardly, and directed against the own self. The work of proclamation, after all, is service in war, arduous service. One who does not want to fight should relinquish this office. This struggle is not your own will but a commission. But—now the *other* prerequisite for this service [Dienst] must be named.

Verse 19. The calling from above, from the church-community, from outside, is to give Timothy certainty, but in his having "*faith and a good conscience.*" That is: 1. The calling from outside does not help if the one who is called does not have faith and a good conscience. No one can stand in the ministry of proclamation without this. Here Paul is not thinking of Judas, who also preached, although provoking a curse upon himself. The *person and the office* depend on each other! No one can preach with joy, commitment, fearlessness, and go around the church-community without standing in faith and being accused again and again by his own conscience. Such a person would be paralyzed in word and deed, exhortation etc., and without strength in the struggle. Timothy destroys his ministry unless he stands

in faith and good conscience. He may not justify himself by means of his office when he lives in unbelief and sin. 2. Joining faith with good conscience, Paul protects his teaching from the misconception that faith goes together with an unclear conscience, with sin. The loss of a good conscience leads necessarily to the loss of faith. Whoever does not want to be obedient but gives free rein to sin can no longer believe, for this arbitrarily destroys the community with God. Faith becomes an empty word; it becomes self-justification. For Paul the requirements for the holder of this office are the
calling from outside and faith with a good conscience. 309

Timothy's enemies have despised a good conscience (perhaps as a kind of moralistic Christianity that relies on a sanctification by works!),[28] so they lost their faith and *blasphemed* God. Indeed, it is a blasphemy of God to use God's grace for a justification of sin. Now they became "teachers of the law" in order to gain what they did not want to receive from Christ. But even this teaching of the law is blasphemy, for it takes the place of the gospel, supplanting divine grace with human will and obedience. It thereby blasphemes God and destroys the human being.

Verse 20. For the first time, Paul gives the names of the apostates. The first lapse from Christ into anti-Christianity as the result of disregard for good conscience! Something to think about. This exclusion has a pedagogical purpose. Excluded from the community for the sake of community.

Chapter 2

Verse 1. Once Timothy is exhorted toward true teaching, Paul speaks of prayer. It is a deeply rooted predicament of the church-community that it repeatedly forgets that the privilege of prayer has been given not only for its own sake but for the sake of the entire world. "Christ came into *the world* . . ." (1:15). That the church-community is rescued from the world does not mean that it should despise the world; instead, it means that its task is to intercede for the world. Precisely because those who have been rescued from the reign of the world truly know the world [(] "all people" [)], they are bound with the world in a new manner. Prayer and the preaching of the gospel serve the world according to the will of God in Jesus Christ. The church-community that denies its responsibility toward the world, toward "all people" ([v.] 1), and withdraws into itself denies the gospel and its commission. The church-community of saved sinners must moreover learn that from now on its prayer
cannot be limited to petitions concerning its own affairs, but that genuine 310

[28.] Uncertain reading.

prayer extends far beyond that. 1. Petitions—in the beginning, this is the proper attitude of the child. 2. Worship, whose gaze is not upon our own needs but on God's majesty and glory. 3. Intercession—entreating for others, by right of the church-community's priesthood. 4. Thanksgiving for everything. In this fullness, congregational prayer belongs to *all people,* without any privilege for the pious over the unbelievers, friends and enemies. How could the church-community of Jesus ever withhold prayer from the enemies who need it in a special way? In the church-community's prayer, all that is human becomes one, without distinctions, one before the grace of God. The fact that the church-community should and can see every person, whether powerful or despised, as in need of God's grace makes it completely *free and fearless* in its encounter with people and takes away any contempt for humankind and all hatred. Because I am "to pray for all people," I therefore cannot despise or hate any person; [otherwise][29] my prayer is a lie. Only in this way does the church-community remain what it is, a church-community of sinners *saved by God's grace.*

Because all humankind needs the prayer of the church-community, this holds true for kings and those in power as well. As human beings they are the objects of intercession. Whether they are Christians [or][30] persecutors (Nero),[31] they are *human beings,* poor sinners in need of salvation and grace. Here, too, Paul always sees the *human being* behind the office. The church-community should bring petition, worship, intercession, *thanksgiving* for all people before God, even for enemies! That authorities must be mentioned in particular is necessitated by the fact that the church-community
311 tends to despise and condemn those in power, especially in times of oppression. But this holds true, even for the authorities: *Petition* = that is, for true order and government, justice and truth. *Worship* = that is, despite enemies and despite the powers that be, do not forget the one who alone has power. *Intercession* = that is, to ask for salvation and grace for those who are[32] in sin, whose conversion would mean much for many people. *Thanksgiving* = that is, for the order and power that remains, as well as for the attack of

[29.] The manuscript erroneously reads "rather."

[30.] The manuscript erroneously reads "and."

[31.] The reference to the Roman emperor Nero, who was obsessed with his own omnipotence and cruelly persecuted Christians, is very likely also a reference to those who held power in the National Socialist regime. Cf. *DBW* 14, 2/10 (homiletic lecture in Finkenwalde), 523, ed. note 205, Otto Dudzus's notes from Bonhoeffer's 1937 lectures: "Prayer for authorities. What is the object of intercession? Do we pray for 'the authorities' or 'the Führer'? This should become neither a confession for nor one against Adolf Hitler."

[32.] The manuscript erroneously reads "not."

the enemy under which the faith of the church-community endures. The church-community is not particularly called to pray for political-worldly objectives. Rather, the aim of this prayer also serves the church-community. The final objective cannot be that the world should remain in its worldly nature and be happy; the aim of God in the world is always God's church-community. That which is done by God on earth is done ultimately for the sake of the church-community of Jesus Christ. The church-community, for its part, does everything to win the world for salvation, and that means nothing other than to serve God. But it is able to do this only when it leads a "quiet and peaceable life, in all piety and dignity" [(] The love of God and neighbor? ἄνθρωπος[33]—anthropological [)]. The church-community asks not for turbulent times of battle but for quiet and rest. Undoubtedly, God may bless even times of battle, but these are also times of temptation that the church-community does not ask for, for it knows how many fall by the wayside in such times and how difficult the ministry of true piety and dignity is in such times. So much prayer gets lost here, prayer for the oppressors becomes hard for the church-community, and much danger lies in this shortcoming! In a time of chaos the orders of the Christian life dissolve; the temptation to disorder and the frenzy of battle become so grave, shattering the measure of σεμνότης[34] and inflicting harm on the church-community.

Verse 3. Such prayer for all people is pleasing to God, since God's salvatory will embraces all people. From this it becomes clear that the content of prayer is the salvation of all people, including kings and authorities [Obrigkeit].[35] The church-community asks for *salvation* and *knowledge of the truth*
for all people, that is, for *conversion*. Verses 5ff. God's salvatory will is unlim- 312
ited; no person should be privileged over another person, for they are all human beings, and God is the one and only God, who is above everyone, to whom everyone must be converted. Therefore, pray for all people because they have the same God as you, even if they practice idolatry. There is only one mediator between God and *human beings* (!) who is there for everyone and who alone is able to save, the *human being* (!) Jesus Christ. He has given himself for *all* to be saved and has instituted the preaching of this. Now is the time of proclamation. The apostle has become the teacher for the nations. The universal preaching of salvation corresponds to the universal prayer of the church-community.

[33.] "Person, human being."

[34.] "Reverence, respectfulness."

[35.] [Bonhoeffer defined *Obrigkeit* as "the power that creates and upholds the order." (*DBWE* 16:503). For the different nuances in Bonhoeffer's understanding of *Obrigkeit*, see his essay "State and Church," *DBWE* 16, 2/10.—VB]

This needs to be said in particular [(] against the genealogists who break open the differences among people, [)] against the teachers of the law who desire to erect boundaries between the pious and sinners, and who claim for themselves a privilege with God. The gospel belongs to all people *because* it belongs to sinners. How and if the universal salvific will of God will be achieved is no longer the objective of proclamation. Unaffected by this secret (which can easily lead again into ζητήσεις),[36] proclamation is to be issued universally, preaching law and judgment to those who transgress, and the gospel to sinners.

Verse 8. *Men* are to pray wherever there is public prayer, not only in the church-community but also at home. The husband is the head of the wife and the family. He is the priest. He speaks with God on behalf of his own. The hands that he lifts up to God are to be holy, blameless, having done good works; they are not to be the defiled hands of the murderer, the thief, the adulterer, the perjurer. Paul does not ask whether and how this is possible, nor does he say that the holy, pure hands are merely the unclean hands of the sinner who seeks forgiveness. He speaks quite undialectically.—Every defilement comes from the heart. So the heart of the one who prays is to be *without anger and contradiction.* Whoever is in
313 anger against his brother not only ruins his intercession but also prevents the forgiveness being asked for. How can I myself ask God for forgiveness while refusing forgiveness to my neighbor or the enemy? I shall not receive it. Here Paul comes close to the words of Jesus in Matt. 5:24 and Mark 11:24–25. Nor can prayer exist in contradiction against the word of God or in uncertainty. Only the one who prays with confident certainty that God hears and fulfills the prayer will receive what is prayed for. The one who prays without believing makes prayer empty chatter (Mark 11:24; James 1:6). Again, Paul does not say that every prayer will indeed be a prayer for faith or that true certainty of prayer involves complete human uncertainty. He does not want ζητήσεις to arise again at this point, which is why he speaks so simply and undialectically.

Verse 9. In every teaching of the law lies the danger of establishing new laws, thereby rendering the ordinances of God powerless. Human and pious ideals are the enemies of divine ordinances and commandments. Thus, a new teaching of the law easily leads to disorder in the relation between man and woman. Often it is the case that overzealous [schwärmerisch][37]

[36.] "Controversies, debates." Cf. 1 Tim. 1:4, ἐκζητήσεις.

[37.] [Very often in Bonhoeffer's writing he refers to the *Schwärmer* movement, which was the radical stream within the Reformation, translated as the "Enthusiasts." The

teachers will try to win women over by promising them special rights. For Paul the order is clear: Women have a full part in salvation and truth. But they have a different vocation from that of men. Woman's finery is not to be sought in public but in modesty and in moderation, that is, in the very hiddenness[38] of what is inconspicuous. Nothing else should be said about her other than that she lives in good works. "ἡσυχία"—to live quietly and in peace is woman's privilege. She should and can learn, but in submission. Learning should not make her quarrelsome. She is not supposed *to teach and to dominate.* Paul says: *I* do not allow this. She will be able to display greater wisdom in submission than in dominion. This is not merely conservatism but biblical order: 1. The man was created first and, from him, the woman. 2. The woman was seduced by the devil; she is more susceptible to the temptations of Satan. It follows from this not that the woman has *lesser value* but that she has a different *calling.* (For God made Adam accountable! and he
became the father of all sinners!) God gave the woman her calling in sub- 314
mission to the man so that she is not exposed to temptation but is under her husband's protection. Therefore, the woman should not leave her calling in order to be blessed, thus[39] dissolving the ordinances of God. She will be blessed in the midst of her calling, of which she does not need to be ashamed. διά = through giving birth (not "because of"), not the reason for salvation, but the place where salvation happens. διά = rather even in spite of—σωθήσεται! She will be saved *in spite of* and in her calling of submission. Her deliverance [Errettung], to be sure, must be proven not through her natural being,[40] but through her being in faith, love, and sanctification; otherwise she will forfeit her salvation [Heil].[41]

1 Timothy. Chapter 4

Verse 1. Prophecy about apostasy, otherwise the incomprehensibility would be too great. Not to come to faith is already an enigma for the church-community, but *to fall from the faith received* fills it with fear and might lead to

---

German word can also mean fanatic or zealot, and the translator and the editor believe that here he is using the adjectival form, *schwärmerisch*, in that sense.—VB]

[38.] [Cf. *DBWE* 4:149.—VB]

[39.] The manuscript erroneously reads "she."

[40.] Here the manuscript is incomplete; perhaps the word "submission" should be added.

[41.] Bonhoeffer's notes on 1 Tim. 1 and 2 end here, on a sheet of paper numbered "8." Notes on 1 Tim. 3 do not exist. The following four sheets—on 1 Tim. 4—are unnumbered. [Ilse Tödt suggests that this may be an indication that Bonhoeffer planned a later exposition of chap. 3.—VB]

unbelief. Paul reckons with this as a fact; cf. 1:6 and 1:19. This is exhortation to keep the faith in fear and trembling.

Apostasy is the work of the devil, who chooses human instruments.

Verse 2. As such, human beings serve with a "branded conscience," that is to say, with unforgiven guilt that hinders them from faith. Being unable to believe in the gospel of sinners and unable to repent, they consequently strive to become saints and seduce others to strive to become saints.[42]

Verse 3. Therefore, they establish laws (the same persons who despise God's commandments!) (νομοδιδάσκαλοι—antinomians).[43] The devil
315 always tries to entice a person into wishing to be a saint. But Christ tells us that we are to participate in the gospel as sinners and only as sinners. All of us must become sinners!—Hypocritical asceticism arises from the branded conscience. Asceticism is to replace what is not received through Jesus Christ. *Asceticism against Jesus Christ*! But: God has created food *for believers*, who receive it with thanksgiving, and not for unbelievers, who disdain it.

Verse 4. *Everything created by God is good*! This stems from the universality of the gospel. The people of Israel distinguished between clean and unclean creatures according to God's will [(] Lev. 11ff. [)]. This was a clear symbol for the separation of the people of God from the world of the Gentiles. In *Christ* salvation belongs to *all people*. Peter learns this from the vision of the clean and unclean animals in the cloth (Acts 10). Because the gospel belongs to the whole world, therefore, all creatures must serve the gospel. For those who have recognized themselves as flesh and sinners under the gospel and were accepted by God as sinners, there was no longer any distinction between clean and unclean among creatures. Everything was unclean through sin and clean through grace. *Through Jesus Christ God's creation is good.*

Verse 5. This means that the creature's goodness no longer lies in its *naturalness*; it is good not *as such* but through *thanksgiving*, through *word* and *prayer*. The *prayer at table*! The goodness of the creature is that which the word of God gives me free use of and about which I can pray, asking and thanking God for it. That which is contradicted by the word of God, for which I may not give thanks and for which I may not ask according to God's

[42.] [See also p. 333 below and Bonhoeffer's comment in his July 21, 1944, letter on the "dangers" of trying to become a saint, *DBWE* 8, 4/178, esp. p. 486.—VB]

[43.] Here Bonhoeffer correlates the (false) teachers of the law, 1 Tim. 1:7, with the "antinomians," that is, those who claimed in the "antinomian controversies" that the "law" (the Decalogue) no longer had any validity for the Christian life; it would pertain solely to the city hall, but not in the pulpit (cf. *WA* 39/1:344,30, attributed to Johann Agricola). See also *DBW* 14:420 and *DBWE* 16:547, 592.

word, is unclean. All of creation exists in order that God be honored, and that the giver of the gift be adored.

Verse 6. When Timothy teaches these things, he will prove himself as a *servant of Jesus Christ* who is nourished (has his food) by the word of faith and this teaching.

Verse 7. Not *myths* but revelation is the foundation of this teaching. Myths 316
are childish prattle, old women's prattle, because they seek to edify life on the basis of speculations, uncertainties, fables. The exercises of a Christian must be aimed at the entirety of worshipping God (εὐσέβεια), and not just at a partial goal. Paul ended up denying that physical abstinence has a place here too! (1 Cor. 7:9, 25ff.). But the aim is a different one!

Verse 10. For the servant of Jesus Christ, enough effort and struggle arise from his service to the message and his hope in God. Such effort is better than self-inflicted asceticism, for it is taken in a necessary service!

Savior of *all people*—the service and life of the Christian have as their aim not separation but devotion to the Savior of *all* people, to whom the believer belongs in a special way.

Verse 12. Timothy's statement might be impeded by his youth (he is at least between thirty and forty!). Three things should protect him against reproaches and discouragement. 1. He is to be an example, which even a young person can be. *By word*, in what he says and how he says it, he is to instruct the community in the use of God's word; in conduct, his behavior must correspond to the word, a conduct firmly bound to the word of God in which created things are freely used; *in love*, not condemning and judging sinners, as false teachers do; in *faith*, in *chastity*. Be an example to your church-community if you do not wish to hinder your ministry. This does not exclude (!) but includes humility, for it is conduct in deference to the word that I preach. 2. He is to perform his service faithfully and not be distracted by all kinds of conflicts:

Verse 13. *Reading* of the Old Testament, *exhortation* (comfort), (pastoral care), *teaching* (law and gospel).

Verse 14. 3. Ordination. It is his ministry. Even when he speaks to the experienced, he has the commission.

Verse 15. He is to be *concerned* about these three things (and not about other things), be found performing them reconciled to this, and make his improvement evident. προκοπή[44]—even the minister should continue to
grow! The community should know this. [(] No stagnation, possessing, but 317
each day anew. [)] This progression will focus the church-community not on the person but on the message.

[44.] "Advancement, progress."

Verse 16. Take care of yourself and of the teaching—the inseparability of the two. Both the salvation of the church-community and of the minister depend on the true performance of the service. (1 Cor. 9:23).[45]

2 Timothy. Chapter 1.

Verses 1, 2. "Paul, an *apostle*"—he always writes as *such.* He does not separate his ministry from his person. "*For the sake of the promise of life*"—the tone of one who envisions death as a martyr [(] Paul is imprisoned, awaiting the verdict and death [)]—otherwise as 1 Tim.

Verse 3. ἀπὸ προγόνων[46] Cf. 1 Tim. 1:15!—Phil. 3:5![47] Rom. 10:2! Gal. 1:15; 2 Cor. 11:21ff.—the connection to the past, the unity of Paul's life, which incorporates the break, forgiveness. [(] Acts 24:14 φαρισαῖός εἰμι;[48] 23:6 ἀγνοῶν; 1 Tim. 1:13 [)]. In 1 Timothy, Timothy is to recognize the power of preaching the gospel from the case of Paul's life.[49] Here he is to gain strength for his own path of suffering from the unified strength of Paul's life (cf. also 2 Tim. 4:7!).—The memory of the ancestors strengthens responsibility and drive. This is the *true* genealogy, κατὰ πνεῦμα![50] For Timothy, cf. Acts 16:1; his father was a pagan. It is *not* stated that Lois and Eunice were *Christians.*—ἐν καθαρᾷ συνειδήσει Rom. 1:9; Acts 23:1; Acts 24:16; the exhortation toward having a pure conscience also applies to Paul.

The *unceasing* memory of Timothy in prayer. "Participating in the life" of the other person about whom we know something (Niemöller) will be espe-
318 cially intense in the total seclusion of a prison,[51] and particularly so when suffering for the sake of Christ—consciously and unconsciously, day and night. This prayer is guided by two things: first, *by thanksgiving*—the prisoners' thanksgiving for faithful work is an impetus for those who are free.

[45.] No manuscript exists for chaps. 5 and 6. The following three sheets—on 2 Tim. 1—are numbered, but the remaining pages are not.

[46.] "From the parents of old."

[47.] Later deleted: Acts 23:1.

[48.] "I am a Pharisee."

[49.] [I.e., this emphasizes the continuity of Paul's life on the basis of his Jewish heritage and calling. Bonhoeffer is using Paul as an example and model. The editor thanks Christiane Tietz for this insight.—VB]

[50.] "According to the Spirit."

[51.] Martin Niemöller, incarcerated on July 1, 1937, became "Hitler's personal prisoner" from March 1938 onward (until 1945) in the concentration camps of Sachsenhausen and Dachau; cf. 1/4, p. 27, and 1/12, pp. 41–42.

Verse 4. Second, *by the desire to see Timothy again.* Such physical community *fills with joy*, for the nature of our physical existence is that we need visible community for our *joy* and *strength.* Paul needs Timothy not only to be strengthened personally but also for his *service* (4:9, 21). The tears of Timothy. Heavy-hearted good-bye. Many went with Paul (cf. 4:9ff.); Timothy stayed behind.

Verse 5. Paul's memory of Timothy prompts gratitude in Paul and fosters the desire to see him again, because he knows Timothy's faith and longs to be strengthened by it.

Verse 6. Paul *desires Timothy to be with him.* He calls him into the community of his sufferings. "*Therefore,*" Timothy is to let the gift of grace be *aflame* (1 Thess. 5:19). Everything that he needs is given to him. It rests in him.

Verse 7. The spirit Timothy has received is a spirit not of cowardice but of *strength* (especially in suffering), of *love* (for the suffering brethren), of discipline (toward wise decisions and true judging of a situation, the renunciation of his own comfort).

Verse 8. For this reason no being ashamed of the μαρτύριον[52] of Jesus nor of the one bound with him (both belong together), but rather *suffering together with the gospel* according to the power of God. The power of God is revealed in suffering. Suffering is *deed, not exclusion,* but utmost participation in the gospel.

Verses 9–11. *The gospel.* Deliverance, the *holy calling* of grace, before the existence of time, in Jesus Christ, *who overcame death, who gives life.* Paul is his apostle and teacher.

Verse 12. *Because of this* he suffers. No shame; he knows *in whom* he entrusted himself, to the *crucified* and *resurrected* Lord. He is able to preserve the παραθήκη[53] until the last day. (?)

Verses 13–14. The *example,* the *form*—ὑποτύπωσις—Timothy should be 319
found in this example (cf. τύπος,[54] 1 Tim. 4:12). He is to preserve the παραθήκη through the Holy Spirit, ἐνοικοῦντος.[55]

Verse 15. The suffering of the apostle is exacerbated by the behavior in Asia. They have abandoned him (cf. 2 Tim. 4:16); they did not deny their faith. *He calls them by name!*

Verses 16ff. Onesiphorus—eulogy for the faithful brother who died. Mercy upon his house! Mercy upon him on the last day!

[52.] "Witness, testimony."

[53.] "That which is entrusted, a deposit."

[54.] "Pattern."

[55.] "Indwelling."

2 Timothy. Chapter 2

Verse 1. Timothy needs strength—*in grace*—in order to do what Onesiphorus did. The strength to suffer comes only through *grace*. How can grace become strength? The vocation, *forgiveness*, gracious *help and presence of God*. God is with me—in Christ Jesus.

Verse 2. Timothy must consider that he might not return. The proclamation must not depend on him as a person. The *gospel* [(] not as an opinion of Paul, but as witnessed by many! [)] must go forward, from person to person, generation to generation; wherever one of them falls, another one must stand. "Faithful people"—faithful to the cause. "Able to teach others"—not all faithful people are capable of this. Timothy is supposed to choose them.[56]

Verses 3, 4. "Share in suffering"—now Timothy is free for the community of shared suffering of Paul. A good soldier is not concerned about his own property, but he stands for his lord. He is ready to suffer. This is part of his vocation. In this way he will be pleasing to his lord. And this is what counts, for he is in the service of the Lord.

Verse 5. An athlete receives the prize only when competing according to the rules of the competition and cannot make up rules. Accordingly, suffering belongs to the rule of Christian struggle. Timothy cannot exempt him-
320 self from this rule, especially now, since he is called. He cannot choose the moment when he wishes to fight. The "*Nomos*" of the struggle determines this for him.

Verse 6. ? Does γεωργός[57] refer to Paul? or to Timothy? [(] πρῶτον—in the very first place; δεῖ = ought = by virtue of the promise! [)]

Verse 7. Paul does not say anymore. Timothy will understand him; the Lord will determine his decision. Paul does not command. He leaves Timothy to the Lord, who will give him direction and understanding.

Verse 8. Timothy will find strength for all this if he only thinks of Jesus Christ, the victory over [(] all suffering [)] death and of the divine promise meant for him—as Paul has proclaimed to him. From this[58] Timothy will receive the willingness to suffer and strength.

Verses 9–10. Paul suffers already for the sake of the gospel, as a "criminal," without honor, like Jesus Christ himself, but the Word continues. It is not bound either to the freedom or to the bondage even of the apostle (how much less so to Timothy, how much less even to us!). The church-

---

[56.] Crossed out in the manuscript: "The ministry carries the ministry further."

[57.] "A worker of the land."

[58.] Uncertain reading.

community might have complained that everything is over; Paul is imprisoned and is being treated as a criminal. He is not even granted the honor due a Roman citizen! Paul says, the Word carries on. Indeed, his suffering is suffering for the sake of the elect,[59] who will receive the message only through Paul's suffering. In this way, Paul's suffering is for their salvation. [(] Phil. 1:14, σωτηρία[60] *eschatologically*? No! καὶ αὐτοί[61] [)]

Verses 11–13. [(] Past, present, future. [)] To die with Christ—to live; to endure (to be beneath)—to reign (to be above). If we deny, he also denies. Are we *unfaithful*, he remains πιστός[62]—our unfaithfulness does not annul his faithfulness (cf. Rom. 3:4).

Verses 14–15. Timothy is to remind those who remain behind not to engage in quarrelsome disputes with the false teachers. Instead, he must distribute the *Word* in faithfulness and do his work without disrepute. This is steadfastness.

Verses 16–17. Empty chatter will increase and thus magnify godlessness; 321
such talk will spread like cancer. Sin is also an organism that grows and destroys the healthy body of the church-community and the individual. In the meantime, Hymenaeus has become the leader (1 Tim. 1:20) of the sectarians and teaches:

Verse 18. The resurrection has already happened—the essence[63] of Enthusiasm,[64] the disdain for the carnal nature of the world—perfection here [on earth]—abuse of the Pauline teaching in Rom. 6. The dawn of the kingdom of God on earth—rejection of the expectation, of eschatology.

Verse 19. The apostasy of some false teachers and the loss of faith never invalidate the firm foundation of the gospel—it has the seal of God's *election*. On earth, belonging to the church is based on human judgment, and thus there are many false Christians. But "God knows those who are his" [(] *Matt. 7:21*! "I have known you"[65] [)].

Verse 20. It is therefore not surprising that both good and bad vessels are in the same house. Matt. 13. *Fish, seeds. mali admixti sunt*[66]—"to cleanse oneself," "to separate oneself."[67]

[59.] Deleted in the manuscript: "it is in itself a service to the church-community."

[60.] "Salvation."

[61.] "They also." (See 2 Tim. 2:10.)

[62.] "Faithful."

[63.] Difficult to decipher in the manuscript.

[64.] [Here the reference is to the perspective of the radical Reformation—VB]

[65.] Cf. Matt. 7:23. Bonhoeffer formulates here as in *DBWE* 4:180.

[66.] Cf. Augsburg Confession, Article 8 (Kolb and Wengert, *Book of Concord*, 43): "Many false Christians and hypocrites . . . remain among the faithful" *(multi hypocrite et mali admixti sint)*.

[67.] No manuscript exists for vv. 22–26.

2 Timothy. Chapter 3.

Verses 1–5. Despite all hope that some will still come to repentance (2:26), Paul does not leave Timothy with any illusions. The last days will be even worse than the present ones. That is the common teaching of the New Testament. The world will become not better but more evil. The world intrudes
322 *upon the church-community* and mixes truth with lies. All this is found among Christians ([v.] 5).[68] People will not become more pious and more trustworthy, but they will "fall in love with themselves"[69] become *addicts of money* (1 Tim 6[:6], πορισμός).[70] They will think only of themselves and their advantages; *boasters, arrogant* [(] (Bedouin proverb: "Who says, I am better than you, deserves hell!). Contempt for the weak, the small ones [)] before people and God; therefore *blasphemers* (against God), *disobedient to their parents* (against people). All bonds and order are dissolved. People are unwilling to bow and be submissive any longer. The lack of respect for parents is always a sure sign of godlessness! *Ungrateful, wicked*; gratitude is always a sign of humility. Boasting does not know gratitude. [(] No thanks, but *mine by* right! [)] Everything else is nothing; only I am something. They know no reverence. *Heartless, implacable.* In their dealings with others, they are inconsiderate toward their neighbors. They do not desire peace. Instead they are *slanderers* [(] Derisive toward other believers! [)], *profligates;* the other person is dishonored, while one's own lust is unleashed. *Savage, without benevolence,* without concern for the other, without asking about good and evil; *treacherous, reckless* [(] Judas! [)]—they know no loyalty to higher obligations; they do rashly whatever pleases them. *Swollen with conceit*—and they are proud of it. *They love pleasure rather than God.* They have lapsed into lust, egotism [(] love of self [)] and do not know the love of God. In all of this they have the outward form of *saintliness*! They do all that under the guise of religiosity. *But* they deny *the power—the reality*, the power of repentance, of faith, of humility, of the *love for their fellow human beings.*

Verse 6. [(] Spiritual exuberance [Schwärmertum] and sexual excess [)]. The secrecy of the homes, instead of the publicity of the assembled congregation. They captivate dubious women who vacillate between a lascivious life and religious needs,[71] who prefer to *learn* and to *ask*, rather than to *understand* the truth and *do* it. [(] "Womanish times" [)] The *problematic* for the sake of the *problematic.* "The seekers of God."

[68.] In the manuscript the preceding two sentences replace "the contrasts become sharper."

[69.] This phrase replaces "self-absorbing."

[70.] "Moneymaking."

[71.] Substituted for "interests."

Verses 7–9. They ape the truth with all kinds of deceitful sorcery and thereby resist the truth, as the Egyptian sorcerers resisted Moses.[72] "Corrupt minds"—sick, at variance with themselves and with God. Their mind 323
no longer has any clarity. It is destroyed by desire. Therefore, they lack the capacity to believe,[73] have not stood the test. But they will fail because their lack of reason must become evident to all.

Verses 10–12. *The endurance of the community of apostolic teaching and apostolic life through* Timothy. Not his own theology, but the teaching of Paul; *not his own* lifestyle, not his own plans; he desired to remain in the community of apostolic life; that was all. A good beginning in Iconium and Lystra (Acts 13–14). Persecutions! But the Lord was always mightier. *All* the pious must be persecuted, *even Timothy*!

Verse 13. The wicked people move ahead, but from bad to worse. Deceived deceivers. The one deceives the other.

Verses 14–15. σὺ δέ—*but you* (2:1; 1 Tim. 6:11) *continue in* (keep!) what you have *learned* and found to be certain! *From childhood you have known the Old Testament, for salvation through faith in Jesus Christ.* The Old Testament becomes a means toward salvation of the believer!

Verse 16. θεόπνευστος[74]—Scripture from *God's* spirit—for the *teaching* that Timothy needs. No teaching without *reproof* for errors; this reproof leads to betterment, to *chastisement* in righteousness. The aim: in a proper condition, ready for *good work. Prepared* to do what God desires. Timothy will be able to withstand the powers of deception only on the basis of Scripture.

2 Timothy. Chapter 4.

Verses 1–2. This is the apostle's last summons to Timothy to be faithful in his ministry. Look to God! to Jesus Christ, the judge over the living and the dead! Look to his appearance, which means the end of all things! Look to his kingdom, which destroys the kingdom of Satan in spite of its splendor! "*Proclaim* the message"—publicly, loudly, a messenger of the coming of the Lord. The *Word*! that is all. *Stand to it*! The *Word*, not the situation, determines the καιρός[75] when it is proclaimed! *Convey*, do not try to convince, for only when the heart is overcome can the Word be received. *Rebuke,*
exhort, with personal encounter. Not in fanaticism, but with *patience* and 324
teaching.

[72.] Cf. Exod. 7–9. Bonhoeffer's Greek text mentions Exod. 7:11, 22.

[73.] [Luther's translation of this biblical text, which Bonhoeffer is repeating here, is *untüchig zum Glauben.*—VB]

[74.] "Inspired by God."

[75.] "Moment."

Verses 3–5. They "will not *put up* with sound teaching"—too harsh! they are softened. Thus they will "accumulate" for themselves teachers "to suit their own desires"—these teachers will have to serve their desires. They want teachers, but these must only say what they already know, what they want to hear. They only want their own opinions confirmed, their own longings satisfied, and their own existence justified. For these purposes, there are *many* teachers. There are not many true preachers of the Word, while there are plenty of those who are servile to human wishes. It is easy to do what is necessary for people, but not for the truth. Servility to human wishes preaches *myths,* but the true preacher proclaims the *truth.* The first creates ecstasy, excitement, emotional thrill—the latter, *soberness.* Sober with respect to both what is to be said and what is expected. Everything is placed in the hand of God. *Willingness to endure suffering*—on the other side there is addiction to pleasure, satisfaction of desires. The *work* of the evangelist. Complete *service* [diakonia]—πληροφόρησον![76] is the final summary of all the exhortations. Timothy is to *complete* his service.

Verse 6. Paul is already consummating it. σπένδομαι[77]—the libation poured out on the altar, points to Paul's blood, which is soon to be poured out. He is awaiting his execution, but as a *sacrifice* for the Lord (Rom. 12:1)! The hour of *departure* has come (Phil. 2:17).[78]

Verse 7. Thanksgiving for his life. He has reached the goal. His life was complete and whole. "By the grace of God I am what I am." But this grace does not prevent him from now looking back at his life with thanksgiving and confidence. Only at the *very end,* however, not before that. (He served since the time of his ancestors!)[79] He can be certain of receiving the wreath [(] of *righteousness*—the great desire, the eternal gift! The Pharisee, the believer [)]. He will finally receive the wreath—with all those who love the *second coming* of Christ! including *Timothy*!

325 Verse 8. The life of Paul is approaching its end. "Come *soon.*" This is the situation: Demas (Col. 4:14; Phlm. 24). He wants to establish himself in the world, while Paul is leaving it. Crescens has gone to *Galatia to work*! *Titus* to Dalmatia! The work continues even from prison. Luke is alone with Paul (Col. 4:14; Phlm. 24). *Mark* is in *Colossae* (Col. 4:10) εἰς διακονίαν[80]—for work in the church-community, not for personal reasons. Mark belongs to

[76.] "Fulfill, complete!" (imperative).

[77.] "I am sacrificed; I am poured out as libation."

[78.] The citation of this verse covers up numbers that Eberhard Bethge identified for the first edition in 1961 as "1:23" (cf. the mention of this verse in Bonhoeffer's letter to Elisabeth Zinn, dated January 27, 1936, *DBW* 14:114).

[79.] 2 Tim. 1:3.

[80.] "For service."

Peter and Barnabas, Jerusalem. *Tychicus* to *Ephesus* (Acts 20:4; Eph. 6:21—Col. 4:7). He is supposed to ease Timothy's coming[81] and to replace him.

Verse 13. The cloak, parchments! The *poverty* of Paul, he requires his cloak. *Books* and *parchments*!? Verses 14–15, *Alexander*, the smith—Timothy must beware of him. No further attempt at conversion. Christ will repay him according to his deeds. A harsh experience (1 Tim. 1:20?), a very harsh experience!

Verses 16–17. A grave experience. Interrogation. All the brothers deserted him. They separate themselves from Paul. Jesus! The greater the witness, the more fall away. But just as Jesus forgave Peter, so also Paul forgave his brothers. Heavy judgment upon the Roman church-community! But the Lord was there, and *all the Gentiles had to listen*! The *consummation* of the proclamation! The end of Paul's apostolic proclamation. *Everyone had to listen*! The Word is proclaimed. Thanks be to God!

Verse 18. The Lord will help in all things. Doxologies!

Verses 19–20. *Aquila* and Prisca. Acts 18:18 Corinth—Ephesus (Rom. 16:3 Rome. Now Ephesus). *Onesiphorus* (see above).[82] *Erastus* (Acts 19:22; Rom. 16:23). *Trophimus* (Acts 20:4). Greetings from Rome, where Timothy is known.

Verse 21. *Timothy should come before the winter*![83] The last summons. Linus, the first successor of Peter. The Roman bishop.[84]

[81.] [To Paul.—VB]

[82.] See above on 2 Tim. 1:16–18.

[83.] [One year later, this verse would have special significance for Bonhoeffer in his decision to return to Germany from New York. See the June 26, 1939, entry in Bonhoeffer's New York diary, 1/137, p. 232.—VB]

[84.] On the reverse of this sheet (written in ink, like the manuscript), Bonhoeffer's assignments for the candidates of the collective pastorate in Groß-Schlönwitz in the summer of 1938 follow (the names are added in pencil). 1. "The chronology of the Letters to Timothy. [Gerhard] Schulze 2. Timothy. Life and Work. [Adolf] Buchmann 3. Pastoral care between Paul and Timothy. [Ulrich] Nithack. [Erwin] Sander 4. The false teachers in 1 and 2 Timothy and how to deal with them. [Walter] Schultz. [Helmut] Kiausch 5. The order of the church-community in Ephesus. [Rudolf] Lynker." On a separate sheet Bonhoeffer noted in pencil (questions that are preceded by "/" in the following list were designated by lines in the margin): *Questions regarding 1 and 2 Timothy. Aim of the Letters?* Who is Timothy? His life? / His task in Ephesus? / The false teachers in Ephesus? Myths, genealogies, ascetics, resurrection, (Titus) 2:13). / The offices in Ephesus? Bishops, deacons, elders, widows. / Ordination? 1 Tim. 1:18; 4:14; Titus 1:6. Paul's imprisonment in Rome? 2 Tim. 1:15–16. Onesiphorus. Phygelus and Hermogenes turned away. 4:10 Luke; Tychicus; Mark[.] Alexander 4:16! The proclamation of the gospel in the pastoral letters? 1 Tim. 1:15; 2:5; 3:16; 2 Tim. 2:8ff. [–13]; 2 Tim. 1:9. The first bishop of Rome? Linus 2 Tim. 4:21. / Pastoral care between Paul and Timothy: *ordination*! 2 Tim. 2:22 ff[–24] flee . . . 2:3 share in suffering 1:8 do not be ashamed . . . 1 Tim. 4:12. Exercise 4:8; 1:19

326 The Letter to Titus. Chapter 1

Verses 1–3. [(] (The situation 3:12. Paul is free) [)] servant of God = neither driven by nor looking after his own affairs. [(] 1. The elect are to come to *faith* and to the knowledge of *truth* that is in accord with εὐσέβεια.[85] (No spirit speculation!) *Hope.* Connection between the four terms! [)] Paul is a *member* in God's *plan of salvation,* the *apostle* of Jesus Christ—V. 3 the *Word of God* is revealed to the world today in his preaching.[86] On the aim of εὐσέβεια—of the worship of God; this exists through *faith* and the *knowledge* of truth, but it has a goal: *the hope for eternal life—promised* by the one who does not lie—hope, and not an ideal picture, but God's promise, and therefore more.

Verse 4. Titus—connection with Paul Gal. 2:1, 3. Antioch, he takes him along to Jerusalem. It follows from the letter to the Galatians that Titus is also known there. Task 2 Cor. 2:12; 7:6–16—converted by Paul.

Verse 5. *Crete.* When? after the first imprisonment. Paul was in Crete. He leaves Titus behind. Paul is a missionary. His companions are responsible for the building up and nurturing of the church-community.—*Elders* in every town.

Verse 6. Blameless—as seen from outside. They are not to burden their difficult office even more through being reproached with personal guilt.
327 *Marriage* must be *holy.* Children should be believers.[87] Whoever is unable to create space and authority for the gospel in his own house will likewise be unable to do so in the church-community. (The pastor's devotions at home, household congregation!) Rude and disrespectful children bring dishonor to the minister and defile his ministry.

Verse 7. "Bishop" = "elder!"[88] (cf. Acts 20:17, 28; 1 Tim. 5:17). Blameless as a *steward*[89] of the house of God. Only someone who is pure can be steward of what belongs to God. Not "self-willed"[90]—he must not rule by tyr-

---

good conscience." [According to Ilse Tödt, this separate sheet appears to have been used for a first draft of the second version on the reverse of the manuscript sheet.—VB]

[85.] "Piety" is Bonhoeffer's translation for 1 Tim. 2:2 (see above); Luther translates it as "worship of God" (*Gottseligkeit*).

[86.] Deleted: "Promised before the ages."

[87.] In his Greek text, Bonhoeffer underlined in pencil the word πιστά, which Luther translated as "believing [children]."

[88.] Bonhoeffer underlined in pencil the words πρεσβυτέρους in v. 5 and ἐπίσκοπον in v. 7 in his Greek text and connected them with a line in the margin.

[89.] In Bonhoeffer's Greek text, the word οἰκονόμον, "economist," which Luther translated as "householder," is underlined in pencil.

[90.] [Bonhoeffer's word (*eigenwillig*) means literally "from one's own will" and is thus different from the "arrogant" of the NRSV.—PF]

anny (2 Cor. 1:24, helpers of *your joy*!), not "irascible"—which would spring from self-will!—not unbridled in drinking, quarreling, dealing with *money*. *Friend to the stranger*[91]—sensible—prudent; righteous: in the church-community without prejudice; *devout, dignified* when dealing with holy things (sermon, sacrament, church-community), not out of *routine* but in *discipline*!

Verse 9. The service for the *word*. *To hold on to the reliable* word; *to exhort* [(] to comfort (the church-community!) [)]; *to convict, to put right those who contradict*.

Verses 10–11. Jewish opponents, *disobedient, idle talkers, deceivers*—περιτομή[92]—the glory of the Jews, the law! *self-sanctification*. To shut up their *mouths*—to *silence* them. Like 9.[93] Through open words on repentance, punishment, and through refutation. For they *overthrow whole households*. Often one family member pulls the others into sectarianism. They operate in the houses, in secret. In the dangerous atmosphere of personal encounter. They teach that which should not be taught. What? Everything for the sake of shameful gain, lust for honor, financial gain (*quite otherwise the bishops*! see above).[94]

Verses 12–14. The national defects of the Cretans: *lies, brutishness, lazy sensuality*. Harsh. They threaten to meddle in Christianity. *Therefore*, because of these dangerous qualities, punish them *severely*. Mild words are of no avail here. It is necessary to use sharp language against these vices, through which they are sick. They are to become *sound* through the gospel, through faith. Not cling to Jewish legalism.

Verse 15. To the pure all things are pure; *defiled* = *unbelieving*! Nothing is 328
pure for them. They are defiled and seek purity; they think the world makes them unclean. For this reason, legalism. Impurity lies within themselves, in their mind and conscience.

Verses 15–16. Conscience is impure [(] defiled [)] = it accuses them constantly and pushes them toward the way of works, but it keeps them from attaining purity through forgiveness and a new life closing them off from the gospel.

Verse 16. Confession and works fall apart. But confession does not justify where there are no works. Those who take trouble about works cannot achieve them. Their works testify against them because they are works of *disobedience*, therefore *detestable* and *contrary to any good work*.[95]

[91.] [Bonhoeffer literally translates this: "a friend of strangers."—PF]

[92.] "Circumcision."

[93.] Cf. Titus 1:9.

[94.] See above on Titus 1:7.

[95.] Bonhoeffer's manuscript ends here; the rest of the page is blank.

329 **2. Biblical Study Seminars on**
Basic New Testament Concepts, 1938–1939[1]

2.1 Notes on the Concept of "Sin"[2]

Sin

ἁμαρτία, ἁμαρτίαι, (ἄφεσις ἁμαρτιῶν!)[3] παράπτωμα, παράβασις, ἀνομία (1 John 3:4).[4]

1. *Sin as a concept of separation*: Rom. 14:23. / *Faith—sin* a—non a }[5] a paradoxical contradiction.

no neutral zone—not even eating and drinking

/ σάρξ and πνεῦμα[6]—John 3:6; Rom. 8:5ff.; Gal. 5:16ff.

/ σκότος—φῶς[7] John 1:5; 3:19; 8:12; 12:46; Rom. 13:12; 2 Cor. 4:6; 6:14; Eph. 5:8, 11; Col. 1:13; 1 Thess. 5:4; 1 John 1:5; Heb. 12:18

/ κόσμος—μαθηταί/[8] John 12:31; 15:18–19; 17:9; 18:36; Rom. 12:2;
330 1 Cor. 1:20; 4:13; 7:31; 10:11; 11:32; Gal. 1:4; 6:14; 2 Tim. 4:10; 2 Pet. 1:4
flee . . . James 1:27; 4:4 world, friendship . . .

[1.] There is a continuity between the work on basic New Testament concepts in the collective pastorates and the seminars in Finkenwalde; see the example on the "Holy Spirit" in *DBW* 14, 2/9.1. On a separate sheet titled "office" (διακονία) (*NL*, A 55,4 (1), there is a reference to notes from Finkenwalde: "6. The Offices—*see enclosure*"; cf. *DBW* 14, 2/8.6. Similarly, the note *NL*, A 55,1 resumes the discussions on "sin" in Finkenwalde. Bonhoeffer started working more intensely on biblical concepts after his extensive Bible study on the theme of "Temptation," held for the former candidates at the preachers' seminary in Zingst in late June 1938. Several of Bonhoeffer's notes are extant, some containing names of the candidates from the winter term of 1938–39. Cf. the letters to the Finkenwalde brothers of November 20, 1938, and February 14, 1939 (1/36 and 1/75). As examples of the teaching done in the collective pastorates, the documents in this section deal with Bonhoeffer's notes on sin, temptation, patience, probation, joy, peace, abstinence, death, gratitude. Foreign terms are not translated in the editorial notes when they are explained by Bonhoeffer in the text. Bonhoeffer's later additions to his notes are indicated by parentheses enclosed in brackets, [() [)].

[2.] *NL*, A 55,1 (2); handwritten in ink; three pages, DIN A4 [this is the international standard page size used throughout Europe—VB]; not previously published. See also *NL*, B 9,1; notes made by Eberhard Bethge, pp. 21–22, dated January 9, 1936, in Finkenwalde.

[3.] "Sin," "sins," "forgiveness of sins" (the plural is underlined in the manuscript). Bethge: "difference between singular and plural. Usage of the concept—never ἄφεσις ἁμαρτίας ['forgiveness of sin']."

[4.] "Trespass," "transgression," "lawlessness"; 1 John 3:4, in Bonhoeffer's Nestle New Testament, Luther's translation: "sin is injustice [ἀνομία]."

[5.] In the manuscript, the preceding contrasts are linked with "}."

[6.] "Flesh" and "spirit."

[7.] "Darkness—light."

[8.] "World—disciples."

/ ἁμαρτία—δικιαοσύνη[9]—Rom. 6:16ff., to be the servant of only *one* (δοῦλος). Matt. 6:24! John 8:34ff.

/ διάβολος—υἱός[10]—1 John 3:8; John 8:44. Humanity breaks apart into those who belong to the *devil* and those who belong to *Christ*. Two humanities

in Adam—in Christ, Rom. 5:12ff. ἐφ ᾧ . . .[11] 1 Cor. 15:22 (πάντες!)[12] Here only the division is to be stated! Christ is without sin, John 8:46.

Consequence: where Christ rules, sin cannot rule and vice versa (κυριεύσει εἷς κύριος) Rom. 6:14; 8:2.[13] Whoever is in Christ does not sin, 1 John 3:6, 9. *World—church-community = rule of sin—rule of righteousness.*

However: 1 John 1:8, 10; 2:1; Rom. 7! 5. Petition![14]

Question: what is sin?

2. *Sin as condemned godlessness*[15]

Gen. 3. Disobedience against the commandment of God—*wishing to be oneself sicut deus*[16] *through the knowledge of good and evil*—of one's own accord, wishing to live in one's own power, wishing to decide between good and evil, but not to live only by the commandment (Matt. 19, young man, children)[17]—to obtain καύχημα[18] for oneself (Rom. 3:27) (δόξα[19] Rom. 3:23) 4:2; Gal. 6:4. Rom. 2:23; 1:30; 11:18; 1 Cor. 1:29ff.; 4:7; 2 Cor. 5:12–13; 11:16ff.; Eph. 2:9; 2 Tim. 3:2. Such boasting breaks through the boundaries established in the commandment of God; hence, *sin* = breaking of the boundaries that have been established by God, of the νόμος (scilicet 331

[9.] "Sin—righteousness."

[10.] "Devil—son." In Bethge's notes, the first two (of five) pairs of contrasts in this sequence are "light—darkness"; "spirit—flesh."

[11.] Cf. Rom. 5:12. Luther translates "because they have all sinned."

[12.] In Bethge's notes: "(all!?)." In the Greek text of his New Testament, Bonhoeffer underlined parts of 1 Cor. 15:21–22 in pencil.

[13.] "Only one Lord will rule"—in the manuscript, the word εἷς (one) is underlined—synopsis of both references. In Bethge's notes: "Rom. 6:14! 8:2! κυρειύσει—ἐλευθεροῦν free from the νόμος of ἁμαρτία [to set free from the law of sin], most sharply in 1 John 3:5ff. and 9!! σπέρμα [seed] 2 Pet. 1:4; here Rom. 14:23 most radically applied."

[14.] The fifth petition of the Lord's Prayer. In Bethge's notes: "Matt. 6:12; Forgive us our debts." Bethge's 1936 notes end here.

[15.] This replaces the heading deleted in the manuscript: "The Content of Sin. [Addition:] as Godlessness."

[16.] "Like God" (Gen. 3:5). Cf. *DBWE* 3:111–14 and other passages, and *DBWE* 4:282.

[17.] Matt. 19:13–15: "Let the children . . ." Matt. 19:16–26: "The rich young man."

[18.] "Boasting."

[19.] "Glory."

Χριστοῦ)[20] = ἀνομία 1 John 3:4. νόμος πίστεως[21]—Rom. 3:27—*sin is unbelief* Rom. 14:23, it is ἐχθὰ εἰς θεόν[22] Rom. 8:7; James 4:4 τὸ ἑαυτοῦ ζητεῖν[23] 1 Cor. 10:24; Phil. 2:4, 21. ἐπιθυμία[24] Rom. 7:7; Gal. 5:16; James 1:14–15, sin is at the same time[25] *"habitus"—actus*—actus and habitus belong together.[26] Flesh must sin, "in Adam"—"in Christ" it *cannot* sin. That is, not as if there were in Christ only the actus and with Gentiles the habitus and actus. Sinful actus is impossible, except if it springs from a sinful habitus. Therefore, for a Christian: neither habitus nor actus; for a Gentile: habitus and actus and nonetheless: 1 John 1:8, 10; Rom. 7 etc.![27]

Because the essence of sin is to obtain praise for itself and to judge over good and evil, sin can never recognize its own sinfulness. Sin is thus not a person's judgment over one's actions, but sin is *a judgment of God*, who calls sin that which people call good, namely, one's own righteousness. The human being under habitus and actus is judged or is accepted. Sin's ignorance of its own sinfulness is not an excuse but is in itself guilt, Rom. 1:19–20; Luke 23:34 ". . . for they do not know" means: they are blind, so *greatly* sinful, that they know nothing anymore and thus need forgiveness all the more.

3. *Sin "in Adam."*[28] φύσει τέκνα ὀργῆς[29] Eph. 3:3; Rom. 5:12; 1 Cor. 7; Matt. 19:11—sin as guilt—the law as power.—Valid *law*—an *act* of the will![30] All are sinners Rom. 3:23; 5:12ff.; Isa. 64:5; Job 25:4. Ps. 143, catalog of vices Gal. 5, Eph. 5.[31] Human beings commit sins 1 Cor. 7:31; 1 Cor. 2:1–4.

4. Sin "in Christ" in faith, in love—Rom. 7.[32]

[20.] "Law (namely, of Christ)."

[21.] "Law of faith."

[22.] "Enmity against God."

[23.] "To seek one's own, to be selfish."

[24.] "Desire."

[25.] Deleted: "—both *Being* and *Act*—."

[26.] "Condition, state"—"act." [Bonhoeffer referred elsewhere to the Catholic understanding of *habitus* as a deeper, permanent metaphysical quality in contrast to the more transitory *dispositio*, or disposition of a human being. Cf. esp. Bonhoeffer's discussion of *actus, habitus*, and *dispositio* in his "Dogmatic Exercises on 'Theological Anthropology,'" *DBWE* 12:218–26 and 231.—VB]

[27.] The following paragraph was later added in the margin.

[28.] Replaces: "*The Sin of the Gentiles.*"

[29.] "By nature children of wrath."

[30.] Beginning at "—Valid . . ." there is an addition in pencil (including that which follows under point number 3), uncertain reading.

[31.] Cf. Ps. 143:2 in Luther's translation: "Before you, no one among the living is righteous," Gal. 5:19–21; Eph. 5:3–8.

2.2 Notes on the Concept of "Temptation"[33] 332

πειρασμός[34]

Temptation, tribulation.
1. Sixth petition Matt. 6:13. Not probation [Bewährung] of strength, but protection [Bewahrung] against temptation.

2. Temptation of Adam and Jesus 333

a. The origin of the temptation? Serpent, Satan, are suddenly there, without explanation. Where *innocence* is. The denial of the origin belongs to the essence of the tempter. Adam's anxiety.

[32.] There are five pages on the theme "Sin from Weakness?" in *NL*, A 55,1 (3). The handwriting, in fine ink, corresponds to the separate sheet on "office" (*NL*, A 55,4) and can thus be dated to the period after Finkenwalde had been closed. Some of Bonhoeffer's notes concern the traditional dogmatic distinction between *peccata voluntaria* ("voluntary" or "knowingly committed sins") and *peccata involuntaria* ("involuntary" or "ignorantly committed sins"; cf. 1 Tim. 1:13 ἀγνοῶν: "What does ignorantly mean? Paul knew the proclamation and saw the martyrdom of Stephen (Acts 7)! From a psychological point of view he was 'knowing,' but from God, Christ, and grace he was nonetheless *ignorant*! [The German here is *wissend* (knowing) and *unwissend* ('ignorant,' or 'unknowing').—VB] Whether 'ignorance' or not can only be said after receiving grace. It is not a psychological but a theological judgment The state of 'ignorance' can be inferred from the fact of forgiveness. 'Knowing' would mean that person has been encountered by Christ, 'ignorant,' that a person had not yet been encountered by Christ. But only *Christ* himself can know this! A person can know everything and still be 'unknowing' (Paul); and a person can know everything and be made responsible [(] but: Peter's speech in Acts 3:17 [)] for his knowledge (John 9:41; 15:22). One can speak of 'ignorance' only after one has received knowledge, that is, grace has been received. But then ignorance is no longer an excuse but the greater reward of mercy that judges such a *sinful life* as '*ignorant*'! Nowhere does anyone claim 'ignorance' to be an excuse!" Moreover, in *NL*, A 55,1 (3) we read: "Is it possible for Christians to commit sins ignorantly? Gal. 6:1? What is a willful sin? To know the truth and to deny it (Heb. 10:26). [In the Greek text in Bonhoeffer's New Testament, the words Ἑκουσίως (willfully) and τὴν ἐπίγνωσιν (the knowledge) in Heb. 10:26 are underlined in pencil.] Biblically, ignorant sin is always in the past; a willful sin is always in the future! Forgiveness and warning ['Biblically . . . warning' is an addition, bracketed and heavily marked, next to the line.] In systematic terms, every past and confessed sin is an 'ignorant sin.' Every future and unconfessed sin is a sin deliberately committed. [Replaces (in pencil): 'Every future sin may be a willful sin.'] Will God forgive sins of the future? (ἐξουσίαι etc.?) The distinctions between knowing and willful sin are the means to proclaim God's mercy and earnestness! The sin of the Christian is no less serious than the sin of the non-Christian! Quite the opposite (Luke 12:47–48)! Even the Christian lives only by grace. But the difference is that a Christian accepts grace and truly desires to live only by grace."

[33.] *NL*, A 55,11 (1) and (2), handwritten on two DIN A4 sheets; not previously published.

[34.] A sheet with writing in pencil, *NL*, A 55,11 (1). [This is an outline for 2/4.—VB]

b. Temptation of *Jesus* weighs heavier than that of Adam; Jesus bears the burden of sinful flesh.

Matt. 4:1 the Spirit leads Jesus into the desert so that he will be tempted; cf. 2 Chr. 32:31. No being equipped with strength, but desert, loneliness.

1. The temptation of the flesh.

2. The spiritual temptation to tempt God = the desire for more than faith.

3. The perfect [vollkommen] temptation to sin against the Holy Spirit.

The *strengthening* Luke 22:43.

3. Christ is tempted in us. Luke 22:29. Participation in the temptation of Jesus Christ has the promise. Matt. 26:41—the temptation of the disciples = to refuse to participate in the temptation of Jesus. How does a Christian behave in temptation?

4. The author: devil, desire, even God.

a. Devil. Job ([his][35] work!)

b. Desire, James 1:13ff.

1. one's own guilt

2. in covetousness, the ground

3. the conception of covetousness. Covetousness as *Id* and as *Ego* [(] christological psychology ἐπιθυμία [)][36]

c. God (Gen. 22:1; 2 Sam. 24:1; 1 Chr. 21:1) Israel (Exod. 16:4 . . .) 1 Pet. 4:2, 17.

1. nothing happens without God's permission. Abandonment.

2. in Satan's raging a Christian recognizes God's chastisement, Heb. 12:4ff., and God's gracious judgment (1 Pet. 4:17).

3. 1 Cor. 10 ἐάσει—ποιήσει[37] In this way temptation becomes joy (James 1:2ff.)

5. The Temptation of the Christian

334 In general terms 1 Cor. 10:12–13 against false *security and* against *despair*

a. Carnal temptation

1. through *lust*—escape to Christ: "*flee*" in the hour of temptation; no other resistance. 1 Cor. 6:18 fornication, 10:14 idolatry. 1 Tim. 2:22; 2 Pet. 1:4. *Patience*—not arrogant revolt, but endurance.

[35.] The original manuscript reads "s." for *seine*, "his," i.e., the devil's.

[36.] "Christological . . . ἐπιθυμία" [desire] is written in the margin with ink.

[37.] The expression "3. 1 Cor 10[:13] ἐάσει [God permits]—ποιήσει [God will do]" is written in ink between the text written in pencil.

2. through *suffering.* Lust is suffering for Christians. *General* sufferings: Job, in the right against his friends, but not in the right before God. 1 Pet. 4:1 suffering = dying to sin.

Suffering for the sake of Christ: 1 Pet. 4:12–17 πρὸς πειρασμόν[38] Suffering for the sake of righteousness (*not in spite of* righteousness!) χαίρετε, *joy,* ὡς Χριστιανός—*innocent. Honoring* God (δοξάζω)[39] ("for Christ" Phil. 1:25). *Judgment of God.* How can suffering be *innocent* and yet be *judgment*? *Christ*! Judgment for all flesh, even in the house of God, a judgment of *grace.*

In this way, a Christian who suffers for the sake of Christ recognizes:

1. the temptation of the devil
2. the *joy* to suffer for Christ
3. the judgment of grace. A Christian suffers "according to God's will"[40]

b. Spiritual temptation. *To tempt God.*

Through contempt for the law[41] (Jude 4; Acts 5:3, 9; 1 Tim. 1:19) comes spiritual *superbia* [(] *securitas* [)][42]

Through contempt of grace[43] comes *desperatio*:[44] no experience, 2 Cor. 12:7

c. The last temptation. The worship of Satan. Antichristians.

6. Overcoming

1. through the blood of the lamb (Rev. 12:11)
2. the *example* James 5:11, the end of the Lord
3. the prayer of Jesus Luke 22:31

Defenselessness and the *heavenly* robe of armor. Christ puts it around us. 335

7. Eschatological. Rev. 3:10; 2 Pet. 2:9—for us James 1:12; Luke 22:28–29

[38.] "For temptation."

[39.] "Rejoice," "as a Christian," "I glorify."

[40.] 1 Pet. 4:19.

[41.] Replaces the phrase "abuse of *grace.*"

[42.] "*Securitas*" (security) is added above "*superbia*" (arrogance).

[43.] Replaces the phrase *"abuse of the law."*

[44.] "Desperation, despair."

πειρασμός[45]

πειράζειν—δοκιμάζειν—to tempt
more effort required—more intellectual, examining.
hostile against—positive—approving. δοκιμάζεσθαι—having stood the test also as synonyms.[46] 2 Cor. 13:5; Rev. 2:2

To tempt to sin[47]
πειράζειν τινά[48]—in the sense of mistrust. 1 Cor. 10:9
—suffering 1 Cor. 10:10
—devil Matt. 4:3; 1 Cor. 7:5; 1 Thess. 3:5; Gal. 6:1; James 1:13

πειρασμός—sensual Matt. 26:41 ? 1 Cor. 10:13; Gal. 4:14
—moral, religious 1 Tim. 6:9; Matt. 6:13

I. To tempt, to put to the test, to examine.
a. To tempt *God.* From mistrust or from bold sinning. To tempt *Christ* Acts 5:9; 1 Cor. 10:9
b. God puts people on trial in order to test and purify them, John 6:6
c. *To ask* for *testing* (Psalter)[49] for sparing and protection *Matt. 6:13*
1. Consciousness of human weakness.
2. God leads into temptation.
336 3. God's hidden act of love.
4. not avoiding suffering.
5. The sixth and seventh petition . . .[50]
[1 Cor. 7:5 Satan can turn abstinence into temptation to sin
1 Thess. 3:5 falling back into paganism.]

[45.] This sheet *NL*, A 55,11 (2) is written in ink. The heading in the manuscript also shows the corresponding Hebrew word.

[46.] Bonhoeffer relates this comment [i.e., that the two terms are also used as synonyms—VB] (with lines drawn) to both sides of the comparison; to both πειράζειν (to tempt) and δοκιμάζειν (to examine).

[47.] Here a line is drawn to "*hostile* against."

[48.] "To tempt someone."

[49.] Cf. Ps. 139:23.

[50.] Several (Latin?) words are illegible. The following square brackets were inserted by Bonhoeffer.

II. Temptation as an assault on faith.

James 1:13 *God* does not tempt into evil, but *1.* Satan, see above. *2.* the world 1 Cor. 10:13 ἀνθρώπινος—"of human origin" (?). "The nature of temptation, that is, bearable." ἐάσει—ποιήσει.

1 Tim. 6:9 The decisive will to become *rich.* Out of new desires emerge.

Gal. 4:14 The temptation to turn away from those who are sick; this is the same as turning away from Christ.

3. from the flesh. Gal. 5:17; James 1:14.

καιρὸς πειρασμοῦ Luke 8:13 revelation ὥρα τοῦ πειρασμοῦ[51]

2.3 Notes on the Concept of "Patience"[52]

ὑπομονή[53]

Steinert.[54]

Heb. 12:1–2 ἀγών[55] (Phil. 1:30; Col. 2:1)

προσείμενος—ἀγών is "put upon" us 337

χαρά[56] is "put upon" Jesus

He who begins and perfects "our" faith?

ὑπέμεινεν τὸν σταυρόν—remained under the cross. Here is humiliation.

ὑπομε[μενηκότα][57] ἀντιλογία[ν] contradiction

Jesus could achieve his goal only by "remaining below." What does this mean for our ὑπομονή? V. 1 to remain with Christ under the cross . . . to look away *from us*! ἀφορῶντες . . .[58]

[51.] "Moment of temptation," Rev. 3:10: "hour of temptation."

[52.] *NL*, A 55,12 (three DIN A 4 sheets) and *NL*, A 55,20 (two DIN A 4 sheets); handwritten in ink; not previously published.

[53.] Heading ("patience; steadfastness") for *NL*, A 55,12 (1+2); Bonhoeffer numbered the second sheet "2."

[54.] Steinert, Jensen, Staude, Maltusch, von Hanstein, and Kraemer were candidates who participated in this seminar and made presentations on the respective terms. Wherever these names appear in the text, the notes that follow are mostly Bonhoeffer's notes on their presentations. It is not always clear which comments are his. Hans Steinert was in Groß-Schlönwitz in 1938–39.

[55.] "Struggle."

[56.] "Joy."

[57.] Bonhoeffer abbreviated the verb form in Heb. 12:3, "the one who endured [contradiction]."

[58.] Heb. 12:2. Luther's translation is "(those) who look up to Jesus."

ὑπομένειν the perseverance of the καινὸς ἄνθρωπος in the world of σάρξ;[59] ὑπομένειν because we are looking not at ourselves but *toward Jesus*! Not merely in an ethical sense, but only because of *Christ*; the natural person has no hope and therefore is not able to[60] ὑπομένειν; only the Christian has both.

I. a. // ὑπομονή is indissolubly bound with the ὑπομονή of Christ.// *2 Thess. 3:5; Rev. 2:3*—to bear, to suffer as a display of patience διὰ τὸ ὄνομά μου βαστάζω[61] (cf. Luke 14:27) bearing the cross Acts 9! [vv.] 15–16; Gal. 6:17; Rom. 15:1

2 Thess. 3:5; Rev. 2:3

Rev. 1:9 ἐν Ιησοῦ we also ὑπομονή. To remain below in Jesus, to be in the body of Christ and to demonstrate ὑπομονή, yoked in between θλῖψις and βασιλεία![62]

1 Pet. 2:20 Christ has left us the injunction to walk in his footsteps[63]—ὑπομένειν for the sake of *Christ* because *Christ* is for us.

James 5:11 τὸ τέλος κυρίου[64] the *end of Christ*? or the *goal of God*?

II b. // "ὑπομονή of Christ is also manifest in his word" // Rev. 3:10 τὸν λόγον τῆς ὑπομονῆς—cf. 3:8b *do not deny*. The *word* of his *cross*! ? or λόγον μου[65]

338 Rom. 15:4–5 ὑπομονή τῶν γραφῶν? The Scriptures describe the gospel of the cross[66] (Ps. 69 and others). In this way Scripture teaches the patience of Christ.

The God of "ὑπομονή"—his son *or*: Scripture, words themselves patient? *or*: διὰ τῆς ὑπομονῆς = absolute?[67] (Rom. 15:1 βαστάζειν)

[59.] "To remain under," "the new human being," "flesh."

[60.] [The Greek word is an infinitive, hence the structure.—PF]

[61.] "For my name's sake," "I endure"; cf. Rev. 2:3.

[62.] "Tribulation" and "kingdom."

[63.] 1 Pet. 2:21. Luther's translation is "that you shall follow in his footsteps."

[64.] "The end" or "the goal" "of the Lord."

[65.] Bonhoeffer's letter of November 20, 1938, to the Finkenwalde brothers gives "Rev. 3:7–12 (patience)" as the text for meditation for the week of November 27–December 3. See 1/36, pp. 82–84. Luther's translation of v. 10 is "the word of my patience."

[66.] "Gospel of the cross"; uncertain transcription.

[67.] Here it is considered how to interpret the phrase in Rom. 15:4 "through the patience . . . of the Scripture(s)."

I c. // even among the members of the body of Christ there is vicarious ὑπομονή //

2 Cor. 1:5–6 *the suffering that Christ endured*!

2 Tim. 2:10 to endure for the sake of the elect, vicarious representation because of the ὑπομονή Χριστοῦ

II. The *object* of ὑπομονή, the "below what" of ὑπομονή, is summarized as σταυρός, the humility [Niedrigkeit] of the flesh of Christ.

Heb. 12:1–2 σταυρός ἀντὶ[68] Χριστός James 1:2, 12; 5:11 πειρασμός Rev. 3:10 πειρασμοῦ 1 Pet. 2:20 πάσχειν[69] Heb. 10:36 ἄθλησιν παθημάτων[70] Rom. 12:12 θλῖψις 5:3; 2 Thess. 1:4 διωγμὸς[71] καὶ θλῖψις Rev. 13:10 αἰχμαλωσία μάχαιρα[72] 1 Cor. 13:7 πάντα[73]

III. *It is impossible to think of* ὑπομονή *apart from* ἐλπίς,[74] ἐλπις only in ὑπομονή. Septuagint 70. To hope—ἐλπίς and ὑπομονή to abide—James 5:11 the proof. 1 Thess. 1:3 ὑπομονή τῆς ἐλπίδος periodic[75] πίστις, ἀγάπη, πίστις toward God, but unless it becomes a work, it bears no fruit. ἔλπίδος (confession?), κόπος ἀγάπης, ὑπομονή ἐλπίδος;[76] would here be the ἐλπίς radiating in the *flesh*, [(]! good! [)][77] the *remaining* in the cross . . . the view fixed upon *Christ*. Hope leads not away from but into the vocation; hope leads to *perseverance*. // ὑπομονή is the earthly side of ἐλπίς! [(] *good*! [)][78] 339
Rev. 2:2 ἔργον, κόπον, ὑπομονήν. Rom. 8:25; Rom. 5:3; 15:4; 2 Cor. 1:6.

[68.] "Cross, instead of [joy]."

[69.] "To suffer."

[70.] "Struggle with sufferings." The quotation is found in Heb. 10:32.

[71.] "Persecution."

[72.] "Captivity in war"; "sword."

[73.] "All things."

[74.] "Hope."

[75.] Uncertain transcription.

[76.] "Work of faith," "labor of love," "steadfastness of hope"; the phrases are found in 1 Thess. 1:3.

[77.] A note in the margin.

[78.] A note in the margin.

2.[79] (Steinert on ὑπομονή)

IV. *The goal of* ὑπομονή *is* σωτηρία[80]

Matt. 10:22 to maintain ὑπομονή in hatred. Until the *end.* 24:13[81]

Ps. 21:19 you will save your souls *in remaining below.* Rev. 14:12; 3:10; Rom. 2:7; Heb. 10:36; 2 Tim. 2:12.

V. *The life of a Christian can bear fruit only in* ὑπομονή

Luke 8:15 καρποφοροῦντες[82] . . . cf. John 12:24 the *grain of wheat.*

James 1:3–4.

Rom. 2:7 and 2 Cor. 12:12. Deeds and miracles of the apostles. "ἐν ὑπομονῇ"—in weakness.

VI. μακροθυμία[83]—to be slow to wrath.

See above. God's μακροθυμία is the foundation for our μακροθυμία

1 Thess. 5:14

2 Tim. 3:10 μακροθυμία—ἀγάπη—ὑπομονή

1 Cor. 13:4–7 μακροθυμεῖ—ἀγάπη—ὑπομένει (!)

The ἀγάπη of Christ: 1. slow to wrath. μακροθυμεῖ . . . 2. all things borne. ὑπομένει . . .

2 Pet. 1:6 πίστις—ἀγάπη

Jensen[84]

ἀνοχή,[85] μακροθυμία, ὑπομονή

μακροθυμία = opposite ὀργή[86]—refers to persons

ὑπομονή = refers to circumstances—

70. ἐλπίς = ὑπομονή

[79.] This number is at the top of the second sheet in *NL*, A 55,12 (1 and 2).

[80.] "Salvation."

[81.] In Bonhoeffer's letter of November 20, 1938, to the Finkenwalde brothers, "Matt. 24:1–14 (patience)" is mentioned as the text for meditation for the week of November 20–26. See 1/36, p. 85.

[82.] "Those who bear fruit."

[83.] "Patient endurance, long-suffering."

[84.] Hans-Werner Jensen was in Groß-Schlönwitz in 1938–39. The name appears at the top of the reverse side of the sheet numbered "2." The front side of the sheet is not fully covered with writing.

[85.] "Holding back."

[86.] "Wrath."

In Paul Rom. 8:25 eschatological expectation 340

The *burden* lies in the tension between the future of salvation and the empirical present.

To remain is what preserves us. *Content* of hope, strength. The burden is taken away.

Rom. 5:1–5

ὑπομένειν[87]

ὑπό—to remain under, to bow, as under a blessing of God. *Under what?* Under all things that God puts on us.

μένειν—to remain, not to yield, not to give in, not to break down, but to *stand,* to go, to "run." To remain *how long*? Until the end. . . .[88]

μακροθυμία = waiting, long delay

of God 2 Pet. 3:15; Matt. 18:26; Luke 18:7; Rom. 2:4; 9:22

[(] (cf. Rom. 15:5 θεὸς ὑπομονῆς 1 time!) 1 Pet. 3:10; 2 Pet. 3:9 [)]

of Jesus Christ 1 Tim. 1:16.

of Christians toward *one another* Gal. 5:22; Eph. 4:2; Col. 3:12; 2 Tim. 4:2; 1 Thess. 5:14

[(] Col. 1:11 ὑπομονή and μακροθυμίας not *yielding,* (long-suffering) not *angry*! [)]

there is no ὑπομονή toward one another because it refers here to adverse conditions and circumstances

[(] 1 Thess. 5:14 against everyone *Heb. 6:15* μακροθυμία[89] *Abraham*—for God!? James 5:7ff. and for the promise

of the Christian toward *God* James 5:7ff., and toward the future

ἀνοχή—forbearance, reticence; Rom. 2:4; 3:26 in relation to sin, only of *God*

ἀνέχεσθαι—to endure, to bear Eph. 4:2; Col. 3:13; 2 Cor. 11:19; 2 Thess. 1:4; Heb. 13:22[90]

[87.] This is the beginning of the third sheet listed in *NL,* A 55,12 (3). The front page contains many later additions.

[88.] Several illegible (Latin?) words.

[89.] "Having waited patiently."

[90.] This paragraph is written in pencil and marks the end of this only partially completed page. The notes on the reverse of this third sheet are apparently those of two candidates (one of them Hans-Werner Jensen); the notes are from a discussion of their sermon sketches on Rev. 22:1–5.

341 *Only patience wins the promise.*[91] (πίστις = faithfulness)

Matt. 10:22 and 24:12 ὁ δὲ ὑπομείνας εἰς τέλος οὗτος σωθήσεται, the believer comes to salvation only through perseverance, patience.

Heb. 10:36—ὑπομονῆς χρείαν ἔχετε,[92] so that you receive ἐπαγγελία.[93] Without perseverance there is no promise.

2 Tim. 2:12 εἰ ὑπομένομεν καὶ συμβασελεύσομεν[94]

Rom. 2:7 glory and honor to those καθ' ὑπομονὴν ἔργου ἀγαθοῦ[95]

Rev. 13:10; 14:12 patience and faith of the saints, in the last days—of the beast and in the kingdom of God—Zion.

Patience results in the good work.

Luke 8:15 καρποφοροῦντες ἐν ὑπομονῇ

James 1:3–4 . . . ἔργον τέλειον ἐχέτω[96]

The work through suffering.

The patience of Jesus Christ

Heb. 12:2 ὑπέμεινεν σταυρόν

[V.] 3 ἀντιλογίαν

Rom. 15:5 ὁ θεὸς τῆς ὑπομοῆς . . . ?

1 Thess. 1:3?

2 Thess 3:5 εἰς τὴν ὑπομονὴν τοῦ Χριστοῦ

? (Rev. 1:9 συγκοινωνὸς . . . ἐν τῇ ὑπομονῇ ἐν Ἰησοῦ[97]

3:10 ἐτήρησας τὸν λόγον τῆς ὑπομονῆς μου[98]

2 Cor. 1:6ff.[99]

Patience in struggle[100]

Heb. 12:1 (10:36) "*to run*," to hurry, to lose no time

"*Struggle*," to overcome obstacles

[91.] This is the beginning of *NL*, 55,20 (2). The upper left margin of the sheet, where "Only . . . promise" is written, is almost disintegrated.

[92.] "You are in need of patience."

[93.] "Promise."

[94.] Luther's translation: "If we suffer patiently, we will also rule together."

[95.] "Patient in good work."

[96.] The words in James 1:4 are underlined with pencil in Bonhoeffer's Greek New Testament: "let endurance have its full effect."

[97.] "The comrade who shares . . . in the patience in Jesus." The question mark and parenthesis were added later.

[98.] "You have preserved the word of my patience."

[99.] This is the end of *NL*, A 55,20 (2).

[100.] This is the beginning of *NL*, A 55,20 (1). The paper is the same as that of the three sheets in *NL*, A 55,12.

"*through patience*" The goal is far away; let us not think that we can seize it 342
today; let us not give up if it takes a long time; let us not despair even if we experience a setback; let us not lose trust in the goal.

To look toward Christ and his patience. This is the only possibility to run and at the same time to be *patient.*

Patience in suffering

2 Cor. 1:6 παθήματα τοῦ Χριστοῦ εἰς ἡμᾶς—Christ's sufferings are upon us. ἐν ὑπομονῇ τῶν αὐτῶν παθημάτων—patient bearing of Christ's sufferings.[101]

Rom. 12:12; 5:3

Patience emerges out of communion in the sufferings of Jesus Christ.

Discipline is the preparation for patience (ἐγκράτεια) (2 Pet. 1:6).

Patience and the time of testing [Bewährung]. *Patience as the way out of suffering to hope,* through a period of testing. Without patience there is no hope; without a time of testing there is no hope; without patience there is no time of testing (Rom. 5:3). We call blessed . . . (James 5:11).[102]

Patience as the way out of temptation to perfection,[103] to the complete, perfected work. Such patience comes out of the faith that is proven true[104] in temptation. τὸ δοκίμιον τῆς πίστεως [105] in connection with "*temptations*" cf. 1 Pet. 1:6.

Patience out of love. 1 Cor. 13:7.

343

2.4 Notes on the Concept of "Probation"[106]

δόκιμος[107]

2 Cor. 13:7—held in esteem, diligent

[101.] Citations are from vv. 5 and 6. Bonhoeffer's November 20, 1938, letter to the Finkenwalde brothers mistakenly cites "1 Cor. 1:6ff." instead of 2 Cor. See 1/36, p. 83.

[102.] "We call blessed . . ." is added in pencil.

[103.] Bonhoeffer changed the word "perfection" to "completeness" but reversed the change again.

[104.] Replaces "the testing of the faith that comes from the genuineness of faith."

[105.] "The means for testing faith"; cf. 1 Pet. 1:7.

[106.] *NL*, A 55,6 (1) and (2): handwritten on paper size DIN A 5 for (1) and DIN A 4 for (2); previously unpublished. [*Bewährung* is a key term here that means "probation," a "time of testing" or having passed such a time of testing.—VB]

[107.] *NL*, A 55,6 (1) begins with this word, "well proved."

[108.] "Pleasing to God and approved [as trustworthy] by people."

Rom. 14:18 εὐάρεστος τῷ θεῷ, δόκιμος τοῖς ἀνθρόποις[108]
2 Tim. 2:15 σεαυτὸν δόκιμον παραστῆσαι . . .[109]
Rom. 16[:10] . . . τὸν δόκιμον ἐν Χριστῷ . . . well proved
James 1:12 tested and approved
2 Cor. 10:18 ὃν ὁ κύριος συνίστησιν[110]
1 Cor. 11:19 those well proved, genuine

ἀδόκιμος[111] Rom. 1:28! οὐκ ἐδοκίμασαν τὸν θεὸν . . . παρέδωκεν . . . εἰς ἀδόκιμον νοῦν[112]

1 Tim. 6:5; 2 Tim. 3:8 ἀδόκιμοι περί τὴν πίστιν[113] Titus 1:16
2 Cor. 13:5

That which does not stand the test, which is not genuine, only appearance.

δοκιμάζειν Luke 12:56; 1 Cor. 11:28; 2 Cor. 13:5; Gal. 6:4; Phil. 1:10; Rom. 2:18; Eph. 5:10; Rom. 12:2; 1 Thess. 5:21; 1 John 4:1; 1 Tim. 3:10; 2 Cor. 8:8 = to put to the test.

of God 1 Thess. 2:4
= to approve = 2 Cor. 8:22; Rom. 14:22
= to prove when put to the test 1 Pet. 1:7; 1 Cor. 3:13
= to choose 1 Cor. 16:3; 1 Thess. 2:4

δοκιμασία[114]—only Heb. 3:9; against God.

δοκιμή—actively 2 Cor. 8:2

passively = that which has stood the test Rom. 5:4; 2 Cor. 2:9; 13:3; 2 Cor. 9:13; 8:2

ἀγών[115]—The task of a Christian, to prove his faith 1 Tim. 6:12; 2 Tim. 4:7; Heb. 12:1–2; 11:39–40; 10:36ff.

[109.] "To show yourself as having stood the test."

[110.] "The one whom the Lord commends."

[111.] "Unproven, not standing the test."

[112.] "They did not see fit to acknowledge God. . . . [He] gave them up to a debased mind."

[113.] Luther's translation: "not diligent in the faith."

[114.] "Testing."

[115.] "Struggle."

(*Staude*)[116] 344

δόκιμος—tested in struggle, capable

δοκιμή—not passively, only Paul[117]

δοκίμιος—having stood the test

δοκιμάζειν—70. . . .[118]—prophetic—Ps[alter]

to ask, to pray for the testing eye of God . . .

religious meaning first in the New Testament . . . *as those who stand proven in judgment*

1. *Proven before God* =[119]

in judgment 1 Cor. 3:13. James 1:12

in πειρασμοῖς to be patient = approved. δόκιμος as consequence of *patience* (cf. Rom. 5:3!)

1 Peter 1:7—in temptations "proven in faith." Faith becomes praise, the glory of Christ . . . through a time of testing. εἰς ἔπαινον . . . that he may *receive praise*! τὸ δοκίμιον ὑμῶν τῆς πίστεως—*you*[120] are being tested, *not faith*. Faith does not need to be tested, only the human being. Faith—testing, like hope—patience.

2. *Proven in life*.—1 Thess. 2:4 God has examined Paul. δεδοκιμάσμεθα—*proven* or *tested*? 1 Cor. 9:27. || *2 Cor. 13:3ff.* || *Probation* is *Christ*; *the crucified*![121] Christian stands in faith.

a. Of what does standing the test consist? In θλῖψις—Rom. 5:3 and James 1:3.

// τὸ δοκίμον ὑμῶν = Christ (?) //

= means of testing (?)

= proven in faith

The time of testing is always aimed toward judgment, once related to ἐλπίς (Rom. 5:3) and once related to πίστις (ἔργον) (James 1:3).

b. Standing the test in active love (2 Cor. 9:13; 8:8; 2:9)

[116.] *NL*, A 55,6 (2). Joachim Staude was in Groß-Schlönwitz in 1938–39.

[117.] Cf. in *NL*, A 55,6 (1) on δοκιμή: "actively 2 Cor. 8:2."

[118.] Two Hebrew terms are omitted here.

[119.] Deleted: "probation in life."

[120.] In the Greek text in his New Testament, Bonhoeffer underlined in ink ὑμῶν in 1 Pet. 1:7.

[121.] Bonhoeffer marked "*2 Cor. 13:3ff.*" with two vertical lines on the left and right and underlined the terms in the following text three times.

345 c. Standing the test in office. (Phil. 2:22; 2 Tim. 2:15; *2 Cor. 10:18*). δόκιμον is a predicate, which is given by God. Rom. 14:18; 16:10 δόκιμον ἐν Χριστῷ

As a human judgment 1 Cor. 16:3; 2 Cor. 8:22; *1 Tim. 3:10*!

III. To examine oneself.

a. to examine the will of God Eph. 5:9;[122] Rom. 12:2
b. situation Phil. 1:10; 1 Thess. 5:21; 1 John 4:1; Rom. 2:18; Luke 12:56
c. oneself 2 Cor. 13:5; (Gal. 6:4?); 1 Cor. 11:28

(IV. Profane usage Luke 14:19)

The Christian is always only δόκιμος in an ultimate decision made by God.

δόκιμος is the one whose faith proves true in temptation and who passes examination under judgment.

δόκιμος already begins here. The entire life is testing and probation in tribulation, temptation, love, and the service of proclamation.

Here a *penultimate* decision can be made whether another person is δόκιμος.

In examining the *will of God* one is to ask about etc. . . .

2.5 Notes on the Concept of "Joy"[123]

χαρά[124]

(Jensen)[125] *philological?*

1. Joy is the most prominent word pronounced on *Jesus's* birth, his earthly
346 life, resurrection, ascension. Matt. 2:10; Luke 2:10 | Mark 2:19; Luke 15:7, 10; 19:6 | Matt. 28:8; Luke 24:41, 52; John 20:20[126]

[122.] [The actual verse is 10.—PF]

[123.] *NL*, A 55,15 (1) and (2); handwritten in ink and pencil; previously unpublished. On this topic, see also Bonhoeffer's contribution to the *Festschrift* (commemorative paper) for Adolf von Harnack's seventy-fifth birthday in 1926, in *DBWE* 9:370–85.

[124.] This is the heading (joy) of the double sheet *NL*, A 55,15 (1). The sheet contains notes written in ink on "(Jensen)" and "(Maltusch)" and notes in pencil on scriptural references.

[125.] Hans-Werner Jensen was in Groß-Schlönwitz in 1938–39.

[126.] Bonhoeffer mentions part of these scriptural references in his letter of February 14, 1939, to the Finkenwalde brothers, on the themes of "the birth of Christ," "Christ's fellowship with his disciples," and "Christ's resurrection and ascension." See 1/75, p. 145. There are further agreements between the letter and the following text.

2. Joy not only among human beings, but also with God. It is the joy *of God* that stands over Jesus's work. Luke 15:7, 10; Matt. 25:21, 23; Eph. 4:31. The joy of the disciples is the joy of Jesus (John 15:11). The joy of God—of Jesus comes through the word of Jesus to the disciples. (16:22, 24; 17:13)

3. Therefore, the one who walks with Jesus participates in joy. Mark 2:18ff.; Matt. 13:44! Joy, for which a person gives everything. Luke 10:17. Matt. 5:12 (6:17)

4. Who does not walk with Jesus is *sad.* Matt. 19:22 (26:22? *17:23*)

5. Because of this Jesus enters into mourning and sorrow. Matt. 26:37; Heb. 12:2 Jesus is sad because he is distant from God. (Nearness to God is joy.)

6. The foundation for joy is

a. the coming of the Redeemer (Luke 1:47; 1 Sam. 2:1; Luke 19:37; John 3:29)

b. God's deeds done through the Redeemer (Luke 13:17)

c. the names written *in heaven* Luke 10:20; Phil. 3:20–4:4

d. the proclamation of the gospel (Acts 8:8; 13:48; 2 Cor. 1:15 VB.)[127]

e. the foundation for the joy of the apostle is the church-community and vice versa 2 Cor. 1:14 (?); Phil. 4:1;[128] 1 Thess. 2:19–20 | Phil. 1:25; 2 Cor. 1:15 through faith 1 Thess. 3:9; 3 John 4 because of the salvation of the other (Luke 15:32; 2 Cor. 7:9!)

f. the nearness of God Phil. 4:4 (Luke 21:28)

g. χαρά and λύπη[129] relate in the same way as belief and unbelief,[130] but χαρά will break right through the λύπη (John 16:20ff.) in the *midst* of *persecution* and in the *midst* of *anxiety* (Matt. 5:12; Luke 6:23; Phil. 1:18; Col. 1:24–25; Rom. 12:12, 14; 1 Thess. 5:16). The consequence 1 Pet. 4:13 is joy 347
at the revelation of the glory of God. 1 Pet. 1:8; Rev. 19:7 eschatological.[131]

[127.] The apparatus to the Greek New Testament text lists as a variant reading χαράν in Codex Vaticanus and other manuscripts.

[128.] In Bonhoeffer's November 20, 1938, letter to the Finkenwalde brothers, "Phil. 4:1–9 (joy)" is listed as the meditation text for the week of December 11–17. See 1/36, p. 85.

[129.] "Grief, mourning."

[130.] Replaces "are not mutually exclusive."

[131.] Up to this point the writing was in ink; now it changes to pencil.

John 16:22 αἴρει[132]—present tense—*present joy.*
1 Pet. 1:6–8 church-community is sad and joyful
2 Cor. 6:10 ὡς[133]—in fact.

The Letter to the Philippians.
1:4 joyful prayer for the congregation. Joy over[134] community
1:18 rejoices at the progress of the proclamation
1:25 rejoices at being alive for the congregation's sake
1:27ff. congregation should be a source of joy for him
2:2 petition for the fulfillment of joy
2:17 joy on the part of apostle and congregation—συγχαίρειν[135]
2:28 . . .[136]
2:29 a fresh start: τὸ λοιπόν—χαίρετε[137]
3:1—χαίρετε ἐν κυρίῳ—righteousness in Christ
4:1—congregation "his joy"—στήκετε[138]
4:5—the result of joy: gentleness toward human beings
[4:6] Thanksgiving toward God
4:10—thankfulness

Col. 1:24—"to make full use of everything" [ausschöpfen]—ὑπέρ[139]
(2 Tim. 2:10; 2 Cor. 4:12; 1:5)

θλῖψις—45 times χαρά 56
θλίβειν[140]—10 times χαίρειν[141] 53
θλῖψις—1. suffering, affliction 2. inner affliction, anxiety 3. affliction of the pious

[132.] This word, "(no one) takes away," is underlined in ink in Bonhoeffer's Greek New Testament text.

[133.] "As."

[134.] Replaces "Thankfulness for." The words "Thankfulness . . ." and "Joy . . ." are added in ink.

[135.] "To rejoice with."

[136.] Illegible; perhaps "Ex mortuis" ("From the dead"), since in v. 27 there is a reference to [a brother—VB] who was sick, "near death"; similarly in v. 30.

[137.] The citation (as well as in the next line) is Phil. 3:1: "finally—rejoice in the Lord."

[138.] "Stand firm."

[139.] "For."

[140.] "To press upon, to afflict or become afflicted, distressed."

[141.] "To be joyous."

Acts 20:37[142] Paul expects θλῖψις 2 Cor. 1:5[143] 348

1. for the sake of his proclamation 2 Cor. 4:8; Mark 4:18;[144] 1 Thess. 1:6; Col. 1:24

2. eschatological Matt. 24; Mark 13 μεγάλη θλῖψις[145] Rev. 14

James 1:1 χαίρειν; 1:2 χαρά, 4:9 false joy[146]

1 Pet. 4:13, 14; Rom. 12:12, 13; 1 Thess. 5:16

Heb. 10:34; 12:2! ἀντί = "for, for the sake of" or "instead"?[147] 12:11

(Maltusch)[148]

εὐφραίνειν[149]—. . .[150] [(] 16 times [)] to be smooth (Glad)[151] Isa. 65[:19]—God exults

New Testament profane. Joy of the world. Acts 14:17; 7:14; Rev. 12:12; 18:20

ἀγαλλιάσθαι[152]—. . .[153]—cultic dance—not classical

New Testament cultic inspired joy, John 5:35 religious rapture (critical?) Luke 10:21; Acts 2:46; Jude 24; Matt. 5:12; Luke 1:14; Luke 8:56; Rev. 19:7; omits P[aul], instead καύχησις[154]

χαίρω/χαρά—(ready, gladly, greedy)[155] 115 times

1. As a formula for salutations: the greeting of Judas Matt. 26:49; Matt. 27:29; Luke 1:28 angel.

2. Of Jesus John 15:11; *16:24!* Complete joy—*an answer to prayer.* 17:13: *Preservation* of the disciples in Jesus. (1 Cor. 13:6; 1 Pet. 4)[156] Heb. 12:2 χαρά of Jesus.

[142.] "7" uncertain transcription.

[143.] See v. 6.

[144.] Cf. v. 17.

[145.] "Great affliction."

[146.] Deleted: "(5:13)."

[147.] In Bonhoeffer's Greek New Testament text, the word ἀντί in Heb. 12:2 is underlined in pencil.

[148.] The writing on the fourth page of the double sheet begins here; in ink. Gottfried Maltusch was in Köslin in 1938–39.

[149.] "To make glad, joyful."

[150.] Omission of a Hebrew word.

[151.] [The German word *glatt* ("flat" or "smooth") has the same root as the English "glad," which Bonhoeffer inserts here.—VB]

[152.] "To rejoice, exult."

[153.] Omission of a Hebrew word.

[154.] "Boasting." Beginning at "Matt. 5:12 . . ." the notes are added in pencil.

[155.] [The three German words here (*gar, gern, gierig*) are derived from χαρά.—VB]

[156.] "1 Pet. 4" uncertain transcription and later addition in pencil; cf. 1 Pet. 4:13.

3. Joy over Christ.—(Luke 24:41! Matt. 28:8) χαρά and φόβος[157]

4. Joy of heavenly beings John 8:56; Luke 15:7; 2 Cor. 7:4ff.

349 5. Joy, result of proclamation—from the word John 3:29; *4:35*! λευκός[158] of the garments of the Samaritans! Matt. 13:44—over the deed of redemption John 14:28; 16:20; 20:20

6. Joy about the community. Phil.; 2 Cor.2; 2 and 3 John 4;[159] Heb. 13

7. Joy for the sake of persecution. Matt. 5:12; Acts 5:41; Phil. 2:17; Col. 1:24; 1 Thess. 1:6 joy from the Holy Spirit. Heb. 10:34; James 1:2[160]

συγχαίρω Luke 1:58; 15:6, 9; 1 Cor. 12:26; 13:6; Phil. 2:17, 18 joy with God, Christ, and the brothers and sisters.

false joy see Mark 14:11; Luke 22:5; John 16:20; Luke 10:17, 20 (Luke 24:51![161] (Luke 23:8; James 4:9; Luke 15:29; John 5:35 [ἀγαλλιασθῆναι])

Matt. 25:21![162]

Matt. 25:21; 18:13

Luke 15:7; 10:20 (13:17); 15:32; *24:41*?; 19:6, 37; 23:8

John 16:24, 22

Acts 13:52

2 Cor. 2:3

Phil. 1:25; 2:17

Col. 1:11

1 Thess. 1:6; 5:16

1 Cor. 13:6

Col. 1:24

[157.] "Fear."

[158.] "White."

[159.] 2 John 4 and 3 John 4.

[160.] "James 1:2" is added in pencil. Below this addition is a line in pencil as wide as the page; the notes below the line are also in pencil.

[161.] Deleted: "?" ("Joy" is in v. 52.)

[162.] Regarding Matt. 25:21, Bonhoeffer quotes from Augustine in his letter of February 14, 1939, to the Finkenwalde brothers (see, however, 1/75, ed. note 9!). This biblical reference in ink is the only entry on the one page of the DIN A5 sheet (*NL*, A 55,15 (2), which is otherwise blank. On the other side of this sheet, there are biblical references on the left side, notes on the right side, both in pencil, which are reproduced above.

The joy of God, of Jesus Christ (John) over us[163]
Our joy over God, Christ
our joy over one another 350
our joy in suffering
the eternal joy

Luke 15 the joy over the conversion of a sinner—rejoice with me! We are to share in Jesus's joy.[164]

2.6 Notes on the Concept of "Peace"[165]

εἰρήνη (v. Hanstein)[166]

46 times (except[167] in parallel Scripture references)

1. εἰρήνη the *peace with God* (Rom. 5:1) Luke 2:14; 19:36; Eph. 2:14ff. *the gospel of peace*: Acts 10:36; Eph. 6:15; Eph. 2:18
2. εἰρήνη as formula of salutation
3. εἰρήνη eschatological 2 Pet. 3:14; Rom. 8:6 Old Testament Lev. 26:6 / prophetic 1 Kings 22; Micha ben[168] Jemla Jer. 28! 29:11
4. Peace as the opposite of dispute Matt. 10:34 par.; 1 Pet. 3:10[169]
5. Peace among human beings James 3:18; Rom. 14:17–18; 1 Cor. 7:15; 2 Tim. 2:22; Eph. 4:3; Heb. 12:14

εἰρήνη Rom. 12:18

εἰρηνεύειν—to *have* and to keep peace! New Testament? On the *basis* of *having* also *keeping*! ?

εἰρηνοποιεῖν—of *Christ* and of[170]

[163.] See Bonhoeffer's letter of February 14, 1939, to the Finkenwalde brothers: "The origin of all true joy is God's joy in us"; see 1/75, p. 146. The letter mentions also "John 15:11; 17:13."

[164.] Cf. in Bonhoeffer's letter of February 14, 1939, to the Finkenwalde brothers: "The entire chapter of Luke 15 stands under this call" for "rejoicing together"; see 1/75. p. 146.

[165.] *NL*, A 55,7 (2) and (1): (2) is handwritten in pencil on a sheet of DIN A 5 linen stationery; (1) mostly written in ink on a DIN A 4 sheet, which is folded over to make it a double DIN A 5 sheet; previously unpublished.

[166.] Heading: "Peace." This is the beginning of the notes in pencil on the sheet *NL*, A 55,7 (2). Hans-Joachim von Hanstein was in Groß-Schlönwitz in 1938–39.

[167.] Uncertain reading.

[168.] Uncertain reading. 1 Kings 22:8: "Micaiah son of Imlah."

[169.] The word "peace" is found in 1 Pet. 3:11.

[170.] Incomplete. The verb "to make peace" is used in view of Christ in Col. 1:20. Cf. Matt. 5:9, the beatitude of "those who make peace."

Eph. 6:23! εἰρήνη καὶ ἀγάπη μετὰ πίστεως![171] 1 Pet. 1:2 πληθυνθείη—peace should be increased (!)

351 John 14:27 "Jewish wish for peace" | unsystematic[172]

Eph. 2:14

6. θεὸς εἰρήνης Heb. 13:20; 1 Thess. 5:23 "God, whose manner is peace," Rom. 16:20; 15:33; *2 Cor. 13:11*! Heb. 7:1ff. βασιλεὺς εἰρήνης[173]

7. εἰρήνη Χριστοῦ—Ἰησοῦ Col. 3:15; John 14:27; 16:33; Phil. 4:7

εἰρηνοποιεῖν—*Greek*: a matter of power

in the Old Testament:[174] Act of humility, suffering

in the New Testament: Act of love

external, internal struggles of the conscience?[175]

εἰρήνη[176]

Greek: the state of rest

pax: the current legal condition

שָׁלוֹם: salvation, well-being.

LXX: εἰρήνη must be understood on the basis of שָׁלוֹם.[177]

[1.] *False peace*[178]

Luke 2:14 and Matt. 10:34;[179] Matt. 10:34; Luke 12:51 οὐ εἰρήνην ἀλλὰ μάχαιραν[180]

1 Thess 5:3 εἰρήνη καὶ ἀσφάλεια[181] (*ludus de a . . .*)[182]

[171.] "Peace and love with faith!"

[172.] [This may be Bonhoeffer's critical comment about Hanstein's presentation. —VB]

[173.] V. 3: "king of peace."

[174.] Uncertain reading.

[175.] Uncertain reading.

[176.] Heading of the double sheet *NL*, A 55,7 (1), written in pencil.

[177.] The explanations of the four terms ("shalom" is written in Hebrew) are written in ink in the upper right corner beside the heading.

[178.] The heading of this paragraph replaces "1" and is written in pencil, as are the following lines, up to and including the heading of paragraph "2."

[179.] "Luke 2:14 and [repeated] Matt. 10:34" is a later addition in ink above the line.

[180.] "Not peace but the sword," a citation from Matt. 10:34.

[181.] "Peace and security," in Bonhoeffer's Greek New Testament text; both terms are underlined in pencil.

[182.] Illegible.

False peace as ἀσφάλεια, as a secure possession on earth, as an anticipation of eschatological peace.

Christ brings γῇ *to the earth*[183] "dissension." For and against Christ. He 352
brings decision and separation. ([Luke] 2:14?)[184]

This happens for the sake of true "peace on earth" (Luke 2:14) εἰρήνη ἐπὶ γῆς

2. *True peace*

Christ brings peace to his own.[185]

1. *What is "peace"?*[186]

1./ *Peace as objective gift of salvation. The making and essence of peace*

Christ is our [(] personal! [)][187] peace (Eph. 2:14)

We have peace "*in Christ*" (John 16:33)

"Christ has made peace through the blood of his cross" (Col. 1:20; Heb. 13:20)[188]

Peace, then, is nowhere in the world, *only in Jesus Christ* ἐμὴ[189] εἰρήνη (John 14:27). It is "*his*" peace, his possession.

In the world there is: θλῖψις (John 16:33) θάνατος (Rom. 8:6) σατάν (Rom. 16:20) ἀκαταστασία (1 Cor. 14:33) ἔχθρα (Eph. 2:16) ταράσσειν—δειλιᾶν (John 14:27) μάχαιρα (Matt. 10:34) διαμερισμός (Luke 12:51) 1 Pet. 3:11 κακόν[190] Gal. 5:22 ἔρις, ζῆλος[191]

Peace is thus the end of affliction, of death, of Satan, of disorder, of enmity, of confusion, of fear, of the sword and dissension. Peace means *becoming whole in Jesus Christ.*

This happens 1. Through reconciliation with God in the blood of Jesus Christ (Col. 1:20) (Rom. 5:1)[192] 2. through the founding of the church
through the cross of Jesus Christ (Eph. 2:14–15). Peace is being reconciled 353

[183.] The Greek word for "earth" from Matt. 10:34 is added above the line.

[184.] Deleted: "Christ brings *peace* to his own."

[185.] This line is the beginning of writing in ink.

[186.] What follows is set apart from the preceding notes by lines. The heading "1./ . . ." is an addition, the "/" is written in pencil; cf. below ed. note 197, under number "2./."

[187.] "Personal!" is written in pencil above "our."

[188.] The reference to Hebrews is added in pencil.

[189.] "My" (i.e., Christ's peace).

[190.] "Morally bad." Bonhoeffer translates the preceding Greek terms in the paragraph that follows.

[191.] "Strife," "jealousy"; the terms are mentioned in Gal. 5:20 (not v. 22). The references to 1 Peter and Galatians are added in pencil.

[192.] Cf. v. 9.

with God and human beings in the body of Jesus Christ. Here our relation to God and human beings has become whole.[193]

Therefore, peace as a comprehensive term

Gospel as "the gospel of peace" Eph. 6:15; Acts 10:36; Rom. 10:[15][194]

God as "God of peace" Rom. 15:33; 16:20; 2 Cor. 13:11; Phil. 4:9; 1 Thess. 5:23; Heb. 13:20 king of peace Heb. 7:2[195]

"*Way of peace*" (Rom. 3:17) Luke 19:42

God as the origin and giver of peace[196]

2./[197] *The attainment of peace.*

He is *our* peace Eph. 2:14. We have no other peace except him alone. We *receive* this peace, which he is, as *our* peace:

I. 1. through justification (Rom. 5:1)

2. as the fruit of the Spirit (Gal. 5:22); we know through the Holy Spirit of the peace made between God and human beings and we *have* it.

3. as a gift of Christ (John 14:27). It remains "his" peace, which he alone has made and that we have "in him" alone (John 16:33). He is the "Lord of peace" (2 Thess. 3:16; 1 Thess. 5:23), and it is "the peace *of Christ*" (Col. 3:15).[198]

4. as a gift of God (Rom. 15:13). He is the "God of peace" (see above), and it is the peace *of God* (Phil. 4:7).

5. as the fruit of faith (Rom. 15:13). We have peace only *in faith*; cf. Eph. 6:23.

6. as the reality of the kingdom of God (Rom. 14:17).

[193.] Deleted: "What is the consequence of peace? Phil. 4:7; Col. 3:15; 1 Thess. 5:23."

[194.] Incorrectly cited in the manuscript: "v. 36."

[195.] "King . . . 7:2" is added in pencil.

[196.] Deleted: "2. *The attainment of peace* [replaces: '*The peace in us*']. Peace as the fruit of the Spirit (Gal. 5:22) Peace as the fruit of faith (Rom. 15:13) ἐν τῷ πιστεύειν ['in faith'] Peace as an element of the kingdom of God (Rom. 14:17)."

[197.] The numbering "2./" is added in pencil.

[198.] The standard Greek text reads εἰρήνη τοῦ Χριστοῦ, whereas Luther's translation follows a variant reading ("the peace of God").

II. What does peace effect in us? 354

1. It guards in Jesus Christ (Phil. 4:7). What reason cannot accomplish is possible for the peace of God. φρουρεῖν (Gal. 3:23)—to lock up,[199] to remain in the body of Christ. He makes us firm.

2. "He rules our heart as a referee" Col. 3:15. Hence, the heart is in conflict within itself.[200] What is in agreement with the peace of God is right; what is not, is wrong.

3. He makes us into εἰρηνοποιοί (Matt. 5:9) (Rom. 12:18; 14:9; 2 Cor. 13:11; 1 Thess. 5:13; 2 Tim. 2:22; Heb. 12:18; Eph. 4:3) (Mark 9:50!). εἰρηνοποιήσας *as Christ*![201] James 3:18! τοῖς ποιοῦσειν τῆν εἰρήνην[202]

III. The *greeting of peace* ἀσπάζεσθαι, χαίρειν. *"To greet"* is an act of worship. Where one person meets another, one honors God and wishes the other the help of God [for this reason 2 John 11–12!][203] (the removing of one's hat). A greeting places salvation in God between human beings. Prayer.

The greeting of peace effects the real communication of peace to the other. (Luke 10:5ff.) Only the "*son of peace*" will receive peace, and it will remain with him.[204] ([Sons] τοῦ φωτός (Luke 16:8; John 12:36; 1 Thess. 5:5) τέκνα τῆς σο^φ^ας (Matt. 11:19) ἀναστάσεως (Luke 20:36) βασειλείας (Matt. 8:12) παρακλήσεως (Acts 4:36).[205] Thus, whoever is "from peace" (ἄξιος[206] Matt. 10:13) will receive peace through the greeting. The Christian greeting stands under the salvation brought about by God. Greeting of Christ! John 10:19–20; Mark 5:34; Luke 8:48; 7:50; Acts 16:36; James 2:16; 1 Cor. 16:11!

IV. Peace—eschatological in heaven Luke 19:38; Rom. 2:10 ἀνάπαυσις, κατά-[παυσις] Heb. 4 ἡσυχία[207]

[199.] [Cf. *DBWE* 4:260.—VB]

[200.] This sentence is written with pencil in the margin.

[201.] Col. 1:20.

[202.] The reference from James—"to those who make peace"—is added in pencil.

[203.] Bonhoeffer added the square brackets. Second John 10–11 (not v. 12) forbids giving a greeting to the deceiver.

[204.] Luke 10:6.

[205.] "[Sons] of the light," "children of wisdom," "of resurrection," "of the kingdom," "of consolation."

[206.] "Worthy."

[207.] "[To come to have] rest," "rest [getting rested]," "Sabbath rest," "rest [silence]."

355 **2.7 Notes on the Concept of "Abstinence"**[208]

ἐγκράτεια[209]

ἐν—κράτος—to control oneself—Greek philosophy . . .[210]

ἐγκράτεια (ἀκρασία)[211]
Greek: self-control
Matt. 6:16; *9:14*!; Luke 18:12; Mark 9:29; Matt. 19:12

νηστεύειν νηφαλέος—νήφειν ἁγνεία γρηγορεῖ ἀγρυπνεῖν[212]
(ἀπέχεσθε, ἀρνήσασθαι, φεύγειν, ἀποτάσσειν)[213]
The brother
The second coming

1 Cor. 9:25, exercising self-denial for the sake of the goal. (The entire context deals with the self-denial of the apostle.) Gal. 5:23, no false freedom, v. 13; 1 Cor. 7:9, Titus 1:8; 2 Pet. 1:6; 1 Cor. 6:9

Crämer ἐγκράτεια[214]

[Sir.[215] 8:16?; Sir. 26:15]
Vulgate: ἐγκράτεια = *abstinentia, continentia, caritas*[216]
1 Cor. 7:9 = to abstain. *7:32*! Is marriage impure? (Kittel)
356 Acts 24:25, sexual ἐγκράτεια is not an end in itself, but for the sake of the Lord and the kingdom

[208.] *NL*, A 55,14 (1) + (2) + (3); handwritten on two sheets of DIN A 5 paper, sheet (1) is written in pencil, sheet (3) in ink. Sheet (2), DIN A 4, is folded once into a double sheet. Previously unpublished.

[209.] Heading—"self-control" or "abstinence"—of the double sheet *NL*, A 55,14 (2), written in pencil.

[210.] Omitted are terms and scriptural references on three pages.

[211.] This is the beginning of the sheet *NL*, A 55, 14 (3), written in ink. The term in parentheses means "lack of self-control" or "lack of restraint."

[212.] "To fast," "sober"—"to be sober," "purity," "to watch, be alert," "to be watchful."

[213.] "To be abstinent," "to deny," "to flee," "to renounce."

[214.] Heading of the sheet *NL*, A 55,14 (1), written in pencil. Wilhelm Kraemer was in Groß-Schlönwitz in 1938–39.

[215.] Uncertain transcription. Square brackets were inserted by Bonhoeffer.

[216.] The Latin terms for "abstinence," "self-control," "love," respectively.

1 Cor. 9:24 ἐγκράτεια *in general*: σῶμα for the sake of the στέφανος[217]
ὑπωπιάζω—metaphorically or literally? To strike under the eye with fists.[218]
Titus 1:8—through Christ, ἐν—κράτος, *in power*, thus positively in contrast to above—*negatively*. [219]

ἁγνεία νηστεύειν *Contradiction* between Matt. 6:16 and Matt. 9:14–15?[220]

Asceticism[221] for the sake of the death of Jesus? for the sake of his *going*! *a time of waiting*! *a time of repentance*!
Asceticism for the sake of the future, Luke 12:37
Asceticism from faith (Matt. 9:15ff. new wineskins)[222]
Asceticism for the sake of the goal,[223] 1 Cor. 9:25
Asceticism for the sake of the kingdom of God, Matt. 19:12
Asceticism for the sake of the struggle against the devil, Mark 9:29
Asceticism for the sake of the Lord, 1 Cor. 7:32
Asceticism no work (Luke 18:12), not legalistic (1 Tim. 5:23) Matt. 6:16
Asceticism in everything, sexuality, eating, drinking, sleeping, possessions, chastity, fasting, soberness, wakefulness.
To be wakeful with Jesus—"participate in Jesus's sufferings"
To be wakeful and *sober* for the sake of the end; it is still the *time of waiting*.

2.8 Notes on Death[224] 357

θάνατος[225]

I. Death outside Christ

a. Came into the world through sin. The sinner cannot live before God. Adam sinned and thus brought death to himself and all other human beings. Ever since, death has dominion; all human beings sin and have

[217.] "Body," "crown"; the terms are found in 1 Cor. 9:27, 25.

[218.] In his Greek text Bonhoeffer underlined in pencil the terms ἐγκρατεύεται (he abstains) in 1 Cor. 9:25 and ὑπωπιάζω (Luther: "I paralyze") in v. 27. Bonhoeffer considers the literal meaning of the verb, which derives from Greek fistfighting.

[219.] After this point there is a horizontal pencil line across the page.

[220.] This is heavily underlined in pencil.

[221.] Replaces "abstinence."

[222.] Matt. 9:17.

[223.] Replaces "service."

[224.] *NL*, A 55,2; handwritten in ink (linen stationery, one DIN A4 sheet folded into a double DIN A5) and pencil (on two DIN A5 sheets); previously unpublished.

[225.] Heading—"death"—written in ink on the folded sheet of linen stationery (*NL*, A 55,2).

fallen prey to death. Rom. 5:12, 14, 17, 21; 1 Cor. 15:21–22; Rom. 1:32; 6:16, 23; 8:6; James 1:15;[226] John 8:21, 24.[227]

b. Ever since, the human being is mortal in body and flesh and cannot obtain salvation by human means, Rom. 7:24 (Acts 14:15) *Rom. 6:12*;[228] 8:11, 13; 1 Cor. 15:53; 2 Cor. 4:11; Heb. 9:27.

c. Sin makes death an enemy (1 Cor. 15:56; 15:26; Rev. 20:14; 6:8). Personified.

d. Death casts its *shadow* on life (Luke 1:79; Matt. 4:16). The fear of death (Heb. 2:15; Luke 12:4), bondage.

e. Life must serve death (2 Cor. 7:10; Rom. 7:5). Even works are dead (Heb. 9:14); indeed, the human being is dead even before physical death (Eph. 2:1, 5; Matt. 8:22; 1 Tim. 5:6; Rom. 7:10). Death has engulfed life; death has power over it (2 Tim. 1:10).

f. Death is not nonbeing but a new mode of existence [(] one fraught with pain, Acts 2:24[)],[229] namely, corruption (Gal. 5:19). No one can escape judgment through death (Heb. 9:27). See also Rev. 9:6. In the last days of hardship, death becomes desirable, but no one can find it; those who do find it face judgment. (Today there is a widespread weariness of life, but death flees!) (On the *condition of being dead*, later!)

358 II. *Christ and Death.*

Jesus Christ actually dies, struck by the wrath of God over sin (Mark 15:34).[230] His death is not the *wage of his*[231] sin, but a freely willed death as one without sin *for us* (Rom. 5:6, 8; 2 Cor. 5:21; Gal. 3:13). God has allowed Christ to die for us (Rom. 8:3). In this way sufficient satisfaction has been given for human sin. Death has no right and no power over the innocent. *Only the innocent one could overcome death.* He died willingly, and death's grip could not hold him (Acts 2:24). He has broken the power of death (2 Tim. 1:10; Heb. 2:14).[232] The resuscitation and resurrection of Christ is the foundation for the reign of Christ over death. He had the keys of death and hell (Rev. 1:18). Therefore, law, sin, and death have lost their

[226.] Deleted: "Eph. 2:1, 5."

[227.] Deleted: "Heb. 9:27."

[228.] The parentheses around the reference to Acts 14:15 and the underlining of Rom. 6:12 are in pencil.

[229.] "One fraught with . . . 2:24" is an addition above the line.

[230.] Replaces "a. He has broken the power of death 2 Tim. 1:10; Heb. 2:14." At the beginning of the next line, "b" is deleted. [NRSV translation altered here to conform to Bonhoeffer's German.—VB]

[231.] "Of his" is written in pencil and replaces "of" (sin).

[232.] Deleted: "Christ will be raised, Christ *arises*."

power over humankind once and for all. From now on Christ reigns. The βασιλεία[233] of death yields to the βασιλεία of Christ. νίκη Χριστοῦ[234] 1 Cor. 15:55.

III. *Christians and Death.*

a. Death in baptism; the old human being dies with Christ on the cross Rom. 6:1ff.; Rom. 8:10. Now, the human being is dead to sin (to the world) but lives for God; in the past it was vice versa. 2 Cor. 5:14, 15; Col. 3:3ff.; 2:12.

b. Daily dying 1 Cor. 15:31.[235] 2 Cor. 4:10, 11, 12; 2 Cor. 6:9; Col. 3:5. It is the communion of the death of Christ (Phil. 3:10ff.!). Formerly dead even while alive, now ἐκ νεκρῶν ζῶντας Rom. 6:13![236]

c. The martyr's death 2 Tim. 2:11; Rev. 14:13; 2:13; 2:10.

d. Physical death: *a longing for death* (2 Cor. 5:1ff.; Phil. 1:21; Rom. 8:18ff.; Phil. 3:20). *Dying for the Lord* (Rom. 14:7ff.). The dead are in Christ (1 Thess. 4:16, 14; 1 Cor. 15:18). The twofold cancellation of death: 1. the second coming (Mark 9:1ff.; John 21:23) 2. having passed through death already (John 5:24; 8:51, 52).[237]

Intermediary state. κοιμᾶσθια[238] (θάνατος continuation) 359

profane *to sleep* Matt. 28:30; Acts 12:6 to have fallen asleep Acts 7:60; 13:36; 1 Cor. 7:39; 1 Cor. 15:6 the moment of death.

Those who have died are sleeping: Matt. 27:52 the bodies of the departed sleeping saints. John 11:1 is intentionally ambiguous: "Lazarus is sleeping" 1 Cor. 11:30 (15:6); 1 Thess. 4:13.

Not all will fall asleep 1 Cor. 15:51; 1 Thess. 4:15. Christ is the first risen one among those who are sleeping 1 Cor. 15:20, asleep in *Christ* 1 Cor. 15:8. This is to say that not all will experience the intermediate state between death and resurrection.[239]

[233.] "Kingdom, reign."

[234.] "Victory of Christ."

[235.] Deleted: "[v. 36]."

[236.] This sentence is an addition in the margin. The Greek words—Luther's translation: "(made) alive from the dead"—are underlined with pencil in Bonhoeffer's Greek text.

[237.] Here the text ends on the partially written third page of the folded paper. The linen paper is folded around a plain sheet that is also folded to a DIN A5–size page, the contents of which follow.

[238.] "To sleep."

[239.] This sentence is written in the margin next to the following deleted passage: "After death, immediately into paradise (Luke 23:43; Luke 16:19–31)."

What happens immediately after death to those who have departed into sleep?

Luke 23:43 in paradise with Christ

Acts 7:59 Jesus receives the spirit; (the body sleeps)

Phil. 1:23–24 to be with Jesus

Rev. 6:9ff. the souls of the martyrs wait before the altar for the Last Judgment

Luke 16:19ff. poor Lazarus is carried away by the angels to be with Abraham

2 Cor. 5:1ff. 8!! to be with Christ outside the body

The spirit (soul) is sheltered in Christ while the body is asleep. To be sleeping is the state of rest [(] but at the same time participation in God's good works on earth, hence not idleness (Rev. 6; 2 Cor. 5:9) [)][240] of peace, nothing new happens, the time of decision is past, that which exists previously is kept (Wisdom 3:1ff. "the souls of the righteous . . ."). Paradise = thus blessedness, community with Christ. "To be home" in paradise "*with Christ*" (2 Cor. 5:8), to be sheltered (Luke 16),[241] *waiting* for the Last Judgment (Rev. 6:9).

The *godless*? In the New Testament, "to sleep" is not mentioned in this respect. They have no rest (Luke 16); they suffer torment and cannot return, no conversion. ὠδῖνας—woes of death that Christ suffers for the godless.[242]

360 Is it possible to conceive of *body and soul* in the New Testament as being separate?

Rev. 6:9; 20:4

Matt. 10:28 ψυχή and σῶμα.[243] ψυχή cannot be killed.

Matt. 16:26?[244]

Resurrection of the Body:

1. the miracles of the resurrection Luke 7:11; Mark 5:23–24; John 11
2. the empty tomb of Jesus
3. from the tombs Matt. 27:52–53; John 5:28; 1 Cor. 15:35ff.

[240.] "But at the same time . . ." is an addition in the margin; there is no mark to indicate where to insert it. Cf. Rev. 6:9–11.

[241.] Cf. v. 23 (Lazarus with Abraham).

[242.] The sentence regarding "woes" is added in the margin.

[243.] "Soul" and "body."

[244.] After this point there is a horizontal line across the page.

There is no purgatory after death. 1 Cor. 3

There is still a certain connection between the dead and life [the living], 1 Sam. 28

Christ's Descent into Hell

1 Pet. 3:18ff.; 4:4–6 suffering is grace. The sufferings of Christ are a sermon to the generations in the days of Noah. Which one? Descent into hell after being brought to life "in the spirit." Who are the dead? Has the gospel been preached to them before their death or only as dead ones? The preaching of the gospel.

Rom. 10:7

Eph. 4:8–10. He has received power over everything through his death. The triumphal procession.

There is no information regarding the state of the dead, but information only regarding *the grace* and *righteousness of God* that acts on them; hence, no occultism, no Gnosticism.[245]

The One-Thousand-Year Kingdom[246]

Sign of the end, catastrophes, conversion of the pagans, Jews, Antichrist, Parousia, resurrection of believers ("first resurrection"), *millennium*.

Rev. 20:1–6; 1 Cor. 15:23–24 361

1. Christ will rule on earth.

2. The right and victory of the church-community will be made manifest on earth.

3. A time of grace for all peoples has begun under the governance of Christ and the believers.

4. Satan's right over the earth and humankind is taken from him.

5. The church-community will be strengthened for the final struggle.

Matt. 16:28; Luke 23:42 Christ comes again *himself* "in" *his kingdom* 2 Tim. 4:1. The lordship of believers with Christ: 2 Tim. 2:12; Luke 22:30. "Resurrection of the righteous" Luke 14:14; Matt. 24:31; 1 Thess. 4:16; 2 Thess. 1:7ff.? 1 Cor. 15:23, 52?

[245.] On the following fourth page of the double sheet, Bonhoeffer initially wrote three lines in pencil: "What God does is not revealed to us! *Peace.* Without *contours.*" Later he crossed through these lines in ink that obscures the penciled writing.

[246.] [The German title of this section, *Das 1000jährige Reich*, is striking, both because it uses the same wording of the Nazi claim that Hitler's rise to power marked the beginning of a "thousand-year Reich" for Germany, and because it concludes with Bonhoeffer's refutation of Paul Althaus's eschatological perspective on this history as "unbiblical." (Althaus became a theological apologist for National Socialism.)—VB]

1. The Reformation's rejection[247] of chiliasm included the Anabaptists' attempt to establish the kingdom themselves. But this rejection is worded too generally (CA XVII).[248]

2. The attempt to find the one-thousand-year kingdom in the history of the church (since Constantine, Charlemagne, etc.) fails because of the preceding *resurrection*.

3. Althaus's critique is a necessary consequence that stems from his abolishing the notion of eschatology at the end of history, but it is unbiblical.[249]

The dying of persons mentioned in the New Testament[250]

Simeon Luke 2:29

Stephen Acts 7:56ff.

Ananias and Sapphira Acts 5:6. James Acts 12:2

Judas Matt. 27:5; Acts 1[251] (cf. Abimelech J[udges] 9:54; Saul 1 Sam. 31:4; Ahithophel 2 Sam. 17:23; Zimri 1 Kings 16:18; Ptolemy 2 Macc. [Maccabees] 10:13)

Herod Agrippa Acts 12:23

John the Baptist Matt. 14[:1–12]

362 The two criminals Luke 23:34–35, 42

suddenly, terribly, violently as an example[252]

to struggle to find death (Jer. . . .)[253] Sir. 40.

Death from outside[254]

Death as the end [(] never naturalistically [)],[255] as the *power* over me, being at the mercy of. Cutter, sting.

[247.] Deleted "solely."

[248.] Augsburg Confession, Article 17 (*Book of Concord*, 48).

[249.] In his dissertation Bonhoeffer dealt with Paul Althaus's eschatological conception, "Die letzten Dinge" (The Last Things), the third edition of which was published in 1926; see *DBWE* 1:282–89.

[250.] The writing on the fourth page of the linen double sheet begins here.

[251.] The reference to Acts 1 (v. 18) is added in pencil.

[252.] This line is written in pencil.

[253.] Cf. Wis. 1:16: "ungodly men . . . struggled to find death" [NRSV translation revised—VB]. The expression "struggle to find death" is cited in Bonhoeffer's 1943 drama fragment in *DBWE* 7:58.

[254.] In his letter of September 20, 1939, to the Finkewalde brothers, Bonhoeffer wrote about "death from outside" and "death within us." See 1/160, p. 276.

[255.] "Never naturalistically" is added above the line without an indication of where to insert it.

Sudden death [(] being dead Luke 12 [)].[256] Claudius,[257] Luther, (Hofmannsthal)[258]

Death as the question about life, as *judgment*, as the question about sin unique, irreversible (no transmigration of souls)

Death as the *never-ending*, not as nonexistence

Death from within

Forgiveness of sin, *death* of the I, dying in the love for Christ and for all human beings.[259]

Death as a friend, With peace and joy.[260] Redemption, reconciliation with Christ, bitter and sweet.

Christ. Simeon, the criminal, Stephen.

Death[261]

natural death
spiritual death Eph. 2:1; Rom. 6:11; Luke 15:24
eternal death Rev. 20:6, 14; 2:11; 21:8 363
death is the penalty for sin Rom. 5:12; 6:23
death is the enemy 1 Cor. 15
death personified Rev. 9:6; 6:8
death is the boundary Luke 12:35ff.; Mark 13:33: John 9:4

[256.] "Being dead" (uncertain transcription) and "Luke 12" (cf. v. 20) are added above the line.

[257.] See, for example, Matthias Claudius's poem "Der Mensch" (The Human Being) in the fourth section of *Wandsbecker Boten* (1783). Bonhoeffer cites this poem in a manuscript of his "Ethics" in 1943 (*DBWE* 6:383–84).

[258.] Cf. Hugo von Hofmannsthal's "Jedermann" (Everyman) (1911).

[259.] Cf. Bonhoeffer's letter of September 20, 1939, to the Finkenwalde brothers, 1/160.

[260.] Luther's hymn on dying (1524): "Mit Fried und Freud ich fahr dahin," in *EG*, 519. [The English translation is "In peace and joy I now depart," in *Lutheran Hymnal*, 137.—VB]

[261.] Heading on one of the two sheets in *NL*, A 55,2; both written in pencil.

Death[262]

θάνατος ἐχθρός[263] 1 Cor. 15:26; Rev. 20:14 personified Rev. 6:8
mortal Acts 14:15; Rom. 6:12; 8:11; 1 Cor. 15:53; 2 Cor. 4:11
θάνατος came into the world through Adam's sin Heb. 9:27; John 8:21, 24; 1 Tim. 5:6; Col. 2:13; James 1:15; Eph. 2:1, 5
through the law Rom. 7:10, 13, 24; 8:2, 6; Gal. 2:19 (Rom. 5:12, 14, 17, 21) 1 Cor. 15:21–22; Rom. 1:32; 6:16, 21, 23
indeed, for all human beings ἐφ' ᾧ πάντες[264]
sadness of the world 2 Cor. 7:10, flesh Rom. 8:13
universality of death but Matt. 16:28 *par.*[265]
shadow of death Luke 1:79; Matt. 4:16
the pain of death Acts 2:24[266]

Not dying Matt. 16:28 par. John 21:23; John 5:24; 8:51, 52
death in baptism *Rom. 6:3, 4, 5, 9. The body is dead* Rom. 8:10
sting of death 1 Cor. 15:55
redeemed from death 2 Cor. 1:10. Martyrs 2 Cor. 11:23
The daily death[267] 2 Cor. 4:10, 11, 12; 1 Cor. 15:31, 36; 2 Cor. 6:9
Similar to the death of Jesus Phil. 3:10
death's power is broken 2 Tim. 1:10; Rom. 6:9; Heb. 2:14–15
sin unto death 1 John 5:17
364 the "other" death Rev. 2:11; 20:6, 13, 14; 21:8
to seek death Rev. 9:6

Old Testament
Death as fulfillment and end: Gen. 15:15; 25:8; Job 42:17
Death as frightening experience 2 Sam. 3:33; 14:14 et passim (2 Sam. 21:10)
Death as distance from God Isa. 38:18; Ps. 88:12; 6:6

[262.] Heading on the other of the two sheets in *NL*, A 55:2, both written in pencil. The first lines are extended by many later additions.

[263.] "Death [as] enemy."

[264.] Rom. 5:12; Luther's translation is "since they all (have sinned)."

[265.] The parallel references are Mark 9:1; Luke 9:27.

[266.] The following line is crossed out in ink: "to struggle with death Luke 22:44."

[267.] Cf. Bonhoeffer's letter of September 20, 1939, to the Finkenwalde brothers: "We die this death [in us] daily"; see 1/160, p. 276. *Discipleship* contains many references to this "daily dying" (see the *DBWE* 4 index of subjects [death, daily]) and to death in baptism.

2.9 Notes on the Concept of "Gratitude"[268]

Gratitude

(Heim: Jesus's dealing with those who doubt. First the deed, then a reproach and encouragement.)[269]

Old Testament

Gratitude. Ps. 50:14, 23 to offer thanks to God

Thanks as a way to salvation   *to forget* God—whoever offers thanks . . . show the salvation of God

Thanks more than an offering   69:31—thanks better than offerings[270]

Gratitude of the *redeemed*   107:1–3 give thanks to the Lord—this is how those who are *redeemed* through the Lord should speak; cf. 116:17 you have torn my bonds[271]

Gratitude and *proclamation*   107:22; 116:17; 106:2; 105:1; 108:4; 9:2

Gratitude and *Juda*(s)   Gen. 29:35. The *kiss of Judas.*

Gratitude and *remembrance*   Deut. 32:6–7 Is this how you give thanks . . . ? Remember . . .

Thanksgiving in the morning and evening through the Levites   1 Chr. 23:30. *At midnight* Ps. 119:62.

Gratitude of the *living*, and not the dead   Ps. 6:6; 30:10; 88:11 365

Gratitude for the sake of *God's righteousness*   Ps. 7:18

Gratitude in the *gates of God*   Ps. 100:4

Gratitude for *humiliation*   118:21   cf. Isa. 12:1

[268.] *NL*, A 55,13 (1+2); handwritten on two sheets of DIN A4 paper, numbered by Bonhoeffer as "1.)" and "2)"; written in pencil and ink; previously unpublished. Cf. also his July 1940 theological letter "On Gratitude among Christians" (*DBWE* 16:489–92).

[269.] Cf. Karl Heim, *God Transcendent*, vol. 2, section 20: "Das Zeugnis von der Gottesoffenbarung in Christus" (The Testimony of God's Revelation in Christ).

[270.] See v. 31.

[271.] See v. 16.

Thanksgiving even before the sun rises Wis. 16:28. The *hope* of the *ungrateful* may vanish.[272]

Continual thanksgiving. Tob[ias] 2:13; 4:20 For three hours 12:22.[273]

New Testament See page 2.

Thomas à Kempis[:] "Be grateful, then, for even the least gift and you will be worthy of receiving greater ones," page 159.[274] This means to be thankful even [for] the *weak beginnings* of faith and not always to desire in discontent the greater things. It is easy to close off God's path to greater gifts of grace because of our ingratitude for small things, for the beginning.

Larochefoucauld: Gratitude is often nothing more than the expressed willingness to accept further acts of kindness.

Rousseau: Wherever the act of kindness is done only from selfish motives, the reproach of ingratitude is just as right as when a fisher reproaches the fish because it only took the bait and did not also swallow the hook (Paulsen *Ethics* II 193–94).[275]

Nietzsche: "Gratitude . . . is a milder form of revenge"—"through his good deed, his benefactor has, as it were, violated the powerful man's
366 sphere and penetrated it . . ." (*Human—All Too Human* I 44 [page 66 (edition) Kröner]).[276]

Calvin: "We never lack reason and occasion for praise and thanksgiving" (III.20).[277]

All the gifts of God are to be *transformed* into *thanksgiving*! They are given for this purpose. In thanksgiving we give back to God what he gave us. In this

[272.] See v. 29. Bonhoeffer marked both verses (Wis. 16:28–29) in his Bible (Luther translation) in pencil. He also marked other verses from Wisdom that are mentioned in this manuscript.

[273.] [This is a reference to Luther, who was said to have prayed three hours each day. Cf. *DBWE* 9:267, ed. note 43. The editor thanks Ilse Tödt for this reference.—VB]

[274.] Thomas à Kempis, *Imitation of Christ*, 62. [Bonhoeffer cites here from his 1904 edition.—VB] Bonhoeffer cites several passages from *The Imitation of Christ*, by Thomas à Kempis, in his book *Life Together* (cf. *DBWE* 5:96 and 98, as well as the references on pp. 81, 85, and 89).

[275.] Bonhoeffer quotes these aphorisms by François VI, Duke La Rochefoucauld, and Jean-Jacques Rousseau from Paulsen's *System der Ethik* 2:193–94.

[276.] Bonhoeffer quotes from *Menschliches, allzumenschliches* [in Nietzsche's *Werke*, published by C. G. Naumann in 1899; "Kröner" refers to the name of publisher after 1910. The translation here is from *Human—All Too Human*, 46—VB].

[277.] John Calvin, *Institutes*, book 3, 888.

sense we desire help so that gratitude to God may be increased. Ps. 106:47; Hos. 14:2 "the fruit of our lips" Ps. 102:18-19, 22; Isa. 38:20; Jonah 2:10.

The "*new* song" Ps. 40:4 and more often

Goethe: "In the clear depths of our soul there springs an impulse to give ourselves *freely, in gratitude,* to something higher, purer, and unknown, and thus to unriddle the eternal Unnamed: this we call piety." (Elegy 1823)[278]

Gratitude

New Testament

Luke 17:11 the thankful *Samaritan.* Only to him: your faith has saved you. The turning back to Jesus. Give God the honor.

Luke 18:11 thanksgiving of the Pharisee. False thanksgiving (humility)

Matt. 14:19 par., *Jesus's* thanksgiving over the bread

Rom. 1:8 gratitude of the *Apostle*—the beginning of the letters 1 Cor. 1:4; 1 Tim. 1:12; 2 Tim. 1:3; Phil. 1:3; Col. 1:3; Philm. 4; (Rom. *14:6*?); Rom. 16:4!

The doxologies. Everything culminates in thanksgiving.

Thanksgiving "through Jesus Christ" Rom. 7:25; 1:8

For what do we give thanks? "that your faith becomes known throughout the world" Rom. 1:8

"that you, having once been slaves of sin, have become obedient" Rom. 6:17. Even for the sinful past! The "yes" to the past because of the new present!

"for you, for God's grace that has been given you in Christ Jesus" 1 Cor. 367
1:4

"thanks be to God, who in Christ always leads us in triumphal procession" (2 Cor. 2:4)[279]

The collection leads to "many thanksgivings to God" 2 Cor. 9:12

"for you, faith, love" Eph. 1:16; Col. 1:3

"for your community in the gospel" Phil. 1:3;[280] 1 Thess. 1:2; 2 Thess. 1:3; Philm. 4

[278.] [Translation from *Goethe: Selected Verse,* 313.—VB] Bonhoeffer wrote this citation from Goethe's 1823 "Marienbad Elegy" in ink; everything preceding it is written in pencil. End of sheet "1.)"; what follows on sheet "2)" is written alternately in ink and pencil.

[279.] Not v. 4, but 2 Cor. 2:14.

[280.] [This should be Phil. 1:5.—VB]

2 Cor. 4:15 that grace abundant may increase thanksgiving, to the glory of God.[281]

Eph. 5:20 give thanks to God all the time, for everything, in the name of Jesus Christ.

Col. 1:12 give thanks with joy . . . empowered to share in the inheritance in the light.[282]

2 Cor. 9:11 to give in sincerity,[283] which will produce thanksgiving (accusative) to God.

Phil. 4:6 in everything let your requests . . . with thanksgiving be made known before God. Thanksgiving is the foundation for all prayer.[284]

Col. 4:2 be wakeful in prayer, with *thanksgiving.*[285]

1 Tim. 2:1 . . . thanksgiving for all human beings . . .

4:3–4 . . . to receive with thanksgiving

διὰ Ἰησοῦ Χριστοῦ[286] Rom. 1:8

Rom. 1:21 to know God through thanksgiving

(Luke 17. To honor Jesus through thanksgiving, stubbornness in ungratefulness [Judas!])

1 Tim. 4:3; 1 Cor. 10:30 transformation of all gifts in thanksgiving. The goal of all divine gifts is *thanksgiving* (doxologies)

Luke 18:9ff. thanksgiving and humility

Luke 17:11ff. thanksgiving and faith; only a thankful person is saved by faith! Salvation

1 Thess. 5:18 thanksgiving in all things (without worry Phil. 4:6)

1 Cor. 1:30 freedom finds its boundaries in the ability to give thanks[287]

εὐχαριστεῖν—*"to give thanks for oneself in Jesus Christ"*

[281.] [NRSV translation altered here to conform to Bonhoeffer's wording.—VB]
[282.] [NRSV translation altered here to conform to Bonhoeffer's wording.—VB]
[283.] [NRSV translation altered here to conform to Bonhoeffer's wording.—VB]
[284.] [NRSV translation altered here to conform to Bonhoeffer's wording.—VB]
[285.] [NRSV translation altered here to conform to Bonhoeffer's wording.—VB]
[286.] "Through Jesus Christ."
[287.] Not "1:30," but 1 Cor. 10:30.

3. Lecture on Marriage, 1939–1940[1] 368

Marriage Consecration[2]

1. Marriage is a worldly matter,[3] various forms, affection, status, rational reasons, polygamy;[4] *concrete* marriage is the creation of God (preservation) [Erhaltung].[5]

2. Marriage is constituted by means of a *mutuus consensus* made known in public.[6] Not *through* the state, but *before* the state.[7]

3. Even the marriage before the civil servant is a marriage commissioned by[8] God. The two enter the church as a married couple. For this reason, the liturgical formula should omit everything that gives the appearance of a repetition of the marriage covenant (the exchange of rings etc.!). [No] making the order of marriage into a sacramental church function through[9] the Word (confusing of—nature—grace!).[10]

4. The consecration[11] of the church wedding has a threefold purpose: proclamation, intercession, blessing.

[1.] *NL*, A 54,4; handwritten; DIN A5 sheet, written in ink on the front, in pencil on the reverse side and in the additional notes; previously unpublished.

[2.] This word is an addition in pencil and is evidently meant to clarify that the church wedding is the consecration of the marriage previously conducted before a civil servant (cf. points 2 and 3).

[3.] In his 1530 treatise "Von Ehesachen" ("On Marriage Matters," in *LW* 46:259–320), Luther characterized marriage as "an external worldly matter . . . like clothing and food, house and property, subject to temporal authority." He also rejected a sacramental understanding of marriage (*LW* 46:265). Cf. also the "Traubüchlein" (Marriage Booklet) in the *Small Catechism* (1529): Wedding and matrimony "are worldly affairs" (Kolb and Wengert, *Book of Concord*, 367).

[4.] The words beginning at "affection" are added in pencil.

[5.] This is a reflection of Bonhoeffer's central concern, from the early 1930s onward, to resist the theological legitimization of the misused term "order of creation" in *völkisch* thinking and to replace it with the term "orders of preservation." "The concept of order of preservation differs from that of order of creation in that historical orders as such do not possess ontological validity as such (*keine Daseins- oder Soseinswertigkeit*) in an absolute sense, but are only preserved by God for the sake of their openness toward the gospel" (1931–32, *DBW* 11:237); cf. *DBWE* 3:139–40. Cf. also Chr. Strohm, *Theologische Ethik im Kampf gegen den Nationalsozialismus*, 36–39.

[6.] "Mutual agreement."

[7.] Cf. the passage written early in 1941 for his *Ethics*: "Marriages are concluded neither *by* the church nor *by* the state . . . [but] only *in the presence of* the state and *in the presence of* the church. . . . This is Lutheran teaching" (*DBWE* 6:205–6).

[8.] Replaces "name" in pencil.

[9.] Uncertain reading.

[10.] Addition in the margin, written in pencil, after [No].

[11.] This word is written in pencil above "church wedding"; cf. ed. note 2 above.

369 5. This can be done only if both partners are Christians. If not, an admonition [Mahnung] for the Christian partner.

6. Proclamation *Text* and *Casus*:[12]

(1) God's "yes" to his creation, to the will of his creatures! Joy.

(2) God's order—not to be alone. Marriage cannot be annulled. Ordered as the one above, the one below.[13] The grace contained in this order.

(3) God's *command* for the married life. Man and woman, to be lord and the subordinate, Col. 3 to live in the order as Christians according to the commandments of God. Love. Forgiveness. To carry one's cross.

(4) The *grace* of community. Marriage may can[14] become church.[15] The covenant of baptism is realized in marriage. The blessing of children.

Mebes[16] John 15:16 *Choice of text*? The order of redemption.

1. As if you still wanted to include him, to choose. *The one who chooses = creator*—life as a gift. His love first.

2. Ready for each other—God laid within you. Sin.

3. How we can live with each other? Fruit,[17] to live as *Christians* in marriage. *Christ between* you.

4. Prayer. *Folding hands together.*[18]

Election in *Jesus* Christ (Jesus says it) here: election = creation, fruit = Christ
the one is the conscience of the other?
from the problematic of sin.[19] Marriage

[12.] "*Text* and *Casus*" are added in pencil. Here Bonhoeffer underscores—as he did during the Finkenwalde period with respect to the pastoral duties documented in *DBW* 14:738–48—the homiletical aspect of official pastoral acts. [The German here, *Kasualien*, refers to such pastoral duties as performing marriages and funerals.—VB]

[13.] *Über- und Unterordnung*; "*Über*" has been added in pencil. [Literally, this means "an order of over- and beneath," phrased differently under point 3 in the text as "lord and the subordinate." Bonhoeffer uses a somewhat similar phrase in *Ethics*, *oben und unten* (above and below), to delineate the realms of authority and responsibility. Cf. *DBWE* 6:23.—VB]

[14.] "May" ("can" is written above "may," both words in pencil) replaces "is to."

[15.] On Bonhoeffer's understanding of marriage, which he sees in an eschatological perspective as becoming church, see *DBWE* 1:226 and 282–89 [as well as *DBWE* 3:100—VB].

[16.] Max Mebes was in Sigurdshof in 1939–40. Here—as well as with Karl-Heinz Probsthain, mentioned below—we have Bonhoeffer's notes, taken when the candidates presented their thoughts on the *casus* of the "marriage sermon." The question marks evidently indicate Bonhoeffer's questions concerning the presentations.

[17.] Cf. John 15:16: "choose . . . so that . . . you should bear fruit."

[18.] The following is bracketed and written below the word "fruit" next to "3. . . ."

[19.] Uncertain reading.

Marriage is here essentially as? community between the two, not so much an order. *Subordination.* House—*church.*

? *not the one to be the lord over the other.*

Probsthain[20] Ps. 84:6 370

1. Praise and thanksgiving. Education—faith. Joy.
2. As a warning and a blessing—.

?? || you *vow* fidelity to each other, and discipleship to God. Isa. 40[21] . . . Phil. 4:13.

Becoming engaged.

[20.] Karl-Heinz Probsthain was in Sigurdshof in 1939–40.

[21.] Possibly a reference to Isa. 40:31.

B. Lectures and Essays

371 **4. Bible Study on Temptation, June 20–25, 1938**[1]

Do not lead us into temptation,
but deliver us from evil.[2]

I.[3] 1. The natural human being and the ethical human being cannot understand this prayer. The natural human being seeks the testing of his strength in adventure, struggle, and the encounter with the enemy. This is life. "If you never risk your life, you can never win life."[4] Only life that is endangered[5] to the point of death is won. This is the knowledge of the

[1.] *NL*, 58,1 (2); handwritten; published as a two-part volume in 1968 as *Schöpfung und Fall—Versuchung* (Creation and Fall—Temptation); also as a separate volume in 1953 as *Versuchung* (Temptation) and *Predigten—Auslegungen—Meditationen* [*Sermons—Interpretations—Meditations*], 2:247–85. Footnotes are in *NL*, B 9,7: stenographic notes taken by Erich Klapproth, "June 21, 1938 Bonhoeffer: The concept of πειρασμός in the New Testament and the petition: Do not lead us into temptation" (Klapproth). Bonhoeffer gave this Bible study on Matt. 6:13a, the sixth petition in the Lord's Prayer, during a retreat in Zingst, June 20–25, 1938 (see *DB-ER*, 518 and 593, for the participants of all five Finkenwalde courses. The concrete background of Bonhoeffer's urgent exhortation to resist, in a narrower sense, "temptations," was the offer made by the regional church consistories to "legalize" the illegal theologians of the Confessing Church. In a wider sense, there were temptations to succumb to the National Socialist ideology with its pseudo-messianic "Führer" cult and its Germanic myths of struggle and redemption. There are also twenty-four extant pages (according to the archival pagination) of Bonhoeffer's handwritten notes and preliminary drafts, *NL*, A 58,1 (1), especially on the biblical concepts of ὑπομονή ("patience," "steadfastness") and πειρασμός ("testing," "temptation"); cf. above 2/2.3. and 2/2.2.

[2.] Matt. 6:13 [NRSV: "And do not bring us to the time of trial, but rescue us from the evil one"—VB]. Another alternative beginning of the text, deleted, is found later in this manuscript; see ed. note 50 on point "III.5"

[3.] This Roman numeral—as also "II" below etc.—is added in the margin with pencil. Klapproth's numbering—"1)," "2)," "3)," [IV] "c)." "V."—corresponds to Bonhoeffer's Roman numerals.

natural human being. The ethical human being also knows that human insights become true and convincing only when tested and proven, that what is good can only live from what is evil, and that the good person would no longer be good without what is evil. In this sense the ethical person challenges evil, praying daily: lead me into temptation in order that [I] may 372
prove the power of goodness in myself.[6]

If temptation truly were how the natural and the ethical human being think of it, namely, the testing of one's own strength—be it vital or ethical or even *Christian* strength—against opposition, the enemy, then this prayer of Christians would make no sense. For it is certainly not a uniquely Christian insight, but also one of the world, that life is won only from death, and good only from evil. But all of this has nothing to do with the temptation Jesus is speaking about. It does not in any way touch upon the reality that is meant here. The temptation of which the entire Holy Scripture speaks does not at all concern the probation of my own strength. For the nature of biblical temptation is such that here—to my own alarm and without being able to do anything about it—all my strengths are turned against me. Indeed, truly *all* my strengths, even my good and pious strengths [(] strengths of faith [)][7] have fallen into the hands of the enemy power and are now enlisted in the fight against me. But even before I can test my strength, I am already robbed of my strength. "My heart throbs, my strength fails me; as for the light of my eyes—it also has gone from me" Ps. 38:11.[8] This is the decisive fact in the temptation of a Christian, namely, that one is being *forsaken*, forsaken by all his strengths, indeed attacked by them, forsaken by all human beings, forsaken by God himself. The heart trembles and is engulfed by total darkness.[9] The self is nothing. The enemy is everything.[10]
God has taken his hand away, "has pulled away his hand" (CA XIX),[11] has 373
forsaken the Christian for a brief moment (Isa. 54:7). The human being is

[4.] The final chorus in Schiller's drama *Wallensteins Lager* (Wallenstein's Camp) (1798), scene 11.

[5.] Deleted "submerged into death."

[6.] Cf. Bonhoeffer's interpretation of Gen. 2:8–17 in *DBWE* 3:80–93, esp. 88ff. Concerning the person in the "situation of 'ethical conflict,'" cf. *DBWE* 4:71–76 (the citation is from p. 71).

[7.] The penciled addition "strengths of faith," written above the line, was apparently meant to replace the words "good and pious strengths."

[8.] [Ps. 38:10 NRSV.—VB] The citation from Psalm 38 replaces: "the strength of the recognition of my sins rises against me, the strength of my faith in forgiveness by grace, given into the hand of the enemy, becomes . . ."

[9.] Replaces: "A Christian who is tempted is engulfed in nothingness."

[10.] Deleted: "in this nothingness."

[11.] The citation from *The Book of Concord* is an addition in pencil.

alone in temptation. There is no support. For a brief moment, the devil has his way. But how should a forsaken person encounter the devil? How can one resist him? It is the prince of this world[12] who stands here against the Christian. The hour of apostasy, of irrevocable, eternal fall, has arrived. For who will free us again from the claws of Satan?

A defeat shows vital and ethical human beings that their strength must increase if they are to pass the test. Because of this a defeat is never irreversible. The Christian knows that his strength will desert him each time in the hour of temptation. Therefore, temptation for him is the dark hour that may prove *irrevocable.* For this reason, a Christian does not seek the perseverance of his own strength but prays: *do not lead us into temptation.* In a biblical sense, then, *temptation* does *not* mean: *testing of strength,* but the loss of all strength, *the defenseless deliverance into Satan's hands.*[13]

2. Temptation is a concrete event, a sudden deviation from the normal course of life. For the vital human being, all of life is a struggle, and for the ethicist *every* hour is a time of temptation. A Christian knows of hours of temptation,[14] which are distinct from the hours of gracious protection, guarded from temptation, just as the devil is distinct from God. The sentence that every moment of life is a time of decision does not make sense as an abstraction to the Christian.[15] A Christian can view life not on principle but only from the perspective of the living God. But God, who gives
374 both day and night, also gives times of comfort after times of thirst; God gives storms and a peaceful journey; God gives times of worry and anxiety and times of joy. "Weeping may linger for the night, but joy comes with the morning" Ps. 30:6.[16] "For everything there is a season, and a time for every matter under heaven: a time to be born, and a time to die; a time to plant, and a time to pluck up what is planted; a time to kill, and a time to heal; a time to break down, and a time to build up; a time to weep, and a time to

[12.] Cf. John 12:31 and other references.

[13.] Klapproth: ". . . into darkness!" See also *DBWE* 4:157–58.

[14.] Replaces "being assailed."

[15.] In his 1930 inaugural lecture in Berlin (*DBWE* 10, 2/7), Bonhoeffer had characterized human existence according to Heidegger's understanding in *Being and Time* (1927) with the sentence that "every moment is a decision for the possibility of authenticity and inauthenticity" (*DBWE* 10:396). See also the more substantial discussion in *DBWE* 2, esp. 67–73.

[16.] [Ps. 30:5 NRSV.—VB] Bonhoeffer had noted this reference in 1935 for his biblical meditation on "the morning"; see *DBW* 14:871. The citation appears in *Life Together*, written in autumn 1938; see *DBWE* 5:112.

[17.] On Bonhoeffer's lifelong insistence on concrete speech, cf. the use of the phrase "here and now" throughout Feil, *Theology of Dietrich Bonhoeffer.*

laugh. . . . He has made everything suitable for its time" (Eccl. 3:1–4, 11). The Christian's concern is not life as such but how God is dealing with me now.[17] God casts me away and he welcomes me back again, he destroys my work and he rebuilds it. "I form light and create darkness, I make weal and create woe; I the Lord do all these things" (Isa. 45:7).

So the Christian lives by God's appointed times and not from his own notion of life. The Christian does not claim to live continually in temptation or continually in probation, but one prays in the time of safekeeping that God will ward off the time of temptation.

Temptation comes suddenly over the pious. "They shoot suddenly and without fear" (Ps. 64:5)[18] in the hour when one expects it the least. "For no one can anticipate the time of disaster . . . so mortals are snared at a time of calamity, when it suddenly falls upon them" (Eccl. 9:12) ("Suddenly the wrath of the Lord will come upon you, and at the time of punishment you will perish" Sir. 5:9).[19] Herein the Christian recognizes Satan's cunning. Suddenly doubt is sown in the heart; suddenly everything is so uncertain; what I do so senseless; suddenly past sins become alive in me again as if they had happened today, and they torture and accuse me. Suddenly my whole heart is filled with the deepest sadness about myself, about the world, about God's powerlessness over me.[20] Suddenly the weariness with life tempts
me to commit a terrible sin,[21] suddenly evil lust awakes, and suddenly the 375
cross comes over me, and I begin to waver. This is the hour of temptation, of being helplessly delivered into darkness,[22] to Satan.

3. But: Is not the coming of the hour of temptation inevitable? Is it for this reason not permitted to pray in this way? Should we not pray far more that we will be given strength to overcome in the hour of temptation, which indeed is bound to come? By such thinking one pretends to know more about temptation[23] than Christ and wants to be more pious[24] than he who experienced the most grievous temptation. "Does temptation not have to come?" Yes, but why? Does God have to deliver his own to Satan? Does he have to lead them to the edge of the abyss? Does God have to grant such

[18.] [Ps. 64:4 NRSV.—VB]

[19.] [Sir. 5:7 NRSV.—VB]

[20.] [The theme of sadness was a recurring and a personal issue with which Bonhoeffer struggled throughout his life. See, for example, p. 411 below about *acedia*; see also *DBWE* 7:38, *DBWE* 9:280 and 198, and *DBWE* 8:70 and 180.—VB]

[21.] Substitute for "to commit a sin unto death."

[22.] "Darkness," is written in the margin with pencil.

[23.] Replaces "wishes to be more intelligent."

[24.] Replaces "more experienced."

power to Satan? Who are we that we could be entitled to say that temptation *must* come? Do we sit on the council of God? And even if temptation must come—because of an ineffable *divine* must—then Christ, the most tempted of all, summons us to pray against this divine must. We are not to yield to temptation stoically and in resignation, but to flee from that dark must, in which God allows the devil's will, to the revealed divine freedom, in which the devil is trod under God's feet, imploring: Do *not* lead us into temptation!

II. 4. After these first preliminary questions, we now begin tentatively to approach the subject of the prayer itself. The one who teaches the disciples to pray in this way is Jesus Christ, who alone must know what temptation means. And because he does know, he wants his disciples to pray: do not lead us into temptation. We can understand what temptation means for us solely by the *temptation of Jesus.*[25]

Holy Scripture does not tell us many stories of human temptations and
376 how they were overcome, as a devotional book would do. Strictly speaking, it reports *only two stories of temptation,* the temptation *of the first human beings and the temptation of Jesus Christ,* that is, the temptation that led to the fall of humankind and the temptation that led to the fall of Satan.[26] Everything else that happened in terms of human temptations must be understood in relation to these two stories of temptation. We are either tempted *in Adam,* or we are tempted *in Christ.* Either Adam in us is tempted, then we are the ones who fall, or Christ in us is tempted, then Satan must fall.

The temptation of the first human beings puts before us the riddle of the tempter in paradise. This easily leads us to turn our eyes back to that event, which should hold for us the mystery of the unrevealed, namely, the origin of the tempter.[27] We learn only three things from this event in paradise: (1) that the tempter is always already present *where there is innocence.* Indeed, the tempter is in any case only present where there is innocence; for where there is guilt, he has already won the power.[28]

[25.] On "the temptation of Jesus Christ," see the two devotions for students that Bonhoeffer presented at the Technical College in Berlin in February 1932 (date somewhat uncertain), *DBW* 11, 3/3.

[26.] On "the temptation of the first human beings," see the 1932–33 lecture "Creation and Fall," *DBWE* 3:103–20.

[27.] Replaces "Our view is thereby immediately directed to the coming of God's kingdom in which there will be no longer any temptation 'because the accuser has been rejected.'"

[28.] Deleted: "Innocence, however, is where a human being holds on to God's word and commandment with a pure and undivided heart. How, then, can the tempter approach the innocent one?" Cf. below, point 3.

(2) It is the entirely unmediated appearance of the tempter in the voice of the serpent in paradise, the presence of Satan in paradise, for which there is no reason or justification (not even through a metaphysics of Lucifer),[29] which constitutes the tempter's essence as such. It is an impenetrable, contingent suddenness of which we spoke before. The voice of the tempter does not come from what I know to be the abyss of hell; rather, it completely hides its origin; it is suddenly beside me and speaks to me. In paradise it is the serpent, obviously also a creature of God, through whom
the tempter speaks to Eve. Thus the origin of brimstone and fire remains 377
completely invisible. *The denial of the origin belongs to the essence of the tempter.*

(3) But in order to gain access to innocence, the origin must be denied to the very end. For innocence means to hold on to the word of God with a pure, undivided heart. Thus the tempter must introduce himself in the name of God. He has God's word at his disposal and becomes its interpreter. "Did God say?"[30]—Did you understand God, the Lord, here correctly? Is there not some other spirit behind God's words?[31] We cannot imagine the unspeakable anxiety the first human beings must have felt in facing such a possibility. Innocence confronts the abyss of unknown guilt; faith confronts the abyss of unknown doubt; life confronts the abyss of unknown death. This anxiety of innocence, which the devil wants to rob of its only power, the word of God, is the hour of temptation. It is no longer an issue of mustering courage for the struggle or a matter of a free decision for good or evil—the aforementioned ethical notion of temptation. Quite to the contrary, Adam is defenselessly at the mercy of the tempter. He lacks any insight, strength, or knowledge that might have enabled him to struggle with his enemy. He is completely forsaken. The abyss has opened up beneath him. Only one thing remains: in the midst of this abyss, he is held by God's hand, by God's word. Thus Adam can only close his eyes and let himself be held and borne by the grace of God in the hour of temptation. But Adam falls. "Did God say?"—Adam, and all humankind with him, tumbles into the abyss of this question. Ever since Adam was expelled from paradise, every human being is born with this question, sown by Satan in Adam's heart. This is the primordial question of all *flesh*: "Did God say?" This question causes all flesh to fall. *Adam's temptation entails death and rejection for all flesh.*

[29.] Replaces "Satan." Here, as already in *Creation and Fall*, Bonhoeffer rejects the traditional dogmatic view that the fall of angels preceded the fall of humanity. Cf. *DBWE* 3:105, ed. note 8.

[30.] Gen. 3:1.

[31.] Deleted: "This question: "Did God say?"—causes Adam to fall and with him all his descendants."

378 *The Son of God, Jesus Christ, our Savior, came to earth, however, in the flesh of sin.* All covetousness and all the fear of the flesh, all the flesh's condemnation by and distance from God was also in him. "He has been tempted in every respect as we are—yet without sin" (Heb. 4:15).[32] If he wanted to help the human being in the flesh, he had to completely take upon himself the flesh's susceptibility to temptation. Even Jesus Christ κατὰ σάρκα[33] was born with the question: Did God say?—yet without sin.

The temptation of Christ was more difficult, inexpressibly more difficult than the temptation of Adam, for Adam bore nothing in himself that could have given the tempter any right or power over him.[34] But Christ bore with him the entire burden of the flesh under the curse and condemnation, and yet his temptation was intended to obtain future help and salvation for all flesh that was to be tempted.

The Gospel reports that Jesus was led into the desert by the Spirit so that he would be tempted by the devil (Matt. 4:1). Thus the beginning of temptation is not that the Father arms the Son with all the strength and weapons he will need to endure in the struggle, but the Spirit leads Jesus into the desert, to be alone, to be forsaken. God takes from his Son all human and every creaturely help. The hour of temptation must find Jesus weak, lonely, and hungry. God leaves the human being alone in temptation. Thus Abraham had to be alone on the mountain Moriah.[35] Indeed, God himself forsakes the human being before temptation. Only in this sense may we understand 2 Chr. 32:31: God forsakes Hezekiah, in order to tempt him; as well as the psalmists who repeatedly call out: God, do not forsake us (Pss. 38:22; 71:9, 18; 119:8). "Do not hide your face from me. . . . Do not cast me off, do not forsake me, O God of my salvation" (Ps. 27:9). All human, ethical, and religious thinking cannot fathom this: that God is not revealed in temptation as the gracious and near God, the one who gives us the gifts of the Spirit, but he forsakes us, he is far away from us, we are in the desert. (Later we will have more to say about this.)

379 In contrast to Adam's temptation and all other human temptations, Jesus here is approached by the *tempter himself* (Matt. 4:3). While otherwise he uses created beings, here he himself must engage in the struggle. Thus it is clear that in the temptation of Jesus, everything is at stake. In this instance, the tempter's essence must consist in the most complete denial of the ori-

---

[32.] [The NRSV has "tested," but Bonhoeffer's German here is *versucht*, or "tempted."—VB]

[33.] "According to the flesh"; see Klapproth and his reference to Heb. 1:5.

[34.] Klapproth: ". . . that would have given Satan a claim [*Anrecht*]."

[35.] See Gen. 22.

gin. It may be with reference to Satan's denial of the origin in the temptation of Jesus that Paul said: even Satan disguises himself as an angel of light (2 Cor. 11:14). We should take this to mean not that Jesus did not recognize Satan but that Satan was so tempting because through this he wanted to bring Jesus to the fall.

Jesus fasted for forty days in the wilderness, and he was hungry. Then the tempter approached him. The tempter begins with the acknowledgment of Jesus as the Son of God. While he does not say: You are the Son of God—that he cannot say!—but he says: if you are the Son of God, speak now as the one who suffers *hunger* so that these stones are turned into bread. Satan tempts Jesus here in the weakness of his human flesh. He wants to pit his divinity[36] against his humanity. He wants to make the flesh rebel against the spirit. Satan knows that flesh does not want to suffer. But why is the Son of God to suffer in the flesh? The intent of this question is clear: if Jesus were to withdraw from the suffering in the flesh through the power of his divinity, then all flesh would be condemned. The path of the Son of God on earth would come to an end. The flesh would belong again to Satan. Jesus's answer with the word of God shows, first, that even the Son of God stands *under God's* word and that he does not have to nor want to have his own right beside this word. Second, Jesus's answer shows that he wants to abide by this *word alone.* Even the *flesh belongs under* God's word, and when it must suffer, then it is true: the human being does not live from bread alone. Jesus has preserved his humanity and his path of suffering in the temptation. The first temptation is the temptation of the flesh.

In the second temptation, Satan begins as he did in the first one: if you are the Son of God—but now he intensifies the temptation in that he uses
God's word against Jesus. Even Satan can use God's word in his struggle.[37] 380
Jesus is to confirm his divine sonship. Jesus is to demand a sign from God. This is the temptation of Jesus's faith, the temptation of the spirit. If the Son of God is already immersed in the suffering of humankind, then [he] should demand a sign of God's power that can save[38] at any time.[39] Jesus's answer sets God's word against God's word, not in such a way that results in unholy uncertainty, but in a way such that here truth stands against lie. Jesus calls this temptation a tempting of God. He desires to abide alone by the word of his Father; this is sufficient for him. If he were to desire more

[36.] Replaces "divine sonship."

[37.] Replaces "in his mouth."

[38.] Deleted with pencil: "him."

[39.] Klapproth: "If you wish, then, to suffer, ask for a sign of power that can save you at any time. Ask for an experience surmounting faith."

than this word, then he would have given room to his doubt about God. The faith that desires more than the word of God in commandment and promise becomes the *temptation of God.* But to tempt God means to project guilt, unfaithfulness, and a lie into God himself rather than Satan. To tempt God is the gravest spiritual temptation.

In the third instance, Satan approaches in a different manner, without affirmation of divine sonship, without God's word. Now he comes—and this is the alarming thing—in a total and unconcealed demonstration of his power[40] as the prince of this world. Now Satan fights with his very own weapons. There is no longer any concealment, any dissembling. Satan pits his power directly against God's power. Satan risks his all. His gift is great and beautiful and enticing beyond measure, and he demands the gift—worship. He demands the open apostasy from God, which has no justification other than the grandeur and beauty of Satan's kingdom. What is at stake in this temptation is the final apostasy from God, perpetrated in full clarity and awareness, and the submission to Satan. It is the temptation into the sin against the Holy Spirit.[41]

Because here Satan has revealed himself completely, he must here be
381 addressed, refuted, and rejected by Jesus himself: go away from me, Satan.
For it is written: You shall worship God your Lord and serve him alone.

Jesus is tempted in *flesh,* in faith, and in his *divine sonship.* In all three instances there is *one* temptation, namely, to tear Jesus away from the word of God: Satan pits the nature of the flesh against the divine commission. For if Satan gains power over the flesh of Jesus, then Jesus is in his hands. If Jesus does not want to suffer, then he is not the Christ. In Gethsemane we hear again of Jesus's anxiety that his flesh might fall prey to Satan.[42] In the second temptation, Satan leads the human being's spiritual yearning for experience, affirmation, miracles, and visions of all kinds against faith, by which alone the human being can endure before God. If Satan gains power over Jesus's[43] piety and spirituality, then Jesus is in his hands. If Jesus does not abide solely by the word, have faith only, blind faith and obedience, then he is no longer the Christ and Redeemer of humankind, who will find salvation only by faith in the word. Thus Satan has tempted the flesh and spirit of Jesus against the word of God. The third temptation affronts the entire bodily-spiritual existence of the Son of God. "If you do

---

[40.] Replaces "nakedness and unveiled [*Unverhülltheit*]."

[41.] Replaces "Jesus himself later calls the decision that is imminent here the sin against the Holy Spirit." Cf. Mark 3:29; Matt. 12:32; Luke 12:10.

[42.] See Matt. 26:39–44.

[43.] Replaces "the human being's."

not want to be torn apart in your inner life, then give yourself entirely to me—and I shall make you great in this world, in hatred against God and in power against him." In this manner Jesus suffers *the temptation in the flesh, the lofty spiritual temptation*, and finally the *total temptation* as such, and yet in all three instances only the *one* temptation against the word of God.

Even Jesus's temptation is not a heroic struggle of the human being against evil forces, as we gladly and lightly would like to understand it. Even Jesus is robbed of all his own strengths in his temptation; he is left alone; he is forsaken by God and human beings; even he must endure the assault of Satan in anxiety; he is held in complete darkness. Nothing is left for him except the saving, enduring, and uplifting word of God[44] that holds
him,[45] fights, and wins the victory for him. The night of Jesus's last words, 382
"My God, my God, why have you forsaken me?"[46] has begun. This night must follow the hour of this temptation as the ultimate, bodily-spiritual, consummate temptation of the Redeemer. In that Jesus suffers this total abandonment by God and humankind, God's word and judgment are for him. As he succumbs defenselessly and powerlessly to Satan's power, the temptation is overcome. He was tempted as we are—and yet without sin.[47]

Thus, in Jesus's temptation nothing truly remains other than God's word and promise, not in any strength and delight of his own in fighting evil. Rather, God's power and victory alone remain, God who holds me in his word and through this word robs Satan of his power. Temptation can be overcome only through the word of God.

"Then the devil left him"—just as initially God left him, now the devil leaves him—"and suddenly angels came and waited on him."[48] In the garden of Gethsemane, too, "an angel from heaven appeared and gave him strength" (Luke 22:43). This is the end of temptation, namely, that the one who became utterly weak but was held by the word receives renewed strength for the vitality of body, soul, and mind through an angel of God.

III. 5. Adam's temptation has been brought to an end through the temptation of Jesus Christ. Just as all flesh fell in Adam's temptation, so likewise all flesh has been extricated from Satan's power in the temptation of Jesus

[44.] After this Klapproth notes the following: "Then the angels of God. Thus always after a temptation!" On a new page, in smaller shorthand: "The spiritual temptation." Cf. p. 409.

[45.] Replaces "But he holds on to the word."

[46.] Mark 15:34; Matt. 27:46; cf. Ps. 22:2.

[47.] Heb. 4:15.

[48.] [Matt. 4:11.—VB]

Christ. For Jesus Christ bore our flesh, he suffered our temptation, and he has gained the victory. Therefore, all of us today bear the flesh that overcame Satan in Jesus Christ. In the temptation of Jesus, even our flesh, we ourselves, have overcome. Because Christ has been tempted and has overcome, therefore, we pray: do not lead us into temptation! For temptation has already come and been overcome; he has done it in our stead. "Look at the temptation of your son Jesus Christ and do not lead *us* into temptation." We may and ought to be certain that this prayer is heard; we should affirm it by our amen, for it *is* heard in Jesus Christ himself. From now on *we* shall
383 no longer be led into temptation, but all temptation that still now happens is the temptation of Jesus Christ in his members, in his church-community. It is not we who are tempted, *but Jesus Christ who is tempted in us.*

Because Satan was unable to bring the Son of God to fall, [he] now persecutes him in his members with all kinds of temptations. But these last temptations are merely the aftermath of Jesus's temptation on earth, for the power of temptation *is* broken in the temptation of Jesus. His disciples ought to be found in this temptation; then the kingdom is surely theirs. This is the foundational word of Jesus to his disciples: "You are those who have stood by me in my temptations[49] and I confer on you the kingdom" (Luke 22:29). Here the promise is meant not for the temptations of the *disciple,* but for the participation and communion in the temptation of *Jesus.* The temptations of the disciples fell on Jesus, and Jesus's temptations came over the disciples. To participate in the temptation of *Christ,* however, means at the same time to participate in the overcoming and the victories of Christ. This does not mean that the temptations of Christ had come to an end and the disciples would no longer experience anything of these; rather, they will experience temptations, but what will come over them will be the temptations of Jesus Christ. In this way, Christ will carry the victory over these temptations as well.

It accords with the disciples' participation in the temptations of Jesus Christ that Jesus wants to spare his disciples other temptations: "Stay awake and pray that you may not come into the time of temptation" (Matt. 26:41).[50]
384 Which temptation threatens the disciples in this hour of Gethsemane if

[49.] Replaces "trials [*Anfechtung*]" (this is the term in Luther's Bible in Luke 22:28). [The NRSV here reads "trials."—VB]

[50.] [The NRSV here reads "time of trial," but Bonhoeffer's Luther Bible uses *Versuchung,* or "temptation," in both instances.—VB] At this point the manuscript has another beginning, which is deleted: "*Do not lead us into temptation, but deliver us from the evil.* Tentatio facit theologum ('temptation makes a theologian')." Cf. Martin Luther's preface to the first volume of his works in German, Wittenberg edition (1539), in which he mentions three rules "to study theology in a proper manner": *oratio, meditatio, tentatio*

not the one that affronts them in the suffering of Christ, *that is, that they do not wish to participate in his temptations*? Thus Jesus here affirms the petition in the Lord's Prayer: "Do not lead us into temptation." The same thing is expressed in Heb. 2:18, where it says, "Because he himself was tempted by what he suffered, he is able to help those who are being tempted."[51] Here the talk is not only of the help that only the one who has personally experienced the suffering and pain of others is able to offer. Rather, the essential meaning is that in my temptations really *only his temptation* is my help; *to participate in his temptation* is alone a help in my temptation. Thus I ought to understand my temptation as nothing other than the temptation of Jesus Christ in me. In his temptation is my help, for only here is victory and overcoming.

The practical task of the Christian, then, must be to understand all temptation that befalls him as the temptation of Christ in him, and then he will be helped. But how does this happen? Before we can speak of the Christian's concrete temptations and how these are overcome, the question of *the author of the Christian's temptation* must be posed here. For only when the Christian knows what temptation is all about can he respond properly in the concrete case.

The Holy Scripture mentions three different authors of temptation: *the devil*, the *desires of human beings, God himself.*

a. *What does Scripture say when the devil* is called the author of temptation? *First*, it says that temptation is entirely *contrary to God*. For it is incomprehensible from God's own nature that the human being would be led to doubt the word of God and be led to apostasy. The tempter is always the *enemy of God*. *Second*: In temptation, God's enemy demonstrates his power to do something that is not the will of God. What is impossible for a creature to accomplish, the evil enemy is capable of doing! That means, temptation is a 385
power that is stronger than any creature. It is Satan's power breaking into the world of creation. If the tempter is the devil, then no creature's strength can

(prayer, meditation, temptation). *WA* 50:657–61, esp. 660. Cf. also *WA.Tr*, 1.16:13 (no. 46, 1531): "Sola . . . experientia facit theologum" (only experience makes a theologian). Bonhoeffer's deleted text continues: "Whoever engages the word of God in a correct manner must soon experience that the word of God will begin to engage him. Whoever works with the word of God [replaces: 'whoever sets in motion [*treiben*] the word of God'] will soon realize that God's word will work in him. For God's word is a living thing. It not only wants to be learned and proclaimed; it wants to be proven in the heart, that is to say, in all of life. Only the person who has come to know the living word of God can speak of it properly."

[51.] [The NRSV here uses "tested," but Bonhoeffer's Luther Bible continues to use *versuchen*, or "to tempt."—VB]

withstand his temptation. The creature must fall. This is how strong Satan's power is (Eph. 6:12). *Third*: Temptation is *seduction*, leading astray. For this reason temptation is from the devil, for he is a *liar.* "When he lies, he speaks according to his own nature, for he is a liar and the father of lies" (John 8:44). Sin is deceitfulness (Heb. 3:13).[52] The deception, the lie of the devil is that he makes human beings believe that they can live without the word of God. Satan presents the human imagination with an illusory kingdom of happiness, power, and peace, which can be entered only by yielding to temptation. And the devil conceals from the human being that he himself is the most disheartened and most unhappy being, eternally rejected by God. *Fourth*: Temptation comes from the devil, for here the devil becomes the *accuser* of the human being. There is a twofold aim to every temptation: that a person ought to fall away from God's word and that God *must* condemn a person, since the accuser has revealed the person's sin. The second aim here is crucial. Here Job's temptation is the prototype of all temptations. Satan's question is "Does Job fear God for nothing? Have you not put a fence around him and his house and all that he has, on every side? You have blessed the work of his hands, and his possessions have increased in the land. But stretch out your hand now, and touch all that he has, and he will curse you to your face" (Job 1:9–11).[53] Here the meaning of all temptation becomes evident. This human being is robbed of all he has and is made utterly defenseless in the extreme. Poverty, sickness, mockery, and rejection by the pious cast him into the deepest night. As the prince of this world, Satan robs him of all he can. He casts Job into desolation that leaves him nothing except God. In precisely this situation, Satan wants to reveal that
386 Job does *not* fear God *for naught,* that he loves God not for God's sake but for the sake of the world's possessions. Satan is determined to find some place where it becomes clear that Job does not fear, love, and trust God above all things.[54] Thus every temptation turns into a revelation of sin, and the accuser appears more righteous than God, since he has revealed the sin. He compels God into judgment.

The devil thus shows himself in the temptation as the *enemy of God, as power, as liar,* and *as accuser.* For the human being in temptation, this means: the enemy of God must be recognized in the temptation; the power that contradicts God must be overcome in temptation; the lie must be exposed

[52.] Deleted: "To doubt God's word is the lie as such."

[53.] In his Luther Bible, Bonhoeffer underlined v. 9 twice in pencil.

[54.] Cf. Martin Luther's explanation of the first commandment in his 1529 *Small Catechism* (Kolb and Wengert, *Book of Concord,* 347–48).

in temptation; the accuser must recognize his injustice.[55] We will discuss later how this can happen in practice. For now we ask further

b. What does Scripture say when human desires are made the author of temptation? "No one, when tempted, should say, 'I am being tempted by God'; for God cannot be tempted by evil and he himself tempts no one. But one is tempted by one's own desire, being lured and enticed by it; then, when that desire has conceived, it gives birth to sin, and that sin, when it is fully grown, gives birth to death" (James 1:13ff.[–15]). *First*: Whoever ascribes the *guilt* [Schuld] for *temptation* to someone else thereby justifies his own fall, for if I have no guilt in my own temptation, then I am also not guilty when I perish in it. *Temptation is guilt,* inasmuch as the fall is inexcusable. If it is thus impossible to blame the devil for one's temptation, then it is even more sacrilegious to make God responsible for it. This might seem pious, but in reality it implies the assertion that God would somehow be accessible to evil. But this only postulates a division in God and renders his word and will questionable, ambiguous, and doubtful. Because even the very possibility of evil cannot have a place in God, therefore, the tempta- 387
tion to evil must never be attributed to God. God himself tempts no one.[56] The origin of temptation resides in myself. *Second*: *Temptation is punishment* [Strafe].[57] The locus where all temptation arises is desire. My own craving for pleasure and the fear of suffering entice me to let go of the word of God. The inherited, corrupted nature of the flesh is the origin of evil inclinations in body and soul. Neither the beauty of the world nor suffering are evil and tempting as such, nor are the human beings or things that might tempt me. Rather, temptation occurs when all these things become pleasurable, arousing and enticing through our evil desires.[58] While the objectivity of the temptation becomes evident in its origin in the devil, here we are stressing the full subjectivity of temptation. Both are equally necessary. *Third*: Even desire as such does not make me sinful. But "when that desire has conceived, it gives birth to sin, and that sin, when it is fully grown, gives birth to death." The conception of desire occurs when my ego identifies with it, that is to say, when the word of God that holds me is surrendered. As long as my self does not bring the desire to fruition, the desire remains an "Id." But sin

[55.] The lines in the manuscript that follow "this means" up to this point are marked with a vertical line in the margin.

[56.] Deleted: "*Temptation is my own guilt.*"

[57.] This sentence is written in the margin with pencil.

[58.] [The German word used here is *Begehrlichkeit,* which can also mean "covetousness."—VB]

occurs only through the "ego" as such.[59] In this sense, the origin of temptation lies in ἐπιθυμία, the origin of sin in myself and in me alone. Hence I must know that the guilt is my very own and that I have become guilty of eternal death when I have succumbed to sin in temptation. Of course, Jesus threatens severe judgment upon the one through whom temptation comes, who tempts the innocent, who scandalizes[60] one of the little ones. "Woe to the one who tempts the other to sin"[61] is the word of God to everyone who tempts, but you alone are guilty of sin and death if you give in to the temptation of desire—this is God's word to the one who is tempted.

388 c. What does Holy Scripture say when it says that *God is the author of temptation*? This is the most difficult and final question. James says that God tempts no one. But Scripture says also that God tempted Abraham (Gen. 22:1), that Israel was tempted by God (Exod. 16:4; Deut. 8:2; Judg. 2:22; Ps. 66:10), likewise that Hezekiah was tempted by God (2 Chr. 32:31), but David "was incited by God's wrath" to arrange a census (2 Sam. 24:1), according to 1 Chr. 21:1 "by Satan." In the New Testament, the temptation of Christians is also seen as God's judgment (1 Pet. 4:11,[62] 17). What does all this mean?

First: Scripture makes it clear that nothing can happen on earth apart from God's will and permission. Even Satan is in the hands of God. He must serve God against his will. Satan does have power, but only where God grants it to him. This serves as a comfort for the tempted Christian. Satan had to get God's permission to tempt Job. He can do nothing from himself. For this reason, God must first forsake the human being in order that Satan find room for temptation. "God left Hezekiah to himself, in order to tempt him"[63] (2 Chr. 32:31). Everything that was said earlier about the desertedness of those being tempted applies here. God gives the one tempted into the hands of Satan.

Second: The question put by children: Why does God not simply kill Satan? demands an answer. We know that the same question could also be phrased as: Why did Christ have to be tempted, suffer, and die? Why did Satan have so much power over him? God gives Satan room *for the sake of* human *sins*. Satan must carry out the death of the sinner, for only when the sinner dies can the righteous live; only when the old human being perishes

[59.] Cf. Sigmund Freud's essay "The Ego and the Id" (1923) and his structural distinction of the psychic organism into the elements "Id," "Ego," and "Superego" (*Standard Edition of the Complete Psychological Works of Sigmund Freud*, no. 12).

[60.] Luke 17:2; cf. Matt. 18:6.

[61.] [Matt. 18:7 NRSV: "Woe to the one by whom the stumbling block comes."—VB]

[62.] Correct: v. 12.

[63.] [The NRSV has "to test him."—VB]

daily and completely can the new human being rise to life. By fulfilling his office [Amt], Satan serves the purpose of God, who "kills and brings to life; he brings down to Sheol and raises up" (1 Sam. 2:6).[64] Thus against his will Satan must serve God's plan of redemption; Satan is left with death and sin, but God with life and righteousness. Satan is active in temptations
in a *threefold* manner: He leads to the *recognition of sin.* He *causes the flesh to* 389
suffer. He *gives death to the sinner.* (a) 2 Chr. 32:31: "God left him to himself, in order to test[65] him and to know all that was in his heart." The human heart is revealed in temptation. The human being recognizes his sin, which he could not have recognized without the temptation, for in temptation the human being recognizes where his heart lies.[66] The sin's coming to light is the work of the accuser, who thinks he has thereby been victorious. But sin that has been revealed can now be confessed and therefore also be forgiven. Thus the revealing of sin belongs to God's soteriological purpose with the human being that even Satan must serve. (b) Satan gains power over the believer in the temptation of a person in the flesh. He torments the believer by inciting the desires, through the pain of privation and through inflicting suffering of body and soul. He takes away everything a person has and thereby entices him at the same time to seek forbidden pleasures. In this manner he pushes the believer, like Job, toward the abyss, into darkness where the tempted person is held only by God's grace, which is no longer felt and experienced but is nonetheless firm. So it seems as if Satan has gained total power over the believer, but again, this victory turns out to be his complete defeat. For the killing of the flesh is merely the path to life in the Spirit; as Satan pushes the tempted one into utter emptiness and defenselessness, he pushes the human being directly into God's own hands. Hence a Christian recognizes in Satan's rage God's gracious *chastisement* (Heb. 12:4ff.[–11]), of the Father with his child; God's *gracious judgment* (1 Pet. 4:17) that saves from God's wrathful judgment. Hence the hour of temptation becomes the hour of greatest joy (James 1:2ff.[–4]). (c) The last enemy is death. It is in Satan's hand. The sinner dies. Death is the last temptation. But precisely here, where the human being loses everything, where hell reveals openly all its horror, life has begun for the believer. So Satan here forfeits his last power and his last right to the believer.

Now we ask once more: why does God grant Satan room for temptation? 390
First, in order to *overcome* Satan finally. In that he receives his rights, Satan is

[64.] Deleted: "As Satan kills the righteous."

[65.] [Bonhoeffer's German Bible uses *versuchen*, or "to tempt."—VB]

[66.] Cf. Luther's explanation of the first commandment in his 1529 Large Catechism (Kolb and Wengert, *Book of Concord*, 386–90).

annihilated. Just as God punishes the godless by granting them their godlessness, by granting them their right and freedom—and the godless die in this freedom (R[om]. 1:19ff.)—so likewise God does not annihilate Satan by an act of power, but Satan must annihilate himself. *Second*: God gives Satan room in order to bring *believers to salvation*. The new human being can live only through recognizing sin, through suffering and death. *Third*: The overcoming of Satan and the salvation of believers are true and real in Jesus Christ alone. All sin, all suffering, and the death of humankind were visited upon Jesus by Satan. But that was the end of Satan's rights. He had taken everything from Jesus Christ and thereby had handed him over to God alone.[67] Thus we are led back to the insight from which we began: the faithful must learn to understand all their temptations as the temptation of Jesus Christ in them, and thus they will partake of his overcoming.

How, then, can Scripture speak of God's temptation of human beings? It speaks of God's wrath, whose executor is Satan (see 1 Sam. 24;[68] 1 Chr. 21:1). God's wrath was upon Jesus Christ from the hour of temptation. God chastised him for the sake of sin and the flesh that he bore. But since God's wrath was met with obedience for the sake of sin—an obedience unto the righteous death of the one who bore the sin of all the world—the wrath was stilled. God's wrath drove Jesus toward the gracious God; here God's grace had defeated the wrath. Satan's power was overcome. Wherever all temptation of the flesh and God's wrath is borne obediently by Jesus Christ, there the temptation is overcome in Jesus Christ. Behind the wrathful God who tempts, the Christian now finds the gracious God who tempts no one.

IV. 6. The *concrete temptation of the Christian* always requires making the
391 distinction between the hand of the devil and the hand of God. In other words, it is a matter of *resistance* and of *submission* at the right moment; resistance to the devil is possible precisely in complete submission under God's hand.

The details of this must be made clear. Because all temptations of believers are temptations of Christ in his members, the body of Christ, we speak of these temptations in analogy to the temptation of Christ: 1. *Of the temptation in the flesh*. 2. *Of the lofty spiritual temptation*.[69] 3. *Of the ultimate temptation*.

[67.] A deleted note in the margin: "Satan has made himself an instrument of God's wrath."

[68.] Correct: 2 Sam. 24:1.

[69.] Replaces "Trial [*Anfechtung*]."

Every temptation must be seen in light of 1 Cor. 10:12–13: "So if you think you are standing, watch out that you do not fall. No temptation[70] has overtaken you that is not common to everyone. God is faithful, and he will not let you be tempted beyond your strength, but with the temptation he will also provide the way out so that you may be able to endure it." This counteracts, first, *every false sense of security*, but also a *false despondency* in the face of temptation. No one should be sure even for a moment that he will be spared temptation. There is no temptation that could not come over me even in this hour. No one should presume that Satan is far away. "Like a roaring lion your adversary the devil prowls around, looking for someone to devour" (1 Pet. 5:8). In this life there is no moment in which we are safe from temptation and fall. Therefore, do not look down on others when you see them stumble and fall.[71] Such security will become a snare causing your own downfall. "So do not become proud, but stand in awe" (Rom. 11:20). Rather, be alert at all times so that the tempter finds no power over you. "*Stay awake and pray* that you may not fall into temptation" (Matt. 26:41).[72] The attitude of a Christian in the face of temptation is *to be wakeful* in view of the cunning enemy and *to pray*[73] to God that he may hold us firm in his word and grace.

But the Christian too is not supposed to be afraid of temptation. If temptation overcomes the Christian in spite of watchfulness and prayer, then he should know that it is possible to overcome every temptation. There is no
temptation that could not be overcome. God knows our capacities and does 392
not permit us to be tempted beyond our strength. It is "human temptation," which means temptation that is not too much for us human beings. God deals out according to the measure of how much each person can endure. This is certain. The person who despairs because of the suddenness and horror of a temptation has already forgotten the main thing, namely, that he will most certainly endure in the temptation because God will not allow us to be tempted beyond our strengths. There are temptations that we fear especially because we have often failed in them. When they suddenly reappear before us, we often give ourselves up for lost right away. But we may face these particular temptations in great calmness and tranquility, for they can be overcome and are overcome by virtue of God's faithfulness. *Temptation should find us in humility and the certainty of victory.*

[70.] [Here and throughout the 1 Corinthians passage the NRSV reads "testing," but the German text here has *Versuchung*, or "temptation."—VB]

[71.] Replaces "Therefore, beware of false pride and false judgment over those who have fallen."

[72.] [NRSV translation altered.—VB]

[73.] Deleted: "in order to abide firmly by God's word."

The temptation in the flesh. We will first discuss the temptation through *lust* and then the temptation through *suffering.*

1. Lust. The yearning for lust that slumbers in our bodies may be suddenly and wildly aroused. With irresistible force, lust seizes power over the flesh. A hidden smoldering fire is suddenly set ablaze. The flesh is burning and aflame. There is no difference here whether [it] is the sexual desire for lust,[74] whether it is ambition, vanity, whether it is lust for revenge, the thirst for fame and power, whether it is greed, or whether it is, finally, even the indescribable lust for the beauty of the world, for nature as such. The joy in God is quenched in us, and now we seek all joy in created being. In this hour, God appears totally unreal to us; he loses all reality, and the only reality is lust offered by the created being; the only reality is the devil. Satan fills us here not with hatred against God but with forgetfulness of God. Satan adds to this demonstration of power also a lie. Desire that has been set aflame enshrouds human thinking and willing in deep darkness. We are
393 robbed of our clarity in distinction and decision. Should it really be sin that the flesh here desires? Should it not be fully allowed, even demanded, right now, right here, right in my situation, to still my lust? The tempter places me under a special law, just as he wanted to place the hungry Son of God under a special law. I insist on my special rights against God.

Everything within me stands up against the word of God. The powers of the body, of thinking, and of willing—which were once kept in obedience under the discipline of the word over which I believed I had control—make it clear to me that *I* in no way had power over them. "All my strength fails me," laments the psalmist.[75] They all went over to the side of the enemy. The enemy uses my own strengths against me. Here indeed I can no longer fight against them as a hero; here I am a defenseless and powerless man. God himself has forsaken me. Who can here overcome and be victorious?

None other than the crucified Jesus Christ himself, for the sake of whom all this happens to me; because he is with me and in me, temptation has come over me just as it came over him.

Against the sole reality of lust and Satan, there is only one stronger reality: *the image and presence of the Crucified One.*[76] This power shatters the power of lust into nothingness, for here that power is overcome. Here the flesh has received both its right and wage, namely, death. Here I recognize that the desire of the flesh is nothing but the flesh's fear of dying. Because Christ is the death of the flesh and because this Christ is in me, therefore

[74.] Deleted: "the body of other people."

[75.] Cf. Ps. 38:10.

[76.] Cf. also the end of the book *Discipleship* (1937), *DBWE* 4:281–88.

the dying flesh revolts against Christ. Now I know that the dying of the flesh is evident in the temptation of the flesh. The flesh is dying and thereby inflames desire and lust. Thus in the temptation of the flesh I share in Jesus's dying in the flesh. The temptation of the flesh, which tried to draw me into the death of the flesh, thus draws me into the death of Christ, who
dies according to the flesh, but is resurrected according to the spirit. Only 394
the death of Christ saves me from the temptation of the flesh.[77]

For this reason, Scripture teaches us to *flee* in the hour of carnal temptation: shun fornication (1 Cor. 6:18)—idolatry (10:14)—youthful passions (1 Tim. 2:22)[78]—the fleeting passions of this world (2 Pet. 1:4). Here Satan can no longer be resisted other than by fleeing. Every attempt to fight the desires with our own strength is doomed to fail. Flee—that can only mean flee to the place where you can experience protection and help, flee to the Crucified One. Alone his image and his presence help. Here we see the martyred body and recognize therein the end of every lust; here we see through the deception of Satan to the last detail; here our spirit becomes sober again and identifies the enemy. Here I recognize the full extent of my carnal nature's being forlorn and forsaken, the righteous judgment of God's wrath over all flesh. Here I know that, in my forlorn state, I could never have helped myself against Satan, but that it is the victory of Jesus Christ that comes to me. Here I find also the basis for the stance from which I can alone overcome all temptation, *for patience* (James 1:2ff.[–4]). I should not even rebel against the temptations of the flesh in impermissible arrogance, as if I were too good. Especially here I must and can only submit myself under the hand of God and patiently endure the humiliation of such temptations.[79] Thus, in the middle of Satan's deathly work, I recognize God's judging and gracious discipline. In the death of Jesus, I find refuge from Satan and the communion of both, dying according to the flesh and of living in the spirit through his victory.

2. Suffering. It has thereby already become clear that for the Christian, temptation through lust means not lust but suffering. A temptation toward lust always includes the renunciation of lust, that is to say, suffering. The
temptation toward suffering always includes the longing for freedom from 395
suffering, that is to say, lust. This is to say that carnal temptation through lust and suffering is ultimately one and the same.

[77.] New paragraph, deleted: "Hence, in the hour of temptation, it is a good thing to keep in mind the image of the Crucified One. Here I see the martyred body, I recognize the end of all lust, and I see through the deception of Satan."

[78.] Correct: 2 Timothy.

[79.] Replaces "trials [*Anfechtungen*]."

We will first discuss the *temptation of the Christian through general suffering*, such as sickness, poverty, and misery of all kinds, and then of the temptation of the Christian *through suffering for the sake of Christ.*

When the Christian falls into severe sickness, bitter poverty, or other kinds of grievous suffering, it is important to know that the devil has a hand in this. The stoic resignation that sees everything as taking its necessary course[80] is human self-protection, which refuses to acknowledge the devil and God. This attitude has nothing to do with Christian faith. The Christian knows that suffering in this world is connected with the fall into sin and that God[81] does not will sickness, suffering, and death. Thus the Christian recognizes in suffering a temptation by Satan to separate him from God. Here lies the origin of murmuring against God.[82] Whereas God vanishes from human sight in the fire of desires, the heat of affliction easily leads to anger toward God. The Christian's trust in God's love is jeopardized. Why does God allow such suffering? God's righteousness becomes incomprehensible: Why does suffering have to befall me? Why do I deserve that? The intent is to make God our enemy through suffering. Job is the biblical archetype of this temptation. Satan robs Job of everything so that he would finally curse God. Agonizing pain, hunger, and thirst can rob a person of all strength and may bring him to the edge of the abyss of apostasy.

How can a Christian overcome the temptation[83] of suffering? The conclusion of the book of Job provides us here with an important aid. Until the very end, Job maintained his innocence in the face of suffering and refused the speeches of repentance from his friends, who wanted to explain his misery because of a particular, perhaps hidden, sin he may have committed. In doing so, Job spoke proudly about his own righteousness. After God's appearance Job declares: "Therefore I have uttered what I did not
396 understand, . . . therefore I despise myself, and repent in dust and ashes" (Job 42:3, 6). But God's wrath is now kindled not against Job but against his friends: "for you have not spoken of me what is right, as my servant Job has" (v. 7). Even though Job is pronounced to be in the right before God, he himself confesses his guilt before God. This is, indeed, the solution. Job's suffering has its origin not in his guilt but precisely in his righteousness. Job is tempted for the sake of his piety [Frömmigkeit]. Thus Job is right to murmur against suffering since he appears as the guilty one. But even for Job this right comes to an end when he faces God and no longer

[80.] Replaces "sees all this as that which is natural."

[81.] Deleted: "God does not will that his children."

[82.] Deleted: "Whereas lust is to lead to forgetfulness of God."

[83.] Replaces: "Trial [*Anfechtung*]."

human beings. Before God even the pious and innocent Job must confess his guilt.

For the Christian tempted by suffering this means: it is permissible to murmur against suffering insofar as one murmurs against the devil and maintains one's innocence. The devil has broken into God's order and brought about suffering (Luther at the death of Lenchen!).[84] But before God Christians recognize their own suffering as God's judgment over the sins of all flesh, which also dwell in their own flesh. The Christian recognizes his own sins and confesses his guilt. "Your wickedness will punish you, and your apostasies will convict you. Know and see that it is evil and bitter for you to forsake the Lord your God; the fear of me is not in you, says the Lord God of hosts" (Jer. 2:19; cf. 4:18). So suffering leads to the recognition of sin and thus a turning toward God. Once we recognize our suffering as God's judgment on our flesh, we find the reason for thanksgiving. For judgment on the flesh, which is the death of the old human being, is merely the side of the new human being's life that is turned toward the world. For this reason, it says: "for whoever has suffered in the flesh has finished with sin" (1 Pet. 4:1). So all suffering must lead the Christian not to apostasy but to the strengthening of faith. While the flesh shies away from and rejects suffering, the Christian recognizes his own suffering to be just the suffering of
Christ in himself. For he has also borne our infirmities and taken our suf- 397
ferings upon himself.[85] In doing so he bore God's wrath over sin. He died according to the flesh, and we likewise die according to the flesh because he lives in us.

Now the Christian understands his own suffering as the temptation of Christ in the self. This leads him to *patience*, to endure temptation in stillness and silence, and fills him with thanks, for the more the old human being dies, the more certainly the new one lives; the deeper one is cast into suffering, the closer one comes to Christ. Precisely because Satan took everything from Job, he pushed him toward God alone. Hence, for the Christian, suffering is *murmuring against the devil, knowledge of his own sin and of God's gracious judgment*, the death of the old human being, and communion with Jesus Christ.

Whereas the Christian must experience the sufferings of this world just like the godless ones, a Christian also experiences a suffering that is foreign to the world: *the suffering for the sake of the Lord Jesus Christ* (1 Pet. 4:12–17).

[84.] On the grief of Katharina and Martin Luther over the death of their daughter Magdalene (1529–42), see Luther's letter to Justus Jonas, September 23, 1542 (*WA.Br* 10:149–50); cf. also *DBWE* 9:262, esp. ed. note 21.

[85.] Cf. Isa. 53:4; Matt. 8:17.

Even this suffering happens as *temptation* (πρὸς πειρασμόν 1 Pet. 4:12; cf. Judg. 2:22). The Christian may understand all general suffering as the consequence of sharing in the general sinfulness of the flesh, but the fact that one may suffer for the sake of righteousness, that is, for the sake of one's faith, must indeed seem a strange thing. It is still comprehensible that the righteous person suffers for the *sake of his own sin*, but that the righteous person should suffer for the *sake of his own righteousness* may easily become a stumbling block for one who believes in Jesus Christ. The temptation becomes even more onerous since general suffering (sickness, poverty, etc.) is unavoidable, whereas suffering for the sake of Christ could immediately find an end with the denial of Christ. In a sense, it is a voluntary suffering that I could avoid. And precisely here Satan has an open field for his activities. He incites the yearnings of the flesh for happiness and turns the Christian's own pious insights against him, by pointing out the folly and godlessness of voluntary suffering as well as the pious way out, the special
398 solution to his conflicts. Since unavoidable suffering is already[86] an exacting temptation, how much more so is a suffering that is avoidable in the eyes of the world, my flesh, and even my pious thinking. *Human freedom is mustered* [for battle] *against the Christian's bond.*

This is a genuine temptation toward apostasy. The Christian, however, should not be surprised about this temptation but rather understand that precisely here he is led into the communion of the sufferings of Jesus Christ (1 Pet. 4:13). Even here Satan's temptation pushes the Christian again into the arms of Jesus Christ, the Crucified One. Precisely where Satan robs a human being of his own freedom and leads it against Christ, the Christian's bond with Jesus Christ will become most gloriously visible. What does it mean to be in communion with the sufferings of Christ? In the first place, it means *joy* (χαίρετε 4:13).[87] It means *recognition of the innocence* where the Christian suffers as a Christian ὡς Χριστιανός (v. 15).[88] It means the *honor of God* in the name by which I am called a Christian (δοξαζέτω v. 16).[89] The Christian suffers "for Christ" (Phil. 1:29). Finally, it also necessarily means recognition of the *judgment* that here begins at the house of God (v. 17). But this thought is difficult; how can the suffering that I experience precisely as a Christian, *as a justified one*, be at the same time understood as a *judgment*

[86.] Bonhoeffer inadvertently repeated the word "already."

[87.] In his Greek New Testament text, Bonhoeffer underlined the two verb forms of χαίρω (to be joyful), which are included in pencil.

[88.] Correct: v. 16 ("as a Christian").

[89.] Here Bonhoeffer does not follow Luther's translation of a variant reading of the Greek text ("to give honor to God in such a case"), but follows the main Greek text ἐν τῷ ὀνόματι τούτῳ ("in this name").

passed on sin; and yet, everything depends on the correlation of these two insights. *Suffering* for the sake of Christ that does not acknowledge God's *judgment* in it is mere fanaticism [Schwärmerei]. How must we understand judgment here? It is God's *only* judgment that came over Christ and that will come in the end over all flesh, namely, God's judgment over sin. No one can stand on Christ's side without also partaking in this judgment by God, for here lies the difference between Christ and the world in that he bore 399
the judgment that is despised and shaken off by the world. This is not the distinction, namely, that there was judgment not over Christ but over the world. Rather, Christ, the innocent one, bears God's judgment on sin. This means "to belong to Christ": *to submit to God's judgment.* This is also the difference between suffering in the communion with Jesus Christ and suffering in the community of some ethical or political hero. The Christian, however, recognizes in suffering that there is guilt, judgment. What kind of guilt is it that [Christians] recognize in judgment? It is the guilt of all flesh that the Christian bears until the end of life, but beyond this it is at the same time the guilt of the world in Jesus that Christians must bear and endure in suffering. In this way the Christian's suffering of judgment in communion with Jesus Christ becomes a vicarious suffering for the world.

Because Christ submitted himself to God's judgment, he is "taken *out of* God's judgment" (Isa. 53:[8]). And since Christians also submit to judgment, they are kept from the coming wrath and judgment. "If it is hard for the righteous to be saved" (namely, from the temptation that comes with this suffering), "what will become of the ungodly" (v. 18)? So judgment beginning at the house of God is God's gracious judgment over Christians, followed by the last judgment in God's wrath on the ungodly.

Thus, the Christian recognizes in his own suffering for the sake of Jesus Christ, *first,* the devil and his temptation toward apostasy from Christ, *second, the joy* to be granted to *suffer* for Christ, *third,* [the] judgment of God that begins at the house of God. The Christian knows that he suffers *according to God's will* (v. 19) and acquires God's grace in the communion of the cross.

[IV b.][90] *Spiritual Temptations.*

Jesus rebutted Satan's second temptation with the words, "*You must not tempt the Lord your God.*"[91] But Satan had tempted Jesus to long for a visible 400

[90.] The Roman numeral "V" is added in pencil in the manuscript; "IV b." is a later correction by the editor corresponding to the following "IV c." Cf. also at "IV. [=] 6." (see above p. 402) the introduction of the subsection "2. *Of the lofty spiritual temptation.*" Here Klapproth's notes resume.

[91.] Matt. 4:7; Deut. 6:16. [The NRSV here reads: "Do not put the Lord your God to the test."—VB]

affirmation of his divine Sonship and thereby not to be satisfied with God's word and promise, and to desire more than faith. Jesus calls such a desire a tempting of God, that is to say, to put to the test God's faithfulness, God's truth, God's love. This, in turn, means to locate faithlessness, lies, and absence of love in God rather than seeking them within oneself. Every temptation that is directly aimed at our faith in salvation entails the danger of tempting God.

The spiritual temptations by which Satan assails Christians have a double aim: the believer should either succumb to the sin of spiritual pride (*securitas*)[92] or should perish in the sin of sadness (*desperatio*). Both sins are the *one* sin of *tempting God.*

Satan tempts us to the sin of spiritual pride by *deceiving* us regarding *the seriousness of the law of God and the wrath of God.* He takes the word of God's grace in his own hands, intimating that God is a gracious God who will not take our sins so seriously. Thus he arouses our desire to sin deliberately while relying on God's grace and to declare that we are forgiven even before we have sinned. He makes us secure in grace. We are, after all, his children; we have Christ and his cross; we are the true church; nothing evil can now happen to us. God will no longer count our sins against us. What makes others perish is no longer any danger for us. Because of grace we have special rights before God. Here is *the willful sin while relying on grace* (Jude 4), here it is said: "where is the God of punishment"[93] (Mal. 2:17), and "now we count the arrogant happy; evildoers not only prosper, but when they tempt God[94] they escape" (Mal. 3:15). Such words only breed spiritual lethargy in prayer, in obedience, lead to indifference toward God's word, the deadening of the conscience, and scorn for a good conscience (1 Tim. 1:19, shipwreck in the faith). Moreover, such words lead to the total hardening
401 and stubbornness of the heart in the sin of fearlessness and security before God; the human being persists in unforgiven sin and daily adds guilt upon guilt[95]—hypocritical piety (Acts 5:3 and 9!). Now there is no longer any room for repentance; the human being can no longer be obedient.[96] This

[92.] "Security." Cf. the distinction in Luther's *Lectures on Romans* of 1515–16 (*LW* 25:20 [*WA* 56] between *securitas* (false security) and *certitud* (certainty); *DBWE* 4:44, esp. ed. note 4.

[93.] [The NRSV here reads "justice."—VB]

[94.] [The NRSV here reads "put God to the test."—VB]

[95.] "He persists . . . guilt" is added in the margin and connected with a line in pencil to "stubbornness." Klapproth's notes read: "Persistence in unforgiven sin, finally the sin of hypocritical piety."

[96.] Initially the phrase "he persists . . . guilt" was marked to be inserted here, but then crossed out again in pencil.

path ends in idolatry. The gracious God has become my idol that I serve. But this is a revealed *temptation of God* that challenges the wrath of God.

Spiritual pride stems from the neglect of God's law and wrath, whether it be that I think I can endure according to the law because of my piety (*righteousness by works*) or that I claim special privilege through grace with regard to sin (nomism and antinomism).[97] In both cases the temptation of God consists of my putting to the test the seriousness of God's wrath and asking for a sign beyond his word.

The temptation toward *securitas* corresponds to the temptation toward *desperatio, sadness* (*acedia*).[98] Here it is not the law and wrath but grace and God's promises that are to be attacked and put to the test. In order to do this, Satan robs the believer of all joy in God's word, *every experience of the goodness of God,* and instead fills the heart with the horror of the past, the present, and the future.[99] Old, long-forgotten guilt stands suddenly before me as if it had happened today, resistance against God's word and the obstinate refusal to be obedient increase, and the completely desolate state of my future before God overpowers my heart. *God was never with me, God is not with me, God will never forgive me,* for my sin is too large to be forgiven. And so the spirit of the human being revolts against the word of God. The human being now demands experience and proof of God's grace, once
and for all. Otherwise, despairing of God, the human being will refuse to 402
listen to the word of God. Despair may push the human being either into the sin of *blasphemy against God* or even into self-destruction in the most extreme act of despair, namely, suicide, like Saul and Judas.[100] Or else the human being, in despair of God's grace, will attempt to bring about the sign that God withholds, namely, to become a saint—in spite of God—by means of one's own strength in self-destructive asceticism and reliance on works [Werkerei][101] or even *sorcery.*

In *thanklessness,* in *disobedience,* and in *hopelessness,*[102] the human being stubbornly refuses God's grace. Satan requests a sign that the human being

[97.] The parenthetical terms are written (without parentheses) in the margin with pencil. Klapproth's notes: ". . . temptation of God—be it through nomism or antinomism."

[98.] Cf. *DBWE* 9:280.

[99.] Here begins a new page in the manuscript with the note in the margin: "2 C[or.] 12!"

[100.] Cf. 1 Sam. 31:4–5; Matt. 27:3–10.

[101.] [Bonhoeffer in Finkenwalde spoke often about *Werkerei* (reliance on works); it is translated in *DBWE* 4:155 as "false belief in works."—VB]

[102.] In the lecture on pastoral counseling in Finkenwalde, Bonhoeffer mentioned, in the section "The Tempted One," thanklessness, hopelessness, and disobedience; cf. *DBW* 14:585.

is a saint. God's promise in Christ is no longer sufficient. "And this is the most severe and highest assault and suffering by which God sometimes chastises and tests his saints, what is usually called *desertionem gratiae*,[103] and in which human hearts feel nothing except that God has deserted them, along with his grace, and no longer shows any concern."[104] "But the human heart receives comfort only with difficulty when our Lord God dotes upon one to such an extent that the soul nearly expires, the eyes become dull, and a cold sweat covers one" (Luther on Gen. 35:1).[105]

When here Satan brings the word of God in the law against the word of God in Christ, and when he here becomes the accuser who takes away all comfort from people, we should know the following: *First*, it is the devil himself who uses the word of God. *Second*, we should never discuss our sin with the devil, but rather we speak about our sin with Jesus alone. *Third*, we should confront the devil with the fact that Jesus called not saints but
403 sinners to himself and that we—in spite of the devil—would like to remain sinners in order to remain with Jesus, rather than be saints with the devil. *Fourth*, we should recognize how in such a temptation our own sin is punished by God's wrath and brought to light, namely, *foremost* as our *thanklessness* against everything that God has done for us up to this hour ("do not forget all his benefits" [Ps. 103:2]). Those who bring thanksgiving as their sacrifice honor me, and I will show them my salvation, speaks God (Ps. 50[:23]); *next, our current disobedience*, which is the refusal to repent unforgiven sin and to refrain from our favorite sin[106] (for an unforgiven and treasured sin is Satan's best entrance gate into our heart); *finally, our hopelessness*, as if our sin were too big for God, as if Christ would have suffered only for small sins [Puppensünden][107] but not for the truly big sins of the whole world, as if God does not also have great things in store for me, and as if he did not also prepare for me an inheritance in heaven.[108] *Fifth*, I should thank God for his judgment of me, for it shows that he "dotes upon me" and loves me. *Sixth*, in all of this, however, I should recognize that Satan has pushed me here into the deepest temptation of Christ on the cross

[103.] "Deserting (running away) from grace."

[104.] From Luther's sermon on Luke 2:42–52 in the *Fastenpostille* (*WA* 17 2:16–32).

[105.] According to Ulrich Köpf of the Luther-Archives at the University of Tübingen, this citation could not be verified (letter to the German editor, October 26, 1995).

[106.] Klapproth: *"Schoßsünde,"* or "pet sin."

[107.] Allusion to the warning that the vicar Johannes von Staupitz gave Luther, namely, that the latter should confess only his true sins and not the many that he merely imagines; he should "not deal with such nonsense and pretend sins [*nicht mit solchem Humpelwerk und Puppensünden umgehen*]." Cf. Köstlin, *Martin Luther*, 1:70.

[108.] Cf. 1 Pet. 1:4.

when he cried: My God, my God why have you forsaken me?[109] Where God's wrath and judgment are realized, there is reconciliation. Where I am hit by God's wrath and lose everything,[110] there I can now hear: my grace is sufficient for you, for my power is made perfect in weakness (2 Cor. 12:7).[111] *Last,* in my thanksgiving for temptation that has been overcome, I know at the same time that there is no temptation more dreadful than to be without temptation.[112]

IV c.[113] *The Last Temptation* 404

Not much should be said about how Satan repeats Jesus's third temptation in believers. Here what is at stake is, after all, Satan's unconcealed appearance as he tempts us to fall away—knowingly and definitively—from God by promising us all power and happiness on this earth if only we worship him. Just as spiritual temptations are not experienced by all Christians because they are beyond their capabilities, this last temptation will certainly come over only a few human beings. Christ has suffered this temptation and overcome it, and we may well say that the Antichrist and the ἀντίχριστοι must have had to suffer this temptation and have fallen. Whenever there is a covenant with Satan knowingly agreed upon through spirit or blood, the night that Scripture calls willful sin has come. There is no repentance of that sin that tramples on the Son of God, which repeats for its own sake the crucifixion of the Son of God, the derision of the spirit of grace (Heb. 10:26–27 and 6:6); it is the sin unto death for which we should no longer pray (1 John 5:15–16), the sin against the Holy Spirit for which there is no forgiveness (Matt. 12:31–32). But one who has experienced and overcome this temptation can be certain to have victoriously overcome every temptation.

Verse 7. All temptation is the temptation of Jesus Christ, and all victory is [the victory] of Jesus Christ. All temptation leads the believer into deepest loneliness, into being forsaken by both human beings and by God. But in

[109.] Mark 15:34; Matt. 27:46. Klapproth: ". . . (Ps. 22[:2]—here again the Christ is tempted in me."

[110.] Klapproth: "must lose all experience."

[111.] The reference is found in 2 Cor. 12:9.

[112.] Cf. *DBW* 14:584 and Luther's statement (*WA* 3:420): "To experience no temptation is the worst temptation of all." [Bonhoeffer also discusses this in his exercises on "Theological Anthropology"; see *DBWE* 12:217, including ed. note 29.—VB]

[113.] This addition in pencil ("IV c.") relates back to "IV. [=] 6" (see pp. 348–49), the sections introduced as a. *"carnal,"* b. *"spiritual,"* and c. *"last temptation."* Klapproth: "c) 1 III."

this loneliness the believer finds Jesus Christ, who is both human being and God. *The blood of Christ* and *the example of Christ* and *the prayer of Christ*[114] are the believer's help and strength. Revelation says of the redeemed: "they have conquered him by the blood of the Lamb" ([Rev.] 12:11). The devil
405 is overcome not by the spirit but by the blood of Jesus.[115] Therefore, in all temptation we must return to this blood in which is all our help. Moreover, in the hour of temptation let us look to the image of Jesus Christ: see "the purpose of the Lord" (James 5:11).[116] His patience in suffering will kill the lust of our flesh, will make the sufferings of our flesh appear less severe, will keep us from all arrogance,[117] and will comfort us in all sadness. *The prayer of Jesus Christ,* which he promised to Peter (: Simon, listen! Satan has demanded to sift all of you like wheat, but I have prayed for you, Luke 22:31[–32]) represents our weak prayer before the Father in heaven, who does not let us be tempted beyond our capability.[118]

Only once it is clearly understood that the one whom God has forsaken must overcome the temptation can it now be recalled that Scripture [speaks] of the *struggle* of Christians.[119] Believers suffer the hour of temptation defenselessly. Their protection is Jesus Christ. But down from heaven, the Lord gives the defenseless the *heavenly* robe of *armor,* invisible to human eyes but from which Satan flees.[120] *He* clothes us with God's armor; *He* gives us the shield of faith in our hands;[121] He places the helmet of salvation on our head; He gives us the sword of the Spirit in our right hand. It is the garment of Christ, the garment of victory[122] that he puts around his struggling church-community.

The Spirit teaches us that the time of temptations is not yet over and that the hardest of all temptations still lie ahead for those who are the Lord's. But he also promises us: "Because you have kept my word of patient endurance, I will keep you from the hour of temptation[123] that is coming on the

---

[114.] Addition, but deleted: "and *the promise of Jesus Christ.*"

[115.] Klapproth: "(the bodily shed blood, not the spirit as such overcomes sin)."

[116.] Deleted: "Regard the patience of our Lord as salvation" (2 P[et.] 3:15).

[117.] Replaces "all security."

[118.] Deleted: "The *promise of Jesus Christ is this*: 'you are those who have stood by me in my trials, and I will confer on you the kingdom' (Luke 22:28–29)."

[119.] "Only after . . . Christians" is added in pencil in the margin.

[120.] Deleted: "the shield of faith and the helmet of salvation and the sword of the Spirit, which is the word of God" (Eph. 6:16–17).

[121.] Addition "left hand" canceled out again.

[122.] Replaces: "the Crucified and Resurrected One."

[123.] [The NRSV here reads "trial."—VB]

whole world to tempt[124] the inhabitants of the earth. I am coming soon" 406
(Rev. 3:10–11), and "the Lord knows how to rescue the godly from temptation" (2 Pet. 2:9).[125]

Thus we pray to the Father in heaven as Jesus Christ has taught us: "do not lead us into temptation," and we know that our prayer has been heard, for all temptation has been overcome *in Jesus Christ* for all time until the end.[126] Yet at the same time we speak with James: "Blessed is anyone who endures temptation. Such a one has stood the test and will receive the crown of life that the Lord has promised to those who love him" (James 1:12). But the promise of Jesus Christ is this: "You are those who have stood by me *in my temptations* and I will confer on you the kingdom" (Luke 22:28–29).[127]

[124.] [The NRSV here reads "test."—VB]

[125.] [The NRSV here reads "trial."—VB]

[126.] Klapproth: "There remain only the temptations of Jesus Christ in us, temptations in Christ. For this reason we may say with, not in contradiction to, Matt. 6[:13a]: James 1:12."

[127.] [NRSV translation altered to conform to Bonhoeffer's wording.—VB] At the end of the manuscript are several notes in pencil. Under the heading πειρασμός ("trial," "temptation"), Bonhoeffer noted the terms corresponding with two Hebrew concepts: "*to tempt* . . . to let go, *to test*"; also: "Luke 8:13. Acts 20:19 served in—temptations 1 Pet. 1:6 ποικίλοι ['manifold' temptations] as in James 1:2 1, from the καινὸς ἄνθρωπος. Members of the body. ἐν Χριστῷ but still in *the world*. Separation only through a *constant* struggle 1 Cor. 15:31. James 1:14 ἐξελκόμενος—to tear out [or to pull] out, 'from Christ,' 1 Cor. 10:13."

407 **5. Lecture on the Path of the Young Illegal Theologians of the Confessing Church, October 26, 1938**[1]

Our Path according to the Testimony of Scripture

The question that was raised among you and that serves as an introduction to this lecture seems rather straightforward to me. It is this:[2] Has the synod[3] of Barmen and especially of Dahlem taught[4] according to Scrip-

[1.] *NL*, A 56,5 a; mimeographed version of Bonhoeffer's lecture of October 26, 1938, at an extraordinary meeting of the Confessing Church Council of Brethren in Pomerania. The controversial question under discussion was the issue of "legalization," i.e., the process by which young theologians placed themselves under the jurisdiction of the regional church consistories, which were controlled by German Christians (cf. *DB-ER*, 607–20, and Klän, *An der Wegscheide*, 147–52). [See also Barnett, *For the Soul of the People*, 94–98.—VB] Previously published in *GS* 2:320–45. An expanded version of the speech was circulated as a typewritten circular letter to the "young brothers in Pomerania" (*NL*, A 56,5 b); any significant differences between these two texts are indicated in the notes below. A general change in the circular letter was a change from the third-person plural addressee, the formal "you," to the second-person plural, the informal "you." Cf. also in this volume Bonhoeffer's circular letter to the Pomeranian illegal pastors from the end of January 1938 (1/7); his circular letter of August 23, 1938 (1/24) to the Finkenwalde students; the introduction to the German *DBW* 15:1–3; and the German editor's comments in the afterword, pp. 565–68. [See also the circular letter from Werner de Boor and Gerhard Sass to the Pomeranian group (1/74).—VB]

[2.] Here Bonhoeffer's circular letter (*NL*, A 56,5 b) reads: "Dear brothers! We would like to summon you through this statement to serious reflection and new joyfulness in the path of the church of Jesus Christ. Only the Holy Scripture will be able to guide our reflection properly and give us full joyfulness and confidence. For this reason we ask you to examine together with us the path of our church in its accordance with scriptural testimony, so that you may thereby stand on the solid ground of the divine word. The question that must be our concern today is this: . . ."

[3.] Here Bonhoeffer's circular letter (*NL*, A 56,5 b) reads consistently in the plural: "Have the synods . . ."

[4.] Cf. the statements issued by the Barmen synod (which met May 29–31, 1934, in Wuppertal-Barmen), "Theologische Erklärung zur gegenwärtigen Lage der Deutschen Evangelischen Kirche" (Theological Declaration on the Current Situation of the German Protestant Church), and the Dahlem synod, "Botschaft der Dahlemer Bekenntnissynode der Deutschen Evangelischen Kirche" (Message of the Dahlem Confessional Synod of the German Protestant Church), issued on October 20, 1934, in Berlin-Dahlem. English translations of both texts have been published in Maclear, *Church and State in the Modern Age* (the Barmen Declaration appears on pp. 379–83, and the Dahlem statement on pp. 383–86). On Bonhoeffer's appraisal of the synodal resolutions and the consequences he drew for a consistent course for the Confessing Church, see especially his 1935 essay "The Confessing Church and the Ecumenical Movement" (*DBW* 14, 2/6) and the 1936 essay "On the Question of Church Fellowship" (*DBW* 14, 2/19) with his related discussion questions (*DBW* 14, 2/19.3).

ture? The fact that this question must be addressed in your circle[5] after four years must above all give us cause for concern. It is truly possible that four years of work and action have passed without this question having been 408
decided[6]—that is, that you allowed yourselves to be trained, examined, and ordained by the Council of Brethren without having been compelled to do so by the word of God. If so, today we stand in our province[7] as we did in 1934. This situation, then, would be unambiguous, and the question concerning Barmen's and Dahlem's accordance with Scripture has indeed arisen somewhat late, but nonetheless, the question would be a genuine one. It is also possible that we were led on the path to Barmen and Dahlem by Scripture alone, and that today it is once again Scripture alone that compels us to object to our former knowledge. We would then have to summon people away from a path contrary to Scripture and toward the path according to Scripture. In other words, we need to bring a deeper knowledge of Scripture to Barmen and Dahlem. If so, it was not only a thoughtless but a false path that led you to the Council of Brethren. This situation would be equally unambiguous, and our question that we bring to Scripture today would be genuine. It might also be that, while previously we were convinced that the confessional synod[8] was in accordance with the Scriptures, we have fallen into pervasive doubt, given the numerous circumstances such as the failure of church leadership, the departure of esteemed brothers, and hindrance and oppression from all sides. To escape further theological, ecclesial, and human difficulties, and moved by a resigned relativism, we hold on to what alone remains positive;[9] we grapple for whatever we can hold on to with certainty, what is still meaningful such as stability, work, and security, namely, the ministry under the leadership of the consistory. But in this situation we must be very clear[10] about the object of our doubt. Are we doubtful that as weak human beings we are unable to fulfill our task?
Or have we begun to doubt whether the confessional synod conformed to 409

[5.] Here Bonhoeffer's circular letter (*NL*, A 56,5 b) deletes the phrase "in your circle."

[6.] Here Bonhoeffer's circular letter (*NL*, A 56,5 b) adds the phrase "before God."

[7.] Here Bonhoeffer's circular letter (*NL*, A 56,5 b) deletes the phrase "in our province" (this refers to the Pomeranian church province of the Confessing Church, within the Old Prussian Union Church).

[8.] Here and elsewhere Bonhoeffer's circular letter (*NL*, A 56,5 b) consistently uses "confessional synods."

[9.] Here Bonhoeffer's circular letter (*NL*, A 56,5 b) substitutes the phrase "from resignation."

[10.] Here Bonhoeffer's circular letter (*NL*, A 56,5 b) substitutes the following: "in any case, however, we have today realized clearly. . . ."

Scripture? Or are we already so far gone that we doubt whether the Holy Scriptures can give us the clarity[11] today that we seek?

You will understand that the kinds of questions we bring to Scripture also determine the kind of answer we receive. If we doubt our ability to proceed along the path assigned to us, then we must examine Scripture for the promises it has given those who are unsure and downcast. Thus we ask for strength and comfort for the hearts and hands that are tired, and we hear that all things are possible with God.[12] If we doubt altogether that today God still gives us clear knowledge of his will through Scripture and if we say that today we should be guided by our personal assessment of current circumstances, then we must examine Scripture to see whether God ever thus deserted his people, or whether it is not more the case that he punished this kind of lament in particular, pointing to his eternal covenant. Here, then, our entire personal attitude toward the Bible and salvation would indeed be at stake. But if our doubts in the present situation are in fact directed not at human beings or at God's word in general, but at[13] the very question as to whether B[armen] and D[ahlem] were in accordance with Scripture, then we must show once again on the basis of Scripture that to which we have witnessed untiringly—and must continue to witness to—for the last four years in the Confessing Church.

It is not for me to decide whether the question I was given to address here is in fact your question.[14] All the questions named above are genuine, but they cease to be genuine the moment they are mixed together. The one who doubts—be it because of worry or anger against the Council of Brethren or the understandable desire for a peaceful ministry—that the confessional synod is according to Scripture will not be able to receive an answer from Scripture. For such a one is not looking seriously for that answer. Whoever,
410 in a state of general temptation of his faith, doubts God's revelation to his church[15] and rejects with it the insights of the confessional synod[16] is in dire need of all the comfort and patience of Scripture, but referring such a person to the scriptural testimony of Barmen and Dahlem will be

[11.] Here Bonhoeffer's circular letter (*NL*, A 56,5 b) adds the phrase "concerning the will of God."

[12.] Cf. Mark 10:27.

[13.] Here Bonhoeffer's circular letter substitutes "against" for "at" in the last three instances in this sentence.

[14.] This sentence is omitted in Bonhoeffer's circular letter.

[15.] Here Bonhoeffer's circular letter replaces the expression "to his church" with "according to the testimony of Scripture."

[16.] Here Bonhoeffer's circular letter substitutes "Confessing Church."

of little help. Perhaps today it would be more necessary[17] to speak about these things within the C[onfessing] C[hurch]. You will have to do this among yourselves.[18] We must now turn to the question of whether the confessional synod[s] of Barmen and Dahlem are in accordance with the Scripture.

What is scriptural evidence?

1. Scriptural evidence can be procured only for the truth of a doctrine.

2. Scriptural evidence is provided where a doctrine is grounded in individual texts and within Scripture as a whole. In other words, scriptural evidence must correspond to the so-called formal and material principles of our church.[19]

The earliest scriptural evidence that Christianity had to bring forward was for the statement: "Jesus is the Christ." In those days, Scripture was exclusively the Old Testament. Next came the scriptural evidence[20] for the dogmas of the early church. Our own scriptural evidence can be extended only to the truth of the teaching[21] of Barmen and especially of Dahlem. Scriptural evidence applies only to the truth of a doctrine, but never to the correctness of a path. With that we reject two dangerous misunderstandings:

1. Scriptural evidence can never be used as the self-justification of one's 411
own path. God alone knows whether our paths are right since he alone sees our faith. Whatever does not proceed from faith is sin (Rom. 14:23), be it even the most consequent path of Dahlem. Our paths are never justified in any way other than by faith. Hence, it is not our Dahlem path but the truth that was pronounced and witnessed to in Dahlem that is justified by Scripture. Our path does not really deserve particular interest. Our path comes into consideration[22] insofar as it is in the truth, that is, insofar as it is for the sake of the truth to which it witnesses. The Bible knows nothing of the pathos and problem of [the question][23] about "our path." Our path follows self-evidently, plainly, and necessarily from the truth that is witnessed to.

[17.] Here Bonhoeffer's circular letter substitutes "a need."

[18.] This sentence is omitted in Bonhoeffer's circular letter.

[19.] The Formula of Concord (Epitome) states that the Holy Scripture consisting of the Old and New Testaments is the "the only rule and guiding principle according to which all teachings and teachers are to be evaluated and judged" (*Book of Concord*, 486).

[20.] Here Bonhoeffer's circular letter substitutes "evidences of Scripture."

[21.] Here Bonhoeffer's circular letter adds the phrase "of the synods."

[22.] Here Bonhoeffer's circular letter adds "only."

[23.] This addition by Bonhoeffer is also in the circular letter.

Our path does not have its own weight, its own problem, and certainly not its own particular tragic aspect. It is simply "the doing of the truth" (John 3:21), whereby the emphasis is entirely on the truth. Because we know that our path is always in need of forgiveness, the question of our path does not need to be as important to us as the question of the truth. If we abide in truth and in truth alone, our path will be the right one.

Since the theme that you have asked me to discuss is the path according to the testimony of Scripture, I can only refer back to[24] the quest for truth[25] at Barmen and Dahlem, in accordance with the testimony of Scripture. Our path is justified only in this truth. Christ is *the* way.[26] He is also our way. Strictly speaking, there really is no other way. Scripture is not interested in the multiplicity of human ways and objectives. Our path is that we let ourselves be found in this way of Jesus Christ.[27] Whoever looks to Scripture for a justification of one's own ways is seeking a justification through one's[28] works.

412 2. The other misunderstanding concerning scriptural evidence stems from the same root: one now looks to justify our paths not for the past but for the future. We expect from Scripture such concrete directives that we are released from acting on faith; one wants to see the path before walking on it. One demands the certainty that the path will certainly be pleasing to God before starting the journey. One says: if we could be absolutely certain on the basis of Scripture that the path of the Council of Brethren is pleasing to God, then we would follow it. Demonstrate this from Scripture and we will follow. Thus I want to have the scriptural evidence in my pocket as the guarantee for my path. But the Bible can never fulfill this kind of request either, because it is not intended to be an insurance policy for our paths, which may become dangerous. The Bible does only one thing: it calls us to faith and obedience in the truth that we know in Jesus Christ. Scripture points not to our paths but to the truth of God. Let no one among you think after this meeting today that he can go home armed with scriptural evidence that justifies his decision for the Council of Brethren; if so, he misunderstands both the Scripture and the essence of faith.[29] The scriptural

[24.] Here Bonhoeffer's circular letter substitutes the following: "The question of 'our path' thus must not consider anything other than . . ."

[25.] Here Bonhoeffer's circular letter adds the phrase "of the confessional synods."

[26.] Cf. John 14:6.

[27.] Here Bonhoeffer's circular letter adds the following: "Christ is the truth [John 14:6]. That we let ourselves be found in this truth, this alone constitutes the truth of our way."

[28.] Here Bonhoeffer's circular letter adds "own."

[29.] This sentence is omitted in Bonhoeffer's circular letter.

evidence does not spare us from faith but actually leads us into the venture of faith and obedience to God's word, and it strengthens us in this. According to Scripture we do not first know and comprehend the way and then decide to follow it; it is rather the one who is on the journey who knows that he is on the right way. Knowledge comes only in action and decision. Only he who is in truth will recognize the truth. Jesus says: "Anyone who resolves to do the will of God will know whether the teaching is from God" (John 7:17). For this reason, scriptural evidence can be provided only along the way, that is, for the one who believes.

Whoever expects from scriptural evidence the justification of a past or future path wishes to be saved on the basis of his work, not to live in faith.

The scriptural evidence is addressed to those who believe. There is there- 413
fore a certain attitude for which scriptural evidence is useless from the outset. By this I mean the attitude that may be characterized by the following sentences: "It is possible to prove anything from Scripture," or "Scripture provides[30] no information for our situation," or "Yes, this is quite correct in theory but as to praxis . . . the congregation, finances, the state, etc." Whoever thinks like this needs first a lecture regarding the Reformers' position on Scripture as such, before he can comprehend the essence of scriptural evidence.[31] But whoever approaches Scripture in faith for information[32] will not be left in silence.[33]

We must now deal specifically with the resolutions of the Dahlem synod. It has now become customary to criticize Dahlem while at the same time reaffirming agreement with Barmen. This is a contradiction that stems mostly from a lack of knowledge of the Barmen and Dahlem resolutions; no one so far has attempted to prove the theological contradiction or difference between Barmen and Dahlem. Dahlem is nothing other than the exposition of the third and fourth theses of Barmen.[34] There is no doubt

[30.] Here Bonhoeffer's circular letter adds "us."

[31.] Here Bonhoeffer's circular letter substitutes the following: "Whoever speaks like this shows unbelief against God's revelation in Scripture, perhaps without even knowing it. He undermines the ground on which one can alone stand, and invalidates the power of Scripture. How should the evidence of Scripture help him?"

[32.] Here Bonhoeffer's circular letter substitutes "direction."

[33.] Cf. the entry for June 21, 1939, in Bonhoeffer's American diary (1/137). See also Feil, *Theology of Dietrich Bonhoeffer*, 20–27 and 49–52.

[34.] Cf. the third and fourth theses of the Barmen Theological Declaration of the first confessional synod of the German Evangelical Church, held in Wuppertal-Barmen, May 31, 1934. [Thesis 3: "We reject the false doctrine, as though the church were permitted to abandon the form of its message and order to its own pleasure or to changes in prevailing ideological and political convictions." Thesis 4: "We reject the false doctrine,

that whoever attacks Dahlem thereby attacks Barmen as well. Dahlem rightfully invokes Barmen, and Barmen itself explicitly established the crucial scriptural ground for the decisive statement at Dahlem: Eph. 4:15 "But
414 speaking the truth in love, we must grow up in every way into him who is the head, into Christ, from whom the whole body is joined and knit together." On this basis, Barmen bore witness that the order in the church is bound to Jesus Christ alone and consequently rejected the false teaching that the order in the church could be left at random to the church's own discretion or the prevailing political or ideological convictions.[35] Barmen was correct in holding to the central New Testament concept of the church as the body of Christ. Church is not a community of souls, as is claimed today, nor is church merely the proclamation of the gospel; that is to say, church is not only the pulpit, but church is the real body of Christ on earth. Church is an ordered and differentiated commonwealth [Gemeinwesen] constituted on this earth by, and grounded in, God.[36] Just as Jesus Christ was not a truth or an idea[37] but flesh, that is to say, a human being in the body, likewise the church is the earthly body of the heavenly head. The entire body with all its members is obedient to its[38] head. The body grows in every way onto him who is the head. There is thus no part of the church that is not entirely and exclusively subject to Christ. It is an unbelievable diminishment of the New Testament when today church is seen only as proclamation and administration of the sacraments. The church is essentially an assembly around the word and sacrament, but in addition it is the fullness of the gifts, offices, and powers that are effective within the church-community. Ultimately, the church means the life of the church-community according to the commandments of God. The church is thus the space of proclamation, the space of order, the space of Christian life. It is all these things as the body of Christ. When the proclamation becomes false, the church's concern must be true proclamation; when the church's order is destroyed
415 by force, then the church's concern must be true order; when the practice of Christian life or love is hindered, then the church must nonetheless follow God's commandments alone.

---

as though the church, apart from this ministry, could and would be permitted to give to itself, or allow to be given to it, special leaders vested with ruling powers." Translations from Hockenos, *Church Divided*, 179–80.—VB]

[35.] Cf. Thesis 3 of the Barmen Theological Declaration (ibid.).

[36.] Here Bonhoeffer's circular letter substitutes "constituted on this earth." [Cf. *DBWE* 4:229 and 261.—VB]

[37.] For Bonhoeffer's thorough critique of the "idea" or "principle" in theology, see Feil, *Theology of Dietrich Bonhoeffer*, 32–37.

[38.] Here Bonhoeffer's circular letter substitutes the phase "to the one."

The Dahlem synod faced the situation of a church whose proclamation and order had been destroyed by the German Christian regime of violence.[39] Hence, it accepted God's word as the commission to call for correct proclamation and to correct church order. This was not just a theoretical matter but one that needed to be put into practice. Dahlem did nothing but this. Referring to Barmen, the synod reestablished the church's correct order, installing the Councils of Brethren as governing bodies of the church, in order to grow in all things onto the one who is the head, Christ.[40] These are the simple facts. All the[41] objections that you undoubtedly wanted to raise: how will the state, how will the consistory, how will the pastors and congregations react; what consequences will this have for the assignment of the coming generation of theologians, for finances, for the conflict with the neutrals,[42] etc.—these were all questions that the Dahlem synod deliberately didn't pose, because it wanted nothing else but to affirm obediently what it recognized as the clear and very simple commission of its Lord. If here was truly God's commission, then all further worries could be left confidently to God.

If the simple fundamental insight of Dahlem is further analyzed for theological clarification, one could do so along the lines of the following sentences:

In the Dahlem declaration the following is being expressed:

1. We are one church.

2. The church needs church leadership.

3. Church leadership[43] exclusively serves the proclamation of the gospel and the correct life of the church-community.

[39.] Regarding the situation in the fall of 1934 preceding the Dahlem synod, see *DB-ER*, 392–94, and Scholder, *Churches and the Third Reich*, 2:244–65.

[40.] Cf. Eph. 4:15–16.

[41.] Here Bonhoeffer's circular letter adds "worrisome."

[42.] See Bonhoeffer's plea in his June 1936 essay "On the Question of Church Fellowship" in *DBW* 14:675: "A special problem are the neutral ones. Tentatively I would say that in reality there are no neutrals. They simply belong to the other side." [In the Church Struggle, the "neutral" or "intact" churches were the Lutheran regional churches, whose governance structures had not been taken over by German Christians. This enabled them to avoid some of the conflicts and decisions that were forced upon the churches in Prussia, but it also meant (according to Bonhoeffer and others who adhered to the "Dahlem" line) that they undercut the solidarity with the Confessing Church. Regarding the anger of Bonhoeffer and others toward these "neutral" leaders, see Barnett, *For the Soul of the People*, 59 and 72.—VB]

[43.] Here Bonhoeffer's circular letter adds the following: "can only be called by the church itself; it . . ."

416 4. Proclamation in the church is tied to the church's commission.[44]

5. Obedience to the heretical church regime is disobedience against Christ.[45]

6. The church leaves the concerns about the future in the hands of its Lord.

1. We are one church.

Dahlem has acted on behalf of [stellvertretend] the entire church. Dahlem spoke "on the matter of the church," thereby announcing that the church does not consist as the sum of individual congregations but is church as such. Every individual congregation is only a part or a member of the entire church, just as the Confessing Church is a part of the one Christian church. In responsibility to Scripture, Dahlem thought not in congregationalist terms, that is, from the perspective of the individual congregation, but from the perspective of the entire church. The church is originally and essentially *one.* The members are not independent of the body but are only members as members of the one body. Paul writes to the "church of God that is in Corinth" (1 Cor. 1:1). He includes the congregation he writes to as one with his own: "to be saints, together with all those who in *their and our* place call on the name of our Lord Jesus Christ" (1 Cor. 1:2).[46] For the sake of church unity, Dahlem did not leave the struggle against the destruction up to the individual congregations but acted in responsibility for the entire church. The entire church was threatened, so action was required for its sake. Let us remember that we stood up for the sake of church unity, in order to ward off schism and division. But who is causing the division: those who dissolve and destroy the teaching and order of the church or those who affirm and uphold it? Let us do away with the erroneous self-accusations[47] that the Confessing Church causes division.[48] That is a false call to repentance.
417 It comes from the mouth of the German Christians. "One body and

[44.] Here Bonhoeffer's circular letter substitutes the following: "the ecclesial [*kirchlich*] commission."

[45.] Cf. Bonhoeffer's 1936 essay ("On the Question of Church Fellowship") mentioned in ed. note 42 above, with its provocative and clarifying thesis (*DBW* 14:676): "Whoever consciously parts with the Confessing Church in Germany parts with salvation."

[46.] [Bonhoeffer's German differs slightly here from the NRSV, which reads: ". . . together with all those who in every place call on the name of our Lord Jesus Christ, both their Lord and ours."—VB]

[47.] Here Bonhoeffer's circular letter substitutes "self-reproaches."

[48.] Here Bonhoeffer's circular letter adds the following: "we will confess where we have sinned. But . . ."

its[49] spirit," this was the question, *but* how is this possible other than that there be also "one Lord, one faith" (Eph. 4:5)? The unity of the church was genuine only and exclusively when it stood before Jesus Christ.[50] There is unity[51] only where it corresponds to the one Lord in one faith, and such unity was and is there to this present hour. Any self-made unity, whether it is based on organization or on pietistic emotions[52] or tactical reasons, was unmasked as fanaticism [Schwärmerei]. Unity exists only in the unity of faith, expressed in *confession.* Dahlem has called the church to[53] unity on the basis of the word: Everyone therefore who acknowledges me before others, I also will acknowledge before my Father in heaven.[54]

From this position, Dahlem claimed—for the new and true[55] church leadership—the validity of the entire church, thereby from the outset objecting against all congregationalist and free-church tendencies. Because the Confessing Church wanted to be the one and true church of the gospel, it could not and cannot merely become a sect that gives up the claim upon the entire church, seeking only to nourish its own existence. As long as the church holds on to the insights of Dahlem, it can never take the path of[56] self-sufficiency in separation from the church in general, even if it becomes a persecuted and suffering church. It will not succumb to any enticement and harassment. But as soon as the church gives up the insights of Dahlem, it is bound to become a sect, for it thereby separates from the one true church and should be content if its status as sect[57] is not taken from it. The true church leadership must claim validity—by virtue of the authority of the confessions of the church as validated in the church constitution—upon the entire church,[58] in the same way that the apostolic council[59] once decided for the entire church.

Because the true unity of the church in the sense of John 17 was here 418
at stake, and because here the right word was found and expressed for the

[49.] Here Bonhoeffer's circular letter corrects with "one."

[50.] This sentence is missing in Bonhoeffer's circular letter.

[51.] Here Bonhoeffer's circular letter adds "of the church of Jesus Christ."

[52.] Omitted in Bonhoeffer's circular letter.

[53.] Here Bonhoeffer's circular letter adds "true."

[54.] Matt. 10:32.

[55.] Here Bonhoeffer's circular letter substitutes "newly constituted."

[56.] Here Bonhoeffer's circular letter substitutes "within."

[57.] Here Bonhoeffer's circular letter corrects with "naked life."

[58.] The first confessional synod of the German Protestant Church, in its Barmen Theological Declaration, had referred to Article 1 of the statutes of the German Protestant Church, July 11, 1933, as providing the legal foundation [for its position at Barmen—VB]. Cf. Maclear, *Church and State in the Modern Age*, 381.

[59.] Cf. Acts 15:1–29; Gal. 2:1–10.

entire church, for these reasons there had to be a corresponding community of action and suffering. God has made the church into one body "that there may be no dissension within the body, but the members may have the same care for one another" (1 Cor. 12:25). This care for one another corresponds to common suffering and joy. "If one member suffers, all suffer together with it . . ."[60] Part of the nature of the body is that here there is no question, no problem, no reflection on whether one member should care for the other or suffer with the other; the very *question* will already dissolve the membership of the body. As a member of the body, one cares for, suffers with, and shares joys with the other naturally. The care for one another and the being there for one another are simply there.[61] Whoever wants to avoid this will separate from the body. Among you the question has been discussed[62] as to whether the church must always act in unity. The New Testament does not recognize this question. It knows that members can care for one another only as long as they are members. Isolated action, that which is not done for one another, divides us from the church as the body of Christ. For the New Testament, being for one another usually means common action. The Corinthians are exhorted to be one not only in their faith but also in νοῦς and γνώμη[63] (1 Cor. 1:10). They are to speak the same; they should think the same (2 Cor. 13:11; Rom. 15:5; Rom. 12:16). The unified decision of the apostolic council arose from the being for one another of Jewish and Gentile Christians. It is self-evident that this being for one another can and will take various forms. Those who are weak act differently than those who are strong.[64] But the limit to these differences is clear: everyone acts in obedience to the one Lord. Disobedient action separates one from the community of the one body. On what constitutes disobedience, more later.

Let me also say a quick word here concerning the frequently dispar-
419 aged[65] expression of "brotherly solidarity." The word itself is not the problem. We are speaking of active brotherly love. It is curious that we theologians repeatedly seem to forget that our obedience to Jesus Christ also demands the simple brotherly love for those who hold the same office, for those who suffer, and for those who fight on the front lines. That we do not abandon a brother in need, that we stand by a brother who is attacked

[60.] 1 Cor. 12:26.

[61.] Cf. *DBWE* 1:182.

[62.] Here Bonhoeffer's circular letter substitutes the following: "The question was raised . . ."

[63.] [Translated as "mind" and "purpose" in the NRSV—VB]

[64.] Cf. 1 Cor. 8:9–12.

[65.] Here Bonhoeffer's circular letter substitutes "misunderstood."

for the sake of the gospel—even if we ourselves happen not to be under attack—that we stand up for each other in danger, struggle, and suffering, is such a self-evident thing that we should not even have to mention it. The questioning of whether these things are demanded unconditionally introduces a set of problems that can only lead to[66] an escape. We are therefore once more posing the question of good works, rather than doing good works in such a way that the left hand does not know what the right one does.[67] I would like to remind you of the lovely testimony of the Old Testament concerning the tribes east of the Jordan, but only as an example, not as scriptural evidence. At issue is the conquering of the promised land. The offspring of Reuben and Gad want to remain east of the Jordan and settle there. They come to Moses and ask for permission. But Moses makes it conditional for them, that they first help their brothers to enter their lands and lead them in the fight on their behalf, before they themselves may conquer their own lands. I ask you to read Num. 32:5–6, 16–24 and Josh. 22:3–4 thoroughly. Please remember as well how the imprisoned Paul called for Timothy to come to him in his sufferings in Rome, not be ashamed of his fetters, but to suffer with him. "Suffer with me" is principally the entire content of the second letter to Timothy. It is also the last word that we have from the apostle Paul.[68] So much for the question of so-called solidarity. We have been speaking of the proper unity and the true community of the church, and we now proceed to the second statement.

2. The church needs church leadership. 420

For the sake of church unity, Dahlem established true church leadership in place of a leadership that had become heretical. It did this for the sake of the responsibility for the entire church. Why and in what sense does the church need church leadership? Just as every congregation needs leadership, so likewise the church in its entirety needs leadership. Even the incipient church-community in the New Testament knows of such common leadership. All that were part of the Jerusalem church, and here we are speaking of several congregations (Acts 21:20: "thousands of believers," including Samaria, Galilee, Damascus!), were under the leadership of James. Similarly, the leadership of the church-community in Ephesus would have been responsible for a wide region. Paul is very clearly in charge of his congregations (1 Cor. 11:1; 1 Cor. 14:34 and 6:1; 1 Tim. 3:2ff.; 2 Cor. 10:6

[66.] Here Bonhoeffer's circular letter substitutes "serves."

[67.] Cf. Matt. 6:3.

[68.] Here Bonhoeffer's circular letter substitutes the following: "it is the last summons that we know from the apostle Paul."

and 13:10). The most telling example of an overarching church leadership is the apostolic council[69] at which the Jewish ceremonial law was formally declared nonbinding for all the Christian congregations. The church needs church leadership for it to be led in unity according to the word of God and to prevent schisms. For the Dahlem synod the situation was plain and simple insofar as the individual congregations had conferred certain rights (training, examination, ordination of preachers) on the entire church, which for this reason now had to administer these rights for the congregations.

Should the church have endured the heretical church regime of the German Christians as that of the "strange [wunderlich][70] masters"? (cf. 1 Pet. 2:18). The ability to make distinctions is sadly lacking if we confuse the "strange masters" with those who destroy the church, that is to say, if we can no longer distinguish between the obedience that is owed to even a "strange" secular authority and the church's responsibility to serve as guardian [Wächteramt]. According to the teaching of Scripture, false teachers must be[71] disciplined and removed from the church-community.
421 This is necessary for the church-community's sake; let us today read once more those sentences that were in everyone's mouth at the beginning of the church struggle, Ezek. 33:2ff.,[72] words that we all too easily prefer not to hear today.

In what sense does the church need church leadership? Is it not able to exist without leadership? To this we must say: The church lives not by church leadership but by the gospel, but the church leadership must care for the proper proclamation of the gospel. Without church leadership the congregations are in[73] danger today of not receiving proper preachers of the Christian truth.[74] Therefore, church leadership is needed precisely for the sake of[75] the congregations.

[69.] Cf. above ed. note 59.

[70.] [The cited verse from 1 Peter refers to "harsh" masters: "Slaves, accept the authority of your masters with all deference, not only those who are kind and gentle but also those who are harsh." Translator Peter Frick notes that the best translation for the original Greek is "crooked," "unscrupulous," or "dishonest."—VB]

[71.] Here Bonhoeffer's circular letter adds "severely."

[72.] Cf. Ezek. 33:2–7: the sentinel who is called by God to blow the trumpet in the face of danger threatening the people of God.

[73.] Here Bonhoeffer's circular letter adds "utmost."

[74.] Here Bonhoeffer's circular letter adds the following: "Without proper church leadership, the holy office of preaching is placed in the service of foreign powers. Without proper church leadership, the congregation's salvation—which has its foundation in the unabbreviated and pure proclamation of the gospel for all times—is wantonly endangered."

[75.] Here Bonhoeffer's circular letter adds "the office of preaching and."

3. Church leadership can be called only by the church itself, for it serves the gospel alone.

According to Scripture the ministries of the church-community as διακονίαι[76] are ordered and appointed by the triune God (1 Cor. 12:38[77] God has appointed . . . ; Eph. 4:11 Christ has appointed . . . ; Acts 20:28 the Holy Spirit has appointed . . .). The apostles or the congregations accomplish this will of God (Acts 1:23; 6:5; 13:3). The formation of the ministries may vary (Jerusalem, Ephesus), but common to all is their appointment by the congregation and their exclusive commitment to the objectives of the gospel.

It is thus the essence of proper church leadership to bind the congregation and its offices to Jesus Christ alone; it is the essence of a heretical church leadership to bind [the] congregation and its ministries to itself. Dahlem rejected the church regime of the German Christians because it bound those holding church office to the church regime instead of to Jesus Christ (Dahlem 1:5).[78] The church leadership of the Confessing Church 422
is not an end in itself but exclusively a means to an end, namely, service to the proclamation.[79] But an attack on the means to the end is an attack on the end itself. The attack on the proper church leadership is an attack on the proclamation. Church leadership is the protective wall for the proper proclamation in the congregation. When this wall is broken through, the proclamation[80] itself is in danger. Where the concern for the proper proclamation is hindered, the proclamation itself is hindered. For the sake of the proclamation, those who hold office in the Confessing Church must continue their service to the body of Christ.

4. *The proclamation in the church is bound to the church's commission.*[81]

The proclamation of the gospel is a matter not of one's own choice and inner drive but of a commission. All depends on whose name, that is, in whose authority I preach. Even the most fervent love for the people, for the church-community, or for the task of preaching can never replace the

[76.] "Services." In Bonhoeffer's circular letter the phrase "as διακονίαι" is missing.

[77.] [Translator Peter Frick notes that the correct reference is 1 Cor. 12:28.—VB]

[78.] See the fifth article of the Dahlem declaration: "The anti-Scriptural introduction of the temporal leadership-principle into the Church and the consequent demand of an unconditioned obedience has bound the office-bearers of the Church to the Church Government instead of the Christ" (in Maclear, *Church and State in the Modern Age,* 384).

[79.] Bonhoeffer's circular letter adds "that brings salvation."

[80.] Here Bonhoeffer's circular letter adds "and the congregation."

[81.] Here Bonhoeffer's circular letter substitutes the following: "the ecclesial [*kirchlich*] commission."

commission. Since preaching should never be my own ever so serious, ever so honest, or ever so faithful word about God, but rather God's own word, preaching therefore exists only where there is divine commission, that is, where there is ministry in its essential sense. The *vocatio interna* cannot replace the *vocatio externa*;[82] otherwise we succumb to Enthusiasm and sectarianism. Precisely this is the danger for all those who enter into the pastorate without a proper *vocatio externa*, namely, those who seek a legal pastorate but not the legitimate preaching ministry.[83] In this respect we must examine the great significance of the Old and the New Testament concept of "sending." Whoever preaches without sending misleads the con-
423 gregation. Of false prophets it is said: "I did not send the prophets, yet they ran; I did not speak to them, yet they prophesied" (Jer. 23:21), and "I am against those who lead my people astray by their lies and their recklessness, when I did not send them or appoint them; so they do not profit this people" (v. 32),[84] and "how are they to proclaim him unless they are sent?" (Rom. 10:15). When Jesus sees the people [Volk], he has compassion for them, because they are parched with thirst and scattered, like sheep without a shepherd. But he does not awaken his disciples' own offer to proclaim the gospel, nor does he appeal to their love for the people [Volk] and the church-community, but he says: "*Ask* the Lord of the harvest to *send* out laborers into his harvest" (Matt. 9:38). In a situation that is very similar to ours, Jesus calls not for self-empowered action but to prayer, asking God to send preachers. For we do not know what is good for the church-community; God alone is to act on his own counsel with the church-community. God alone knows what truly serves the church-community. The fire that burns in us is not supposed to burn in the church-community. God himself wants to kindle the fire on the altar. The fire that Aaron's sons tried to kindle on God's altar by their own initiative has to destroy them, because it is "unholy fire before the Lord, such as he had not commanded them" (Lev. 10:1ff.). Miriam's rebellion against the one who was sent by God, Moses, "Has the Lord spoken only through Moses? Has he not spoken through us also?"

[82.] "Internal" and "external vocation." This is a distinction made by Luther in his interpretation of the *rite vocatus* (proper vocation) in the Augsburg Confession, Article 14 (*Book of Concord*, 47).

[83.] The distinction here between a ministry for preaching and a legal pastorate must be understood against the background of the illegality of the Confessing Church; see the beginning of Bonhoeffer's 1935–36 lectures on homiletics, *DBW* 14:479–81.

[84.] [Bonhoeffer's text differs from the NRSV, which reads: "I am against those who prophesy lying dreams, says the Lord, and who tell them, and who lead my people astray by their lies and their recklessness, when I did not send them or appoint them; so they do not profit this people."—VB]

(Num. 12:2) is punished with leprosy. Likewise, when the Levites Korah, Dathan, and Abiram aspire to the priesthood because "all the congregation are holy,"[85] this is called a rebellion against the Lord and leads to destruction (Num. 16:11). God appoints prophets and priests. "Then some itinerant Jewish exorcists tried to use the name of the Lord Jesus over those who had evil spirits . . ." (Acts 19:13), but they are convicted and punished.

The Word must not be spoken without commission, for it is God's property. When Paul travels through Phrygia and Galatia, he is hindered by the Holy Spirit from speaking the Word (Acts 16:6). Jesus forbids his disciples to go into the cities of the Samaritans even though they needed the gospel according to the disciples' opinion (Matt. 10:5–6). But Jesus knows why it 424
must be this way; the disciples understand only much later. Matt. 28:20 will be fulfilled by God in his own manner. Even if there should be a time when Amos 8:11 comes true, namely, that an insatiable hunger and thirst for the word of God will come over the land, there will be a seeking but no finding. God builds his kingdom, not we. Nowhere in Scripture does someone come to his ministry without being called, since this is not a matter of pious behavior but God's own work. Why was Jeremiah hesitant;[86] why was Jonah disobedient[87] and did not accept God's sending? Why does James have to exhort: "Not many of you should become teachers, for you know that we who teach will be judged with greater strictness" (James 3:1)? And we want to become preachers of the gospel by virtue of our own authority? Do we know what this entails? Dare we usurp this office? Do we really want to do what no man in the Bible did, namely, to assume personal responsibility for the doing of God's work? And[88] if God should not like what we did, to bear the guilt? Do we want to send ourselves because we do not want to pray and wait for God's sending? Since in ministry all depends on the sending, on the commission, we can only receive it with certainty for ourselves when it comes from God's hands, namely, by virtue of a commission in God's true church where we have been correctly instructed in the pure gospel, where our proclamation has been correctly examined and tested (cf. 1 Tim. 3:10; 3:2; 2 Tim. 2:2), both of which serve not only the judgment of the church that does "not ordain anyone hastily" (1 Tim. 5:22) but also our own certainty. Without a proper understanding of the truth and testing of our ministry, we should not even desire to become preachers! To receive the commission to proclaim the gospel from the hands of a heretical church

[85.] [Num. 16:3.—VB]

[86.] See Jer. 1:4–8.

[87.] See Jonah 1:1–16.

[88.] Here Bonhoeffer's circular letter adds the following: "Do we also intend . . ."

regime is a dangerous thing, self-authorization, contempt for God's sending. But what if otherwise we would not receive a ministry? Do we not have to bring the *sacrifice*, for the sake of the church-community, to place ourselves
425 under the authority of the consistory? Scripture says: "To obey is better than sacrifice" (1 Sam. 15:22), for only in obedience do you allow God alone to reign. He says: "I will give you shepherds after my own heart" (Jer. 3:15), for God knows what he wants. What, then, should we do? "Ask the Lord of the harvest"[89]—this is the first thing. And God has many ways to send you. It is better for the sake of the gospel and for the sake of the church-community to receive a lesser office from the hand and by commission of the church of God than to receive a secure office from the hands of the enemies of the church. For in view of all the responsibility and the seriousness of our office, we can even today be fully certain: Christ has sent me.[90]

5. *Obedience to the heretical church regime is disobedience against Christ.*

Based on this insight, Dahlem has summoned us to withdraw from the church regime of the German Christians and warned against cooperation with those who are still obedient to this church regime. A church regime is bound to become heretical when it acknowledges other bonds for its ministries [Amtstätigkeit] than that to the gospel alone. It thereby necessarily becomes the oppressor of those who act only out of this bond, and it becomes the promoter of false teaching and lies. The fact that some individual members of the church regime fight a desperate and hopeless fight against these bonds imposed upon them and against their commission has no effect on the office of church government as such. We are interested here not in persons but in the false commission, the misuse of the office. As those commissioned by a false church, they are bound to become enemies of the church, whether they want to acknowledge this or not. In fact, they themselves become false teachers in that they are no longer permitted to distinguish between truth and lie; they have to justify false teaching. But from the concealed sin of Jeroboam necessarily follows the open sin of Ahab. One should read again very carefully 1 Kings 12:25–33 and what follows. When Saul no longer asks God for wisdom in all things but acts from the thoughts
426 of his own heart, he goes to the witch, who foretells his own destruction to him.[91] But for the sake of God's will, for the sake of the salvation of the

[89.] Matt. 9:38.

[90.] On this section on "sending," see also Bonhoeffer's interpretation of Matt. 10 in *DBWE* 4:183–98.

[91.] Cf. 1 Sam. 28:3–25.

church-community, and for the sake of the salvation of the soul, Christ's church-community must not become entangled with false teachers and with those who introduce and excuse them. "Have nothing to do with a heretical person"[92] (Titus 3:10), for such a person misleads the congregation (2 Tim. 3:6–7). "Everyone who does not abide in the teaching of Christ does not have God" (2 John 9). A congregation[93] that no longer takes seriously its separation from false teaching no longer takes truth seriously, that is, it does not take salvation seriously, and ultimately that means it does not take itself seriously, regardless of how pious or how well organized it is. Those who obey false teachers, and even promote and encourage them, are no longer obedient to Christ. Here it is said: "No one can serve two masters. You cannot serve God and Mammon"[94] (Matt. 6:24), for Mammon has been in the hands of the world all along. "Do not pull together under one foreign yoke with unbelievers. For what partnership is there between righteousness and lawlessness? What agreement does Christ have with Beelzebub?" (2 Cor. 6:14ff.).[95] Obedience to a heretical church regime and[96] disobedience against Christ. We must disobey a heretical church regime for the sake of Christ even if it is appointed by the state.[97] But the disobedience against a false church regime must correspond to the right obedience to right church leadership, namely, as obedience that is expressed through active commitment to this church leadership for the sake of the gospel. Indeed, church leadership is not the gospel; it is in its respective form merely an adiaphoron.[98] But when church leadership is placed by external forces under a law

[92.] [The NRSV here reads: "Have nothing more to do with anyone who causes divisions."—VB]

[93.] Here Bonhoeffer's circular letter substitutes "church."

[94.] [The NRSV here has "God and wealth," but Bonhoeffer's German text is "Mammon"; he is referring here to the German Christian–controlled finance departments that were putting pressure on Confessing congregations. Cf. also *DBWE* 6:421.—VB]

[95.] [The NRSV reads: "Do not be mismatched with unbelievers"; here we have translated more literally the text from Bonhoeffer's Luther Bible.—VB]

[96.] Here Bonhoeffer's circular letter corrects with "is."

[97.] Already in September 1935, Bonhoeffer vigorously resisted the church leadership of the Reich and provincial church committees that had been appointed by Hanns Kerrl, the National Socialist Reich minister for church affairs (cf. *DBW* 14). In February 1937, after the failure of the church committees and the conferring of the power on Friedrich Werner, the president of the High Church Council of the Old Prussian Union Church in Berlin, Bonhoeffer further rejected any cooperation with these church committees that were appointed and controlled by the [German Christian—VB] church authorities.

[98.] An "indifferent matter," i.e., something that is "neither forbidden nor commanded by God"; cf. *Formula of Concord*, Solid Declaration X (*Book of Concord*, 635).

alien to it, then it must stand firm[99] (cf. Paul and Titus, Gal. 2:3ff.). Who-
427 ever thinks, however, that he could be obedient to a heretical church regime with a free conscience and in obedience to Christ should be aware of the crisis into which he leads his colleagues. He should take to heart the word of Jesus, which warns with great gravity against troubling the least of these.[100]

Only when this presupposition is clear once and for all, namely, that the word of God prevents us from following the path to a heretical church regime, can we fruitfully ponder the new paths that open up before us. If we still hold on to the thought in our hearts that we might ultimately be able to go back, then the future will appear bleak, for we now become responsible for what will happen.

6. The church leaves the worry for the future to its Lord, who leads it.[101]

I believe that we have come only now to the point that is fundamental to you; what is going to happen? you are asking.[102] There is much worrying, and this has taken on a dreadful power. Dahlem was able to leave the worry for the future up to God because it wanted to be obedient to him alone. We will become free of worry only when we abide firmly in the truth that we know and let ourselves be guided by it alone. But if we stare at the waves rather than looking to the Lord, then we will be lost.[103] For many of us it is a huge temptation—we need to say this—when again and again brothers
428 are urgently telling us: look at the waves; see the storm; there can be no happy end. This is the temptation toward unbelief. We do not wish and cannot deny that there are waves, but we want not to look at them but at Christ, who is stronger than them. If only this could finally be understood! In the world it is different, but in the church it can only be this way.

Since the beginning of the Church Struggle, the other side has reminded us of Jesus's word (Luke 14:28ff.) to calculate the cost before something is

[99.] Here Bonhoeffer's circular letter adds the following: ". . . and bear witness in word and deed to its freedom from an alien law and to its exclusive bond with Jesus Christ. In a *statu confessionis nihil est adiaphoron* [in a matter of confession there is no indifferent thing]." This is an allusion to the main thesis of Matthias Flacius Illyricus in his dispute with Philipp Melanchthon regarding the Interim 1548–52; cf. Solid Declaration X (*Book of Concord*, 635–40).

[100.] Cf. Matt. 25:31–46.

[101.] Here Bonhoeffer's circular letter corrects with "who alone leads it."

[102.] Here Bonhoeffer's circular letter substitutes the following: "It may be that only now have we come to the point that concerns us today most of all. What is to happen? we are asking."

[103.] Cf. Matt. 8:23–27. Cf. also Bonhoeffer's sermon on the second Sunday after Epiphany, January 15, 1933, *DBWE* 12, 3/4.

started, but for the most part[104] people do not know what this really means. Jesus is speaking here not about a decision about a certain path but about discipleship in its entirety. Jesus coerces no one into discipleship, but he demands that each person consider the consequences of discipleship. But if this reflection reaches a negative conclusion, then there is not another easier path, that is, a path under the consistory's guidance, but everything is at stake. Scripture says very plainly: "None of you can become my disciple" (v. 33). Jesus does not propose here to weigh various possibilities, but he demands a decision: entirely with Jesus Christ or entirely without him. This question definitely confronts us today as well.[105]

One asks: do you really have nothing else to tell us today that goes beyond Barmen and Dahlem? Today we need to go beyond that. Today we need something new! Only those who are totally committed to the declarations of the confessional synod may speak like this, but one thing is certain: we in our place[106] are not in that situation. What is the real situation? It is not that we took Barmen and Dahlem too seriously, but that since 1935 we did not take it seriously at all. I see and confess a great guilt of the Confessing Church among ourselves and beyond:[107] we have[108] rejected God's grace and call. We thought we could do without them. What do Barmen and Dahlem mean? The concern for right proclamation and the true building up of the church-community. Where is this now? We have rejected[109] God's gracious offer, and now it is unimaginably difficult to turn back.[110] 429
Guilt is[111] manifest in two things: 1. We followed the path of Dahlem[112] only with the young theologians; that is, we did not dare to stand entirely by Dahlem.[113] 2. Since 1935, there were constant and substantial efforts to keep those who were undecided, to find a broader front, to listen more

[104.] This is omitted in Bonhoeffer's circular letter.

[105.] This is omitted in Bonhoeffer's circular letter.

[106.] In Bonhoeffer's circular letter the phrase "in our place" is omitted.

[107.] Here Bonhoeffer's circular letter omits the phrase "among ourselves and beyond."

[108.] Here Bonhoeffer's circular letter adds "widely."

[109.] Here Bonhoeffer's circular letter substitutes the following: "thought too low of."

[110.] Here Bonhoeffer's circular letter substitutes the phrase "to start anew." It then adds the following: "Only God himself in his forgiving grace can lead us back to the right path."

[111.] Here Bonhoeffer's circular letter adds "especially."

[112.] Here Bonhoeffer's circular letter adds "strictly speaking."

[113.] Here Bonhoeffer's circular letter adds the following: "This means we put too heavy a burden on you young brothers! But it was still the right path, and for that we give sincere thanks with you to God, our Lord, in this hour."

to and accommodate those who were tossed back and forth, rather than listening to those who wanted to continue faithfully on the paths of the Confessing Church. Through all of this, both were lost, and the Confessing Church's concern for proclamation and the building of the church-community was pushed into the background, and increasingly the question of the church regime became central. That was not only unhealthy; it was also guilt. For the past three years nothing else has been debated here but the question[:] Council of Brethren or consistory. This has gradually become an unbearable burden for those who would like to move on. They are hindered by those who consistently pose this question. The guilt here is not that Dahlem was implemented, but only that it was not implemented. The other provinces[114] teach us these things very clearly. They have long arrived at the crucial theological questions [Sachfragen] of the proclamation and building of the church-community and are doing fruitful work. Essentially everyone here would welcome it today if we would not speak of the old question but discuss together the questions of gospel and law, proclamation and youth, church and synagogue,[115] baptism and godparenting, confession and the Lord's Supper, mission work [Volksmission][116] and
430 congregational discipline. Why are we unable to do this? Because some consistently raise doubts about the confessional synods.[117] Let us not believe

[114.] [The other church provinces in the Old Prussian Union church.—VB]

[115.] The phrase "church and synagogue" points to a question that became increasingly urgent to Bonhoeffer: what is the church's position toward the existence next to it of the Judaic faith; how does it relate to a Judaism that is not in the past, but rather a living Judaism? Cf. E. Bethge, "Dietrich Bonhoeffer and the Jews," 235–36.

[116.] [*Volksmission* has been translated in different ways throughout *DBWE*, but it essentially refers to the mission and evangelization movement within the German Protestant church that became more organized and widespread in the first half of the twentieth century.—VB]

[117.] In Bonhoeffer's circular letter, section "2" instead reads: "Since 1935, we have asked more about how we can win those who are wavering, how we can keep those who want to leave, how we can gain a wider front, rather than continue on the path of Barmen and Dahlem in faithfulness and deed. Through this, the very urgent concerns for the proclamation of the Confessing Church and the building up of the congregations were often pushed too much into the background, and the question of the church regime was placed more and more in the center of our thoughts and conversations. That was not only an unhealthy development, but it was guilt. For all those who wanted to continue in faith on the path of Barmen and Dahlem, it became an almost unbearable burden when the question: Council of Brethren or consistory overshadowed all discussions and meetings. We were hindered on the path along which we had to go. The guilt here is not that Dahlem was implemented, but that it was not implemented. Some of the provinces, church districts, and congregations demonstrated this to us. For the most part they have long since arrived at the theological questions [*Sachfragen*] of proclamation

that on the other side, in the consistories, we would be able to do this. There we have lost all inner authority because we did not abide in the truth. The entire path is at stake, even today, as was the case in Barmen and Dahlem.

But those who come with us on this path[118]—and only those—will become free of all worry about the future, for the worry will be taken from them—and only from them.[119] I want to summarize in six sentences the promise of Scripture that is given to those who follow in faith:[120] 431

1. God does not leave us without guidance (Deut. 30:11ff.).
2. God gives us enough work (Acts 18:19; Rev. 3:7 ff.).[121]
3. God has both the means and the ways to preserve his own (Matt. 6:32).
4. God gives us joy and certainty (Josh. 1:8).
5. God freely gives us perseverance and patience (James 1:12).
6. God grants us victory (Luke 12:32).

When I took on this lecture, I asked a brother—who today finds himself in the difficult position of making a decision—what I should say. He answered: "Take up your cross and follow me."[122] I think that this brother was correct.[123]

---

and building up of the congregations, and their work bears fruit. Would you not welcome it today if—rather than speak about the old question—we could finally discuss matters that really concern us, namely, what the Confessing Church has to say about gospel and law, proclamation and youth, church and synagogue, baptism and godparenting, confession and the Lord's Supper, mission work and congregational discipline? Why are we unable to do this? Because we let ourselves be held back by doubt about the truth that we already know, because we have not already 'acted' on the 'truth' of Barmen!"

[118.] Following Bonhoeffer's circular letter this text corrects "do not come along."

[119.] In Bonhoeffer's circular letter this subordinate clause reads: "those who experience that the path of the church is a joyful way also learn that Jesus's yoke is easy and light for those who do not rebel against it (Matt. 11:30). 'Hear, you servants of the Lord . . . you may be suspended, removed, lose your income, be deprived of your office, bereft of your house, but you will once again be preachers: that is the word of promise! . . . And if one is thrown out of twelve places and receives a new position, then one is preacher in thirteen congregations, for in all the previous our innocence, our cross, our faith, preaches more powerfully than if we had been there' (Zinzendorf on Jer. 15:19 [in Zinzendorf, *Jeremias*, 36–37])."

[120.] Instead of this sentence, Bonhoeffer's circular letter substitutes the following: "Dear brothers, let us be certain of the promises of God."

[121.] In Bonhoeffer's circular letter, this sentence reads: "God will give shepherds to his congregations according to his heart (Jer. 3:15)."

[122.] Cf. Matt. 16:24.

[123.] This last paragraph is omitted in Bonhoeffer's circular letter.

6. Essay about Protestantism in the United States of America, August 1939[1]

Protestantism without Reformation

There are two obstacles to the proper assessment of a foreign church, and they repeatedly hinder the genuine encounter with it:

First: The observer has the tendency to attribute the strangeness of another church to the peculiarities of its geographical, national, and social location, that is, to understand it in terms of its historical, political, and sociological context. The great revivalist and sanctification movements[2]
432 and Puritanism are thus "typically Anglo-Saxon," the "social gospel"[3] is thus "typically American," and conversely, the Reformation is "typically Continental or German." Such an observation is as common as it is ultimately boring and false. It has become common since there is a greater interest in the historical peculiarities of Christianity than in its truth; it is boring because it leads to a dead and convenient schematization. It is false because it dissolves from the outset the mutual obligation that churches have for each other's proclamation and doctrine. For why should a Christian in Germany be concerned with something typically American, and why should a Christian in America be interested in the typical Continental Reformation? At most it may be possible to take a certain aesthetic joy in the variety of appearances and forms of Christianity; it is also possible to

---

[1.] The original of this essay has been lost and therefore is not listed in the *NL*. [Bonhoeffer's notes for this essay, however, are included in the last five pages of his American diary, published here as document 1/137a; these five pages were omitted from *DBW* 15.—VB] The first printing appeared in *Unterwegs* 2, no. 1 (1948):3–17. Previously published in *GS* 1:323–54. Bonhoeffer wrote this essay when he returned from the United States in August 1939 (*DB-ER*, 658–60). [According to Bethge, he wrote most of it at Union Theological Seminary; cf. *DB-ER*, 659.—VB] See also the documents from the period of Bonhoeffer's stay at Union Theological Seminary in New York in 1930–31 in *DBWE* 10, particularly his reports of his studies (1/181 and 1/182) sent to the Church Federation Office in Berlin.

[2.] [The roots of the sanctification movements can be traced back to the Reformation. In the United States, it was called the Holiness movement and grew out of the so-called Second Great Awakening during the nineteenth century. It emphasizes the role of grace and the Holy Spirit in the sanctification of the faith and witness of the individual Christian. Because Bonhoeffer here speaks of these movements in the plural, referring to developments both in Europe and in North America, *Heiligungsbewegung* has been translated here as "sanctification movement."—VB]

[3.] This essentially North American movement within Protestantism was crucially shaped by Walter Rauschenbusch. Cf. *DBWE* 10:317–18 and Bonhoeffer's draft for an article [based on a draft by Paul Lehmann—VB] on the "social gospel" in the fall of 1932 (*DBWE* 12, 2/4).

welcome the other church as a complement to one's own church. But in this way it is impossible to come to a genuine encounter or to have an exchange that leads to commitment. As long as we are interested in American peculiarities, we are merely operating in the realm of detached observations. It is a different question what God does to and with his church, in and with America, how God reveals himself to the church and whether and how we may recognize God in that church. With that, the question of God's word, of God's will, and of God's action is raised between us. It is the same word, the same commandment, the same promise, the same office, the same church-community of Jesus Christ that is at stake, both in America and among us. And only the quest for this does justice to the matter. Indeed, the Reformation is not to be understood as a typically German event; it does not work this way. The same is true with respect to the forms and events of foreign churches. They cannot be explained objectively on the basis of the characteristics of other peoples. There is something more, and that is the issue here.

Second: The observer of a foreign church is all too easily content with 433
the current picture of that church's situation. One can easily forget how important it is to take the history of that foreign church seriously. God speaks differently to his church in different times. God spoke to the church in Germany during the Reformation in a different manner, that is, more urgently, clearly, and publicly than in any other subsequent period. Just as the German church cannot be understood apart from the Reformation, so likewise American Christianity remains concealed from those who do not know the beginning of the Congregationalists in New England, the Baptists in Rhode Island, or the revival movement led by Jonathan Edwards. American Christianity is also and especially what happened in those days, but it bears as little resemblance to American Christianity today as our church at the turn of the century did to the church of the Reformation.

What is God doing to and with his church in America? What is he doing through this church to us and, through us, to it? The following observations seek to contribute an answer to this question.

I. The Unity of the Church and the Denominations[4]

Americans have been less able than any other people on earth to realize the visible unity of God's church on earth. Americans have been more able than any other people on earth to envision the variety of Christian forms

[4.] [Throughout this section, particularly in Bonhoeffer's discussion of the significance of confession of authentic Christian faith in the unity of the church and the issue

of knowledge and community. Statistics show that there are more than two hundred different denominations (church-communities), with approximately fifty of them having more than fifty thousand members. Apparently, on one street in Minneapolis there are four different Lutheran churches with different affiliations. American Christendom[5] has no central organization, no common confession, no common ritual practices [Kultus], no common church history, no common ethical, social, or political principles. North and south (the question of slavery) but also the migration from east to west (the "boundary = frontier") signify changes and separations of the denominations. In addition there is the segregation of the races (color-line)
434 between Negroes and whites, which repeats itself even within the churches; finally, the denominational forms have also been determined by social differences. The "Federal-Council of the Churches of Christ in America"[6] is an association of twenty-nine denominations for common public action. It does not, however, represent *the* church of Jesus Christ in America but is representative of the *churches.*

Even the term "church" is often viewed with suspicion. The characteristic term is "denomination." For many American Christians, church is associated with too much clericalism, autocracy, confessional conceit [Dünkel], intolerance, persecution of heretics, a desire for worldly power and political favors. To be sure, Episcopalians, Lutherans, and Presbyterians are consciously churches, but in the eyes of the others, they are merely denominations. The remaining communities have more a denominational than an ecclesial [kirchliches] self-understanding.

The concept of denomination is not entirely clear. It is not a theological concept. It says more about historical, political, and social conditions.

---

of the "one true church," readers must keep in mind the bitter arguments over these very issues in the German Church Struggle, especially in 1933 and 1934, and the way in which the Confessing Church articulated its claim as the "true church" based explicitly on confession and Scripture. These were central issues for Bonhoeffer during the Church Struggle and later in his teaching of the seminarians in Zingst and Finkenwalde. See, for example, *DBW* 14, 2/6 (where he wrestles with these issues with respect to the Confessing Church and the ecumenical churches) and 2/19. See also *DB-ER*, 444–50.—VB]

[5.] [The German word here is *Christenheit* (Christendom); Bonhoeffer also speaks in this essay of *Christentum* (Christianity). "Christendom" as he uses it here refers to the larger unity of all Christians; "Christianity" refers more to the belief or faith itself. Because of the important different nuances, we have translated both terms as indicated in this note.—VB]

[6.] [In English in the original.—VB] Cf. 1/137, ed. note 15 (Bonhoeffer's diary entry for June 12, 1939, during his trip to America). [In the 1930s, the Federal Council of Churches actually had thirty-three member churches.—VB]

The denomination is a free association of Christians on the basis of certain shared Christian experiences as well as historical, political, and social ones. From the outset it allows for the possibility of other such associations. There is a certain humble hesitation in the denominations' self-understanding not to claim the name of the church of Jesus Christ for themselves, because that name seems too big and too dangerous to them. The church is beyond the denominations. In this respect, the concept of the invisible church is bound to come to mind. Denominations are the visible member bodies of the invisible church.

The deeper sources of denominational self-understanding in the history of the church need to be indicated. *First,* the origins of the Presbyterian-Congregationalist denominational formation in England were determined by the message of the exclusive reign of God on earth. All human claims must bow before the sovereign reign of God. Thus the denomination in
America is the negative stamp of the onset of God's reign. *Second,* one 435
must also see how the concept of tolerance of Congregationalist-Baptist Enthusiasm [Schwärmertum],[7] influenced especially by Roger Williams in Maryland,[8] was responsible. Here the reign of God is equated with the individual's freedom to follow only the inner voice and inner light. This paves the way for the formation of denominations without confession. *Third,* the denominational self-understanding implies a certain relation to the state. An American denomination is not a state church, but it is also not a free church in the sense of the English free church, which is a conscious counterpart to the state church. The American denomination is independent from the state and yet understands itself—in spite of its own internal limitations—as a piece of God's free church on earth. Nowhere does the denominational self-understanding come as close to the self-understanding of the church as in the denomination's relation to the state.

The denomination is not primarily determined by a confession. Most denominations do not have a firmly articulated confession. The *Lutheran and Episcopalian churches,* however, demand in their ordination formulas a binding pledge to their respective confessions. The *Presbyterians* are satisfied—strangely enough—with the commitment to the Scriptures. The *Congregationalist* ordination formula is entirely free; it requires only a confession of one's personal commitment to the Lord Christ in personal experience,

[7.] [Here and throughout this essay, "Enthusiasm" refers specifically to the so-called left wing of the Reformation—the movement within the Reformation that split early from Luther's followers. See also Bonhoeffer's comment on the distinction between the two groups in 1/182, p. 302.—VB]

[8.] [Williams was in Rhode Island, not Maryland.—VB]

in the certainty of the call to ministry and in belief.[9] But even in cases where there are confessional obligations, these are limited to a certain degree since most denominations mutually recognize the administration of the sacraments, of the ministry, and ordination. This is true for Presbyterians, Methodists, Congregationalists, Reformed, United Lutherans, Northern Baptists, evangelicals [Evangelische].[10] Only the Episcopalians,
436 the Missouri Lutherans, and the Southern Baptists have resisted such recognition to this day. The doctrinal differences are often more significant within denominations (e.g., Baptists, Presbyterians) than among the different denominations. Denominations are not churches based on a confession, and where an individual denomination makes such a claim, it is limited denominationally by the others. Today the relationship of the denominations with one another is less than ever a struggle about the truth of proclamation and doctrine.

This situation might suggest that American Christendom offers preconditions that are especially advantageous for a proper understanding of the unity of the church of Jesus Christ. Where churches are not divided by the struggle about the truth, the unity of the church should already be won. But the real picture is exactly the opposite. Precisely here, where the question of truth does not become the criterion either for community or for church schisms, there is greater fragmentation than anywhere else. Hence, precisely where the struggle for a true confession is not decisive, the unity of the church is further away than where the confession alone unites and divides the churches. Why is this so? In order to answer this question, we must turn our attention to a deeper distinction.

The churches of the Reformation start from the assumption of the unity of the church of Christ. There can be only one church on earth. And this one church is alone the true church constituted by Jesus Christ. Church schism means church apostasy, unfaithfulness against the true church of Christ. The division of the church that came about in the Reformation can only be understood as a struggle for the true unity of the church. For this reason, the churches of the Reformation understand themselves as the One Church on earth, not as splinter groups of individual Christians driven from the one church by personal conscience, nor are they individual manifestations

[9.] During his stay in the United States in 1939, Bonhoeffer wrote on a piece of paper (*NL*, A 54,2) some notes on "Training and ordination" for "*Presbyterians*," "*Congregationalists*," and "*Baptists*." See 1/137, ed. note 94 (diary entry for June 26, 1939).

[10.] [The German *Evangelische* usually means Protestant; here, however, since Bonhoeffer is referring to a number of different U.S. Protestant churches, he probably means "evangelical" in the U.S. sense.—VB]

of the one church. The Reformation was about the one, universal, holy church of Jesus Christ on earth.

The denominations in America are faced from the start with an unimaginable variety of Christian communities. None of them can dare to make the claim to be the one church. It is part of Christian humility not to make 437
such a claim, given this astonishing picture of fragmentation. American Christendom has experienced the consequences of church schism, but not the act of the schism itself. For that reason they are no longer themselves engaged in the struggle for the one church; rather, they stand astonished before the results of that struggle and can merely accept with great humility what they find and heal the wounds. For American Christendom, the unity of the church of Jesus Christ is not so much something that is given originally by God and already exists [Seiendes] as it is something that is demanded and should be [Sein-sollendes]. Church is less origin [Ursprung] than it is goal [Ziel]. The unity of the church here thus belongs in the realm of sanctification.[11]

Here it should be pointed out—although this comment does not suffice—that since Occam[12] *nominalism* has been rooted in Anglo-Saxon thinking. This means that the existing particular has priority before the whole in the sense that the particular and empirically given is the real, while the whole is merely a notion, a name. The particular stands at the beginning, unity at the end. Conversely, the German-Continental philosophical tradition is determined by *realism and idealism*, for which the whole is the original reality, and the particular is merely that which has fallen away from the unity [das abgeleitete Abgefallene]. But these conceptual formulas cannot be taken as sufficient explanations for the different ways of thinking about the unity of the church, because they themselves are based on philosophical-methodological demands derived from theological insights. Nominalism and the philosophy of realism cannot be understood without the background of theology, and therefore they cannot provide a fundamental interpretation of the theological question.

Only the truth revealed in Holy Scripture can and must decide between the existing differences. Churches must allow themselves to be questioned by one another on the basis of Holy Scripture. *The denominations in America confront the German churches with the question of the multiplicity of churches*: What 438
is the significance of church fragmentation? Is only a church that is based

[11.] On Bonhoeffer's understanding of the unity of the church that is constituted (realized) in Christ, see *DBWE* 1:192–204 and his 1932 lecture "The Nature of the Church," *DBW* 11, 2/9, esp. 275–77.

[12.] William of Occam (Ockham).

on confession a true church, and, therefore, are American denominations not churches because for the most part they are not based on a confession? Is only the church that has a specific confession church, over against which the other confessional churches are false churches? Does one church on earth become the measure by which all others can and must be measured, for their justification or condemnation? Does multiplicity of churches imply only apostasy; do we have here only the harsh contrast between true and false? Is the unity of the church given only through the confession, or to what degree can actual common action be the foundation for fellowship between churches?[13]

Conversely, the church of Jesus Christ in Germany poses the question of the unity of the church on earth to the American denominations: May one simply accept the multiplicity of the churches as a given and therefore God-intended fact? Can there be a unity of the church other than in the unity of faith and confession in the one Lord? Isn't all the unity in action and organization merely a self-deception that covers up the true divisions in faith? Isn't the indifference or resignation toward the question of truth a guilt that has as its consequence the disintegration of the churches through organizational, ritual [kultisch], and political contradictions? Why is it that the fragmentation of the churches is greatest precisely where the confessional question is relativized? Is not the unity of the church first and foremost origin and only afterward goal?[14]

From over there[15] they say to us: you overestimate reason, theology, dogma; these are only one among many expressions of the church and not even the most important ones. We reply: it is a matter not of reason but of
439 the truth of the word of God with which we wish to live and die. It is a matter of salvation. The unity of the church is surely based not on human thinking nor on human "life and work" (Life and Work!),[16] but solely on the life and work of Jesus Christ in which we participate in faith. Unity in thought is not superior to unity in work, but unity in faith, namely, confession, breaks through both and thus creates the precondition for common thought and action.

[13.] On these questions, see Bonhoeffer's essay "On the Question of Church Fellowship," June 1936, *DBW* 14, 2/19.1, esp. 655–67.

[14.] On the method and content of a theological conversation between different churches, see Bonhoeffer's August 1935 essay, "The Confessing Church and the Ecumenical Movement," *DBW* 14, 2/6.

[15.] [I.e., across the Atlantic.—VB]

[16.] This is an allusion to the ecumenical organization "Life and Work," which was established at the 1925 world church conference in Stockholm.

This conversation cannot take place here. But this much can be said:

First: The unity of the church is both origin and goal, both fulfillment and promise; it belongs to both faith and sanctification. Where the unity of the church as origin is forgotten, human organizations that seek unity take the place of the unity in Jesus Christ; the spirit of the times, which aims toward harmonization, takes the place of the Holy Spirit, which unites only in truth; and the life and work of Jesus Christ is pushed out by human "life and work." Conversely, where the unity of the church as goal is forgotten, the living contradictions become lifeless; the work of the Holy Spirit, which seeks to bring about the fulfillment of the unity of the church, is no longer taken seriously; and the divine unity of the church is replaced with a separatist pharisaic[17] claim. But where unity is understood as origin and goal alike, the life and work of Christendom, which seeks and finds the unity of the fragmented church, grows from the foundation of the life and work of Jesus Christ, in whom all unity of the church is fulfilled.

Second: The claim to be the church of Jesus Christ has nothing to do with pharisaic conceit; rather, it is an understanding that humbles because it moves toward penance [Buße]. Church is the church of sinners and not of the righteous. There may be more self-righteousness in the claim to be church than in the claim itself. It may conceal a false humility that desires something better and more pious than the church that God has elected 440
from among sinners. Denominational self-understanding does not protect from spiritual arrogance. Conversely, ecclesiastical self-understanding must let itself be summoned, again and again, to penance and humility. It remains a fact that the New Testament gives legitimacy to the concept of church, not to the one of denomination.

Third: The unity of the church as promise, as future, as the fruit of sanctification, is a work of the Holy Spirit. This unity cannot be forced, either through theological discussion or through common action. But we know that God may bring the churches together, through both the path of common understanding and the path of common action. Often, common understanding is granted only through common action, and common action from common understanding. There are no methods that lead to the unity of the church. Only total obedience to the Holy Spirit will lead us to common understanding, confession, action, and suffering.

Fourth: The particular problem for an understanding between the churches of the Reformation and the American denominations is that

[17.] [Bonhoeffer's pejorative use here and below of the word "pharisaic" reflects the theological biases of his generation.—VB]

they cannot simply encounter one another on the level of the confessional question. The reason for this is that the confession is not the constitutive moment for the denomination, whereas, conversely, it is the only relevant ecumenical element for the Reformation churches.[18] In the denominations, church ritual [Kultus], liturgy, the life of the congregation, and the church constitution occupy the same place that confession has for us. This encounter is fruitful for this very reason, however, because it calls into question the entire existence as church or, respectively, as denomination. If we ask American denominations first and foremost about their confession, the question is as unessential as the question of constitution and the relation to the state is for the churches of the Reformation. And yet to ask essential questions of the other church opens up unknown riches for one's own church. For the one side, it opens up the full richness of various forms of worship and liturgy, active congregational life, rich experiences of the
441 meaning of the church constitutions; for the other, it reveals the urgency of the question of truth, the riches of Christian knowledge that are in the church's confession—and what is most important—in this encounter both are brought to humility and the expectation of salvation not from their own form [Gestalt] but from the grace of God alone. It is a difficult task for American denominations to understand properly the struggle for a confessional church;[19] and it is no less difficult for the churches of the Reformation to understand the path of American denominations. Precisely because a common level of understanding seems to be missing in this encounter, it becomes easier to envision the only level on which Christians can encounter one another, the Holy Scripture.

II. The Refuge of Christians

The distinctiveness of the history of the church of Jesus Christ in America, in comparison with all other churches on earth, lies in the fact that America was from the very beginning a place of refuge for the persecuted Christians of the European continent. Since the seventeenth century, America has been the asylum for the victims of religious intolerance, for those who desired to live and serve God in freedom. To be sure, America is consciously

---

[18.] [See here Bonhoeffer's 1935 essay, "The Confessing Church and the Ecumenical Movement," *DBW* 14, 2/6, esp. pp. 387–88, where he questions the authority of the ecumenical movement precisely because of the overriding authority (for the churches of Reformation) of the Scriptures and confessions.—VB]

[19.] [This can certainly be seen as a more specific reference to the German Church Struggle.—VB]

a "Protestant" country. Americans have been captivated from the beginning by the notion of a special providence that reserved the discovery of America until the emergence of Protestantism. America is thus the only country in which the concept of "Protestantism" gained church-historical significance and reality, for America wants to be not the country of the Lutheran or the Reformed church but precisely the country of "Protestantism" in its full denominational breadth. Perhaps it is true to say that the Lutherans of America conform the least to American Protestantism. The notion of America as the place of refuge for persecuted "Protestants" is what constitutes the church-historical uniqueness and, indeed, even today the continuing church-historical self-understanding of American Christendom.

A large sector of the American denominations began with voluntary or involuntary flight and the entire complex of problems this poses for Christians. Throughout
the history of the church, endurance and flight in times of persecution 442
have been the two Christian possibilities, since the days of the apostles. Endurance to the point of last resistance may be commanded; flight may be permitted or perhaps even commanded. The flight of a Christian in times of persecution is not apostasy and disgrace as such, for God does not call every person into martyrdom. Not flight but denial is sin, although there may be a situation where flight is the same as denial or, conversely, where flight itself may be a part of martyrdom.[20] Protestant refugees who traveled to the unknown America came not to a paradise but to a place of hard work. They tackled the struggle of colonizing a country in order to be able to live their faith in freedom without a fight. This sheds some light on the plight of the Christian refugee. He has claimed the right to avoid ultimate suffering in order to serve God in quietness and peace. But now, in the place of refuge, the continuation of the fight has no right to exist. Here are gathered Protestants of all confessions who have already renounced the ultimate fight about confession. There is no room for strife in asylum. Confessional stridency [Schärfe] and intolerance must cease for the one who has left intolerant conditions. By virtue of using the right of flight, the Christian refugee has forfeited the right to fight. This, at least, is how the American Christian understands it. Certainly, there has been strife among American churches and even instances of severe persecution, especially in the beginning. But in American Christendom the deep abhorrence that always meets every kind of confessional discrimination can essentially be explained by the Christian right of the refugee, by the American character of political asylum.

[20.] Cf. *DBWE* 4:193–95.

For the first generation of refugees, the path to America was a decision of faith for their entire life. For them, the renunciation of the confessional battle was a Christian possibility they had fought for. Here, however, a danger exists for the coming generations who are born into a situation without
443 struggle and for whom a life decision is no longer at stake. Sooner or later they will misunderstand their situation. What for the fathers was a right of their Christian faith, which they acquired at the risk of their lives, will be regarded by the sons as a general Christian rule. The confessional battle for the sake of which the fathers fled has become for the sons something that in itself is not Christian. The absence of a struggle will be the normal and ideal condition for them. The peace in which the descendants of the refugees grow up has been not fought for but inherited.

Hence, the notion of *tolerance* becomes the fundamental notion of everything Christian for American Christendom. All intolerance is un-Christian as such. Understanding and empathy are aroused not by a confessional struggle as such but rather for the victims of such a struggle. This must remain unsatisfactory for the victims themselves, since they are not so much concerned for their personal plight as they are for the truth of their cause. For the Christian refugee, the renunciation of the fight to the end for the truth remains a most troubling and lifelong issue. Only the deep sincerity and unlimited scope of compassion and the right to asylum in his country of refuge can be convincing in Christian terms. His yearning to decide for the truth against its distortion remains unfulfilled and must remain so. It is ultimately the faithfulness toward one's own church history that is expressed in this strange relativization of the question of truth in the thinking and action of American Christendom.

III. Freedom

America calls itself the land of freedom. Today this means the right of the individual to think, speak, and act independently. In this framework, religious freedom is a self-evident possession for the American. The church's proclamation, organization, and congregational life can flourish in complete independence and without interference. The praise of freedom can be heard everywhere from the pulpit, coupled with the sharpest condemnation
444 of any attempt to curtail such freedom anywhere. Here freedom entails the possibility—as a possibility for the church offered by the world—for unhindered effectiveness.

But as long as the freedom of the church is essentially understood as this possibility, the concept of church freedom remains unrecognized. *The freedom of the church is not where it has possibilities, but only where the gospel is truly*

effective in its own power to create space for itself on earth, even and especially when there are no such possibilities for the church.[21] The essential freedom of the church is not a gift of the world to the church but the freedom of the word of God to make itself heard. The freedom of the church is not the unlimited fullness of possibilities. Rather, freedom is only there where a "must" compels it, if need be against all possibilities.[22] The praise of freedom as the possibility that the world offers the church for its existence might stem precisely from a bond with the world, entered into by the church, which has thereby given up the genuine freedom of God's word.[23] It may happen that a church that praises its freedom as a possibility offered by the world succumbs to the world to a particular degree, that is, a church that is free in this way may be secularized faster than a church that does not possess freedom as a possibility. The American praise of freedom is more a tribute to the world, the state, and society than it is a statement concerning the church. Such freedom may be a sign that in truth the world belongs to God. But whether the world belongs to God in reality depends not on freedom as a possibility but on freedom as a reality, as urgency, as factual event.[24] Freedom as an institutional possession is not an essential predicate of the church. Freedom may be a gracious gift to the church given by God's provi- 445
dence, but it may also be a great temptation to which the church succumbs when it sacrifices its essential freedom to an institutional freedom. Only the actual proclamation of the word of God determines whether the American churches are essentially free. Only where this word can be concretely proclaimed in the midst of historical reality as judgment, commandment, gracious salvation of the sinner, and deliverance from all human ordinances is there freedom of the church. But where the gratitude for institutional freedom must be paid for through the sacrifice of the freedom of proclamation, there the church is in chains, even if it believes itself to be free.

[21.] On the power of the gospel *to create its own* "space" on earth, cf. *DBWE* 4:225–30 and 236–37.

[22.] [This is the freedom demanded by *necessitá*; see *DBWE* 6:272–75 on freedom and "the structure of responsible action" (275). The editor thanks Ilse Tödt for this reference.—VB]

[23.] [Again, this appears to be a direct reference to the controversy about the legalization of Confessing Church pastors by the church authorities.—VB]

[24.] On Bonhoeffer's consistent polemic against the category of "possibility" in theology, see the thesis in his 1930 inaugural lecture, "The Anthropological Question in Contemporary Philosophy and Theology": "*The concept of possibility has no place in theology and thus no place in theological anthropology*" (*DBWE* 10:403). Cf. the fourth thesis of his doctoral promotional theses from 1927, *DBWE* 9:440. See also Feil, *Theology of Dietrich Bonhoeffer*, 30–32.

IV. Church and State

Nowhere does the principle of separation of church and state have such a general, almost dogmatic, significance as in American Christendom, and arguably, nowhere is the participation of the churches in political, social, economic, and cultural affairs as lively and influential as in the country that does not have a state church. This seems to be a contradiction; the only explanation for this is to be found in the uniqueness of the American separation of church and state.[25]

Church and state were not always separated in America. In the seventeenth century, in New England the Congregationalists were a state church, likewise the Anglicans in Virginia and the Catholics in Maryland. However, these were instances of civil bodies controlled by the church more than of churches controlled by a state. *The state church privileges gradually ceased only after the foundation of the federal government following the American Revolution,* for the union is on principle religionless. Questions of religion are left to the individual states. The first major interstate unions of the denominations have their beginnings in these years. In 1784 the *Methodists* established the Episcopal-Methodist Church, in 1788 the *Presbyterians* established the General Assembly, and in 1789 the *Anglicans* united, but—to
446 this day—without electing an archbishop. The political movement toward union corresponds to these church unions. The complete separation of church and state was achieved and generally accepted by the nineteenth century. Not only the union but also the states are religionless. There are no public statistics on religion, religion is not taught in public schools, and in hiring for civil service positions there are no questions about confession. All of this originally was done in agreement with the denominations, for in this way competitive proselytization in state institutions, particularly in the schools, is obstructed. Also, denominational influence determines the lives of Christians to such an extent that there is no need for federal aid. Above all, however, one fact manifests itself in the state's separation from religion, and that is of fundamental importance to American Christendom, namely, that the churches mark the boundaries of the state. From this perspective, the state's religionlessness [Religionslosigkeit] is not so much a triumph of secular powers over Christianity as it is rather the victory of the churches over any unlimited claims of the state.[26]

[25.] [This is a reference to the First Amendment of the U.S. Constitution: "Congress shall make no law respecting an establishment of religion, or prohibiting the free exercise thereof."—VB]

[26.] [Bonhoeffer's use of the words "religionless" and "religionlessness" in this section

Here we find the key for understanding the original meaning of the American separation of church and state as well as that of the American constitution.[27] Even though they are nearly contemporaneous and are not connected politically, there is a profound difference between the American and the French revolutions. *American democracy is founded not on humanitarian principles or human right, but on the kingdom of God and the limitation of all earthly powers.* It is significant when eminent American historians can say that the American federal constitution was written by men who knew about original sin. Those who hold human power, as well as the populace itself, are put in their place because of the wickedness of the human heart and for the sake of the exclusive sovereignty of God. This notion, which stems from *Puritanism*, is connected to another consideration that stems from *spiritualism*,[28] namely, that the kingdom of God on earth can be built not by the state but solely by the church-community of Jesus Christ. Hence, the 447
church has clear priority before the state. The church proclaims the principles of social and political order, while the state merely lends the technical means to achieve these. These original and essentially different rationales for democracy offered by Puritanism and spiritualism soon become almost imperceptively intertwined; for American Christendom it is the latter,[29] however, that becomes more influential than the former. "Christians nowadays think in terms of Christian principles (the sphere of the church)[30]

---

of his essay is striking, since the phrase "religionless Christianity" in his prison letters (cf. *DBWE* 8, 3/137 and 139, and his "Outline for a Book," 4/187) has been one of the most provocative and variously interpreted aspects of his thought. It is an unusual word in German, and clearly Bonhoeffer does not merely mean secularism (since he uses that word elsewhere) but is describing something about the nature of the church-state relationship. His description here of a "victory of the churches over any unlimited claims of the state" suggests that *Religionslosigkeit* may not mean the absence of religion or religiosity, but rather implies a true independence of church and state from each other.

[27.] Regarding the passage that follows, cf. the section in *Ethics* titled "Heritage and Decay," *DBWE* 6:124–27. [The wording of the section in *Ethics* is clearly drawn from this earlier essay; several sentences are almost verbatim. See esp. *DBWE* 6:126, ed. note 102.—VB]

[28.] [This is a reference to the "spiritualists" of the Reformation period. Considered part of the radical, or left, wing of the Reformation, they included figures such as Thomas Müntzer and Kaspar Schwenckfeld von Ossig. As the name implies, the spiritualists were skeptical of external institutions and authority, even that of Scripture, focusing instead on the importance of inner spirituality and the work of the Holy Spirit. See Spitz, *Renaissance and Reformation Movements*, 404–8.—VB]

[29.] [I.e., spiritualism.—VB]

[30.] [Quotation in English in the original; both passages in parentheses were inserted in German by Bonhoeffer as additions to Brown's text.—VB]

and of technical policies whereby they can be put into practice (the sphere of the state)" (W. A. Brown).[31]

The fundamental difference between this church-state relation[32] and that of the churches of the Reformation is obvious. *The American separation of church and state is not based on the doctrine of two offices or the two kingdoms* that were ordered by God to remain until the end of the world, each serving in a fundamentally different way. The dignity of the state, nowhere else more strongly emphasized than in the teaching of the Reformation, fades into the background in American thinking. The juxtaposition of state and church becomes a subordinate relationship wherein the state becomes merely the executive of the church. *State* is essentially a technical organization and administrative apparatus. But the dignity of the state to wield the divine power of the sword "to avenge the evil ones, to reward the good"[33] seems to have been lost. American thinking is governed by the Enthusiast doctrine of the state as being destined in this earthly life to be integrated into the church, but it is at the same time a teaching that places American
448 democracy on firm Christian ground. This should make us think about why on the European continent it has never been possible to base a democracy on Christian principles, about why on our continent democracy and Christianity are always seen somewhat in opposition to each other, while in America democracy can be glorified as the epitome of a Christian form of government. In answering this question, one must recall that the European continent ruled out this possibility when it persecuted and expelled the spiritualists. But the country that offered hospitality to the Enthusiasts has been shaped fruitfully by them, even in its political thinking.

It lies in the uniqueness of the relation of church and state in America that, despite the fundamental separation of the two institutions, there is still cause for conflict. The *church* claims the right for itself to address and act on almost any topic in public life, since only in this way can the kingdom of God be built. In the process, the distinction between the offices is not recognized, on principle. The life of the state and public life in general are subsumed under the judgment of the church without distinction; hence, there can be no significant public decision in which the church would not raise its voice and issue pronouncements. Therefore, the sermons coming

[31.] William A. Brown, *Church and State in Contemporary America*, 140–41.

[32.] [In the United States.—VB]

[33.] Cf. Luther's functional classification of the "temporal authority and the sword it bears" in "Temporal Authority: To What Extent It Should Be Obeyed" (1523), as it is a divine ordinance (*ordinatio*) "to punish the wicked and to praise the righteous"(*LW* 45, II; *WA* 11:247,21–23, and 248,31).

from American pulpits deal usually with thematic discussions of certain public events or conditions. A glance at the New York church bulletins is evidence enough.[34] But it would be a false verdict if we were to appraise this type of sermon merely as a manifestation of secularization. It is that indeed, but behind this stands the old spiritualist claim to build the kingdom of God, publicly and visibly. *The European-continental* secularization of the church stems from the—misinterpreted—Reformation distinction of the two kingdoms; *the American secularization* stems precisely from the lack 449
of the distinction of the kingdoms and the offices of state and church, as well as from the Enthusiast claim that the church is the agent of the universal formation of the world. This is a significant difference. While the churches of the Reformation need a new examination and correction of the doctrine of the two kingdoms,[35] the American denominations must learn the necessity of this distinction today if they are to escape complete secularization.

Our knowledge of the American church situation can teach us the following lesson: *a church that is independent of the state is no more protected from secularization than a state church.* Whether the church is connected to the world or independent of it, the threat of infringement in the church remains the same. There is no form of church as such that preserves it fundamentally from secularization.

The following list of decisions in matters public and political, as recorded in a report by the *General Council of the Presbyterians*, is representative of the state of affairs in America. It should also be noted that we are dealing not with a spiritualist denomination but with the Presbyterians, who hold a Reformed position regarding state and church.[36] The starting point of the report is the refutation of the state's right to curtail religious freedom. The government agreement with Uruguay in this matter is seen positively.[37] Moreover, it includes steps for the colonization of American Negroes in Africa, the demand for a new marriage and divorce law, as well as laws for vaccinations and the right of women to vote. It takes a stand against gambling, lotteries, horse racing, and the practice of lynching. The government is asked to recognize Liberia as an independent republic; better race relations, old-age pensions, and unemployment aid, and simplification of civil

[34.] Bonhoeffer provides a few examples in his report on his academic year at Union Theological Seminary in New York in 1930–31; see *DBWE* 10:312.

[35.] This was one of the tasks Bonhoeffer saw himself faced with in writing *Ethics* (*DBWE* 6), which he began in 1940.

[36.] Cf. the report of the 1932 General Council of the Presbyterian General Assembly, cited in Brown, *Church and State in Contemporary America*, 152.

[37.] [The reference here is unclear.—VB]

legal proceedings are all demanded. The church conferences also deal in general with the International Court of Justice, disarmament, natural-
450 ization laws, etc. This corresponds to a Congregationalist statement: "We have stood resolutely for the separation of state and church but with equal insistence have we stood for the continuous impact of the church upon the state" (cited in W. A. Brown).[38] Brown summarizes the position of American denominations toward the state in three points: 1. all proclaim the separation between state and church as a prerequisite; 2. all recognize state authority as instituted by God; 3. all claim the self-evident right to speak to social, political, and economic questions insofar as these entail general ethical issues.[39]

At the moment there are two questions of special importance that are strong sources of conflict between state and church in America. First, the question of schooling, second, the question of peace.

The question of schooling: The absence of religion [Religionslosigkeit] in the public schools is a matter of serious concern today for the denominations. What the churches once endorsed as the limitation of the state's power[40] now begins to be an instrument against the denominations. Today, the more the pedagogical tasks of the schools expand, the more the denominations find it necessary to have their input. It is possible today in a public school to speak out deliberately against the church, while it is impossible to speak in the public schools in the name of the church. Hence, there is a growing movement within American Christianity against the absence of religion [Religionslosigkeit] in the schools. Curiously, among the Protestants, only the Lutherans opposed from the beginning the absence of religion in the schools and thus maintained their own confessional schools. This is all the more noteworthy since it was the American Lutherans in particular who never adopted a spiritualist understanding of the state and church relationship and who decided, unlike the large denominations, to
451 refrain from any kind of interference in the realm of the state. They alone kept the schools under the authority of the church, and to this day they support their own schools, even if that means paying twice as much.[41]

The peace question in America primarily concerns the issue of whether Christians and the clergy of various denominations should serve in the

[38.] [Quotation in English in original.—VB] See Brown, *Church and State in Contemporary America*, 148.

[39.] See Brown, *Church and State in Contemporary America*, 154–55.

[40.] Cf. 1/137, diary entry for July 4, 1939, p. 236.

[41.] [I.e., they would be paying state taxes to support public schools and private donations and tuition to support their own confessional school.—VB]

military.[42] Today there are three conditions in the United States under which a person can be released from military service: first, by virtue of being a member of a church that refuses military service on the grounds of Christian convictions (Quakers and others); second, by virtue of being a member of a church (for example, the Protestant Episcopalians since 1936, Methodist Episcopalians since 1932, Northern Baptist since 1934, Unitarians since 1936) that affirms the right of a "conscientious objector" (one who refuses to fight in a war on the grounds of conscience); third, for personal convictions of conscience. The decision in each individual case depends on whether the personal hearing clearly establishes that the decisive motive for objection is genuinely a religious or a conscientious one. The struggle concerning this question has been particularly fierce during the last ten years.

A question of somewhat lesser significance concerns *the display of the American flag in churches*, a practice that began during the war[43] but is widespread today. Public opinion polls have shown it is more the desire of laypeople than pastors to continue with the practice. In any case, it is a surprising custom in the land of church-state separation.

The strongest influence of the church on the state comes in America not through the congregation or the pulpit but *through the considerable power of the free Christian associations that are not denominationally connected.* It is impossible to understand the picture of American Christendom apart from this decisive link[44] that connects congregation and public life. These are private associations that have been established by individual Christians with some kind of specific purpose for the work of the kingdom of God in America. Great financial sacrifices are made for these organizations, and there is no comparison between their extent and influence and that of similar European associations. There are associations for evangelization, for social purposes, 452
the YMCA (Young Men's Christian Association), YWCA (Young Women's Christian Association), temperance and abstinence associations, groups for keeping the Sabbath holy, for prison reform, for the fight against vice, for unemployment aid, for the improvement of race relations, especially for the

[42.] [As World War II loomed, this issue was hotly debated in U.S. church circles; Bonhoeffer would have heard a great deal on this topic during his brief stay in New York. It was also a theme elsewhere in his writing; see, for example, *DBWE* 6:407 and *DBWE* 10:27, ed. note 130.—VB]

[43.] [The widespread practice of displaying a U.S. flag in church sanctuaries dates back to the Civil War, when it was adopted by some churches in the Union states as a symbol of their support; it became more widespread during the First World War (this is what Bonhoeffer is referring to here) and even more so during the Second, when President Franklin Roosevelt asked churches to fly the flag.—VB]

[44.] [I.e., the "free associations."—VB]

promotion of the living conditions of Negroes; there is also an overwhelming number of peace movements, and many others. The legal enactment of Prohibition in the Eighteenth Amendment was largely achieved by the relentless work of the Methodist-sponsored Women's Christian Temperance Union and the Anti-Saloon League, which were supported by all denominations except the Lutherans and the Episcopalians.[45] With regard to this, however, American Christendom has had a unique and probably a very consequential experience. It had to realize that the imposition of Christian principles on the life of the state led to a catastrophic collapse. The Prohibition legislation caused an unprecedented upsurge in crime in the large cities. A "Christian" law had brought disaster for the state and had to be rescinded—with the consent of the churches. This reality gave American Christians food for thought, as it should also cause us to reflect.[46]

V. The Negro Church[47]

For American Christendom *the racial issue* has been a real problem from
453 the beginning. Today almost every tenth American is a Negro. The young, forward-looking generation of Negroes are turning away from the faith of their elders because they view its strong eschatological orientation as an obstacle to the progress of their race and rights. This is one of the dangerous signs of the church's guilt in past centuries and a grave problem for the future. The fact that today the "black Christ" of a young Negro poet[48] is pitted against the "white Christ" reveals a destructive rift [Zerstörung] within the church of Jesus Christ. It cannot be overlooked that many white

[45.] After around 1900, several states legally prohibited the production, transport, and sale of alcoholic beverages; in 1919–20, with the passage of the Eighteenth Amendment to the U.S. Constitution, Prohibition was in force throughout the United States. In 1933, however, the Twenty-first Amendment rescinded Prohibition, and control of alcohol consumption was then left up to the individual states.

[46.] Cf. *DBWE* 6:355, esp. ed. note 11.

[47.] The situation of the "church of the outcasts of America" and their social discrimination was a burning issue for Bonhoeffer already in 1930–31 (see *DBWE* 10:314, and *DB-ER*, 150–51, 154–55). [In fact, the situation and church life of African Americans in the United States became a primary focus for Bonhoeffer during his 1930–31 stay at Union Theological Seminary. See the editor's introduction to *DBWE* 10:28–33, esp. ed. note 146. See also Young, *No Difference in the Fare*, for a contemporary evaluation of how this affected Bonhoeffer's theology.—VB]

[48.] *The Black Christ and Other Poems* is the title of a collection of poetry (1929) by the black poet Countee Cullen (cf. *DBWE* 10:315, esp. ed. note 31). [See also Bonhoeffer's reading notes on "Negro Literature," *DBWE* 10:421–22, and the editor's introduction to *DBWE* 10, 30–31.—VB]

Christians through influential organizations do whatever they can to improve the relations between the races and that discerning Negroes recognize the serious difficulties. But today the general picture of the church in the United States is still one of racial fragmentation. Blacks and whites come separately to word and sacrament. They have no common worship.

Historically, this stems from the following development: when the first larger transports of Negroes—who had been stolen from Africa as slaves—arrived in America, the slave masters were generally opposed to the christianization of the slaves. They justified slavery by citing the slaves' paganism. Baptism, however, would have called into question the legitimacy of slavery and brought undesirable privileges and rights to the Negroes. The slave masters agreed that the gospel could be preached among the slaves only after the bishop of Lo[n]don wrote a fateful letter to calm things down. In it he reassured the white masters that nothing whatsoever had to change in the outward conditions[49] of the slaves who were baptized, since baptism signified the deliverance from sin and evil lust, and not so much a release from slavery or any other such external fetters. After all, it brought with it the advantage of having more control over the slaves than would leaving them to their pagan rituals. So it happened that Negroes became 454
Christians and were allowed to attend the worship services of the white people while sitting in the balconies; they were also allowed to partake of communion—as the last guests. Any further participation in the life of a congregation was ruled out; all the offices of the congregation and ordination remained the privilege of the whites. Under these conditions, the common worship service became for Negroes more and more a farce. Once all attempts had failed to be recognized as equal members in the church of Jesus Christ, Negroes made an effort to organize themselves in their own congregations. This was both a forced and a free decision on the part of the Negroes. A number of incidents, particularly during the time of the Civil War, which also brought the abolition of slavery, led to the independent organization of the Negro church. Since then, the large denominations are split; here we have a telling example of the formation of denominations in the United States. The strongest contribution of the Negroes for American Christendom lies in their spiritual songs ("Negro spirituals"), in which they sing with moving expression about the distress and liberation of the people of Israel ("Go down, Moses . . ."), the misery and distress of the human heart ("Nobody knows the trouble I have seen . . .") and love for

[49.] Cf. *DBWE* 4:234–35 and the 1727 pastoral letter of Bishop Edmund Gibson in Dalcho, *Historical Account*, 104–12. See also Feil, "Bishop Edmund Gibson."

the Redeemer and yearning for the kingdom of heaven ("Swing low, sweet chariot . . .").[50] Every white American knows, loves, and sings these songs. It is difficult to understand how famous Negro singers can sing these songs in the overcrowded concert halls of white people and receive resounding applause, while at the same time the same men and women find no acceptance in the communities of the whites because of social discrimination. We should furthermore point out that nowhere else is revivalist preaching still so alive and widespread as it is for Negroes; here the gospel of Jesus Christ, the Savior of sinners, is truly preached and received with great welcome and visible emotion [spürbarer Bewegung]. The issue of the Negro is one of the most decisive future tasks for the white churches.[51]

455

VI. Theology

Given everything that has been said up to this point, it should not come as a surprise that we are discussing theology last. This is not to imply that American theology as such is insignificant. It merely reflects the fact that American denominations must be understood primarily in terms of their church services, their practical work in the congregation, and their public engagement rather than their theologies. The same is true for almost all Anglo-Saxon churches, and this poses a great difficulty for us. No one can do justice to these churches as long as they are judged by their theology. The order and tradition pertaining to the worship services, offices, and congregations carry such weight here that even a bad theology cannot do too much damage. But it is not only this—viewed from the perspective of intellectual history—conservative background that explains this peculiar situation; rather here we find a virtually irreconcilable contrast between the churches of the Reformation and the "Protestantism" without Reformation. We will return to this at the conclusion.

At the beginning of this year, the journal *Christian Century* published a series of essays on the topic: "How my mind has changed in the last decade."[52] *Men of the church and teachers of theology* are asked to give a brief

[50.] [Parenthetical text in English in original.—VB] On Bonhoeffer's deep appreciation for Negro spirituals, see also *DBWE* 10:269 and 315 [as well as *DBWE* 10:30–31—VB].

[51.] The text in *GS* includes the following note: "Even in America it is little known that it was the Lutherans in Fort Christina who first abolished slavery in their colony in 1638 and declared religious toleration for America in 1642!" [*GS* 1:349n1; it is unclear whether this note was also included in *Unterwegs*.—VB] Cf. Qualben, *Lutheran Church in Colonial America*, 138–39.

[52.] Cf. 1/137, ed. note 36 (diary entry for June 17, 1939).

autobiographical and theological report [Rechenschaftsbericht] *on their own development in the last ten years* for the Christian public. A *common* thread in all these essays—with the exception of the fundamentalists, who deliberately declare that nothing essential could have changed in their thinking since they espouse the same teaching then and now—is the admission of a decisive theological turn in the last ten years. *Common* is also the direction in which the turn is seen: it is a return to revelation from secular- 456
ism in its many forms as modernity, humanitarianism, and naturalism. While ten years ago there was a predominant interest in the "social gospel," today there is an awakening of a greater interest in dogmatics, a fact that is especially noticeable in one of the most prestigious theological institutions of the country, namely, at Union Theological Seminary in New York. German theology, inasmuch as it is translated into English—mainly the works of Barth, Brunner, Heim, and a somewhat undifferentiated Tillich as well[53]—has left deep impressions. Kierkegaard[54] is being introduced to wider circles through new translations. There is also—with an almost stronger effect—the new English theology with its strong emphasis on the necessity of a natural theology. *Common* is also the explanation for this shift, namely, the collapse of the old social orders in America and other countries and the ensuing critique of a liberal, optimistic faith in progress [Fortschrittsglaube], which until now dominated theology. Prompted by this new insight is now the *common* speech, more than ever, of sin and God's judgment, as is evident in the current world crisis. Finally, *common* is also the deliberate rejection of Barth's critique of natural theology. Within these boundaries there are all kinds of nuances of theological thinking; this is possible given the combination of a new search for a Christian theology of revelation with the tradition of American thinking.

The essays of the following authors are especially worthwhile reading: *W. L. Sperry* (professor of practical theology at Harvard),[55] whose views may be summarized in these words: "American life has been until most recently, optimistic, once-born . . . our once-born America is changing 457
before our eyes"; *H. N. Wieman* (professor for philosophy of religion in Chicago),[56] an advocate of "theistic naturalism," whose definition of sin is a

[53.] Karl Barth, Emil Brunner, Karl Heim, Paul Tillich.

[54.] Søren Kierkegaard.

[55.] Willard L. Sperry, "How My Mind Has Changed." [The quotation is in English in Bonhoeffer's original.—VB]

[56.] See Henry Nelson Wieman, "Some Blind Spots Removed," from which the following quotations [in English in Bonhoeffer's original—VB] are taken.

strange mixture of Reformation insight and the naturalistic anthropology of James[57] and Whitehead:[58] "Therefore, he, who makes ideas supreme over his life, no matter how lofty and no matter how perfectly he may live up to them, is sinning."[59] Similarly remarkable is the following sentence about grace: "The grace of God is the good which God puts into each concrete situation over and above all that man can do or plan or [even] imagine"; by contrast, the text becomes completely obscure in treating the living Christ as the "working of a process of history which used that human personality" (of Jesus), or as "the growth of a community" that breaks through all natural human communities; similarly weak is the definition of the church as "a new way of living." On the other hand, there is a notable remark concerning the otherness of God: "God alone is concrete in his working . . . man must work abstractly"; and based on this a special appreciation of the apostle Paul. The failure in Christology is characteristic of all current American theology (with the exception of fundamentalism).
458 *Reinhold Niebuhr* (professor at Union Theological Seminary),[60] one of the most important and creative theologians in America today, whose main work one should know in order to appreciate the theological landscape (*Moral Man and Immoral Society, An Interpretation of Christian Ethics, Beyond Tragedy*),[61] is the sharpest critic of current American Protestantism and the contemporary social order. For years now he has left a deep impression by strongly emphasizing the cross as the center and the end of history, tied to a strong and active political theology. He sees the right way between neo-orthodoxy, for which Jesus Christ becomes the basis for human despair, and a true liberalism, for which Christ is the Lord, the norm, the ideal, and the revelation of our essential being. Both are equally necessary. But even here a doctrine on the person and the work of salvation of Jesus Christ is missing. *W. M. Horton* (professor at Oberlin College)[62] wants to work out a synthesis among Augustine, Calvin, Barth, Wieman, and the "social gospel." *E. S. Ames* (former professor and pastor in Chicago) refuses as the only liberal to recognize a change in his thinking through recent develop-

---

[57.] William James. Bonhoeffer studied James and American pragmatism during 1930–31 (cf. *DBWE* 10:310–12 and 438–40).

[58.] Alfred North Whitehead.

[59.] The first printing here erroneously had "sinking."

[60.] See Reinhold Niebuhr, "Ten Years That Shook My World."

[61.] Cf. 1/137, ed. note 71 (diary entry for June 22, 1939).

[62.] Walter Marshall Horton, "Between Liberalism and the New Orthodoxy."

ments and defiantly gives his article the title "Confirmed Liberalism."[63] According to him, new theology is and remains an atavism, because it is unscientific. "God is life as you live it" (!). "Worship as praise and adulation does not fit with my idea of either God or man. It tends to separate them, to exalt one too much and to debase the other too much." It is hardly comprehensible how someone can be a pastor for decades with such a teaching! On the other hand, however, he is stating with frank openness what others, past and present, may be thinking.

With few exceptions, current American theology presents a fairly uni- 459
form picture, at least for someone who comes from the churches of the Reformation. This brings us to the last point.

God did not grant a Reformation to American Christendom. He gave strong revivalist preachers, men of the church, and theologians, but no reformation of the church of Jesus Christ from the word of God. Those churches of the Reformation that came to America either stand in deliberate seclusion and distance from general church life or have fallen victim to Protestantism without Reformation. There are Americans who announce with certainty and pride that they build on principles that are pre-Reformation and radical Reformation [nebenreformatorisch][64] and see in this their essential nature. It cannot be denied that the dangers for American Christendom today are seen clearly by some of the leading theologians. Reinhold and Richard Niebuhr, Pauck,[65] Miller,[66] and several others among the younger theologians speak largely in the spirit of the Reformation. But these are exceptions. American theology and the churches as a whole have never really understood what "critique" by God's word means in its entirety. That God's "critique" is also meant for religion, for the churches' Christianity, even the sanctification of Christians, all that is ultimately not understood.

[63.] Edward Scribner Ames, "Liberalism Confirmed."

[64.] [The term *nebenreformatorisch* is unusual; in the rare instances where it is used (e.g., Hans-Jürgen Goertz, *Innere und äussere Ordnung in der Theologie Thomas Müntzers*) it refers to the radical Reformation. One possible source of Bonhoeffer's thinking on this is Thomas Cuming Hall's 1930 book, *The Religious Background of American Culture*, which he had read during his 1930–31 stay at Union. He referred to it in his final report to the Church Federation Office, continuing: "Even though I cannot check its historical accuracy, the thesis developed there, that American Protestantism developed essentially untouched by Reformation Protestantism as a continuation of Wycliffean ideas and of radical dissent, was very informative for my understanding of the American church situation" (*DBWE* 10:316). "Wycliffean ideas" are pre-Reformation; the "radical dissent" would presumably refer to the ideas of the radical Reformation.—VB]

[65.] Wilhelm Pauck.

[66.] Francis Miller.

[67] One sign of this is the general insistence on natural theology. Christendom in American theology is essentially still religion and ethics. Hence, the person and work of Jesus Christ recedes into the background for theology and remains ultimately not understood, because the sole foundation for God's radical judgment and radical grace is at this point not recognized.
460 The decisive task today is the conversation between the Protestantism without Reformation and the churches of the Reformation.

[67.] On Bonhoeffer's earlier critique—drawing on Karl Barth—of "religion" and the cultural-Protestant synthesis of religion and ethics, see especially his lecture "Jesus Christ and the Essence of Christianity," delivered to the Barcelona congregation in December 1928 (*DBWE* 10:303–59). See also his New York seminar paper from 1930–31 "The Theology of Crisis and Its Attitude toward Philosophy and Science" (*DBWE* 10:462–76); and Feil, *Theology of Dietrich Bonhoeffer*, 67–74.

PART 3
Sermons and Meditations

A. Sermons and Drafts for Worship Services

1. Sermon on Romans 12:17–21, Groß-Schlönwitz, 463
Third Sunday after Epiphany, January 23, 1938[1]

Romans 12:16c–21.[2] [. . . do not claim to be wise. Do not repay anyone evil for evil, but take thought for what is noble in the sight of all. If it is possible, so far as it depends on you, live peaceably with all. Beloved, never avenge yourselves, but leave room for the wrath of God; for it is written, "Vengeance is mine, I will repay, says the Lord." No, "if your enemies are hungry, feed them; if they are thirsty, give them something to drink; for by doing this you will heap burning coals on their heads." Do not be overcome by evil, but overcome evil with good.][3]

"Mercy has befallen me"[4]—as we just sang. The same hymn is sung by the entire Christian church-community on each new day. "Mercy has befallen me"—when I still closed my heart before God, when I walked on the path of my own sin, when I loved my sin more than God, when through my sin I lived in pity and misery, when I had gone astray and could not find my way back—this was when God's word met me and I heard: God loves me. This was when Jesus found me. He was with me—he alone—he comforted me

[1.] *NL*, A 51,4; handwritten. Previously published in *GS* 4:427–34 and *PAM* 2:89–96.

[2.] [In Bonhoeffer's Luther Bible this is v. 17; the NRSV reads: ". . . do not claim to be wiser than you are." Because Bonhoeffer repeats this verse throughout the sermon, we have followed the German closely here.—VB]

[3.] The sermon text does not appear in the original manuscript. [Luther's translation includes the citation of Isa. 5:21 in v. 17 (NRSV: v. 16c).—VB]

[4.] This is the title of a 1767 chorale by Philipp Friedrich Hiller (*Evangelisches Gesangbuch für Brandenburg und Pommern*, 153; *EG*, 355).

and forgave all my sins and did not count the evil against me.[5] "Mercy has befallen me."

When I was hostile toward God because of his commandments, he dealt with me as one would with a friend. When I committed evil against him, God did only good to me. He did not make an accounting of my evil; he looked for me tirelessly and without bitterness. He suffered with me; he died for me. Nothing was too difficult for him for my sake. This is when he overcame me. God had won over his enemy. The father had found his child again. Is that not what we mean when we sing this hymn? Even though I do
464 not understand why God loves me so much, why I was so precious to him, even though I cannot grasp that he could and wanted to overcome my heart through his life, but now I can say: "[Mercy has befallen] me. . . ."

Yet precisely because I do not grasp and understand any of this, our text states: "Do not claim to be wise"—that is, you may be very smart and competent people in your business, at your work, but there is one thing that by nature you do not know anything about at all. There is one aspect where you are as unwise and as foolish as an underage child—namely, in the divine things of mercy or, much more, in how an enemy turns into a friend, how an enemy of God is overcome.[6]

Our text for today[7] speaks about the *behavior of the Christian in relation to his enemies* or *how the Christian "overcomes" his enemies.* This question [will] always be of great importance for the life of the individual and of a Christian church-community.[8] Yet we are so absolutely ignorant about this, and we have such completely wrong thoughts, that our text begins with: "Do not claim to be wise." First and foremost, this might be *a reminder of* how incomprehensible God's way with us was to our wisdom. Truly, it is foreign and inaccessible to our wisdom that God sought us, forgave us, that he sacrificed his Son for us, and thereby won over and converted our hearts. With that we

[5.] Cf. 1 Cor. 13:5.

[6.] Replaces the following text: "if we sing 'mercy has befallen me'? Does this not at the same time say that we were unable to understand on our own why God treated us with such unending kindness, why he dealt with us in such a way. God's mercy with his enemies surpasses all our wisdom. That is the reason why today's Epistle reading begins with the words: 'Do not consider yourselves to be wise.' [new paragraph] It is good that we are reminded of this. Our wisdom is indeed entirely useless in matters of divine mercy and in the art of turning people from evil to good."

[7.] Deleted: "does not quite speak about God's mercy toward his enemies but it."

[8.] Deleted in the manuscript: "to be. But he will not find an answer for it if he does not ask first how God dealt with him when he was God's enemy. Therefore, the first admonition and reminder of our text reads:"

are told: If you meet an enemy: think first about *your own enmity against God and about God's mercy toward you.*[9]

"Do not claim to be wise"—this then is an important reminder about the 465
beginning of our human race. The devil promised wisdom to Adam and Eve. He wanted to make them as wise as God, and they were to know what is good and evil. With that they were supposed to become judges over good and evil. Since the time when Adam accepted the devil's gift of wisdom, all human beings think that they know something about all divine things and have something to say about them.[10] They imagined that they would now know how to deal with God and with humankind. With the aid of their wisdom, they would now certainly build a good world. But what happened? The first son of Adam and Eve was Cain, the murderer of his brother.[11] The first human being born of humans on this earth was a murderer of his brother. This is when the seeds of evil sprouted. This was the fruit of the wisdom of the first human beings! Does this give us something to think about? "Do not claim to be wise"—lest you become murderers of your kin. Do not believe that you know how to deal with human beings, with enemies, or that you know what is good or evil, or otherwise human beings will devour each other. "Do not claim to be wise"—but focus on God's path to humankind, to his enemies. That path that Scripture itself calls foolish,[12] the path of God's love toward his enemies, the love that he extends to them all the way to the cross. It is wisdom at its best to recognize the cross of Christ as the invincible love of God for all humankind, for us as well as for our enemies. Or do we think that God would love us more than our enemies? Do we think that we of all people are the favorite children of God? If we thought that way, then we would be deeply rooted in pharisaism, then we would have ceased being Christians. Does God love our enemies less, having come for them, suffered for them, died for them as well as for us? The cross is not the private property of any human being, but it belongs to all human beings; it is valid for all human beings. *God loves our enemies*—this is what the cross tells us. He suffers for their sake; he experiences misery and pain for their
sake; he has given his dear Son for them. Everything depends on this: that 466
whenever we meet an enemy, we immediately think: this is someone whom

[9.] Replaces the following text: "first and foremost remember that you were God's enemies and that he has forgiven and accepted you out of pure mercy."

[10.] Cf. *DBWE* 3:111 on Gen. 3:4–5: Eve has "the first conversation *about* God" with the serpent.

[11.] See Gen. 4:1–16.

[12.] Cf. 1 Cor. 1:18.

God loves;[13] God has given everything for him. *Therefore, do not consider yourselves to be wise.* Concerning our attitude toward our enemies, this means first and foremost: Remember that *you as well were God's enemy* and *mercy* has happened *to you* without your merit or deserving.[14] Second, that means: Remember that God also *went to the cross* for your enemy and that he *loves your enemy as he loves you.*

Therefore, "do not repay anyone evil for evil, but take thought for what is noble in the sight of all. If it is possible, so far as it depends on you, live peaceably with all." Let's be very clear: there is a person, a neighbor, or someone else who continuously speaks ill of me, who vilifies me, who openly wrongs me, who plagues and tortures me wherever he can. We only have to see this person, and our blood boils and we are filled by a terrible, threatening anger. The one who causes that within us is the enemy. But now one has to be careful. Now one needs to remember quickly: *mercy has happened to me,* not by human doing, no, but *by God,* and *for this person* Jesus Christ *died*—and suddenly everything changes. Now we hear: *do not repay anyone evil* for evil. Do not lift your hand for a blow; do not open your mouth in anger but instead be quiet. What can the evildoer do against you? Evil done to you harms not you but the evildoer. Suffering injustice does not hurt any Christian. But the doing of injustice causes harm. The evil one wants to instill one thing in you, namely, that you will also become evil. But with that he would surely win. Therefore, do not repay anyone evil for evil. You will harm not the other but yourself. You are not in danger when evil is done to you, but the other person is in danger, the one who perpetrates evil against you and will die in it unless you help him. Therefore, for the sake of the other and for the sake of your responsibility for the other[15]—do not repay anyone evil for evil. Has God ever repaid you in such a way?

"Take thought for what is noble in the sight of all . . . live peaceably with all." With *everybody*, with *all* people—there is no exception. Be *worthy of respect,*
467 not only toward the *respectable* but also toward those who are not respectable; be *peaceable* not only with *the peaceful ones* but especially with those who do not want to let us live in peace. The heathens can do the opposite as well. But Jesus Christ died not for the respectable and for the peaceful ones but especially for the sinners and the enemies, for those who are not respectable, the haters, the killers. Our heart always yearns to dwell among friends, among the just and the respectable. But Jesus Christ was in the midst of his

[13.] Deleted: "just as *I* am."

[14.] Allusion to Article 4 of the Augsburg Confession (Kolb and Wengert, *Book of Concord*, 147).

[15.] Replaces the following text: "for the sake of yourself."

enemies. He wanted to be precisely there. This is where we also should be. This is what distinguishes us from all other sects and religions. Their devout members want to be among themselves. But Christ wishes that we be among our enemies as he was. Amid his enemies he died the death of God's love and prayed: Father, forgive them, for they do not know what they do.[16] Christ wants to win his victory among the enemies.[17] Therefore, do not retreat, do not isolate yourselves, but "take thought for what is noble" for everybody, create peace with all people so far as it depends on you. "So far as it depends on you"—it is not in your hands if you are not left in peace, if you are vilified and persecuted. But "so far as it depends on you," that means that you shall never be the source of strife. Your heart should always be full of peace. Does that mean that we should also leave the word of God unspoken[18] for the [sake] of peace? Never—for is there a more peaceful word and deed than preaching about the peace that God has made with his world, with his human beings? "So far as it depends on you"[—]one thing does not depend on you, namely, to leave God's word unsaid, but it does depend on you to speak it for the purpose of peace, to speak it for the purpose of the peace of humankind with God, in the midst of a torn-apart and divided human [world]. Jesus made peace with us when we were enemies.[19] He has also created peace with all our enemies on the cross. Let us witness to this peace in front of everyone!

"Never avenge yourselves . . ." Whoever takes revenge into his own hands
makes himself the judge of the world and of humankind. The revenge he 468
wanted to take will come upon his own head. Whoever wants to take revenge takes the life of his enemy into his own hands and forgets that God's hand already rests upon this person for whom God died on the cross. Whoever seeks revenge on a human being undoes the death of Christ and becomes guilty of the blood of reconciliation. Christ died for me and for my enemy, for the salvation of both of us. If I seek revenge, I disregard the salvation of the other. That might not harm the other person, but by that very act I would break with the deeds of Christ.[20]

Christ demands a difficult sacrifice from us, namely, to let go of our revenge, perhaps the most difficult, for all of human nature screams for revenge against enemies. The lust for revenge is stronger in our human

[16.] Luke 23:34.

[17.] With the allusions to Ps. 110:2 ("Rule in the midst of your foes!") in this paragraph, also cf. the beginning of *DBWE* 5:27–28 [see also *DBWE* 4:40.—VB].

[18.] Replaces the following text: "that we should be silent."

[19.] Cf. Rom. 5:10.

[20.] Replaces the following text: "I lose my salvation in Christ."

blood than any other addiction. But this we know: we cannot take revenge anymore. If the enemy stands before my eyes and the craving for revenge overcomes me, at once Jesus Christ stands behind my enemy and bids me: do not lift your hand, vengeance is mine, I will take it.

". . . Leave room for the wrath of God . . . [I will] repay, says the Lord." What a terrible word. Can we hear it and know what it means that God will take vengeance without asking at once: "No, do not take revenge; no, I do not and cannot wish that even my enemy would fall into God's wrathful hands." But God says: "Vengeance is mine, I will repay"—God wants to and has to wreak vengeance upon the evil ones. But—miracle upon miracle—God has already wrought vengeance in an incomprehensible way, not upon us who were his enemies and who still sin against him every day, and not upon our enemies, but instead upon himself, upon his dear Son. Upon him God visited all our sins and punished them. God cast him out into the hell of despair and of abandonment by God. And in the same hour, Jesus prays: Father, forgive them . . .[21] This is God's vengeance, namely, that he inflicts pain and suffering upon himself but spares and accepts us. This is God's vengeance, namely, that he carries the suffering on his own shoulders and forgives his enemies. Does it not resonate in us: Do not consider yourselves
469 to be wise! God's paths to you are too wonderful and too superior, too merciful and too loving.

It remains astonishing that this word about this vengeance of God is followed immediately by the statement: "If your enemies are hungry [feed them; if they are thirsty, give them something to drink. For by doing this you] will heap burning coals upon their heads."[22] For the enemy, God gave his life, his everything; now you give to him what you have: bread if he is hungry, water if he is thirsty, help if he is weak, blessing, mercy, love of the enemy. Is he worth that? Yes. Who would be worthy of our love, who would need our love more than the one who hates? Who is poorer than him, who is more in need of help, who is more in need of love than your enemy? Have you ever looked at your enemy in this way, as the one who basically stands in front of you, poor as a beggar, and who asks you, without being able to say it himself: help me, grant me the one thing that can still lift me out of my hate, grant me love, the love of God, the love of the crucified Savior. Indeed, all threats and all showing of fists stem from this poverty, and at its root is a begging for the love of God, for peace, for brotherliness. You repudiate the poorest of the poor when you repudiate your enemy.

[21.] Matt. 27:46; Luke 23:34.

[22.] [Rom. 12:20. Cf. also Prov. 25:21–22.—VB]

Burning coals. Coals burn and hurt when they touch us. Love can burn and hurt as well. It teaches us to realize that we are poor as a beggar. It is the burning pain of repentance that appears in the one who finds love, nothing but love, despite hate and menace. God has taught us to know this pain. When we felt it, the hour of repentance had come.

Now you are at the goal: "Do not be overcome by evil, but *overcome evil with good.*" This is what Christ did for us. He did not become confused by our evil; he did not let himself be overcome by it. He *overcame our evil* with good. Let's repeat how [that] happens: not by feeding the other person's evil with our evil, the hatred of the other person with our hatred. Rather, it happens when the evil hits emptiness and finds nothing on which it can ignite. How do we overcome evil? By forgiving without end. How does that
happen? By seeing the enemy as the one he truly is, the one for whom 470
Christ died, the one whom Christ loved. How will the church-community win victory over its enemies? By letting the love of Christ win victory over the enemies. Amen.[23]

2. Sermon on Romans 5:1–5, Groß-Schlönwitz, September 3, 1938[1]

Sermon on Romans 5:1–5 (D. Bonhoeffer)

"Therefore, since we are justified by faith, we have peace with God through our Lord Jesus Christ, through whom we have obtained access by faith to this grace in which we stand; and we boast in the hope of the future glory that God is to give. And not only that, but we also boast in our afflictions, knowing that affliction brings patience, and patience brings experience; experience, however, brings hope, and hope does not disgrace,

[23.] The sermon ends on the last page of the (twice folded) manuscript in the upper half of the page. In the lower half are penciled notes by Bonhoeffer: "*it is written*[—]introduction too long[—]If righteousness of God—on us—on our enemies 2 Cor. 6:14[—]The love of Christ[—]Every human being is our enemy[—] 'Do not lead us . . . [into temptation]' Saved together with the enemy or lost with him. Maybe *the enemy* is saved.[—]One *cannot* do otherwise[:] not ontological but *promise*! Coming from the *fulfilled* commandment." These are probably notes taken during a discussion of a sermon draft in the "homiletic exercises" [which was part of the young pastors' training—VB].

[1.] *NL*, A 51,5; typewritten; mimeographed copy. Addendum to the circular letter of March 14, 1938, to the Finkenwalde seminarians (1/11). Previously published in *GS* 4:434–41 and *PAM* 2:97–103. Bethge's changes to the mimeographed text for the 1961 printing in *GS* have been dropped, with the exception of the corrections of clear mistakes. The sermon was preached during evening worship on March 9, 1938.

because God's love has been poured into our hearts through the Holy Spirit that has been given to us."[2]

"We have peace with God." Thus our struggle with God has now come to an end. Our rebellious heart has thus acquiesced to the will of God. Our own wishes have become quiet. God's is the victory, and our flesh and blood that hate God are now destroyed and must be silent.

471 "Therefore, since we are justified by faith, we have peace with God." God was right. He alone. We speak with the hymn that we have just sung: You are righteous whatever may happen.[3] God is righteous whether we understand his ways or not. God is righteous whether he punishes and disciplines us, or whether he pardons us. God is righteous; we are the transgressors. We do not see it, but our faith must confess it: God alone is righteous. Whoever thus submits in faith to God alone has come into the right standing before God. He has been made ready to pass God's judgment, justified in the faith in God's righteousness.[4] He has found peace with God.

"We have peace with God through our Lord Jesus Christ." So also God's struggle against us has now come to an end. God hated the will that did not wish to submit to him. Countless times God called, urged, pleaded, and threatened until his wrath over us no longer knew any patience. This is when he swung back for a blow against us, when he struck and hit. He hit the only innocent being on the entire earth. It was his dear Son, our Lord Jesus Christ. Jesus Christ died on the cross for us, being struck by the wrath of God. He had been sent by God himself for that purpose. Then, when God's Son had submitted to his will and right unto death, God's wrath was stilled. Miraculous mystery—God had made peace with us through Jesus Christ.

"We have peace with God." Underneath the cross there is peace. Here is the submission to God's will; here is the end of our own will; here is rest and quiet in God; here is peace of conscience in the forgiveness of all our sins. Here, below the cross, is the "access to the grace in which we stand"; here is the daily access to peace with God. Here is the only way in the world to find peace with God. God's wrath is stilled in Jesus Christ alone, and there we are overcome in the will of God. Therefore, for the church-

---

[2.] [The NRSV translation has been altered to conform more closely to the German text, since Bonhoeffer refers to certain key terms throughout the sermon.—VB]

[3.] From the second stanza of the evening hymn by Joachim Neander (1680), "Der Tag ist hin; mein Jesu, bei mir bleibe" (*Evangelisches Gesangbuch für Brandenburg und Pommern*, 283). ["The day is over; my Jesus, stay with me." No English translation appears to exist.—VB]

[4.] [Cf. *DBWE* 4:256, esp. ed. note 11. The editor thanks Ilse Tödt for this reference.—VB]

community of Christ, his cross has become the eternal source of joy and
hope in the coming glory of God. "We boast in the hope for the future 472
glory." Here, in the cross, God's right and victory on earth have begun. Here he will one day be revealed to all the world. The peace that we receive here will become eternal glorious peace in the kingdom of God.

And while we would love to end here, filled with the highest bliss that human beings can receive on this earth, namely, filled by the knowledge of God in Jesus Christ, with the peace of God in the cross, Scripture does not let go of us yet. "And not only that—" it says now. Not everything has been said yet. What else is there to be said after speaking of the cross of Jesus Christ, of the peace of God in Jesus Christ? Yes, dear congregation, there is still one word to be said. There is one word about you, one word about your life under the cross, one word about how God wants to test your life in the peace of God, so that peace may be not merely a word but reality. One word remains to be said, that you will live on this earth for a while and how you will preserve the peace.

Therefore, Scripture says: "And not only that, but we also boast in our afflictions." Whether we have truly found the peace of God will be proven by the way we deal with the afflictions that come upon us. There are many Christians who certainly bend their knees before the cross of Jesus Christ but who refuse and struggle against any affliction in their own lives. They think that they love the cross of Christ, but they hate the cross in their own lives. Thus in truth they also hate the cross of Jesus Christ; in truth they, who try to escape the cross by all means possible, are despisers of the cross. Whoever recognizes that he considers sorrow and suffering in his life to be something hostile and evil can know by this that he has not yet found peace with God. He essentially has only searched for peace with the world, perhaps thinking that he could cope with himself and all his questions by means of the cross of Jesus Christ, that is, in order to find an inner peace of mind. He has used the cross but did not love it. He has sought peace only for his own personal sake. But when affliction comes, this peace disappears quickly. It was not peace with God, because he hated the affliction sent by God.

Therefore, whoever hates affliction, renunciation, crisis, slander, and 473
imprisonment in his life might otherwise talk about the cross with big words, but nonetheless he hates the cross of Jesus and has no peace with God. But whoever loves the cross of Jesus Christ, whoever has found peace in his cross, also begins to love the affliction in his life. And finally he will be able to speak with Scripture: "but we also boast in afflictions."

Our church has suffered great affliction during the last few years: destruction of its order, the incursion of false proclamation, much enmity, evil words and slander, imprisonment and distress of all kinds, up to this very hour. And nobody knows what afflictions still lie ahead for the church. However, have we understood in all this that God himself wanted to and still wants to test us with this, and that in all of this there was only one important question, namely, whether we have peace with God or whether we have so far lived in an entirely worldly peace. How much murmuring and resisting, how much contradiction and hatred against affliction has been uncovered among us! How much denying, standing on the sidelines, how much fear when the cross of Jesus began to overshadow only a small portion of our personal life! How often did we think that we could preserve our peace with God and at the same time still avoid suffering, renunciation, venom, and the endangerment of our existence! Indeed, what is worse, did we not have to hear from our Christian brethren over and over that they despised the suffering of the brothers—and that only because their own conscience did not give them any rest.

But God will not take into his kingdom anyone whose faith he has not confirmed as genuine in affliction. "We *must* enter into the kingdom of God through much affliction." Therefore, we must learn to love our afflictions, even to rejoice in them and boast of them, before it is too late.

How is this to happen? "We know that affliction produces patience, and patience produces experience, and experience produces hope, and hope does not disgrace." Thus, God's word teaches us to regard and understand affliction[5] in the right way. The affliction that appears to us to be so hard
474 and repulsive is in truth filled with the greatest treasures that a Christian can find. It is like a shell in which lies a pearl. It is like a deep shaft in which one thing after another is found the deeper one descends: first ore, then silver, and finally gold. Affliction produces patience, then experience, then hope. Whoever avoids affliction discards along with that God's greatest gifts for his creatures.

"Affliction produces patience." Patience[6] if translated literally means: to remain below, not to throw off the load but to bear it. In the church today, we know much too little about the strange blessing of bearing something.[7] Bearing, not shaking it off, bearing, but also not collapsing underneath, bearing as Christ bore the cross, remaining below, and there below—finding Christ. If God puts a burden on someone, the one who is patient bends his head and believes that it is good for him to be humbled—

[5.] This and the next sentence of the manuscript use the plural *Trübsale* (afflictions) by mistake.

[6.] ὑπομονή. Cf. the notes concerning the term "patience," 2/2.3.

[7.] Cf. the chapter titled "Discipleship and the Cross," *DBWE* 4:84–91, esp. 89–91.

remaining *below it*! But *remaining* below it! Remaining firm, remaining strong also means not giving up weakly, giving way, not dwelling in affliction, but under the burden gaining strength as a grace by God and preserving the peace of God without being shaken. The peace of God is with the patient ones.

"Patience produces experience." The life of a Christian consists not of words but of experience. No one is a Christian without experience. We speak here not of life experience but of the experience of God. But it is also not about various experiences of God but about the experience that lies in the probation [Bewährung] of the faith and of the peace of God, the experience of the cross of Jesus Christ. Only the patient ones experience. The impatient ones do not experience anything. Whomever God wants to send such experience—an individual or a church—God sends much temptation, unrest, and fear, so that daily and hourly he must scream for the peace of God. The experience that is being spoken of here leads us into the depths of hell and into the jaws of death and into the abyss of guilt and into the night of unbelief. But in all of this, God does not want to take his peace
away from us. In all of this we experience, more and more every day, the 475
power and the victory of God, the peacemaking at the cross of Christ.

Therefore, experience produces hope. For each trial that is overcome is already the prelude to the ultimate overcoming; each wave defeated brings us closer to the desired land. Therefore, with experience grows hope, and within the experience of affliction there is already foreshadowed the reflection of eternal glory.

"And hope does not disgrace." Where there is still hope, there is no defeat. Even if there is much weakness, much crying and lamenting, much anxious calling, the victory has already been grasped. This is the secret of suffering in the church and in the Christian life: the same gate on which is written: abandon all hope! The gate of sorrow, of loss, of dying shall become for us the gate of the great hope in God, the gate of honor and glory. "Hope does not disgrace." Do we still have this great hope for God himself in the church and for our church? Then everything is won. Do we no longer have it? Then everything is lost.

"Affliction produces patience, and patience produces experience, and experience produces hope, and hope does not disgrace." But this is only true for the one who has found and keeps the peace of God in Jesus Christ. About this person it is written: "because God's love has been poured into our hearts through the Holy Spirit that has been given to us." Whoever is loved by God, and therefore loves God alone and above all things, is the only one who may speak this way. No, the sequence from affliction to hope is no earthly matter, of course. Luther said that it might be totally different:

affliction produces impatience, impatience produces hardness of heart, hardness of heart leads to despair, and despair brings ruin.[8] Yes, this will occur if we lose the peace of God, if we prefer an earthly peace with the world to the peace with God, if we love the securities of our life more than God. Then affliction will turn into our ruin.

476 But the love of God is poured out into our heart. Whomever it is granted by God through the Holy Spirit that the incomprehensible happens within him, namely, that he begins to love God for the sake of God and not for the sake of earthly goods and gifts, nor for the sake of peace, but truly and only for the sake of God, whomever the love of God in the cross of Jesus Christ befalls so that he begins to love God for the sake of Jesus Christ, whomever is led through the Holy Spirit to yearn for nothing more than to participate in God's love for eternity—this person speaks out of this love of God, and together with him the entire church-community of Jesus Christ: We have peace with God. We boast in our afflictions. The love of God is poured out into our heart. Amen.

3. Confirmation, Kieckow, April 9, 1938[1]

3.1. Confirmation Sermon on Mark 9:24

Mark 9:24. I believe, dear Lord, help my unbelief.

Dear confirmation pupils! This is a very sober word. But it is good that from the very beginning we get used to not bragging about our faith. Faith is not like that. Precisely because all depends today on our *really* keeping the faith, all desire for great words fades away. Whether we believe or not will be evident every day; protests do not change a thing. You know from
477 the Passion story that Peter says to Jesus: "Even though I must die with you, I will not deny you," and Jesus answers: "Before the cock crows twice, you will deny me three times." And the story ends: "And Peter went out and wept

[8.] Cf. the interpretation of Rom 5:3 in Luther's lecture on Romans 1515/1516 (*LW* 25, and *WA* 56:300–303, quote on 303,3–5).

[1.] *NL*, A 51,6 (1); typewritten; mimeographed copy (with later corrections by Eberhard Bethge), addendum to the July 18, 1938, circular letter to the Finkenwalde seminarians (1/21). Previously published in *GS* 4:441–47 and *PAM* 2:104–10. The text here omits several changes made by Eberhard Bethge in the mimeographed copy for the 1961 printing in *GS*. Worship service held on the occasion of the confirmation of Maximilian von Wedemeyer, Spes von Bismarck, and Hans-Friedrich von Kleist-Retzow in Kieckow, at the estate of the Kleist-Retzow family, on April 9, 1938. After Hans-Friedrich von Keist-Retzow died in July 1941 in Russia, Bonhoeffer held the memorial service for him in Kieckow with a homily based on his confirmation verse, Prov. 23:26 (*DBWE* 16, 3/2).

bitterly."[2] He had denied his Lord. Great assertions, even if they were said truthfully and were meant seriously, are always closest to denial. May God protect you and all of us from this.

This confirmation day is an important day for you and for us all. It is not an insignificant thing that you profess your Christian faith today before the all-knowing God and before the ears of the Christian church-community. For the rest of your life, you shall think back on this day with joy. But for that very reason I admonish you today to full Christian soberness. You shall not and may not say or do anything on this day that you will remember later with bitterness and remorse, having said and promised more in an hour of inner emotion than a human being can and may ever say. Your faith is still weak and untried and very much at its beginning. Therefore, when later on[3] you speak the confession of your faith, do not rely on yourselves and on your good intentions and on the strength of your faith, but rely only on the one whom you confess, on God the Father, on Jesus Christ, and on the Holy Spirit. And pray in your hearts: I believe, dear Lord, help my unbelief. Who among us adults would not and should not pray the same with you?

Confirmation day is a serious day. But truly, you know that it is still easy enough to confess one's faith in the church, in the fellowship of Christians, your parents, siblings, and godparents, in the undisturbed celebration of a worship service. Let us be thankful that God grants us this hour of common confessing in the church. But all of this will only become utterly serious, utterly real after confirmation, when daily life returns, our daily life with all its decisions. Then it will become evident whether even this day was serious. You do not have your faith once and for all. The faith that you will confess today with all your hearts needs to be regained tomorrow and the 478
day after tomorrow, indeed, every day anew. We receive from God only as much faith as we need for the present day. Faith is the *daily* bread that God gives us. You know the story about manna.[4] This is what the children of Israel received daily in the desert. But when they wanted to store it for the next day, it was rotten. This is how it is with all the gifts of God. This is how it is with faith as well. Either we receive it daily anew or it rots. One day is just long enough to preserve the faith. Every morning it is a new struggle to fight through all unbelief, faintheartedness, lack of clarity and confusion, anxiety and uncertainty, in order to arrive at faith and to wrest it from God. Every morning in your life the same prayer will be necessary: I believe, dear Lord, help my unbelief.

[2.] Cf. Matt. 26:34–35, 75.

[3.] See 3.2 below: Confirmation Question.

[4.] Exod. 16.

"I believe." Today, when the Christian congregation acknowledges you as autonomous members of the church, it expects that you begin to understand that your faith must be your very own individual decision. The "we believe" must now grow more and more into an "I believe."

Faith *is* a decision. We cannot avoid that. "You cannot serve two masters";[5] from now on either you serve God alone or you do not serve God at all. Now you only have *one* Lord, who is the Lord of the world, who is the Savior of the world, who is the one who creates the world anew. To serve him is your highest honor. But to this Yes to God belongs an equally clear No. Your Yes to God demands your No to all injustice, to all evil, to all lies, to all oppression and violation of the weak and the poor, to all godlessness and mocking of the Holy. Your Yes to God demands a brave No to everything that will ever hinder you from serving God alone, whether it be your profession, your property, your house, your honor before the world. Faith means decision.

But *your* very own decision! No person can relieve you of it. It must arise from loneliness, from the solitude of the heart with God. It will be born out
479 of the hot struggles against the enemy in your own bosom. You are still surrounded by a church-community, by homes that carry you, by parents who pray for you, by people who help you wherever they can. Thanks be to God for this! But God will lead you more and more into loneliness. He wants to prepare you for the great hours and decisions of your life when no human being can stand by your side and when only one thing is true: I believe, yes, I myself, I cannot do otherwise; dear Lord, help my unbelief.

Dear confirmation pupils, the church therefore expects of you that you will come of age in your dealings with the word of God and in prayer.[6] Your faith today is a beginning, not a conclusion. First, you must dive into Scripture and into prayer, you alone, and you must learn to fight with the weapon of the word of God wherever it is needed. Christian fellowship is one of the greatest gifts that God gives us. But God *can* also take this gift away from us as it pleases God, as he has done already to many of our brethren today. Then we stand and fall with our very own faith. Someday, however, each and every one of us will be placed in this solitude even if he has evaded it throughout life, namely, in the hour of death and the Last Judgment. Then God will not ask you, have your parents believed, but: have *you* believed? May God grant that in the loneliest hour of our life we can still pray: I believe, dear Lord, help my unbelief. Then we shall be blessed.

[5.] Matt. 6:24.

[6.] Cf. *DBWE* 5:91–92.

"I believe, *dear Lord* . . ." In life, it is not always easy to say, "Dear Lord." But faith must learn this. Who would not wish sometimes to say: I believe, harsh Lord, severe Lord, terrible Lord. I submit to you. I will be silent and obey. But to learn to say "dear Lord" is a new and difficult struggle. And yet we will have found God, the father of Jesus Christ, only when we have learned to speak that way.

Your faith will be led into difficult temptations. Jesus Christ was tempted as well, more than all of us. At first, temptations will come to you not to obey God's commandments any longer. They will assault you with great force. Satan, Lucifer, the bearer of light, will come to you, handsome and alluring, innocent and with the appearance of light. He will obscure God's 480
law and call it into doubt. He will want to rob you of the joy you have in God's path. And once the evil one has caused us to waver, he will tear our entire faith out of our hearts, will trample it underfoot and cast it away. Those will be difficult hours in your life, when you tend to become weary of God's word, when all is in revolt, when no prayer passes your lips anymore, when the heart refuses to listen any longer. As certain as your faith is alive, all of this must happen. It must happen so that your faith is tested and strengthened, so that you will be able to cope with increasing tasks and struggles. God works on us through these temptations. He never plays a game with you, you can be confident of that, but the father wants to make fast the hearts of his children. That is the reason why all of this will come over you. And even if the temptation is very confusing, if our resistance threatens utter collapse, indeed, even if defeat has already arrived, then we may and should cry out with the final remnant of our faith: I believe, dear Lord, help my unbelief. Dear Lord, it is after all the Father who tests us and strengthens us in such a way. Dear Lord, it is after all Jesus Christ who has suffered all temptations like us, yet without sin,[7] to be an example and a help for us. Dear Lord, it is after all the Holy Spirit who wants to sanctify us in this struggle.

Your faith will be tested through sorrow. You do not yet know much about this. But God sends sorrow to his children when they need it the most, when they become too overly sure on this earth. Then a great pain, a difficult renunciation, a great loss, sickness, death, enters our life. Our unbelief rears up. Why does God demand this of me? Why has God allowed this to happen? Why, yes, why? That is the great question of unbelief that wants to suffocate our faith. No one can avoid this calamity. Everything is so enigmatic, so dark. In this hour of being forsaken by God, we may and

[7.] Heb. 4:15.

shall say: I believe, *dear* Lord, help my unbelief. Yes, dear Lord, also in the dark, also when in doubt, also in the state of being forsaken by God. Dear
481 Lord, you still are my dear father who makes all things serve my benefit. Dear Lord Jesus Christ, you yourself have cried out: My God, why have you forsaken me?[8] You wanted to be where I am. Now you are with me. Now I know that you won't leave me even in the hour of my need. I believe, dear Lord, help my unbelief.

Your faith will bring you not only temptation and suffering but, above all, struggle. Today's confirmation pupils are like young soldiers who march into war, into the war of Jesus Christ against the gods of this world. This war demands the engagement of one's entire life. Should our Lord God not be worthy of this engagement[?] The struggle is already being fought, and you shall now join in. Idolatry and fear of human beings confront us everywhere. But do not think that great words here can accomplish anything. It is a struggle with fear and trembling, for the hardest enemy stands not opposite us but within ourselves. You shall know that precisely those who stood and still stand in the middle of this struggle have most deeply experienced this: I believe, dear Lord (yes, dear Lord!), help my *unbelief*. And if we, despite all temptation, do not flee but stand and fight, then this is not due to our strong faith and our courage in battle, our valor, but rather it is the sole fact that we cannot flee anymore because God holds on to us so that we can no longer disengage from him. God leads the struggle within us and against us and through us.

"Help my unbelief." God answers our prayers. Amid temptation, suffering, and struggle, he has created a sanctuary of peace. This is his Holy Eucharist. Here there is forgiveness of sins; here is conquest of death; here are victory and peace. It is not we who have won it. God himself has done it through Jesus Christ. Righteousness is his; life is his; peace is his. We exist in unrest, but rest is with God. We exist in strife, but victory is with God. You are called to the Lord's Supper. Come and receive in faith forgiveness, life, and peace. Ultimately, only this remains for you in the world: God's word and sacrament. Amen.

[8.] Mark 15:34; Matt. 27:46.

3.2. Confirmation Question[9] 482

Dear confirmation pupils. You have confessed your Christian faith with the creed of the church. You know that your entire life belongs to God and that God wants to grant you the gift of eternal life. But you also know that trials and temptations try to tear your faith out of your hearts and that it is not within human power to keep faith. You know that our heart is unfaithful, yet God is faithful. Therefore, do you want to turn to the sole help and grace of God? Do you want to hear and receive God's word and sacrament for the strengthening of your faith? Do you want to call to God and pray that he may purify, strengthen, and preserve your faith? If so, speak: *Yes, God help me. Amen.*

Confirmation pupils: Yes . . .

Yes, may God the almighty Father support you in this for Jesus Christ's sake and through his Holy Spirit. May God grant you the desire to fulfill this, so that in all of this you may remain, grow, and increase. Amen.

3.3. Confirmation Verses[10]

Maximilian von Wedemeyer: Ps. 73:25–26. Whom have I in heaven but you? And there is nothing on earth that I desire other than you. My flesh and my heart may fail, but God is the strength of my heart and my portion forever.

Spes von Bismarck: 1 Pet. 3:4. Let your adornment be the inner self with the lasting beauty of a gentle and quiet spirit, which is very precious in God's sight.

Johann Friedrich von Kleist: Prov. 23:26. My son, give me your heart, and let your eyes take pleasure in my ways.[11]

[9.] *NL*, *A* 51,5 (2); handwritten in Bonhoeffer's precise Latin script [as opposed to the German handwriting he used otherwise in his manuscripts and which is barely decipherable.—VB]. Previously published in *GS* 3:368. Bonhoeffer addressed the confirmation pupils with this question, which he formulated himself, during the worship service in Kieckow on April 9, 1938.

[10.] *NL*, A 51,6 (2); handwritten (in Bonhoeffer's German handwriting). Previously unpublished.

[11.] Cf. ed. note 1. [The NRSV text has been altered here to conform more closely to the German.—VB]

483 4. Confession Homily on Micah 4:9, Groß-Schlönwitz, Saturday before the Second Sunday in Advent, December 3, 1938[1]

Mic. 4:9: Why are you now crying so loudly? Is the king not with you?[2]

Let us prepare for the Lord's Supper. Before the Lord's Supper, there is penitence [Buße]. No one who has not passed through the slashing sword of penitence can properly enter the kingdom of grace. Before the supper of peace, there is the screaming of the human heart in fear of sin and death. We cannot avoid serious and thorough penitence. But penitence is a dangerous matter. In it one can perish. How do we pass through the slashing sword to reach the kingdom of grace and life? This is where our text wants to help us: *it warns us against penitence without Jesus. It helps us toward penitence with Jesus.*

"Why are you now crying? Is the king not with you?" Thus says the Lord God. God hears a hue and cry on earth coming from his church-community. It is a scream for help, for deliverance, not only from the external miseries that have befallen the church-community but also deliverance from sins, from the overwhelming power of the devil, from damnation through the law. It is a crying for righteousness, sanctification, victory, and overcoming. Is this not a proper cry from the church-community? Yet—how strange—God does not like it. "Why are you now crying aloud? Is not the king with you?" It is the cry of penitence without Jesus, which God hears yet does not want to hear, for it is a crying, a penitence against God. Your heart cries as if God had not helped you long ago. Your heart cries as if you
484 had been forsaken. "Is not the king with you?" Not all crying against one's own sin and weakness is to God's liking. You want to repent; you submit under God's holy commandments; you begin to reproach yourself; you even revolt against the power of sin that you had to experience in your life so far. Now come the severe self-accusations, the rebellion against our daily failings. Our indolence in prayer, for worship, our carelessness in our use of God's name, the sins committed during the time devoted to meditation and prayer, our wrong behavior toward our parents, teachers, and superiors, our

---

[1.] *NL*, A 51,9; handwritten. Previously published in *GS* 4:450–52 and *PAM* 2:110–13. The upper left edge of the manuscript's first page has the following note: "2. Sunday of Adv[ent] 1938. Confession." Concerning the practice of confession at Finkenwalde and in the collective pastorates, cf. *DB-ER*, 465–66, *DBWE* 5:108–18, and *DBW* 14, especially 2/12.2 and 2/24. [The German title, *Beichtansprache*, refers to the act of confessing one's sins (*Beichte*) as opposed to a confession of faith (*Bekenntnis*).—VB]

[2.] The manuscript erroneously cites v. 19. In Bonhoeffer's Luther Bible, the beginning of v. 9 is marked in pencil with the comment "Advent!" above in the margin. [The NRSV wording has been altered here to conform more closely to the German.—VB]

murderous and adulterous thoughts, our untruthful and slanderous words, our heart that is filled with covetousness[3]—all these things accuse us terribly and offend us deeply. Why are we so incapable of dealing with ourselves? Why are we so incapable of coping with our sin? Are we still Christians at all? Have we been converted at all? Do we believe at all? And now there follows one of the countless attempts and beginnings that we already have behind us in our lives. This time it must succeed. Things cannot continue like this. God will help, starting today, from tomorrow forward. This can be a loud cry of the heart for new life, for righteousness and sanctification. Yet God does not like this kind of penitence, for it is penitence out of one's own defiant and despondent heart, out of pride and despair, out of discontent and new resolutions. But: "Is the king not with you?" You want to repent; you look for help from afar and forget that the king is with you, that help was given to you already long ago. You repent without Jesus. Yet this penitence can only push you deeper into sin and misery. The new beginning will be followed by new failure, and your cries will become louder and even more godless.[4] Therefore, beware of penitence without Jesus!

Repent with Jesus! "Is not the king with you?" Yes, he is with you, and together with him is all the help[5] that you require. He has brought it to you. Do not cry as if help were far off. It is very near, so near that you can grasp it. The king is with you and has brought and granted you everything,
peace and righteousness and purity and truth, the gospel! In addition to 485
all of this, he has granted you an immeasurably great gift that, more often than not, you have so far disdained. He has given you the brother who can help you in the misery of your sin and who can forgive you in his name. God knew your sin and your yearning. God has already fulfilled it some time ago. Now look at Jesus Christ, your king who is with you, and all that he grants you. Now look at God's deeds and mercy for you and "do not cry as if the king were not with you." And now repent. Now you can no longer become proudly outraged about your own sin. Now you no longer want to make your own decision[6] for a new beginning that is bound to be followed by an even deeper defeat. Now you recognize your sin humbly and quietly to be your own great fault for which your king has atoned and because of which he is now with you. Now you hand over all your sin, really all of it and with it your whole heart, to the one who alone can deal with you and with your sin. You wanted to know how things with you will finally change? How

[3.] Cf. the Decalogue, especially Exod. 20:7, 12–17.

[4.] Uncertain reading.

[5.] Deleted in the manuscript: "all righteousness, all purity, love, and truth."

[6.] Substituted for "own strength."

you will finally deal with yourself and your sin? Things with you can only change if you realize today that your king is, in fact, with you. None other than your king Jesus Christ can deal with you and your sin. Come and let us bring it to him. He will relieve us of it fully and wholly, and he grants us a new beginning, a beginning that he himself made with you when he came to you. That was the new beginning. It has long been made. Believe me, He has already been with you a long while on the path to his kingdom. Amen.

486 5. Draft for Worship Service on 2 Corinthians 2:14, 6:10, 6:1, Groß-Schlönwitz, February 25, 1939 (?)[1]

Confession[2]

"I trust, O Christ, in You Alone"[3]

2 Cor. 2:14 [But thanks be to God who in Christ gives us victory at all times.][4]

(1) Thanks be to God—for all things, even for the painful hours, for the unpleasant things,[5] for each disappointment, for each criticism, for the brothers, for the work, for the Word—Without thankfulness, a Christian does not progress.

[1.] *NL*, A 53,7. Not previously published. The document indicates that there were two separate stages of writing; the later additions are made in very small writing. The text is probably part of a worship service in Groß-Schlönwitz during which Bonhoeffer preached on 2 Cor. 6:1–10, as Eberhard Bethge recalled in his letter to Bonhoeffer on March 2, 1944 (*DBWE* 8:313): "I've been thinking of you a good deal these days. It started early Sunday morning when the Epistle reading was 2 Cor. 6:1–10, and I saw you standing in the pulpit in Schlönwitz and remembered your splendid long sermon. For the brothers it was an event. I was playing the organ that day." The year is uncertain—either 1938 or 1939—probably in a worship service near the end of that collective pastorate that included confession of sin and the Lord's Supper. On the upper right edge of the manuscript "25/2" is handwritten in the same handwriting as the first section. This suggests it was 1939, since the lectionary epistle for the first Sunday of the Passion (Invocavit) on February 26, 1939, was 2 Cor. 6:1–10.

[2.] [The German here is *Beichte*, or confession of one's sins.—VB]

[3.] The German hymn "Allein zu Dir, Herr Jesu Christ," by Konrad Hubert (1540) (*Evangelisches Gesangbuch für Brandenburg und Pommern*, 141; *EG*, 232). [English translation in *Lutheran Hymnal*, 319.—VB]

[4.] The manuscript does not quote 2 Cor. 2:14. [The NRSV wording has been altered to follow the German more closely.—VB]

[5.] In the manuscript this is substituted for "days"; above "unpleasant" is added "words." The phrase that now follows "disappointment . . . criticism" was added at the later stage.

(2) The one who always wins the victory over us in Christ. *Defeated by God in Jesus Christ.*

1. Defeated: We lie on the ground. Not what we have accomplished and achieved, but what God has accomplished over us, and this is: that we lie on the ground and are overcome: we recognize our sin, God's holy commandments, Christ.

2. Defeated by *God*: God leads us in the triumphal procession of the defeated; we as the defeated participate in his victory. We no longer come free from him. His victory is our victory. Luther's text.[6]

3. Thanks be to God.

How does Christ stay victorious over us?[7] 487

(1) He leads us to the recognition of our sin. Not of our victories! How much failure there is in faithfulness, service, in personal sanctification, etc.! Shuddering! Mea culpa! No excuses.[8]

(2) We cling to him. *Forgiveness* of our sins; brotherly forgiveness! (as long as we are not forgiven, Satan has power over us) be reconciled—sacrifice—.[9] The fact that we conclude in forgiveness, this is the victory of Christ over us.

(3) He leads us in his triumphal procession as prisoners, bound ones. We take part in his victory. Luther's text. Our ministry!

(4) Thanks be to God. To the Lord's Supper as the ones defeated by God![10]

[6.] Departing from Luther's translation ["God gives victory"—VB], Bonhoeffer understood θριαμβεύω ("to parade in triumph," or "to make triumphant") in 2 Cor. 2:14 as it is used in Col. 2:15. Bonhoeffer alluded to the meaning in which the Greek word is used in the Letter to the Colossians in his sermon on Jer. 20:7 in London on January 21, 1934 (*DBWE* 13:351; cf. the reference there to the "victory procession").

[7.] This question, as well as the following four points, was added at the second stage.

[8.] The words "Mea culpa! No excuses" are added in pencil in the margin.

[9.] The allusion to Matt. 5:23–24 (". . . first be reconciled to your brother and then come and offer your gift" on the altar) is added in pencil. [See also *DBWE* 4:124.—VB]

[10.] The sentence "To the Lord's Supper . . ." is added in pencil. The following passage on the Lord's Supper was written in the first stage.

Lord's Supper. 138, 1.7.8.[11]

2 Cor. 6:10 having nothing, and yet possessing everything.[12]

1. having nothing—no merit, no right, nothing that is good. But also [(]this is especially true for you:[)][13] no hope, no security, no future.

2. possessing everything—cross, body, blood "that I have a savior."[14] Incomprehensible for the world. Forgiveness, future, brothers.

488 *Baptism.* 2 Cor. 6:1[15]

I. Now is the day of salvation[16]

1. Thanks be to God the creator—so many children, so many Lord's Prayers—the *salvation* of the soul.

2. Salvation: death = eternal life, birth = rebirth, flesh = spirit, sin = forgiveness

3. "not in vain"—do you know that baptism can be a great injustice? If the child does not come to have faith. Therefore,[17] your confession, faith. God will demand the soul of this child from you. He has entrusted it to you.

4. Receive salvation with fear and trembling! It is the salvation of God!

[11.] The communion hymn "Komm, mein Herz, in Jesu Leiden" ["Come, my heart, into Jesus's suffering"—VB], by Ernst Gottlieb Woltersdorf (*Evangelisches Gesangbuch für Brandenburg und Pommern*, 138). The seventh stanza begins: "Holy bread, be blessed for me"; the eighth stanza: "Holy cup, be blessed for me." (The hymn is not included in the more recent *Evangelisches Gesangbuch.*)

[12.] The end of the verse.

[13.] The later addition in small writing, "this is especially true for you," apparently relates to the ministerial candidates who would have to be ministers illegally. [Cf. 2/5, ed. note 1, and elsewhere, including the editor's introduction to this volume, for discussion of the "illegal" candidates in the Confessing Church.—VB]

[14.] "Daß ich ein Heiland habe," a line in the first stanza of "Komm, mein Herz, in Jesu Leiden" (*Evangelisches Gesangbuch für Brandenburg und Pommern*, 138).

[15.] This is the beginning of the final addition to the later section. In the German text in Bonhoeffer's Nestle New Testament, the phrase "not in vain" in 2 Cor. 6:1 is underlined in pencil. [The Nestle edition of the New Testament included both Greek and Luther's German translation.—VB]

[16.] 2 Cor. 6:2, where Isa. 49:8 is cited. In Bonhoeffer's German text, the italicized phrases are underlined: "I . . . helped you on *the day of salvation*. Behold, *now* is the acceptable time; behold *now* is *the day of salvation*!"

[17.] Uncertain reading.

6. Communion Homily on 1 Corinthians 15:55, Sigurdshof, Remembrance Sunday, November 26, 1939[1]

Worship Service for Remembrance Sunday 1939 in Tychow

1 Cor. 15:55 [Death is swallowed up in victory. O Death, where is your sting: O Hell, where is your victory?][2]

It was a strange and dreadful strife, when life and death contended.
The *victory* remained with life, the reign of death was ended.[3]

You are invited to a *victory celebration*—to the celebration of the greatest victory won in the world, the victory of Jesus Christ over death. *Bread and wine,* body and blood of our Lord Jesus Christ are the *signs of victory,* for Jesus lives and is present in these signs today, the same Jesus who almost two thousand years ago was nailed to the cross and laid in the grave. Jesus arose from the dead, burst asunder the rock before the tomb, and remained the victor. 489
Today, you are to *receive the signs of his victory.* And later, when you receive the blessed bread and blessed chalice, you should know: *just as certainly* as I eat this bread and drink this wine, *just as certainly* has Jesus Christ remained the victor over death, and *just as certainly* is he the living Lord who meets me.

We *do not like to speak of victories in our lives.* It is too large a word for us. We have suffered too many defeats in our lives. Too many weak hours and too many crude sins have reduced victory to nothing. But, isn't it true, *the spirit within us longs* for this word, yearns for the final victory over sin, over the anxious fear of death in our lives. And now God's word does not speak to us about *our* victory. It does not promise us that from now on *we* will be victorious over sin and death. It does say with all power, however, that someone has won this victory, and that this one will also win the victory over us when we have him as our Lord. It is not we who are victorious but Jesus.

Today, *we proclaim and believe that: against everything that we see around us,* against the graves of our loved ones, against the dying nature outside, against the death[4] that the war casts over us once again. We see the reign

[1.] *NL*, A 51,10; handwritten. Previously published in *GS* 4:453–55 and *PAM* 2:115–18.

[2.] The text of 1 Cor. 15:55 has been inserted here; it is not in the original manuscript. Cf. Isa. 25:8 and Hos. 13:14.

[3.] These are the opening lines of the fourth stanza of the Easter hymn "Christ lag in Todesbanden" by Martin Luther (1524; *EG*, 101). [The translation here is by Richard Massie from "Christ Jesus lay in death's strong bands" (*Lutheran Book of Worship*, 134).—VB]

[4.] Deleted: "in us and of our soldiers." [Cf. also 1/160.—VB]

of death, but we preach and believe in the victory of Jesus Christ over death. Death is swallowed up in victory. Jesus is victor, resurrection of the dead, and eternal life.

It is like a *mocking song of triumph* over death and sin that the Holy Scripture sings here: O Death, where is your sting? O Hell, where is your victory? Death and sin puff themselves up and instill fear in humankind, as if they were still the rulers of the world. But it is only an illusion. They have long since lost their power. Jesus has taken it from them. Since then, anyone who is with Jesus no longer needs to fear these dark lords. Sin, that sting of death with which death causes us pain, has no more dominion. Hell no longer has any power over us who are with Jesus. They are powerless. They still rage like a vicious dog on a chain, but they cannot get at us, because Jesus holds them fast. He remains the victor.

490 But, we ask ourselves, if that is the case, why *does it appear so completely different in our life?* Why does one see so little of this victory? Why do sin and death rule so terribly over us? Indeed, this very question is God's question to you: I have done all this for you, and you live as if nothing has happened! You submit yourselves to sin and fear of death as if they could still enslave you! Why is there so little victory in your life? Because you do not want to believe that Jesus is the victor over death and sin, over your lives. Your *unbelief* brings about your defeat. But now the victory of Jesus is proclaimed again to you today in the Lord's Supper: the victory over sin and death for you, too, whoever you may be. Seize it in faith. Today, Jesus will once again forgive all your heavy and manifold[5] sins. He will make you wholly clean and innocent. From now on, you need not sin anymore. Sin need not rule over you any longer. Jesus will rule over you, and he is stronger than every temptation. Jesus will be victorious in the hour of your trial and fear of death, and you will confess: Jesus has become the victor over my sin, over my death. Whenever you abandon this belief, you will have to sink and succumb, sin and die. Whenever you seize this belief, Jesus will keep the victory.

On Remembrance Sunday, we are asked at the graves of our loved ones: for what are you, too, willing to die? *Do we believe* in the *power of death* and sin, or do we believe in the *power of Jesus Christ*? There can be only one of these two beliefs. In the past century, there was a man of God who during his life had often preached the victory of Jesus Christ and done wonderful things in his name. As he lay in great torment and distress on his deathbed, his son bent over toward his ear and screamed to the dying man, "Father, *victory is*

[5.] Uncertain reading.

won."[6] When dark hours and when the darkest hour comes over us, then 491
[we] want to hear the voice of Jesus Christ calling in our ear: *victory is won.* Death is swallowed up in victory. Take comfort. And may God grant that then we will be able to say: I believe in the forgiveness of sins, the resurrection of the body, and life everlasting. It is in this faith that [we] want to live and die. It is to that end that the Lord's Supper helps us. Amen.

7. Liturgy Fragment for Christmas, Sigurdshof (?), December 24, 1939 (?)[1]

Now the salvation, and the power, and the kingdom of our God and his Christ have come. For a child has been born for us, a son has been given to us, authority rests upon his shoulders, and he is named Wonderful, Counselor, Mighty, Hero, Everlasting Father, Prince of Peace. His authority shall grow continually, and there shall be endless peace from this time onward and forevermore.[2] He is our peace.[3]

Let us pray: Lord, God of all peace and all love;
you have come to us, so that we should come to you.
You became human, so that we would become godly.
In grace, you took on our flesh and blood, so that we might partake of you.
Through your most holy birth, may we be born anew in peace and love, and turn us poor sinners into children of your mercy.
Lord Jesus Christ, come stay with us. Amen.

[6.] These were the words of Johann Christoph Blumhardt Jr. to his father, Johann Christoph Blumhardt Sr. Cf. Zimmermann, *Bruder Bonhoeffer,* 74: "I [Zimmermann] brought from Berlin [to Finkenwalde 1936] the 'account of the illness of Mrs. Gottliebin Dittus in Moettlingen by Johann Christoph Blumhardt, an official report of this pastor to his superiors on phenomena of possession by and exorcism of spirits." [Blumhardt's account of his father's death immediately follows the passage about the exorcism of Mrs. Dittus; Blumhardt's actual words are "Jesus is victor." See Lejeune, *Christoph Blumhardt and His Message,* 25–26.—VB]

[1.] *NL,* A 54,19; handwritten in ink on one side of a DIN A5 sheet [an international standard size, approximately 5.8 x 8.3 inches—VB]. While the location and year are uncertain, the similarity of this fragment with other texts from the collective pastorates suggests that it was written in Sigurdshof in 1939. Previously unpublished. Cf. the 1939 Christmas letter to the brothers (1/169) ("May God bless you this Christmas time, you personally, your homes, and your congregations").

[2.] Cf. Isa. 9:5–6.

[3.] Eph. 2:14.

Let us give thanks to the Lord our God, who has called us[4] to peace into
492 his eternal kingdom. In the light of the Christmas tree, we pray to him for our homes, for all whom we hold dear, near and far, big and small, for all who would like to be with us today[5] and who think of us, for all who, on this day in the church, have sought the word of God's peace anew, for all who spend this night in poverty, misery, and need, for all those who are afraid and[6]

8. Sermon for the Lector on Matthew 2:13–23, Sunday after New Year's Eve, 1940[1]

Hymn: "Help us, O Lord! Behold, we enter" (23, 1–4).[2]

Matt. 2:13–23. [Now after they had left, an angel of the Lord appeared to Joseph in a dream and said, "Get up, take the child and his mother, and flee to Egypt, and remain there until I tell you; for Herod is about to search for the child, to destroy him." Then Joseph got up, took the child and his mother by night, and went to Egypt, and remained there until the death of Herod. This was to fulfill what had been spoken by the Lord through the prophet, "Out of Egypt I have called my son." When Herod saw that he had been tricked by the wise men, he was infuriated, and he sent and killed all the children in and around Bethlehem who were two years old or under, according to the time that he had learned from the wise men. Then was fulfilled what had been spoken through the prophet Jeremiah: "A voice was heard in Ramah, wailing and loud lamentation, Rachel weeping for her children; she refused to be consoled, because they are no more." When Herod died, an angel of the Lord suddenly appeared in a dream to Joseph in Egypt and said, "Get up, take the child and his mother, and go to the

[4.] Addition, subsequently deleted: "from all peoples."

[5.] Substituted for "who are with us in their thoughts."

[6.] The text ends here at the end of the completed page. [It is possible that the text continued on another page that has been lost.—VB]

[1.] *NL*, A 5,17; published version (original manuscript not preserved) from Beckmann and Linz, *Meine Worte werden nicht vergehen*, 42–46. Previously published in *GS* 4:473–79 and *PAM* 2:288–94. The text of the biblical reading has been inserted here. [The heading indicates that Bonhoeffer didn't preach this himself but wrote it to be read by a lector. Once the war began, many clergy were drafted into the military, and the number of Confessing Church clergy and seminarians drafted early was particularly high. As ministers became scarce, trained lectors were often asked to read prepared sermons. See also Barnett, *For the Soul of the People*, 159–72.—VB]

[2.] "Hilf, Herr Jesu, laß gelingen," the New Year's hymn by Johann Rist (1642) (*Evangelisches Gesangbuch für Brandenburg und Pommern* 23; *EG*, 61). [The English version of this hymn is in *Lutheran Hymnal*, 120.—VB]

land of Israel, for those who were seeking the child's life are dead." Then Joseph
got up, took the child and his mother, and went to the land of Israel. But when 493
he heard that Archelaus was ruling over Judea in place of his father Herod, he was afraid to go there. And after being warned in a dream, he went away to the district of Galilee. There he made his home in a town called Nazareth, so that what had been spoken through the prophets might be fulfilled, "He will be called a Nazorean."][3]

Dear congregation! In reading this story about the flight to Egypt, the slaughter of the children of Bethlehem, and the return of the holy family to Nazareth, we will certainly have noticed that each story concludes with a passage from the Old Testament, and that each of these passages is introduced with the short sentence: "so that what had been spoken might be fulfilled." We have probably often overlooked it, thinking it simply an irrelevant formula. However, by doing so we overlook something especially important and lovely about our text. "So that it might be fulfilled"—this means that nothing can happen to Jesus that God has not resolved beforehand, and likewise, nothing can happen to us when we are with Jesus other than what God intends for us and has promised. Even if influenced by all kinds of human thoughts, plans, and errors, even if a murderous Herod puts his cruel hands in play, in the end everything will go as God has seen, intends, and spoken. Governance will not be taken from God's hands. This is a great consolation: God only fulfills what God himself has promised. Whoever holds the Holy Scripture in hand and in heart will find confirmation of this consolation in it again and again.

The wise men from the East had worshipped Jesus and brought him precious gifts. Can there be a more terrifying contrast than to read in the same sentence that the king of the Jews, Herod, is searching for the child in order to slay him? Herod, who sits on the throne of David, king and at the same time tyrant over the people of God, Herod, the one who knows the history,
the promise, and the hope of this people, plots murder when he hears that 494
God wants to make his promises come true and wants to give his people the king of righteousness, of truth and peace. The mighty, brutal ruler who has often been stained with blood seeks to kill the helpless, innocent child because he is afraid of it. All worldly means of power are on Herod's side. Yet God is on the child's side.

And God has means other than Herod. He sends an angel into Joseph's dream and commands him to flee to Egypt, where the power of Herod

[3.] The German text follows the translation from the Nestle edition. Above the text in Bonhoeffer's Luther translation is written: "Gospel for the Sunday after New Year's."

meets its limit. God's means are mysterious, like God himself. He does not lack invisible powers and servants through whom he can let his people know his ways. He has certainly given us his word and therein revealed his entire will. Yet in special hours he helps us in special ways so that we will not miss the right path. Who among us has never experienced such special help and guidance by God? At night, in a dream, God commands Joseph to flee to Egypt. And without hesitating for a moment, Joseph obeys the divine command and sets out to flee with the child and his mother—this is the order in which our story names Jesus and Mary twice! If God's word to us is to be fulfilled, we must be obedient and if necessary get up at night in order to do his will. This is what Joseph did.

The child Jesus had to flee with his parents. Could God not have protected him from Herod in Bethlehem as well? Certainly, but we are supposed to ask not what God could have wanted and done but what is truly God's will. God's will is that Jesus flee to Egypt. With this, he shows that Jesus's path from the beginning is a path of persecution. But God also shows that he can keep Jesus safe and that nothing will happen to him as long as God does not allow it. Jesus now lives in Egypt, where his people once had to live in servitude and misery. The king should now be where his people had been. He is to experience the history of his people himself, bodily. In Egypt, Israel suffered. In Egypt, the sufferings of Jesus began. In Egypt, God's people and their king had to live as foreigners and in misery. Yet out
495 of Egypt God led his people into the promised land. Out of Egypt, God called his son back into the land of Israel. What the prophet once said about the people of Israel is now fulfilled in Jesus: "Out of Egypt I have called my son."[4] The flight to Egypt was no mere chance but divine promise and fulfillment. In Egypt, Jesus became completely one with the suffering and the joy of his people, of the people of God, of us all. In Egypt, he is in a foreign land, with us. With him, we will also leave the foreign land to go to the land of God. The wrath of Herod grew when the wise men from the East, following God's command, did not travel back through Jerusalem in order to inform him where he could find Jesus. Filled with immeasurable fear and jealousy, he now orders the slaughter of all children in Bethlehem younger than three years of age. He considers this to be the only certain way to get the divine child. But even though his strike is clever and cruel, it misses its target. Herod wants to destroy Christ, but Christ is alive, and in his place and for him the first martyrs are struck down and die. The innocent children of Bethlehem protect the life of their king and Lord who is their age.

[4.] Hos. 11:1.

They become the first martyrs of Christendom, the dying witnesses for the life of Jesus Christ, their savior. All persecution aims at the final destruction of Jesus Christ. Its purpose is to murder Christ, yet it cannot harm Christ. Christ lives, and with him live the martyrs of all times.

Great sorrow, screaming, lamenting, weeping, and wailing come over the people whenever the Lord Jesus Christ is persecuted, as it came over all Bethlehem when the innocent children had to die. Over and over again tears were shed when the people of God suffered misery and distress. Back then it was as if mother Rachel, the mother of Israel, arose from her grave close to Bethlehem and wept for the sorrow of all her children. This is what the prophet Jeremiah once beheld in the last hour before the destruction of Jerusalem. But only now, when Bethlehem's mothers wept for their children who had died for Jesus Christ, did the word of the prophet come to fulfill-
ment: "A voice is heard in Ramah, lamentation and bitter weeping. Rachel 496
is weeping for her children; she refuses to be comforted for her children, because they are no more."[5] The lament for the martyrs of Jesus Christ begins, and it will not quiet down until the end of time. It is the lament for the world estranged from God and an enemy of Christ, for the blood of the innocents, for our own guilt and sin for which Jesus Christ himself experienced suffering. But within this inconsolable lamentation, there is one great consolation: Jesus Christ lives, and we will live with him if we suffer with him.

The slaughter of the children of Bethlehem, as ungodly and gruesome as it was, nevertheless had to serve God, who brings his promises to fulfillment. Sorrow and tears come upon God's people, but they are precious to God, for they are offerings for Christ's sake, and Christ will take them up in eternity.

Day after day, year after year, Joseph in Egypt awaits the divine order to return. Joseph does not want to act from his own decisions. Joseph waits for God's directive. Then God once more sends into Joseph's dream at night the order to rise and to return home with the child and his mother. "Those who were seeking the child's life are dead." The mighty Herod is dead without having attained his goal, but Jesus lives. This keeps happening in the history of the church. First misery, persecution, mortal danger for the children of God, for the disciples of Jesus Christ, but then came the hour in which it was said: "They are dead." Nero is dead, Diocletian[6] is dead, the

[5.] Jer. 31:15.

[6.] [The Roman emperor Diocletian, who ordered widespread persecution of Christians.—VB]

enemies of Luther and the Reformation are dead, but Jesus lives, and with him live those who are his. The age of persecution suddenly comes to an end, and it becomes clear: Jesus lives.

Called by God, the child Jesus returns to the land of Israel. Jesus comes to make the kingdom his, to ascend to his throne. Joseph first wants to bring Jesus to Judea, from whence the king of Israel is expected to come. But a special divine directive prohibits him and orders him to go to Naza-
497 reth instead. To the ear of the Israelite, Nazareth is a lowly place, of ill repute. "Can anything good come out of Nazareth?"[7] Despite this, or precisely because of it, Jesus was to grow up in Nazareth "so that what had been spoken through the prophets might be fulfilled, 'He will be called a Nazorean.'" This prophecy seems hard to understand, all the more because we do not find it anywhere in Scripture in this form. But we must learn to pay close attention to the biblical text. It does not say here that one single prophet but that *all* prophets receive this prophecy. This is certainly a reminder of the recurring promise in the Old Testament that the future king will appear in lowliness and plainness. True, nothing is said here about Nazareth. However, Matthew the evangelist finds this reference in the well-known verse of Isaiah in which it is written that a branch will spring from the root of Jesse, a shoot, an unsightly twig, and that this weak, minor branch growing out of the stump of a root will be the messiah of Israel.[8] The Hebrew word for branch is *nezer*, and the consonants in the related place name Nazareth are the same.[9] Thus, the Gospel finds the promise that Jesus will be poor, despised, and of humble origins deeply hidden in the Old Testament. In the path to humble Nazareth, a path so hard for Joseph and for the whole world to comprehend, God's path with the Savior of all the world is fulfilled once more. He is to live in deepest poverty, hidden and humble. He is to share the life of those who are disregarded and despised, so that he may bear the misery of all human beings and become their Savior.

We have learned from our story how God makes three great promises come true in the child Jesus: Jesus bodily experiences the history of the people of God himself; he brings to those who belong to him not only joy but also suffering and death for his sake; he lives hidden and in humility,

---

[7.] John 1:46.

[8.] Isa. 11:1–9.

[9.] In their interpretation of the place name Nazareth in Matt. 2:23, early Christian exegetes such as Jerome already referred to the Hebrew term *nezer* in the messianic passage in Isa. 11:1. Cf. Luz, *Matthew*, 1:149, with note 41.

in order to become a helper to all human beings. But all of this happens
according to the promise of God. It is the fulfillment of what God decreed 498
for the salvation of the world.

We are entering a new year. Many human plans and mistakes, much animosity and misery will determine our path. Yet as long as we remain with Jesus and walk with him, we may be assured that nothing can happen to us that God has not foreseen, willed, and promised beforehand. The consolation of a life that is lived with Jesus is that of this life, too, it will be said: It was fulfilled what the Lord has spoken. Amen.

Prayer: We praise you, Lord, that you have everything in your hand and that you reign with such glory. You safely lead those who are yours through all oppression and animosity for Christ's sake and according to your counsel. Lead your church-community and all its members in the new year as well, along the right path for your name's sake. Amen.

Hymn: "From God shall naught divide me" (213,1–4).[10]

[10.] The hymn "Von Gott will ich nicht lassen," by Ludwig Helmbold (1563) (*Evangelisches Gesangbuch für Brandenburg und Pommern*, 213; *EG*, 365). [The English translation of this hymn is in *Lutheran Hymnal*, 393.—VB]

B. Meditations

499 **9. Meditation on Psalm 119, 1939–1940**

9.1. Bonhoeffer's Meditation (Fragment)[1]

Verse 1. [*Happy are those* whose way is blameless, who walk in the *law* of the Lord.][2]

Whoever speaks this way presumes that the beginning has already occurred. He points out that the life with God consists not only and not essentially of ever-new beginnings. Therefore, the psalmist calls it a change,
500 a walking in God's law. Thus he confirms the beginning that has occurred,

[1.] *NL*, A 58,2 (2a); handwritten. Previously published in *GS* 4:505–43 and *PAM* 2:398–436. In the winter of 1939–40, Bonhoeffer intensified his long-practiced meditation on the Psalms and considered an interpretation of Ps. 119 "the climax of his theological life" (*DB-ER*, 667). [See also *DB-ER*, 412, where Bethge notes that this psalm was "the biblical passage quoted most frequently by Bonhoeffer."—VB] Bonhoeffer writes about his "favorite psalm" in his American diary (1/137, p. 238, entry for July 9, 1939), which he had previously worked on intensively (cf. especially the 1936 "Lesson Plan for Confirmation Classes" [*DBW* 14, 2/27]). In his introduction to the Psalms (*Prayerbook of the Bible*, 1940), he writes: "Psalm 119 becomes especially difficult for us perhaps because of its length and uniformity. Here a rather slow, quiet, patient movement from word to word, from sentence to sentence is helpful. We recognize, then, that the apparent repetitions are in fact always new variations on one theme, the love of God's word. As this love can have no end, so also the words that confess it can have no end. They want to accompany us through all of life" (*DBWE* 5:164–65). Deletions in the manuscript are noted here selectively. There are additional extant notes and drafts made by the candidates Hellmuth Birk and Karl-Heinz Probsthain (both were members of the collective pastorate in Sigurdshof in the winter of 1939–40), by Eberhard Bethge, and by Bonhoeffer himself; these are listed in *NL*, A 58,2 (1). They include (1) a list of Hebrew terms that recur in the psalm, studied lexically and in the form of a concordance; (2) notes taken on Sellin, *Theologie des Alten Testaments*, and Gunkel, *Die Psalmen*, about the term "Law" and the era in which the psalm originated; (3) main statements and prayer concerns that recur in the psalm; (4) a list of the stanzas used in antiphonal singing during horary prayers at the

accepts it as valid, does not want to go back before it.[3] Because God's beginning with us has already occurred, our life with God is a path being walked within God's law. Is that the servitude of human beings under the law? No, it is the freedom from the murderous law of never-ending beginnings. To wait for a new beginning, day after day, thinking that one has found it countless times[4] only to declare it lost in the evening: this is the complete destruction of faith in that God who set the beginning once through his forgiving and renewing[5] word in Jesus Christ, that is, in my baptism, in my rebirth, in my conversion. God has converted me to himself once and for all; I was not the one who converted myself to God once and for all. God has set the beginning; this is the joyful certainty of faith. Therefore, I am not to attempt setting countless beginnings of my own next to the *one* beginning of God. From that very thing I have been freed; the beginning, God's beginning, lies behind me once and for all. Now the members of the church-community are not to demand of one another a new beginning; rather, they address one another as those who *have already been* granted a new beginning and who walk together on the path that began with God finding those who are his, and the end of this path always can only consist in God's seeking them again (v. 176).[6]

The path between this beginning and this end is the turn [Wandel] within God's law. It is the life under the word of God in its utter multitude of forms, in its richness, in its inexhaustible fullness of knowledge and experiences. In truth there is only one danger on this path, namely, to want to step back behind this beginning or to lose sight of the goal, which is the same thing. In that moment the path ceases to be a path of grace and of faith. It ceases to be God's own path.

Thus, we are being addressed as those who are on the same path as the 501
psalmist. The question whether it is really true, whether the right beginning

---

first, third, sixth, and ninth hours [in religious orders the horary prayers are short liturgies, held each hour, that usually include a biblical text, a psalm reading, and a canticle from the New Testament—VB]; (5) several attempts to supply headings for each eight-verse stanza. For Bonhoeffer's two attempted outlines, see 3/9.2.

[2.] The manuscript does not cite the verse. Words underlined in Bonhoeffer's meditation Luther Bible edition appear here in italics. Next to v. 1 in the Luther Bible, "I" is penciled in the margin to mark the first eight-verse stanza.

[3.] Deleted in the manuscript: "Because of the beginning of our life with God that has taken place, or as we now say in a better way:"

[4.] Replaces "daily."

[5.] Replaces "sanctifying."

[6.] The last verse of the psalm, marked in Bonhoeffer's Luther Bible. It ends (Bonhoeffer's marks in italics): "*seek out your servant*, for I do not forget your commandments."

has truly happened with us, is no longer asked, on principle, because it would drive us into fruitless fear. We are to learn to understand ourselves as people who have been placed on the path and now cannot do otherwise than walk the path as well. Therefore, there is good reason to avoid speaking about the beginning, instead presupposing that it has simply happened, making it indisputable, and thereby addressing and claiming human beings on the basis of this beginning. Whoever is caught in the search for a new beginning is *under* the law and is worn down and killed by it. Whoever comes from the found beginning is *within* the law of God, is upheld and preserved by it for life.[7]

Now it is understandable why our psalm begins with a beatification of those who accept what God made happen as having happened to them, who no longer live in revolt against God's doing but who instead are borne by this doing, who are sheltered in it, who walk "within the law." Yet the praise is due not to the human beings but to the law of God alone in which human beings can attain such salvation.

What is this "law"? "When your children ask you in time to come: 'What is the meaning of the decrees and the statutes and the ordinances that the Lord our God has commanded you?' then you shall say to your children, '*We were Pharaoh's slaves in Egypt*, but the Lord brought us out of Egypt with a mighty hand. The Lord displayed before our eyes great and awesome signs and wonders against Egypt, against Pharaoh and all his household. He brought us out from there in order to bring us in, to give us the land that he promised on oath to our ancestors. Then the Lord commanded us to observe all these statutes, to fear the Lord our God, for our lasting
502 good, so as to keep us alive, as is now the case. If we diligently observe this entire commandment before the Lord our God, as he has commanded us, we will be in the right.'" (Deut. 6:20–25).[8] This, therefore, is the answer to the question about the law: God's act of redemption,[9] God's law, and God's promise. No one understands the law of God who does not know of

[7.] Cf. *DBWE* 5:164: "Under 'law,' then, is to be chiefly understood the entire redemptive act of God and direction for a new life in obedience. Joy in the law, in the commands of God, fills us when God has given to our life the great transformation that comes through Jesus Christ."

[8.] Bonhoeffer slightly altered the Deuteronomy citation. Phrases underlined by Bonhoeffer in his Luther Bible are italicized here. [In Bonhoeffer's manuscript] vertical lines mark vv. 20 and 21–23, next to which "history" has been penciled in the margins and "law" penciled next to v. 24. The verse begins in the Luther Bible: "And the Lord has commanded us"; in the manuscript "A strange answer!" follows this and has been deleted.

[9.] Deleted: "and judgment."

the redemption that has already occurred and the future promise. Whoever asks about the law will be reminded of Jesus Christ and the redemption from servitude in sin and death that in him has been accomplished for all human beings and will be reminded of the new beginning set by God in Jesus Christ for all human beings. The question about the law of God is answered not by a moral doctrine [Sittenlehre], a norm, but by a historical event, not by an unfulfilled[10] ideal but by an act completed by God. If we ask how we can begin a life with God, Scripture answers that God has already begun life with us; if we ask how we can live without sin before God, then forgiveness of all sin in Jesus Christ is proclaimed to us; if we ask what we can do for God, then we will hear what God has done for us. If we turn our eyes toward our future doing, then God's word calls us back to the past and says: remember! (Deut. 7:18;[11] 8:2; 32:7–18). Only when we realize that the decision has already been made, that the beginning has already occurred, that the deed has already been done by none other than God, only when we know that we have been affected and drawn into the decision, the beginning, and the deed of God, can we hear God's commandment as the law for life [Lebensgesetz] of those for whom God has already done everything and who now are "within the law."

God's law is inseparable from his redemptive deed. The God of the Ten Commandments is the God who has led you out of the land of Egypt (Exod. 20:2). God gives his law to those whom he loves, whom God has chosen and accepted (Deut. 7:7–11). To know God's law is grace and joy (Deut. 4:6–
10). It is the way of life for those who accept the grace of God (Lev. 18:5). 503
"Indeed, O favorite among peoples, all his holy ones were in your charge; they marched at your heels, accepted direction from you" (Deut. 33:3).[12]

The original meaning of Torah, the law, is that which has been determined by lot.[13] It is God's verdict that is sought and pronounced wherever human capability has reached its limit, where God alone must act and decide. The Torah is God's casting over humankind, beyond all human expectations and thinking. "The boundary lines have fallen for me in pleasant places; I have a goodly heritage" (Ps. 16:6). God's verdict meant grace

[10.] Replaces "unreal."

[11.] Replaces "5:15."

[12.] Bonhoeffer's manuscript erroneously cites Deut. 32:3.

[13.] This etymological derivation of "torah" as "that which has been determined by lot" [Bonhoeffer's German here is "das Los Geworfene," which literally means throwing or casting the lot—VB] probably was introduced by Julius Wellhausen (*Prolegomena to the History of Israel*, 468). This interpretation has been generally discarded in more recent scholarship (cf. Botterwerk, Fabry, and Ringgren, *Theological Dictionary of the Old Testament*, 15:609–46).

and life for human beings, life before God and with God, through forgiveness of sins.

Therefore, "happy are those who walk in the law of the Lord." Truly, these are the ones who have ventured to accept God's deeds as having happened for them, who proceed from the beginning that God has accomplished. They are like the victors after a battle won. They are like the living who have come through the valley of death. They are like the wanderers for whom the sun rises after a dark night and who have found their way. Now they reach forth toward a new future; now they walk from victory to victory; now they are on the path in the light.

Happy are those, for they are freed from the agony of their own beginnings; happy are those because they have overcome all the internal divisions that arise from the discrepancy between their own beginnings and the beginning by God;[14] they are "complete," "whole," undivided, unas-
504 sailable.[15] Luther says "the wholly healthy ones" in his first translation of the psalm in 1521 and correctly recalls Paul's use of this word in his pastoral letters, "that is, those without fault, who do not patch themselves up with other human teachings."[16] Happy are those because this law of their own decision[17] has been taken from them. They live in the law of God.

"Happy are those"—here the talk is of happiness and bliss of the life in the law of God. It is God's will that those who walk in his commandments fare well. It is not a sign of a strong and mature faith if we are embarrassed by this sentence, if we say that God intends greater things with us than to care for our well-being.[18] There are Christians who want to be more spiritual than God himself. They like to talk about struggle, asceticism, suffering, and cross, yet it is almost embarrassing to them that the Holy Scripture does

---

[14.] On the "breaking apart" inside the "human beings in their dividedness," cf. *DBWE* 3, esp. 68–92, 122–24, 133–35.

[15.] Replaces the following text: "without fault, that is, in literal translation: complete, whole, undivided, not subject to punishment." In the New Testament lectures in Finkenwalde in 1936 and 1936–37, Bonhoeffer emphasized in James: "τέλειος important [James] 1:4[;] 3:2 complete (*entire*) human being" as opposed to δίψυχος James 1:8 (double-minded). See *DBW* 14:614, also *DBWE* 4:137–45 and 276–79.

[16.] Martin Luther, "Der Hundertt und achtzehnte Psalm [Ps. 118—VB] nuezlich zu betten fur das wortt gottis tzur hebenn wider den grossen feynd des selben, den Bapst und menschen leren" (To pray the one hundred and eighteenth psalm usefully to raise the word of God against his great foes, the pope and human dogma) (1521), *WA* 8:186–204. The citation in Bonhoeffer's text is from 187:7–10. Cf. the use of the verb ὑγιαίνω (I am healthy) in the pastoral letters, such as in 1 Tim. 6:3.

[17.] Replaces "their own pious life."

[18.] Penciled in the margin: "Deut. 27:9 (*today*—my people)."

not talk exclusively about that, but that it cannot speak often enough about the happiness of the pious, about the well-being of the righteous. They may say that this comes from the Old Testament and is outdated. However, the real reason for their embarrassment lies in the narrowness of their hearts, which cannot grasp the entire kindness of God, being too narrow to praise God in the fullness of the worldly gifts that God bestows on those who live in his laws. They want to be the schoolmasters of the Holy Scripture and thus deny themselves the full joy of their Christianity and deny God the thanksgiving that is owed to his great kindness.

When our psalm promises well-being, happiness, and bliss to those who live in God's law, this should be taken at its word. One may certainly think here of the earthly life as well. Or is it not the case, do the pious want to deny the fact that they[19] already fare well on this earth (Ps. 37:37), that they lead a life full of deepest happiness and bliss (Ps. 37:25), that they 505
do not lack any good thing (Ps. 34:10),[20] that they have "good days" (Ps. 34:12),[21] yes, that the Lord gives them what their heart desires (Ps. 37:4). "Did you lack anything?—No, not a thing."[22] Only the one who is satisfied to receive God's gifts, however they come, as long as they make his life possible, can speak this way. Only the satisfied heart will always enjoy well-being. "But if we have food and clothing, we will be content with these" (1 T[im.] 6:8).

It is a surprising observation that it is precisely in the psalms lamenting the oppression and the suffering of the righteous that praise for the kindness of God, who bestows well-being on his own, emerges most strongly. The person who prayed our psalm has experienced misery and affliction as well. But ought not the pious one who has experienced misery have special reason to be thankful for all previous safekeeping and for every gift that is still preserved for him to this hour. For "better is a little that the righteous person has than the abundance of many wicked" (Ps. 37:16). Is this not the very person who should know that the judgment starts in the house of God (1 Pet. 4:[17]),[23] that he would have earned nothing but wrath and judgment if God wanted to deal with him according to his merit and his deserving?[24]

[19.] Replaces "the believing pious."

[20.] [V. 11 in the German Bible.—VB]

[21.] [V. 13 in the German Bible.—VB]

[22.] Luke 22:35; cf. *DBWE* 4:168.

[23.] The quote from 1 Peter (the verse number "12" is deleted in the ms.) is written in the margin of the manuscript without any indication where to insert it.

[24.] An allusion to the Augsburg Confession, Article 4 (*Book of Concord*, 39–40).

"Happy are those"—"blessed," says Jesus. Luther also translated this word with "blessed" [selig] in his first translation of this psalm in 1521.[25] The term is the same in Hebrew. Blessed—not because they do not lack anything, but because they receive all from God's hand. "Be still before the Lord, and wait patiently for him" (Ps. 37:7). They gratefully eat the daily bread that God "created to be received with thanksgiving by those who believe and know the truth" (1 T[im.] 4:3). They know that the good gifts of creation are there for their sake so that they confess Christ in praise and thankfulness and proclaim him as the Lord of the world. They also experience daily the truth of Jesus's saying that everyone who leaves their house, their brother, or sister, or father, or mother, or children, or fields for the
506 sake of the gospel will receive it back hundredfold "in this time," namely, in the community of the congregation of the faithful—and they believe that in addition they will receive "in the age to come eternal life" (Mark 10:29–30).[26] Thus they know and also confess that "God's steadfast love is better than life" (Ps. 63:4).[27] In their heart, they are thankful for all good gifts, but their hearts belong to the giver alone.

But if God should indeed give the cup of suffering for Christ's sake to one of his own to drink, to the bitter end of the cross and death, with which God has honored only a few throughout the ages, he will have certainly prepared their hearts in such a way that it will be these who will witness with a strong faith in a new and powerful way: "Happy are those who walk in the law of the Lord."

What is true for the individual also holds true for the community, the house, the people. Happy will be the house, the people who walk in the law of the Lord (read Ps. 112!). Because it is the same God who has given the law and rules the world (read Ps. 19!), the earth will belong to those who live in the law of God (Matt. 5:5; Ps. 37:9, 11). Pride, arrogance, and injustice will perish by themselves, but humility and the fear of the Lord, discipline and order, justice and truth are enduring, for God is a "God in heaven above and on earth below" (Josh. 2:11).

[25.] Cf. Luther, "Der Hundertt und achtzehend Psalm," *WA* 8:186,20–23.
[26.] Mark 10:29–31. Cf. *DBWE* 4:98–99.
[27.] [V. 3 in the NRSV.—VB]

[Verse 2.] *Happy are those who keep his decrees, who seek him with their whole heart!*[28]

A second beatitude follows the first. The testimonies [Zeugnisse] are the reminders that God has erected on the path of his people lest they lose their way. This term comes into more frequent use only during the Babylonian captivity. There, in the time of judgment and repentance, it is recognized that the path of the people of God is to bring testing and probation, and that the law was given as a warning for the Lord God (Neh. 9:34). Now, the 507
ark of the covenant is called the "ark of admonition [Mahnung]" (Exod. 25:22), the Ten Commandments "the tablets of admonition [Mahnung]" (Exod. 31:18), the tabernacle the "tent of admonition [Mahnung]" (Num. 9:15) or the "tabernacle of admonition [Mahnung]" (Exod. 38:21).[29] This was an expression that all these things do not have their ultimate meaning in themselves but rather admonish and witness to God himself. Only the one who would find and honor God himself and God alone in the Ten Commandments, in the ark of the covenant, and the tabernacle of the covenant would understand their essence. God gives such reminders to the people along their path so that they may prove true in times of testing, "that in the end he would do you good" (Deut. 8:16). Because his commandments are supposed to remind us daily and witness to us that God is the Lord, a purely external fulfillment of the commandments is not enough. Not only lips and hands but the entire undivided heart must be involved. It must search continuously for the one of whom the testimonies speak. In commandments, worship services, and prayers, the heart is seeking the one who has given everything. Thus it is not idle and satiated, but it continuously seeks[30] God in his revelation, for the Word in the words, and for the gospel in the law. Blessed is the one who holds to the testimony of God in such a way, who seeks God with all his heart. For he can only search because

---

[28.] The words "Happy are those" and "decrees" are underlined in Bonhoeffer's Luther Bible. [The word translated here as "decrees," following the NRSV text, is *Zeugnis*, which means "testimony" or "witness." The passage from the Luther Bible could be translated as "Happy are those who keep his witnesses." Accordingly, in the passages that follow, *Zeugnisse* (plural) is translated as "testimonies."—VB]

[29.] [Bonhoeffer uses the word *Mahnung* (which can mean "reminder," "warning," or "admonition") here throughout as indicated in the text. It is not used, however, in the German Luther Bible translations of the passages cited in this paragraph. The NRSV translations of all these passages use the word "covenant": ark of the covenant; tabernacle of the covenant, etc.—VB]

[30.] Replaces the following text: "but because it has found, or rather, because it was found, therefore it seeks."

it was previously shown to him where he must seek and whom he will find, because it was promised to him that seeking will be followed by finding.

[Verse 3.] "*who also do no wrong, but walk in his ways.*"[31]

God's ways are the ways that he has tread before and that we are to walk with him now. God does not allow us to walk a path that he has not walked before and on which he would not precede us. It is the way cleared by God and protected by God on which he calls us. Thus it truly is His way. "The Lord went in front of them in a pillar of cloud by day, to lead them along
508 the way, and in a pillar of fire by night, to give them light, so that they might travel by day and by night. Neither the pillar of cloud by day nor the pillar of fire by night left its place in front of the people" (Exod. 13:21[–22]). "Your way, O God, is holy. What god is so great as our God? . . . Your way was through the sea, your path, through the mighty waters; yet your footprints were unseen. You led your people" (Ps. 77:13, 19–20).[32]

With God, one does not just mark time but one walks along a path. Either one moves ahead or one is not with God. God knows the entire way; we only know the next step and the final goal. There is no standing still; every day, every hour, one progresses. The life of whoever has set his foot on this path has become a wandering. He walks through the lush pastures and through the dark valley, but the Lord will always lead him on the right path (Ps. 23) and "he will not let your foot be moved" (Ps. 121:3).

The entire gospel message of salvation can be called simply "the way" (Acts 19:9; 22:4; 24:14) or the "way of God" (Acts 18:25, 26). In this way it becomes clear that the gospel and faith are not a timeless idea but an action of God and of the human being in history. As a path, it cannot remain hidden before the eyes of other human beings. It becomes obvious whether good or evil happens on this path. And it does matter whether occasionally evil is done on this path, as if one could then retreat from the imperfect reality to the perfect ideal, or that one is content with knowing the right path and having the right faith, even if one cannot always act accordingly. "Who also do *no wrong* but walk in his ways." To know the way, to be on the right path, never alleviates responsibility and guilt; rather it renders them more severe. God's children are under no special law except the one to know about God's grace and God's way and to do no evil. Or does God's word say too much: they do *no* evil? Is there one Christian for whom this is true? But if we ask this question, we have already turned our attention from God's word to ourselves, from the mighty promise of God to our inability.

[31.] In the Luther Bible "ways" (*Wegen*) is underlined.

[32.] [These verse numbers in the German Bible are Ps. 77:14, 20–21.—VB]

With this we come instantly under the influence of sin, which wants to keep 509
us from trusting God's word. If it is really *his* way on which we walk, we will certainly do "no evil." But if we suppose for just a moment that God's path has now become our path, we have already fallen and do much evil. For "everyone who commits sin is guilty of lawlessness; sin is lawlessness" (1 John 3:4). Do we Christians no longer sin? Yes, we have sinned and do not deny it (1 John 1:8–9). But after we have confessed this, our gaze belongs no longer to our sin and our weak nature but to Christ and the word of God alone, which determines our future and states: "Those who have been born of God do not sin, because God's seed abides in them; they cannot sin, because they have been born of God" ([1] John 3:9).

The way of God is God's way to human beings, and only in this way is it the way of human beings to God.[33] Its name is Jesus Christ (John 14:6). Whoever is on this way, whoever is in Jesus Christ, does no evil.

Verse 4. *You have commanded your precepts to be kept diligently.*[34]

Literally: "You have ordered your commandments so that they will be kept in earnest." The "you" with which the person praying addresses God indicates that throughout this psalm it is not the human being who is addressed but God. Moreover, the one who commands, not the commandments, is the focus. We are encountered by a You, not an It [Es], an idea, in the commandments.[35] This is also illustrated by the Hebrew term [for] "commandment" in this place, which cannot be translated by one single word: it derives from the verb for "to seek," "to visit," "to attend." Thus it
refers to that to which God pays heed, looks to, that by which he visits and 510
besets human beings. Thus the direction toward human beings is included in the commandments. They have a certain purpose, a goal, for me. They are not given for their own sake but for our sake, namely, that we "keep them diligently." We are to hold on to the commandments when they come from God to us, diligently, earnestly, with all our strength, so that they cannot be lost to us or torn away from us. God's commandment is there not only for the moment but permanently. It wants to enter us deeply and wants to be held fast in every condition of life.

[33.] Cf. Bonhoeffer's lecture "Jesus Christ and the Essence of Christianity" held in Barcelona on December 11, 1928 (*DBWE* 10, 2/2), especially 352–58. See also section 13 on "Preaching" from his 1931–32 Berlin lectures "The History of Twentieth-Century Systematic Theology" (*DBW* 11, 2/3, pp. 204–9, esp. 204–5). Cf. also Feil, *Theology of Dietrich Bonhoeffer*, 68–69.

[34.] In the Luther Bible "commanded," "kept," "precepts" are underlined.

[35.] Cf. *DBWE* 5:75 as well as *DBWE* 8:304.

Verse 5. *O that my life might keep your statutes completely in earnest!* [36]

Literally: "O, that my way would be directed toward keeping your statutes." The sigh "O!" might express a small displeasure but also a nameless woe, indeed, at times an entire life story that otherwise is not allowed to be expressed out loud. If the poor and miserable person must swallow his pain, the "O!" arises from the anxious soul, and when the eye looks up toward the great helper, then the "O!" by itself has the power of a mighty prayer" (P. Geyser: *Pia desideria,* 1878).[37] The O! of our wishes and the O! of our prayers are two different things. One arises out of our need as we ourselves understand it, the other out of our need as God has taught us to see it. One is pretentious or desperate, the other humble and confident. We cannot bring forth even the right "O!" from our own heart. God has to teach us through the Holy Spirit how to call it out. In the right "O!" that which words cannot express out of the depth of our need is summed up before God; it is
511 the "sigh too deep for words" of the Holy Spirit, who intercedes for us before God (Rom. 8:26). This right sighing, however, does not remain hidden to God (Ps. 38:9).[38]

Our wishes are directed toward improving the world; our prayer begins with ourselves. How longingly do we often desire that humankind would change, that evil in the world would cease and new righteousness would enter in. But we do not bring anything about with all this. All conversion and renewal must start with me myself. "O, that *my* way would be directed toward keeping your statutes!" This is a prayer for which there is promise. "The craving of the lazy person is fatal, for lazy hands refuse to labor" (Prov. 21:25).[39] Here, however, all hands must get busy. This prayer immediately leads to action at the place where it is needed the most, myself. Certainly, this action can arise only out of prayer; otherwise it is for naught. "O that *my* life . . ." Just as the look at the misdeeds of others does not help me, neither does the mere admiration of their piety if *my* own life is not lived right, if I cannot be pious myself. The many goals of my life's path must become one goal; the many directions that I walk must become one single direction: God's statutes. The crooked and winding path should become

[36.] The word "my" is underlined twice. In the Luther Bible (with Bonhoeffer's underlined words in italics): "O *that* my life your *laws* . . ." Here and in the following verses, Bonhoeffer's translation of Ps. 119 differs considerably in some places from the Luther Bible but follows Gunkel's *Die Psalmen,* 516–19. [The NRSV here reads: "O that my ways may be steadfast in keeping your statutes!"—VB]

[37.] In Geyser, *Gesammelte Schriften,* 5:49.

[38.] [V. 10 in the German Bible.—VB]

[39.] Prov. 21:25 is notated in the Luther Bible with indelible pencil.

straight and "not become obstructed and crooked through human teaching" (Luther).[40] God's "statutes," this is what stands fast, what has been determined by God for all time. The course of heaven, earth, and humankind has been irrevocably prescribed by these statutes. God's covenant with his people is as unchanging as the change from day to night is. "Only if I had not established my covenant with day and night and the ordinances (statutes) of heaven and earth, would I reject the offspring of Jacob and of my servant David" (Jer. 33:25–26; 31:35–36). Creation and the law are the two great inviolable statutes of God that belong indissolubly together, since the same God has given them (Ps. 19). God keeps his statutes; he is faithful. O, if only my life would enter into this firmness and faithfulness.

Verse 6. *Then I shall not be put to shame, having my eyes fixed on all your* 512
commandments.[41]

Being put to shame is the opposite of being blessed. My life is put to shame when that which I relied upon breaks apart. For then I have nothing left that could give my life its meaning and due, nothing to which I could appeal. My[42] life becomes a mockery and shames me. I relied upon my own strength, and I became weak and sick. I counted on my property, and it was taken from me overnight. I trusted in reputation and power, and I fell deep. I took pleasure in my honesty, and was overcome by sin. In the same way, anyone's life can be put to shame if they consider "mere flesh their strength" (Jer. 17:5). The world mocks its own by pointing its finger at them. Whoever wants to find honor with the world will be put to shame with it. But if my gaze seeks not people, honors, and riches in the world but God's commandments alone, then I will not be put to shame. For God's commandments cannot break apart because God himself holds on to them and with them everyone who looks to them. I will never have to be ashamed of heeding God's commandments. My life will never again be without an intercessor. Even if the world's judgment is against me, God's judgment speaks for me. I look at God's commandments when I base my decisions neither on other people nor even on my own thoughts or experiences, but rather when I ask ever anew, even if contrary to my pious thoughts and experiences, for what God commands me. I can be put to shame even by my most pious decisions and ways but never by God's commandment. God

[40.] Cf. Luther's marginal note to v. 5, *WA* 8:187,15.

[41.] In the Luther Bible it reads (Bonhoeffer's underlining italicized): "When I look solely at your *commandments*."

[42.] Bonhoeffer had originally used the plural "our" here and in the preceding sentences.

alone, not my piety, will preserve me from shame and dishonor. "*All* your commandments"—our life is so colorful, the temptations and dangers are so manifold, each moment is so new, that none of God's commandments
513 has been given in vain. Instead, only the entire richness of God's commandments can guide me safely through my life. Thus I can be certain that there is no situation in my life for which God's word would not give me the necessary advice. But serious attention, tireless asking, and learning[43] are necessary to recognize the right commandment and to recognize the inexhaustible kindness of God in all his commandments. The harder the world confronts and judges me, the more dire and miserable my way becomes, the firmer my gaze must stay directed toward God's commandments, so that I do not come to run but belong to those of whom I say: Blessed are[44] those who walk in the law of the Lord.

Verse 7. "I will praise you with an upright heart, when I learn your righteous ordinances."[45]

Gratitude can arise only now, when the gift of the divine word has been recognized, even more so when I stand in the midst of the learning about the divine word. How could someone for whom God's word is of no personal concern thank God? What kind of thanksgiving would it be that receives the gifts but refuses the obedience that is owed to the giver? It would be a heathen thanksgiving, which is a widespread custom. But this is thanksgiving not to the Lord God but to a friendly, impersonal destiny or to my luck to which I do not feel any obligation. Gratitude to God that does not come from an obedient heart is hypocrisy and audacity. Only where the revealed word of God has overcome the heart so that it wants to obey him, can the heart thank God for worldly and heavenly gifts. But the heathens, though they received the gifts of creation and "though they knew God, they did not honor him as God or give thanks to him" (Rom. 1:21).[46] The
514 thanksgiving of the world always refers ultimately to itself; through gratitude one seeks merely the higher confirmation and consecration of one's

[43.] Addition, subsequently deleted: "in the Scripture."

[44.] Replaces "Happy are those."

[45.] This replaces the following text: "from a true heart, so that you teach me the rights." This verse is not underlined in the manuscript. Ps. 119:7 in the Luther Bible (Bonhoeffer's underlined terms are italicized): "I *will praise* you with an upright heart, when I learn your righteous ordinances. [The Luther Bible German text reads "I will thank (*danken*) you."—VB]

[46.] Deleted: "Thus, there is a thanksgiving of the insincere [replaces 'untrue'] heart and one of the upright [replaces 'true'] heart."

own happiness.[47] To have given thanks conveys the satisfaction of feeling the received gifts to be one's rightful possession from now on. Yet even among the faithful, impermissible thanksgiving occurs. Even the Pharisee thanked God and sinned (Luke 18[:11]) because in his thanksgiving he saw only himself and did not receive the gift in humility but abused it against his neighbor. Thus he could not give thanks with an "upright heart"; otherwise he would have forgotten himself. He would have presented himself not as one who already has merit to show God but instead as someone who, like the person who prayed our psalm, is still only "learning" of the "demands of righteousness." What God has given and what I am not able to give, God's abundance for me and my poverty before God, are necessarily interconnected in thanksgiving "with an upright heart." Here too, then, the person giving thanks encounters the law not so much as gift but rather in its form as God's just demand. I thank God because I know his demands and want to learn them, but I thank him as one who is still only learning, as one who still lacks everything when measured by the demands of God's righteousness. Thus thanking leads me back to the giving God and in turn again forward to the demanding God, so that in him I finally find God's righteousness, which in turn is righteousness given to me.[48]

Verse 8. *I will keep your statutes; do not utterly forsake me.*[49]

First, we need to unlearn completely saying: "I want,"[50] before God teaches us through the Holy Spirit to say it new and correctly. Precisely in
matters of piety, this "I want" can have disastrous effects—"I want to be 515
pious, I want to be sanctified, I want to keep the commandments"—first, we must understand thoroughly that in this matter, too, it is not our will but God's will alone that counts. We must also renounce our pious ego so that God can do his work with us. Otherwise, the consequence of our "I want" is certainly bankruptcy. But when through God's grace we have stopped saying, "I want," when through God's new beginning with us in Jesus Christ we have been brought onto his path—despite all our "I want" and "I do

[47.] Marginal note in ink: "*Nietzsche*." This might refer to Nietzsche's allusion to the Pharisees in *Thus Spoke Zarathustra*, pt. 3, sec. 26, "On Old and New Tablets" (*Portable Nietzsche*, 324). Cf. *DBWE* 6:313, ed. note 51.

[48.] Marginal note in ink: "Ps. 50. To give thanks!" Cf. especially Ps. 50:14–23.

[49.] Replaces "nevermore." In the Luther Bible, the verse reads: "Your rights . . . nevermore."

[50.] [The German verb here is *wollen*, which in its transitive form is usually translated as "to want," but in its intransitive form it can also mean to "will" to do something, and that sense seems implicit here. It is translated here as "to want," however, since the English "I will" has a very different meaning.—VB]

not want"—then the Holy Spirit begins to speak within us, and we will say "I want" in a quite new and quite different way. "As soon as the Holy Spirit has begun his work of rebirth and renewal in us through the Word and the holy sacraments, it is certain that on the basis of his power we can and should be cooperating with him, though still in great weakness" (Formula of Concord, Solid Declaration II, 65).[51] As the blessed ones, as those who call upon God's help, who praise God and thank him, we may now say: "I want." Yes, I want to keep your statutes, I am not compelled to do it, but you have freed me so that I can want what I had hated. You have bound my will to your statutes. It is God, the Holy Spirit himself, who makes for me the reality of what was true for Jesus Christ alone: my will is your word. [52] But because I am not the Holy Spirit or the Lord Jesus Christ himself, I quickly have to add the request to my "I want": "do not forsake me too much" (Luther, 1521).[53] Otherwise, my weak will would soon come to an end. But one should not think here that God would withdraw the Holy Spirit from us; then the prayer would have to be: do not forsake me *for one moment.* For without the Holy Spirit, our good will cannot exist even for a moment. But instead it says: "do not forsake me too much," "not utterly,"
516 and thus we must think about a kind of forsaking through which God tests the faith of his own, as is said about Hezekiah: "God left him to himself, in order to test him[54] and to know all that was in his heart" (2 Chr. 32:31). This is how to think about misfortune, misery, and crises of all kinds in which God forsakes us for a brief moment. We should ask God in prayer not that he should spare us all misfortune but rather that he may come back to us soon and end the time of testing and not forsake us completely, for we are weak and quick to fail. Thus we will only be able to keep God's statutes, we can only remain steadfast, through the grace and help of God's presence. We pray for a steadfast heart that proves true in God's statutes, and we know that the heart does not become steadfast except through God's grace (Heb. 13:[9]).[55]

[51.] *Book of Concord*, 556.

[52.] Cf. the third stanza of Paul Gerhardt's 1647 hymn "Ein Lämmlein geht und trägt die Schuld," in *Evangelisches Gesangbuch für Brandenburg und Pommern*, 44 (*EG*, 83): "Mein Wollen hängt an deinem Mund, mein Wirken ist dein Sagen" (My will depends on your lips; my doing is your saying). [The English translation of the hymn is "A lamb goes uncomplaining forth," in *Lutheran Hymnal*, 142.—VB]

[53.] This is Luther's translation ["verlaß mich nit allzusehr"—VB] of v. 8b in "Der Hundertt und achtzehend Psalm" (*WA* 8:187,6).

[54.] Replaces "so as to tempt him" (as in the Luther Bible).

[55.] The manuscript erroneously cites v. 8.

Thus the circle is completed. God's grace stood at the beginning; it makes our beginning so that we may be freed from our own beginnings. Grace put us on the way, and it is grace that we call upon, step-by-step.

Note the recurring phrases in these verses and in what now follows: *Your* law, *your* commandment, *your* witnesses, etc. It is not human beings who are praised here but God and his revelation.

Blameless[56]

Verse 9. *How can young people keep their way pure? By guarding it according to your word.*[57]

A young man has prayed this psalm and this verse (cf. vv. 99–100). Thus this is not the question of an old person looking at the terrible young people; rather, this question arises here out of self-experienced trials and an individual encounter with the word of God. A young man stumbles here upon the question of his life, not out of enthusiasm [Begeisterung] for the good and the noble in general, not because of Enthusiastic[58] idealism, 517
but out of his own experience with the power of God's word and with the powerlessness of his own life. Does this question about the blameless, pure way sound unyouthful to us, unfree, life-negating? If so, then only because we have become accustomed to a very godless concept of youth and are no longer able to understand the strength and full vitality of life that lies in innocence. It is a very presumptuous and perverted thought that a human being first needs to become deeply entangled in life's guilt before coming to know life and finally God. We never recognize life and its guilt from life itself but solely [through] God's judgment over humankind and his grace in the cross of Jesus Christ. To want to include sin as a pedagogical moment in upbringing is an irresponsible[59] idea that exacts a terrible revenge. "Remember your creator in the days of your youth, before the days of trouble come, and the years draw near when you will say, 'I have no

[56.] In the Luther Bible, the following notes are penciled in the margin next to v. 9: "II" (cf. ed. note 2 above [with v. 9, the second stanza of eight verses begins—VB]), "Eccles. 12:1; Sir. 18:21." [The German word here and in the biblical v. 9 is *unsträflich*, which means not punishable in a criminal sense. A more literal translation of the Luther Bible v. 9 would be: "How can a young man walk his path without transgression? When he conducts himself according to your word."—VB]

[57.] The Luther Bible reads: ". . . your words."

[58.] Replaces "youthful." [The German here is *schwärmerisch*, a reference to the Enthusiast movement within the Reformation.—VB]

[59.] Addition deleted: "sacrilegious."

pleasure in them'" (Eccles. 12:1). "Before falling ill, humble yourself; and when you have sinned, repent" (Sir. 18:21).[60] "Shun youthful passions" (2 T[im.] 2:2[2]). To be pure where impurity is still a danger, to be blameless not out of bourgeois satisfaction but because of love for God, this is no renunciation of life but its fulfillment; this is not disregard for God's creation but its sanctification through obedience to the creator. "Rejoice, young man, while you are young, and let your heart cheer you in the days of your youth. Follow the inclination of your heart and the desire of your eyes, but[61] know that for all these things God will bring you into judgment" (Eccles. 11:9). Whoever lives with his crass sins until he becomes a mature man will often try too late to master them. God is Lord of the human being from the first breath, and he does not want to abdicate his rule, even for
518 one moment. God does not ask about our more or less modern ideals of youthfulness, but he asks only whether a life is submitted to his rule.

By asking the question about the blameless way, the young man recognizes the sin that lives within him. Otherwise, he would not need to ask. Only because he has recognized sin in all its power over his heart and his nature does he cease to look for human remedies. Neither good intentions, nor rousing ideals, nor even work and the fulfillment of one's duties can keep the way pure, but rather God's word alone, because only God is a match for sin. He has already done so in Jesus Christ by forgiving us all our sins (cf. John 15:3!); he still does it by letting us know his word of grace and of judgment and by judging and being merciful to us with every new day. What should I hold on to in the hour of trial and temptation? To God's word alone. In this way my path will remain pure.

Verse 10. *With my whole heart I seek you; do not let me stray from your commandments.*[62]

Whoever has received God's word must begin to seek God; he can do nothing else. The clearer and deeper God's word shows itself to us, the more vivid the desire in us becomes for the consummate clarity and inexhaustible depth of God. Through the gift of his word, God drives us to seek ever richer knowledge and an ever more glorious gift. He does not like false

[60.] [V. 22 in the German Bible.—VB]

[61.] Replaces "and" (as in the Luther Bible). With this one exception, Bonhoeffer cites Eccles. 11:9 without any changes according to the Luther Bible (there is a penciled exclamation mark in the margin next to the first part of this verse).

[62.] Underlined in the Luther Bible: "seek"; Bonhoeffer has made an "x" in the margin.

contentment. The more we receive, the more we have to seek God, and the more we seek, the more we will receive from him. "To those who have, more will be given."[63] God wants to be fully glorified in us and be revealed in
his full abundance.[64] Certainly, we can never seek God anywhere else but 519
in his word, but this word is alive and inexhaustible, for God himself lives in it. When God's word has struck us, we may say: I seek you *with my whole heart.* For we would seek an idol halfheartedly, but never God himself. God needs the whole heart. God wants nothing (not something) from us; rather he wants us ourselves, entirely. God's word has told us so. Therefore, we seek him with all our heart. There remains only one worry for us, namely, that we stray from the way that we started out on, away from the commandments that we heard. The person who is praying[65] says "stray." He is no longer considering an intentional, deliberate transgression of the recognized divine commandments. But how easily[66] do we stray when evil fogs our vision. We go astray and no longer know the way forward or backward, and do not find our way back to God's commandments. We must ask God daily to preserve us from the sin of straying, from the sin committed unwittingly (Num. 15:22ff.), for as soon as we unknowingly stray into evil ways, we might quickly enjoy this path, and error turns into evil intention. But whoever seeks God with all his heart will not go astray.

Verse 11. *I treasure your word in my heart, so that I may not sin against you.*[67]

When God's word comes to us, it wants to be secured in fertile ground. It does not want to lay by the wayside so that "the devil comes and takes away the word from their hearts, so that they may not believe and be saved." It
does not want to fall on the rocks where it cannot take root even though 520

[63.] Matt. 13:12.

[64.] The above sentences for v. 10 replace the following text: "We have received God's word, yet it is a strange law that lies within this gift, namely, that the more God allows us to know about him, the more we begin to seek God. A possession of the word that does not immediately lead us to seek is already lost. Through the word that God gives us, he turns our hearts to himself and awakens the longing in us to seek him [deleted: 'and to find. So it does not work to begin our life's path with firm possession, that we gradually']. Thus, we cannot gainsay our life's path with such knowledge of God that we think we possess. We must seek God daily."

[65.] [I.e., in Ps. 119.—VB]

[66.] Deleted: "the error creeps up on us."

[67.] The Luther Bible has "I keep your word in my heart, so that I do not sin against you." [A more literal translation of Bonhoeffer's German text here would be "I hold your saying in my heart, so that I might not trespass against you."—VB]

"they hear the word, receive it with joy. But these have no root; they believe only for a while and in a time of testing fall away." It does not want to fall among the thorns where it is choked "by the cares and riches and pleasures of life" and does not come to fruit (Luke 8:11ff.). It is a great miracle that the eternal word of the almighty God seeks a dwelling within me, wants to be held within me like seed in the soil. God's word is held not within my intellect but within my heart. The aim of the saying that comes from God's mouth is not to be thought to pieces but to be moved by the heart, just as the word of a beloved person dwells in our heart,[68] even when we do not think about it consciously. If I have God's word only in my mind, my mind will often be preoccupied with other things, and toward God, I will be missing. Therefore, it is never enough to have read God's word. It must enter us deeply, dwell in us like the Holiest of Holies in the sanctuary, so that we do not stray in thoughts, words, and deeds. Often it is better to read little and slowly in the Scriptures, and to wait until it has penetrated into us, than to know much about God's word but not to "treasure" it.

Verse 12. *Blessed are you, O Lord; teach me your statutes.*[69]

Are we praising human sanctity and piety? Are we preoccupied with ourselves and our faultlessness? Is this so conspicuously repeated "I" in this stanza of the psalm[70] self-reflection, self-criticism, self-righteousness? Praised be you, Lord! No other praise can count here. The Lord alone be praised, who has made the new beginning with us, who has revealed to us his word, who allows us to seek and serve him, who lets his word live in us,
521 and who preserves us from sin. On the path of the faithful, there is only the praise of God. In this praise of God lies all their strength and hope. God be praised! We, however, must repeatedly ask like beggars: teach me your statutes! By bringing God all the praise, we are confessing what we have received; by asking God, we are confessing our poverty. Never, as long as we live, will the begging for enlightenment, knowledge, for growth in learning the word now cease. But the praise of the one who has given us enough and more than enough out of his grace will not fall silent, neither in this world nor in the next.

[68.] Cf. Bonhoeffer's reference to Mary [treasuring the words in her heart—VB] (Luke 2:19) in the 1936 "Instruction for Scriptural Meditation" (*DBW* 14:947).

[69.] The Luther Bible has "rights" instead of "statutes." [The literal translation of Bonhoeffer's German verse is "Praise be to you, Lord! Teach me your statutes."—VB]

[70.] Bonhoeffer is referring to vv. 9–16, over which he has written: "blameless."

Verse 13. *With my lips I declare all the ordinances of your mouth.*[71]

God's demands come out of God's mouth and want to come upon my lips. Often it is easy to bear God's word in the heart, but how difficult is it sometimes to make it pass the lips! What is meant here is not empty lip service but the voicing of that which fills the heart. Do our lips not often seem locked, in the face of great woe, because we fear that a pious formula will take the place of the divine word?[72] Is there not an atmosphere of thoughtlessness and ungodliness, in which we simply do not find the right word and remain silent? Does [not],[73] often enough, a false shyness and a fear of people close our mouth? Warnings and admonitions remain unspoken; consolation and encouragement are withheld. How forced and anxious the name of Jesus Christ has passed our lips on occasion! It demands a great measure of spiritual experience and practice as well as childlike faith and confidence to be able to speak "all demands" of God with one's lips without succumbing to a spiritual routine, without becoming a moralizer or an obtrusive babbler. The whole heart must belong to the word of God before we learn to place our lips also entirely into the service of Jesus Christ.

Verse 14. *I delight in the way of your decrees as much as in all riches.*[74] 522

I rejoice—here is the grand word without which there is no walking the way of God. "In his joy he went," it is said of the person who had found the treasure in the field, "and sold all that he had and bought that field" (Matt. 13:44). All riches and possessions meant little to him compared to the divine treasure. Yes, in it he found all the riches that he could possibly wish for. Whoever finds the way of God must first have lost all his own riches in order to win the full abundance of God and within it "manifold riches" in general. God's word creates joy in the one who takes it in. It is the joy about

[71.] The Luther Bible has "With my lips, I want to tell of all the rights of your mouth." Bonhoeffer's note in ink on the upper margin, "Job 23:12," probably refers to this verse. [The German text reads literally: "With my lips I tell of all the demands of your mouth."—VB]

[72.] [Cf. *DBWE* 6:152: "Why, precisely in completely serious situations—for instance, when facing someone grieving deeply over a death—do I often decide on a 'penultimate' response, such as a kind of helpless solidarity . . . instead of speaking the words of biblical comfort familiar to me. . . . Why is my mouth often closed when it should give voice to the ultimate, and why do I opt for a thoroughly penultimate human solidarity?" Thanks to Ilse Tödt for alerting me to this cross-reference.—VB]

[73.] The manuscript includes an erroneously deleted "not."

[74.] In the Luther Bible, the verse is underlined starting at "way." In the margin next to vv. 13–14 Bonhoeffer has written an exclamation mark. [The German text reads literally: "I rejoice in the way of your witnesses as much as in all riches."—VB]

the fellowship with God that has been given once again. It is the joy about the redemption from fear and sin. It is the joy of the one who has lost his way and after a long night has found the right way once again. God prepares festive joy for human beings. God is the source of all joy; indeed, God himself knows joy.[75] "As the bridegroom rejoices over the bride, so shall your God rejoice over you" (Isa. 62:5).[76] "He will rejoice over you with gladness, he will renew you in his love; he will exult over you with loud singing" (Zeph. 3:17). We are invited to festively participate in God's joy at the delivery and the faith of his people. God's word itself is full of this joy of God, which is to break forth in us. The proclamation of great joy stands above the becoming flesh of the word of God in Jesus Christ (Luke 2:10); the Lord's days on earth are like the dawn of a single wedding day (Mark 2:29; cf. Luke 19:6); the conversion and salvation of each repentant sinner through Jesus Christ is celebrated in heaven.[77] The resurrection and ascension of the Lord fill the disciples with joy (Matt. 28:8; Luke 24:41, 52; John 20:20), and
523 the young church-community receives the Eucharist of Jesus with exultation (Acts 2:46). Where the word of God is, there is joy. As Jesus leaves the disciples to go to his father, he nonetheless leaves them his word, and in it his joy. "I have said these things to you so that my joy may be in you, and that your joy may be complete."[78] Complete joy is the gift of the word of God to its listeners.[79] God wants joy. But it is a joy "with trembling" (Ps. 2:11), simply because it is joy before the holy God.

God's word is the source of all joy, and the paths of his witnesses are full of such joy[80] because they are the paths that God himself has walked and still walks with us. But wherever God is with us, there is joy, and no one can take this joy from us (John 16:22). In days of affliction and persecution, this joy grasps the promise of the one who goes before us: "Rejoice and be glad, for your reward is great in heaven."[81] These are the riches of the ones who follow Jesus.

[75.] Deleted: "It is God himself who rejoices in his people."

[76.] In the Luther Bible, Isa. 62:5b is marked with indelible pencil. There is a cross-reference [in the Luther Bible next to the Isaiah verse—VB] to Zeph. 3:17.

[77.] Replaces "with the angels" (Luke 15:7, 10; Bonhoeffer has penciled a line next to both verses in his Nestle edition).

[78.] John 15:11.

[79.] Replaces the following text: "Complete joy, this is what the word of God brings to human beings, divine joy. God is not like the tyrant who wants to see only terror and fear in the faces of his underlings."

[80.] Deleted: "for on these paths, we find God with each step."

[81.] Matt. 5:12.

But whoever cannot or does not want to go on the path of God will be sad (Matt. 19:22; 17:23). "But I fear that we have neither the joy nor the cross, since we concern ourselves so little with the Gospel. We remain evermore in our old ways and thus despise the exquisite treasure of the Gospel" (Luther selection p[age] 204).[82]

Verse 15. *I will meditate on your precepts,*[83] *and fix my eyes on your ways.*

There is no standing still. Each gift, each realization that I receive, only drives me more deeply into the word of God. I need time for God's word and often have to ponder the words for a long time in order to understand the precepts of God correctly. Nothing would be more mistaken than that 524
kind of activity or sentimentality[84] that devalues pondering and reflection. It is also a matter not only for those especially called to this but rather for everyone who wants to walk in God's ways. True, God often demands fast and immediate action, yet he also demands silence and contemplation. Thus I may and must often stay for hours and days with one and the same word before I am enlightened with the correct realization. No one is so far advanced that he would no longer be in need of this. No one may think that he is exempt from it because of strong demands on him. God's word claims my time. God himself entered time and now wants me to give him my time. To be a Christian is not the matter of a moment but takes time. God gave us Scripture in which we are to recognize his will. Scripture needs to be read and pondered anew every day. God's word is not the sum of a few general sentences that could be in my mind at any time; rather it is God's daily new word addressed to me, expounded in its never-ending wealth of interpretation. Meditation, that is, prayerful consideration of the Scriptures, and exegesis are indispensable for the one who honestly seeks God's precepts, not his own thoughts. A theologian who does not practice both denies his office. But every Christian[85] will be granted the time that he needs if he truly seeks it. Meditation means to take God's word prayerfully into my heart; exegesis means to recognize and understand God's word in Scripture as God's word. The one does not exist without the other. But both are reflection, which needs to be practiced on a daily basis.

[82.] Cf. Witte, *Nun freut euch lieben Christen gmein*, 204, from the postscript of the *Rothschen Sommerpostille* of the sermons of Luther (1531): "Another sermon on the third Sunday after Easter on John 1:16–23" (*WA* 22:432,24–27).

[83.] Replaces the following text: "I speak of that which you have commanded" (beginning of the verse in the Luther Bible, continuing: "and fix my eyes on your ways").

[84.] Replaces "sentimental Enthusiasm."

[85.] Replaces "also the member of the congregation."

If I want to recognize God's commands, I must look not at myself and my situation but at God's paths alone. My way should be determined solely by what God did for me when he acted on his people and in Jesus Christ, by what God's deeds in becoming human, the cross and resurrection of Jesus Christ as divine actions mean for me. "For you were bought with a price; therefore glorify God in your body" (1 C[or.] 6:20). "You were bought with a price; do not become slaves of human masters" (1 Cor. 7:23).

525 Verse 16. *I will delight in your statutes; I will not forget your word.*[86]

Why is it that my thoughts deviate so quickly from God's word and that the right word for the right time does not occur to me? Do I forget to eat and to drink and to sleep? Why do I forget God's word? Because I cannot yet say as the psalm says: I delight in your statutes. I do not forget the things in which I delight. To forget or not to forget is (not) a matter (of the intellect but)[87] of the whole human being, of the heart. I can never forget that on which body and soul depend. The more I begin to love God's orders in creation and in word, the more present they will become to me in every hour. Only love protects us against forgetting.

Because God's word has spoken to us in history, that is, in the past, remembering and the repetition of what has been learned is a daily, necessary exercise. Every day we need to return once again to the saving deeds of God in order to move forward. Therefore, Scripture warns gravely, again and again, against forgetting: "Do not forget all his benefits" (Ps. 103:2). "Take care that you do not forget the Lord, who brought you out of the land of Egypt, out of the house of slavery" (Deut. 6:12; read the entire chapter!). "Remember Jesus Christ" (2 T[im.] 2:8). Faith and obedience live out of remembrance and repetition. Remembrance becomes the power of the present because it is the living God who has acted for me once and assures me of that today. In and of itself, the past is irrelevant. But because something decisive happened "for me" in the past, the past becomes present for the one who grasps the "for me" in faith, "for the words *For you* require altogether believing hearts" (Luther).[88]

526 Because my salvation lies not within me but outside myself, because my righteousness is the righteousness of Jesus Christ alone, because this can

[86.] Replaces the Luther Bible wording (Bonhoeffer's underlining italicized): "I *delight* in your rights and do not *forget* your words." Next to this verse in the Luther Bible is written: "!x."

[87.] Bonhoeffer added these parentheses later (deletion was considered).

[88.] See Luther's explanation of the sacrament of the altar in the Small Catechism (1529), in *Book of Concord*, 607.

only be proclaimed to me in the word, therefore, remembering and repeating are necessary for the sake of blessedness, and therefore, forgetting has the same significance as falling away from faith.

In the daily remembering of Jesus Christ, however, I am promised that God has loved me from eternity and has not forgotten me (Isa. 49:14ff.). If I know that God does not forsake me because he loves me, I rejoice, and new love for God's faithfulness in his word fills me, and I learn to say: I will not forget your words.

Opened Eyes

Verse 17. *Deal bountifully with your servant, so that I may live and observe your word.*[89]

I ask for life, as the servant asks his master. Life is a benefaction from God. Life is not a means to an end but is fulfillment in itself. God created us so that we may live; he reconciled us and redeemed us so that we may live. He does not want to see the triumph of ideas over a devastated field of corpses. Ideas exist for the sake of life, not life for the sake of ideas. Where life is turned into an idea, there the truly created and redeemed life is destroyed more thoroughly than through any other idea. Life is God's goal with us. If it becomes a means to an end, then a contradiction enters life that makes it a torment. Then the goal, the good, is sought in the hereafter, and that can be acquired only by the negation of life. This is the circumstance in which we find ourselves before we receive life in God, and we have been taught to call this circumstance "good." We became haters and despisers of life and lovers and devotees of ideas.

I ask God for the benefaction of life. Only the life that he gives is a bene- 527
faction. All other life is torment. Only life from God is goal and fulfillment, is the overcoming of the contradiction between "is" and "ought."[90] Life is the time of grace; death is judgment. Therefore, life is divine benefaction because I am given time for the grace of God. Such time is given as long as the word of God is with me. To hold on to this word is life from God that is affirmed. God's word is not in the hereafter; it does not lower life to a means to an end; rather, it protects life from succumbing to the contradiction, to the lordship of ideas. God's word is the fulfillment of life beyond

---

[89.] In the Luther Bible "Deal bountifully" is underlined. Next to the verse is written: "III."

[90.] [Quotation marks have been added here to make Bonhoeffer's distinction clearer; they are not in the original German.—VB]

which there is no other goal. Therefore, I ask God for the benefaction of life that has succumbed to him, as the life of the servant before the master, and which will be fulfilled through the observance of the word of God.

Verse 18. *Open my eyes, so that I may behold the wonders in your law.*[91]

I must close the eyes of my senses when I want to see what God shows me. God blinds me when he wants to let me see his word. He opens the eyes of the blind. Now I see what I would not have recognized otherwise, namely, that God's law is full of wonders. How could I walk along the long path of this psalm and begin it ever anew, how could I not tire of these unceasing repetitions, if God had not shown me that each of his words is full of undiscovered and unfathomable wonders? How could I preserve God's word day after day without the opened eyes that want to see their fill of the glory and depth of this word? To the eyes of my intellect, God's law must appear as a
528 possibly necessary but quickly learned and understood rule of life, about which there is not much to think, talk, or marvel anymore. As long as I think that I see with these eyes, I have no longing for the opened eyes. But if I have become blind, if God has led me into the deep night, if I am caught in dark misery and guilt so that my natural eyes no longer recognize and understand anything, then I cry out for better eyesight. Only the blind person cries for opened eyes. But is the person who prays our psalm, who is so capable of praising God's word, is he blind? Precisely the one who has glimpsed the wondrous world of the law of God knows how blind he still is and how much he needs to have his eyes opened, lest he sink back into utter night. Each day it is a new prayer, when we open our eyes in the morning and when we close them at night, that God may give us illumined eyes of the heart, eyes wide open when the day wants to deceive our natural eyes and when night dupes us with bad dreams, eyes opened and enlightened, filled at all times with the wonders of God's law.

We must emulate the blind Bartimaeus. When he hears Jesus walking past him on the road of Jericho, he lets nothing silence him, instead crying for help until Jesus hears him. Responding to Jesus's question: what do you want me to do for you? he answers: My teacher, let me see again! Thus, he receives healing (Mark 10:46ff.). But just as the blind man of Bethsaida (Mark 8:22ff.) receives only a gradual, step-by-step recognizing and seeing,

---

[91.] Underlined in the Luther Bible: "Open," "wonders." Next to the verse is written: "x," "F.C." (Formula of Concord). This possibly refers to the beginning of the Formula of Concord that determines Scripture to be *unicam regulam et normam*, "the only rule and guiding principle" (*Book of Concord*, 486). [NRSV: "Open my eyes, so that I may behold wondrous things out of your law."—VB]

so too our eyes will only be opened slowly and advance from one recognition to the next.

But whoever thinks he can see, even though he is blind, cannot be helped anymore, but will perish in his blindness (John 9:40–41). It is a gift of grace to recognize one's own blindness to God's word and to be able to pray for opened eyes.

One whose eyes God has opened to his word will see into a world of wonders. What had appeared dead to me is full of life; contradictions resolve themselves into a higher unity; harsh demands become gracious commands. Within the human word I hear God's eternal word; in past
history I recognize the present God and his working for my salvation. The 529
merciful consolation becomes a new claim of God; the unbearable burden becomes an easy yoke.[92] The great wonder in God's law is the revelation of the Lord Jesus Christ. Through him, the word receives life, contradictions receive unity, revealed things receive unfathomable depth. Lord, open my eyes.

Verse [19.] *I am a guest on earth; do not hide your commandments from me.*[93]

When God's word first encountered[94] me, it made me a stranger on this earth.[95] It put me into the long line of the fathers of the faith who lived as strangers in the promised land (Heb. 11:9). Abraham believes the call that commands him to go from his father's land into the land of promise. At an old age after the death of Sarah, he—as a "stranger and resident alien" in this land—buys a burial place as his only possession in the land of the covenant (Gen. 23:4). Jacob confesses before Pharaoh that his entire life has been a pilgrimage, shorter and worse than even the pilgrimage of his fathers Isaac and Abraham (Gen. 47:9). When the land of Canaan has come into the possession of the children of Israel, they are never allowed to forget that they, too, were and are strangers. They were strangers in Egypt (Exod. 22:20 et passim), and they are until now "strangers and guests" in the land that belongs not to them but to God (Lev. 25:23). In a great and festive hour of his life, David connects himself to the fathers: "For we are

[92.] Cf. Matt. 11:30. Also *DBWE* 4:39.

[93.] In the Luther Bible, "do not hide" is underlined. An "x" is written next to the verse, and a dividing line extending into the margin is drawn underneath it. The cited verse (its number, "19," is missing) is the first line written on an extra sheet that Bonhoeffer numbered "9" and inserted into his manuscript. [NRSV: "I live as an alien in the land; do not hide your commandments from me."—VB]

[94.] Deleted: "and opened my eyes for God."

[95.] [Cf. *DBWE* 4:251.—VB]

aliens and transients before you, as were all our ancestors; our days on the earth are like a shadow, and there is no hope" (1 Chr. 29:15).

I am a guest on earth—with this I confess that I cannot remain here,
530 that my time here is short. Neither am I entitled to possessions and a house here. All the good that I experience I must receive with thanksgiving, but I must suffer injustice and violence without anyone standing up for me. I do not have any strong support, neither in people nor in things. As a guest, I need to submit to the laws of my shelter. The earth that feeds me has a right to my work and my strength. It is not my prerogative to despise the earth that sustains my life. I owe it faithfulness and thanksgiving. I may not evade my destiny to be a guest and a stranger, and thereby God's call into this sojourner status, by dreaming away my earthly life with thoughts about heaven. There is a very godless homesickness for the other world that will certainly not be stilled by a homecoming. I am meant to be a guest, with all this entails. I should not close my heart apathetically to the tasks, pains, and joys of the earth, and I should wait patiently for the divine promise to be redeemed, but truly wait for it, and not rob myself of it in advance, in wishes and dreams. Nothing is said here about the homeland itself. I know that it cannot be this earth, yet I know nonetheless that the earth is God's and that I am already on this earth not just as a guest of the earth but as a pilgrim and a sojourner[96] (Ps. 39:13). But because I am nothing on earth but a guest, without rights, without support, without security, because God himself has made me so weak and lowly, therefore, he has given me one single firm pledge for my goal:[97] his word. This one certainty will not be withdrawn from me; God will keep this word and through it will let me feel his strength. Wherever the word of home is with me, I will find my way in the strange land; I will find my rights in the midst of injustice, my support in the midst of insecurity, my strength in my work, patience in the midst of suffering.[98]

[96.] Replaces: "'your [replaces '*God's*'] pilgrim and citizen'" (allusion to Ps. 39:13 in the Luther Bible).

[97.] Replaces: "my goal and my homeland."

[98.] From the beginning, Bonhoeffer's theology is directed against "fleeing the world" and is a christologically mediated plea for "faithfulness to the earth." Cf. his 1929 "Basic Questions of a Christian Ethic" (*DBWE* 10, esp. 374–77); his 1932 sermon on Col. 3:1–4 (*DBW* 11, 3/12); "The Human Being of Earth and Spirit" (*DBWE* 3:74–79); his 1932 essay "Thy Kingdom Come!" (*DBWE* 12, 2/11); *DBWE* 4:163–64 et passim; *DBWE* 6, especially 146–70 ["Ultimate and Penultimate Things"]; *DBWE* 8, 2/84 and 3/170.

"Do not hide your commandments from me." This is the prayer of the pilgrim in a foreign land.[99] 531

For the one who has become a stranger on earth according to God's will and call, there is in truth only *one* thought that can fill him with deep fear, namely, to no longer recognize God's will, to no longer know what God demands of him. Certainly, God is often hidden to us in our personal lives or in his action in history; this is not what is alarming. But when God's revealed commandment is obscured, so that we no longer recognize from God's word what we are to do, it is a severe trial. In the middle of the joyous certainty of God's commandments, we are overcome by this fear: what if God willed one day to hide his commandments from me? I should fall into nothingness; I should fall with the very first step; I should perish in the foreign land.[100] Or is it already the case—as I must ask myself now as well—do I already live so much by the skeleton of my own principles[101] that perhaps I would no longer even sense it were God one day to withdraw his living commandment from me? Perhaps I would then act according to my principles as I always had, but God's commandment would no longer be with me. God's commandment is God's word to me personally for this day and for my life today; certainly what God wants from me is not one thing today and another tomorrow. God's commandment is at one with itself. But the decisive difference is whether I obey God or my principles. If my principles are sufficient for me,[102] then I cannot understand the prayer
of the psalmist. But if I permit God himself to show me the way, then I 532
am completely dependent on the grace that either reveals or denies itself to me; I tremble with each word that I receive from God's mouth and in anticipation of the next word and the continuation of grace. Thus I remain bound wholly to grace in all my ways and decisions, and no false security can beguile me out of the living community with God.

[99.] End of inserted sheet "9." Sheet "10" [replaces: "9"] begins with the deleted citation from v. 19.

[100.] Deleted: "Two things are said here: first: it is grace that God makes his commandments known to us; second: we know God's commandments."

[101.] The phrase "Or is it . . . principles" replaces the following text: "We learn from this: it is grace when God makes his commandments known to us, and we need this grace daily. We cannot know God's will once and for all. We cannot deduce it from general insights or experiences; rather God himself must say it to us daily. One can have the skeleton of general Christian principles any time, but God's commandment is not dead but is a living word addressed to me. We will have to examine ourselves concerning whether we already live so heavily from the skeleton of principles."

[102.] Insertion deleted: "which I can have at any time."

The cry, may God not hide his commandment from me, comes only from the heart of someone who knows God's commandments. There is no doubt: God *has* given his commandments for us to know and we have no excuse, as if we did not know the will of God. God does not allow us to live in irresolvable conflicts; he does not turn our lives into ethical tragedies; rather, he lets us know his will, demands its fulfillment, and punishes disobedience. Things here are much easier than we like. Our distress is not that we do not know God's commandments but that we don't do them—and that as a result of such disobedience, we are gradually unable to recognize them. It is said here[103] not *that* God hides his commandments but: God is beseeched for the grace not to hide his commandments. It is within God's freedom and wisdom to deny us the grace of his commandment; then, however, there is for us not resignation but far more the urgent and persistent prayer: Do not hide your commandments from me.[104]

533 Verse 20. *My soul is crushed by longing for your demands at all times.*[105]

The longing for God's demands is mightier than our soul. The soul perishes, overcome, when from God the great longing for his word comes over us. This longing to know God's demands, whatever it may cost, is not a

[103.] Deleted in the margin, uncertain reading: "But [v.] 20?"

[104.] Deleted notes in the margin: "God, you let me become a guest . . ." "Guest = only for a short while[—]hurried[—]not at home." Sheet "10a" begins with twenty lines that were deleted: "Because and as long as I am on earth I must cry in such a way. It is the cry of the sojourner [*Fremdling*]. In the foreign land, I seek the right path. In the loneliness, I yearn for a word from home. 'I am a guest on earth.' With that I confess that I will not stay here, indeed, that my time here is short. As a guest, I am subject to the laws of the earth [replaces 'of the land']. The earth has a claim on me, and I do not want to and should not deny that to it. I live by its fruits; therefore, I need to work for it. But my goal is elsewhere, and the earth never shows me the way there. Even if I serve the laws of the earth, my heart depends solely on the laws of God, which show me the way to a home where I can remain permanently. Since I know the commandments of God, I know that I can be only a guest on earth. God's commandments have taken from me my right to a home on earth and have turned me into a sojourner, a pilgrim, a guest on earth. But having become a guest and a sojourner through God, being led to the way home through him, I grasp him by his word and help, asking: now do not hide your commandments from me? You have separated me from the earth, you have made me lonely, you have made the earth a foreign land to me; now be with me and do not hide your commandments from me." In the upper margin, next to the deleted part, is written: "1. short 2. no claims 3. what he [the guest] has received, only as a fief. 4. Because so weak, God will help you 5. No support, home." This was apparently Bonhoeffer's preparation for the added sheet "9"; see the beginning of the meditation on v. 19.

[105.] In the manuscript "demands" replaces "rights"; the Luther Bible reads "rights." [NRSV: "My soul is consumed with longing for your ordinances at all times."—VB]

strength of the soul but, on the contrary, its death. It is not the soul with its manifold inclinations and wishes that lives in me, but the one longing for God's word, which silences all else. My soul is unable to withstand it, as every thought, every moment is filled with it. The soul must sacrifice everything in order to perceive, to know, to see God's rights over against human rights, God's demands over against the claims of human beings. When this longing for God comes over us, the soul suffers torment, is devastated; the fine creation is crushed. Whoever makes the pilgrimage to the promised land heeds not the dust, sweat, and wounds that cover him but only the goal.[106]

Because the yearning for God's word is not born of the soul, it does not
pass like a trembling or a frenzy of the soul in an hour or a day. It cannot be 534
compared to the longing of the soul for a beloved person, because this only lasts for a while, whereas the longing for God, which crushes the soul, is "at all times." It cannot be otherwise, when it comes over us from God himself. It must be everlasting. It has nothing at all to do with a sudden surge, with a one-time dedication of the heart to God's word. The "at all times" is decisive. The longing for God's word is distinguished, not by the heat of piety, but by the perseverance to the Word until the end.

This is precisely why it would be wrong to mistake religious euphoria for this longing. On the contrary, what is being spoken of here is precisely the experience of being crushed under the burden of this longing. This longing is less likely to consist in the bliss of religious exuberance than in seeing the triumph of the presumed right of human beings, yet hoping for God's right and relying on it; of living in a foreign land and yet being unable to forget the homeland; in misery, need, and guilt of being unable to come free of God; of having to seek God where intellect and experience reject him; of having to call to God when all strength sinks in death; of experiencing God's word as the power over our life that does not release us, even for a moment. Thus, the "at all times" is not an exaggeration but can be understood as a reality.

[106.] The following new paragraph is deleted: "This is how things stand with us, not for an hour or a day but 'at all times.' Precisely because it is not thrills and emotions of the soul but the divine longing for the divine word that is at stake, it seizes our whole life. Longing for God is different from longing for a beloved person. The former is permanent; the latter is fleeting. The former comes over the soul like death; the latter comes from the soul like life."

Verse 21. *You have threatened the haughty; cursed are those who deviate from your commandments.*[107]

God hates the haughty, those who are self-satisfied, who do not heed divine and human right, for whom mercy means nothing, the despisers of
535 the word of God and of the faithful. Haughtiness before God is the root of all disobedience, of all violence, of all thoughtlessness. Haughtiness is the source of all rebellion, of all tumult, of all destruction.[108] But a terrible threat looms over all haughtiness, which the haughty themselves do not grasp, but the faithful recognize it:[109] the gospel. "God opposes the proud, but gives grace to the humble" (1 Pet. 5[:5]). The fact that God is with the weak and the humble—in a word, the cross of Jesus Christ—is God's threat against the haughty. God will put them to shame, even if they carry the victory over all human beings. Whoever believes the gospel sees God's sword over the haughty of this earth. The preaching of the word of God is the only serious threat to a humanity that has become haughty. But God has also given the signs of his power to his word. In the middle of history, God's threat has already become reality here and there, and the congregation watches in amazement and shivering as the haughty fall and perish, even in this time. Yet the congregation is preserved from pharisaic security because it must realize that together with the haughty, innocents perish as well. And thus the visible judgments of God remain hidden and obscure, even to believers. Only the word that contains the announcement of the curse over the godless ones remains undeniably clear. "Cursed are those who wander from your commandments." In the law, it says: "Cursed be anyone who does not uphold the words of this law by observing them" (Deut. 27:26).[110] Can we speak this word without knowing that it is directed to us? Should it apply only to others but not to us? The curse over the ones who trespass against God's law is God's right and . . .[111]

[107.] Luther Bible (Bonhoeffer's underlined term is in italics): "You rebuke the *haughty*; cursed are those who stray from your commandments." Deleted in the manuscript: "The haughty ones before God are those who are self-satisfied, who go their own ways and do not ask for justice and mercy. They know no longing for God's word, their soul is not crushed but firm and defiant [replaces 'healthy']. They defy the commandments of God, and the obedient ones are despicable to them." [NRSV: "You rebuke the insolent, accursed ones, who wander from your commandments."—VB]

[108.] Deleted: "But God has threatened the haughty ones!"

[109.] Deleted: "a strange threat, seemingly without measure but of ultimate earnestness."

[110.] In the Luther Bible there is a cross-reference from Ps. 119:21 to this verse in Deuteronomy. The margin of the manuscript shows an unreadable word (perhaps "attachment").

[111.] Bonhoeffer's manuscript ends here.

9.2. Two Structural Outlines of Psalm 119 536

First Outline[112]

1–8	1. Praise of the walking in the law
9–16	2. The blameless way
17–24	3. Illumination—wonder of the eyes opened by law
24–32	4. The power[113] refreshment
33–40	5. (Steadfastness) Firmness
41–48	6. Confession (gladness)
49–56	7. Those who mock?
57–64	8. The congregation of the faithful. Community
65–72	9. (Thanksgiving for) humiliation
73–80	10. (Asking for) consolation—comfort
81–88	11. How long?
89–96	12. Transience [(]of the world), eternity (of the law)
97–104	13. Wisdom (through the law)
105–12	14. *The vow* (of faithfulness to the law)
113–20	15. Shiver before God's judgments—horror
121–28	16. Love for the despised law—love of the law
129–36	17. Hunger (for the law)—hunger for the law
137–44	18. Eagerness (in vain) (for the law)
145–52	19. Day and night (in the service of the law)
153–60	20. God's matter
161–68	21. Peace through the law
169–76	22. (God seeks those who seek him.) God in search

Second Outline[114]

1. Praise
2. Blameless
3. Opened Eyes
4. Refreshment 537
5. Firmness
6. Confession
7. Experience
8. Community

[112.] *NL*, A 58,2 (1); handwritten in ink, additions with indelible pencil; previously unpublished. Archival pagination pp. 15–16: Bonhoeffer's headings for the psalm stanzas, next to last draft.

[113.] In parentheses and deleted: "of the law."

[114.] *NL*, A 58,2 (1); handwritten in ink, additions with indelible pencil. Archival pagination p. 16: Bonhoeffer's headings for the psalm stanzas, last draft.

9. Humiliation—Conversion?
10. Comfort through judgment, consolation, destruction of enemies, formation of community
11. How long? longing—passion?
12. Eternity—what remains? "I *am yours*"
13. Wisdom
14. Vow
15. Horror—Simplicity?—Fear of God
16. Love of the law
17. Hunger for the law
18. Eagerness
19. Day and night. Enemy is near, but God is closer (Birk)[115] [—]validity, binding
20. God's matter—enliven me
21. Peace—waiting—joy—great reward
22. God in search

10. Supplements to the Monthly Letters from the Confessing Church Council of Brethren in Pomerania to Its Pastors

10.1 Meditation on Christmas, December 1939[1]

Theological Letter on Christmas

No priest, no theologian stood at the cradle of Bethlehem. And yet all Chris-
538 tian theology finds its origin in the miracle of miracles, that God became human. "Next to the splendor of the holy night burn the unfathomable mysteries of theology" (Hello).[2] *Theologia sacra*[3]—it originates in prayerful kneeling before the mystery of the divine child in the stable. Israel had no theology. It did not know God in the flesh. Without that holy night, there is no theology. "God revealed in the flesh," the God-human Jesus Christ, that

[115.] Hellmuth Birk, candidate in Sigurdshof, 1939–40.

[1.] *NL*, A 62,1; hectograph copy. Previously published in *GS* 2:382–88 and *PAM* 2:343–49. Probably written at Sigurdshof and sent on December 15, 1939, as a supplement to the monthly letter sent by the Council of Brethren of the Confessing Church in Pomerania to its pastors (Superintendent Friedrich Onnasch was responsible for the editing of this letter).

[2.] About the French author Ernest Hello, see *DBWE* 5:84, esp. ed. note 7, and *DBWE* 6:141, ed. note 30.

[3.] "Sacred theology."

is the holy mystery, which theology was instituted to preserve and protect.[4] What foolishness, as if it were the task of theology to decode God's mystery, pulling it down to the commonplace, miracle-less words of wisdom based on human experience and reason! Whereas this alone is its charge—to keep the miracle of God a miracle, to comprehend, defend, and exalt the mystery of God, precisely as mystery. The early church meant the very same thing when it concerned itself with the mystery of the Trinity and the person of Jesus Christ with tireless fervor. What superficiality and thoughtlessness, particularly among theologians, when theology is disparaged,[5] when they boast about not being and not wanting to be theologians, ridicule their own office and ordination, and nonetheless at the end of it all, they have and advocate a bad theology instead of a correct theology! But then, where among the theological professorships has the mystery of God in the flesh, of the birth of Jesus Christ, as God-human and Savior, been depicted and taught to us as the unfathomable mystery of God? Where do we hear it preached?

If Christmastide does not succeed in kindling in us anew something like a love toward holy theology, so that we, captured and overcome by the miracle of the cradle of the Son of God, must devoutly ponder the mysteries of 539
God—then it might well be the case that the fire of the divine mysteries is already extinguished and dead, even for our hearts.

The early church pondered the Christ question over several centuries. In so doing, it made reason captive to obedience to Jesus Christ and vividly testified, in stern and contradictory statements, to the mystery of the person of Jesus Christ. It did not yield to the modern illusion that this mystery could only be felt and experienced, because it knew about the corruption and egocentricity of all human feeling and experience. The church did not mean, of course, that this mystery could be logically conceived, but in that it did not shy away from uttering the ultimate conceptual paradoxes, it declared and glorified the mystery as mystery for all natural thinking. The early church Christology really originated at the cradle of Bethlehem, and the splendor of Christmas lies on its eroded countenance. Even today, this

[4.] Regarding "the mystery" as the leitmotif in all speech about Jesus Christ, see Bonhoeffer's lectures on Christology in Berlin during the 1933 summer semester (*DBWE* 12:299–308) and his sermon on 1 Cor. 2:7–10 on May 27, 1934 (*DBWE* 13:360–63). See also Feil, *Theology of Dietrich Bonhoeffer*, 5–16 and 27–29, and Abromeit, *Das Geheimnis Christi*, esp. 35–63.

[5.] The German text here reads: "die Theologie auf den Schindanger zu werfen," literally "to throw theology on the *Schindanger*." This archaic term designated the place where tanners skinned dead animals. It was considered a cursed place, connected in folklore to witches' and devils' cults.

Christology wins the hearts of those who come to know it. So during the time of Christmas, let us take a lesson once again from the early church and try to understand devoutly what it thought and taught about the glorification and defense of the faith in Christ. The stern concepts from that age are like the flints from which one makes a spark of fire.[6]

We would like to consider briefly three well-known teachings on Christology that continue to live on in our Lutheran confessions,[7] not in order to preach them to the congregations, but in order to place our thinking and our recognition as preachers of the word in the light of the holy night.

First. It was of utmost importance to the church fathers to state that God, the Son, had taken on *human nature* but not a human being. What does
540 that mean? God became human by taking on human nature, rather than taking on a single human being. This distinction was necessary for the preservation of the universality of the Christmas miracle. "Human nature" is nature, being, flesh of all human beings, thus includes my nature, my flesh; human nature is the epitome of all human possibilities altogether. Perhaps we today would say as intelligibly as possible: in the birth of Jesus Christ, God took on [annehmen] humanity, not just a single human being.[8] This taking on happened in a bodily way—and this is the unique miracle of the incarnation. The body of Jesus Christ—that is our flesh. He bears our flesh. Therefore, where Jesus Christ is, we are, whether we know it or not. This is so by virtue of God's becoming human;[9] what happens to Jesus Christ,

[6.] Cf. Bonhoeffer's agreement with Karl Barth concerning the appreciation for the Christology of the early church, *Church Dogmatics* 1/2:122–26, especially concerning the category of the "mystery" of revelation.

[7.] Cf. Formula of Concord, Epitome, Article 8 ("The Person of Christ," in *Book of Concord*, 508–14) and Formula of Concord, Solid Declaration, Article 8 ("The Person of Christ," in *Book of Concord*, 616–34).

[8.] Cf. the discussion of the doctrine on the two natures of Christ in Bonhoeffer's Christology lecture in the 1933 summer semester (*DBWE* 12:315–18 and 353–60) and in *DBWE* 4:213–16. [The German verb *annehmen* can mean assuming, taking on, accepting; Bonhoeffer uses it throughout his christological writings to describe God's "taking on" full humanity. Cf. the following note, as well as *DBWE* 6:134, ed. note 2.—VB]

[9.] [In the German text of this sermon, Bonhoeffer uses several different terms (*Inkarnation*, *Menschwerdung*, and *fleischgeworden*) and their cognates to describe God's becoming human in Christ. Throughout his writings, Bonhoeffer's entire Christology is strongly shaped by this emphasis that God has become "fully human," and his usual word to describe this is *Menschwerdung*, or "becoming human." The word *fleischgeworden* (becoming flesh) highlights the physicality or bodily nature of Christ's human existence. Although "incarnation" is the word more commonly used in English, Bonhoeffer uses it rarely. It is striking in this sermon that he uses all three terms, each with its own particular nuance, and careful attention has been paid here to translate them accordingly. For

happens to us. It is truly the "poor flesh and blood"[10] of all of us that lies there in the manger. It is our flesh that he sanctifies and cleanses in obedience and suffering. It is our flesh that dies with him on the cross and is buried with him. He took on human nature so that we can be with him in eternity. Wherever the body of Jesus Christ is, there we are. Indeed, we are his body. Therefore, the testimony of Christmas for all human beings is you have been accepted; God has not despised you but bodily bears the flesh and blood of you all. Look to the manger! In the body of the little child, in the incarnate Son of God is your flesh, all your misery, fear, temptation, even all your sin, borne, forgiven, and sanctified. If you lament: my nature, my entire being is without salvation, and I must be lost forever, then the message of Christmas answers: your nature, your entire being has been accepted; Jesus bears it, so he has become your Savior. Because Christmas is the bodily assumption of all human flesh by the God of grace, therefore it must be said: God's Son took on human nature.

Second. "Two natures and one person"—in this paradoxical dogmatic
formula, the early church dared to express its knowledge of Christmas. 541
Dared, because it knew that something inexpressible had been expressed here, expressed simply because one could not be silent about it (Augustine).[11] Both were found and witnessed to in the manger: the humankind that was taken on in the flesh and the eternal Godhead, both joined together in the one name, Jesus Christ, human and divine nature joined in the person of the Son of God. Divine nature—that is the Godhead, which unites the Father, the Son, and the Holy Spirit in eternity. It is the eternal power, glory, and majesty of the triune God. Wherever the Son is, he brings this divine nature, because he remains true God from eternity to eternity. If the Son of God has truly become human, the divine nature is certainly present in all majesty; otherwise Christ would not be true God. In fact, if Jesus Christ is not true God, how could he *help* us? If Christ is not true human, how could he help *us*? Of course, the divine nature is hidden in the manger; only here and there in the life of Jesus does it shine through the beggar's garment of human nature. But although mysteriously hidden, it is nonetheless present; it is hidden for our sake, it is present for our sake.

---

more discussion of the significance of this language in Bonhoeffer's Christology, see also *DBWE* 6:6–7 and *DBWE* 12:46.—VB]

[10.] From the second stanza of Martin Luther's 1524 Christmas hymn "Gelobt seist du, Jesu Christ," in *Evangelisches Gesangbuch für Brandenburg und Pommern*, 10 (*EG*, 23). [The English translation is "All Praise to Thee, Eternal God," in *Lutheran Hymnal*, 80. —VB]

[11.] See, for example, Augustine, *De trinitate* 5.10 (CCSL 50:218, 22–27). See also Formula of Concord, Solid Declaration, Article 8, 19 and 30 (*Book of Concord*, 596 and 598).

Divine and human nature are united in Christ, yet without becoming one. Otherwise the great difference between Godhead and humankind would have been abolished. Therefore, it must never be said: the divine nature took on human nature. That would include the Father and the Holy Spirit becoming flesh as well. That would mean the final (modalistic—idealistic—pantheistic—Schleiermacher-like)[12] blending of God and humankind.[13] Rather, the Son of God, the divine person of the Logos, took on human nature. But Godhead and humankind, divine and human nature, meet and unite in the *person* of the Son of God, in Jesus Christ. Nowhere else but
542 in and through the person of Jesus Christ are Godhead and humankind united with each other, "[which] can never more be separated nor mixed together with each other, nor can one be transformed into the other,"[14] as stated at Chalcedon, as the utmost paradox and at the same time most reverently preserving the mystery of the person of the mediator. Seldom was reason so willing to humiliate itself and surrender itself before the miracle of God as happened in these words. For this very reason, seldom has reason been made into a better tool for the glorification of the divine revelation than happened then. The christological formula of two natures, one person, therefore, at the same time contains the highest soteriological significance: Godhead and humankind separated from each other before Christ came, united with each other alone in the becoming human of the Son of God. Only through the person are the natures in communion with each other. That means: only through Jesus Christ are Godhead and humankind united.

Third. The contribution of the Lutheran Church to the Christology of the early church consisted of the teaching of *genus majestaticum*, that is, the impartation during the incarnation of the attributes of the divine nature to the human nature (the Reformed Church vehemently disputed this teaching). "For the ability to give life, to execute all judgment, and to possess all power in heaven and on earth, to have all things in his hand, to have everything subjected to him under his feet, or to cleanse people from their sins, etc., are not created gifts, but divine, infinite characteristics. According to the statements of Scripture these are given to and imparted to the *human* Christ" (Formula of Concord, Solid Declaration, 8, 55).[15] While

[12.] Friedrich Schleiermacher. [Cf. *DBWE* 12:322, esp. ed. note 64, and 336.—VB]

[13.] Bonhoeffer rejects this chain of the tradition in his lectures on Christology in 1933, calling it a "docetic heresy." See *DBWE* 12:332–38.

[14.] ἀδιαιρέτως, ἀσυγχύτως—ἀωρίστως, ἀτρέπτως; Council of Chalcedon (451). Cf. also Formula of Concord, Solid Declaration, Article 8, 7 (*Book of Concord*, 617). Bonhoeffer treats this text in his 1933 lecture on Christology (*DBWE* 12:342).

[15.] *Book of Concord*, 626; italics are Bonhoeffer's.

it certainly remains incomprehensible how human nature, which is our nature, could partake in the attributes of the divine majesty, the Scripture teaches it, and with this teaching the deepest and ultimate union of God with the human being is expressed, so that with Luther it can now be said, "Wherever you can say, Here is God, there you must also say, Then Christ
the man is also there. And if you would point out a place where God is, 543
and not the man, the person would already be divided. . . . No, my friend, wherever you place God for me, there you must also place the humanity for me."[16] "It is the honor of our God, however, that, in giving the divine self for our sake in deepest condescension, entering into the flesh . . ."[17] The Lutheran teaching withstood the Reformed argument, that human nature is no longer taken seriously here, by pointing to the unique miracle and to Scripture. Indeed, from here the proper understanding of the Lord's Supper and the words of the Lord, "this is my body!"[18] is first disclosed to Lutheran teaching. When Christ speaks this way, he knows better than any other human being what his body is and can bring about. Thus incarnation and the Lord's Supper are intimately related. The doctrine of *genus majesticum* brings this correlation to light. The same God who came into the flesh for our sake gives himself to us through his flesh and blood in the sacrament. "The end of the ways of God is bodiliness [Leiblichkeit]" (Oetinger).[19]

These are ancient thoughts that we have expressed here, the smallest fragments of the edifice of ecclesiastical Christology. But the point, of course, is not that we admire this edifice, but that through one or another of these thoughts we will be led to read and contemplate the biblical testimony to the mystery of God's becoming human with more reverence and adoration, and perhaps even to sing Luther's Christmas hymns[20] more thoughtfully and joyously.

[16.] Luther, "Confession concerning Christ's supper" (1528) (*WA* 26:332,31–34 and 333,6–7). [This document can be found in *LW* 37:161–372; the parallel passage is on pp. 218–19. This wording, however, follows much more closely that in the Solid Declaration, which is cited here: 8:82 and 84, in *Book of Concord*, 632.—VB]

[17.] Luther: "That these words of Christ, 'this is my body,' still stand firm against the fanatics" (1527), *WA* 23:157,30–31; *LW* 37:72, trans. altered.

[18.] Mark 14:22 and pars.; 1 Cor. 11:24.

[19.] Oetinger, *Biblisches und emblematisches Wörterbuch* (1776), 407: "Leiblichkeit ist das Ende des Wege Gottes" (Bodily existence is the end of God's ways). Quoted in Zinn, *Die Theologie des Friedrich Christoph Oetinger*, 152, as the summary of Oetinger's teachings about salvation. Also cf. *DBWE* 3:78 and 121.

[20.] See the hymn "Gelobet seist du, Jesu Christ," quoted above (*Evangelisches Gesangbuch für Brandenburg und Pommern*, 10; *EG*, 23 ["All Praise to Thee, Eternal God," in *Lutheran Hymnal*, 80) as well as "Vom Himmel hoch da komm ich her" (1535), *Evangelisches*

544 **10.2. Meditation on Epiphany, January 1940**[21]

Epiphany: A Theological Reflection

The strange indeterminacy that lies over the feast of Epiphany is as old as the festival itself. It is certain that long before Christmas was ever celebrated, Epiphany was considered the highest festival of the winter months in the churches of the Orient and the Occident. Its origins are in the dark. We know that initially four different events were commemorated on this day: the birth of Christ,[22] the baptism of Christ,[23] the wedding at Cana,[24] and the arrival of the magi from the East.[25] In his essay "The Origin of the Feast of Epiphany" (*Gesammelte Aufsätze* 2, pp. 123ff.),[26] Karl Holl has attempted to trace this peculiar feast back to the Egyptian Aion festival, which was celebrated on the night from the fifth to the sixth of January and coincided with drawing water from the Nile and a wine miracle. Be that as it may, beginning in the fourth century, the church celebrated the birth of Christ on December 25 and separated it from Epiphany. Rome further moved the blessing of the water, which stood in connection with Christ's baptism, to the Saturday before Easter. The wedding at Cana was moved to a later festival season. Thus the adoration of Christ through the wise men of the East, the "appearance of the star before the Gentiles," became the focus of the feast of the Epiphany. Yet the liturgies of the churches in the West still show that the original content of the festival was not lost altogether. Because of this, a certain indeterminacy remains about the feast
545 of the Epiphany. In light of church historical findings, it is a dogmatic and pedagogical simplification when we say today that Epiphany is the festival of the appearance of the divinity of Jesus Christ before the world. Nonethe-

Gesangbuch für Brandenburg und Pommern, 11; *EG*, 24) ["From Heaven Above to Earth I Come," in *Lutheran Hymnal*, 85] and "Vom Himmel kam der Engel Schar" (1543), *Evangelisches Gesangbuch für Brandenburg und Pommern*, 12 (*EG*, 25) ["To Shepherds as They Watched by Night," in *Lutheran Hymnal*, 103].

[21.] *NL*, A 62,2; hectograph copy. Previously published in *GS* 3:388–92 and *PAM* 2:349–54. This text was probably written in Sigurdshof. It was sent in January 1940 as a supplement to the monthly letter of the Council of Brethren of the Confessing Church in Pomerania to its pastors. The last paragraph contains particularly numerous abbreviations of words (e.g., definite articles, adjectives, etc.) that have been written out here. [Because paper was scarce during the war, the text of the monthly letters was kept as short as possible, hence the frequent use of abbreviations.—VB]

[22.] See Matt. 1:18–25; Luke 2:1–21.

[23.] See Mark 1:9–11 and pars.; John 1:32–34.

[24.] See John 2:1–11.

[25.] See Matt. 2:1–12.

[26.] Holl, "Der Ursprung des Epiphanienfestes."

less, the content of the feast can indeed be described with this or a similar formula.

The detaching of the celebration of the birth of Christ from the day of Christ's baptism was of great importance. In gnostic and heretical circles of the East, the notion had developed that the day of Christ's baptism was, strictly speaking, the day of the birth of Christ as the Son of God. As an afterthought, an artificial calculation had been employed, according to which Jesus would have been thirty years old on the very day of his baptism.[27] This gives us an occasion to ponder for a moment the relationship between the birth and the baptism of Jesus Christ. It had become common in ancient Christianity, a custom still cited by Augustine, to celebrate the day of rebirth, of baptism, instead of one's own birthday.[28] So it seemed natural to deal with the day of the baptism of Jesus in the same way and to declare it the main festival. Yet this allowed for the possibility of a dangerous error, namely, disregard for God's becoming flesh. The birth of Jesus is not the natural beginning of a human life that would have had to be followed later by a spiritual rebirth; rather, the birth of Jesus is the Son of God becoming flesh for the salvation of all flesh. As we have already seen in our meditation on Christmas,[29] God chose to take on human flesh, human nature, but did not simply "adopt" the human being Jesus Christ as son, as the false teachers taught in opposition to the early church.[30] Had God accepted only the human being Jesus as his son in baptism, we would remain unredeemed. Then although Jesus would indeed be the singular, unreachable One, the superhuman [Übermensch] who won salvation for himself, he would have been incapable of helping us. Only if from his very conception and birth onward Jesus is the Son of God who has taken on and bears our own flesh and blood, then alone is he truly human and truly
God, then alone can he help us. Then, however, it is truly in his birth that 546
"the hour of salvation"[31] has tolled, then the birth of Christ is the salvation of all humanity, then precisely the day that God's Son became flesh

[27.] See Holl, "Der Ursprung des Epiphanienfestes," 143–44, on the Basilidians [a gnostic sect that celebrated Jesus's baptism—VB].

[28.] See Lietzmann, *History of the Early Church*, 2:309, and Dürig, *Geburtstag und Namenstag*, 36–38.

[29.] See Bonhoeffer's Christmas meditation (3/10.1).

[30.] In order to uphold strict monotheism (monarchy of the Father), some Judeo-Christians of the second century (Ebionites, Theodore the Tanner, Paul of Samosata, and others) considered the divinity of Christ to be the consequence of his adoption through God at his baptism in the river Jordan.

[31.] Cf. the third stanza of Joseph Mohr's Christmas hymn "Stille Nacht, heilige Nacht" (1818/1838), *Evangelisches Gesangbuch für Brandenburg und Pommern*; *EG*, 46. [This

is the day that makes our rebirth possible. Christ's birth and our rebirth belong together, but not Christ's baptism and our baptism. This now sheds light on the meaning of the baptism of Jesus. If it is not the day of the adoption of the Son of God, then what is it? When Jesus desires baptism, he does it as the sole good one, the one without sin, the one who does not need forgiveness, different from all other human beings. As the good one, he desires baptism, even though he does not need it for himself, for the sake of those who need it, for the sake of sinners. Precisely because he is the sole good one, he doesn't allow himself to be separated from sinners; he does not become a Pharisee who wants to claim what is good for himself. The sinlessness, the goodness of Jesus, is attested precisely in his unconditional love for sinners. Jesus goes to baptism not out of penitence but out of love and in this way takes the side of the sinners. When John wants to deny baptism to him, he does so because he does not grasp here what Jesus is doing.[32] The baptism of Jesus is self-humiliation for the sake of sinners. As the sinless one, he becomes a sinner for the sake of his brothers. Nowhere in the entire Scriptures is there an indication that Jesus needed baptism for his own sake. Instead, there is emphatic testimony everywhere to the contrary. Jesus desires baptism alone as the one whose goodness consists of being in community with sinners. Thus he submits to baptism, "for it is proper for us in this way to fulfill all righteousness" (Matt. 3:15). This "full" righteousness is not selfish sanctity but perfect love for humanity, for sinners. It is this moment of the Son of God's association with sinners in
547 baptism, in which his heavenly Father confirms to him (and to the bystanders; cf. John 1:31ff. and Matt. 3:17 and apparatus!)[33] that he is *his* beloved Son. As the sinners' savior, Jesus is proclaimed as the one he has been from the beginning, namely, the Son of God. The baptism is a confirmation of what Jesus is in the eyes of God. It does not add anything new to his being, but it brings something entirely new into his doing, for from now on Jesus acts before the whole world as the one he is in all eternity. The appearance of Jesus as the Son of God, as it is celebrated on Epiphany in remembrance of the baptism of Jesus, is the appearance in lowliness, ranking equally with sinners. Companion to tax collectors and sinners[34]—that is the Son of God, whose appearance we are to love.

---

is the hymn "Silent Night, Holy Night" in English. The wording of this phrase in the English translation is "with the dawn of redeeming grace."—VB]

[32.] Matt. 3:13–17.

[33.] In the critical apparatus in Bonhoeffer's Nestle edition, there is a list of manuscripts that prove the variant reading συ εἰ ("You are" instead of "This is [my beloved son]") in Matt. 3:17.

[34.] Matt. 11:19.

It is no different with the two other aspects of the feast of Epiphany, namely, the appearance of the star to the magi and the wedding at Cana. The star is not a sign that would have visibly announced the birth of the King of Jews to the world. It must be recognized and believed in. Herod did not see it. It rose to the Gentiles and called them to Jerusalem. Therefore, Epiphany is the festival of Gentile Christianity; it is "our" festival. But even the Gentile magi would not have found the way without the guidance of Holy Scripture.[35] The wonderful summons by the star is followed by the call to believe in God's promise in Scripture. Otherwise, they would not have recognized and honored the King in the child of Bethlehem. Here, too, the appearance of the Godhead of Jesus Christ is only a call to believe in the poor child in the manger.

The wedding at Cana is a report of the "first sign that Jesus did"[36] for the revelation of his glory, a most miraculous, and for our understanding, almost unnecessary sign of his divine glory in light of such an unimportant occasion. What is decisive, however, is that this sign of the divine power of Jesus remains hidden from the guests, from the chief steward, and from the bridegroom of the wedding; instead, it serves the faith of the disciples
alone. Jesus does not force recognition as the Son of God through magic, 548
but he wants to be believed as the Son of God. "His disciples believed in him."[37] The glory of Jesus is hidden in his humility and is perceived only in faith. Here, the content of the feast of Epiphany is closely connected again with the Christmas story, so that it becomes understandable that at one time the day of Epiphany was also the appearance of the one who had "no form or majesty."[38] With this, Epiphany points to the next season in the church year: to the Passion. It makes good sense that the last pericope of the season of Epiphany is the transfiguration of Jesus on his way to Jerusalem.[39]

Signed Dietrich Bonhoeffer

[35.] Cf. Matt. 2:4–6.

[36.] John 2:11.

[37.] Ibid.

[38.] Isa. 53:2.

[39.] According to the Protestant order of the church year, the sixth (last) Sunday after Epiphany is celebrated in remembrance of Jesus's transfiguration (see Matt. 17:1–9) (Bieritz, *Das Kirchenjahr*, 202–3).

10.3. Theological Reflection on the Lord's Supper, February 1940[40]

On the Lord's Supper: A guide to the study of Article 7
of the Lutheran Formula of Concord[41]

Before us is the season of frequent and grand celebrations of the Lord's Supper, the last hours of confirmation instruction, during which many thousands of young Christians are to be prepared for their first partaking of the sacrament. This and Lent itself often become an occasion for the pastor to ponder the last gift of Jesus to his disciples. Reflection on the Lord's Supper—are we still supposed to do that? Has it not been this very
549 thinking about the Lord's Supper that has brought more division than clarity into the church for the past one thousand years? Has this not turned the meal of reconciliation and brotherly love into a sign of disruption and strife? Has not everything been said over the course of the centuries that could possibly be said about this issue? Would it not be better to simply use and receive this sacrament and refrain from all thoughts about it? It is certainly true that the primary damage in this whole issue lies in the imperfect use of confession and the Lord's Supper and in the imperfect preaching about them. Proper thoughts only come from proper practice. But what is the proper practice of the Lord's Supper? What can we expect from receiving the sacrament? What is the gift in which we partake? What has Jesus promised with the institution of the Lord's Supper? And what is the proper sermon that invites to the Lord's Supper? We cannot evade the fact that the Lord's Supper is about not an unclear, mystical experience but rather the clear word of God that has become flesh, about the consolation and claim of Jesus Christ.[42] Jesus himself did not give bread and wine to the disciples in silence but spoke his word to it. When the Lutheran Church,

---

[40.] *NL*, A 62,3; hectograph copy. Previously published in *GS* 3:393–98. This text was probably written in Sigurdshof. It was sent in February 1940 by the Council of Brethren of the Confessing Church in Pomerania to its pastors. Throughout the text numerous words are abbreviated [see first ed. note for the previous document, 10.2—VB] that have been written here in full. The accompanying text by Superintendent Friedrich Onnasch reads as follows: "We send this letter to the brethren as a greeting for Lent and as a stimulus for theological work." Bonhoeffer's text triggered an exchange of letters between Friedrich Onnasch, Eberhard Baumann, and Bonhoeffer in March 1940 (see *DBWE* 16, 1/1, 1/2, 1/4, and 1/8).

[41.] See the Formula of Concord, Epitome, Article 7, and the Formula of Concord, Solid Declaration, Article 7 (*Book of Concord*, 503–8 and 591–615).

[42.] Cf. the second thesis of the Barmen Theological Declaration: "As Jesus Christ is God's assurance of the forgiveness of all our sins, so, and with equal seriousness, he is also God's mighty claim upon our whole life" (translation from Hockenos, *Church Divided*, app. 1).

with great emphasis and gravity, elaborated the doctrine on the Lord's Supper, it was concerned with the correct reiteration of this word of Jesus (as with all preaching, this cannot be simple repetition and declamation of the biblical verses!); it was concerned that the sacrament remain Jesus's own word and deed for all time. Nothing in the church should count and happen other than Jesus's word and deed. But because the Lutheran Church saw the entrance of human thinking into the Lord's Supper in both the Roman and the Reformed teachings on the Lord's Supper, the Lutheran Church fought for the cause of Jesus Christ with utmost determination. The Lutheran Church entered this fight not in order to express its own deep thoughts about the Lord's Supper but rather, on the contrary, to ward off all willful human thoughts, allowing that only the word and deed of 550
Jesus Christ stand and be valid in their original purity. Here all theological thinking stood in the service of the proper and unadulterated *use* of the sacrament in the church. Only where the church—in spite of all ridicule and horror of a modern world—rests on the pure word of God and the sacraments instituted by Christ himself, does it have the promise that the gates of hell will not prevail against it.[43] There is a dogmatic pharisaism, but just as frequently, today even more so, there is an antidogmatic pharisaism. There is an intellectual justification through works. But, likewise, there is an intellectual licentiousness and insincerity that can certainly not last before God. In its doctrine on the Lord's Supper, the Lutheran Church has gone between the two with sure steps, led by the word of God alone. It thought where thinking was necessary, and yet it strictly respected the limits of thinking. It was enabled to do so by allowing the only goal of its thinking to be that the miracle and mystery of the Lord's Supper of Jesus Christ should stand as such and be adored.

1. The point of departure for everything is the words of Christ: This is my body.[44] Here there are no ifs and buts. The bread that we eat in the sacrament is the body of Jesus Christ. This is so by virtue of the almighty word of Jesus, and not by something like the virtue of our faith (vs. the *"respectu fidei"*[45] of the Reformed). The sacrament is made by the word alone, not by faith. It is irrelevant before the word of Jesus whether our reason finds it plausible or whether the world is outraged. The word of Jesus needs no

[43.] Reference to the Augsburg Confession, Article 7, in *Book of Concord*, 42.

[44.] Mark 14:22 and pars.; 1 Cor. 11:24.

[45.] "With respect to faith"; see Formula of Concord, Article 7 ("Holy Supper"), in *Book of Concord*, 593. The Latin expression and the page numbers from the German *Bekenntnisschriften der evangelisch-lutherischen Kirche*, "973–74," are written on note *NL*, A 54,9 (notes on "Holy Supper. Lutheran concepts. Reformed concepts"). It also includes what follows in the text.

confirmation through us. Either the word of Jesus is valid in and of itself on into eternity, or it is an empty sound.

2. Because Jesus's word is valid by its own power, it is also valid whether we receive the sacrament in faith or unbelieving. The bread is the body
551 of Christ even for the one who eats in unbelief. This is the Lutheran doctrine on the *manducatio impiorum*, which is contested by the Reformed.[46] It expresses that the sacrament is founded on and exists by the word of Christ alone. Even Judas received the body of Christ, though as a curse upon himself. Whoever eats unworthily, "eats it to his own damnation" (1 Cor. 11:29).[47]

3. Since the word of Christ is true, we receive the body of Christ not only spiritually but "orally." Where this is denied, the word of Christ is no longer taken seriously. Christ humiliates himself so thoroughly, his fellowship with us is so intimate, he manifests himself so immediately to each one of us, that we receive his body with our mouths and drink his blood. This is the Lutheran doctrine on the *manducatio oralis*, which was denied by the Reformed.[48] This teaching desires nothing other than to take Christ at his word and let it be effective, in spite of all the arrogance of human reason.

4. The body of Jesus Christ is present in the sacrament "truly and essentially" "in, with, and under" the bread. The bread does not turn into the body (transubstantiation)—this would be human interpretation and do violence to the miracle of omnipotence, which is founded on the word of Christ alone!—but the *bread* is the body. The bread is not the "sign for the absent body of Christ" (against the Reformed), but the bread *is* the body. This is what the word of Christ says and creates.[49]

5. The body of Christ is eaten in the bread, orally and spiritually (*oraliter et spiritualiter*). Not only orally ("Capernaetic"—against Rome), as if the body of Jesus Christ had become a "thing." But also not only spiritually (against the Reformed), as if, again, the sacrament had been created by faith and not the word of Christ alone.

6. The union of bread and body cannot be comprehended by human concepts. It should neither be magically materialized (Rome) nor spiritualized (Reformed). In both cases, the miracle that is accomplished by the
552 word of Christ alone would be denied, dissolved, and rationalized. In both

[46.] For the teachings on the "eating by the unfaithful," see Formula of Concord, Article 7, in *Book of Concord*, 593. Note *NL*, A 54,9 reads: *"manducatio indignorum"* (eating by the unworthy).

[47.] [The NRSV reads: "eat and drink judgment against themselves."—VB]

[48.] See Formula of Concord, Solid Declaration, Article 7, in *Book of Concord*, 604, for the teachings about "oral eating."

[49.] See Formula of Concord, Solid Declaration, Article 7, in *Book of Concord*, 601–5.

cases, the sacrament would fall under the power of the human being. The union is something utterly unique, incomparable, and is therefore designated as *unio sacramentialis.* Likewise, the eating of the body is neither a purely bodily nor a purely spiritual act. It is something unique, incomparable, and is therefore designated as “sacramental eating.”[50] Here is the limit of the thinking that serves only to defend the word of Jesus in its purity. The concepts of *unio sacramentialis* and sacramental eating, which are not to be resolved further but express the irresolvable miracle itself, bear witness to the word of Jesus. The issue, however, is not the doctrine on the Lord’s Supper but the Lord’s Supper of Jesus Christ itself.

7. As the logos entered the flesh, the entire Christ is present in bread and wine. It is his honor to enter the human essence deeply and wholly out of his love for sinners (against the Extra-Calvinisticum).[51] Christ wants to live among us bodily. Only in the body is he our savior. In the Lord’s Supper, therefore, not only “the power, effect, and merit of Christ” are present, but Christ himself is present in the body, that is, in his human nature. When Oecolampad challenged Luther in 1529 not to cling to the humanity of Christ but to arise to Christ’s divinity, Luther answered that he did not know and worship any other God but the one who has become human, who is present in the sacrament and is the only one who can save.[52] In the Lutheran Church’s struggle against any type of spiritualism, the issue is about the genuine presence of the Son of God who became human in his community; it is about Christ in the flesh.

8. “Nothing has the character of a sacrament apart from the use insti- 553
tuted by Christ.”[53] Only where the “entire action or administration of the Lord’s Supper” is being kept according to Christ’s command: “Do this,” where “in a Christian assembly bread and wine are taken, consecrated, distributed, received, eaten, and drunk, and that thereby the Lord’s death is proclaimed,”[54] does the sacrament of Jesus Christ exist. With this, the Lutheran Church staves off all curious questions concerning the moment

[50.] Ibid., 604.

[51.] The opinion of the Reformed theologians that the body of Christ remains in its heavenly dwelling and thus outside (Latin: *extra*) the event of the Lord’s Supper was called “Extra-Calvinisticum” by the Lutheran theologians. Cf. A. Adam, *Lehrbuch der Dogmengeschichte,* 2:354. See also the treatment of the internal Reformation controversies concerning the question of the Lord’s Supper in Bonhoeffer’s 1933 Christology lectures from the summer of 1933, *DBWE* 12:319–21.

[52.] See the disputation between Johannes Oecolampadius and Luther during the Marburg Colloquy, second disputation on October 2, 1529 (*WA* 30/3:131,4–132,8; *LW* 38:19).

[53.] Formula of Concord, Solid Declaration, Article 7, in *Book of Concord,* 608.

[54.] Ibid., 607.

and the length of time of the *unio sacramentialis*. The Lutheran Church closely connects everything to the command and institution, to the word of Christ. The sacrament exists only in the "use" (*usus*) or the "action" (*actio*). With that, all questions and thoughts are strictly directed toward and limited by the use of the sacrament in worship. To ponder the Lord's Supper in this way and to protect it from abuse, secularization, superstition, and impertinence are not only permissible but necessary in order to use the Lord's Supper properly and thankfully. Thus proper thinking comes from proper use and again leads back to the proper use of the sacrament.

Everything said here has been summarized by Luther in the Small Catechism, "What is the Sacrament of the Altar? It is the true body and blood of our Lord Jesus Christ. . . ."[55]

554 **11. Sermon Meditations, 1940**[1]

11.1. Sermon Meditations on John 20:19–31 for Quasimodogeniti Sunday[2]

John 20:19–31

[When it was evening on that day, the first day of the week, and the doors of the house where the disciples had met were locked for fear of the Jews, Jesus came and stood among them and said, "Peace be with you." After he said this, he showed them his hands and his side. Then the disciples rejoiced when they saw the Lord. Jesus said to them again, "Peace be with you. As the Father has sent me, so I send you." When he had said this, he breathed on them and said to them, "Receive the Holy Spirit. If you forgive the sins of any, they are forgiven them; if you retain the sins of any, they are retained."

[55.] The Small Catechism, "The Sacrament of the Altar," in *Book of Concord*, 362.

[1.] *NL*, A 63,2; printed copy (original manuscript not extant) from Eichholz, *Herr tue meine Lippen auf*, vol. 1. As in the sermons, the biblical text according to the Luther Bible has been inserted at the beginning of each meditation (this was not the case in the text printed in Eichholz). The four sermon meditations here are the last published texts by Bonhoeffer. After he was prohibited from public speaking on September 9, 1940, throughout the entire German Reich, due to "activity subverting the people" (cf. Bonhoeffer's letter of September 15, 1940, to the Reich Central Security Office, *DBWE* 16, 1/20), the president of the Reich Chamber of Literature forbade Bonhoeffer "every activity as a writer" "due to lack of the requisite political reliability" (cf. *DBWE* 16, 1/100) on March 19, 1941.

[2.] Eichholz, *Herr tue meine Lippen auf*, 1:120–24; Bonhoeffer sent this to Eichholz on January 24, 1940. Previously published in *GS* 4:480–86 and *PAM* 2:311–17.

But Thomas (who was called the Twin), one of the twelve, was not with them when Jesus came. So the other disciples told him, "We have seen the Lord." But he said to them, "Unless I see the mark of the nails in his hands, and put my finger in the mark of the nails and my hand in his side, I will not believe."

A week later his disciples were again in the house, and Thomas was with them. Although the doors were shut, Jesus came and stood among them and said, "Peace be with you." Then he said to Thomas, "Put your finger here and see my hands. Reach out your hand and put it in my side. Do not doubt but believe." Thomas answered him, "My Lord and my God!" Jesus said to him, "Have you believed because you have seen me? Blessed are those who have not seen and yet have come to believe."

Now Jesus did many other signs in the presence of his disciples, which are 555
not written in this book. But these are written so that you may come to believe that Jesus is the Messiah, the Son of God, and that through believing you may have life in his name.]

1. Verses 19–20. The miracle happened at morning. In the evening, the disciples are together. And as night falls, when the shadows of unrest want to cover the disciples, when in light of the new situation they carefully close the doors to be safe from the agitated Jews, not considering that they might close the door to the Lord, "Jesus came and stood among them." Strange that in the hour when we most hope for Jesus's presence, we always seem to close the door out of fear of all kinds of other things. But far more miraculous that Jesus does not let himself be hindered by these locked doors. On his way to the people, the Resurrected One does not let himself be stopped by human beings. His new body does not hinder or limit him anymore, as our body does, but Jesus's body has now become the consummate tool of his spirit. The Resurrected One steps among his fearful disciples. He speaks: *"Peace be with you."* Certainly, this used to be the common greeting and an appropriate greeting, for it contains everything that people might say in greeting one another. But even among us, it makes a difference who utters a greeting. The pious greeting of a mother or an elderly Christian has a different weight than if someone simply uses it as a formula. "Peace be with you"—(instead of "be" it would be better to add "is"!)[3]—on the lips of the

[3.] The greeting of peace does not contain a verb in the original Greek (εἰρήνη ὑμῖν). Bonhoeffer here refers to the exegetical dispute about Rom. 5:1. Luther translated with the poorer version: "Now that we have been made justified through faith, we *have* (ἔχομεν, indicative) peace with God" and not "we *are to* have peace with God (ἔχωμεν, subjunctive). In Bonhoeffer's Nestle New Testament, ἔχομεν in Rom. 5:1 has been changed to ἔχομεν in pencil.

Resurrected One, this means: the end of all your fears, the end of the reign of sin and of death over you, now you have peace with God,[4] with human beings, and therefore with yourselves. Thus speaks the very one who has
556 won this peace for us, and like a visible sign of the battle fought and the victory won, he shows his pierced hands and his wounded side. "Peace with you"—that means: He, who himself is this peace,[5] Jesus Christ is with you, the Crucified and Resurrected One. Word and sign of the living Lord give the disciples joy. The community with the Lord is found again after days of fear and darkness.

2. Verses 21–23. But there is no community with Jesus that is not at the same time *a call to service.* The community with Jesus is fulfilled only in service to him. Jesus has always told his disciples this (cf. John 15:1ff.). Now, as the Transfigured One, he reveals to them the highest charge, namely, the one in which they are to prove and preserve the community with him. "I send you" (present tense!). The sending of the disciples through Jesus parallels the sending of Jesus through the Father. Jesus places his work into the hands of his disciples before he goes to the Father. The same peace that has been granted to the disciples shall be the force of their service. This is why Jesus speaks to them "again": "Peace with you." The peace that comes forth from the resurrection of Jesus is the potent force for the commission. Here, too, the word and the sign meet.[6] Jesus does to his disciples what the Creator did to the first human being.[7] The breath of new life and of the new commission, the breath of resurrection touches, fills the disciples. The one who has fought with sin and death, the one who comes forth from the battle won, from the resurrection morn, is able to bring to the disciples what no human being could obtain: the Holy Spirit. "Receive the Holy Spirit." There is no dilution or deception here. It is the Holy Spirit himself, the spirit of Pentecost, that the Resurrected One gives to those who are his and with whom he equips them for their commission. Only in the possession of the Holy Spirit can the work of Jesus be done. That means: forgiving and retaining sins in divine authority. This was Jesus's work on earth; this is the task of the disciples and with them all believers (cf. Matt.
557 16:19; 18:18). The disciples are now charged to do that which had—in the

[4.] Cf. Rom. 5:1.

[5.] Cf. Eph. 2:14.

[6.] Cf. Augustine's definition of the sacrament: "Accedit verbum ad elementum et fit Sacramentum" (The word is added to the elemental substance, and it becomes a sacrament, also itself, as it were, a visible word) (Tractate 80, *Tractates on the Gospel of John*, 117).

[7.] Cf. Gen. 2:7.

eyes of the pious—made Jesus the thief of the honor that was God's alone, namely, that he forgave sins. Previously, only the one who bore the curse of sin on his own body and yet was without sin[8] was allowed to forgive sins in the name of God; from now on, the disciples do this in Jesus's name and spirit. Yet because the forgiveness of sins is a gift of the free and pure grace of God, wherever sin may not be forgiven due to the hardness of heart, sin must be retained; that is, God's judgment must be proclaimed. Wanting to forgive sins but not wanting to retain sins turns divine forgiveness into a human work, a dalliance with sin. The squandering of grace dishonors God and does damage to human beings.[9] Nonetheless, the proclamation of judgment serves the proclamation of grace; the retention of sin serves the future repentance, conversion, and forgiveness. The disciple shall forgive and retain sins with great certainty and joyfulness by Christ's authority, for this is the work of his Lord that has been entrusted to him. He may not shy away from it. Both will be carried out in the public proclamation of the word and in personal confession. The breath of the Resurrected One blows through both of them. Divinely authorized preaching and confession exist because Christ lives and has given us the Holy Spirit.

3. Verses 24–29. What good to me is the news of the most glorious miracle if I cannot experience and examine it myself? Dead is dead, and a wish makes people gullible. So speaks doubt in all ages, and this is what Jesus's disciple *Thomas* thinks. From the few words that we have from him (John 11:16; 14:5), we know him as a disciple ready for any sacrifice, who openly acknowledged his questions for Jesus and desired clear answers. After the death of Jesus, he had separated himself from the other disciples and also kept his distance on Easter day. He did not want to be drawn into sick fanaticism. "I will not believe it," he says firmly when the news from the other 558
disciples reached him, "before I have seen it and touched it myself." Thomas is right when he either wants to find his faith on his own or is not willing to believe at all. But the way in which he seeks it is wrong. Despite his refusal to believe, Thomas comes to the circle of disciples on the following Sunday evening. This is important since it shows the readiness of Thomas to be convinced; it shows the sincerity of his doubt. Yet it is the free grace of the Resurrected One that now pursues the individual, overcomes the doubter, and creates in him the Easter faith. Jesus comes, again through locked doors. There could be no doubt about the miraculous nature of his presence.

[8.] Cf. Heb. 4:15.

[9.] See Bonhoeffer's understanding of "cheap grace" in *Discipleship*, *DBWE* 4:49–55.

He speaks the greeting of peace that is directed to all, but this time it is directed in particular to the peaceless heart of Thomas. Jesus comes for the sake of his doubting disciple. He knows the whole process that has unfolded within him; he knows him through and through. This is shown by his first word to Thomas. Jesus calms the doubtful yearning[10] of the disciple by granting him what he denied Mary ([John] 20:17). There is a difference between our wanting to take something and the Lord granting something to us. Mary is rebuffed; Thomas is allowed to hear, see, and touch. To allow himself to be put to the test is an incredible courtesy on the Lord's part for the benefit of his doubting disciple. "Do not *become* unbelieving, but believe"—Christ woos his disciples; the final decision has not been made yet but is dangerously close. But when Jesus addresses the disciple as one who has not yet decided against him, he gives him the freedom to change his ways. But whether Thomas dared to stretch out his hand remains unsaid. It is not important. What is important is that the Easter faith breaks through in Thomas: "My Lord and my God." This is the entire confession of Easter. No one had spoken in this manner before this doubter. The conquest is complete. Jesus's answer does not glorify doubt, seeing, or touching, but glorifies faith alone. Faith can find assurance in or rest on not that which
559 we see but the word of God alone. Millions of doubters will follow Thomas. Their doubt will be overcome not through seeing or touching but through the witness of the living Christ. Even Thomas could trust not his eyes and his hands but Christ alone. Hence the silence about what he did and the straightforward narrative about his Easter confession.

4. Verses 30–31. Is less given to us than to the disciples, than to Thomas? Does Jesus make access to him more difficult for us? Did we not receive only shards of the deeds of Christ so that the full richness of his miracles as the disciples experienced them is lost to us? John says: it is true that Jesus did many more things than we know today. But what is written is enough for us, enough in view of the one thing that is most important: that we believe Jesus to be the Christ, God's Son, and in his name we have eternal life. He instituted for us word and sign, sermon and sacrament, in order to help us believe. The disciples did not receive more than that either, nor did Thomas. What they saw, Jesus in his poverty, in his death, and his transfig-

[10.] This is a modification of a phrase in Paul Gerhardt's 1667 hymn on Luke 2:15–20, "Kommt und laßt uns Christum ehren" (1667; *Evangelisches Gesangbuch Brandenburg-Pommern*, 16, and *EG*, 39), fifth stanza: "Jacob's star has risen and calms the urgent yearning." [The English translation is "Come, Your Heart and Voices Raising," in *Lutheran Hymnal*, 90.—VB]

ured form, was no less exposed to doubt than what we see. Only when they themselves believed Him was he the Lord for them. They could ground their lives only in him, based not on how they saw him but on how they believed in him as the Christ, the Son of God, and not some supernatural appearance, and so they could have eternal life in his name. This is also the reason why word and sacrament are given to us, that we may become blessed by believing, not seeing.

The following three points informally relate to Quasimodogeniti[11] Sunday: that the resurrection of Jesus is our new life, that from now on we live in service to Jesus, and that both only become real for us in faith.

11.2. Sermon Meditation on John 10:11–16 for Misericordias Domini Sunday[12] 560

John 10:11–16[13]

[I came that they may have life, and have it abundantly. I am the good shepherd. The good shepherd lays down his life for the sheep. The hired hand, who is not the shepherd and does not own the sheep, sees the wolf coming and leaves the sheep and runs away—and the wolf snatches them and scatters them. The hired hand runs away because a hired hand does not care for the sheep. I am the good shepherd. I know my own and my own know me, just as the Father knows me and I know the Father. And I lay down my life for the sheep. I have other sheep that do not belong to this fold. I must bring them also, and they will listen to my voice. So there will be one flock, one shepherd.]

1. Verses 11–13. Jesus, the good shepherd—this has nothing to do with common idylls and poetry about shepherds and sheep. Everything of that sort ruins the text. *Ego eimi*[14]—"I am"—with this it becomes clear that it is not about shepherds and their work in general but about Jesus Christ alone. I am *the* good shepherd—not *a* good shepherd, as if Jesus compared himself with other good shepherds and learned from them what a good shepherd should be (cf. in the original the double article: *the* shepherd, *the* good

[11.] "Like the newborn children" (cf. 1 Pet. 2:2). A name for the first Sunday after Easter based on the opening words of the Latin Introitus.

[12.] From Eichholz, *Herr tue meine Lippen auf*, 1:124–27; Bonhoeffer sent this to Eichholz on January 24, 1940. Previously published in *GS* 4:486–91 and *PAM* 2:317–22.

[13.] [In the NRSV, this passage begins with verse 10b.—VB]

[14.] Greek: ἐγώ εἰμι.

one!).[15] One can only experience what a good shepherd is from *the* good shepherd to whom there is no comparison, from the "I," from Jesus.

All the other shepherd ministries in the church of Jesus Christ are not the establishing of a second or third shepherd next to *the* good shepherd, but rather allow Jesus alone to be *the* good shepherd of the congregation. He is the "chief shepherd" (1 Pet. 5:4); it is his shepherd ministry in which the "pastors" participate, or else they ruin the ministry and the herd. That it is about *the* good shepherd as such, and not about one shepherd among others, immediately becomes obvious because of the unusual work that he calls his own. It is not about grazing, watering, helping, but "the good shepherd
561 (again note the article!)[16] lays down his life for the sheep." Steinmeyer states correctly: "Truly, the shepherd cares for his flock with all loyalty. But his shepherding duty never demands that he sacrifice himself for them."[17] But Jesus calls himself the good shepherd because he dies for his sheep. This is only true for *the* good shepherd. If one understands this sentence in light of Jesus, it gains an even richer meaning: *First,* if Jesus speaks of the giving of his life as something present (present tense!), then we may say with Bengel: "That entire life was a walk toward death."[18] *Second,* when Jesus gives his own death significance "for the sheep," then one sees in this dying one final, saving deed for the flock, namely, a freely given and not a forced deed. *Third,* when the dying of the shepherd is for the sake of the sheep, it is not disputed that Jesus died for all humanity, but it is pointed out that only the sheep of his flock take part in the fruit of his dying. The view is not on the world, but solely on the good deed of Jesus for the sake of his congregation. The good shepherd and his congregation belong together.

"But the hired hand"—what distinguishes him from the shepherd? That the sheep are not his own. For they belong to the good shepherd alone. Because they are his property and his life as shepherd depends on them, that is why he never lets himself be separated from them, instead saving them though his death. The hired hand is a hired hand (v. 13); he only serves for his wage, and therefore in the hour of danger he deserts the flock and flees. A hired hand can deceptively resemble the shepherd for a long time. But in the hour of danger, it will come to the light of day. Why should the hired hand stay with the flock? Nothing can keep him when he sees that his gain is in danger. What does it matter to him that the wolf attacks the flock, steals and kills some, scatters the others so that they can no longer

[15.] Greek: ὁ ποιμὴν ὁ καλός.

[16.] See the preceding ed. note.

[17.] Steinmeyer, *Der homiletische Gebrauch der Evangelischen-Altkirchlichen Perikopen*, 67.

[18.] Latin: "Tota illa vita Christi erat itio in mortem" (Bengel, *Gnomon*, 237).

find one another and have to die alone, in misery, and without protection? That is what the wolf, the enemy of the church-community of Jesus, will always do. He snatches some, the others scatter—but what does this concern 562
the hired hand to whom belongs not the flock but only his own life and his wages. He flees "because he is a hired hand." Is everyone who flees a hired hand? No, the prophets and the apostles fled as well; even Jesus ordered his disciples to flee when it became necessary for the sake of the proper service.[19] Not everyone who flees is a hired hand, but it is certain that every hired hand flees. It is also flight if one is silent where one should speak, if one neglects doing what one should do. The hireling flees just as surely as the good shepherd dies for his sheep. Even the most faithful pastor is not the good shepherd, but because he knows that "his" congregation is not his own but is the Lord Jesus's own congregation and that Jesus died for this congregation and alone is its good shepherd, he allows Jesus to be the sole good shepherd of his congregation and therefore does not flee. But the pastor for whom ministry, himself, and his gain are more important than the congregation of the good shepherd is a hired hand and flees. Sometimes he may even flee by staying with "his" congregation, which he considers his property. At this point, one could point to the shepherd ministry of the Evangelical preacher.[20]

2. Verses 14 and 15. Note the weighty importance of the new beginning! The second thing that the good shepherd Jesus says about himself is that he knows his own. That seems somewhat insignificant and yet is indeed the greatest thing of all. We fathom this when we consider what it would mean if Jesus would not know us when he spoke to us: "I have never known you" (Matt. 7:23; 25:41). This would be our end, our damnation, our eternal separation from him. Therefore, being known by Jesus means our blessedness and our community with him. Jesus recognizes only those whom he loves, those who belong to him, his own (2 Tim. 2:19). He recognizes us as those who are lost, as sinners who need and receive his grace, and by recognizing us as the forgiven sinners whom he has claimed as his own,[21] by
knowing that we ourselves are recognized by him and him alone, he reveals 563
himself to us, and we recognize him as the only one to whom we belong in eternity (Gal. 4:9; 1 Cor. 8:3). The good shepherd recognizes his sheep

[19.] See Matt. 10:5–25.

[20.] Cf. *DBWE* 4:185.

[21.] Cf. Thesis 3 of the Barmen Declaration: The church "as the church of pardoned sinners, . . . has to testify in the midst of a sinful world . . . that it is solely his property" (from Hockenos, *Church Divided*, 179).

and only them, because they belong to him. The good shepherd, and only he, recognizes his sheep, because only he knows who belongs to him in eternity. The sheep recognize the good shepherd, and only they, because they alone know how good he is. They recognize him as the only good shepherd, because they belong to him alone. To recognize Christ means to recognize and do his will for us and with us; it means to love God and the brethren (John 4:7–8; 4:20). It is the blessedness of the father when he recognizes the son as son, and it is the blessedness of the son when he recognizes the father as father. This mutual recognition is love and community. And so it is the blessedness of the Savior when he recognizes the sinners as his acquired property, and it is the blessedness of the sinner when he recognizes Jesus as his savior. Because Jesus is connected to the father (and to his own) in such a community of love and mutual recognition, that is why the good shepherd can give his life up for the sheep (note the first-person singular!) and can thus win for himself the flock as eternal property. "Through the love in which I die for the sheep, I show how much I love the Father" (Gregorius).[22]

3. Verse 16. Because Jesus alone knows his own, that is why he alone can say that he has the sheep of his flock in the middle of the heathen world. The love and the dying of the good shepherd are not only for the chosen people. The good shepherd Jesus also has his own in the places we are least likely to think of, where up to now there has been only heresy and idol worship. Jesus does not belong only to us, and he is not dependent on us. That is said to the church as a warning against hubris and as consolation. To "lead" those other sheep also belongs to the mandate of the good shepherd. Literally, it does not say "lead here," meaning to Israel, but he must "lead"[23] them, that is, save them from the isolation and lack of leadership in their
564 existence. The good shepherd must lead all his sheep so that they know the right way and be preserved from danger and harm. It will be the consummation of the congregation of Jesus when they all hear his voice. No other voice will then mean anything or will be able to lead the sheep astray. The voice of the good shepherd will not be hidden from a single person. Everyone will live from its command, its guidance, and its comfort.[24] The voice

[22.] Pope Gregory I, Homily 14 for the second Sunday after Easter on John 10:14–15 (Latin: "Ea charitate qua pro ovibus morior, quantum Patrem diligam ostendo").

[23.] The Greek text features an aorist infinitive of ἄγω.

[24.] Cf. Thesis 3 of the Barmen Declaration: The church witnesses that it "lives and wants to live solely from his comfort and his direction" (from Hockenos, *Church Divided,* 179).

of the good shepherd will be the only thing that unites them. The word of God will be the unity of the church on earth. The unity of the church will consist not of organizations, of dogmas, of liturgies, of pious hearts, but in the word of God, in the voice of Jesus Christ, the good shepherd of his sheep. That is how the hope of all the faithful will be fulfilled. All division within Christianity will come to an end when all hear his and only his voice, when everything that demands attention and wants to be heard aside from this one voice falls away.[25] Thus they will all be one flock under one shepherd. Then the good shepherd's work on earth will be complete.

The relationship of the gospel to Misericordias Domini[26] Sunday is usually sought with the preaching of the mercy of the good shepherd. But this twists the text in a way that tends to hinder the full recognition of its specific character. One is easily tempted to define the text by a theme that is brought to the text. So it is not recommended to use the name of the Sunday thematically for the sermon. But it is recommended to remember occasionally the inner relationship between the Sunday and the text, which objectively can certainly be justified.

11.3. Sermon Meditation on John 14:23–31 565
for the First Day of Pentecost[27]

John 14:23–31

[Jesus answered him, "Those who love me will keep my word, and my Father will love them, and we will come to them and make our home with them. Whoever does not love me does not keep my words; and the word that you hear is not mine, but is from the Father who sent me.

"I have said these things to you while I am still with you. But the Advocate, the Holy Spirit, whom the Father will send in my name, will teach you everything, and remind you of all that I have said to you. Peace I leave with you; my peace I give to you. I do not give to you as the world gives. Do not let your hearts be troubled, and do not let them be afraid. You heard me say to you, 'I am going away, and I am coming to you.' If you loved me, you would rejoice that

[25.] Cf. the rejection of other sources of proclamation in Thesis 1 of the Barmen Declaration (Hockenos, *Church Divided*, 179).

[26.] "God's mercy" (cf. Ps. 33:5). Name for the second Sunday after Easter, based on the opening words of the Latin Introitus.

[27.] From Eichholz, *Herr tue meine Lippen auf*, 1:141–45. Bonhoeffer sent this to Eichholz on February 20, 1940. Previously published in *GS* 4:491–97 and *PAM* 2:322–28.

I am going to the Father, because the Father is greater than I. And now I have told you this before it occurs, so that when it does occur, you may believe. I will no longer talk much with you, for the ruler of this world is coming. He has no power over me; but I do as the Father has commanded me, so that the world may know that I love the Father. Rise, let us be on our way."]

The old gospels for both days of Pentecost[28] keep us from delivering general festival or doctrinal sermons. These difficult texts do not allow for any veering away; they command complete attention. While the old epistle speaks of the first singular Pentecost event,[29] our gospel lesson talks about the current, remaining Pentecost, about the Pentecost that the church-community experiences throughout all ages. When we hear this text as a Pentecost text, we do not read anything into this text that is excerpted from Jesus's farewell discourse. It indeed speaks of Pentecost even if the focus of the text is not the Holy Spirit but Jesus Christ, his departure, and his coming again. But the coming again meant here is indeed his coming in the
566 Holy Spirit, namely, at Pentecost. So at Pentecost, too, one preaches *about Jesus Christ, the one who is present in the Holy Spirit,* and nothing else.[30] In the choice of this pericope from the early church, which celebrated the first half of the church year strictly as *semestre domini,*[31] this has been clearly expressed and rightly so. Because the text speaks about Pentecost within the framework of the farewell discourses, the character of the singular revelatory event is less in the foreground than *Jesus's remaining with his church-community,* even after his departure. If we preach this text as a Pentecost pericope, we may speak about Pentecost in three parts without forcing the text: 1. Concerning the indwelling of the Father and of the Son within those who love Jesus. 2. Concerning the sending of the Holy Spirit to teach and to remind one about the word of Jesus Christ. 3. Concerning the gifts that Jesus gives to his own: peace, joy, faith. The pericope begins with v. 23, and the consideration of v. 22 cannot be recommended because of the already abundantly rich content of the pericope. Likewise, v. 31b is omitted, probably because it would twist the text too strongly toward the Passion.

[28.] [In the church calendar of the German Evangelical Church, worship services are held on both Pentecost Sunday and the following Monday.—VB]

[29.] See Acts 2:1–18.

[30.] This is an allusion to Luther's central homiletical rule: "*Nihil nisi Christus praedicandus*" (Nothing but Christ must be preached), *WA* 16:113,7–8.

[31.] "The first half of the year of the Lord." The distinction between a festive (*semestre domini*) and nonfestive half (*semestre ecclesiae*) of the church year is debated (see Bertheau, "Kirchenjahr," 10:395).

1. Verses 23, 24. Pentecost comes to those who love Jesus Christ and keep his word. Just as the disciples were once with one another and in one mind before the rushing of wind[32] came from heaven, so today it will be Pentecost everywhere where there is love for Jesus Christ. Wherever people love him, there his entire word (note the singular!),[33] his promise, and his command will be preserved and kept. What does it mean to love Jesus? Wanting to belong to him alone who has given his word to us and kept it, to seek community with him more than anything else, to desire his presence. Whoever loves this way, keeps the word of the beloved, clutches it, does not let it go, and does it wherever one can. Such love for Jesus shall experience the most complete fulfillment.

The whole love of God, the father of Jesus Christ, will be completed in 567
the one who loves the Son of God: God and Jesus Christ come to him and *dwell within him.* Whoever loves Jesus will become a holy dwelling place in body, soul, and spirit, and will become the temple of God and Christ on earth. Jesus's coming in the flesh was for the world; his coming in the spirit is for those who love him. Here nothing should be softened or explained away. It is about the real, full indwelling of God and Christ in the human being. It is not like the picture of a beloved person that takes possession of us, not like a new power that fulfills us; rather it is the personal God and Christ himself who dwell within us. God and Christ are not only with us, next to us, around us, above us, but—in us. It is not the gifts of God and Christ that we receive, but we partake of God and Christ himself; we carry them within us as the highest sanctuary. Nor does this apply here to the church-community; rather it is truly for the individual. This promise goes far beyond that which the disciples had in Jesus during his time on earth; it is for the benefit of all who love him. When Jesus goes away from them, he gives to his own not less but incomparably more. When God and Christ dwell in us, then all other lords for whom we have made room in our hearts must yield. Now Christ himself lives and reigns in us; from now on our life becomes a Christ-life within us. But all this only becomes true, and we are only able to witness to it, if we love the Lord Christ and keep his word. The more our life reaches toward Christ, the more Christ will enter into us. The more we seek our entire salvation in him and not in ourselves, and the more we allow him to be Lord over us, the more fully will he be in us and take possession of us. But whoever loves not Christ but only himself, whoever enjoys Christ but does not want to serve and obey him, that person

[32.] See Acts 2:1–2.

[33.] Greek: ὁ λόγος ὃν ἀκούετε (the word that you hear).

also does not keep his words (note the plural!)[34] and for that reason will experience nothing of all this. For the word of Christ (note the singular![35]
568 the one, undivided word stands opposite the divided words!)[36] is the word of the Father, and God only grants his blessed presence to the keeping of the word of Christ.

In the sermon it should be noted that John adds another thought to the one already familiar to us, that only the one who is loved and "drawn in" by the Father and has been taken possession of by Jesus is able to love Jesus—John adds that God does not leave our love toward Jesus unanswered and unfulfilled (*agapesei*—future tense!).[37] "I love those who love me" (Prov. 8:17).

It should be further noted that while the indwelling of Christ is promised to this kind of love as its fulfillment, this is only possible through faith, as Eph. 3:17 decisively adds. Only where faith reaches for the *iustitia extra nos*,[38] Christ will be *in nobis*.[39]

2. Verses 25 and 26. With this promise of the indwelling, Jesus says that he remains with his disciples (this is how one can also understand the *par' hymin menon*!)[40] despite his departure. But this will happen in such a way that the Father *will send* assistance [Beistand], the *Holy Spirit*, in the name of Jesus. The Holy Spirit only comes in the name of Jesus, from the Father and from the Son (*filioque*).[41] How the indwelling of the Father and of the Son relates to the sending of the Holy Spirit is not elaborated on. Next to this, however, which may not be overlooked, is the fact that the indwelling is conceived more strongly in terms of the individual, but here it is the disciples. The Paraclete[42] (the "one who has been called" and the "one who speaks on behalf of" = *advocatus*), the assistance, comes to the church-

---

[34.] Greek: τοὺς λόγους μου οὐ τηρεῖ (who does not keep my words).

[35.] In v. 23: "the word" (cf. ed. note 33).

[36.] Cf. Thesis 1 of the Barmen Declaration, which calls Jesus Christ the "one Word of God" (Hockenos, *Church Divided*, 179).

[37.] Greek: ἀγαπήσει (he will love).

[38.] "Justification outside ourselves."

[39.] "In us."

[40.] Greek: παρ' ὑμῖν μένων (remaining with you).

[41.] "And from the Son"; an addition by the Western churches to the text of the Nicene Creed at Constantinople in 381 CE. It was originally believed that the Holy Spirit came *ex patre* (from the Father). Since the sixth century, the perception that the Holy Spirit comes *ex patre filioque* (from the Father and from the Son) became increasingly prevalent in the Western churches. See Hauschild, "Geist/Heiliger Geist/Geistesgaben," 203.

[42.] Greek: ὁ παράκλητος.

community. The Holy Spirit is not some neutral power (as the Pneuma-
tomachians teach),[43] but a person just like the Father and the Son (*ho* 569
parakletos).[44] (At this opportunity, it would be helpful to point out that we should pray more often for the Holy Spirit rather than for "strength.") The Holy Spirit provides assistance to the church-community and thus is also its "comforter." The office of the Holy Spirit is twofold: *teaching* and *reminding*. On its path through the world, the church-community always needs renewed guidance and knowledge. When faced with new enemies, new questions, and new needs, the congregation finds its teacher in the Holy Spirit, who "teaches" it "everything." At no stage that is important for it will the church-community remain without guidance and knowledge, and it may be assured of this knowledge, since the Holy Spirit and not human understanding is its teacher. Thus the church will receive new knowledge in the course of its history; it will not cease to learn and listen to the Holy Spirit. The Holy Spirit is not a lifeless word on a page but the living God.[45] Thus the church-community can entrust itself to the Holy Spirit in every decision and firmly believe that the Holy Spirit is present and works upon and in it, and does not let us stumble along in the dark[46] as long as we only and earnestly wish to hear the Spirit's teaching. All teaching of the Holy Spirit, however, remains bound to the word of Jesus. The new firmly stands on the old. Thus teaching is joined by remembrance. If there were only remembrance in the church, it would fall prey to a dead past; if there were only teaching without remembrance, the church would fall prey to Enthusiasm. Thus the Holy Spirit, as the proper assistant of the church-community, does both: it leads the church forward and at the same time holds it fast to Jesus (cf. Matt. 13:52).

3. Verses 27–31. In addition to the indwelling of the Father and the Son,
and the sending of the Holy Spirit, now come the gifts that Jesus gives to 570

[43.] The Pneumatomachians [a fourth-century sect—VB] denied the *homousia* of the Holy Spirit with the Father and the Son (i.e., that the Holy Spirit is of the same divine essence). The third article of the Nicene Creed is directed against them when it confesses that the Spirit "adored and glorified together with the Father and the Son" (*qui cum patre et filio simul adoratur et glorificatur*); see Hauschild, "Geist/Heiliger Geist/Geistesgaben," 200n39.

[44.] Greek: ὁ παράκλητος ("*the* comforter"—to be understood on a personal level).

[45.] Cf. 2 Cor. 3:6.

[46.] Cf. the first stanza of the evening hymn by Nikolaus Herman (1560) "Hinunter ist der Sonne Schein" (*Evangelisches Gesangbuch Brandenburg-Pommern*, 276; *EG*, 467): "Shine upon us, Lord Christ, your true light, let us not blunder in the darkness." [The English translation is "The Sun's Last Beam of Light Is Gone," in *Lutheran Hymnal*, 563. Trans. altered to follow the German more closely.—VB]

the disciples when he leaves them. First, *peace.* Jesus clearly repeats that it is His peace that he gives to his own so that the disciples know what he means here. Otherwise, how easily deception and false hope could arise here! It is the peace of the one who had nowhere on earth to lay his head[47] and had to go to the cross. Peace with God and humanity is even there where the wrath of God and of humanity threaten to destroy us. Only this Christ-peace endures. What the world offers can only be a dream from which we awaken filled with confusion and fear. But whoever receives the peace of Jesus Christ no longer needs to let himself be confused or hunted down by fear whenever the peaceless world is in uproar. That is the peace that Jesus gives to his congregation. No one but Jesus can give it.

The second gift is *joy.* When Jesus goes to the Father, who is greater than he (beware here of Arianist thoughts!),[48] because he is in glory and transfiguration, he gives joy to those who love him, for now their Lord himself is transfigured and glorified. If the heart of the disciples is really with Christ, they partake in his glorification in adoring jubilation, because they also know that the Transfigured One will return and stay with them (note that the return here refers to the church-community!). This is the church-community's joy in Christ.

Jesus's promise grants the power of *faith* to his own. This is the third gift. Nothing happens that the Lord has not foretold. Everything happens according to his word. The prince of this world will come, but he will not be able to do anything against Jesus because he finds no sin in him. Jesus will go to the cross, not because of the power of the devil, but as a sign for the world that Jesus loves his Father and is obedient to him alone until death. In all this, however, the church-community always knows through the word of Jesus that its Lord goes to his Father and returns. The church-community
571 believes in his word and awaits his promise. In this faith in Christ, however, and in it alone, the church-community has the peace of Christ and the joy of Christ. In faith, the church-community is certain of the sending of the Holy Spirit and receives the Father and the Son, who will dwell in those who love Jesus Christ and keep his word.

[47.] Matt. 8:20 and par.

[48.] Arius argued against the true divinity of Jesus Christ. The Nicene Creed (the first version, from 325 CE) condemned his teaching that the Son of God (ὁ λόγος [the Word]) is dissimilar from the Father (ἀνόμοιος); see Ritter, "Arianismus," 704–6.

11.4 Sermon Meditation on John 3:16–21 for the Second Day of Pentecost[49]

John 3:16–21

[For God so loved the world that he gave his only Son, so that everyone who believes in him may not perish but may have eternal life.

Indeed, God did not send the Son into the world to condemn the world, but in order that the world might be saved through him. Those who believe in him are not condemned; but those who do not believe are condemned already, because they have not believed in the name of the only Son of God. And this is the judgment, that the light has come into the world, and people loved darkness rather than light because their deeds were evil. For all who do evil hate the light and do not come to the light, so that their deeds may not be exposed. But those who do what is true come to the light, so that it may be clearly seen that their deeds have been done in God.]

A Pentecost gospel without a single word about the Holy Spirit is a somewhat surprising and seemingly unfortunate choice. It would indeed be appropriate to ask whether today, when the teaching about the Holy Spirit has largely faded and been forgotten, we should not choose a text for the second Pentecost sermon that contains full and clear statements about the Holy Spirit. Nonetheless, the old gospel reading is not without connection to the feast of Pentecost. Whereas the gospel reading for the first day of Pentecost speaks of the Pentecost gift to the church-community, the second day of Pentecost shows that the love of God in Jesus Christ, as witness to the Holy Spirit,
brings forth a division in the world between faith and unbelief. On the first 572
day of Pentecost, we hear about Pentecost and the church-community. Pentecost in the world is the topic of the second day of Pentecost. In this regard it makes good sense that precisely on the second day, before the feast day is over, we speak about the most serious matter that hovers over the Pentecost sermon. In this way the gospel anchors itself better in our hearts and cannot be so easily forgotten. The very selection of a text for the second day of Pentecost in which there is a great deal said about Jesus Christ but nothing about the Holy Spirit reflects a great awareness that the only ministry of the Holy Spirit consists *in the witness to Jesus Christ.* "Shine in our hearts, O most precious Light, That we Jesus Christ may know aright."[50]

[49.] From Eichholz, *Herr Tue meine Lippen auf,* 1:145–50. Bonhoeffer sent this to Eichholz on February 20, 1940. Previously published in *GS* 4:496–504 and *PAM* 2:328–35.

[50.] Second stanza of Martin Luther's 1524 Pentecost hymn, "Nun bitten wir den

1. Verses 16–18a. (a) For a person who does not want to speak in formulas it is difficult to speak of God's love for the world. It is certainly clear enough that God's love for the world does not consist of bringing an end to wars and taking poverty, need, persecution, and catastrophes of all kind away from us. We are used to looking for God's love in these very things, and yet we do not find it. However difficult it is for us, however deeply we are shaken that God's love hides itself from the world in this manner, we may be especially thankful in precisely such times that we no longer need to seek God's love in places where it does not exist for us, rather that it shines all the clearer for us in the only place where we are to find it: in Jesus Christ. "For . . . so"—that excludes all our own wishes and thoughts about God's love; it points to Jesus Christ alone. God's love toward us is to be found in him alone. (b) When God has loved the world, the entire creation that has fallen away, then God has not preferred us over others; he has not loved my worst enemy less than me; Jesus Christ has died for his and our enemies. If we wanted to consider ourselves the special, favored children of God, we would be the worst Pharisees and enemies of God and of the cross. When God
573 loved the world, he also loved us. We have already closed ourselves off from blessedness if we do not want to become blessed through the same love that applies to our enemies as well. (c) God's love toward the world could not be such that God forgot about creation that had fallen away, as if loss and sin did not exist, or that he declared, in his divine omnipotence—or better in divine discretion—that what he had called sin in his revealed word has not happened or does not matter. Why did God not simply forgive sin or do away with it through a word of power? Because God is God and hates sin and punishes the sinner in holy anger, because before him the sinner is lost and damned. This is why God gave his Son for us, in the death of a sinner. He suffered with us and for us out of love. God the Father separates himself from God the Son and lets him suffer and die for our salvation. God's love for the sinner costs him his eternal, divine, only-begotten Son. The Holy Spirit teaches us to recognize Jesus Christ, the Crucified One, as the Son of God, as the sole revelation of God's love for the world. (d) Because God did not exclude any human being from his love, we are not allowed to exclude ourselves. When God sent the Son, he also thought about me. Therefore, "all"—there is no gap here!—who find the love of God in Jesus Christ, "who believe in him," have eternal life. Only *they* have it, but they *have* it because they have been saved from ruin through Jesus Christ. There is only the one

Heiligen Geist" (*Evangelisches Gesangbuch Brandenburg-Pommern*, 76; *EG*, 124). [Translation here from "We Now Implore God the Holy Ghost," in *Lutheran Hymnal*, 231.—VB]

or the other: ruin or eternal life, faith or getting lost. Both are decided in Jesus Christ. (e) The one and only goal of the sending of Jesus is the salvation of the world, not its condemnation. If we think that it is the ministry of Jesus to put us, the faithful, into the right before the world and to condemn and destroy the godless, then we place ourselves outside God's love for sinners, through which we alone can be blessed, and then we summon the righteous judgment of God upon us. Only if Jesus Christ came to make the *world* blessed can we too be blessed. Salvation in Christ must be proclaimed to all the world, because it is for all the world and thereby in the end for me. This is an essential thought of Pentecost. Whoever allows himself to be saved by Jesus from eternal destruction, whoever has found in him the love
of God for the sinner, no longer stands under judgment (*krinetai*[51]—note 574
the present tense!). Sin, the law, conscience, and God's wrath can no longer accuse him. They have no power over and no claim on him any longer, for he is protected by the love of God in Jesus Christ (cf. Rom. 8:1). Faith brings an end to judgment; it prides itself in the Savior from all judgment.[52] The sin that has been forgiven can no longer hurt me, can no longer accuse me, it will no longer be a force against me, not even on the last day. The Holy Spirit assures me of this.

2. Verses 18b–20. (a) If Jesus came into the world not to judge but to save, then through his coming there is necessarily a separation and, therefore, also a judgment. The goal of the sending of Jesus must be distinguished from its effect. Whoever does not believe in Jesus, whoever does not find the love of God in him, closes himself off from this love of God and hands himself over to judgment. He condemns himself. Jesus does not even need to proclaim the judgment. "Who does not believe" has already said and done it, namely, the one who "has not believed in the name of the only Son of God." This remarkable repetition (the *hoti* sentence)[53] shows that there must have been an encounter between the human being and the name of Jesus, and that it is the conscious rejection (because of either pride or destitution) of this name that signifies self-judgment. Thus the preaching of the name of Jesus Christ becomes the decision about eternal life and judgment. (b) Even though Christ came to save and not to judge, the judgment of the world came with him. That Jesus came as the savior—precisely this was the judgment. That the light came into the world—precisely this was the

[51.] Greek: κρίνεται (he is judged).
[52.] Rom. 5:2, 11.
[53.] Greek: ὅτι (because).

judgment over darkness. The judgment is not an ideal, not a new norm or a law, but Jesus Christ.[54] This is the judgment for all times: that a human being was born for the salvation of all humanity, that the light entered the dark world, and that humanity avoided the light and preferred to remain
575 in darkness. Therefore, Jesus did not come to judgment; he was the light that wanted to save, but through this light the darkness of human beings became obvious. They had learned to love their darkness and wanted to remain in it (the *mallon*[55]—"more"—should here, as so often, be understood not comparatively but exclusively!). How can it be that human beings loved the darkness more than the light? Because that which is darkness in Jesus's judgment is bright light for our eyes, while the light of Jesus appears dark to our eyes. On the one hand: the splendid works of human beings, their goods, knowledge, their ethical accomplishments, their religions. On the other hand: the poor child in the feeding trough, the friend of sinners, the criminal on the gallows. Where is the light? Where is the darkness? But because Jesus called himself the light, and called everything else darkness, this is why human beings hated this light and loved their shining darkness. They rejected Jesus, they killed Jesus, and so they damned themselves. But this could not be any different because "their deeds were evil." Whether these evil deeds consisted of coarse sensual transgressions or of secret spiritual sins—perhaps precisely in their fine form they had to avoid the light of Christ and love darkness even more. Not only past evil deeds, however, but the present or intended evil deeds, the wanting-to-remain-in-the-evil (note the present participle *prasson*),[56] make the light hateful and hinder access to it, because even in its most shining form evil fears its disclosure. In the light of Jesus, the works of human beings are recognized and handed over as evil; the darkness feels this. The name of Jesus: that means the uncovering and confessing of sin, taking upon oneself the shame of evil. But since evil exists only as long as it can justify its evilness in the shining of its own light (which is still darkness in the light of Jesus), it fights with utmost power against the light of Jesus. This fight, however, is the self-judgment of the human being who avoids Jesus.

576 3. Verse 21. Who comes to the light? The one who does the truth! What does that mean? Truth shall happen; it should not only be thought about or intended; rather it should be done. Truth arises through the doing, which

[54.] Regarding the critique of the discussion about Jesus Christ as "ideal" or "norm," see *DBWE* 4, esp. 57–59.

[55.] Greek: μᾶλλον.

[56.] Greek: πράσσων (in doing).

stands in contrast to illusion, to darkness, in which evil happens. But how should one who lives in darkness do the truth? Does this not reverse the following sentence of the catechism: "I believe that by my own understanding or strength I cannot believe in Jesus Christ my Lord or *come to him*, but instead the Holy Spirit . . ."?[57] We must realize that this strange word is directed to Nicodemus,[58] to whom the word of the Scriptures is not unknown and yet who had still not come to the light. He and now we are supposed to move on to the doing of the divine word soon and without delay, as far as it has been revealed to us, not to torment ourselves with unanswered or difficult thoughts, not to be satisfied with questions and problems. By focusing on problems we hide from the seriousness of the deed. You will come to the light not by thinking, says Jesus, but through that which you do; of course not just any kind of doing, but the doing of *the truth*. The truth itself will bring you to the light through your doing. In the word of Jesus, one first needs to emphasize the word "truth" and only subsequently the word "doing." In all of this, one should not think of a justification through works; neither should one think of a justification through thinking. It is said, however, that if we want to come to the light, that if we want Pentecost to come for us, there is no time to waste; rather, the moment of acting, of obeying, as much as we are able to obey the word of God, has come. This stops our escape into endless questions and forces us to serious action in the here and now, to living under the word. If you want to go to the light and have not yet found it, "do the truth," and it will be shown that you will be led to the light in this way. Because the truth in your doing will yearn for the light on its own, in which it wants to be revealed. Yes, this is how it
will be revealed, that your words, which you have done on the path to the 577
light, "have been done in God": because they happened in obedience to his word under the guidance of the truth. In this way the text, which initially threatened to leave us in the open question of how we can participate in the light, summons us clearly to doing. Coming to the light is only possible because the light, because the truth, has come to us. On the other hand, we will not come to the light in any different way than through acting, obeying, and doing the truth.

This truly difficult text can be treated in a Pentecost sermon in three sections. Vv. 16–18a: The Holy Spirit reveals Jesus Christ to us as the love of

[57.] Cf. Luther, the Small Catechism (1529), explanation of the third article, in *Book of Concord*, 355.

[58.] John 3:1–21.

God for all the world and in us brings about faith in him. Vv. 18b–20: The Holy Spirit, the sermon about the salvation in Christ, becomes the judgment of the unbelieving world. V. 21: The Holy Spirit shows us the way of the truth to the light.

Dirk Schulz

Editor's Afterword to the German Edition

I 578

In his 1937 Christmas letter to the former Finkenwalde candidates, Dietrich Bonhoeffer wrote: "The balance sheet for this year is rather clear and unambiguous. Twenty-seven from your circle have been in prison; for some it lasted several months. Some are still detained at present and have spent the entire Advent in prison. Among the others there won't be a single person who has not experienced the impact, in his work and his personal life, of the increasingly impatient attacks of the anti-Christian forces."[1]

Here Bonhoeffer was succinctly describing the National Socialist regime's twofold strategy for finally resolving the "church question" in its own favor.

On the one hand, the regime had sought quietly to regulate and control the still intractable circles of the Confessing Church through church administrative and secret police measures. Within the framework of the National Socialist state, these circles continued to represent a disruptive element. With the resignation of the Reich Church Committee on February 12, 1937, Reich minister for church affairs Hanns Kerrl's plan to "restore order in the German Evangelical Church"[2] had finally failed.[3] With the March 20, 1937, "thirteenth implementation decree" of the "Law to Restore Order

[1.] 1/2, pp. 20–21.

[2.] See the *Gesetzblatt der Deutsche Evangelische Kirche* (1935), 99.

[3.] Regarding the heated disputes within the Confessing Church about the question of possible cooperation with the committees, resulting in a de facto split within the Confessing Church itself in January 1936, see the portrayal in *DB-ER*, 419–24 and 495–506.

in the German Evangelical Church," Kerrl appointed the jurist Friedrich Werner, president of the Evangelical High Church Council [Evangelischer Oberkirchenrat] in Berlin, to oversee the ongoing church governance.[4] Werner was now the new strongman intent on realizing Kerrl's vision of a
579 Reich church loyal to the state in which a state-controlled administration would empower and indeed prompt the "securing of the religious freedom of the Germans." That meant the cultivation of the "spiritual affairs of the faithful" in a manner that conformed to the regime.[5]

On the other hand, one had to contend with "the increasingly impatient attacks of the anti-Christian forces." This was a reference to the radical powers hostile to Christianity in the state and party around Joseph Goebbels, Alfred Rosenberg, and Martin Bormann, who were increasing the ideological and administrative pressure on the churches under the guise of a "deconfessionalization of public life." At the very latest, from the spring of 1937, even Adolf Hitler himself was "finished with the churches."[6] His hopes of bringing the two great churches into the service of his own goals had come to nothing, eliminating the need for any further constructive policies concerning those churches. From now on, the determinative strategy became one of a complete exclusion of ecclesiastical influence from public life and the liquidation of Christianity. At the latest, the "deconfessionalization of public life" was a decided matter as of October 1937. It was only the preparations for war that made it seem prudent to postpone the final assault on the churches and Christianity until after the war, not least because the more radical powers in the party did not want to discourage the churches' alliance with the interests of the nation in the event of war. As a result, at the beginning of the war Hitler prohibited "any action against the Catholic
580 and Protestant churches for the duration of the war."[7] Although this prohibition did indeed put a stop to the more spectacular acts of violence on the part of the state and party against the churches in the "old Reich,"[8]

[4.] *Gesetzblatt der Deutsche Evangelische Kirche* (1937), 11. [The so-called muzzling decree.—VB]

[5.] According to Kerrl, in a memorandum concerning an edict he wanted Hitler to promulgate for "securing the religious freedom of the Germans"; cited from Baumgärtner, *Weltanschauungskampf im Dritten Reich*, 79–81.

[6.] So the assessment of Klaus Scholder in "Politics and Church Politics," in *Requiem for Hitler*, 155; see also 152–56.

[7.] Scholder, "The Church Struggle," in *Requiem for Hitler*, 117. Cf. also Röhm and Thierfelder, *Evangelische Kirche zwischen Kreuz und Hakenkreuz*, 122–24, and H. E. Tödt, *Komplizen, Opfer und Gegner des Hitlerregimes*, 324–32.

[8.] Hence the plans for a strict separation of church and state, pursued especially by Bormann, whose goal was to force all the churches into the legal status of private

it did not stop the National Socialist church jurists from pursuing a relentless policy of reining in and repressing church activities. Deciding how to deal with the churches and with religious matters remained a ticklish business for the regime, not least because according to the 1940 census, at least 95 percent of the population belonged to one of the churches,[9] and the regime wanted to avoid unnecessarily upsetting this potentially powerful group. (Pre)war conditions required calm on the home front.

II

It was primarily two of Friedrich Werner's initiatives in 1938 that prompted Dietrich Bonhoeffer's resolute objections.

1. From 1935 to 1936, the territorial consistories had been offering young illegal theologians various ways to become "legal," offering each of them a legal pastorate, with the attendant privileges and security associated with "the office of ministry," albeit at the price of each candidate agreeing to turn away from the leadership of the Confessing Church and instead to recognize the consistory as the legitimate church government and to follow its orders.[10] These offers had already generated painful disputes among the community members as early as the Finkenwalde period. Bonhoeffer's provocative assertion that "those who knowingly separate themselves from the Confessing Church in Germany are also separating themselves from salvation"[11] was aimed not least at helping "his" candidates stay the course, that is, to remain loyal to what he considered to be the only legitimate gov- 581
erning body, namely, the Confessing Church, and to warn them against the seductive offers of the other side. With Werner's central "order concerning the admission of unofficially examined theologians into the service of the regional churches" of February 26, 1938, this explosive theme was once more on the agenda. In the period that followed, the number grew of the "illegals" who sought an individual compromise with the consistory and accordingly negotiated the conditions for such "legalization."[12] The present volume contains impressive documentation of Bonhoeffer's rigorous

---

associations. This was implemented only in Austria after the *Anschluß* in March 1938 and in the newly created Reich district [Reichsgau] Wartheland in 1940 (Scholder, "The Church Struggle," in *Requiem for Hitler*, 114–15).

[9.] Cf. Thamer, *Verführung und Gewalt*, 446.

[10.] See *DB-ER*, 498–506.

[11.] In Bonhoeffer's June 1936 essay, "The Question of Church Fellowship," *DBW* 14, 2/19, p. 676.

[12.] Cf. *DB-ER*, 607–20; see also 1/74 and 1/76.

opposition to these attempts at ideological synchronization [Gleichschaltungsversuche] by Werner and those under him.[13] Bonhoeffer's position was provocatively unequivocal: Only adherence to the unity of the synodal resolutions of Barmen *and* Dahlem, that is, only adherence to the unity of the correct doctrine and correct church law, determined the existence of the Confessing Church. Those who revised their previous decision for Barmen *and* Dahlem and became "legal" were taking a position apart from or against the Confessing Church, denying the previously acknowledged legitimacy of its church government and deviating from the certainly narrow but only promising path within the Church Struggle.[14] Only by remaining on this path was it possible to risk and bear together the "Church Struggle as gospel."[15] In this respect, Bonhoeffer's resolute summons back to Barmen *and* Dahlem was a call forward borne by trust.

2. The *Anschluß* of Austria in March 1938 unleashed a grandiose feeling of joy and a wave of enthusiasm for "unification" in the "Third Reich." The "Führer" had finally brought to reality the vision of a "Greater German Reich" of which so many had dreamed since the assembly at the Church of Saint Paul in Frankfurt in 1848, an accomplishment for which he was also
582 commensurately lauded.[16] Because Friedrich Werner had no intention of being left behind on such an occasion, he wanted to include in his own words of thanks to Hitler the pastors of "his" Evangelical Church of the Old Prussian Union. Thus on April 20, 1938—as a birthday present for Hitler, as it were—Werner decreed that pastors and church officials had to take a loyalty oath to document their "personal attachment [Bindung] to the Führer under the solemn appeal to God."[17] Because Werner quite correctly assumed that many pastors would have enormous reservations against taking this oath for theological and political reasons, he helped them along by threatening removal from office. This cheap gesture plunged the Confessing Church into a state of profound perplexity.[18] Alongside Karl Barth, it was Dietrich Bonhoeffer who protested unequivocally against the required oath, an oath for which even the Confessing Church itself ultimately gave permission.[19] He saw here a fateful situation in which pastors were being

---

[13.] See esp. 1/7, 1/19, 1/24, 1/94, and 2/5.

[14.] See the editors' afterword to the German edition in *DBWE* 4:296–99, and Ludwig, "Die 'Illegalen' im Kirchenkampf," 41–48.

[15.] 1/7, p. 32.

[16.] See Fest, *Hitler*, 569–73, and Hildebrand, *Das vergangene Reich*, 644–51.

[17.] See 1/22 with ed. note 8.

[18.] See *DB-ER*, 599–603.

[19.] See esp. 1/22, 1/24, and 1/28. Cf. also Busch, *Unter dem Bogen des einen Bundes*, 316–17.

coerced to conform ideologically with the National Socialist regime, or an equally fateful situation in which pastors would be inclined to bring themselves into conformity, as it were, and in any case a situation that must be rejected for both theological and political reasons. The idea that the state would preempt and basically dislodge the vows of ordination and the idea of a personal oath of loyalty to Adolf Hitler were a complete impossibility for him and utterly unacceptable. After all, at the very beginning of the "Third Reich," he had already seen through the pseudo-messianic character of the "Führer" myth and rejected the temporally and qualitatively unrestricted claims to authority of the National Socialist "Führer" principle.[20] Consequently, a bit later it was especially the "military oath" that prompted him to look for a way to avoid being called up for military service.[21] Similarly, under changed conditions during the period of the conspiracy, he tried to assuage the moral and social scruples plaguing
some members of the military at the idea that a coup would involve the 583
assassination of Hitler, and to extricate them ethically from the inner loyalty to the Führer, to whom they felt bound precisely by their soldier's oath of loyalty.[22] He demanded that those responsible freely risk this deed and accept the culpability associated with it, since an emergency situation in which criminal violence reigns as a principle also annuls the obligations of a military code of honor.[23]

Werner's provocative actions were a constant topic of discussion and disputes in the collective pastorates. Other topics of discussion included the conflicts surrounding the potential reorganization of the church government in the Old Prussian Union ("Essen III"),[24] the rifts in the Confessing Church regarding Karl Barth's letter to his Prague colleague Josef Hromádka during the Sudeten crisis in the autumn of 1938, the courageous prayer liturgy of the Provisional Church Administration and its warning against impending war,[25] and the profound distress prompted by the Jewish pogrom in November 1938.[26] Discussions of the burning ecclesiastical-political and general political issues of the day were an integral part of instruction in the collective pastorates. Members of Groß-Schlönwitz and Sigurdshof managed to inform themselves more fully by listening to the

[20.] See esp. the important March 1933 lecture, "The Führer and the Individual in the Younger Generation," *DBWE* 12, 2/9.

[21.] See 1/82.

[22.] See Fest, *Plotting Hitler's Death*, 239–41 and 332–33.

[23.] Cf. *DBWE* 6:272–74 and 282–84.

[24.] See esp. 1/26 and 1/27.

[25.] See *DB-ER*, 605–6.

[26.] See section V below.

forbidden newscasts of the British Broadcasting Corporation at night on a carefully guarded, battery-powered receiver. Free speech was now obviously to be found only with the "enemy"—despite some of the propaganda even there.

III

The book *Life Together*, which Dietrich Bonhoeffer wrote during the tense months of September and October 1938, essentially documents his experi-
584 ences with the *praxis pietatis* in Finkenwalde, which also shaped the candidates' lives together in the collective pastorates.[27] Bonhoeffer viewed these two situations—the preachers' seminary in Finkenwalde and the new form of collective pastorates that had been forced upon them—as his contribution to the authentic shaping of the doctrine and life of the church amid the present danger and persecution.[28] At the same time, they also represented a significant element of the synodal church structure associated with the Council of Brethren as created by the resolute Confessing Church, commensurate with its own synodal resolutions in Dahlem. Bonhoeffer's plans were to incorporate this heritage into what he hoped would be a complete reorganization of the church after the anticipated war. To that extent both the Finkenwalde seminar and the collective pastorates represented a future-oriented model of ecclesiastical and theological education.[29]

The statement from the proposal for "establishing the House of Brethren," which can serve as a superscription for the entirety of spiritual life in Finkenwalde, also applies without change to the collective pastorates: "The goal is not monastic seclusion but intense concentration in preparation for service on the outside."[30] Although the end of the "House of Brethren," the move to the eastern Pomeranian forests, the perpetual shuttling between Köslin and Groß-Schlönwitz or Sigurdshof, and especially the necessity of disguise all brought about certain changes in the style of instruction, they changed nothing about the programmatic goals of the illegal training of theological students.

[27.] See also 1/26 with ed. note 2 and 1/29.

[28.] Cf. Bonhoeffer's preface to *Life Together* (*DBWE* 5), 25, and his reflections on community, 29–30.

[29.] See Bonhoeffer's "Draft Proposal for a Reorganization of the Church after the 'End of the Church Struggle,'" written at the end of 1942 (*DBWE* 16, 2/16).

[30.] Letter to the Council of the Evangelical Church of the Old Prussian Union, September 6, 1935, *DBW* 14, 1/24, p. 77.

To a great extent the content of instruction remained the same as during the Finkenwalde period, albeit with a certain shift of focus in individual instances. Bonhoeffer continued his lectures on homiletics, pastoral care, and catechetics in almost unaltered form. The candidates' lecture notes
that have been preserved are extremely fragmentary.[31] Although they do 585
often preserve some of Bonhoeffer's more pointed formulations and also reflect the excitement his listeners experienced, they do not really document any discernible, internally cohesive train of thought. For this reason they could not be included in the present volume.[32] After Bonhoeffer finished his book *Discipleship,* which grew out of his Finkenwalde lectures on the New Testament, he now focused more on examining New Testament concepts and clearly referring these discussions to the particular situation now faced by the candidates themselves and the Confessing Church.[33] In his exegetical work, the Psalms acquired an even greater significance than had already been the case in Finkenwalde.[34] The small piece *The Prayerbook of the Bible: An Introduction to the Psalms,*[35] published in 1940, probably represents the immediate results of these psalm studies, studies for which Bonhoeffer drew on his own experience with the Psalms during years of daily devotional study. Indeed, Bonhoeffer now viewed the interpretation of Psalm 119 in particular as the "climax of his theological life."[36] Here he sought to discover the idea of discipleship in the Old Testament as well. Although his meditation on his "favorite psalm"[37] remained fragmentary, it does demonstrate in an exemplary fashion how intensive work on the biblical text can generate new insights, which then in their own turn become fruitful in a systematically theological fashion. In this context one might mention especially Bonhoeffer's search for an appropriate biblical-
Reformational understanding of the "law" and his increasingly clear assess- 586
ment of the "natural" (as he later called it in the *Ethics* fragments),[38] and his ongoing turn toward the "profound this-worldliness of Christianity."[39]

[31.] See appendix 3 for the list of unpublished *Nachlaß* material from 1937–40.

[32.] The notes to the lectures in *DBWE* 14 refer to variants from the period of the collective pastorates. For a precise analysis and systematic classification of these praxis-oriented theological lectures, see Bobert-Stützel, *Dietrich Bonhoeffers Pastoraltheologie.*

[33.] See, e.g., 2/2.2, 2/2.3, and 2/2.8, also 2/4.

[34.] See the 1935 lecture on "Christ in the Psalms," *DBW* 14, 2/5.

[35.] Now published in *DBWE* 5:141–78.

[36.] *DB-ER,* 667.

[37.] See Bonhoeffer's entry for July 9, 1939, in his American diary, 1/137, p. 238.

[38.] See *DBWE* 6:171–218.

[39.] Letter of July 21, 1944, to Eberhard Bethge, *DBWE* 8, 4/178, p. 485.

"The life of a Christian consists not of words but of experience. No one is a Christian without experience. We speak here not of life experience but of the experience of God. But it is also not about various experiences of God but about the experience that lies in the probation [Bewährung] of the faith and of the peace of God, the experience of the cross of Jesus Christ. Only the patient ones experience. The impatient ones do not experience anything." These are Bonhoeffer's thoughts in a sermon on Romans 5:1–5 in March 1938.[40] The sermons and sermon drafts that have come down to us are also an important witness to the instruction and shared attempts at reassurance in the Christian training centers in Köslin, Groß-Schlönwitz, and Sigurdshof. These materials are also closely related to the "homiletic exercises" in which individual candidates or even Bonhoeffer himself discussed basic homiletic principles and sermon drafts.

The directness of Bonhoeffer's sermons is riveting and is grounded first of all in his understanding of the preaching of God's word as a word directed to the church-community by its very nature; the biblical word "moves on its own into the community," and the preacher thus must take as the point of departure this "basic orientation of the text toward the community"—thus the thetic conclusion of Hans-Werner Jensen in his notes to the "Lecture on Homiletics" from the winter session 1938–39.[41] On the other hand, Bonhoeffer was speaking not from the position of a spectator in which he might stand over against the candidates and their own, special experiences of illegality, but rather as one who was himself traveling and enduring the same
587 path of "bearing up" and of being patient in the face of injustice.[42] He was speaking concretely to the situation itself, referring to God's solidarity as revealed in Christ crucified. In prison later in Tegel, he would concentrate this orientation to the Crucified One into the formula "only the suffering God can help."[43] Like the messenger of Marathon, so too the preacher is permitted to speak about God's previous as well as God's anticipated help, mounting the pulpit with the assurance: "Victory has come!"[44]

[40.] 3/2, p. 475; cf. also 3/1.

[41.] *NL*, B 10,1; p. 5. Cf. *DBWE* 4:227: "The word of God . . . moves on its own into the community."

[42.] See esp. 3/2 and 1/36.

[43.] Letter to Bethge, July 16, 1944, *DBWE* 8, 3/177, p. 479.

[44.] Lecture on homiletics, 1938–39, *NL*, B 10,1, p. 1. [These are student notes taken by Hans-Werner Jensen from Bonhoeffer's lecture on homiletics; because of their similarity to the student notes of his earlier (1936) lectures, they were omitted from this volume. See, however, *DBW* 14, 2/3, for the notes of the earlier lecture.—VB]

IV

Because "God does not want the word to be proclaimed by phonograph records, but rather by witnesses,"[45] the theme of the distress and promise accompanying the Christian proclamation also occupies considerable space in the correspondence between Bonhoeffer and the former candidates from Finkenwalde. Many of these young theologians, dispersed as they were throughout the country in their various positions, now suffered from the loneliness generally associated with their uncertain existence. Bonhoeffer's regular circular letters to this group attest his concern with preserving the community of fellowship [brüderliche Gemeinschaft] despite the great distances. One important means to this end was to continue the meditation exercises first practiced in Finkenwalde. The list of meditation texts appended to the circular letters was supposed to help "ground our community even more strongly by listening together to the Word and by prayer," as Bonhoeffer expressed it in his first circular letter after the police had closed Finkenwalde.[46] He also regularly incorporated into these circular letters the results of this work on the central New Testament concepts in order to strengthen the fellowship [Gemeinschaft] between those on the "inside" and those on the "outside," that is, between Bonhoeffer and the candidates in the collective pastorates and the former seminarians from Finkenwalde 588
now out in the field. For "it has become our firm certainty that we will either win the victory in the fellowship of our brethren or not at all. Those who look out only for themselves have been cheated of the community of the church."[47]

The letters included in this volume from former seminarians at Finkenwalde *to* Bonhoeffer clearly show the variety of ways in which he tried to share the particular distress and concerns of their "illegal" existence. They also show that these former seminarians did indeed make use of his offer to send him their sermons occasionally as topics of discussion;[48] they show their exchanges concerning other areas of church life in the communities and circles of the Confessing Church, for example, with respect to confirmation instruction or pastoral care or topics of study required for the second theological examination by the Council of Brethren of the Confessing Church of the Old Prussian Union;[49] they show how Bonhoeffer's

[45.] Ibid., p. 12.

[46.] 1/2, p. 21.

[47.] 1/24.1, p. 60.

[48.] See esp. 1/11 and 1/38.

[49.] See, e.g., 1/21.2, 1/51, 1/59, and 1/32, 1/159.

admonitions and warnings in theological and ecclesiastical-political disputes were received and provide insight into his own praxis of pastoral care.[50] And they also show from the perspective of those involved just how difficult it could be to resist the temptation of "'keeping an eye on' the consistory"[51] with the prospect of a secure salary and a parsonage. In this sense, these letters provide various pieces of a mosaic that illustrates the daily lives of those in the Confessing Church who rigorously adhered to the resolutions of Barmen *and* Dahlem.[52]

589 V

During the night of November 9–10, 1938, the synagogue in Köslin was also burned. The ritual of public humiliation, debasement, and persecution of Jewish citizens[53] was enacted in Bonhoeffer's immediate vicinity as well. Although Goebbels's references to a "spontaneous outpouring of the people's wrath" against the Jews was merely a propaganda lie,[54] the number of spectators during that night (the designation *Reichskristallnacht,* often rendered as "night of the broken glass," glosses over its seriousness) was certainly large enough, the "bystanders," as termed by the renowned American Holocaust scholar Raul Hilberg.[55] Nonetheless, in broad segments of society and the church—even the Confessing Church—the reaction to this regression into barbarism was merely silence.[56] The courageous individuals within the Protestant church who did indeed protest publicly or express their outrage at these events, individuals such as Julius von Jan in Oberlenningen, Helmut Gollwitzer in Berlin-Dahlem, or Karl Immer in Wuppertal-Barmen, did not include Bonhoeffer. Was he, too, silent?

In one sense, certainly, the answer is yes, since he issued no public protest against the pogrom, made no statement against it *publicly*. Why? First, one must remember that during this period he did not really have a pastoral position and thus no access to a pulpit from which he could have made a statement in the sermon on the following Sunday or on November 16

[50.] See esp. 1/50, 1/53, and 1/54.

[51.] 1/69, p. 133.

[52.] Cf. in this regard also the extremely instructive letters from Gerhard Vibrans and from his circle of family and friends in Andersen et al., *So ist es gewesen.*

[53.] See Benz, "Der Novemberpogrom 1938," esp. 541–44.

[54.] See Benz, "Relapse into Barbarism," esp. 7–21, and U. D. Adam, "How Spontaneous Was the Pogrom?"

[55.] See Hilberg, *Perpetrators, Victims, Bystanders.*

[56.] See Gerlach, *And the Witnesses Were Silent,* 143–54, and H. E. Tödt, "The November Crimes of 1938 and German Protestantism."

(the Wednesday eleven days before Advent, a day of penance). Moreover, a public protest would inevitably have drawn the attention of the Gestapo to the illegal collective pastorates, endangering the individual candidates and putting a stop to the entire enterprise. And finally his knowledge of the coup plans in autumn of 1938 would have prompted him to exercise
extreme caution. Hence even though his solidarity with the ostracized and 590
persecuted group, as well as his loyalty to the self-imposed standards he had developed and advocated without compromise, beginning with his April 1933 essay "The Church and the Jewish Question,"[57] would certainly have prompted him to speak out publicly, his own current responsibilities and involvements prohibited it. This dilemma is *one* of the agonizing experiences that prompted Bonhoeffer's question to himself and to his friends in the conspiracy at the turn of the year 1942–43, namely, "Are we still of any use?" For "we have been silent witnesses of evil deeds. We have become cunning and learned the arts of obfuscation and equivocal speech. Experience has rendered us suspicious of human beings, and often we have failed to speak to them a true and open word. Unbearable conflicts have worn us down or even made us cynical. Are we still of any use?"[58]

What Bonhoeffer said *privately* was another matter entirely. Documents show that for Bonhoeffer, the night of burning synagogues represented a key date from the theological perspective as well, important evidence for which can be found in his daily meditation Bible, where he underlined Psalm 74:8b ("they burned all the meeting places of God in the land") and entered the date "November 9, 1938." He variously marked and added exclamation points to the following verses as well.[59] Although Bonhoeffer marked a great many verses and words in his Bible, occasionally even making notes regarding parallel passages or hymn verses, this date entry is unique. It obviously reveals Bonhoeffer's agitation and his horror at the simultaneity of the "terrible devastation of the sanctuary"[60] during the time of the psalm and the devastation in the present. God's earlier written word moves the prayerful reader and in so doing becomes the revealed word of God in the here and now.

Taking this passage as his point of departure, Bonhoeffer prompted 591
the candidates to consider anew the indissoluble link between Christianity

[57.] *DBWE* 12, 2/13.

[58.] "After Ten Years" (1942–43), *DBWE* 8:52.

[59.] See *Dietrich Bonhoeffer: A Life in Pictures* (centenary ed.), 113. On this entire topic, cf. *DB-ER*, 607, and Bethge, "Dietrich Bonhoeffer and the Jews," 75–77.

[60.] [This is the heading of that psalm in Bonhoeffer's Bible. Cf. *Life in Pictures* (centenary ed.), 113.—VB]

and the Jewish people. Bonhoeffer himself now vehemently objected especially to the old anti-Jewish thesis concerning the curse afflicting this people since the crucifixion of Jesus Christ.[61] In two weighty sentences in his November 20, 1938, circular letter to the former Finkenwalde seminarians, he pointed the way to the kind of critical self-reflection and productive renewal that, for him, the synagogue burnings had now made absolutely necessary: "In the last few days, I have thought much about Ps. 74, Zech. 2:8, Rom. 9:4–5, and 11:11–15. That leads deeply into prayer."[62] The profundity of these sentences can be fathomed only when one considers the fundamental significance of prayer in the path of knowledge taken by the theologian Dietrich Bonhoeffer since his turn to the Bible. This path can be visualized as a circle of faith, life, and knowledge, for which prayer provides both the point of departure and the end point of thought. For Bonhoeffer, then, the path that theological thinking must take emerges only after a person regularly spends long periods of time in the cathedral of prayer with its numerous chapels.[63] It is also striking that Bonhoeffer unequivocally associates the passage from Zechariah 2:8 ("Truly, one who touches you touches the apple of my eye") with the discriminated against and persecuted Jews, since just a year earlier, in his December 20, 1937, circular letter, he had associated the same biblical passage exclusively with the persecuted church in order to comfort the besieged brothers and strengthen their resolve.[64]

The conclusion to the October 1938 lecture "Our Path according to the Testimony of Scripture" shows how important the critical self-reflection and
592 productive renewal of the relationship between Christians and Jews had become for Bonhoeffer in the intervening period. Here he views the theme "church and synagogue" as one of the genuinely urgent questions that now had to be addressed, despite the energy now required for the question "Council of Brethren or consistory."[65] The expression "church and synagogue," which Bonhoeffer uses for the first time in this piece, shows that he was concerned with the ecclesiological question of how the church was to respond to the existence of the Jewish faith alongside it. Hence in addition to the necessary charitable aid for the persecuted Jews, he also demanded basic theological reflection capable of overcoming the traditional reserva-

[61.] Cf. Maltusch, "When the Synagogues Burnt," 133, and Jensen, "Life Together," 153.

[62.] 1/36, p. 84. Cf. Bethge, "One of the Silent Bystanders?" esp. 65–67.

[63.] Cf. Bethge, "Der Ort des Gebets," esp. 160–65.

[64.] See 1/2.

[65.] See 2/5.

tion and prejudice against Judaism and capable of countering the systematic move toward inhumanity on the part of the National Socialist rulers.

There is little doubt that the main motivation for Dietrich Bonhoeffer to enter into active political conspiracy was the marginalization and persecution of the Jewish population in the "Third Reich," which also directly affected his own family. Along this path to conspiratorial activity, the night of November 9–10, 1938, became pivotal for Bonhoeffer's thinking and for his biography—precisely because he could not risk making a public statement. Bonhoeffer himself reflected on and articulated most clearly his own culpable involvement in "the lives of the weakest and most defenseless brothers and sisters of Jesus Christ."[66] And with exemplary honesty he incorporated the necessity of accepting guilt into his understanding of a theological ethics of responsibility as a way to counter the "unfruitful self-righteous morality" with the open "confessing guilt face-to-face with the figure of Christ"[67] For in an age in which the "the huge masquerade of evil has thrown all ethical concepts into confusion," one is not allowed to 593
retreat into the "sanctuary of a private virtuousness."[68] The ostracized and persecuted block that path.

VI

Dietrich Bonhoeffer's final crossing of the Rubicon was preceded by a period of hesitation, with the attempt to reflect and clarify for himself the possible consequences his actions might have for himself, his family, and his brothers in the Confessing Church.

It was one thing to participate in the conspiratorial plans against Hitler and his unjust regime in the form of insider knowledge, advice, and pastoral counseling, as he had done since the autumn of 1938, particularly in close contact with Hans von Dohnanyi. It was quite another to participate actively in the duplicity of political conspiracy and to help shape the substantive plans for a coup and for the period after the assassination of Hitler, all this coupled with having to learn the necessary skills of disguise and deception and always dealing with the threat of compromising oneself. The former activities involved his role as a pastor in offering advice and encouragement, the latter the role of the pastor as an agent in the Office of Military Intelligence in the High Military Command.

[66.] As in his 1941 confession of the church's guilt, *DBWE* 6:139, with ed. note 25.

[67.] Cf. *DBWE* 6:125–45; citation on p. 136. See also ed. note 23 above.

[68.] "After Ten Years," *DBWE* 8:38, and *DBWE* 6:80.

The key motivation for Bonhoeffer's trip to America in June–July 1939 and for the preceding trip to England in March–April was to gain time to reflect on this decision to cross that boundary, a decision that, in retrospect, ultimately decided the course of the rest of his life. Other factors included especially the threat of being called up for military service at a time when clear-thinking people could no longer doubt that Hitler
594 intended to start a war. For the Bonhoeffers, in any case, the situation was clear enough: "Uncle Rudi" was already quite ill.[69] Moreover, Bonhoeffer also had to consider what was for him the utterly impossible personal oath to the Führer and the oppressive question regarding the consequences for the Confessing Church, which the National Socialist press was already accusing of engaging in "treasonous activities," if one of its most prominent representatives were to refuse military service. But the tempting prospect of undisturbed theological work abroad also played a role for the passionate ecumenist, not least because despite his joy in participating in the illegal pastoral training, he did not deny to close friends that the rigors of his nomadic existence were also becoming an issue.[70]

The diary Bonhoeffer kept during his trip to America provides a disturbing look at the inner struggles he experienced in determining the path he was to take. This diary vividly reveals not only the background to the public confession "I have made a mistake in coming to America,"[71] but also the relief he felt at having decided—even before the key conversation with Henry Smith Leiper on June 20, 1939—to return to Germany as quickly as possible.

He was bothered first and foremost by thoughts of his friend Eberhard Bethge and his brothers at home: "I am fully with you, today more than ever. If only the doubts about my own path were overcome."[72] Or: "Since yesterday evening my thoughts cannot get away from Germany. . . . How usefully I could spend these hours in Germany. I would have liked to take the next ship. This inactivity, or rather activity spent on trivialities, is simply no longer bearable for us, thinking of the brothers and the precious time. The full force of self-reproaches about a wrong decision comes back up and is
595 almost suffocating. I was filled with despair."[73] After Bonhoeffer reached

---

[69.] Among Bonhoeffer's family and friends, "Uncle Rudi" was the code term used to refer to the status of the National Socialist regime's preparations for war (cf. 1/17 with ed. note 3).

[70.] See esp. the letters to Erwin Sutz on September 18, 1938, and to Paul Lehmann on December 14, 1938 (1/29 and 1/40).

[71.] Letter to Reinhold Niebuhr at the end of June 1939 (1/129), p. 210.

[72.] Diary entry for June 11, 1939, p. 219.

[73.] Diary entry for June 15, 1939, p. 222; cf. also the entry for June 16.

his decision to return, all these doubts and self-accusations disappeared in a sense of relief[74] and were replaced by renewed activity, stimulated by the prospect of returning to his previous work. "The journey is over. I am glad that I was there, and glad that I am on my way home again. I have perhaps learned more in this month than in the entire year nine years ago; at least I have come to realize important things for all future personal decisions. Probably this journey will have a great effect upon me."[75]

Careful analysis shows that during these weeks as well, Bonhoeffer's life theme of "discipleship" remained decisive.[76] The old question, "Who is Jesus Christ?" from his 1933 lectures on Christology[77] remained *the* question in America as well. This question encompasses his understanding of the indissoluble link between faith and obedience from the period in Finkenwalde when he was working on the book *Discipleship*[78] and then emerged anew later in the cell in Tegel: "What keeps gnawing at me is the question, what is Christianity, or who is Christ actually for us today?"[79] Admittedly, at this point the question assumed the specific form of a "where" question. In his meditation on the Daily Text for June 9, 1939, Bonhoeffer wrote in his diary: "God chooses the sinner as servant, in order that God's grace becomes entirely clear. The sinner is to do God's work and spread God's grace. Whomever God has forgiven, God gives this person a service to do. But this service can consist in nothing other than in discipleship. Great programs always lead us only to where we ourselves are; we, however, should be found only where God is. We cannot be anywhere other than where God is.
Whether you work over there or I work in America, we are both only where 596
God is. God takes us along. Or have I indeed evaded the place where God is? where God is *for me*? No, God says: You are my servant."[80]

"*Where* is Jesus Christ for me?"—this question drove Bonhoeffer during these weeks and at the same time articulated the foundation for his entire life and work, for his struggles, his hopes, and his prayers. His attempt to live in discipleship to Jesus was like an ongoing search for the presence of Jesus Christ, and for him—something evident in his diary entries during the next

[74.] See esp. the diary entries for June 20 and 26, 1939.

[75.] Diary entry for July 7, 1939, p. 237.

[76.] In this context the German editor is grateful for several insights communicated by Otto Dudzus in a presentation on April 9, 1995, at the Bischöfliche Akademie of the Diocese of Aachen.

[77.] See *DBWE* 12, 2/12, esp. after p. 353.

[78.] See esp. *DBWE* 4:67–83.

[79.] Letter of April 30, 1944, to Bethge, *DBWE* 8:362.

[80.] See p. 218.

few days—this presence was not to be found abroad in America. Reference to Matt. 18:20 ("for where two or three are gathered in my name, I am there among them") did not help, as he discovered at the common morning prayer with the family of Henry Coffin,[81] nor was he able to incorporate into his own life the knowledge of the church's purpose as found in Article 7 of the Augsburg Confession or of the existence of the Una Sancta.[82] The friendliness and helpfulness of his American friends did not help, for he did "live over there, after all" with his brothers in Germany.[83] References to the daily joy of all Christians at being "on the way home" were painful for him.[84] On June 22, he wrote in his diary that he "sat by the Hudson and thought of Sigurdshof,"[85] an individual repetition of what the exiled Israelites experienced in Babylon: "By the rivers of Babylon—there we sat down and there we wept when we remembered Zion" (Ps. 137:1).

In a word, he increasingly realized that he was in the wrong place, at an "utterly trivial" place.[86] The center of his life—as experienced and lived in Jesus's presence—could be found only in his life together with his besieged
597 brothers at home, not in the external security that America offered him: "For a German over here it is simply no longer to be endured; one is simply torn apart. To be here during a catastrophe is simply unthinkable, unless it is meant to be. But to be guilty of this oneself, to have to reproach oneself for having gone abroad unnecessarily, is certainly crushing. We simply cannot separate ourselves from our fate, here abroad less than ever; here it rests upon one's shoulders alone, and one has no voice and no rights in a foreign land. Moreover, here too the storm will soon break loose. There is seething unrest under the surface. Woe then to them who are here without a homeland! It is so strange, how strongly these very thoughts move me in these days and how all thoughts of the Una Sancta break through only with difficulty."[87] Accordingly he had to return immediately to the "trenches" of the Church Struggle.[88]

[81.] See the diary entry on June 14, 1939.

[82.] See the diary entry for June 22, 1939.

[83.] Diary entry for June 16, 1939, p. 223.

[84.] Diary entry for June 25, 1939, p. 231.

[85.] [P. 230.—VB]

[86.] Diary entry for June 15, 1939, p. 222.

[87.] Diary entry for June 22, 1939, p, 229.

[88.] Letter of June 28, 1939, to Paul Lehmann (1/126); cf. also the letter to Reinhold Niebuhr at the end of June 1939 (1/129). It was Karl Barth who used a bellicose metaphor to refer to the Church Struggle in which one would need "all guns blazing" against those who would destroy the Evangelical Church in Germany; he employed such language in a

During the night of July 7–8, 1939, Dietrich Bonhoeffer and his brother Karl-Friedrich boarded the ship in the New York harbor that would take them back to Europe and toward impending war. He wrote in his diary: "Since I have been aboard the ship the internal tension about the future has stopped. I can think about the abbreviated time in America without reproach."[89] And a short time later, in his London farewell letter to his fatherly friend George Bell, he remarked succinctly, "It was a difficult decision, but I am still convinced, I was not allowed to decide otherwise. That meant my early return to Germany."[90] After arriving in London, he waited until July 25 to return to Germany, not least out of concern for the subse- 598
quent course of "Uncle Rudi's" illness.[91] By the end of July, he was back in Berlin, and a few days later back with his friends and brothers in the collective pastorates, continuing his previous work up until the session concluded on August 24–25.

It is here that one finds the foundation of the inner resolution and strength with which Bonhoeffer, even in Tegel prison, was still able to write that he regretted neither his return from America nor anything that happened afterward:[92] In the summer of 1939, he did not shrink from the special sense of responsibility he felt for the Confessing Church in Germany, for his family, and for his country. By returning from an allegedly secure place to an insecure one, he in fact rediscovered the "given situation" where he knew what he had to do.[93] By returning to his homeland, back to the interpersonal relationships that had come to shape his life, he was returning to himself—precisely in the community of those who were trying together to follow responsibly the path of discipleship to Jesus. And he had also found an answer to the question "where is Jesus Christ for me?" in the conspiratorial resistance to the criminal National Socialist regime that would ultimately end in his own martyrdom.

---

temperamental letter to Bonhoeffer in London on November 20, 1933, in an attempt to persuade the latter to return to his position in Berlin as quickly as possible ("by the next ship!"; *DBWE* 13:39 and 41). In a later letter to Barth on September 19, 1936, Bonhoeffer admitted to himself and to Barth, "The thorn did, by the way, have an effect on me. I think I really did end up returning on the second ship" (*DBW* 14:234–39; citation on p. 235).

[89.] Diary entry for July 9, 1939, p. 238.

[90.] Letter of July 22, 1939, to George Bell (1/147), p. 258.

[91.] See 1/140.

[92.] Letter of December 22, 1943, to Bethge, *DBWE* 8:236.

[93.] See *DBWE* 6:268.

VII

In the meantime, Hitler and his followers in the party, the state, and the armed forces had intensified their efforts to turn "the nation into an unthinking war-machine."[94] Plans for a military attack on Poland had already been drawn up, and the relevant preparations for deployment were concluded in August 1939. Hitler canceled the "Reich Day of Peace" [Reichsparteitag des Friedens] planned for the first week of September in
599 Nuremberg because it no longer fit the programmatic plans of his new, disastrous foreign-policy maxim: "Germany will exist either as a world power or not at all."[95] And after the non-aggression treaty with its secret addendum was signed in Moscow on August 23, the "propagandistic pretext for launching the war"[96] announced by Hitler could be put into motion. A detachment of SS troops feigned a Polish attack on the German radio station in Gleiwitz; a few hours later, in the early hours of September 1, the German armored cruiser *Schleswig-Holstein* opened fire on the Westerplatte near Danzig. Without any official declaration of war, the well-armed German army invaded Poland and advanced with "ruthless efficiency"[97] against the Polish defenders.

In Berlin, where Dietrich Bonhoeffer and Eberhard Bethge experienced the initial days of the war, they found no "great display of emotion," and even publicly things seemed rather unspectacular: "There was no crisis within the population, no intensification of hopes for a coup, no onslaught by the Allied Powers, not even an enlistment order or a halt to the secret training of seminarians."[98]

Their first order of business was to consider whether and how the collective pastorates in the provinces so near the front could be continued. After the quick conquest of Poland concluded on October 6, 1939, however, things there did "indeed become quite peaceful again,"[99] and a new session began in Sigurdshof at the end of October. So many men had been

---

[94.] Thomas Mann in his lectures (published in English as *The Coming Victory of Democracy*, 23) delivered in fifteen North American cities in the spring of 1938.

[95.] Hitler had already used this formulation in 1925 in *Mein Kampf*; cited here in Hildebrand, *Das vergangene Reich*, 570, 577.

[96.] Hitler, in a speech on August 22, 1939, to the military commanders at Obersalzberg (Fest, *Hitler*, 620).

[97.] Craig, *Germany:1866–1945*, 715.

[98.] *DB-ER*, 662–63.

[99.] Cf. Bethge's letter from Berlin to his family and friends on September 21, 1939, in Andersen et al., *So ist es gewesen*, 352–53.

called up for military service, however, that only eight candidates were actually enrolled, and the training in Köslin was halted entirely. Bonhoeffer also spent considerable time and effort avoiding being called up himself by investigating possible engagement as a military chaplain in the army and medical service.[100] Considerable difficulties hampered this course 600
of action as well, despite high-placed supporters among Bonhoeffer's distant family relations and his own personal contacts with the supportive authorities—"the consistories and German Christians are still standing in the way everywhere," as Eberhard Bethge wrote.[101] A few months later, the authorities did indeed reject Bonhoeffer's application.[102]

Indeed, on September 1, 1939, there was a widespread feeling of "grim acceptance of the catastrophe as a necessary judgment"[103] in many Christian circles, including Confessing Church leaders, which prevented them from taking a public position on the issue. Moreover, they were also suffering under the ongoing legal proceedings against those responsible for the courageous prayer liturgy of the Provisional Church Administration in September 1938.[104] The official German Evangelical Church, however, did feel pressed both privately and publicly "to issue a statement on behalf of the entirety of the German Evangelical Church which might include all the individual congregations as well."[105] Hence Friedrich Werner and his Confidential Council of Clerical Advisors [Geistlicher Vertrauensrat] had "brought his name once again to public attention"[106] with a "Summons of the German Evangelical Church" on September 2, 1939: "Since yesterday our German Volk stands in battle for the land of its fathers, in order that German blood may return home to German blood. The German Evangelical Church always stood in loyal solidarity with the fate of the German Volk. It has offered invincible strength from the word of God to augment the weapons of steel. . . . So we unite in this hour as well with our Volk in intercessory prayer for the Führer and Reich, for the entire armed forces and all who perform their service in the homeland for the fatherland."[107]

[100.] See 1/157 and 1/158.

[101.] See ed. note 99 above.

[102.] See 1/179.

[103.] *DB-ER*, 663; cf. also Herbert, *Der Kirchenkampf*, 222–31.

[104.] [See Barnett, *For the Soul of the People*, 88–89 and 142–43.—VB]

[105.] *Gesetzblatt der Deutsche Evangelische Kirche* (1939), 100.

[106.] An ironic remark by former Finkenwalde seminarian Otto Kistner in his letter of September 28, 1939 (1/163), p. 283.

[107.] *Gesetzblatt der Deutsche Evangelische Kirche* (1939), 99. [Cf. 1/163, ed. note 10. As that note indicates, I believe Kistner's reference is actually to Bishop August Marahrens.—VB]

And the appended official "church prayer" concludes: "Lord, it is your will
601 that the nations live in righteousness and freedom according to the eternal laws into which you have placed all human life. Bless this our struggle for honor, for freedom, for the *Lebensraum* of the German people and its daily bread. Bless our armed forces. . . . Bless all engagement and all work in the German land, bless and protect our Führer, just as you have preserved and blessed him until now, and grant him success in winning for us a true and just peace as a blessing for us and for all the nations of Europe and to your glory."[108]

Worlds removed from such blasphemous "gymnastics coach theology,"[109] Bonhoeffer reacted on September 20, 1939, to the beginning of the war in a circular letter to the former Finkenwalde seminarians that was pastoral and admonitory.[110] Quite in contrast to the deceptive propaganda regarding "extremely light German losses" and the "complete admiration" of the rest of the world "for the German successes in Poland," he forcefully directed his readers' attention to the issue of death associated with war. His remembrance of Theodor Maaß, one of the brothers who was killed in action in Poland, expanded into a pastoral reflection on the renewed emergence of the question of theodicy, and his summons to pray for those who had entered military service, "that they can prove themselves at all times to be Christians," goes hand in hand with his urgent appeal to those not yet called up to remain in place and to preach "with a good, free conscience and to be faithful pastors who do not deny their church even in times of need."[111] In one place there is the prayer that God might "bless this our struggle for honor, for freedom, for the *Lebensraum* of the German people"; in another, Bonhoeffer prays for the strength to prove oneself worthy of the beatitudes of the Sermon on the Mount, even as people of war. Bonhoeffer had already clearly articulated his own, personal persuasion regarding the
602 war months before: "It seems to me conscientiously impossible to join in a war under the present circumstances. . . . Perhaps the worst thing of all is the military oath which I should have to swear. So I am rather puzzled in this situation."[112] One wonders whether during these initial weeks of

[108.] *Gesetzblatt der Deutsche Evangelische Kirche* (1939), 101.

[109.] This was Heinrich Böll's accurate characterization of church proclamation aimed at inculcating military obedience and bravery ("Brief an einen jungen Katholiken" [1958], 259).

[110.] See 1/160.

[111.] 1/160, p. 274. See also the letter to the family members of those Finkenwalde seminarians who were called up (October 8, 1939, 1/164).

[112.] Letter of March 25, 1939, to George Bell (1/82), p. 157.

the war, as in the autumn of 1941, Bonhoeffer was already praying for the defeat of his own country.[113]

VIII

After the personal and political turmoil of the preceding months, the final weeks of life together in "snowed-in" Sigurdshof provided Bonhoeffer the peace and quiet needed for intensive theological work.[114] The theologian Dietrich Bonhoeffer once more reflected on the broader issue, meditating anew on the *"guest status" of the Christian*[115] on earth with an eye simultaneously on the "eroded countenance" of early church Christology and its "splendor of Christmas."[116] And influenced by the double experience of "flight" and return from America, he reflected on how the Christian is directed *toward the earth itself* as the "given situation" where one engages in discipleship to Jesus Christ. In his attempt to fathom the mystery of Psalm 119, Bonhoeffer articulated concretely that central statement from his America diary: "We simply cannot separate ourselves from our fate."[117] Commenting on Psalm 119:19, he wrote: "The earth that feeds me has a right to my work and my strength. It is not my prerogative to despise the earth that sustains my life. I owe it faithfulness and thanksgiving. I may not evade my destiny to be a guest and a stranger, and thereby God's call into this sojourner status, by dreaming away my earthly life with thoughts about
heaven. There is a very godless homesickness for the other world that will 603
certainly not be stilled by a homecoming. I am meant to be a guest, with all this entails. I should not close my heart apathetically to the tasks, pains, and joys of the earth, and I should wait patiently for the divine promise to be redeemed, but truly wait for it, and not rob myself of it in advance, in wishes and dreams."[118]

Here Bonhoeffer prefigured almost verbatim his own later description from the cell in Tegel of what it means to be a Christian, namely, prayer and righteous action among human beings and waiting for God's own time.[119] It was characteristic of the urgency with which he searched for a theology

[113.] According to Willem A. Visser 't Hooft immediately after the war (cf. *DB-ER*, 744).

[114.] See the letter to his parents of February 23, 1940 (1/178).

[115.] [3/9, pp. 521–24.—VB]

[116.] See esp. 3/10.1, p. 529, and 3/10.2.

[117.] Diary entry on June 22, 1939, p. 229.

[118.] 3/9, p. 522.

[119.] "Thoughts on the Day of the Baptism of Dietrich Wilhelm Rüdiger Bethge" (May 1944), *DBWE* 8, 3/145, pp. 389–90.

that was close to reality, a theology capable of making the wealth of tradition accessible to the tasks of one's own age, that in his correspondence with the jurist Gerhard Leibholz, his brother-in-law, he thought he had clarified the question that had troubled him concerning the "the relationship of law, righteousness, and love (in the sense of the Sermon on the Mount)."[120] Thus his readings and correspondence, including the insights he committed to writing during these weeks, all flowed into the work he was doing on his anticipated *Ethics.* He would write this in years that followed, during his "participation in the fate of Germany"[121] in his double life as a political conspirator. His own theologically grounded contemporaneity with his age continued in this unusual form, because in the face of the millions of crimes being committed, there was a need for "simple, uncomplicated, and honest human beings" who could put an end to the horror.[122] It was such a human being that Dietrich Bonhoeffer wanted to be and remain.

[120.] Letter to Sabine and Gerhard Leibholz on March 7, 1940 (1/182), p. 301.
[121.] Letter of December 22, 1943, to Bethge, *DBWE* 8, 2/88, p. 236.
[122.] "After Ten Years," *DBWE* 8:52.

Appendices

Appendix 1
Chronology of
Theological Education Underground: 1937–1940

1937		607
August 29	Himmler issues an edict banning the Confessing Church's colleges and preachers' seminaries	
September 11	End of the fifth session at the Finkenwalde preachers' seminary; Bonhoeffer and Eberhard Bethge then spend two months with Bonhoeffer's parents in Berlin, then (in October) travel together on vacation to southern Germany	
September 25–29	Mussolini pays a state visit to Germany; "Axis" alliance is formed [with the signing of the Tripartite Pact between Italy, Japan, and Germany in Berlin—VB]	
September 28	Gestapo closes Finkenwalde	
November 5	Before military commanders and the foreign minister, Hitler announces his intent for the "conquest of new *Lebensraum* in the East" and its "Germanization" (in the Hoßbach Protocol)	
November 6	Italy joins the Anti-Comintern Pact, forming an "international political trio" (Berlin-Rome-Tokyo) to oppose Communism and the Soviet Union	
End of November	Twenty-seven former Finkenwalde seminarians arrested; publication of Bonhoeffer's *Discipleship* (*DBWE* 4)	
December 5	Collective pastorates begin in Köslin and Groß-Schlönwitz; Bonhoeffer's official residence is now in Schlawe, as an "assistant pastor" under Superintendent Eduard Block	
Christmas	Bonhoeffer in the collective pastorate Groß-Schlönwitz	

1938

January 11	Bonhoeffer banned from Berlin and Brandenburg; shortly thereafter Karl Bonhoeffer manages to get permission for Bonhoeffer to visit his family
January 24–25	Meeting of the "Brotherhood of Young Theologians in Pomerania" in Stettin
February 4	Blomberg-Fritsch crisis; Hitler becomes the commander in chief of the armed forces, Ribbentrop becomes foreign minister
February 7	Martin Niemöller's trial begins; he is acquitted on March 2, 1938, but rearrested and taken to the concentration camp in Sachsenhausen
February 10 (?)	Bonhoeffer meets with his parents in Stettin
608 February 26	Central order from Friedrich Werner concerning the "acceptance into regional church ministry of those theologians trained by nonofficial institutions" (legalization)
March 12–13	German troops march into Austria; *Anschluß* (annexation) of Austria into the German Reich
End of March	End of the 1937–38 winter session in the collective pastorates in Köslin and Groß-Schlönwitz
April 9	Confirmation at the Kleist estate in Kieckow; Bonhoeffer and Bethge then take vacation in Friedrichsbrunn (eastern Harz Mountains) until about April 23, 1938
April 10	Referendum on the *Anschluß* of Austria; 99 percent vote "yes"
April 20	Friedrich Werner, president of the Evangelical High Council in Berlin, orders all pastors and church officials to take the oath of loyalty to Adolf Hitler
End of April (ca. April 25)	Beginning of 1938 summer session in the collective pastorates in Köslin and Groß-Schlönwitz
June 11–13	Sixth Synod of the Confessing Church of the Old Prussian Union in Berlin-Nikolassee; discussions about the pastors' required loyalty oath
June 20–25	Study conference for former Finkenwalde participants in Zingst; Bonhoeffer examines the biblical question of "temptation"
End of June	Bonhoeffer vacations with Bethge in Rowe on the Baltic Sea

July 31	Second conference of the Sixth Synod of the Confessing Church of the Old Prussian Union in Berlin-Steglitz; church gives permission to take the loyalty oath
August 6	Karl Barth's "open letter" to the Sixth Synod of the Confessing Church of the Old Prussian Union against granting permission to take the loyalty oath
August 11	Bonhoeffer registers a protest with the Council of Brethren of the Old Prussian Union against granting permission to take the loyalty oath
August 17	Decree concerning middle names in passports, requiring "non-Aryans" to add either "Israel" or "Sarah"
August 18	Ludwig Beck resigns as Chief of the General Staff of the army, succeeded on August 27, 1938, by Franz Halder
End of August	End of the summer sessions in the collective pastorates in Köslin and Groß-Schlönwitz
September	Crisis between Germany and Czechoslovakia regarding 609 the Sudetenland
September 9	Leibholz family emigrates; Bonhoeffer and Bethge accompany them as far as Giessen; thereafter the two stay at the Leibholz home in Göttingen until October 10, 1938; Bonhoeffer writes *Life Together* (*DBWE* 5); attends the music festival in Kassel
September 12	At the Reich party conference in Nuremberg, Hitler announces military assistance for the Sudeten Germans
September 15	[British prime minister] Neville Chamberlain visits Hitler in Berchtesgaden
September 19	Karl Barth's letter to Josef Hromádka in Prague [encouraging the Czechs to stand up against Nazi aggression; Barth said they would be doing so "for the Church of Jesus Christ"—VB]
September 27	Peace prayer liturgy of the Provisional Administration of the Confessing Church for a worship service on September 30, 1938, in the face of impending war
September 29–30	Munich agreement [signed by France, Britain, Italy, and Germany, it ceded the Czech Sudetenland to Germany—VB]
October 1	German troops enter the Sudetenland

October 5	All Jewish passports recalled; any new passports had to be stamped with "J"
October 12	Bonhoeffer and Bethge depart Göttingen
Mid-October	Bonhoeffer meets with Hans von Dohnanyi and several of his colleagues (including Reich Minister of Justice Franz Gürtner) in Berlin
October 17–19	Beginning of the 1938–39 winter session in the collective pastorates in Köslin and Groß-Schlönwitz
October 26	Meeting of the Pomeranian Council of Brethren; Bonhoeffer presents his report "Our Path according to the Testimony of Scripture"
October 31	Theological Society meets at the home of Ruth von Kleist-Retzow in Stettin (until November 2, 1938)
November 3	Bonhoeffer must register at the enlistment office in Schlawe
November 9–10	The "Reich pogrom" (*Kristallnacht*) [destruction of hundreds of synagogues and thousands of Jewish-owned shops in Germany; arrests of an estimated thirty-five thousand Jews—VB]
November 10	Hitler delivers a secret address to members of the German press regarding a shift in propaganda toward preparing the German people psychologically for war
610 November 20	Circular letter to the Finkenwalde brothers giving Bonhoeffer's reaction to the pogrom
Christmas	Bonhoeffer in the collective pastorate in Groß-Schlönwitz; thereafter spends several days with his parents in Berlin

1939

January 9–11	Theological Society meets at the home of Ruth von Kleist-Retzow in Stettin
January 28–31	Seventh Synod of the Confessing Church of the Old Prussian Union in Berlin-Nikolassee ("Epiphany synod"); rejection of the legalization offers from the territorial consistories, declaration of solidarity with the "illegals"
January 30	Hitler's speech before the Reichstag; defends aggressive foreign policy, announces the "destruction of the Jewish race in Europe"
March 8	End of the winter session in the collective pastorates in Köslin and Groß-Schlönwitz

March 10	Bonhoeffer and Bethge leave together for London; meetings there with Bishop George Bell and Willem A. Visser 't Hooft
March 15–16	German troops enter Czechoslovakia ("march to Prague")
March 23	German troops enter Lithuanian region of Memel
March 29	Bonhoeffer meets with Leonard Hodgson (Faith and Order) in Oxford
March 31	Britain and France guarantee Poland's independence
April 3	Hitler instructs the armed forces to prepare for an attack on Poland ("Fall Weiss" directive); Bonhoeffer meets with Reinhold Niebuhr in Sussex, England
April 4	German Evangelical Church issues "Godesberg Declaration," demanding a German national church "free of Jews"
April 18	Bonhoeffer returns from London
April 23	Bonhoeffer applies at the military enlistment office in Schlawe for a leave of absence for a trip to the United States from May 1, 1939, to May 1, 1940
End of April	Collective pastorate at Groß-Schlönwitz relocated to Sigurdshof (Tychow near Schlawe)
April 28	Hitler addresses the Reichstag, renounces the Anglo- 611 German Naval Treaty of 1935 and German-Polish Non-Aggression Pact of 1934
May 6	Establishment of the Institute for the Study and Eradication of Jewish Influence on German Church Life in Eisenach
May 13	Bonhoeffer receives orders to report for duty in the armed forces on May 22, 1939
May 20–22	Eighth Synod of the Confessing Church of the Old Prussian Union in Berlin-Steglitz ("Exaudi synod")
May 22	Military alliance between Germany and Italy ("Steel Pact")
June 2	Bonhoeffer leaves for the United States via London; visits the Leibholz family
June 6	Bonhoeffer meets with George Bell
June 7	Bonhoeffer departs Southampton for New York on the *Bremen*, via Cherbourg
June 12	Arrival in New York
June 13–16	Visit with the Coffin family in Lakeville, Connecticut

	June 20	Bonhoeffer speaks with Henry S. Leiper; decides to return to Germany immediately
	July 6	Meets with Paul Lehmann
	July 7–8	Bonhoeffer and Karl-Friedrich Bonhoeffer depart New York together
	July 13	Arrival in London, where he spends several days with the Leibholz family
	July 18	Confessing Church pastor Paul Schneider murdered in the concentration camp in Buchenwald
	July 25	Bonhoeffer departs London
	July 26–27	Visits to Hans J. Iwand and Hermann A. Hesse in the Rhineland
	July 30	Bonhoeffer arrives in Berlin
	August 4–14	Bonhoeffer attends retreat with members of the Sigurdshof collective pastorate in Jershöft on the Baltic Sea; thereafter spends several days there with members of the Köslin collective pastorate
	August 23	Non-aggression treaty signed between Germany and the Soviet Union with a secret protocol ("Hitler-Stalin Pact")
	August 24–25	End of the summer session of the collective pastorates in Köslin and Sigurdshof
612	August 26	Bonhoeffer and Bethge travel to visit his parents in Berlin
	August 29	Confidential Council of Clerical Advisors established by the German Evangelical church, includes August Marahrens, Johannes Hymmen, Walther Schultz
	September 1	Germany invades Poland
	September 2	Confidential Council of Clerical Advisors, with president Friedrich Werner of the German Evangelical Church, publicly states support for the Führer and Reich
	September 3	Britain and France declare war on Germany
	September 9	Bonhoeffer applies for military chaplaincy with the army and medical service
	September–October	Bonhoeffer visits his parents in Berlin with Bethge
	September 27	Warsaw capitulates; formation of the Reich Central Security Office as the headquarters for all National Socialist repressive measures
	September 28	Soviet-German Friendship Treaty

October	Beginning of the National Socialist "euthanasia" program ("Action T 4")
October 6	Conquest of Poland concludes; Hitler addresses the Reichstag with his "offer of peace" to the Western powers if they will recognize the "new realities"
October 12–17	First deportation of Jews from Austria and the Protectorate of Bohemia-Moravia to Poland
October 26	Establishment of the "General Government for the Occupied Polish Territories"
End of October	Beginning of the 1939–40 winter session in the collective pastorate in Sigurdshof; no longer possible to continue in Köslin
November 8	Assassination attempt on Hitler by Johann Georg Elser in the Bürgerbräukeller in Munich
December	First mass deportations of Jews and Poles from the Wartheland to the "General Government" region
Christmas	Bonhoeffer at the collective pastorate in Sigurdshof, then travels to Berlin to be with his parents. While in Berlin, meeting with Nils Ehrenström, Hans Schönfeld, Helmut Gollwitzer at the Gossner Mission house[1]

1940

Mid-January	Bonhoeffer returns to Sigurdshof from Berlin 613
February 4	Birthday celebration with his family in Berlin
February 13–14	First deportations of Jews from the German Reich territory (Schneidemühl, Stettin, Stralsund) to Lublin
February 27	Bonhoeffer's application for military chaplaincy with the army and medical service rejected
March 15	End of the 1939–40 winter session in Sigurdshof; return to Berlin
March 18	Gestapo closes Sigurdshof

[1.] This information was given to Ulrich Kabitz by Oskar Hammelsbeck. See *Bonhoeffer-Jahrbuch 2003*, 118–25.

Appendix 2
List of Candidates in the Collective Pastorates

614 *Unless mentioned elsewhere in this volume, these names are not included in the index of persons.*

Winter 1937–1938

Groß-Schlönwitz
Inspector: Eberhard Bethge

Heinz Bluhm (b. 1910), Berlin-Brandenburg
Edgar Engler (b. 1911), Pomerania (1941, killed in action)
Heinz Fleischhack (b. 1913), Province of Saxony
Emanuel Kahn (b. 1910), Berlin-Brandenburg (1939, killed in action)
Heinrich Lange (b. 1907), Pomerania
Gerhard Lehne (b. 1910), Berlin-Brandenburg (1942, killed in action)
Hermann Schröder (b. 1913), [?] (1942, killed in action)

Köslin
Inspector: Friedrich Onnasch

Kurt Appold (b. 1907), Saxony
Fritz Dorau (b. 1911), Berlin-Brandenburg
Hans-Otto Georgii (b. 1911), Berlin-Brandenburg (1941, killed in action)
Wolfgang Georgii (b. 1913), Berlin-Brandenburg (1944, missing in action)
Walter Kergel (b. 1908), Pomerania
Otto Kunze (b. 1912), Westphalia
Ernst Nasner (b. 1911), eastern Prussia
Otto Stolzenwald (b. 1906), Berlin-Brandenburg
Artur Theuerkauf (b. 1910), Saxony

Summer 1938

Groß-Schlönwitz
Adolf Buchmann (b. 1914), Berlin-Brandenburg
Helmut Kiausch (b. 1912), Pomerania
Rudolf Lynker (b. 1912), Westphalia (1942, killed in action)
Ulrich Nithack (b. 1913), Berlin-Brandenburg (1941, killed in action)

Erwin Sander (b. 1911), Westphalia (1943, killed in action)
Walter Schultz (b. 1913), Berlin-Brandenburg
Gerhard Schulze (b. 1913), Province of Saxony (1941, killed in action)
Erwin Schutz (b. 1907), Pomerania (1942, killed in action)

Köslin
Heinz Corves [?]
Friedrich Diening (b. 1909), Westphalia
Helmut Lange (b. 1912), Rhineland 615
Walter Schmidt (b. 1913), Province of Saxony
Gerhard Stähler (b. 1911), [?]
Heinz Winkelmann [?], Berlin-Brandenburg
Kurt Zywietz (b. 1910), East Prussia

Winter 1938–1939

Groß-Schlönwitz
Werner Albrecht [?]
Heinz Dobrik [?]
Heinz Emmerich (b. 1910), Berlin-Brandenburg
Joachim-Hans von Hanstein (b. 1914), Province of Saxony
Hans-Werner Jensen (b. 1913), [?]
Wilhelm Kraemer [?]
Joachim Staude (b. 1911), Berlin-Brandenburg (1941, killed in action)
Hans Steinert (b. 1913), [?] (1944, killed in action)

Köslin
Günter Biesental (b. 1913), Berlin-Brandenburg (1943, killed in action)
Heinrich Glücks [?]
[?]Herzog [?]
Gottfried Maltusch (b. 1911), Berlin-Brandenburg
Kurt Nimz (b. 1913), Pomerania
Lothar Rudnik (b. 1910), East Prussia
Albert Teschke, Berlin-Brandenburg
Alfred Viol (b. 1912), [?] (1942, killed in action)

Summer 1939

Sigurdshof
Heinrich Begrich (b. 1912), [?]
Heinz Doebert (b. 1910), Berlin-Brandenburg

Hinrich Korporal (b. 1912), Province of Saxony
Heinz Petermann (b. 1910), [?]
Karl Stephan (b. 1913), [?]
Heinz Tonn (b. 1911), Pomerania

Köslin
Bernhard Burgwitz (b. 1910), Berlin-Brandenburg
[?] Ertel [?]
616 Gottfried Grundmann (b. 1910), Silesia
Arno Pagel [?]
Johannes Städler (b. 1911), East Prussia (1941, killed in action)
Günter Stornowski (b. 1912), Province of Saxony
[?] Vogelweider [?]

Winter 1939–1940

Sigurdshof
Hellmuth Birk (b. 1913), Berlin-Brandenburg
Bruno Kerlin (b. 1913), Berlin-Brandenburg (1941, killed in action)
Hans-Wolf Litterscheid (b. 1912), [?]
Max Mebes (b. 1913), Berlin-Brandenburg
Hans-Dietrich Müschner (b. 1913), Berlin Brandenburg
Karl-Heinz Probsthain [?]
Heinrich Vollriede [?]
Karl-Heinz Ziegler (b. 1913), Berlin-Brandenburg

Because of the massive military call-ups, the collective pastorate in Köslin could not be continued in the winter of 1939–40.

Appendix 3
Unpublished Material from Bonhoeffer's Literary Estate, 1937–1940

The following list of unpublished material includes document numbers as cited in the Bonhoeffer *Nachlaß* volume (these are the numbers as they appear in the Bonhoeffer microfiche collection). 617

I.

Letters and documents from Bonhoeffer

A 45 (46) To Gerhard Krause (four visiting cards with brief references from Bonhoeffer for G. Krause for a trip to Sweden), February 2, 1938

A 60,2 To Georg Eichholz (telegram), January 10, 1940

A 82,5 Bonhoeffer's vehicle registration certificate, issued in Schlawe, May 5, 1938

A 82,7 Receipt of establishment of a military registration record in Groß-Schlönwitz, November 3, 1938

A 82,8 Certificate from the Military Enlistment Office regarding passports (for Bonhoeffer's trip to England in March–April 1939), March 6, 1939

Anh. A13 To Susanne and Walter Dreß, November 11, 1938

Letters to and about Bonhoeffer

A 44,3 (8) From Eberhard Bethge to Wolfgang Staemmler, June 29, 1939

A 45 (44) From Eberhard Baumann to Martin Strege, January 7, 1938

A 50,2 (8) From Henry Smith Leiper to Samuel McCrea Cavert, June 6, 1939

A 50,2 (9) From Henry Smith Leiper to Henry P. Van Dusen, June 15, 1939

A 60,2 From Georg Eichholz, January 31, 1940

C 1 From his parents, May 1939

C 24 From Günter Besch, January 4, 1939

C 25 From Herbert Liedtke, January 3, 1939

C 25 From Hans Georg Berg, February 4, 1939

C 25 From Heinz Doebert, February 16, 1939

C 25	From Otto Dudzus, February 2, 1939
C 25	From Wolfgang Georgii, February 2, 1939
C 25	From Heinz Johannsen, February 3, 1939
C 25	From Gerhard Krause, February 28, 1939
C 25	From Winfried Krause, February 3, 1939
618 C 25	From Otto-Karl Lerche, January 5, 1939
C 25	From Alexander von der Marwitz, February 1, 1939
C 25	From Margret Onnasch, February 3, 1939
C 25	From Eugen Rose, February 2, 1939
C 25	From Erwin Sander, February 4, 1939
C 25	From Albrecht Schönherr, February 1 and 3, 1939
C 25	From Gerhard Stähler, February 3, 1939
C 25	From Friedrich Trentepohl, January 5 and February 3, 1939
C 25	From Eberhard Veckenstedt, February 3, 1939
C 25	From Gerhard Vibrans (and Heinz Fleischhack), February 3, 1939
C 25	From Robert Zenke, February 4, 1939
C 25	From Wolf-Dieter Zimmermann, January 21, 1939
C 25	From Rudolf Weckerling, January 31, 1939
C 25	From Bernhard Riemer, February 3, 1939
C 25	From Herbert Jehle, February 1, 1939 (?)
C 25	From Maria Gersdorff, December 15, 1938
Anh. C 4	From Ruth von Kleist-Retzow, January 7, 1938
Anh. C 5	From Maria von Kleist-Retzow, January 12, 1939
Anh. C 5	From Spes von Bismarck, February 2, 1939
Anh. C 5	From Hans-Friedrich von Kleist-Retzow, February 2, 1939
Anh. C 5	From Max von Wedemeyer, February 2, 1939

II.

Notes (undated)

A 53,10	Rev. 5:8 "When he had taken the scroll . . ."
A 53,12	Easter sayings, "Christ is risen . . ."
A 54,2	"Education and Ordination" (United States, 1939)
A 54,4	Sketch regarding the wedding ceremony
A 54,9	Notes on "Lord's Supper. Lutheran concepts. Reformed concepts"
A 54,10	Citation "Ap. Formula of Concord . . . pp. 193–94"
A 54,11	Citations "Calvin. Institutio IV. Lord's Supper"
A 54,13	"Christology"
A 54,15	"Let us never pity ourselves"

A 54,16	Notes on doing God's will	
A 54,18	"Schleiermacher"	
A 55,4 (1)	"Office"	
A 55,4 (3)	"Teaching Obligation"	
A 55,4 (4)	"Church Discipline"	
A 55, 8	Notes on ὁδός	
A 55,16	Notes on εὐχαριστία	
A 55,17	Notes on ταπεινοφροσύνη	
A 55,18	Notes on νικᾶν	
A 55,21	Notes on 2 Pet. 1:1–7	619
A 55,23 (6)	Brief notes on ἡδονή, καυχάσθαι, παρρησία, χαρά	

Student lecture notes

B 11,6	Heinz Bluhm, Pastoral Care, Groß-Schlönwitz 1937–38
B 12,6	Heinz Bluhm, Catechetics, Groß-Schlönwitz 1937–38
B 10,1	Hans-Werner Jensen, Homiletics, Groß-Schlönwitz 1938–39
B 11,5	Hans-Werner Jensen, Pastoral Care, Groß-Schlönwitz 1938–39
B 12,4	Hans-Werner Jensen, Catechetics, Groß-Schlönwitz 1938–39

Appendix 4
Texts Published in Both *Gesammelte Schriften* and *DBWE* 15

GS	***DBWE* 15**
1:48–49	1/29
1:49	1/135
1:279	1/80
1:279–82	1/82
1:282–83	1/81
1:283–86	1/83
1:286	1/85
1:287–88	1/87
1:288	1/90
1:289	1/97
1:289–90	1/100
1:291	1/103
1:291	1/104
1:292	1/107
1:292–315	1/137
1:316–19	1/111
1:319	1/115
1:320	1/129
1:320–22	1/147
1:323–54	2/6
2:295–96	1/10
2:297–306	1/7
2:307	1/4
2:307	1/12
2:308–15	1/22
2:315–18	1/26
2:318–19	1/28
2:320–45	2/5
2:345–46	1/57
2:347–48	1/40
2:348	1/86
2:348	1/88
2:349	1/89
2:349–50	1/91
2:350	1/95
2:351	1/112
2:351–52	1/114
2:352–53	1/123
2:353–54	1/124
2:354–56	1/125
2:356	1/126
2:357–58	1/128
2:359	1/130
2:359–60	1/131
2:360–61	1/132
2:361	1/133
2:361–62	1/112
2:362	1/146
2:362	1/154
2:524–30	1/2
2:531–33	1/11
2:533	1/17
2:533–35	1/20
2:535–37	1/21.2
2:537–41	1/24
2:541–44	1/36
2:545	1/39
2:546–50	1/75
2:550–51	1/93
2:551–52	1/98
2:552	1/141
2:552	1/145
2:553–58	1/160

GS	***DBWE* 15**
2:559–62	1/169
2:562	1/171
2:562	1/177
2:563	1/178
2:563	1/181
3:31–33	1/55
3:33–36	1/182
3:368	3/3.2
3:382–88	3/10.1
3:388–92	3/10.2
3:393–98	3/10.3
4:358–84	2/1
4:427–34	3/1
4:434–41	3/2
4:441–47	3/3
4:450–52	3/4
4:453–55	3/6
4:473–79	3/8
4:480–86	3/11.1
4:486–91	3/11.2
4:491–97	3/11.3
4:497–504	3/11.4
4:505–43	3/9
6:433	1/3
6:433–34	1/5
6:434	1/6
6:435	1/8
6:435	1/9
6:436	1/13
6:436	1/17
6:437–38	1/14
6:438	1/23
6:439–42	1/76
6:443	1/62
6:443–44	1/143
6:444–45	1/94
6:446–47	1/34
6:447–49	1/37
6:449–50	1/41
6:450–51	1/44
6:451–52	1/42
6:452	1/43
6:453–54	1/61
6:455	1/86
6:455–56	1/92
6:456	1/102
6:456–57	1/108
6:457–58	1/118
6:458–59	1/121
6:459–60	1/122
6:461	1/117
6:461–62	1/134
6:462	1/139
6:462–63	1/140
6:463	1/144
6:464–65	1/141
6:465–67	1/145
6:467	1/153
6:467	1/155
6:469	1/156
6:469–71	1/164
6:472	1/174
6:472–73	1/179
6:473–74	1/180
6:475	1/181
6:478	1/166
6:478	1/167

BIBLIOGRAPHY

Dietrich Bonhoeffer's papers and personal library, as well as correspondence from others and relevant material in other archives, have been cataloged in the *Nachlaß Dietrich Bonhoeffer* volume compiled by Dietrich Meyer and Eberhard Bethge. All such citations in *DBWE* are indicated by *NL*, followed by the corresponding reference code within that published index. Not all this material is part of the actual Bonhoeffer Nachlaß in the Staatsbibliothek in Berlin; footnote citations of *NL* material from other archives also give the numbering from the respective archive. All the material listed in the Meyer and Bethge catalog, however, has been included on microfiches now located at the Staatsbibliothek in Berlin (previously at the Bundesarchiv in Koblenz) and in the Bonhoeffer Collection at Burke Library, Union Theological Seminary, New York. The designation *NL-Bibl.* in some bibliographic records indicates that a copy of the book was found in Bonhoeffer's surviving personal library.

1. Archival Sources and Private Collections

Bundesarchiv Abt. Potsdam (BA Potsdam)
Bestand 51.01: Reichskirchenministerium
Evangelisches Zentralarchiv, Berlin
Nachlaß Walter and Susanne Dreß
Lambeth Palace Library, London (LPL)
Bell Papers, vol. 42 (Dietrich Bonhoeffer) and vols. 9 and 21
Landeskirchliches Archiv der Evangelischen Kirche von Westfalen, Bielefeld (LkA, EkvW Bielefeld)
Bestand 5,1: Sammlung Wilhelm Niemöller
Princeton Theological Seminary, Special Collections
Paul Lehmann Collection

Staatsbibliothek zu Berlin-Preußischer Kulturbesitz-, Handschriftenabteilung
Nachlaß Dietrich Bonhoeffer (Nachlaß 299; fiches)

Private Collections (locations at time of *DBW* publication)
Renate Bethge (née Schleicher), Wachtberg-Villiprott
Literary estate of Eberhard Bethge
Hans-Jürgen Blanck-Lubarsch, Bochum
Ehrentraut Bohren (widowed Eichholz), Dossenheim
Literary estate of Georg Eichholz
Otto Dudzus, Cologne
Ilse Fischer, Berlin
Tony Gambley, Durban
Margret Grude (née Bethge, widowed Onnasch and Grude), Magdeburg
Familie Koch, Emlichheim
Sigrid Krause, Bonn
Wilhelm Niesel
Renate Petras, Schöneiche
Spes Pompe (née von Bismarck), Bonn
Johannes Radtke, Berlin
Gottfried Rieger, Berlin
Albrecht Schönherr, Waldesruh
Familie Sutz, Herrliberg/Schweiz

2. Literature Used by Bonhoeffer

Althaus, Paul. *Die letzten Dinge: Entwurf einer christlichen Eschatologie* (The last things: Outline of a Christian eschatology). Gütersloh: C. Bertelsmann, 1926. *NL-Bibl.* 3 B 3.

———. *Paulus und Luther über den Menschen: Ein Vergleich* (Paul and Luther on human beings: A comparison). Studien der Luther-Akademie, no. 14. Gütersloh, 1938.

Ames, E. S. "Liberalism Confirmed." *Christian Century* (March 22, 1939): 380–82.

Arper, Karl, und Alfred Zillessen, eds. *Agende für Kriegszeiten* (Wartime worship liturgies). 3 vols. Sonderband der Praktisch-theologischen Handbibliothek 3 (Special volume of the practical theology portable library). Series edited by Friedrich Niebergall. Göttingen: Vandenhoeck & Ruprecht, 1915.

Asmussen, Hans. *Theologisch-kirchliche Erwägungen zum Galaterbrief* (Theological-ecclesial reflections on the Letter to the Galatians). 2nd ed. Munich, 1935.

Barth, Karl. *Die Kirchliche Dogmatik.* Zurich: Evangelischer Verlag, 1932–67. Translated by G. W. Bromiley as *Church Dogmatics.* Edited by G. W. Bromiley and T. F. Torrance. 4 vols. Edinburgh: T & T Clark, 1956–77. Vol. 1, pt. 1: *Die Lehre vom Wort Gottes: Erster Halbband.* Translated as *The Doctrine of the Word of God* (I/1), rev. ed. Vol. 1, pt. 2: *Die Lehre vom Wort Gottes: Prolegomena zur kirchlichen Dogmatik; Zweiter Halbband.* 6th ed. Zurich: Evangelischer Verlag, 1975. Translated as *The Doctrine of the Word of God: Prolegomena Part 2* (I/2). Vol. 3: *Die Lehre von der Schöpfung: Dritter Teil.* 6th ed. Zurich: Evangelischer Verlag, 1975. Translated as *The Doctrine of Creation: Part 3* (III/3).

———. *Rechtfertigung und Recht.* Theologische Studien, no. 1. Zürich: Zollikon, 1938. Also published in Barth, *Eine Schweizer Stimme 1938–1945,* 13–57, Zürich: Zollikon, 1945. Translated by G. Ronald Howe as *Church and State,* introduction by David E. Mueller. Greenville, S.C.: Smyth & Helwys, 1991.

Beckmann, Joachim, and Friedrich Linz, eds. *Meine Worte werden nicht vergehen: Ein Predigtbuch über die altkirchlichen Evangelien.* (My words will not pass away: A sermon book about the early church gospels). Gütersloh: C. Bertelsmann, 1940.

Bekenntnisschriften und Kirchenordnungen der nach Gottes Wort reformierten Kirche (Confessional texts and church law of the Reformed Church according to God's law). Edited by Wilhelm Niesel. Zürich: Evangelischer Verlag A. G. Zollikon, 1938.

Bengel, Johann Albrecht. *Gnomon: Auslegung des Neuen Testaments in fortlaufenden Anmerkungen, I: Evangelien und Apostelgeschichte.* Latin edition, 1742. German edition by C. F. Werner. Basel, 1876. Translated by Charlton T. Lewis and Marvin R. Vincent as *Bengel's New Testament Commentary.* Grand Rapids, Mich.: Kregel, 1981.

Benson, R. M. *The Way of Holiness: An Exposition of Psalm CXIX—Analytical and Devotional.* London: Methuen, 1901.

Betts, George Herbert. *The Beliefs of 700 Ministers and Their Meaning for Religious Education.* New York, 1929.

Die Bibel oder die ganze Heilige Schrift des Alten und Neuen Testaments nach der deutschen Übersetzung D. Martin Luthers (The Bible or the entire Holy Scriptures of the Old and New Testaments according to the German translation of Dr. Martin Luther). Durchgesehen im Auftrag der Deutschen Evangelischen Kirchenkonferenz. Stuttgart: Mitteloktav-Ausgabe, 1911. *NL-Bibl.* 1 A 6.

Botterwerk, G. Johannes, Heinz-Josef Fabry, und Helmer Ringgren, eds. *Theologisches Wörterbuch zum Alten Testament.* Stuttgart: Kohlhammer, 1970–. Translated as *Theological Dictionary of the Old Testament.* 15 vols. Grand Rapids, Mich.: Wm. B. Eerdmans, 1974–.

Brown, William Adams. *Church and State in Contemporary America: A Study of the Problems They Present and the Principles Which Should Determine Their Relationship.* New York: Charles Scribner's Sons, 1936.

Brunner, Emil. *Das Gebot und die Ordnungen: Entwurf einer protestantisch-theologischen Ethik.* Tübingen: J. C. B. Mohr (Paul Siebeck), 1932. *NL-Bibl.* 4. 6. Translated by Olive Wyon as *The Divine Imperative,* 1947. Reprint, Philadelphia: Westminster Press, 1979.

Calvin, Johannes. *Institutio Christianae Religionis: Unterricht in der christlichen Religion, nach der letzten Ausgabe übersetzt und bearbeitet von Otto Weber.* Vol. 1. Neukirchen-Vluyn: Neukirchener, 1936. Cf. *NL-Bibl.* 2 C 3. 4 a. (1988 ed. cited). Translated as *Institutes of the Christian Religion,* edited by John T. McNeill, translated and indexed by Ford Lewis Battles, vol. 2, 1960. Reissue, Louisville: Westminster John Knox Press, 2006.

The Christian Century (Chicago) 56 (1939).

Dürer, Albrecht. *Die große Passion* (The great passion). Berlin, n.d. *NL-Bibl.* 9. 7.

Evangelische Christenlehre: Ein Altersstufen-Lehrplan (Protestant Christian doctrine: A lesson plan for different age groups). Prepared by Martin Albertz und Bernhard Heinrich Forck, Wuppertal-Barmen, n.d. [probably 1938].

Evangelisches Gesangbuch für Brandenburg und Pommern (Protestant hymnal for Brandenburg and Pomerania). Compiled by the Provincial Church Council of Brandenburg and Pomerania. Berlin/Frankfurt an der Oder: Trowitzsch, 1931.

Garrod, Heathcote William. *The Religion of All Good Men, and Other Studies in Christian Ethics.* London: A. Constable; New York: McClure, Phillips, 1906.

Geyser, Paul. *Pia Desideria.* 1878. Vol. 5 of *Gesammelte Schriften,* edited by a circle of his friends. Wuppertal-Elberfeld, 1921. *NL-Bibl.* 2 C 4. 15.

Gunkel, Hermann. *Die Psalmen: Göttinger Handkommentar zum Alten Testament.* Abteilung 2, Bd. 2 (The psalms: Göttingen commentary on the Old Testament, section 2, vol. 2). Göttingen: Vandenhoeck & Ruprecht, 1926. *NL-Bibl.* 1 C 8.

Hall, Thomas Cuming. *The Religious Background of American Culture.* Boston: Little, Brown, 1930.

Harnack, Adolf von. *Lehrbuch der Dogmengeschichte.* Vols. 1–3, 1895; Vol. 4, new rev. and enlarged ed. Tübingen: Mohr, 1909. *NL-Bibl.* 2 C 4. 17. Translated by Neil Buchanan as *History of Dogma,* 7 vols. New York: Harper, 1958.

Hegel, Georg Wilhelm Friedrich. *Vorlesungen über die Philosophie der Religion.* Vol. 16 of *Sämtliche Werke.* Leipzig: Meiner, 1929. Cf. *NL-Bibl.* 7 A 26. Translated by R. F. Brown, P. C. Hodgson, and J. M. Stewart, with H. S. Harris, as *Lectures on the Philosophy of Religion,* edited by Peter C. Hodgson, 3 vols. Berkeley: University of California Press, 1984–87. (Vol. 3 of *Die Philosophie der Religion* was previously published as *The Christian Religion,* edited and translated by Peter C. Hodgson, based on the edition by Georg Lasson. Missoula, Mont.: Scholars Press, 1979.)

Heim, Karl. *Glaube und Denken: Philosophische Grundlegung einer christlichen Lebensanschauung.* Vol. 1 of *Der evangelische Glaube und das Denken der Gegenwart: Grundzüge einer christlichen Lebensauffassung.* Berlin: Furche-Verlag, 1931. *NL-Bibl.* 3 B 34. Translated from the 3rd ed. by Edgar Primrose Dickie as *God Transcendent: Foundation for a Christian Metaphysic,* introduced and revised by Edwyn Bevan. New York: Charles Scribner's Sons, 1936.

Der helle Ton: Ein Liederbuch des Reichsverbands der Evangelischen Jungmännerverbände (The clear tone: A songbook of the Reich Association of Protestant Young Men's groups). Edited by Otto Reithmüller. Berlin-Dahlem, 1933.

Holl, Karl. "Der Ursprung des Epiphanienfestes" (The origin of the feast of Epiphany). In *Gesammelte Aufsätze zur Kirchengeschichte* (Collected essays on church history), vol. 2: *Der Osten* (the East), 123–54. Tübingen: J. C. B. Mohr (Paul Siebeck), 1928.

Horton, Walter Marshall. "Between Liberalism and the New Orthodoxy." *Christian Century* 56 (May 17, 1939): 637–40.

———. *Contemporary Continental Theology.* New York: Harper & Brothers, 1938.

———. *Contemporary English Theology.* New York: Harper & Brothers, 1936.

———. *Realistic Theology.* New York: Harper, 1934.

———. *Theism and the Modern Mood.* New York: Harper & Brothers, 1930.

Kohlbrügge, Hermann Friedrich. *Sechs Predigten, gehalten vor der Eröffnung der Kriegsläufte im Jahre 1870* (Six sermons, held at the beginning of the war in 1870). Wuppertal-Elberfeld: Verlag der niederländisch-reformierten Gemeine, 1915. *NL-Bibl.* 5 C 27.

Lewis, Edwin. *A Christian Manifesto.* New York: Abingdon, 1934.

———. "From Philosophy to Revelation." *Christian Century* 56 (June 14, 1939): 762–64.

———. *Jesus Christ and the Human Quest: Suggestions toward a Philosophy of the Person and Work of Christ.* New York: Abingdon, 1924.

———. *A Philosophy of the Christian Revelation.* New York: Harper & Brothers, 1940.

Lietzmann, Hans. *Geschichte der alten Kirche.* Vol. 3: *Die Reichskirche bis zum Tode Julians.* Berlin: W. de Gruyter, 1938. Translated by Bertram Lee Wolf from the 3rd rev. ed. as *A History of the Early Church*, 4 vols. in 2. Cleveland: World, 1961.

Litt, Theodor. *Der deutsche Geist und das Christentum: Vom Wesen geschichtlicher Begegnung* (The German spirit and Christianity: On the nature of a historical encounter). Leipzig: Klotz, 1938. *NL-Bibl.* 7 A 52.

———. *Protestantisches Geschichtsbewußsein: Eine geschichtsphilosophische Besinnung* (Protestant historical consciousness: A historical philosophical reflection). Leipzig: Klotz, 1939. *NL-Bibl.* 7 A 53.

Macartney, Clarence E. "Warm Hearts and Steady Faith." *Christian Century* 56 (March 8, 1939): 317.

Maritain, Jacques. *True Humanism.* New York: Charles Scribner's Sons, 1938.

Niebuhr, Helmut Richard. *The Kingdom of God in America.* Chicago: Willett, Clark, 1937.

Niebuhr, H. Richard, Wilhelm Pauck, and Francis P. Miller. *The Church against the World.* Chicago: Willett, Clark, 1935.

Niebuhr, Reinhold. *Beyond Tragedy: Essays on the Christian Interpretation of History.* New York: Charles Scribner's Sons, 1937.

———. *An Interpretation of Christian Ethics.* New York: Harper & Brothers, 1935.

———. *Moral Man and Immoral Society: A Study of Ethics and Politics.* New York: Charles Scribner's Sons, 1932. *NL-Bibl.* 4. 33.

———. "Ten Years That Shook My World." *Christian Century* (April 26, 1939): 543–46.

Nietzsche, Friedrich. *Werke* (Works). 16 vols. Part 1: vols. 1–8 (containing the works published by Nietzsche himself). Leipzig: C. G. Naumann, 1899. *NL-Bibl.* 7 A 61.

Novum Testamentum Graece et Germanice (The New Testament in Greek and German). Edited by D. Eberhard Nestle and Erwin Nestle. 13th ed. Stuttgart: Deutsche Bibelstiftung, 1929. *NL-Bibl.* 1 A 4.

Paulsen, Friedrich. *System der Ethik mit einem Umriß der Staats- und Gesellschaftslehre.* Vol. 2. (System of ethics with an outline of state and societal doctrine). Berlin: W. Hertz, 1906.

Pringle-Pattison, Andrew Seth. *The Idea of God in the Light of Recent Philosophy: The Gifford Lectures Delivered in the University of Aberdeen in the Years 1912 and 1913.* New York: Oxford University Press, 1920.

Qualben, Lars P. *The Lutheran Church in Colonial America.* New York: Thomas Nelson, 1940.

Sackmann, Jacobus. *Die höchst ergötzlichen Predigten des Jobst Sackmann, weiland Pastor zu Limmer* (The most divine sermons of Jobst Sackmann, pastor of Limmer). Insel-Bücherei 476. Leipzig: Insel Verlag, 1935.

Schmidt, Kurt Dietrich, ed. *Die Bekenntnisse und grundsätzlichen Äußerungen zur Kirchenfrage* (The confessions and fundamental statements on the church question). Vol. 2: *Das Jahr 1934* (The year 1934). Göttingen: Vandenhoeck & Ruprecht, 1935. *NL-Bibl.* 2 C 4. 2b.

Schnepel, Erich. *Als Christ und Kompanieführer im Weltkrieg: Das Fronterlebnis des Christen* (As a Christian and company leader in the world war: A Christian's experiences on the front). Berlin: Furche Verlag, 1938.

Schütz, Paul. *Warum ich noch ein Christ bin: Briefe an einen jungen Freund* (Why I am still a Christian: Letters to a young friend). Berlin: H. von Hugo und Schlotheim, 1937.

Sellin, Ernst. *Theologie des Alten Testaments* (Theology of the Old Testament). Leipzig: Quelle & Meyer, 1936.

Sheldon, Charles M. *In His Steps: What Would Jesus Do*? Philadelphia: American Baptist Publication Society, 1898.

Sperry, Willard L. "How My Mind Has Changed in This Decade." *Christian Century* (January 18, 1939): 82–84.

Steinmeyer, Franz Ludwig. *Der homiletische Gebrauch der Evangelischen-Altkirchlichen Perikopen* (The homiletic use of the Protestant–early church pericopes). Edited by M. Reyländer. Leipzig: Deichert, 1902.

Thomas à Kempis. *Imitatio Christi.* Vol. 2 of the 7 vol. edition of his works. Edited by Michael Josephus Pohl. Freiburg, 1904. *NL-Bibl.* 11. 8. Published in German as *Das Buch von der Nachfolge Christi*, translated by Johann Michael Sailer. Freiburg in Breisgau: Herder, 1916. Translated and edited by Joseph N. Tylenda as *The Imitation of Christ*, preface by Sally Cunneen, Vintage Spiritual Classics Original. New York: Random House, 1998.

Tillich, Paul. "The Social Functions of the Churches in Europe and America." *Social Research* 3 (1936): 90–104. Published in German as "Die Bedeutung der Kirche für die Gesellschaftsordnung in Europa und Amerika," in *Gesammelte Werke*, vol. 3: *Das religiöse Fundament des moralischen Handelns*, 107–19. Stuttgart: Evangelisches Verlagswerk, 1965.

Timmermans, Felix. *Bauernpsalm* (Farmers' psalm). Leipzig: Insel Verlag, 1936.

Troeltsch, Ernst. *Die Soziallehren der christlichen Kirchen und Gruppen.* Vol. 1 of *Gesammelte Schriften.* Tübingen: J. C. B. Mohr (Paul Siebeck), 1912. Translated by Olive Wyon as *The Social Teaching of the Christian Churches*, foreword by James Luther Adams, 2 vols. Louisville: Westminster John Knox, 1992.

Tyrrell, George. *Christianity at the Cross-Roads.* New York: Longmans, Green, 1909.

Vilmar, August Friedrich Christian. *Theologische Moral: Akademische Vorlesungen* (Theological morality: Academic lectures). 3 pts. Gütersloh: C. Chr. Isräel, 1871.

Waetzholdt, Wilhelm. *Dürer und seine Zeit* (Dürer and his era). Königsberg: 1936.

Wieman, Henry Nelson. "Some Blind Spots Removed." *Christian Century* (January 27, 1939): 116–18.

Wieman, Henry Nelson, and Walter Marshall Horton. *The Growth of Religion*. Chicago: Willett, Clark, 1938.

Witte, Karl, ed. *Nun freut euch lieben Christen gmein: Luthers Wort in täglichen Andachten zusammengestellt* (Now rejoice ye good Christians together: Luther's word summarized in daily devotions). Berlin: Wichern-Verlag, 1934. *NL-Bibl.* 5 F 23.

Zischka, Anton. *Wissenschaft bricht Monopole* (Science breaks monopoly). Leipzig: W. Goldman, 1938.

3. Literature Mentioned by Bonhoeffer's Correspondents

Barth, Karl. *Der Römerbrief.* 2nd printing of the new, rev. ed. of 1922. Munich: Chr. Kaiser, 1923. Translated from the 6th ed. by Edwyn C. Hoskyns as *The Epistle to the Romans,* 1933. London: Oxford University Press, 1960.

Bauer, Walter. *Griechisch-Deutsches Wörterbuch zu den Schriften des Neuen Testaments und der übrigen urchristlichen Literatur* (Greek-German lexicon of New Testament and other early Christian literature). 3rd fully revised ed. Berlin: A. Töpelmann, 1937.

Bernanos, Georges. *Der Abtrünnige.* Hellerau: J. Hegner, 1929. Translated from the French original by J. C. Whitehouse as *The Imposter.* Lincoln: University of Nebraska Press, 1999. Originally published as *L'imposture.* Paris: Plon, 1927.

———. *Die Sonne Satans: Ein Roman.* Hellerau: Jakob Hegner, 1927. Translated from the French original by J. C. Whitehouse as *Under Satan's Sun.* Lincoln: University of Nebraska Press, 2001. Originally published as *Sous le soleil de Satan.* Paris: Plon-Nourrit, 1926.

———. *Tagebuch eines Landpfarrers.* Vienna: Thomas Verlag Jakob Hegner, 1936. Translated from the French original by Pamela Morris as *The Diary of a Country Priest,* 1937. New York: Macmillan, 1962. Originally published as *Journal d'un curé de campagne.* Paris: Plon, 1936.

Calvin, Johannes. *Auslegung der Heiligen Schrift in deutscher Übersetzung.* Band V: *Die Psalmen, 2. Hälfte* (Exegesis of the Holy Scripture in German translation. Vol. 5: The psalms, pt. 2). Neukirchen: Verlag der Buchhandlung des Erziehungsvereins, 1930.

Diem, Hermann. *Warum Textpredigt? Predigten und Kritiken als Beitrag zur Lehre von der Predigt* (Why a textual sermon? Sermons and critiques as a contribution to a doctrine of the sermon). Munich: Chr. Kaiser, 1939.

Eichholz, Georg, ed. *Herr, tue meine Lippen auf: Eine Predigthilfe.* Band 1: *Die altkirchlichen Evangelien* (Lord, open my mouth: A preaching aid, vol. 1: The early church gospels). Wuppertal-Barmen: E. Müller, 1941.

Gollwitzer, Helmut. *Coena Domini: Die altlutherische Abendmahlslehre in ihrer Auseinandersetzung mit dem Calvinismus, dargestellt an der lutherischen Frühorthodoxie* (The heavens of God: The early Lutheran doctrine of the Eucharist in its confrontation with Calvinism, portrayed in the Lutheran early orthodoxy). Munich: Chr. Kaiser, 1937. New ed. with introduction by Dietrich Braun: Munich: Chr. Kaiser, 1988.

Harnack, Theodosius. *Die Kirche, Ihr Amt, Ihr Regiment: Grundlegende Sätze mit durchgehender Bezugnahme auf die symbolischen Bücher der lutherischen Kirche, zur Prüfung und Verständigung hinausgegeben* (The church, its office, its governance: Fundamental principles with ongoing reference to the symbolic books of the Lutheran Church, published for examination and understanding). Nuremberg: U. E. Sebald, 1862. Reprint, Gütersloh: C. Bertelsmann, 1934.

Kierkegaard, Søren. "'Zuerst Gottes Reich': Eine Art Novelle." In *Der Augenblick*, vol. 12 of *Gesammelte Werke*, 99. Translated from the Danish by Christoph Schrempf. Jena, 1909. Translated by Howard and Edna Hong as "'First the Kingdom of God': A Kind of Short Story," in *The Moment and Late Writings*, 233–36. Princeton, N.J.: Princeton University Press, 1998.

Kittel, Gerhard, ed. *Theologisches Wörterbuch zum Neuen Testament.* Stuttgart: W. Kohlhammer, 1933–. Translated and edited by Geoffrey W. Bromiley as *Theological Dictionary of the New Testament.* Grand Rapids, Mich.: Wm. B. Eerdmans, 1964–76.

Klabund [Alfred Henschke]. *Dumpfe Trommel und berauschtes Gong: Nachdichtungen chinesischer Kriegslyrik* (Thumping drum and dulled gong: Chinese war poetry). Leipzig: Insel, 1915. *NL-Bibl.* 8 C 28.

Rauschning, Hermann. *Die Revolution des Nihilismus: Kulisse und Wirklichkeit im Dritten Reich.* Zürich: Europa Verlag, 1938. Translated by E. W. Dickes as *The Revolution of Nihilism: Warning to the West.* New York: Alliance Book Corp., Longmans, Green, 1939.

Riecker, Otto. *Das evangelische Wort: Pneumatologie und Psychologie der evangelischen Bewegung; Träger, Rede und Versammlung* (The Protestant word: Pneumatology and psychology of the Protestant movement; Representatives, speech and meeting). Gütersloh: Bertelsmann, 1935.

Schöne, Wolfgang. *Die großen Meister der Niederländischen Malerie des 15. Jahrhunderts* (The great masters of 15th-century Dutch painting). Leipzig: H. Schmidt & C. Günther Pantheonverlag für Kunstwissenschaft, 1939. *NL-Bibl.* 9. 30.

Stuttgarter Jubiläumsbibel mit erklärenden Anmerkungen (Annotated Stuttgart Jubilee Bible). 1912. 2nd ed. Stuttgart: Württembergische Bibelanstalt, 1937.

Vilmar, August Friedrich Christian. *Lehrbuch der Pastoraltheologie: Nach dessen akademischen Vorlesungen* (Handbook of pastoral theology: According to his academic lectures). Edited by K. W. Piderit. Gütersloh: C. Bertelsmann,1872.

———. *Von der christlichen Kirchenzucht: Ein Beitrag zur Pastoraltheologie* (On Christian discipline: A contribution to pastoral theology). Marburg: N. C. Elwert, 1872.

Weber, Marianne. *Max Weber: Ein Lebensbild.* Tübingen: Mohr, 1926. *NL-Bibl.* 10. 67. Translated and edited by Harry Zohn as *Max Weber: A Biography.* New York: Wiley, 1975.

4. Literature Consulted by the Editors

Abromeit, Hans-Jürgen. *Das Geheimnis Christi: Dietrich Bonhoeffers erfahrungsbezogene Christologie* (The mystery of Christ: Dietrich Bonhoeffer's experientially based Christology). Neukichener Beiträge zur Systematischen Theologie 8. Neukirchen-Vluyn: Neukirchener Verlag, 1991.

Adam, Alfred. *Lehrbuch der Dogmengeschichte II: Mittelalter und Reformationszeit* (Handbook of dogmatic history II: The medieval and Reformation eras). 6th ed. Gütersloh: G. Mohn, 1992.

Adam, Uwe Dietrich. "Wie spontan war der Pogrom?" In *Der Judenpogrom 1938: Von der "Reichskristallnacht" zum Völkermord,* edited by Walter H. Pehle, 74–93. Frankfurt am Main: Fischer Taschenbuch Verlag, 1988. Translated as "How Spontaneous Was the Pogrom?" in *November 1938: From "Reichskristallnacht" to Genocide,* 73–94. New York: Berg, 1991.

Alston, Wallace, and Michael Welker, eds. "Dietrich Bonhoeffer: Previously Unpublished Letters to Paul Lehmann." *Theology Today* 55, no. 3 (1996): 289–98. A translation of this article appeared as "Dietrich Bonhoeffer: Bisher unveröffentliche Briefe an Paul Lehmann," *Evangelische Theologie* 56 (1996): 465–75.

Andresen, Carl, ed. *Handbuch der Dogmen- und Theologiegeschichte* (Handbook of dogmatic and theological history). Vol. 2: *Die Lehrentwicklung im Rahmen der Konfessionalität* (The development of dogma in the context of confessionality). Vol. 3: *Die Lehrentwicklung im Rahmen der Ökumenizität* (The development of dogma in the context of ecumenism). Unabridged ed. Göttingen: Vandenhoeck & Ruprecht, 1988.

Andersen, Dorothea, née Vibrans, G. Andersen, E. Bethge, and E. Vibrans, eds. *So ist es gewesen: Briefe im Kirchenkampf 1933–1942 von Gerhard Vibrans, aus seinem Familien- und Freundeskreis und von Dietrich Bonhoeffer* (So it was: Correspondence of Gerhard Vibrans, from his family, friends, and Dietrich Bonhoeffer, during the German Church Struggle). Supplement to *Dietrich Bonhoeffer Werke*. Gütersloh: Gütersloher Verlag, 1995.

Arad, Yitzhak, Israel Gutman, and Abraham Margaliot. *Documents on the Holocaust: Selected Sources on the Destruction of the Jews*. Lincoln: University of Nebraska Press, 1999.

Augustine. *Tractates on the Gospel of John*. Vol. 90 (55–111). Translated by John W. Rettig. The Fathers of the Church series. Washington, D.C.: Catholic University of America Press, 1988.

Aurelii Augustini. *Opera* (Works). Pars XVI, 1: *De trinitate* (The trinity). Libri XV (Libri I–XII). Edited by W. J. Mountain et al. Corpus Christianorum Series Latina 50. Turnhout, Belgium: Typographi Brepols, 1968.

Bagchi, David, and David C. Steinmetz, eds. *The Cambridge Companion to Reformation Theology*. New York: Cambridge University Press, 2005.

Barnett, Victoria. *For the Soul of the People: Protestant Protest under Hitler*. New York: Oxford University Press, 1992.

Baumgärtner, Raimund. *Weltanschauungskampf im Dritten Reich: Die Auseinandersetzung der Kirchen mit Alfred Rosenberg* (Struggle over worldview in the Third Reich: The churches' dispute with Alfred Rosenberg). Veröffentlichungen der Kommission für Zeitgeschichte, Reihe B, Forschungen 22. Mainz: Matthias-Grünewald-Verlag, 1977.

Beckmann, Joachim, ed. *Kirchliches Jahrbuch für die Evangelische Kirche in Deutschland 1933–1944* (Church yearbook for the Evangelical Church in Germany, 1933–1944). 60–71 Jahrgang. Gütersloh: C. Bertelsmann, 1976.

Die Bekenntnisschriften der evangelisch-lutherischen Kirche (The confessional texts of the Evangelical-Lutheran church). Published in the anniversary year of the Augsburg Confession 1930. 2 vols. Göttingen: Vandenhoeck & Ruprecht, 1930. (Bd. II: NL-Bibl. 2 C 3) [Bonhoeffer owned the 2-vol. 1st ed.]. See also Kolb and Wengert, *Book of Concord*.

Bell, George K. A. "Die Kirche und die Widerstandsbewegung." *Evangelische Theologie* 17 (1957): 289–305. Published in English as "The Church and the Resistance Movement," in Bonhoeffer's *Gesammelte Schriften*, edited by Eberhard Bethge, 1:399–413.

Benz, Wolfgang. "Der Novemberpogrom 1938." In *Die Juden in Deutschland 1933–1945: Leben unter nationalsozialistischer Herrschaft* (The Jews in Germany, 1933–1945: Life under National Socialist rule), edited by Wolfgang Benz, 499–544. Munich: Beck, 1989.

———. "Der Rückfall in die Barbarei: Bericht über den Pogrom." In *Der Judenpogrom 1938: Von der "Reichskristallnacht" zum Völkermord*, edited by

Walter H. Pehle, 13–51. Frankfurt am Main: Fischer Taschenbuch Verlag, 1988. Translated as "The Relapse into Barbarism," in *November 1938: From "Reichskristallnacht" to Genocide,* 1–43. New York: Berg, 1991.

Bernard of Clairvaux. *Selected Works.* Translated by Gillian Rosemary Evans. Edited by Emilie Griffin. Classics of Western Spirituality. Mahwah, N.J.: Paulist Press, 1987.

Bertheau, Carl. "Kirchenjahr" (Church year). In *Realenzyklopädie für protestantische Theologie und Kirche,* 3rd ed., 10:393–98. Leipzig: Hinrichs, 1901.

Besier, Gerhard. "Die Gründung der Kirchlichen Hochschule Berlin 1935/45 und ihre 'Väter'" (The founding of the Church College in Berlin 1935–45 and its "fathers"). In *Berlinische Lebensbilde: Wissenschaftspolitik in Berlin; Minister, Beamte, Ratgeber* (Berlin life portraits: Academic politics in Berlin; Minister, civil servant, advisor), edited by Wolfgang Treue and Karlfried Gründer, 325–36. Berlin: Colloquium Verlag, 1987.

Bethge, Eberhard. *Dietrich Bonhoeffer: Theologe—Christ—Zeitgenosse; Eine Biographie.* Munich: Chr. Kaiser, 1967. Translated by Eric Mosbacher, Peter Ross, Betty Ross, Frank Clarke, and William Glen-Doepel as *Dietrich Bonhoeffer: A Biography,* under the editorship of Edwin Robertson. Revised and edited by Victoria J. Barnett, based on the 7th German ed. Minneapolis: Fortress Press, 2000.

———. "Dietrich Bonhoeffer und die Juden." In *Die Juden und Martin Luther, Martin Luther und die Juden: Geschichte, Wirkungsgeschichte, Herausforderung,* 2nd ed., edited by Heinz Kremers, with Leonore Siegele-Wenschkewitz and Bertold Klappert, 211–48. Neukirchen-Vluyn: Neukirchener Verlag, 1987. Also in *Ethik im Ernstfall,* edited by Wolfgang Huber and Ilse Tödt, 171–214. Munich: Chr. Kaiser, 1982. Translated as "Dietrich Bonhoeffer and the Jews," in *Ethical Responsibility: Bonhoeffer's Legacy to the Churches,* edited by John D. Godsey and Geffrey Kelly, 43–96. New York: E. Mellen, 1981.

———. *Erstes Gebot und Zeitgeschichte: Aufsätze und Reden, 1980–1990* (The first commandment and contemporary history: Essays and speeches). Munich: Chr. Kaiser, 1990.

———. "Mein Freund Dietrich Bonhoeffer." In *Theologie und Freundschaft: Wechselwirkungen; Eberhard Bethge und Dietrich Bonhoeffer,* by Eberhard Bethge, Christian Gremmels, and Wolfgang Huber, 13–28. Gütersloh: Chr. Kaiser/Gütersloher Verlagshaus, 1994. A somewhat revised translation appears in *Friendship and Resistance: Essays on Dietrich Bonhoeffer,* by Eberhard Bethge. Grand Rapids, Mich.: Wm. B. Eerdmans, 1995.

———. "One of the Silent Bystanders? Bonhoeffer on November 9, 1938." In *Friendship and Resistance: Essays on Dietrich Bonhoeffer,* by Eberhard Bethge, 58–71. Grand Rapids, Mich.: Wm. B. Eerdmans, 1995.

———. "Der Ort des Gebets in Leben und Theologie Dietrich Bonhoeffers" (The place of prayer in the life and theology of Dietrich Bonhoeffer). In *Bekennen und Widerstehen: Aufsätze, Reden, Gespräche,* (Confession and resistance: Essays, speeches, conversations), by Eberhard Bethge, 159–77. Munich: Chr. Kaiser, 1984.

Bethge, Eberhard, Renate Bethge, and Christian Gremmels, eds. *Dietrich Bonhoeffer: Sein Leben in Bildern und Texten.* Munich: Chr. Kaiser, 1989. Translated by John Bowden as *Dietrich Bonhoeffer: A Life in Pictures.* London: SCM; Philadelphia: Fortress Press, 1986. Translated by Brian McNeil as *Dietrich Bonhoeffer: A Life in Pictures,* edited by Renate Bethge and Christian Gremmels, abridged, centenary ed. Minneapolis: Fortress Press, 2006.

Bethge, Eberhard, and Ronald C. D. Jasper, eds. *An der Schwelle zum gespaltenen Europa: Der Briefwechsel zwischen George Bell und Gerhard Leibholz 1939–1951* (On the cusp of a divided Europe: The correspondence between George Bell and Gerhard Leibholz). Stuttgart: Kreuz-Verlag, 1974.

Bieritz, Karl-Hinrich. *Das Kirchenjahr: Feste, Gedenk- und Feiertage in Geschichte und Gegenwart* (The church year: Festivals, memorials, and holidays in past and present). Munich: Beck, 1988.

Block, Eduard. "Kirchenkampf in Schlawe" (Church Struggle in Schlawe). In *Der Kreis Schlawe: Ein pommersches Heimatbuch* (The district of Schlawe: A book of the Pomeranian homeland), edited by Manfred Vollack, 1:332–36. Husum: Husum Druck- und Verlagsgesellschaft, 1986.

Bobert-Stützel, Sabine. *Dietrich Bonhoeffers Pastoraltheologie* (Dietrich Bonhoeffer's pastoral theology). Gütersloh: Chr. Kaiser, 1995.

Böll, Heinrich. "Brief an einen jungen Katholiken" (Letter to a young Catholic) (1958). In Boll, *Zur Verteidigung der Waschküchen: Schriften und Reden 1952–1959* (In defense of the laundries: Essays and speeches, 1952–1959), by Heinrich Boll, 257–72. Munich: Deutscher Taschenbuch Verlag, 1985.

Bonhoeffer, Dietrich. *Dietrich Bonhoeffer Werke.* Edited by Eberhard Bethge et al. 17 vols. Munich: Chr. Kaiser; Gütersloh: Gütersloher Verlagshaus, 1986–99. Translated as *Dietrich Bonhoeffer Works.* Victoria J. Barnett, Wayne Whitson Floyd Jr., and Barbara Wojhoski, general editors. 17 vols. Minneapolis: Fortress Press, 1996–.

Vol. 1: *Sanctorum Communio: Eine dogmatische Untersuchung zur Soziologie der Kirche.* Edited by Joachim von Soosten. Munich: Chr. Kaiser, 1986. Translated by Reinhard Krauss and Nancy Lukens as *Sanctorum Communio: A Theological Study of the Sociology of the Church,* edited by Clifford J. Green. Minneapolis: Fortress Press, 1998.

Vol. 2: *Akt und Sein: Transzendentalphilosophie und Ontologie in der systematischen Theologie.* Edited by Hans-Richard Reuter. Munich: Chr. Kaiser,

1988. Translated by Martin Rumscheidt as *Act and Being: Transcendental Philosophy and Ontology in Systematic Theology*, edited by Wayne Whitson Floyd Jr. Minneapolis: Fortress Press, 1996.

Vol. 3: *Schöpfung und Fall: Theologische Auslegung von Genesis 1–3.* Edited by Martin Rüter and Ilse Tödt. Munich: Chr. Kaiser, 1989. Translated by Douglas Stephen Bax as *Creation and Fall: A Theological Exposition of Genesis 1–3*, edited by John W. de Gruchy. Minneapolis: Fortress Press, 1996.

Vol. 4: *Nachfolge.* Edited by Martin Kuske and Ilse Tödt. Munich: Chr. Kaiser, 1989; 2nd ed., Gütersloh: Chr. Kaiser/Gütersloher Verlagshaus, 1994. Translated by Barbara Green and Reinhard Krauss as *Discipleship*, edited by Geffrey B. Kelly and John D. Godsey. Minneapolis: Fortress Press, 2001.

Vol. 5: *Gemeinsames Leben: Das Gebetbuch der Bibel.* Edited by Gerhard Ludwig Müller and Albrecht Schönherr. Munich: Chr. Kaiser, 1987. Translated by Daniel W. Bloesch and James H. Burtness as *Life Together* and *Prayerbook of the Bible*, edited by Geffrey B. Kelly. Minneapolis: Fortress Press, 1996.

Vol. 6: *Ethik.* Edited by Ilse Tödt, Heinz Eduard Tödt, Ernst Feil, and Clifford Green. Munich: Chr. Kaiser, 1992; 2nd ed., Gütersloh: Chr. Kaiser/Gütersloher Verlagshaus, 1998. Translated by Reinhard Krauss and Charles West, with Douglas W. Stott, as *Ethics*, edited by Clifford J. Green. Minneapolis: Fortress Press, 2005.

Vol. 7: *Fragmente aus Tegel.* Edited by Renate Bethge and Ilse Tödt. Munich: Chr. Kaiser, 1994. Translated by Nancy Lukens as *Fiction from Tegel Prison*, edited by Clifford J. Green. Minneapolis: Fortress Press, 2000.

Vol. 8: *Widerstand und Ergebung* (Resistance and submission). Edited by Christian Gremmels, Eberhard Bethge, and Renate Bethge, with Ilse Tödt. Gütersloh: Chr. Kaiser/Gütersloher Verlagshaus, 1998. Translated by Isabel Best, Lisa Dahill, Reinhard Krauss, and Nancy Lukens, with Barbara and Martin Rumscheidt and Douglas W. Stott, as *Letters and Papers from Prison*, edited by John W. de Gruchy. Minneapolis: Fortress Press, 2010.

Vol. 9: *Jugend und Studium: 1918–1927.* Edited by Hans Pfeifer, with Clifford Green and Carl-Jürgen Kaltenborn. Munich: Chr. Kaiser, 1986. Translated by Mary Nebelsick, with Douglas W. Stott, as *The Young Bonhoeffer: 1918–1927*, edited by Paul Matheny, Clifford J. Green, and Marshall Johnson. Minneapolis: Fortress Press, 2001.

Vol. 10: *Barcelona, Berlin, Amerika: 1928–1931.* Edited by Reinhard Staats and Hans Christoph von Hase, with Holger Roggelin and Matthias Wünsche. Munich: Chr. Kaiser, 1991. 2nd ed., Gütersloh: Chr. Kaiser/Gütersloher Verlagshaus, 2005. Translated by Douglas W. Stott as *Barcelona, Berlin, New York: 1928–1931*, edited by Clifford J. Green. Minneapolis: Fortress Press, 2008.

Vol. 11: *Ökumene, Universität, Pfarramt: 1931–1932* (Ecumenical, academic, and pastoral work: 1931–1932). Edited by Eberhard Amelung and Christoph Strohm. Gütersloh: Chr. Kaiser, 1994.

Vol. 12: *Berlin: 1932–1933*. Edited by Carsten Nicolaisen and Ernst-Albert Scharffenorth. Gütersloh: Chr. Kaiser/Gütersloher Verlagshaus, 1997. Translated by Isabel Best and David Higgins, with Douglas W. Stott, as *Berlin: 1932–1933*, edited by Larry L. Rasmussen. Minneapolis: Fortress Press, 2009.

Vol. 13: *London: 1933–1935*. Edited by Hans Goedeking, Martin Heimbucher, and Hans-Walter Schleicher. Gütersloh: Chr. Kaiser/Gütersloher Verlagshaus, 1994. Translated by Isabel Best as *London: 1933–1935*, edited by Keith Clements. Minneapolis: Fortress Press, 2007.

Vol. 14: *Illegale Theologenausbildung: Finkenwalde 1935–1937* (Theological education at Finkenwalde: 1935–1937). Edited by Otto Dudzus and Jürgen Henkys, with Sabine Bobert-Stützel, Dirk Schulz, and Ilse Tödt. Gütersloh: Chr. Kaiser/Gütersloher Verlagshaus, 1996.

Vol. 15: *Illegale Theologenausbildung: Sammelvikariate: 1937–1940*. Edited by Dirk Schulz. Gütersloh: Chr. Kaiser/Gütersloher Verlagshaus, 1998. Translated by Victoria J. Barnett, Claudia Bergmann, Peter Frick, and Scott Moore, with Douglas W. Stott, as *Theological Education Underground: 1937–1940*, edited by Victoria J. Barnett. Minneapolis: Fortress Press, 2011.

Vol. 16: *Konspiration und Haft: 1940–1945*. Edited by Jørgen Glenthøj, Ulrich Kabitz, and Wolf Krötke. Gütersloh: Chr. Kaiser/Gütersloher Verlagshaus, 1996. Translated by Lisa E. Dahill, with Douglas W. Stott, as *Conspiracy and Imprisonment: 1940–1945*, edited by Mark S. Brocker. Minneapolis: Fortress Press, 2006.

Vol. 17: *Register und Ergänzungen* (Index and supplements). Edited by Herbert Anzinger and Hans Pfeifer, assisted by Waltraud Anzinger and Ilse Tödt. Gütersloh: Chr. Kaiser/Gütersloher Verlagshaus, 1999.

———. *Gesammelte Schriften* (Collected writings). Edited by Eberhard Bethge. 6 vols. Munich: Chr. Kaiser, 1958–74. English selections edited by Edwin H. Robertson, translated by Edwin H. Robertson and John Bowden in *No Rusty Swords* (New York: Harper & Row, 1965), *The Way to Freedom* (New York: Harper & Row, 1966), and *True Patriotism* (New York: Harper & Row, 1973).

———. *Predigten—Auslegungen—Meditationen 1925–1945* (Sermons, exegeses, meditations). 2 vols. Edited by Otto Dudzus. Munich: Chr. Kaiser, 1984, 1985.

———. "Protestantismus ohne Reformation." *Unterwegs* 2, no. 1 (1948): 3–17.

———. *Schöpfung und Fall: Versuchung.* Munich: Chr. Kaiser, 1968. Translated by John C. Fletcher and Kathleen Downham as *Creation and Fall: Temptation.* New York: Macmillan, 1959.

———. *Versuchung.* Edited and published by Eberhard Bethge. Munich: Chr. Kaiser, 1953. Translated by Kathleen Downham as *Temptation.* London: SCM Press, 1961.

———. *Widerstand und Ergebung: Briefe und Aufzeichnungen aus der Haft.* Edited by Eberhard Bethge. Munich: Chr. Kaiser, 1951; expanded eds., 1970, 1985. Translated by Reginald H. Fuller as *Letters and Papers from Prison,* edited by Eberhard Bethge; translation revised by Frank Clarke et al., additional material translated by John Bowden for the enlarged edition published in London. London: SCM, 1971; New York: Macmillan, 1972; New York: Simon & Schuster, 1995.

———. *Zettelnotizen fur eine "Ethik"* (Working notes for an "*Ethics*"). Supplementary vol. to *Ethik, DBW* 6. Edited by Ilse Tödt. Gütersloh: Chr. Kaiser/ Gütersloher Verlagshaus, 1993.

Büchmann, Georg. *Geflügelte Worte: Der Zitatenschatz des deutschen Volkes* (Familiar quotations: The treasury of sayings of the German people). 33rd printing, newly revised by W. Hofmann. Frankfurt am Main: Haude & Spener, 1981.

Busch, Eberhard. *Karl Barths Lebenslauf nach seinen Briefen und autobiographischen Texten.* 4th ed. Munich: Chr. Kaiser, 1975. Translated by John Bowden as *Karl Barth: His Life from Letters and Autobiographical Texts.* Grand Rapids, Mich.: Wm. B. Eerdmans, 1994.

———. *Unter dem Bogen des einen Bundes: Karl Barth und die Juden 1933–1945* (Under the arc of the one covenant: Karl Barth and the Jews, 1933–1945). Neukirchen-Vluyn: Neukirchener, 1996.

Claudius, Matthias. *ASMUS omnia sua Secum portans oder Sämtliche Werke des Wandsbecker Boten* (The complete works of Asmus, or collected works of the Wandsbeck Messenger). With an introduction by Peter Suhrkamp. Berlin: S. Fischer, 1941. New printing of the 1st ed. (1775–1812): Munich: Winkler, 1976.

Coffin, Henry Sloane. *Religion Yesterday and Today.* Nashville: Cokesbury Press, 1940.

Craig, Gordon A. *Germany, 1866–1945.* New York: Oxford University Press, 1978. Published in German as *Deutsche Geschichte 1866–1945: Vom Norddeutschen Bund bis zum Ende des Dritten Reiches.* Munich: Beck, 1981.

Cullen, Countee. *The Black Christ and Other Poems.* New York: G. P. Putnam's Sons, 1929.

Dalcho, Frederick. *A Historical Account of the Protestant Episcopal Church in South Carolina.* 1820. Reprint, Ithaca, N.Y.: Cornell University Library, 2009.

Dostoyevsky, Fyodor Mikhaylovich. *The Brothers Karamazov.* New York: Knopf, 1992. Distributed by Random House.

———. *The Idiot.* Translated by Constance Garnett. New York: Modern Library, 1962. Published in German as *Der Idiot.* Munich: R. Piper Verlag, 1922.

Dürig, Walter. *Geburtstag und Namenstag: Eine liturgiegeschichtliche Studie* (Birthday and name day: A historical liturgical study). Munich: K. Zink, 1954.

Eichholz, Georg. *Herr tue meine Lippen auf: Eine Predigthilfe* (Lord, open my mouth: A preaching aid). Vol. 1. Wuppertal-Barmen: E. Müller, 1941.

Elisabeth of Berlin. DVD. Directed by Steven D. Martin. Produced by Vital Visuals, Inc. 2008.

Emerson, Ralph Waldo. *Selected Writings of Ralph Waldo Emerson.* Edited by William H. Gilman. With a new introduction by Charles Johnson. New York: Signet Classic, 2003.

Erdmann, Karl Dietrich, ed. *Die Zeit der Weltkriege* (The era of the world wars). Vol. 4 of *Handbuch der deutschen Geschichte* (Handbook of German history). Edited by Bruno Gebhardt and Herbert Grundmann. 9th newly revised ed. Vol. 4. Stuttgart: Union-Verlag, 1976.

Evangelisches Gesangbuch (Protestant hymnal). Berlin: Evangelische Haupt-Bibelgesellschaft; Leipzig: Evangelische Verlagsanstalt, 1993.

Feil, Ernst. "Bishop Edmund Gibson as Author of the Letter on 'Negro Baptism' in Bonhoeffer's America Report of 1939." *Union Seminary Quarterly Review* 54 (2000): 87–96.

———. *Die Theologie Dietrich Bonhoeffers: Hermeneutik, Christologie und Weltverständnis.* Vol. 6 of *Gesellschaft und Theologie: Systematische Beiträge.* Munich: Chr. Kaiser; Mainz: Matthias-Grünewald-Verlag, 1971. Edition abridged by author and translated by Martin Rumscheidt as *The Theology of Dietrich Bonhoeffer.* Minneapolis: Fortress Press, 1985.

Fest, Joachim C. *Hitler: Eine Biographie.* Expanded new edition with a preface. Berlin: Ullstein, 1995. Translated by Richard and Clara Winston as *Hitler: A Biography.* New York, Harcourt Brace Jovanovich, 1974.

———. *Staatsstreich: Der lange Weg zum 20. Juli.* Berlin: Siedler, 1994. Translated by Bruce Little as *Plotting Hitler's Death: The Story of the German Resistance.* New York: Metropolitan Books, 1996.

Fox, Richard Wightman. *Reinhold Niebuhr: A Biography.* New York: Pantheon Books, 1985.

Freud, Sigmund. *Gesammelte Werke, chronologisch geordnet.* Edited by Anna Freud et al. 18 vols. Frankfurt am Main: S. Fischer, 1968–78. Published in English as *The Standard Edition of the Complete Psychological Works of Sigmund Freud,* translated from the German under the general editorship of James Strachey, in collaboration with Anna Freud, assisted by Alix Strachey and Alan Tyson. London: Hogarth Press; Institute of Psychoanalysis, 1962–66.

Friedländer, Max J. *Early Netherlandish Painting.* Translated by Heinz Norden. Preface by Erwin Panofsky. Comments and notes by Nicole Veronee-Verhaegen. Vol. 6, pt. 1. New York: Praeger, 1971. Originally published as *Die Altniederländische Malerei.* Berlin: P. Cassirer, 1934.

Friedrich, Karl Josef. *Die Gemälde Ludwig Richters* (The paintings of Ludwig Richter). Berlin: Deutscher Verein für Kunstwissenschaft, 1937.

Gailus, Manfred. *Elisabeth Schmitz und ihre Denkschrift gegen die Judenverfolgung: Konturen einer vergessenen Biografie (1893–1977)* (Elisabeth Schmitz and her memorandum against the Jewish persecution: Contours of a forgotten biography). Berlin: Wichern Verlag, 2008.

Geismar, Eduard. *Søren Kierkegaard: Seine Lebensentwicklung und seine Wirksamkeit als Schriftsteller* (Søren Kierkegaard: His life and effect as a writer). Göttingen: Vandenhoeck & Ruprecht, 1929.

Genizi, Haim. *American Apathy: The Plight of Christian Refugees from Nazism.* Ramat-Gan, Israel: Bar-Ilan University Press, 1983.

Gerlach, Wolfgang. *Als die Zeugen schwiegen: Bekennende Kirche und die Juden.* Mit einem Vorwort von Eberhard Bethge. Studien zu Kirche und Israel 10. Berlin: Institut Kirche und Judentum, 1987. Translated by Victoria Barnett as *And the Witnesses Were Silent: The Confessing Church and the Jews.* Lincoln: University of Nebraska Press, 2000.

Gerlach-Prätorius, Angelika. *Die Kirche vor der Eidesfrage: Die Diskussion um den Pfarrereid im "Dritten Reich"* (The church and the loyalty oath question: The discussion about the pastors' oath during the "Third Reich"). Arbeiten zur Geschichte des Kirchenkampfes 18. Göttingen: Vandenhoeck & Ruprecht, 1967.

Gesetzblatt der Deutschen Evangelischen Kirche (Legal gazette of the German Evangelical Church). Ausgabe A (Reich) for 1935, 1937, and 1939. Berlin: Deutschen Evangelischen Kirchenkanzlei, 1935, 1937, and 1939.

Gill, Theodore. *Memo for a Movie: A Short Life of Dietrich Bonhoeffer.* New York: Macmillan, 1971.

Glenthøj, Jørgen. "Die Eideskrise in der Bekennenden Kirche 1938 und Dietrich Bonhoeffer" (The 1938 crisis about the oath in the Confessing Church and Dietrich Bonhoeffer). *Zeitschrift für Kirchengeschichte* 96 (1985): 377–94.

Goertz, Hans-Jürgen. *Innere und äussere Ordnung in der Theologie Thomas Müntzers* (Internal and external order in the theology of Thomas Müntzer). Leiden: E. J. Brill, 1967.

Goethe, Johann Wolfgang von. *Selected Verse: Dual-Language Edition with Plain Prose Translations of Each Poem.* Introduction by David Luke. New York: Penguin Putnam, 1964. Reprint, New York: Penguin Classics, 1986.

Graff, Gerti, et al., eds. *Unterwegs zur mündigen Gemeinde: Die evangelische Kirche im Nationalsozialismus am Beispiel der Gemeinde Dahlem; Bilder und Texte einer Ausstellung im Friedenszentrum Martin-Niemöller-Haus Berlin-Dahlem* (On the road to a congregation come of age: The Protestant church during National Socialism and the example of the Dahlem parish; Pictures and texts of an exhibition at the Martin Niemöller House and peace center in Berlin-Dahlem). 2nd ed. Berlin: Alektor Verlag, 1989.

Gregory I, Pope. *Forty Gospel Homilies.* Translated from the Latin by David Hurst. Cistercian Studies Series 123. Kalamazoo, Mich.: Cistercian Publications, 1990.

Greschat, Martin, ed. *Zwischen Widerspruch und Widerstand: Texte zur Gedenkschrift der Bekennenden Kirche an Hitler (1936)* (Between protest and resistance: Texts on the 1936 Confessing Church memorandum to Hitler). Studienbücher zur kirchlichen Zeitgeschichte 6. Munich: Chr. Kaiser, 1987.

Härter, Ilse. "Zuerst kamen die Brüder . . . !" (First came the brothers!) In *Predigtamt ohne Pfarramt? Die "Illegalen" im Kirchenkampf* (Preaching office without ministry? The "illegals" in the church struggle), edited by Karl-Adolf Bauer, with an introduction by Eberhard Bethge, 12–22. Neukirchen-Vluyn: Neukirchener, 1993.

Hauschild, Wolf-Dieter. "Geist/Heiliger Geist/Geistesgaben IV: Dogmengeschichtlich" (Spirit, Holy Spirit, gifts of the spirit IV in the history of dogma). In *Theologische Realenzyklopädie,* 12:196–217. Berlin: W. de Gruyter, 1984.

Heidelberg Confession. In the *Internet Modern History Sourcebook: Reformation Europe,* http://www.fordham.edu/halsall/mod/modsbook02.html.

Helmreich, Ernst Christian. *The German Churches under Hitler: Background, Struggle, and Epilogue.* Detroit: Wayne State University Press, 1979.

Herbert, Karl. *Der Kirchenkampf: Historie oder bleibendes Erbe?* (The Church Struggle: History or enduring heritage?) Frankfurt am Main: Evangelisches Verlagswerk, 1985.

Heschel, Susannah. *The Aryan Jesus: Christian Theologians and the Bible in Nazi Germany.* Princeton, N.J.: Princeton University Press, 2008.

Hilberg, Raul. *Perpetrators, Victims, Bystanders: The Jewish Catastrophe, 1933–1945.* New York: Harper Collins, 1992. Translated by Hans Günter Holl as *Täter, Opfer, Zuschauer: Die Vernichtung der Juden 1933–1945.* Frankfurt am Main: S. Fischer, 1992.

Hildebrand, Klaus. *Das vergangene Reich: Deutsche Außenpolitik von Bismarck bis Hitler 1871–1945* (The past Reich: German foreign policy from Bismarck to Hitler, 1871–1945). Stuttgart: Deutsche Verlags-Anstalt, 1995.

Hildebrandt, Franz. "Kirche und Recht—vor dreißig Jahren: Aus einer unveröffentlichten Vorkriegsstudie über 'Evangelium und Humanität'" (Church and law—30 years ago: From an unpublished prewar study of "Gospel and Humanity"). In *Die moderne Demokratie und ihr Recht: Modern Constitutionalism and Democracy; Festschrift für Gerhard Leibholz*, edited by Karl Dietrich Bracher, vol. 1, 499–505. Tübingen: Mohr-Siebeck, 1966.

Hockenos, Matthew D. *A Church Divided: German Protestants Confront the Nazi Past.* Bloomington: Indiana University Press, 2004.

Hofer, Walther. *Der Nationalsozialismus: Dokumente 1933–1945* (National Socialism: Documents, 1933–1945). Rev. ed. Frankfurt am Main: Fischer Taschenbuch Verlag, 1982.

Hohlfeld, Johannes, ed. *Dokumente der Deutschen Politik: Geschichte von 1848 bis zur Gegenwart, ein Quellenwerk für die politische Bildung und staatsbürgerliche Erziehung* (Documents of German politics: History from 1848 to the present). Vol. 5: *Die Zeit der nationalsozialistischen Diktatur 1933–1945: Deutschland im zweiten Weltkrieg 1939–1945* (The era of the National Socialist dictatorship, 1933–1945: Germany in the Second World War, 1939–45). Berlin: Dokumenten-Verlag H. Wendler, 1952–55.

Huxley, Thomas Henry. *Evolution and Ethics.* Edited by Michael Ruse. Princeton, N.J.: Princeton University Press, 2009.

Iwand, Hans Joachim. *Theologie in der Zeit: Lebensabriß und Briefdokumentation, Bibliographie* (Theology in that era: Biographical overview and documented correspondence, bibliography). Edited by Peter Sänger und Dieter Pauly. Munich: Chr. Kaiser, 1992.

———. *Von der Gemeinschaft christlichen Lebens* (On the fellowship of Christian life). Munich: Chr. Kaiser, 1937.

James, William. *Writings, 1902–1910.* New York: Literary Classics of the United States, 1987.

Jensen, Hans Werner. "Gemeinsames Leben." In *Begegnungen mit Dietrich Bonhoeffer*, edited by Wolf-Dieter Zimmermann, 134–38. Munich: Chr. Kaiser, 1969. Translated by Käthe Gregor Smith as "Life Together," in Zimmermann, *I Knew Dietrich Bonhoeffer*, 152–56.

Kersting, Andreas. *Kirchenordnung und Widerstand: Der Kampf um den Aufbau der Bekennenden Kirche der altpreußischen Union aufgrund des Dahlemer Notrechts von 1934–1937* (Church law and resistance: The struggle to found the Confessing Church in the Old Prussian Union on the basis of the Dahlem emergency law of 1934–1937). Heidelberger Untersuchungen zu Widerstand, Judenverfolgung und Kirchenkampf im Dritten Reich 4. Gütersloh: Chr. Kaiser, 1994.

Klän, Werner. "An der Wegscheide: Die 'Bruderschaft junger Theologen in Pommern' zwischen 'Illegalität' und 'Legalisierung' 1936–1939" (At the crossroads: The "brotherhood of young theologians in Pomerania" between "illegality" and "legalization," 1963–1939). In *Der Kirchenkampf im Osten und in den deutschsprachigen Kirchen Osteuropas* (The Church Struggle in the east and in the west German-speaking churches of eastern Europe), edited by Peter Maser, Kirche im Osten Monographiereihe 22, 136–58. Göttingen: Vandenhoeck & Ruprecht, 1992.

Klemperer, Klemens von. *German Resistance against Hitler: The Search for Allies Abroad.* New York: Oxford University Press, 1992. Translated by Klaus Kochmann as *Die verlassenen Verschwörer: Der deutsche Widerstand auf der Suche nach Verbündeten.* Berlin: Siedler, 1994.

Kolb, Robert, and Timothy J. Wengert, eds. *The Book of Concord: The Confessions of the Evangelical Lutheran Church.* Translation of *Die Bekenntnisschriften der evangelisch-lutherischen Kirche* by Charles Arand, Eric Gritsch, Robert Kolb, William Russell, James Schaaf, Jane Strohl, and Timothy J. Wengert. Minneapolis: Fortress Press, 2000.

Köstlin, Julius. *Martin Luther: Sein Leben und seine Schriften* (Martin Luther: His life and his writings). Completed after the author's death by Gustav Kawerau. 2 vols. Berlin: A. Duncker, 1903.

Leibholz-Bonhoeffer, Sabine. *Vergangen, erlebt, überwunden: Schicksale der Familie Bonhoeffer.* Gütersloh: Gütersloher Verlag, 1968. Translated as *The Bonhoeffers: Portrait of a Family.* New York: St. Martin's Press, 1972.

Lejeune, Robert. *Christoph Blumhardt and His Message.* Translated by Hela Ehrlich and Nicoline Maas. Edited and with an introduction by Robert Lejeune. Rifton, N.Y.: Plough, 1963. Originally published as *Christoph Blumhardt und seine Botschaft.* Zurich: Rotapfel-Verlag, 1938.

Ludwig, Hartmut. "'Christen dürfen zu diesem Verbrechen nicht schweigen': Zum 100. Geburtstag von Pfarrer Dr. Adolf Freudenberg, Sekretär der Flüchtlingshilfe des ÖRK im Zweiten Weltkrieg" ("Christians may not be silent about this crime": On the 100th birthday of Pastor Adolf Freudenberg, secretary for refugee aid at the World Council of Churches during the Second World War). *Ökumenische Rundschau* 43 (1994): 260–74.

———. "Die 'Illegalen' im Kirchenkampf" (The "illegals" in the Church Struggle). In *Predigtamt ohne Pfarramt? Die "Illegalen" im Kirchenkampf* (Preaching office without ministry? The "illegals" during the Church Struggle), edited by Karl-Adolf Bauer, with an introduction by Eberhard Bethge, 23–70. Neukirchen-Vluyn: Neukirchener, 1993.

Luther, Martin. *Briefwechsel.* Edited by E. L. Enders. 1912 ed. Vol. 14. Frankfurt am Main: Schriften-Niederlage des Evangelischen Vereins, 1884–1978. Selected letters translated in *Luther's Works,* vols. 48–50. Philadelphia: Fortress Press, 1963–75.

———. *Luthers Vorlesung über den Römerbrief 1515/1516* . Edited by Johannes Ficker. 2 vols. in 1. Vol. 2: *Die Scholien (Anfänge der reformatorischen Bibelauslegung 1).* 3rd unrevised edition. Leipzig: Dieterich, 1925. *NL-Bibl.* 1 D 24. Translated as *Luther's Lectures on Romans,* Vol. 25 of *Luther's Works.* Philadelphia: Fortress Press, 1972.

———. *Werke: Kritische Gesamtausgabe.* Weimarer Ausgabe (WA). 58 vols. Weimar: H. Böhlau, 1883–2009. Translated as *Luther's Works,* vols. 1–30, edited by Jaroslav Pelikan, vols. 31–55 edited by Helmut Lehmann. Complete works on CD-ROM. Minneapolis: Fortress Press; St. Louis: Concordia, 2002.

The Lutheran Hymnal. St. Louis: Concordia, 1941.

Luz, Ulrich. *Das Evangelium nach Matthäus.* 1. Teilband (Mt. 1–7). Evangelisch-Katholischer Kommentar zum Neuen Testament I/1. Zürich: Benzinger; Neukirchen-Vluyn: Neukirchener Verlag, 1989. Translated by James E. Crouch as *Matthew: A Commentary,* edited by Helmut Koester, 3 vols., Hermeneia: A Critical and Historical Commentary on the Bible. Minneapolis: Augsburg Fortress, 2001.

Maclear, J. F., ed. *Church and State in the Modern Age: A Documentary History.* New York: Oxford University Press, 1995.

Maechler, Winfried. *Ein Christ in den Wirren des 20. Jahrhunderts: Stationen, Reisen, Einsichten* (A Christian in the turmoil of the 20th century: Stops, travels, insights). Stuttgart: Radius Verlag, 1991.

Maltusch, Gottfried. "Beim Brand der Synagogen." In Zimmermann, *Begegnungen mit Dietrich Bonhoeffer.* Translated by Käthe Gregor Smith as "When the Synagogues Burnt," in Zimmermann, *I Knew Dietrich Bonhoeffer,* 150–51.

Mann, Thomas. "Vom kommenden Sieg der Demokratie." In *Gesammelte Werke in 13 Bänden,* edited by H. Bürgin und P. de Mendelssohn, 11:910–41. Frankfurt am Main: S. Fischer, 1960–74. Translated by Agnes E. Meyer as *The Coming Victory of Democracy.* New York: Knopf, 1938.

Meier, Kurt. *Der evangelische Kirchenkampf: Gesamtdarstellung in drei Bänden* (The Protestant Church Struggle: A general account in three volumes). Vol. 3: *Im Zeichen des zweiten Weltkrieges* (Under the sign of the Second World War). Göttingen: Vandenhoeck & Ruprecht, 1984.

Metz, Brigitte, and Karl Pagel. *Wir können's ja nicht lassen: Der Weg des Friedrich Onnasch unter dem Gebot seines Gewissens* (We couldn't let it go: Friedrich Onnasch's path under the command of his conscience). Edited by Matthias Gürtler. Berlin: Verbum, 1995.

Migne, Jacques-Paul, ed. *Patrologiae cursus completus* (Complete patrologia). Paris: Garnier Frères, 1958–; Ridgewood, N.J., Gregg Press, 1965.

Nawyn, William A. *American Protestantism's Response to Germany's Jews and Refugees, 1933–1941.* Ann Arbor, Mich.: UMI Research Press, 1981.

Niebuhr, Reinhold. "The Death of a Martyr." *Christianity and Crisis* 5, no. 11 (June 25, 1945): 6–7.

———. *The Nature and Destiny of Man: A Christian Interpretation.* 2 vols. New York: Charles Scribner's Sons, 1941.

Niemöller, Martin. *Was würde Jesus dazu sagen? Eine Reise durch ein protestantisches Leben* (What would Jesus say to this? A journey through a Protestant life). Edited by Hannes Karnick and Wolfgang Richter. Frankfurt am Main: Röderberg, 1986.

Niesel, Wilhelm. *Kirche unter dem Wort: Der Kampf der Bekennenden Kirche der altpreußischen Union 1933–1945* (Church under the word: The struggle of the Confessing Church of the Old Prussian Union, 1933–1945). Arbeiten zur Geschichte des Kirchenkampfes, Ergänzungsreihe, 11. Göttingen: Vandenhoeck & Ruprecht, 1978.

———, ed. *Um Verkündigung und Ordnung der Kirche: Die Bekenntnissynoden der Evangelischen Kirche der altpreußischen Union 1934–1943* (For the proclamation and order of the church: The confessional synods of the Protestant Church of the Old Prussian Union, 1934–1943). Bielefeld: L. Bechauf, 1949.

Nietzsche, Friedrich. *Human, All Too Human: A Book for Free Spirits.* Translated by Marion Faber, with Stephen Lehmann. Introduction and notes by Marion Faber. New introduction by Arthur C. Danto. Lincoln: University of Nebraska Press, 1996.

———. *Sämtliche Werke: Kritische Gesamtausgabe.* Edited by Giorgio Colli and Mazzino Montinari. Berlin: W. de Gruyter, 1967–77. Translated as *The Complete Works of Friedrich Nietzsche.* Stanford, Calif.: Stanford University Press, 1994–.

———. *Thus Spoke Zarathustra.* Translated by Walter Kaufmann. New York: Random House, 1995.

Pejsa, Jane. *Matriarch of Conspiracy: Ruth von Kleist, 1867–1945.* Cleveland, Ohio: Pilgrim Press, 1992. Translated in German as *Mit dem Mut einer Frau: Ruth von Kleist-Retzow, Matriarchin im Widerstand.* Moers: Brendow, 1996.

Reuter, Fritz. *Sämmtliche Werke: Volks-Ausgabe in 7 Bänden* (Collected works: Popular edition in 7 volumes). Vol. 1. Wismar: Hinstorff, 1877.

Rieger, Julius. *Bonhoeffer in England.* Berlin: Lettner Verlag, 1966.

Ritter, Adolf Martin. "Arianismus." In *Theologische Realenzyklopädie,* 3:692–719. Berlin: W. de Gruyter, 1978.

Rohkrämer, Martin. "Karl Barth in der Herbstkrise 1938" (Karl Barth in the crisis of autumn 1938). *Evangelische Theologie* 48 (1988): 521–45.

Röhm, Eberhard, and Jörg Thierfelder. *Evangelische Kirche zwischen Kreuz und Hakenkreuz: Bilder und Texte einer Ausstellung* (Protestant church between cross and swastika: Pictures and text of an exhibition). Stuttgart: Calwer, 1982.

Scherffig, Wolfgang. *Junge Theologen im "Dritten Reich": Dokumente, Briefe, Erfahrungen* (Young theologians during the "Third Reich": Documents, letters, experiences). 3 vols. Neukirchen-Vluyn: Neukirchner Verlag, 1989–94.

Schleunes, Karl A. "Nationalsozialistische Entschlußbildung und die Aktion T 4" (The formation of the National Socialist decision and the T 4 program). In *Der Mord an den Juden im Zweiten Weltkrieg: Entschlußbildung und Verwirklichung* (The murder of the Jews in the Second World War: The formation of decision and implementation), edited by Eberhard Jäckel and Jürgen Rohwer, 70–83. Stuttgart: Deutsche Verlags-Anstalt, 1985.

Scholder, Klaus. *Die Kirchen und das Dritte Reich.* Vol. 2: *Das Jahr der Ernüchterung 1934: Barmen und Rom.* 2nd ed. Berlin: W. J. Siedler, 1988. Translated by John Bowden as *The Churches and the Third Reich,* vol. 2: *The Year of Disillusionment 1934: Barmen and Rome.* London: SCM Press, 1988.

———. *Die Kirchen zwischen Republik und Gewaltherrschaft: Gesammelte Aufsätze.* Edited by K. O. von Aretin und G. Besier. Berlin: Siedler, 1988.

Schönherr, Albrecht. . . . *Aber die Zeit war nicht verloren: Erinnerungen eines Altsbischofs* (. . . But the time was not lost: Memoirs of a retired bishop). Berlin: Aufbau-Verlag, 1993.

Shapiro, James. *Oberammergau: The Troubling Story of the World's Most Famous Passion Play.* New York: Pantheon Books, 2000.

Snyder, Louis L., ed. *Documents of German History.* 1958. Reprint, Westport, Conn.: Greenwood Press, 1975.

Spitz, Lewis. *The Renaissance and Reformation Movements.* Chicago: Rand McNally, 1971.

Strohm, Christoph. *Theologische Ethik im Kampf gegen den Nationalsozialismus: Der Weg Dietrich Bonhoeffers mit den Juristen Hans von Dohnanyi und Gerhard Leibholz in den Widerstand* (Theological ethics in the struggle against National Socialism: Dietrich Bonhoeffer's path with the lawyers Hans von Dohnanyi and Gerhard Leibholz into the resistance). Heidelberger

Untersuchungen zu Widerstand, Judenverfolgung and Kirchenkampf im Dritten Reich 1. Munich: Chr. Kaiser, 1989.

Thamer, Hans-Ulrich. *Verführung und Gewalt: Deutschland 1933–1945* (Temptation and violence: Germany 1933–1945). Rev. ed. Siedler Deutsche Geschichte 11. Berlin: Siedler, 1994.

Timmermanns, Felix. *Bauernpsalm* (Farmers' psalm). Munich: Deutscher Taschenbuch Verlag, 1977.

Tödt, Heinz Eduard. "Die Novemberverbrechen 1938 und der deutsche Protestantismus: Ideologische und theologische Voraussetzungen für die Hinnahme des Pogroms" (1989). In his *Theologische Perspektiven nach Dietrich Bonhoeffer*, edited by Ernst-Albert Scharffenorth, 217–42. Gütersloh: Chr. Kaiser, 1993. Translated by David Stassen and Ilse Tödt as "The November Crimes of 1938 and German Protestantism: Ideological and Theological Presuppositions for the Toleration of the Pogrom," in *Authentic Faith: Bonhoeffer's Theological Ethics in Context*, edited by Glen Harold Stassen, 232–59. Grand Rapids, Mich.: Wm. B. Eerdmans, 2007.

Tödt, Heinz Eduard, with Jörg Dinger und Dirk Schulz, eds. *Komplizen, Opfer und Gegner des Hitlerregimes: Zur "inneren Geschichte" von protestantischer Theologie und Kirche im "Dritten Reich"* (Accomplices, victims and opponents of the Hitler regime: On the "inner history" of Protestant theology and church during the Third Reich). Gütersloh: Chr. Kaiser, 1997.

Visser 't Hooft, Willem A. *Die Welt war meine Gemeinde: Autobiographie.* Munich: Piper, 1972. Published in English as *Memoirs.* London: SCM Press; Philadelphia: Westminister Press, 1973.

Walker, Williston. *A History of the Christian Church.* 3rd ed. Revised by Robert T. Handy. New York: Charles Scribner's Sons, 1970.

Wellhausen, Julius. *Prolegomena zur Geschichte Israels.* 6th ed. Berlin: W. de Gruyter, 1927. Translated by John Sutherland Black and Allan Menzies as *Prolegomena to the History of Israel.* Atlanta: Scholars Press, 1994.

Wiechert, Ernst. *Wälder und Menschen: Eine Jugend* (Forests and people: A youth). Munich: A. Langen, G. Müller, 1936.

Young, Josiah. *No Difference in the Fare: Dietrich Bonhoeffer and the Problem of Racism.* Grand Rapids, Mich.: Wm. B. Eerdmans, 1998.

Zimmermann, Wolf-Dieter, ed. *Begegnungen mit Dietrich Bonhoeffer: Ein Almanach.* 3rd ed. Munich: Chr. Kaiser, 1965. Translated from the 1st German ed. by Käthe Gregor Smith as *I Knew Dietrich Bonhoeffer*, edited by Wolf-Dieter Zimmermann and Ronald Gregor Smith. London: Collins; New York: Harper & Row, 1966.

———. *Wir nannten ihn Bruder Bonhoeffer: Einblicke in ein hoffnungsvolles Leben* (We called him Brother Bonhoeffer: Insights into a life full of hope). Berlin: Wichern-Verlag, 1995.

Zinn, Elisabeth. *Die Theologie des Friedrich Christoph Oetinger* (The theology of Friedrich Christoph Oetinger). Beiträge zur Förderung christlicher Theologie, vol. 36, no. 3. Gütersloh: C. Bertelsmann, 1932. *NL-Bibl.* 2 C 4. 55.

Zinzendorf, Nikolaus Ludwig von. *Jeremias: Ein Prediger der Gerechtigkeit* (Jeremiah: A preacher of justice). 1741. Ergänzungsbände zu den Hauptschriften 6, series edited by Erich Beyreuther and Gerhard Meyer. Hildesheim: G. Olms, 1965.

Index of Scriptural References

Index of Names

Unless they appear elsewhere in the text, the names of the theological candidates in the collective pastorates (listed in appendix 2) are not included here.

Index of Subjects

μύθοις, 324

Hebrew Terms

Editors and Translators

Victoria J. Barnett (MDiv, Union Theological Seminary, New York) is general editor of the *Dietrich Bonhoeffer Works*, English edition, and director of church relations at the United States Holocaust Memorial Museum. She is the author of *Bystanders: Conscience and Complicity during the Holocaust* (Greenwood Press, 1999) and *For the Soul of the People: Protestant Protest against Hitler* (Oxford University Press, 1992) and the editor and translator of the new revised English edition of *Dietrich Bonhoeffer: A Biography*, by Eberhard Bethge (Fortress Press, 2000), as well as *And the Witnesses Were Silent: The Confessing Church and the Jews*, by Wolfgang Gerlach (University of Nebraska Press, 2000). In addition to numerous book chapters and articles, she is the author of the essay on Bonhoeffer on the U.S. Holocaust Memorial Museum Web site.

Claudia D. Bergmann (PhD, University of Chicago) is an ordained pastor in the Evangelical Lutheran Church in America. She has served in both pastoral and teaching capacities in the United States and Germany, including at Valparaiso University, the University of Chicago, and the Martin-Luther-Institut at the University of Erfurt. She is the author of numerous articles in the field of Old Testament/Hebrew Bible. Her dissertation, titled *Childbirth as a Metaphor for Crisis: Evidence from the Ancient Near East, the Hebrew Bible, and 1QH XI, 1–18*, was published by DeGruyter in 2008. She is currently doing postdoctoral work at the University of Erfurt Graduate School of Religion, writing on the eschatological meal in extrabiblical literature.

Peter Frick is an associate professor and academic dean at St. Paul's University College, University of Waterloo. He teaches a variety of subjects including courses in Western religions, theology, and biblical studies. His main interest lies at the intersection of philosophy and theology, in both ancient and modern times. Recently he published *A Handbook of New Testament Greek*

Grammar (Laodamia, 2007) and *A Dialogue with Dietrich Bonhoeffer: Collected Essays* (Chung Yuan Christian University, 2009). He also edited *Bonhoeffer's Intellectual Formation* (Mohr Siebeck, 2008) and *Dietrich Bonhoeffer: Meditation and Prayer* (Liturgical Press, 2010). Currently he is editing *Interpreting Bonhoeffer: Essays on Methods and Approaches* (Peter Lang, 2011) and *Paul in the Grip of Continental Philosophy* (Fortress Press, 2012). He is a member of the International Bonhoeffer Society and serves on the editorial board responsible for the publication of the Dietrich Bonhoeffer Works English.

Scott A. Moore is a graduate of the University of Maryland, where he studied music education, and the Lutheran Theological Seminary at Gettysburg. He has written in the fields of youth ministry and liturgy. He is an ordained pastor in the Evangelical Lutheran Church in America (ELCA) and has served parishes in Indiana, Illinois, and most recently Lutherstadt Eisleben, Germany. He currently serves as the ELCA representative for the Luther decade and as coordinator of the ELCA Wittenberg Center. He has also translated for films, scholarly journals, and the Luther Memorials Foundation of Saxony-Anhalt. He is currently working on his doctoral dissertation in liturgical studies at the University of Erfurt Graduate School of Religion and is a member of the Theologisches Forschungskolleg.

Douglas W. Stott is a freelance editor and translator. A graduate of Davidson College, Northwestern University, and Emory's Candler School of Theology, he also studied in Germany at the Philipps University in Marburg and at the University of Stuttgart. His translation credits include several volumes of the *Theological Dictionary of the Old Testament* and the *Exegetical Dictionary of the New Testament*; commentaries for the Old Testament Library; *DBWE* 10, *Barcelona, Berlin, New York: 1928–1931*, and *DBWE* 14, *Theological Education at Finkenwalde: 1935–1937*; and F. W. J. Schelling's *Philosophy of Art*. He was also on the translation team of volume 1 of *Religion Past and Present*. He is currently preparing an annotated English edition of the correspondence of Caroline Schelling.

Barbara Wojhoski studied art history at New York University; ancient history at the Philipps University in Marburg, Germany; and anthropology at Georgia State University, and has participated in archaeological excavations of Late Woodland Period sites in the southeastern United States. Since 1995 she has been a fulltime freelance editor for academic and denominational presses and has worked on projects ranging from a dictionary of the Miami-Illinois language to contemporary fiction translated from German to theological commentaries and philosophical works.